The Practical Encyclopedia of Boating

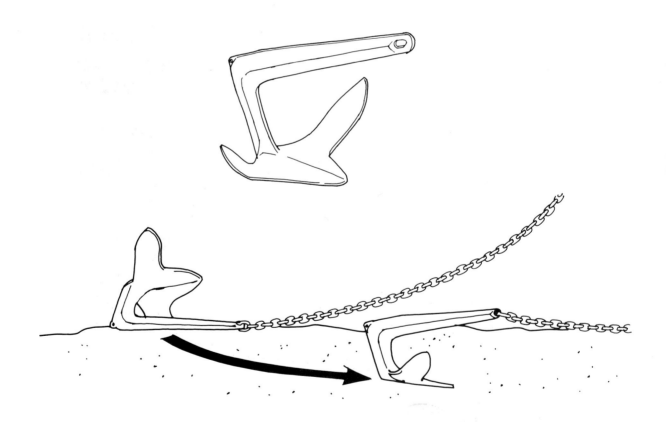

The Practical Encyclopedia
of Boating

An A – Z Compendium of Seamanship, Boat Maintenance, Navigation, and Nautical Wisdom

John Vigor

  INTERNATIONAL MARINE / McGRAW-HILL
Camden, Maine • New York • Chicago • San Francisco •
Lisbon • London • Madrid • Mexico City • Milan • New Delhi •
San Juan • Seoul • Singapore • Sydney • Toronto

The McGraw·Hill Companies

1 2 3 4 5 6 7 8 9 CCW CCW 0 9 8 7 6 5 4 3

The Library of Congress has cataloged the cloth edition as follows:

Vigor, John.
    The practical encyclopedia of boating : an a–z compendium of seamanship, boat maintenance, navigation, and nautical wisdom / John Vigor.
            p.   cm.
Includes bibliographical references and index.
    ISBN 0-07-137885-5 (hardcover : alk. paper)
    1. Boats and boating—Encyclopedias.
I. Title.
    GV775.V53 2004
    797.1´03—dc22   2003016127

Paperback ISBN 978-0-07-149888-3
Paperback MHID 0-07-149888-5

Questions regarding the content of this book should be addressed to
International Marine
P.O. Box 220
Camden, ME 04843
www.internationalmarine.com

Questions regarding the ordering of this book should be addressed to
The McGraw-Hill Companies
Customer Service Department
P.O. Box 547
Blacklick, OH 43004
Retail customers: 1-800-262-4729
Bookstores: 1-800-722-4726

Credits for art and graphics are on pages 343–44.

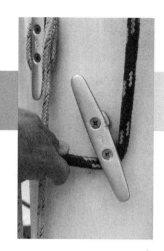

To my sons:
Trent, Terry, and Kevin

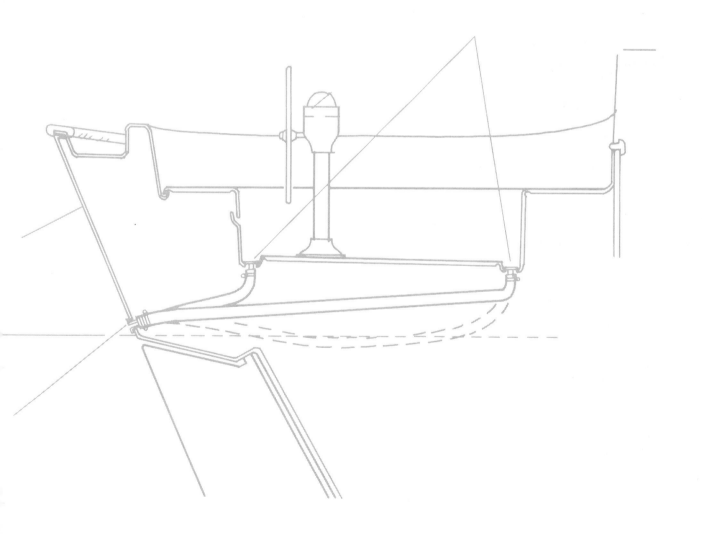

Contents

Acknowledgments

I gratefully acknowledge the help of a host of people in the yachting community all over the world. There are so many that I can't possibly thank them all personally here, but I must admit that I could not have written this book without their invaluable insights and contributions to yachting knowledge and literature over the years. The wisdom is theirs. The mistakes are mine.

Introduction

This is no ordinary encyclopedia. Admittedly, it's encyclopedic in form and content because it touches on every important boating subject from A to Z. But it's not written in the usual dry scholastic prose of an encyclopedia. This one is different. In refreshingly simple language, it informs, entertains, enlightens, and amuses.

It is nevertheless an authoritative, comprehensive guide that will help you solve many everyday boating problems. These alphabetically arranged entries and illustrations cover all aspects of boating, power and sail. They explain the mystery of how boats can sail against the wind, why the sea sometimes speaks with human voices, and why sailors think it unlucky to start a voyage on a Friday. They tell you how to dename your boat (so you can later rename it without suffering bad luck) and they reveal how good sailors *earn* the "luck" that keeps them safe at sea.

The subject matter has been arranged so that you can flip the book open at any page and find yourself following a fascinating trail from entry to entry of your choice. When you have a specific subject in mind, first look it up alphabetically, using the words you would normally use. If you don't find it there, go straight to the comprehensive index at the back of the book, which will guide you to the right place.

Running through the pages of this book is a thread of sensible hints and tips on everything from anchoring to zinc replacement. You'll find the explanations, definitions, and instructions here clear and helpful. This is a practical directory for practical people.

At the end of most entries you'll find a cross-reference. If it says, for example, "See also **Boat Types**," you'll find additional information on a closely related subject.

A

Abandoning Ship

Why it may not be such a good idea in extremely bad weather

You'll often hear the old advice never to abandon your boat until you have to step *up* to the life raft. It sounds deceptively easy, but the only time it works is in reasonably calm water. People who advocate it as a general rule have obviously never seen an inflatable life raft performing its antics alongside a boat in a bad gale, rising and falling like an elevator gone mad, crashing and bashing against the hull, jerking and tugging and doing its best to puncture itself or break the painter and fly away like thistledown in the winter wind. It's up one moment, down the next, and then it's disappearing forever over the swells to leeward.

Nevertheless, the principle is sound: Don't abandon your boat until you are absolutely, positively sure it's going to sink. Too often, a partially waterlogged boat is found still floating months or years after it was abandoned, whereas those who actually managed to get into the life raft are never seen again. Trying to board a life raft in those conditions may

be far more dangerous than staying with the boat.

Fifteen lives were lost during the Fastnet Race in Britain in 1979—many of them when boats were being abandoned. It happened again during the Queen's Birthday storm off New Zealand in June 1994, when three sailors died—the *only* ones who abandoned their boat and got away in a life raft.

Unfortunately, the pressure to abandon ship before it's necessary is often very great. It's not easy to resist, particularly if you have a well-found raft in good condition.

You may be exhausted mentally and physically after fighting a gale, pumping bilges, and possibly suffering a dismasting or other damage. You'll experience a feeling of not being in control, of having made wrong decisions. You may also be frightened if the weather seems to be getting worse. You'll certainly be scared by the noise: the banshee scream of the wind and the bloodcurdling thunder of solid water hitting the hull. In addition, you'll probably be feeling guilty about leading your crew into danger.

It all becomes too much, and the inflatable raft offers a way out—you want nothing more than to curl up in the fetal position in the soft belly of a boat. It offers peace: relief from the great mental strain of making decisions and giving orders to a crew, or trying to quell their panic. The life

raft will look after you. There's nothing to be decided: no more fighting, no more mess of tangled ropes, no more chaos down below—complete and wonderful capitulation. Just lie down and let it carry you away. The lure of the life raft is very strong.

Yet, it's a fact that few boats sink from the stress of storms, even those abandoned with hatches open. Your best bet is to think about the possibility well in advance, to be fully aware of the pressures you'll experience to abandon ship too early, and to fight them until it's quite evident that the raft really is your last refuge.

See also **Life Rafts**.

Accidental Circling

Accepting the inevitable could keep you out of trouble

Well-documented studies carried out in the Northern Hemisphere show that people who are cut off from sensory information about their surroundings tend to move in a circle, usually clockwise. It makes no difference whether they're driving, walking, swimming, or steering a yacht.

So, if you happen to be caught in dense fog in a dinghy—or even in a bigger boat—without a compass, accept that your chances of steering a straight course are slim. You may have a little breeze to

A

guide you, but there's no guarantee it will remain steady in direction. If you have a fishing line, try trailing a length astern to help you keep going straight ahead. However, even if it does keep you straight for a little way, you won't know in what direction you're traveling, and sooner or later you're going to start veering off to the right, even if it does take a little longer.

Merely knowing that you're going to circle clockwise is not much of an aid to practical navigation; its usefulness lies in the fact that you will not fool yourself into believing you can maintain a straight course. That could keep you out of worse trouble.

To my knowledge, no equivalent studies have been carried out in the Southern Hemisphere, where it's possible that you might circle counterclockwise instead of clockwise.

See also **Fog Types**.

Accidents on Board

Dealing with a wide range of calamities that can't be avoided

Like many other sports, boating involves certain risks that can never be entirely eradicated. Despite the best training and precautions, accidents do happen and always will. But you can substantially reduce the risk of death or serious injury by preparing for the worst, installing equipment to handle emergencies, and knowing how to use it.

First, be aware of the wide range of accidents that occur on boats. The major ones involve fire, carbon monoxide, falling overboard from your boat or dinghy, collision, being hit on the head by a boom, getting a finger caught in an anchor chain or a line to a winch, and being run over by a propeller.

Following is what you can do (and what, in some cases, you are *required* to do by federal law) to lessen the consequences of an accident.

Fire

Keep several U.S. Coast Guard–approved fire extinguishers on board. Federal law dictates how many your boat should have, but it's the very minimum. Take at least of couple of extra extinguishers, and check them regularly. Place them near likely spots for fires—the galley and the engine compartment—and along exit routes, where you might have to put out a fire before you can escape into the cockpit. Show all your passengers where they are and how to use them.

Carbon monoxide

This colorless, odorless gas is a killer. It's a by-product of combustion, and it's found in copious quantities in engine exhaust. If exhaust fumes are blowing over the stern into the accommodations, beware. It also forms where open flames are burning—at the galley stove, oil lamps, and heaters. Your charcoal barbecue grill is another prolific producer of carbon monoxide, which, incidentally, has the ability to travel rapidly in a draft of air, even up-

Inflatable life jackets, which the coast guard classifies as type 5 personal flotation devices (PFDs), are convenient to wear (top). In use (above), they provide more buoyancy than most.

stream. Many deaths have occurred in sleeping cabins tightly sealed against cold weather in which open-flame heaters were being used. There have even been reported cases of knee-boarders overcome by carbon monoxide while being towed behind powerboats.

The danger signs are light-headedness, headache, light nausea, dizziness, and unnatural sleepiness. Drag yourself into fresh air immediately. In advanced cases of carbon monoxide poisoning, the skin turns pink.

The best defense is to vent your stoves to the outside atmosphere and maintain a steady flow of fresh air inside the boat, cold as it may be. It's equally important to install a carbon monoxide monitor-alarm. Marine stores sell battery-operated alarms.

Falling overboard

This risk is always present, in big boats and small. Even if you can swim well, it might be a long time before the boat can turn back to rescue you. In cold water, you will quickly become weak and confused as hypothermia sets in.

Most life jackets, as mandated by federal law, don't have to be worn all the time you're aboard. But it's a good idea to don one when the weather turns bad because you're likely to be in the water much longer if you fall overboard. Better still, discipline yourself to wear a slim vest-type life jacket all the time you're on deck. It won't hamper your movement much and, although it's not as buoyant as an offshore-type jacket, it will be ready when you need it. It should have reflective patches, a pocket for a crew-overboard light, and a good whistle.

Inflatable life jackets have now been approved by the U.S. Coast Guard, but you'll notice that guardsmen don't wear them. That's because this type of life jacket is not foolproof: it doesn't always inflate when it should, especially if you fail to maintain it religiously. These life jackets are becoming popular because they look smart, don't get in your way, and can incorporate a harness; however, they're still not as reliable as solid flotation.

Lifelines, the wires running through stanchions at the edge of the deck, are supposed to stop you from falling overboard, but they are often too low to do the job properly, especially on sailboats. Regard them as backup; never rely on them.

In heavy weather, it makes sense to use a harness and tether attached to a jackline running fore and aft so that you're always attached to the boat. Try to arrange it so that the tether is short enough to stop you going overboard—people have drowned from being dragged alongside in harnesses and not being able to scramble back aboard.

A crew-overboard pole, equipped with a flag and a strobe light, is a valuable aid for locating someone in the water, and should be kept ready for use in the cockpit.

A crew overboard pole, when deployed quickly, can guide a boat back to the lost crew.

Collision

Whether you collide with an iceberg, a rock, or another boat, there's always a chance of sinking. A collision mat might stem the

A

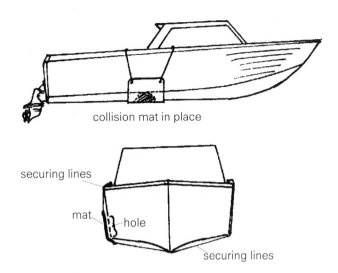

collision mat in place

securing lines

mat — hole

securing lines

A collision mat might slow down a bad leak while you make temporary repairs.

flow of water until you can make temporary repairs, but some alternative form of flotation is advisable just in case: a life raft or a dinghy.

You can avoid collisions by cautious navigation and thorough application of the rules of the road, but primarily by keeping a good lookout at all times.

Head injuries

Your only defense against being hit on the head by the boom is to be aware of the danger and duck at the right time. Accidental jibes happen without notice, so be extra cautious if you're in a sailboat that's running dead downwind. If it's a long leg, pin the boom forward with a preventer line so it can't jibe. Otherwise, it might be a good idea to wear a helmet; an even better idea is to wear a life jacket. If a jibing boom knocks you overboard and you're unconscious without flotation, you'll be lucky to survive.

Finger injuries

Anchor lines and sheets handling heavy loads around winches often cause finger injuries. The immediate cure for a trapped finger is to ease the load on the line or cut it, but prevention is a matter of awareness and caution. Be sure to tell landlubbers to keep their fingers well clear of winches and cleats.

Propeller injuries

If you're in the water being rescued, keep your legs well clear of propellers; they inflict nasty wounds. If you are the rescuer, turn off the motor at the last moment. Don't assume the prop will stop turning in neutral gear because sometimes they don't.

See also **Fire on Board; Harnesses; Heaters; Jacklines; Life Jackets; Lookouts; Preventers; Winches.**

Adhesives

Four types of boat glue and one powerful sealant

Modern glues have proved to be surprisingly efficient and durable, even on boats, where salt, moisture, heat, grime, and the ultraviolet (UV) rays of the sun do their best to degrade them. Many boat parts that formerly required fixing with nails, screws, rivets, or nuts and bolts are now fastened in place with glue only. Indeed, the major hull components of many small plywood boats are now held together solely by fiberglass tape glued in place.

Nearly all glues used in boat work fall into one of the following four categories:

Rubber glues, the basis of contact adhesives, may be natural or synthetic.

Melamine-urea types of glue are water-resistant and very forgiving, which makes them suitable for amateur use. Examples include Weldwood plastic resin, Casco urea-formaldehyde, and Aerolite resin glues.

Epoxies, probably the most popular glues used on boats, also are forgiving in many ways because their curing times can be controlled, and they can be stiffened and strengthened with fillers to avoid dribbling and slumping. Epoxy resin fills large gaps and is an excellent sealer for wood. It is almost exclusively used to laminate new fiberglass to old fiberglass hulls.

In fact, epoxy sounds like the ultimate glue, and it might have been except for two flaws:

in its normal state, it's not water-proof or heatproof; and it can be adversely affected by salt water and sunlight, both of which are plentiful where boats abound. For exterior use, therefore, it should be protected from salt and sunshine by paint, preferably white or a light color. Varnish that contains UV-ray filters offers some protection, but not as much as paint.

Resorcinols have the very qualities that epoxies lack: they are not affected to the same extent by water or sun. Typically a purple-brownish color, they are the glues used in exterior- and marine-grade plywoods. The original resorcinols were not gap-filling and required a good fit between the pieces of wood to be joined. However, newer varieties have the ability to fill gaps and require less clamping, making them the best wood-to-wood glue available for marine use.

Resorcinol comes in two basic forms. One needs temperatures of 70°F (21°C) or higher to effect a cure; the other, an imported version made by Ciba-Geigy and known as Aerodux or Cascophen, will cure in temperatures as low as 50°F (10°C). The U.S. product is known as Weldwood and is available at marine hardware stores.

Polyurethane sealant needs to be mentioned in connection with glues. It's a bedding compound that also has great adhesive powers—so much so that anything you bed down in polyurethane is never likely to come apart. It's used for permanent sealing bonds, such as hull-to-deck joints, or where a ballast keel joins the hull.

The most popular brand is 3M 5200.

See also **Sealants**.

Air Masses

What you can expect when the barometer rises or falls

All forms of boating are directly affected by the weather—but what exactly is weather? It's simply the reaction of the atmosphere—a relatively thin layer of air that surrounds the Earth—to changes in temperature and pressure.

In simple terms, the atmosphere consists of huge invisible bubbles of air, often hundreds of miles in diameter, rising and falling, warming and cooling, like the colored wax in a lava lamp.

The restless motion of the air masses is caused by simple physical laws, but the results are so complicated that even professional meteorologists armed with the latest computer technology can rarely issue a forecast that is valid more than three days ahead. Nevertheless, boaters who know a few basic principles concerning the movement of air masses can often forecast the weather in their immediate vicinity with reasonable accuracy.

Warm bubbles of air are low in pressure and will rise; cold bubbles of air are higher in pressure and will fall. Air in a bubble of higher pressure will try to balance the pressures by moving toward a bubble of lower pressure; the action starts when two bubbles meet. These boundary zones are called fronts.

The larger the difference in pressure between the two air masses, the faster the air will flow from high to low pressure. That's the air movement we call wind.

If your barometer drops 6 millibars (0.177 inch) or more in 12 hours, thus indicating that the pressure is changing rapidly, you may safely assume that a major low-pressure storm system is fast approaching—especially if the cloud cover has been increasing and the winds have either changed direction or increased in speed.

Air that flows into a low-pressure area is forced to ascend; as it rises, it cools, causing the water vapor it contains to condense and form clouds—hence, the increasing cloud cover in the vanguard of a storm. But air descending from a high-pressure area and moving outward from its center tends to be warm and dry, so fewer clouds form. When your barometer is high, therefore, expect fine weather.

See also **Barometer; Buys Ballot's Law; Clouds; Weather Fronts; Weather Maps.**

Air Pressure on Sails

How the wind causes pressure on sails and why that's important

You've probably heard the America's Cup experts talking about the pressure being better over on the starboard lay line. In the language of sailors seeking to dazzle television viewers with their expertise, that means there's more

A

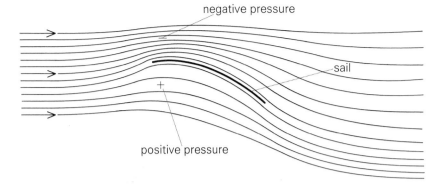

Wind blowing over a sail causes differences in air pressure that provide forward drive for a sailboat.

wind over on the right. How does air pressure equate to wind and what does it mean to ordinary boaters? Well, it should mean something to sailboat owners because, simply put, wind creates areas of high and low pressure on sails, and that's what makes them work when you are sailing across or obliquely into the wind.

When I was a kid, I had no difficulty understanding that an airplane wing, which is simply a horizontal sail, tended to rise if you tilted it slightly upward in front. The air hitting the bottom of the wing simply forced it up like a wedge. But the further I progressed with science lessons, the more ridiculous my theory appeared. What was happening, my mentors explained with great patience, was that air molecules passing over the rounded top of the wing had a longer course to follow than those sliding along the straight bottom, so they had to move faster to meet up with the bottom molecules at the aft edge of the wing. If you speed up a stream of molecules, the pressure drops; therefore, with less pressure on top and greater pressure below, the wing was forced upward.

Unfortunately, no sooner had I learned that theory by rote than they changed it again. These days, the theory of how a sail gains lift to windward is much more complicated.

No matter. For the purposes of celestial navigation, most of us assume that the sun revolves around the Earth. We know it's not true, but it brings the right results. The same applies to yacht sails: one side of a sail sucks (negative pressure), the other side shoves (positive pressure). It's caused by air pressure that depends on the angle of the wind. That's all you really need to know.

See also **Sails and "Lift."**

Albatrosses

Although much admired, these great fliers can bring bad luck

The albatross, the largest of all sea birds, is a wonderful flier. In the "Roaring Forties" south of the equator, the Great Wandering Albatross (*Diomedea exulans*) will follow a vessel for weeks on end, and is even reputed to be able to sleep on the wing. Scientists have recorded specimens with a wingspan of 20 feet (6 m). In the North Pacific, the Blackfooted Albatross (*Diomedea nigripes*) and the Short-Tailed Albatross (*Diomedea albatrus*) are common, and all are members of the web-footed petrel family (genus *Diomedea*).

Understandably, these solitary birds, which are so at home on the vast oceans, have always inspired awe in sailors. For many centuries, European mariners believed that an albatross housed the soul of a dead sailor. Therefore, it was considered bad luck to kill one, as Samuel Taylor Coleridge pointed out in his famous poem, "The Rime of the Ancient Mariner." So beware if you ever find yourself in the Roaring Forties towing a lure for fish. If an albatross takes it, you're in big trouble—one way or another.

Oddly enough, the word *albatross* stems from the Portuguese and Spanish *alcatraz* (a word familiar to Americans), which has actually come to mean pelican. An albatross looks nothing like a pelican, of course; it seems that in the golden days of exploration, Spanish and Portuguese sailors gave the name alcatraz to most new sea birds they came across, just as many English-speaking sailors with scant interest in ornithology referred to all sea birds as seagulls.

Alternators

Rules of thumb concerning horsepower drain and charging

It's easy to regard the alternator as a free source of electrical power,

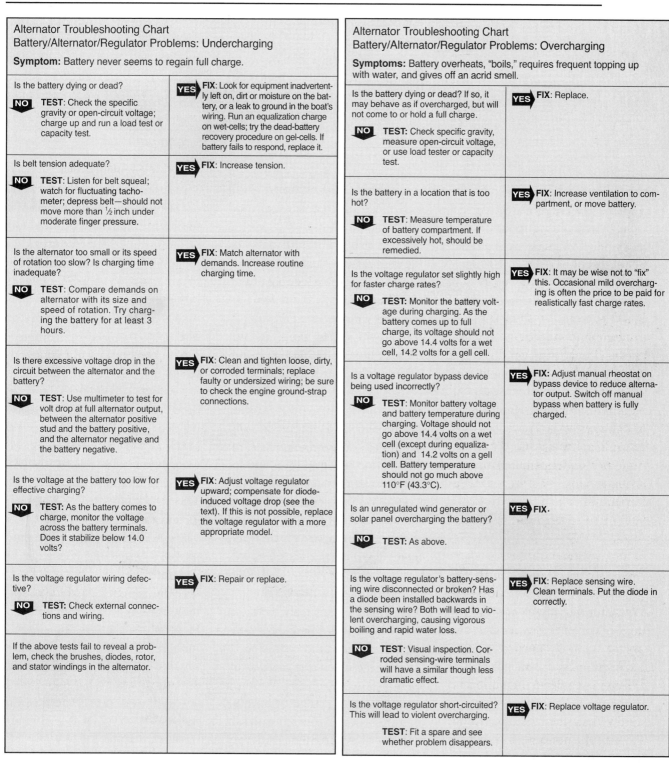

Alternator Troubleshooting Chart
Battery/Alternator/Regulator Problems: Undercharging

Symptom: Battery never seems to regain full charge.

Is the battery dying or dead? **NO** **TEST:** Check the specific gravity or open-circuit voltage; charge up and run a load test or capacity test.	**YES** **FIX:** Look for equipment inadvertently left on, dirt or moisture on the battery, or a leak to ground in the boat's wiring. Run an equalization charge on wet-cells; try the dead-battery recovery procedure on gel-cells. If battery fails to respond, replace it.
Is belt tension adequate? **NO** **TEST:** Listen for belt squeal; watch for fluctuating tachometer; depress belt—should not move more than ½ inch under moderate finger pressure.	**YES** **FIX:** Increase tension.
Is the alternator too small or its speed of rotation too slow? Is charging time inadequate? **NO** **TEST:** Compare demands on alternator with its size and speed of rotation. Try charging the battery for at least 3 hours.	**YES** **FIX:** Match alternator with demands. Increase routine charging time.
Is there excessive voltage drop in the circuit between the alternator and the battery? **NO** **TEST:** Use multimeter to test for volt drop at full alternator output, between the alternator positive stud and the battery positive, and the alternator negative and the battery negative.	**YES** **FIX:** Clean and tighten loose, dirty, or corroded terminals; replace faulty or undersized wiring; be sure to check the engine ground-strap connections.
Is the voltage at the battery too low for effective charging? **NO** **TEST:** As the battery comes to charge, monitor the voltage across the battery terminals. Does it stabilize below 14.0 volts?	**YES** **FIX:** Adjust voltage regulator upward; compensate for diode-induced voltage drop (see the text). If this is not possible, replace the voltage regulator with a more appropriate model.
Is the voltage regulator wiring defective? **NO** **TEST:** Check external connections and wiring.	**YES** **FIX:** Repair or replace.
If the above tests fail to reveal a problem, check the brushes, diodes, rotor, and stator windings in the alternator.	

Alternator Troubleshooting Chart
Battery/Alternator/Regulator Problems: Overcharging

Symptoms: Battery overheats, "boils," requires frequent topping up with water, and gives off an acrid smell.

Is the battery dying or dead? If so, it may behave as if overcharged, but will not come to or hold a full charge. **NO** **TEST:** Check specific gravity, measure open-circuit voltage, or use load tester or capacity test.	**YES** **FIX:** Replace.
Is the battery in a location that is too hot? **NO** **TEST:** Measure temperature of battery compartment. If excessively hot, should be remedied.	**YES** **FIX:** Increase ventilation to compartment, or move battery.
Is the voltage regulator set slightly high for faster charge rates? **NO** **TEST:** Monitor the battery voltage during charging. As the battery comes up to full charge, its voltage should not go above 14.4 volts for a wet cell, 14.2 volts for a gell cell.	**YES** **FIX:** It may be wise not to "fix" this. Occasional mild overcharging is often the price to be paid for realistically fast charge rates.
Is a voltage regulator bypass device being used incorrectly? **NO** **TEST:** Monitor battery voltage and battery temperature during charging. Voltage should not go above 14.4 volts on a wet cell (except during equalization) and 14.2 volts on a gell cell. Battery temperature should not go much above 110°F (43.3°C).	**YES** **FIX:** Adjust manual rheostat on bypass device to reduce alternator output. Switch off manual bypass when battery is fully charged.
Is an unregulated wind generator or solar panel overcharging the battery? **NO** **TEST:** As above.	**YES** **FIX.**
Is the voltage regulator's battery-sensing wire disconnected or broken? Has a diode been installed backwards in the sensing wire? Both will lead to violent overcharging, causing vigorous boiling and rapid water loss. **NO** **TEST:** Visual inspection. Corroded sensing-wire terminals will have a similar though less dramatic effect.	**YES** **FIX:** Replace sensing wire. Clean terminals. Put the diode in correctly.
Is the voltage regulator short-circuited? This will lead to violent overcharging. **TEST:** Fit a spare and see whether problem disappears.	**YES** **FIX:** Replace voltage regulator.

just whirring away as your engine runs. But, in fact, it absorbs a lot of engine power, which you pay for in increased fuel consumption.

The rule of thumb is that the horsepower drain on the engine is twice the number of kilowatts produced. For example, if a 100-amp alternator is charging a 12-volt system at full capacity, it's producing 1,200 watts, or 1.2 kilowatts. Therefore, it steals 2.4 horsepower from the engine.

Another rule of thumb concerns charging capacity. It states that the alternator should have a charging capacity in amps of 25 to 40 percent of the total amp-hour capacity of your batteries. This assumes you're using a modern multistage regulator that won't allow overcharging, particularly when the batteries become warm.

If you don't have a multistage regulator, the rule of thumb for long battery life is to limit the charging rate in amps to 10 percent of available amp-hours. For example, if you have two batteries with capacities of about 100 amp-hours each, your alternator shouldn't have a constant charge rate of more than 20 amps when it's charging the two together.

Because charging at such a low rate takes so long, many boaters ignore the rule, preferring to charge at 20 to 25 percent and to buy new batteries more frequently as a consequence.

See also **Smart Regulators**.

Aluminum Hulls

Pros and cons of building with this strong, light metal

Aluminum has been used for the hulls of small boats ever since the power yacht *Alumina* was built in Switzerland for Prince Wilhelm zu Wied in 1894. This light metal is refined from the mineral bauxite. Although it was discovered early in the nineteenth century, it wasn't until 1886 that the first practical refining methods were developed in France.

Today, aluminum is used to build sailboats and power yachts of all sizes, and it is especially suited to high-speed planing powerboats where weight is all-important.

One of its major characteristics, in addition to its light weight, is its ductility; that is, its ability to stretch without breaking. That means it can be deformed in a collision with a half-submerged container or when grounding on rocks without being holed—as a hull made of fiberglass or wood might be.

It is also strong, stiff, and—in the right alloys—resistant to corrosion. You don't need to paint an aluminum hull, except for cosmetic purposes.

On the other hand, an aluminum hull costs more to build. The metal is hot in summer and cold in winter. It readily transmits wave noise to the interior and it needs insulation in cold waters to prevent condensation. Aluminum is less forgiving of sloppy welding technique than steel, though easier to weld now than formerly. It is otherwise easy to work. For many cutting and fitting operations, hand tools suffice.

Aluminum is low on the galvanic scale—close to zinc, in fact—thus, it is particularly vulnerable to galvanic corrosion, a process by which it is eaten away by more "noble" metals. A copper coin left in the bilge of an aluminum boat and covered with salt water will eventually eat its way through the hull.

Special through-hull fittings are needed for aluminum hulls, as is special antifouling paint, because the typical copper-based paint would react with the hull metal.

See also **Galvanic Corrosion; Steel Hulls; Wooden Hulls**.

America's Cup

Spending millions to capture an old potbellied silver mug

The America's Cup is a baroque silver pitcher with a bulging midriff, curlicue handles, and lots of fussy detail. It is less than 27 inches in height and quite homely to a modern eye, but what it lacks in elegance, it more than makes up for in importance—it is the oldest international sporting trophy in the world still being contested.

Known originally as the Hundred Guinea Cup, the Auld Mug resided most of its life in the New York Yacht Club, having been won by one of the club's yachts, the schooner *America*, in 1851. The club successfully fought off all subsequent challenges for 132 years, and its first loss came only in 1983, when the cup went to Australia.

America belonged to a six-member syndicate led by John C. Stevens, the club's first commodore, who entered her in a race organized by Britain's Royal Yacht Squadron after she had sailed across the Atlantic. The race on August 22, 1851, was a circumnavigation of the Isle of Wight, off the southern coast of England, and the prize was the Hundred Guinea Cup. *America* had trouble raising her anchor and was the last away of 18 entrants, but she finished first in the 58-mile contest, 18 minutes ahead of the cutter *Aurora*. Thereafter, the trophy was known as the America's Cup.

America was designed along the lines of the New York pilot schooners, and was 90 feet long on the waterline. She carried 5,326 feet of sail and cost $20,000. She was designed by George Steers and built by William Brown.

During the Civil War, she became a Confederate blockade runner, but she was captured by Union forces and put to work. Eventually, she became a training ship at the U.S. Naval Academy and served again as a yacht before being broken up in 1945.

Since that first race, the America's Cup has become the most sought-after prize in yacht racing. It is a perpetual challenge trophy open to any yacht club in the world for a match race—that is, a race between only two boats. Early races were dominated by British challengers, but in modern times it has become necessary to run a challengers' regatta to accommodate the many foreign countries vying for the cup. The winner of the challengers' series then races for the cup with the present holder.

Many hundreds of millions of dollars have been spent on yachts especially designed to win the cup, which was deeded to the New York Yacht Club for "friendly competition." On occasion, it has been anything but friendly, and the history of the competition is strewn with controversy, allegations of bad sportsmanship, and even bitter legal battles. Nevertheless, watching the titans of the yachting world outwitting and outspending each other for the

sake of a frilly little pitcher has always provided great entertainment for lesser sailors and landlubbers alike.

Amp-Hour Ratings

An indication of how much energy a battery can store

A battery's amp-hour rating indicates the total amount of energy it will deliver at a constant rate of discharge over a period of 20 hours before it reaches a voltage at which it is stone dead for all practical purposes.

A 12-volt battery, the most common nominal voltage, is fully discharged at 10 volts. A 100-amp-hour, 12-volt battery will run a 5-amp motor (or a 60 watt light) for 20 hours, and a 200-amp-hour battery will run a constant 10-amp (120 watt) load for 20 hours.

That's the theory. In fact, if a 100-amp-hour battery is discharged at a rate greater than 5 amps, it will not deliver all the advertised amp-hours before it goes dead. On the other hand, if you discharge it at a steady rate of less than 5 amps, you'll get more amp-hours than the manufacturer's rating shows—not a whole lot more, but some.

That principle applies to most lead-acid batteries found on boats—the faster the discharge rate, the fewer amp-hours delivered. The more slowly energy is taken from a battery, the longer it will last.

Sometimes a battery's work capacity is given in reserve minutes.

In the absence of any other definition, this is the number of minutes you can discharge a fully charged battery at a whopping 25 amps before its voltage drops to 10.5.

See also **Battery Choices**; **Cranking Ratings**.

Anchoring Rights

What to do if someone anchors too close to you for comfort

The first boat to anchor has certain rights over others who later anchor nearby. These rights spring from common courtesy and practical seamanship, but they are also backed up by law.

A boat already anchored must be given room to swing freely, and she must also be allowed maneuvering room if she wishes to depart. This can mean significant room in the case of an engineless sailboat.

If you, as first boat in the anchorage, notice another boat attempting to anchor too close to you, your first responsibility is to inform the newcomer of the possibility of fouling.

Decision No. 124-5861 (1956) in U.S. Admiralty case law states: "A vessel shall be found at fault if it . . . anchors so close to another vessel as to foul her when swinging . . . (and/or) fails to shift anchorage when dragging dangerously close to another anchored vessel. Furthermore, the vessel that anchored first shall warn the one who anchored last that the berth chosen will foul the former's berth."

Note, however, that if you start to drag anchor and threaten to collide with another vessel, it doesn't matter that you anchored first. A dragging boat must take immediate action to avoid collision and find a new berth.

See also **Anchors, Anchoring**.

Anchors, Anchoring

It all adds up to a bit of science and a lot of art

Anchoring can be a puzzling and sometimes frustrating experience for newcomers to boating. After all, it doesn't look difficult when you see others do it. Simply throw an anchor overboard and tie off the end of the line up in the bow somewhere. Early mariners probably used a big rock, heavy enough to hold by weight alone. Now we use metal anchors shaped to dig into the bottom and grip fast. What's the problem?

Well, there are so many problems that one scarcely knows where to begin—as the neophyte soon discovers—and they all lead to danger or, at least, great excitement when the wind gets up in the middle of the night and the anchor drags.

The truth is, anchoring is as much an art as a science. It's one of those maritime arts you have to perfect by practice. You can tell people how to anchor, but you can't tell them how to *know* when they're properly anchored. They have to find out for themselves what the angle of the anchor line should look like; what the depth of the water should be; what that rumbling noise coming from the forepeak means; why the boat is lying at right angles to the anchor; and why everybody else in the anchorage is shouting, gesticulating, and running for boathooks and fenders.

The mundane art of anchoring does not attract much attention among newcomers to the sport of boating, who are naturally consumed by thoughts of flying over sparkling seas and exploring fascinating new ports. Sooner or later, they'll learn that good anchoring techniques can save their boats and even their lives. Anchors are as important to boats as brakes are to automobiles. You don't use them as often, but when you do, you need them badly.

Sailboats cruising around the world often spend 85 percent of their time at anchor, according to well-known circumnavigators Lin and Larry Pardey. About 10 percent is spent at sea and 5 percent is spent tied to docks.

The practice of anchoring is described in this book under several different headings. You'll find the recommended sizes of anchors and anchor lines. You'll learn how much line to let out and how to get an anchor to set. But that's just the beginning; the next step is to get out there and try it for yourself.

Finally, a note of comfort: nobody gets it right *all* the time. Sometimes even the experts have to make two or three attempts at anchoring before they're satisfied. The trick is to know what's satisfactory.

See also **Anchor Types; Anchoring Rights; Bahamian Moor; Chain Stoppers; Dragging Anchor; Freeing Anchors; Lights at Anchor; Rodes; Safe Anchorage; Scope for Anchors; Setting Anchors**.

Anchor Types

Established favorites—how they compare in performance

An anchor needs to perform several tasks. It must dig into the bottom when a pull is first applied and present as much surface area as possible to the bottom to resist movement under load. It also needs to reset itself quickly when it is uprooted by a change in the direction of pull. It should also free itself easily from the bottom when you pull it straight up, and the anchor line, or rode, shouldn't be able to foul it. It should be easy to handle and stow securely in a bow roller or in chocks on deck. This is a very tall order to fill.

In fact, the perfect anchor has not yet been invented, but small differences in certain dimensions result in large differences in performance, so inventors and engineers are continually developing new ideas.

More than 20 types of anchor already exist. Most fall into one of three categories: anchors with twin pivoting flukes, anchors shaped like plows, and traditional "fisherman" anchors.

For comparatively light weight, pivoting-fluke anchors offer good holding power in mud and sand—provided they can dig in. All are poor performers on rocky bottoms or bottoms covered with thick weed or grass, where penetration is aided by

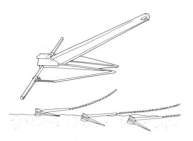

Pivoting-fluke anchors such as the Danforth hold well in mud and sand but often have problems with thick weed or grass.

The C.Q.R. and other plow anchors set quickly by digging their sharp points into the seabed.

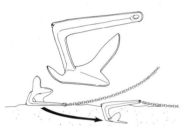

Modified plow anchors, or winged scoops, such as the Bruce, are simple, rugged, and efficient.

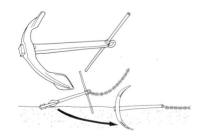

The traditional fisherman-type anchor must be larger and heavier than others, but it excels on rocky bottoms.

sheer weight. They are also easily fouled if the anchor line drags across them, in which case they will be rendered ineffective. Pivoting-fluke anchors are compact and stow flat.

The best-known example is the Danforth; other similar models include the Fortress, the Guardian, and the Performance.

Plow anchors perform much as their name suggests, by digging a sharp point into the seabed. This enables them to penetrate weed and grass. Their surface area is typically smaller than that of a pivoting-fluke anchor, so their ultimate resistance, or anchoring power, is somewhat less. They are better at hooking into a rocky bottom, however, and perform well in sand and adequately in mud. There is little chance of the rode fouling a properly set plow anchor, and they stow neatly in a bow roller, ready for action. The best-known plow is the C.Q.R., which has a pivoting head. The Delta, which offers comparable performance, has a fixed head.

Winged scoop anchors are modified plows with manta-like wings extending from the sides. They were specially designed to anchor oil rigs in the North Sea. They have a reputation for setting quickly and they, too, stow neatly in a bow roller. They perform well in sand and adequately in mud or rock, but often have difficulty penetrating weed and grass. Winged scoop anchors are not easily fouled and their simple construction makes them very rugged. The best known of the winged scoops is the Bruce.

Fisherman, or traditional, anchors must be very large to pro-

vide adequate holding power in sand, mud, or clay bottoms—almost three times as heavy as a plow anchor—but they are the best type on rocky bottoms. They are easily fouled by their rodes, and their projecting stocks and flukes make them awkward to handle, but most fisherman anchors can be dismantled to stow flat. Two well-known makes of fisherman anchors are the Herreshoff and the Luke.

The established favorites mentioned previously are constantly challenged by new designs, the latest of which include the Barnacle, the Bulwagga, and the Spade. All three have proven as good as if not better than the favorites in at least some respects. The Barnacle is an unusual single-fluke anchor with a curved shank that stows flat. The Bulwagga has twin triangular flukes joined to a straight shank, which makes it a problem to handle and stow. The Spade is similar to the venerable C.Q.R., except that the shank is curved and the head does not pivot.

See also **Bower and Kedge; Cruising Anchors; Fisherman Anchor; Holding Power; Lightweight Anchors; New Anchors; Plow Anchors.**

Antifouling Paints

Four types of bottom paint that discourage foul growth

Antifouling paint discourages the growth of barnacles, weed, and other water life on the submersed hull of your boat. If your boat is wooden, it prevents marine borers from eating it for lunch. I use the

A

A

word *discourages* advisedly because there is no acceptable antifouling agent that will stop growth altogether. So if your boat remains in the water year-round, you'll have to scrape the bottom and recoat it with antifouling paint at least every couple of years.

Copper, in one form or another, is the most favored biocide. Tin, in the form of tributyltin, or TBT, was found to be more effective, but its harmful effects on shellfish led to its banning for most marine applications by the U.S. Congress in 1988. It may still be used on aluminum hulls that would react adversely with copper antifouling. The four most common types of antifouling paint are as follows.

Ablative. An ablative paint gradually and constantly wears away to reveal a new surface of copper biocide. It wears from both the chemical reaction with the water and the scouring action of water on the hull. If your boat covers large distances at fast speeds, you can expect to lose a lot of ablative bottom paint.

It has two big advantages: as long as the paint remains, it's 100 percent effective, and it retains its biocidal properties no matter how long it's out of the water.

Most ablative paints are expensive because they need a minimum of two coats, preferably three.

Sloughing. Sloughing paint is similar to ablative paint in that it wears away constantly. However, it comes from a less refined branch of the family because it seems to slough off in coarse flakes rather than disappear discreetly. It uses a softer binder than ablative paint does, and softer translates to less costly. It also loses its potency quickly if it's exposed to air.

Modified epoxy. With modified-epoxy antifouling paint, it's the copper that wears away, not the paint. Copper particles in the epoxy gradually dissolve and allow the water to penetrate deeper and deeper until all the copper biocide is used up. You can scrub epoxy to reinvigorate it, but if you leave it out of the water, it will gradually lose its potency. Although the paint film builds up over the years and occasionally must be removed—an arduous and messy job—epoxy antifouling is a good choice for boats left in the water year-round.

Vinyl. Similar in action to epoxy, vinyl antifouling paint develops a hard smooth finish that you can burnish if you race your boat. Like epoxy, it is non-ablative and it loses efficiency out of the water. You must be careful when applying it because its powerful solvents can soften other undercoats, causing them to bubble. Carefully follow the manufacturer's instructions.

See also **Bottom Painting**.

Apparent Wind

Recognizing the difference that speed makes to wind direction

The wind that blows against you as a result of your passage through still air is known as the apparent wind. Boats create their own wind when they're underway, and if there is a natural wind blowing, it will be modified in force and direction by the boat's forward movement to become the apparent wind, as observed from the boat. The wind hitting a sailboat's sails or her steering vane is the apparent wind, and that—not the "true wind"—is the wind by which she is steered.

In a dead calm, the apparent wind created by a boat's movement comes from dead ahead. The faster she goes, the stronger the apparent wind. Conversely, if a boat lies dead in the water when a wind is blowing, the wind she experiences will come from the true-wind direction. However, as soon as she starts moving forward, the apparent wind direction will draw ahead; the faster she moves, the more it will move ahead.

As the wind moves ahead, a sailboat must pull off more to keep her sails full; therefore, a boat going to windward at 6 knots cannot point quite as close to the true wind as a boat doing only 4 knots. Luckily, the difference is small, so there is no chance of the slower boat reaching a windward destination ahead of the faster boat because she can point slightly higher.

It's interesting to observe the effect of the apparent wind when you're sailing dead downwind in a light breeze. If the wind is blowing at 5 knots from astern and your forward speed is 5 knots, the apparent wind will cancel out the true wind. You will fall into dead air until the boat slows down and the true wind can once more overwhelm the apparent wind. This holds true no matter how much sail you raise. The answer is to change course and tack downwind on a series of broad reaches, thereby generating an apparent wind at an angle that provides useful drive instead of merely canceling out the true wind.

See also **Wind and Altitude**.

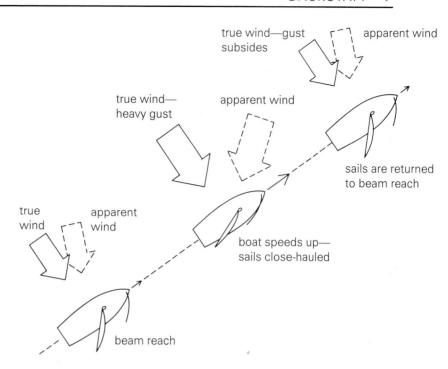

The vector sum of the true wind speed and direction and your boat's course and speed will tell you the strength and direction of the apparent wind. In a simple example, suppose you're motoring north at 4 knots and the true wind is out of the west at 4 knots. The apparent wind—the wind as you observe it on deck—will be from the northwest at 5.6 knots.

B

Backstaff

A giant leap forward in ancient ocean navigation

Around 1590, English seaman and explorer John Davis wrought a revolution in celestial navigation by inventing the backstaff. It was so simple and so practical that it remained in use for more than 200 years. The Davis Strait, between Baffin Island and Greenland, was named in his honor.

The backstaff was an improvement on the old cross-staff because it eliminated parallax errors. In addition, there was no glare to contend with because the user stood facing away from the sun (hence the name). It consisted of three vanes (a sight vane, a shadow vane, and a horizon vane) and a pair of wooden arcs attached to a staff.

Davis's invention was as significant an advance in his time as GPS has been in ours: the backstaff made it possible to read the altitude of the sun and moon in minutes rather than degrees so, for the first time, navigators could consistently find their latitude to

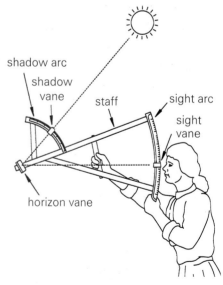

Smoked mirrors on the backstaff solved the ancient navigator's problem of having to look straight at the sun.

within a few miles. Later, the backstaff was fitted with mirrors so it could be used for star and planet sights as well.

Incidentally, the backstaff was the first practical navigational instrument of any importance devised by someone whose name was recorded in history.

See also **Emergency Navigation**; **Quadrant**; **Sextant**.

Bahamian Moor

A safe way to secure a boat left unattended in an anchorage

Strictly and traditionally speaking, to moor is to secure a boat with two anchors whose rodes lead in opposite directions, or nearly so. A boat is not moored when she lies to one anchor only, or even to two anchors lying ahead; she is then at anchor. (In modern parlance, mooring connotes any semipermanent anchoring system.)

If you're planning to leave your boat unattended for a while in an anchorage, both you and she will be happier if she's moored. Some insurance policies will cover your boat if she's moored but not if she's at anchor, so be sure you understand the difference.

To begin the Bahamian moor, set out your bower anchor—your largest working one—in the direction of the prevailing wind or the strongest current. Drift back to the full extent of the anchor line, and drop your kedge anchor. Then haul in on the bower line, snubbing the kedge as you go to set it

into the ground, and center the boat between the two anchors. Now make the end of the kedge line (usually nylon) fast with a rolling hitch to the bower rode (chain or nylon). Ease away the bower rode from the bow roller until the kedge line is well underwater—deep enough not to foul your keel when the boat swings.

In effect, you are now made fast by the bow to a line stretched between two anchors, and the advantages are that your swinging circle is greatly restricted and your rodes cannot foul their anchors.

In practice, don't try to make an absolutely taut line between the two anchors. Leave some slack so that when the wind comes from abeam, the rodes will lie to windward in a shallow V shape and relieve the anchors of considerable strain.

Incidentally, it's not always as easy as it sounds to join the kedge line to the bower line. The longer the length of kedge line above water, the more awkward it is to work with. It's easier if you work the spare line into a tight coil and lash it with a light line to prevent its unraveling before you try tying the rolling hitch and submerging it.

If you have a dinghy, simply anchor with the bower from the bow on a scope of 5 to 1 or so, and take the kedge aft in the dinghy to the full extent of its rode. Then tie the inboard end of the kedge rode to the bower rode and lower the join into the water as before, leaving the boat to swing freely from one rode passing over the bow roller.

When it's time to leave, if you can't recover the kedge with the

dinghy, buoy the end of the line and throw it overboard. Weigh the bower anchor as usual, and then recover the kedge from your boat.

See also **Anchors, Anchoring**; **Bower and Kedge**; **Mooring**.

Balanced Helm

Few sailboats have this much sought-after safety feature

One of the most desirable attributes of a sailboat is a balanced helm. Here's how a prominent British designer, J. Laurent Giles, defined it: "Freedom from objectionable tendencies to gripe or fall off the wind, regardless of angle of heel, speed, or direction of wind."

Laurent Giles tried to design boats with "the utmost docility and sureness of maneuvering at sea, in good or bad weather." His aim was to design hulls that would maintain a steady course with little attention, but that would respond instantly to the helm in heavy weather when there might be large seas to dodge.

A boat with a balanced helm is truly a delight to sail and is easy on her crew, but there are few around. Most boats have weather helm; that is, they require you to pull the rudder to leeward (which, on a tiller-steered boat, means pulling the tiller to windward) to maintain a straight course, particularly in stronger puffs of wind. The tendency of these boats to head into the wind when a puff hits them is what Laurent Giles meant by the old term "griping."

A few boats have lee helm,

which is the tendency to bear away from the wind. On some boats it's constant, on others it occurs only when the wind drops. On all boats, it's dangerous because it can lead to uncontrolled jibes.

C. A. Marchaj, the respected naval architect and research scientist, states bluntly: "Seaworthiness cannot be achieved if the boat is badly balanced."

See also **Center of Effort; Lead Percentage; Lee Helm; Weather Helm.**

Ballast Ratios

The amount of ballast a boat needs for safety, stability

Ballast is weight carried in a monohull vessel to make her stable; that is, to prevent capsize or to help her recover from an accidental inversion. In pleasure boats, ballast most often consists of lead or iron fixed firmly in place, although a mixture of concrete and steel scraps is sometimes used. On some boats, seawater is used for ballast in special tanks that can be pumped dry. Old sailing ships used many kinds of ballast, including gravel, sand, stones, and pig iron. The word *ballast* is derived from the Old Danish *barlast*, which means bare (or waste) load. This ballast was not fixed and would often be jettisoned when the time came to load a cargo, which, properly stowed, would serve as ballast. This is why, for example, English flint is found on the shores of Maine harbors.

Because ballast is dead weight and robs a vessel of speed, yacht designers try to keep the ballast ratio—the weight of ballast divided by the boat's overall weight, or displacement—as low as possible, compatible with seaworthiness. Every hull has its own limits, of course, but here is a rough guide to "normal" ballast ratios for sailing monohulls:

- cruising boats: from 30 to 40 percent of total displacement
- racing boats: from 40 to 50 percent of displacement
- extreme racing boats: As much as 70 percent of displacement

Incidentally, the need for ballast decreases as a boat gets larger because the stability increases with size. Whereas the overturning moment varies as a cube of length, stability (and, therefore, sail-carrying capacity) increases as the fourth power. On the other hand, on racing sailboats, crew members are often treated as moveable ballast and spend much of their time on the windward rail, acquiring the inelegant appellation, "rail meat."

See also **Ballast Taboo.**

Ballast Taboo

Where not to take ballast from and why

Considering that yachts are legally presumed to be permanently in ballast (i.e., not carrying cargo), it's unlikely that you'll ever need to take on ballast the way the old sailing ships did. They did it to maintain stability while they were running light, of course.

However, in the extremely unlikely event that the situation might arise in your lifetime, you ought to know that ballast should never be taken from the seabed. According to ancient tradition, it brings bad luck.

The logic is not quite clear, but seems to spring from the notion that if ever Davy Jones set about to reclaim his property, he would more than likely claim the entire vessel with it, along with the crew.

See also **Ballast Ratios.**

Barge Hazards

The long invisible towline constitutes danger for boaters

Barges towed by tugs constitute a considerable hazard to inexperienced or uninformed boaters. To prevent snatching by waves and swells, tugboats in ocean and semiprotected inland waters often tow large barges at the end of long heavy lines. The weight of these towlines, or hawsers, makes them sink in the water in a shallow curve, or catenary, that absorbs and evens out shock loads. However, the weight also places most of the towline under 1 or 2 feet of water where it cannot be seen.

With a distance of a quarter mile or more between a tug and its tow, it's easy for a boater to make the mistake of cutting between them, resulting in the distinct possibility of striking the towline and becoming disabled in the path of an approaching barge.

Be especially wary at night, and never cut close behind another vessel without being sure

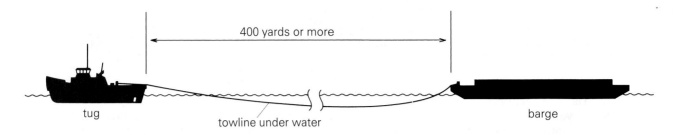

Long, submerged towlines between tugs and their barges can spell danger for unwary boaters.

it's not a tug. Learn to watch out for the two vertically aligned white lights on the foremast that distinguish a tug with a tow whose length does not exceed 200 meters (219 yards); three white lights indicate a longer tow.

Be careful in fog, too. In international waters, a tug with a barge in tow gives the same signal as a sailing vessel: one prolonged blast followed by two short blasts every two minutes. If possible, the barge is supposed to sound its own signal immediately thereafter—one long blast and three short ones—but if it's not manned, it probably won't. If you have serious doubt, put out a call on VHF Channel 16 and ask if there is a tugboat in your immediate vicinity. If there is, ask for her position, speed, and course, and ascertain if she can see you on radar.

Barometer

Simple and reliable, it's your best weather forecaster

The simplest, most reliable aid to forecasting the local weather is your barometer. Along with a magnetic compass, it's the most indispensable of boating instruments.

The kind of barometer used on a boat consists of a metal box with a pleated, flexible top. It's called an aneroid barometer, from the Greek a-, meaning no or not, and neros, meaning wet. That distinguishes it from a mercury barometer, which will not function properly on a bouncy boat.

Air is removed from the aneroid box during manufacture, so the position of the top rises and falls according to the pressure of the atmosphere. That's precisely what you need to know—the pressure of the atmosphere now and several hours, or even days, ago.

The accuracy of the readings is not important unless you are sharing your observations with others—say, in a radio net at sea—for plotting. Otherwise, what you need to know is whether the air pressure is rising or falling and how quickly. An old-fashioned recording barograph, with a graph-paper roll wound by clockwork and a moving pen tracing an inked line, provides a clear picture of pressure changes in graphic form. More modern digital barographs provide the same information on the screen of a small handheld instrument powered by batteries.

If you don't have a barograph, you can make do with graph paper. Simply plot the barometric pressure every 4 hours and join the points with a pencil line.

In the middle latitudes, a high barometer indicates an air pressure of about 30.50 inches of mercury, or 1,033 millibars (mb). A low barometer reads 29.50 inches, or 999 mb. The average reading at sea level is 29.9 inches (1,013 mb). For reference purposes, 3.4 mb equal $\frac{1}{10}$ inch.

Here's what changes in pressure portend:

- steady, persistent decrease in pressure: foul weather is on the way
- steady, persistent increase in pressure: the weather will improve
- pressure remains the same: present conditions likely to continue
- sudden rise or sudden fall: unsettled weather to come

If the pressure falls at least 1 mb per hour for 24 hours, exceptionally bad weather is on the way. This is known as a "weather bomb." The infamous 1979 Fast-

WEATHER FORECASTER

Using the wind as you observe it, and the trend of the barometer for the preceding three hours, you can arrive at a reasonable estimate of the coming weather. This chart is intended for use in continental North America between 30 and 50 degrees north latitudes. Barometric readings are in inches of mercury.

WIND	BAROMETER	FORECAST
SW to NW	30.1 to 30.2, steady	Fair with slight temperature changes for one or two days
SW to NW	30.1 to 30.2, rising rapidly	Fair followed within two days by rain
SW to NW	30.2 and above, stationary	Continued fair with no major temperature changes
SW to NW	30.2 and above, falling slowly	Slowly rising temperature and fair for two days
S to SE	30.1 to 30.2, falling slowly	Rain within 24 hours
S to SE	30.1 to 30.2, falling rapidly	Increasing wind and rain within 12 to 24 hours
SE to NE	30.1 to 30.2, falling slowly	Rain within 12 to 18 hours
SE to NE	30.1 to 30.2, falling rapidly	Increasing wind and rain within 12 hours
E to NE	30.1 and above, falling slowly	Summer: With light winds, no rain for two days Winter: Rain in 24 hours
E to NE	30.1 and above, falling fast	Summer: Rain, probably in 12 hours Winter: Rain or snow with increasing winds
SE to NE	30.0 or below, falling slowly	Rain will continue for one or two days
SE to NE	30.0 or below, falling rapidly	Rain with high winds followed within 36 hours by clearing and colder in the winter
S to SW	30.0 or below, rising slowly	Clearing in a few hours and fair for several days
S to E	29.8 or below, falling rapidly	Severe storm imminent, followed by clearing in 24 hours and colder in winter
E to N	29.8 or below, falling rapidly	Summer: Severe NE gale and heavy rains Winter: Heavy snow and cold wave
Going to W	29.8 or below, rising rapidly	Clearing and colder in the winter

net storm in Britain was one such bomb; the 1994 Queen's Birthday storm off New Zealand was another.

Incidentally, atmospheric pressure changes with the time of day, regardless of local weather patterns, because of atmospheric pressure waves within a period of 12 hours that regularly sweep around the world from east to west. It varies most at the equator, where it rises and falls about 0.15 inch (5 mb); diurnal change is almost nonexistent at the poles.

The approximate times of the diurnal fluctuations are as follows:

- pressure rises between 4 A.M. and 10 A.M., and between 4 P.M. and 10 P.M.
- pressure falls between 10 A.M. and 4 P.M., and between 10 P.M. and 4 A.M.

See also **Air Masses**.

Barrier Coats

Keeping water away from the hull helps prevent blistering

Since the unwelcome discovery that fiberglass gelcoat can be permeated by water vapor, barrier coats for the underwater portions of hulls have assumed greater importance. The theory is that keeping water away from the surface of the fiberglass will prevent osmosis, the formation of high-pressure blisters between the layers of glass mat or cloth.

Some boatbuilders now use expensive vinylester resin in place of polyester resin because it is more water-resistant, but there is no real consensus concerning the best way to waterproof the underwater hull.

Epoxy manufacturers recommend stripping off all old paint and coating the underwater hull with their special epoxy formulations. Ordinary epoxy resin, however, is not waterproof, merely water-resistant. So perhaps it is significant that they recommend as many as seven barrier coats of special epoxy. In fact, osmosis studies conducted by the University of Rhode Island suggest that several coats of marine-grade enamel paint might work just as well.

There is still much to be learned about the formation of blisters in fiberglass, but it is generally agreed that the inside of the hull—the bilges, the walls of lockers, and so on—should not be barrier-coated because that would only trap any water present in the laminate, making matters worse. If the inside of the hull is simply kept dry and well ventilated, it is likely that unwanted water will evaporate faster than it can penetrate the gelcoat.

See also **Blisters in GRP; Epoxy**.

Battens in Sails

You can, in fact, get along without them—and save money

Ever since the Bermuda rig came into general use some 70 years ago, sailors have been discovering one of its major drawbacks—the need for battens to support the roach of the mainsail.

Battens are a curse, but without their support, the roach—the curved sliver of mainsail that ex-

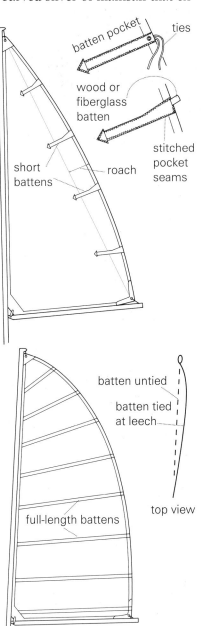

Short battens (top) *extend the leech of a sail into a convex curve, or roach, creating additional sail area but also additional complexity and chafe. Full-length battens* (above) *carry this trend to its extreme, creating a highly efficient airfoil that is also expensive to build and maintain.*

tends above and aft of a straight line drawn from the masthead to the end of the boom—would simply fold over and flap uselessly in the breeze.

Short battens crease and bend the cloth just forward of the pocket, chafing and wearing out the sailcloth. Longer battens put considerable stress on the leech and luff ends of their pockets. Battens of any sort, in fact, add considerably to the cost of maintaining a sail because their pockets so frequently need attention. Sailmakers love battens.

Battens also make handling the sail more difficult—as you know if you've ever tried to douse a mainsail on a dead run—and they often lie awkwardly on the boom when you try to stow the sail.

But if you're not concerned with squeezing the last few ounces of performance out of the mainsail, you don't need battens at all. Many cruising boats choose mainsails with slightly hollow leeches, cut just like headsails. The roach area they lack is only needed off the wind, when you can easily add foresail area to compensate. When you're beating, it's the area near the mast that does nearly all the work, so there's little penalty then.

A mainsail with a hollow leech will clear the backstay more easily when you jibe, and there are no battens to hang up on the spreaders or get caught in the rigging when you want to drop it on a run. It stows better, it's easier to handle, and—here's a bonus—it reduces weather helm in a blow. Its one drawback: without question, it's a

less powerful and efficient sail in a light to moderate breeze.

Battens are also used in performance craft to create better sail shapes, but they come at a price and they're often taken to extremes. There is nothing simple, seaworthy, or inexpensive about a set of full-length battens attached to specially articulated batten cars running up and down the mast. Still, if you do invest in a set, you'll never want for something to fix—or curse—in those moments of boredom.

Battery Choices

How to choose batteries for starting and household needs

There are two main classes of electrical storage batteries for pleasure boats: unsealed and sealed. And there are two main applications: cranking and deep cycling.

Unsealed (or "flooded") lead-acid batteries, the oldest design, operate at atmospheric pressure. They have vent caps open to the air to allow hydrogen and oxygen gases to escape during the charging process. However, because the electrolyte is allowed to "boil away" in this manner, it must be topped off occasionally with distilled water.

Sealed batteries don't allow the electrolyte to escape. They force the gases to recombine, so there is no maintenance to be done. The electrolyte in most sealed batteries is a gel rather than a liquid.

Starting batteries are designed to release a lot of current over a

Gel-cell batteries are sealed, need no maintenance, and will not spill acid if tilted. They make good deep-cycling banks.

short period. They need to be recharged immediately after use and they will be damaged if they are deeply discharged. They are excellent for supplying power to the starter motor that brings a boat's engine to life.

Deep-cycle batteries are designed to deliver current at a lower rate for a much longer period. They may be deeply discharged hundreds of times without damage. They are excellent at supplying the long-term household needs of a boat, but they cannot supply the same huge surge of current to the starter motor that a special starting battery can.

A new generation of batteries tends to blur the distinctions of the various types, combining all the best features. Absorbed glass mat (AGM) batteries are similar to gel batteries, but are not damaged by high charging voltages, as the older gel cells were. Manufacturers claim that they have a high discharge capability but will also withstand deep discharge as well as flooded batteries can. In short, they eliminate the need for two different kinds of battery on board. Some of the batteries manufactured with this new technology are spiral-wrapped, and look like jelly rolls stood on end. They are, of course, more expensive than flooded batteries.

Time will tell how effective and economical AGM batteries are. If you're not willing to experiment, and especially if you're not averse to a little maintenance now and then, the safest bet is still the flooded lead-acid battery in starter or deep-cycle form. For the latter, 6-volt golf cart batteries, linked together for a 12-volt system, will take a lot of abuse and are still an excellent choice.

See also **Amp-Hour Ratings; Battery Needs; Checking a Battery; Cranking Ratings; Locating Batteries**.

AVERAGE DAILY WATT-HOUR TOTALS

Appliance	Watts Consumed	Hours of Use	Daily Watt-Hours
anchor light	10	10	100.0
bilge pump	48	0.2	9.6
cabin fan	12	6	72.0
cabin lights	48	5	240.0
instruments	12	3	36.0
inverter	60	4.3	258.0
AM/FM radio	2	4	8.0
starter motor	2,400	0.006	14.4
SSB radio (on standby)	12	3	36.0
SSB radio (transmit)	240	0.3	72.0
tape deck	15	4	60.0
VHF (receive)	6	12	72.0
VHF (transmit)	60	0.2	12.0
water pump	48	0.25	12.0
windlass	240	0.16	38.4
daily watt-hour total			**1,040.4**

Battery Needs

An easy way to calculate the number of amp-hours required

How many batteries do you need for your boat? It's a simple calculation, but it will take a little time to make a list.

Make a note of the number of watts that each DC electrical item draws and the number of hours, or portions of an hour, it's in use every day. If an item is rated in amps instead of watts, convert to watts by multiplying amps by the battery voltage, which is usually 12 on small boats.

For example, if a cabin light draws 12 watts and it's on for 4 hours each night, list it as 48 watt-hours. If the starter motor draws 2,400 watts and it's used for 20 seconds a day, list it as 20 divided by 3,600 (the number of seconds in an hour) multiplied by 2,400—which is 13 watt-hours.

Divide the total of watt-hours by the voltage of the batteries you want; the answer will be in amp-hours. Batteries are marked with their capacity in amp-hours, so now you know how many you'll need—except for one important step.

The rule of thumb is that *usable* battery capacity is only 40 percent of *stated* capacity. That's because you shouldn't discharge any battery below 50 percent (not even a deep-cycle battery) and because it's difficult to top off the last 10 percent of a battery's charge. Therefore, if you can only use 40 percent of the charge, you need to buy batteries that are 250 percent bigger than your daily requirements. In other words, calculate your need in amp-hours as described previously, and multiply it by $2\frac{1}{2}$.

You might want to increase that final figure by 10 percent to allow for the inevitable increase in demand created by electrical items that find their way onto your boat in the future.

See also **Amp-Hour Ratings; Battery Choices; Checking a Battery; Cranking Ratings; Locating Batteries**.

Beam-to-Length Ratio

See Length-to-Beam Ratio.

Beaufort Scale

An admiral's standardized descriptions of wind speed

In 1805, Sir Francis Beaufort, an admiral and hydrographer in the British navy, established a common scale for wind speeds. It is still widely used by mariners and meteorologists all over the world.

Force 0. Calm. Wind speed less than 1 knot. Sea mirrorlike, smooth. Ideal conditions for seaworthy large powerboats, which are not seriously affected by sea conditions in wind speeds of less than force 7. Sailboats: no steerageway.

Force 1. Light airs. Wind 1 to 3 knots. Small wavelets without crests just forming. Sailboats: just steerageway.

Force 2. Light breeze. Wind 4

FORCE	MPH (KNOTS) *	PRESSURE LBS./ SQ. FT.	DESC.	WAVE PATTERN	WAVE HEIGHTS	EFFECTS ON LAND	SMALL CRUISER
Force 1	1–3 (1–3)	.004–.036	Light airs	Ripples	Flat	Flag hangs limp, windvanes do not respond.	Use motor. Steerageway possible; full main and large drifter.
Force 2	4–7 (4–6)	.064–.196	Light breeze	Small wavelets	0–.5′	Flag stirs, leaves rustle, wind felt on face, wind vanes move.	Boat begins to heel, full main and drifter or #1 genoa.
Force 3	8–12 (7–10)	.256–.576	Gentle breeze	Large wavelets	.5′–2′	Flag occasionally extends, leaves and twigs in constant motion.	Comfortable sailing. Noticeable heeling; full main and #1 genoa.
Force 4	13–18 (11–16)	.676–1.29	Moderate breeze	Small waves; numerous whitecaps	2′–4′	Flag flaps, small branches move, dust and paper raised.	Great sailing. Boat making speed. Full main and #1 genoa.
Force 5	19–24 (17–21)	1.44–2.30	Fresh breeze	Moderate waves; many whitecaps; some spray	4′–8′	Flag ripples, small leafy trees begin to sway.	Leeward rail near water. Single reef in main and #2 genoa.
Force 6	25–31 (22–27)	2.5–3.84	Strong breeze	Larger waves; whitecaps everywhere; more spray	8′–13′	Flag snaps, large branches in motion, whistling in wires.	Sailing becomes strenuous. Second reef in main and working jib.
Force 7	32–38 (28–33)	4.09–5.77	Moderate gale	Sea heaps up; white foam in streaks	12′–15′	Flag extended, whole trees in motion.	Progress to windward impossible. Three reefs in main and working jib.
Force 8	39–46 (34–40)	6.08–8.46	Fresh gale	Waves begin to heighten and roll	14′–19′	Twigs and small branches broken, difficult to walk.	Limit of boat's sailing ability. Use motor or seek shelter.
Force 9	47–54 (41–47)	8.83–11.6	Strong gale	High waves; dense streaks of foam; spray may reduce visibility	18′–24′	Slight structural damage occurs.	Run under bare poles, lie ahull, or sit to sea anchor.
Force 10	55–63 (48–55)	12.1–15.8	Whole gale	Very high rolling waves with long overhanging crests	20′–30′	Trees broken or uprooted, considerable damage.	Swear oaths you will not keep once back on land.

Note: Wind pressure varies greatly according to the shape of an object; pressures indicated are only approximate. Wave patterns are described for large open lakes or oceans. Smaller bodies of water will have diminished wave patterns. Also, wave patterns will be different near abrupt shore features like cliffs, or when the wind is blowing against a current. When judging waves, look into the wind to estimate their size and power, not downwind.

   * MPH: Statute miles (5,280 feet) per hour. Used on inland waters.

    KNOTS: Nautical miles (6,076 feet) per hour. Used at sea or on coastal waters.

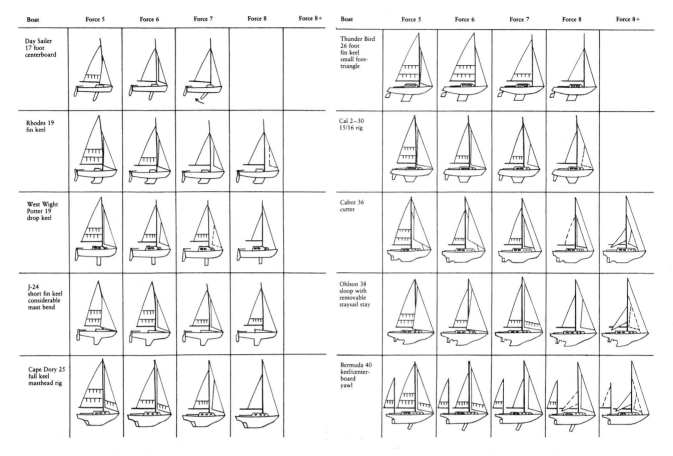

Sail-reduction strategies for representative production boats as drawn by Richard Henderson. These sail reductions are general and need not be relied on literally. Exact strategy would depend on such factors as the number of crew members, sea conditions, whether the boat is racing or cruising, and how the boat is rigged. The reef points illustrated are largely symbolic, since many boats with jiffy reefing use a lacing line rather than reef points to gather the bunt of the sail.

to 6 knots. Short waves with crests. Sailboats handle comfortably and sail 2 to 3 knots.

Force 3. Gentle breeze. Wind 7 to 10 knots. Waves short and more pronounced; their crests begin to break; foam of glassy appearance. Sailboats sail 3 to 5 knots.

Force 4. Moderate breeze. Wind 11 to 16 knots. Waves becoming longer; many white horses formed; breaking seas produce a short, continuous rustling sound. Sailboats sail at hull speed with decided list and some motion.

Force 5. Fresh breeze. Wind 17 to 21 knots. Waves take on a more pronounced, lengthy form with white foam crests. Seas break with a noise like a perpetual murmur. Most sailboats are uncomfortable if close-hauled unless one reef is taken in the mainsail.

Force 6. Strong breeze. Wind 22 to 27 knots. Larger waves, 8 to 12 feet high, begin to form; white foam crests more extensive; seas break with duller "rolling" noise. Sailboats double-reef mainsails and reduce foresail area to working jib or storm jib.

Force 7. Moderate gale. Wind

28 to 33 knots. Seas heap up, with waves 12 to 20 feet high, and spindrift begins to be blown in streaks; noise of breaking seas is heard from a greater distance. A few larger sailboats may make slight progress to windward if seas permit. Most powerboats will be more comfortable running dead downwind. Single-screw vessels might need to stream warps or a storm anchor from the stern to help avoid broaching to.

Force 8. Fresh gale. Wind 34 to 40 knots. Waves still 12 to 20 feet, but growing longer, and spray starts to be whipped off surface. Sailboats heave to under storm trysail or triple-reefed mainsail. Powerboats in danger of broaching to must now be turned head to wind.

Force 9. Strong gale. Wind 41 to 47 knots. Height of waves, and their crests, increases greatly; spindrift occurs in dense streaks; sea begins to "roll"; spray reduces visibility. Sailboats lie ahull or run under bare poles. Powerboats ride most comfortably by taking oncoming waves at about 15 degrees off the bow.

Force 10. Whole gale or storm. Wind 48 to 55 knots. Waves to 30 feet with long, overhanging crests; entire sea surface appears white; rolling of the sea becomes heavy and shocklike. Sailboats run under bare poles, or a storm jib only, using drogues as appropriate to maintain a safe slow speed, and maneuver to avoid the worst breaking seas. Powerboats continue to take oncoming waves at a slight angle at reduced speed.

Force 11. Violent storm. Wind 56 to 63 knots. Waves to 45 feet; seas lengthen; foam patches cover sea. Wind noise intimidating. Sailboats retrieve or cut away drogues and start high-speed scudding downwind under bare

poles. Powerboat skippers no longer try to make forward progress but concentrate on holding a hove-to position 15 to 20 degrees off oncoming waves.

Force 12. Hurricane. Wind 64 knots and higher; noise overwhelming. Waves more than 45 feet; foam and spray fill air; sea completely white. Sailboat crews keep scudding and pray hard. Powerboat skippers make every use of engines and rudders to maintain the hove-to position and avoid at all costs being blown sideways onto the waves.

See also **Drogue; Heavy Weather; Scudding.**

Berths

Making sure you have a comfortable place to sleep

A berth is a sleeping place on a boat, but not all are made equal by any means: many are cramped or too short, some are too wide for comfort and safety at sea, a few are too narrow.

The minimum desirable length for an adult berth is 6 feet, 4 inches (1.93 m), although one berth in four may be only 6 feet, 1 inch (1.85 m) long. The width

should be no less than 21 inches (530 mm), and preferably 24 to 28 inches (610 to 710 mm). At sea, a 21-inch-wide bunk stops you from flopping around when the boat rolls. In harbor, a berth can hardly be too wide for sleeping in, but it can be uncomfortable for sitting on if it doubles as a settee.

The minimum width for a comfortable double berth is 44 inches (1.12 m). The mattress for a double berth is best made in two halves, split down the middle, so that a lee cloth may be brought up between them and made fast overhead for use at sea.

A pipe berth is a more rudimentary type with a frame of light metal supporting a base of canvas. They are often hinged to the side of the boat, folding down flat when not in use. A pipe berth can be a lot more comfortable than its description makes it sound, particularly if you use a 1-inch (25 mm) foam mattress for insulation and a little padding.

Bilge

Defining terms; differences between hard and soft bilges

Strictly speaking, the bilge is the area of a boat's hull between the vertical sides and the bottom. On most sailboats, it's a rounded section; on some sailboats and most powerboats, it's a sharp angle (known as a chine) or series of angles (known as a multiple chine).

A hard or firm bilge defines a section that is sharply rounded. An easy or weak bilge is where the

A reasonably narrow berth of 21 inches (530 mm) or a little more will keep you in place in heavy seas.

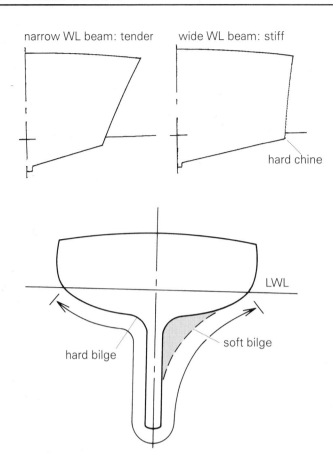

narrow WL beam: tender wide WL beam: stiff

hard chine

LWL

hard bilge soft bilge

The bilge on the powerboats at top is a sharp angle known as a chine. The bilge on a sailboat (bottom) is called "soft" when the curve between the sides and the bottom is gentle, and "hard" when it's sharply rounded.

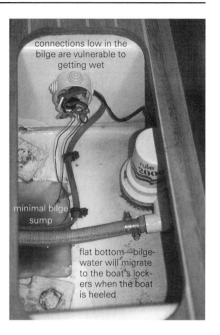

connections low in the bilge are vulnerable to getting wet

minimal bilge sump

flat bottom—bilge-water will migrate to the boat's lockers when the boat is heeled

This electric bilge pump is activated by a float switch when the bilgewater rises to a threshold level. A pump like this will keep your boat afloat when you're away from it, but avoid the installation problems highlighted in this photo.

turn is gentle and through fewer degrees. Hard bilges denote good initial stability; easy bilges indicate a hull that is easily heeled at first.

A second meaning of bilge is the internal part of a boat below the waterline. In this use, we usually speak of the bilges, in the plural. This is where bilgewater collects, as well as anything else that falls (or jumps) out of your hand, including vital parts for the engine you're trying to fix. A magnet on the end of a long dowel is a handy tool for retrieving nuts and bolts that disappear into murky bilgewater.

Many more-or-less flat-bottomed boats (sailboats with dinghylike hull shapes and fin keels, and semidisplacement or planing powerboats) have shallow bilges below the cabin sole. These easily fill with water, which then sloshes around the cabin, making footing treacherous and soaking gear and provisions.

See also **Bilge Pumps; Chines; Deadrise**.

Bilge Pumps

Assessing your pumping needs, both manual and mechanical

Good reliable bilge pumps can save your boat and your life, but they have their limitations. First, few small boats carry pumps that can cope with the flow of water through a fist-sized or bigger hole in the hull. The only way to survive that kind of damage is to repair it immediately, or at least slow the leak so the pumps can handle it.

The normal function of a bilge pump is to remove the water that gathers in the bilges from various sources. Pumps may be worked by electric motors, by mechanical takeoffs from a boat's engine or an auxiliary power plant, or by hand. Most manual bilge pumps are diaphragm pumps; the others are usually rotary pumps of some kind, often turned on and off automatically by a float switch.

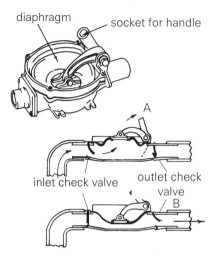

diaphragm   socket for handle

A

inlet check valve   outlet check valve

B

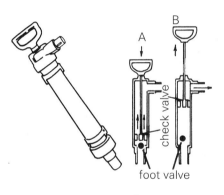

A   B

check valve

foot valve

Most manual pumps operate either with a diaphragm (top) *or a piston* (bottom).

No matter how many mechanical or electrical pumps a seagoing boat might carry, she still needs at least two additional manual pumps. One should be placed handy to the helm in a powerboat, or in the cockpit of a sailboat, so that one person can pump while steering in heavy weather.

It's vital that the intake ends of all suction pipes be fitted with strum boxes—coarse strainers to keep out debris that might clog the pump—that you can reach easily for cleaning.

Don't forget that you would be lucky to pump 15 gallons per minute (GPM) with a manual bilge pump for any extended period, and it takes only a small hole or crack to admit that much water. A 1½-inch (38 mm) hole 6 inches (152 mm) below the waterline admits about 32 GPM. Beware of manufacturers' claimed rates of flow for their pumps. If you have to lift water even a few feet, the flow is drastically reduced.

In an emergency, you might be able to use your toilet pump as a bilge pump. You could also probably use the engine's raw-water pump, but you would need to be extra careful about straining the water; otherwise, you could lose your engine in short order. And never overlook the value of a bucket or two—they move a lot of water and never clog.

Binoculars

Learning what the numbers mean; the classic boat size

The basic rule concerning binoculars is that every boat should carry two pairs: a good expensive pair for your use only, and another inexpensive pair for visitors who keep changing the focus and won't put the strap around their neck.

The classic choice for boat binoculars is 7x50—that is, sevenfold magnification and front lenses 50 mm (2 in.) in diameter. Any greater magnification is counterproductive on a small boat with a lively motion, causing dancing, erratic views in the eyepiece. The larger the front lenses, the better, because they admit more light; 7x50 mm binoculars are good night glasses and will help you locate objects almost invisible to the naked eye at dusk and afterward.

Special image-stabilizing binoculars powered by batteries that use software technology permit magnifications of as much as 14 times, but are not commonly found on small boats because of their expense and extra weight. The same applies to even more expensive night scopes—a spin-off of military applications—that electronically enhance minute amounts of existing light. They don't magnify as much as ordinary night glasses do, but they certainly paint clear pictures of objects you would never otherwise see at night.

Black Box Theory

Earning luck this way will help when the chips are down

You've probably noticed that some boaters have fewer accidents than others. Their boats survive storms in which other boats founder. Their engines keep going when others fail. And when they do get into trouble, it's never serious. Why?

Some people call it luck, but in my opinion, there is no such thing as fortuitous luck at sea. You have to earn your "luck" by constant and deliberate acts of seamanship. If that sounds difficult and complicated, don't let it bother you. This is how I see it:

On every boat there's an imaginary black box. Every time you do something seamanlike, you earn a point for the black box. For example, you get a point for taking the trouble to inspect the chart before you enter an anchorage, and another point for having the right chart in the first place. You earn points for going forward on a cold stormy night to check your running lights, or for changing the fuel filter on your engine on schedule, or for hundreds of other menial and sometimes troublesome little tasks that you would rather not do.

In times of stress—in heavy weather or other threatening circumstances where human skill and endurance can accomplish no more to help the ship—the points are cashed in as protection. You don't have to oversee their withdrawal; they withdraw themselves as appropriate.

Those skippers with no points in the box get into trouble. They're later described as "unlucky"—but we know better. Those skippers with points in the box will survive and be called "lucky," although luck had nothing to do with it. However, having survived, they will need to immediately replenish the points in the black box because the sea offers no credit.

See also **Seamanship; Unlucky Colors.**

Blisters in GRP

The rule? Don't ignore them, catch them at an early stage

If there's one word that can instill fear in the heart of the toughest mariner, it's osmosis. The discovery of osmotic blistering in a glass-reinforced plastic (GRP, or fiberglass) hull often carries the same connotation as a diagnosis of a terminal disease. Boatowners who are advised that the love of their life is suffering from the dreaded boat pox fear the worst. Sometimes their fears are justified because serious cases of osmosis are expensive to cure; however, in many cases, a slight rash of blisters can be no more than a minor nuisance, a problem that you can easily fix yourself.

Because the causes of osmosis are so many and so varied, so too are the results and the cures. There is just one rule that applies to all cases: If you ignore it, it will get worse.

Most blisters start in the outer $1/10$ inch (2.5 mm) of the GRP. One theory is that they're caused by the migration of water vapor through the gelcoat into the laminate, where it reacts with certain chemicals and causes pressure.

Small shallow blisters are more of a cosmetic problem than anything else. They can be drilled out, drained, allowed to dry, filled with epoxy paste, sanded, and sealed. The hull should then be coated with a waterproof barrier and, with any luck, you'll have no more osmosis problems.

Deep blisters that penetrate more than one fifth of the laminate may be structurally serious, leading to delamination. Serious blistering calls for expert attention, and may involve stripping of the gelcoat to allow the laminate to dry out. An experienced surveyor will be able to advise you.

Peeling off the gelcoat and affected laminates and rebuilding with vinylester resin and top coating is an expensive business. It could cost 25 percent or more of the value of a fairly new boat and as much as 75 percent of the value of an older one; therefore, check your hull frequently and catch any blistering at an early stage.

See also **Barrier Coats.**

Block and Tackle

Calculating the mechanical advantage of using blocks

A block is a pulley, or sheave, mounted in a case or frame that's fitted with an eye or shackle to attach it to an object. A second eye or shackle at the opposite end of the block is known as a becket. When two or more blocks are used with a rope or chain for hoisting or hauling, the entire thing is known as a tackle. Sailboats make great use of tackles for trimming sheets and halyards, tightening running backstays, and many other jobs.

The mechanical advantage gained by using two or more blocks in a tackle is known as the purchase. Here's how to calculate the purchase in relative terms: it's equal to the number of lines leading into and away from the moving block only, and includes a line attached to the moving block's

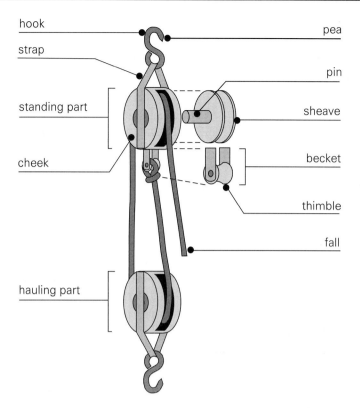

hook
pea
strap
pin
standing part
sheave
cheek
becket
thimble
fall
hauling part

Anatomy of a tackle. This one has a 2:1 advantage since there are two line parts on the moving block or hauling part.

Another way of saying this is that the purchase of a tackle equals the number of parts pulling on the load, with a part identified as either a line leading into or out of the sheave of the moving block or a line attached to the moving block's becket.

In practice, the purchase is never quite that much because of friction in the sheaves, which has traditionally been calculated at one tenth of the load for every sheave over which the line passes. In modern blocks with roller or needle bearings, this figure is probably excessive, but it does build a safety factor into the calculations.

Incidentally, a fixed block adds no power; it merely changes the direction of pull, as does a masthead sheave for a halyard. But when one tackle is applied to the hauling part of another, the total purchase gained is the power of the first multiplied by the power of the second.

See also **Block Sizes; Handy-Billies; Purchases.**

becket. A line attached to the load is not included.

In other words, a moving block with one sheave and a line attached to its becket will give a purchase, or mechanical advantage, of 3 to 1 because there is one line leading into the block, one line leading away from the block, and one line attached.

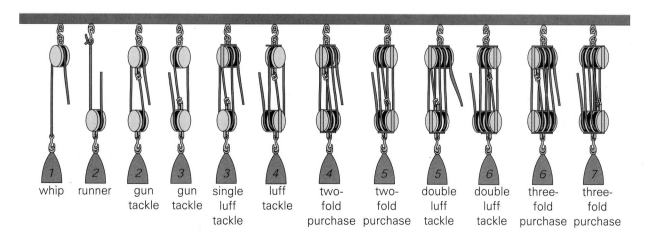

whip	runner	gun tackle	gun tackle	single luff tackle	luff tackle	two-fold purchase	two-fold purchase	double luff tackle	double luff tackle	three-fold purchase	three-fold purchase
1	2	2	3	3	4	4	5	5	6	6	7

A variety of tackles and their associated advantages. Note that the second gun tackle (fourth from left) provides a mechanical advantage of 3:1 because the becket is on the moving block, making three parts at the load. Note that the pull on the fall is in the direction of the lift, meaning that this tackle is rove to advantage.

Block Sizes

Choosing the right size so that lines run free and easy

If the sheave of a block is too small, it forces the line running around it to crimp into an unnaturally tight curve, which can damage and weaken it. Here are the rules of thumb:

- for fiber rope, the sheave diameter should be at least 8 times the diameter of the rope
- for wire rope, the sheave diameter should be at least 20 times the wire diameter, and preferably 40 times

These sizes ensure that the line will render freely through the block, avoiding undue stress on the sheave and obviating the premature wear that results from oversharp turns.

See also **Block and Tackle**.

Boarding Ladders

Why placement is so important for social and health reasons

There are two distinct types of boarding ladder for pleasure boats. One is the familiar stainless steel ladder over the side, or the transom, for recovering swimmers from the sea. The other is a narrow platform consisting of one or two steps, usually slung about halfway up the topsides along the cockpit, for use by crew and guests arriving by boat.

The essential thing to know about the guest ladder is that it should be slung on the starboard side, the superior side of the yacht. The port side of the yacht, as the cognoscenti know well, is used for provisions, fuel, tradesmen, and low-ranking crew members.

The swimmers' ladder is essential equipment unless you tow a dinghy wherever you go, or unless you have a sugar-scoop transom with built-in steps. It is probably the only relatively easy way back on board for someone who has fallen over the side.

Ladders mounted permanently on the stern pulpit may be hinged up out of the water when they're not being used, and they are far more preferable in emergencies than portable side-mounted ladders that must fit into chocks on deck. Incidentally, if you're using a side-mounted ladder, it too should be mounted on the starboard side if the head is to port.

Most ladders are too short. For easier boarding, they should have at least two rungs under water; otherwise, you need significant upper-body strength to haul yourself out of the water, especially if you are wearing heavy sodden clothing.

Many ladders made of stainless steel tubing are also painful to bare feet. For comfort, they need flat teak treads, a couple of inches wide.

On some sailboats with transom-hung rudders, it's possible to carve notches into the rudder itself to form an emergency boarding ladder. On others, hand and foot grips may be bolted to the transom.

See also **Crew Overboard**.

Boat

A yacht by any other name would sound just as sweet

There is some confusion about exactly what constitutes a boat.

Webster's New World Dictionary, Second College Edition, gives these definitions: "1. a small open vessel or watercraft propelled by oars, sails, or engine. 2. a large vessel; ship: landsman's term." (One shouldn't scoff too much, of course. That does at least narrow it down to the fact that a boat is either a small vessel or a large one.)

The Concise Oxford Dictionary is a little less confused: "1. small, open, oared or engined or sailing vessel, fishing vessel, mail packet, or small steamer."

The *Encyclopedia of Nautical Knowledge* describes a yacht as "the term usually given to small craft, although lake, river, and excursion vessels, also ferries, regardless of build or means of propulsion, are generally called boats. As distinguished from a vessel, a boat has no continuous deck . . . "

The *Encyclopedia Britannica* described it in 1771 as "a fmall open veffel, commonly wrought by rowing."

Chapman Piloting: Seamanship and Small Boat Handling freely admits that "The term has no precise definition" and then goes on to define it quite precisely: "It is a waterborne vehicle smaller than a ship . . . one definition of a boat is a small craft, such as a lifeboat, carried on board a ship. Many consider a boat as being not over 65 feet in length. Another dividing point might be 65.7 feet (20

meters) as used in the Navigation Rules."

The body that develops and publishes safe standards for the boatbuilding industry calls itself the American Boat and Yacht Council (ABYC), thereby drawing an undefined distinction between boats and yachts.

In any case, for our purposes a boat is what a yacht used to be before that term fell out of favor. Yachts are not much referred to in these enlightened times because no politically correct term has been found to replace the gender-specific *yachtsman*. We talk now not of yachts and yachtsmen but of boats and boaters, and we do our best to forget that the dictionary definition of a boater is "a stiff hat of braided straw, with a flat crown and brim."

See also **Dinghies**.

Booms

Working out the correct proportions for these spars

The boom is a spar—usually wood or aluminum—along which the foot of a sail is stretched and fastened. Despite what many sailors think, it's not true that a boom is named after the noise it makes when it hits your head during an accidental jibe. The fact is that *boom* is the Dutch word for tree or pole.

Most booms are made of aluminum these days, of course, and here are the recommended minimum proportions:

- simple round aluminum booms: diameter, $\frac{1}{45}$ of over-

all length; wall thickness, $\frac{1}{26}$ of diameter

- elliptical-section booms: width (transverse section), $\frac{1}{50}$ of length; height (vertical section), $1\frac{1}{2}$ times width; wall thickness, $\frac{1}{26}$ of width

See also **Sailboat Rigs**.

Borers

Using preservative to protect wooden hulls from being eaten

Although wood is a wonderful material for boats, it does suffer from the disadvantage that marine borers eat it, leaving long tunnels that destroy its strength.

The carpenter ants of the sea, borers attack any wood that is not protected by paint or a poisonous preservative; even wooden docks and pilings are not immune. It is important, therefore, that a wooden boat be well painted with an antifouling paint, sealed with an epoxy the borers cannot penetrate, or sheathed in fiberglass or similar cloth and resin (traditionally copper was used). Borers are present in almost all salt water and brackish water in the United States, but they breed more prolifically in warmer waters.

Shipworms consist of species of *Teredo* and *Bankia*, which start off as tiny free-swimming creatures that soon attach themselves to wood and then grow a pair of boring shells. These so-called worms are thus, in fact, mollusks. They can bore holes up to 4 feet long and create a virtual honeycomb from solid timber.

Limnoria worms, better known as gribble, are crustaceans less than $\frac{1}{4}$ inch in length that bore into surface wood. Colonies of these worms working close together can remove so much material that the surface sloughs off, creating fresh provender for them.

Clamlike mollusks, which are known as *Martesia* and can grow to a size of $2\frac{1}{2}$ inches long and 1 inch in diameter, are widespread in the Gulf of Mexico, where they burrow deeply into wood creating large holes.

Sphaeroma are like large gribble worms, but fortunately they are not as numerous, although they are also sometimes found in fresh water.

See also **Antifouling Paints**.

Bosun's Chair

Going up the mast requires planning, careful inspection

A boatswain is a warrant officer in the U.S. and British navies, or a subordinate officer in the merchant marine, who is responsible for most things that happen on deck. The word *boatswain* is pronounced *bosun* and has also come to be spelled so.

A bosun's chair is used to haul a sailor up the mast on a halyard to do repair work or inspect the rigging. It was once a wooden plank with stout lines passing underneath it and up into a bridle at chest level. Its weaknesses were that it was hard to sit on for any length of time and there was no back support. You could easily fall backward out of the chair. Consequently, you had only one hand to

B

work with aloft because the other was permanently engaged in a convulsive grip on the nearest spar or rigging wire.

The plank has now largely been ousted by fabric chairs with comfortable backs and cushioned seats for today's pampered derrieres. It's almost impossible to accidentally fall out of one of these bosun's armchairs, so it's much easier to use two hands for the work aloft. These chairs often also incorporate built-in pockets for

tools and gear; there's no need to send all that stuff up in a separate bucket.

Some bosun's chairs are more like circus acrobats' harnesses, attaching near the hips and allowing you to swirl and spin and do cartwheels aloft—if that is what the skipper requires. These are really climbing harnesses, not chairs, and you'll see them in action in the America's Cup series, when some poor foredeck hand has to go up in midrace to untan-

gle a snarl of lines or canvas. They might also have some appeal to athletic sailors seeking a little adventure on otherwise boring trips to the masthead.

No matter what kind of chair you use, you are at the mercy of the winchers and tailers down below. Never trust them. Be sure to take a personal safety tether with you and clip it on at every opportunity. Inspect the halyard thoroughly before you are hoisted on it, and don't trust the clip or shackle that normally joins it to the head of the sail. Use a light line to bind the chair's bridle to the halyard, if possible, and take many turns. Or, if there are plenty of slackers about on deck, have them devise a second safety halyard for you, and clip it on.

Cruising boats often have mast steps that allow you to climb up without having to depend on anyone else for help, but they create significant windage and are expensive to install. There are also temporary steps comprising loops of Dacron tape sewn to stout line. To use them, hoist the line in the mast groove where the mainsail luff or slides normally fit. In theory, it's a good idea; in practice, it's not as easy as you might think. But it's certainly a convenient piece of gear for a single-handed voyager.

Some enterprising sailors haul themselves up the mast in a bosun's chair by using counter-weights. Fill some plastic jugs with water and raise them to the masthead on a halyard. Then attach the chair to the halyard, and let the weight of the jugs pull you up the mast. You no doubt will sense the danger inherent when

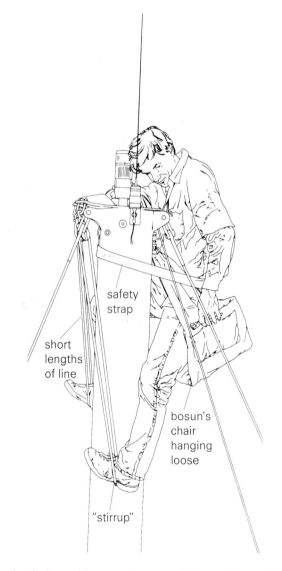

safety strap

short lengths of line

bosun's chair hanging loose

"stirrup"

A bosun's chair enables you to ascend the mast on a halyard for repair work or to inspect the rigging. Modern fabric chairs incorporate pockets for tools.

the water jugs weigh more than you do: you could ascend to the masthead much faster than you anticipated, and spend a lot more time up there than you had planned.

Beware, too, of stepping out of the bosun's chair straight onto the deck. Without your weight to counterbalance them, the water jugs will descend speedily and smite you mightily upon the head. If you're using jugs, be sure to think deeply before you act.

Yet another alternative means of going aloft solo is to ascend a rope by means of rock-climbing aids, such as mechanical ascenders (which slide up the rope, then grip when needed) and prusik knots (which accomplish much the same thing).

See also **Mast Steps**.

Bottom Painting

Treading the fine line between pollution, protection

Painting a boat's bottom was once a comparatively casual affair. People used to put their boats on sandbanks or lean them against posts and paint them between tides; however, now it's a much more high-tech operation in which all old scrapings of bottom paint are carefully collected in dammed enclosures and carefully disposed of as hazardous waste.

There's no doubt that bottom paint is harmful to the environment. That's the whole point. The environment is trying to grow on the bottom of our boats, and we don't want it there because it

slows our boat down and makes it unmanageable.

The pressure from the non-boating community—that is, the majority of the world—is to ban antifouling paints that harm marine life. Tin, probably the most effective biocide ever tried on boats, has already been banned for all except aluminum-hulled boats, and there is now a movement to ban the old standby, copper.

So far, no reasonable alternative to copper has been found for boats that stay in the water year-round. The search continues for a coating that will discourage the growth of barnacles and other mollusks, as well as slime and grass, without harming other marine organisms.

The pollution problem has been exacerbated by the trend to herd ever-greater numbers of boats into the tight confines of marinas, where the water quality is affected by greater concentrations of biocides "leaking" from bottom paint.

On the practical side, the golden rule about bottom painting is to attack marine growths immediately after the boat is hauled out. Don't ever let the bottom get dry before you start scraping. Weed, slime, and barnacles will harden and set like concrete if you let them dry on the hull.

Most boatyards have high-pressure hoses to remove bottom growth straight after haulout; if not, keep the bottom wet with spray from a hose or splashes from buckets until you're ready to scrape. If you're planning to smooth the bottom, use water-

proof paper and wet-sand it; if you dry-sand antifouling paint, the dust spreads everywhere and you'll breathe in more than is good for you. Let the bottom dry well before you paint.

See also **Antifouling Paints**.

Bower and Kedge

Clearing up confusion about two essential anchors on board

The bower is a ship's principal working anchor. The kedge is smaller, often used in conjunction with the bower, but sometimes alone. Kedging is the act of maneuvering a vessel by hauling on a line attached to a light kedge anchor laid out in the direction required.

For some reason, the kedge is often wrongly presumed to be of the traditional fisherman's anchor design, with its spidery shank, stock, and flukes. It could be, but not necessarily.

Eric Hiscock's classic, *Cruising Under Sail*, gives the following definition: "Kedge. An anchor smaller than the bower, often used with a fiber cable instead of a chain. Used for hauling a vessel off when she has gone aground and to prevent her from fouling her bower."

Usually, if the two working anchors are similar types, the kedge is about two thirds the weight of the bower. But if the bower anchor is a plow and the kedge is a lightweight pivoting fluke, the kedge may be about half the weight of the bower.

See also **Anchors, Anchoring**.

B

Brake and Shaft Horsepower

Not all the engine's power reaches the propeller

Manufacturers of marine engines usually quote the horsepower of the engine with its auxiliaries, such as the water pump and alternator, coupled up—but some advertise the horsepower without these loads.

It may be useful to inquire about the terminology the manufacturer is using. Brake horsepower is measured at the crankshaft; shaft horsepower is the actual amount of power delivered to the propeller. The latter will be less than the former because of friction losses in the transmission and the stern gland. If the engine is not correctly aligned, the losses will be greater. As a rule of thumb, shaft horsepower in small craft is usually between 70 and 90 percent of brake horsepower.

See also **Powerboat Engines; Sailboat Engines; Torque.**

Brightwork

Painting wood: the sensible road that's not often taken

The word *brightwork* usually means exterior varnished wood these days but, in fact, it defines all metal objects on a boat that are kept bright by polishing. It also includes wood that is either left untreated or is oiled or varnished but not painted.

Fortunately, few small pleasure boats have metal objects on deck that need regular polishing, although stainless steel stanchions and pulpits usually benefit from a yearly polish to remove brown salt stains. Bronze cleats and port-surrounds develop a patina that most boaters regard as pleasing, and aluminum spars are never polished anyway.

That leaves wood, which is always a problem. Boatbuilders use teak for exterior trim, decks, coamings, caprails, hatchboards, and so on because its natural oils resist rot. Teak looks shipshape even when it's not maintained at all. It mostly turns an attractive silvery gray, except in polluted regions, where it soon turns a murky brown. When teak is oiled or varnished, the effect is magnificent. Thus, few boaters can bring themselves to paint teak, which is really the only sensible thing to do with it.

Untreated teak needs to be

Choosing the Finish

There are countless variations on the varnish and oil themes, and an ideal "finish program" can be formulated only when one understands not just what is *in* the can, but how the contents of that can relate to the wood being finished.

- Varnish brings out the beauty in wood and is the strongest protector of all the bright finishes. Beauty arrives by the third coat, but protection does not come into play until after the eighth. Eight to ten coats of varnish provide the best finish foundation for follow-up varnish management.
- A true oil finish also brings out the beauty in wood but affords exterior wood little if not completely transient protection. Oil finishes require the same amount of prep labor as varnish, then disappear in a matter of months without constant (read: monthly!) refresher coats. I have another name for "oil finish" on exteriors. It is "full-time job."
- A "sealer" is not a finish. It is a thin, solvent-intense formula meant *only* to deliver a "seal" to the deepest reaches of the wood's grain, in preparation for a subsequent application of an oil or varnish. That seal will last fully intact about a week when exposed to the weather.
- Bare wood is the "no-finish" finish option. It looks easy, but it demands initial prep similar to that given wood slated for a finish: properly bleached and sanded, and faithful, appropriate cleaning to forestall mildew. The decision to leave wood bare first requires that it be a wood that can survive without a finish. Teak, with its natural storehouse of oils, is an ideal "bare wood." So is ironwood. Mahogany fares best—and shows off its most beautiful self—with varnish protection. Veneer of any kind should *never* be left bare.

— Rebecca J. Wittman, in *The Brightwork Companion*

scrubbed regularly, preferably with salt water, and bleached occasionally. Oiled teak calls for frequent attention and also needs to be scrubbed down periodically to bare wood. Varnished teak demands considerable attention and many protective coats.

It's the sun that makes varnish deteriorate, of course, so exterior varnish is loaded with filters that trap the damaging ultraviolet rays. However, it's still necessary to give most varnish a rubdown every few months and apply another coat or two.

The more solids there are in the varnish, the better the wood will be protected from the sun. But some longer-lasting wood finishes are so loaded with filters that they take on an orange or brown hue that begins to look like paint.

There is still nothing that emphasizes the natural beauty of teak more than multiple coats of deep, glossy, clear varnish. Thus, despite the drudgery, some boaters continue to apply it . . . and apply it . . . and apply it.

See also **Teak Finishes; Varnishing; Varnishing Details.**

Broaching To

How to avoid being turned sideways to menacing seas

Mr. Webster's admirable dictionary calmly defines broaching to as "to turn or swing so that the beam faces the waves and wind, and there is danger of swamping or capsizing." It's a lot more frightening when it actually occurs.

It can happen to almost any

small boat, power or sail, that's running downwind in heavy weather. A breaking wave rushing up from aft grips the stern, lifting it and pushing it sideways suddenly while the bow digs in deeply and holds its ground. The resulting momentum can easily capsize a powerboat or dismast a sailboat.

Even if the worst doesn't happen immediately, a boat that has broached to will be lying broadside to other approaching waves, and might find herself in a particularly vulnerable position if she is attempting to carve a course through lines of surf while running an inlet.

A small boat is most in danger of broaching to when she is running at about the same speed as the overtaking waves. Slowing her down by reducing engine power or by using drogues (while still maintaining adequate steerageway) will allow the waves to pass beneath her more quickly and affect her course less.

Running straight before breaking waves, rather than taking them at a 45-degree angle to the stern, also usually reduces the chances of broaching to (while possibly increasing the chances of pitchpoling), but it depends on many things, including the underwater shape of the hull and the state of the sea. In fact, the recommendation of some experienced sailors, including Bernard Moitessier, is to bear off slightly—just 20 degrees or so—when taking a wave from astern in "survival weather."

Although it is important to know the general principles, the truth is that every boat is so indi-

vidual that only actual experience in a gale will tell you what is best for your boat.

Some boats are far more prone than others to tripping up on their bows and broaching to, and some sailors are better than others at anticipating that sudden sickening lurch and maneuvering the boat to avoid it. If the situation seems to be getting out of control and broaching to appears inevitable, it is wise to try to face the waves. Powerboats can take the waves slowly at an angle of 20 degrees or so, and sailboats might be able to heave to under a deep-reefed mainsail or trysail. A powerboat or a shallow-drafted multihull might also lie safely to a sea anchor streamed from the bow, but most deep-keeled sailboats will not be happy this way in really heavy weather, lying broadside on no matter what happens.

See also **Heavy Weather; Pitchpoling; Scudding.**

Bulwarks

Keeping gear and people on deck where they belong

Bulwarks are low walls built around the edge of the deck. They're a seaworthy addition to any oceangoing boat, but few production boats carry them because they increase the cost and they appear old-fashioned if they're not well designed.

There's nothing more efficient at preventing gear and sails from sliding overboard, and bulwarks give the crew a better foothold too. Some boats carry bulwarks that are an extension of the top-

B

sides, others have separate wooden bulwarks raised an inch or so from deck level to let water efficiently drain off the decks. Bulwarks provide excellent stiffening for lifeline stanchions and they can be shaped to make a boat's sheerline more attractive.

Almost any bulwark is better than the paltry wooden or aluminum toerail most boatbuilders supply, but the deeper it is, the better: 3 inches (75 mm) is passable, but 4 inches (100 mm) is better; 8 inches (200 mm) is wonderful and can be incorporated on a boat only 30 feet (9 m) in length.

See also **Yacht Design**.

Buoyage Systems

Floating aids to navigation defined by two major systems

Buoys are used by maritime nations as floating traffic signs. They direct you to safe, deep water, and away from dangers such as shoal water, isolated rocks, wrecks, and reefs.

There are two basic systems. Under the lateral system, floating buoys mark the edges of traffic lanes and channels. Distinct shapes, colors, and numbers are used to distinguish between the port and starboard sides of channels. Under the cardinal system, a buoy indicates the direction in which danger lies according to the cardinal points of the compass.

The International Association of Lighthouse Authorities (IALA) drew up two systems of buoyage. Most countries in the world use the IALA-A System, but the IALA-B system is used in North and South America, Japan, Korea, the Philippines, and some parts of the Caribbean. One big difference between the two systems is that the color of the buoys on either side of a channel is reversed.

Under the IALA-B system used in the United States, *green can buoys with odd numbers mark the port side* of a channel leading from the open sea to a harbor. They should be on your port side as you enter harbor. *Red nun buoys with even numbers mark the starboard side* of the safe channel, and should be on your starboard side. Remember the old memory aid: *Red right returning.*

If you have difficulty knowing which side of a channel that a buoy is marking, remember that you can tell from its shape, its number, or its color. Nun buoys are conical, or pointed, on top; can buoys are flat.

A mnemonic that has helped me for many years is: *Even red nuns carry odd green cans.* In my mind's eye, I see Russian nuns carrying large milk cans to the convent. Milk cans aren't normally green; that's what makes them odd.

Unfortunately, buoys with lights on them don't necessarily have to conform to the nun or can shape. From a distance in daylight, most lighted buoys look like can buoys with their middles missing, but their silhouettes give

metal stanchion

hardwood bulwark

heavy-wall tube for stanchion socket

reinforcing pad

A rugged bulwark installation that allows water on deck to drain overboard quickly.

LATERAL MARKS — REGION A

This diagram is schematic and in the case of pillar buoys in particular, their features will vary with the individual design of the buoys in use.

PORT HAND	STARBOARD HAND
Colour: Red.	Colour: Green.
Shape: Can, pillar or spar.	Shape: Conical, pillar or spar.
Topmark (when fitted): Single red can.	Topmark (when fitted): Single green cone point upward.
Retroreflector: Red band or square.	Retroreflector: Green band or triangle.

DIRECTION OF BUOYAGE

LIGHTS, when fitted, may have any rhythm other than composite group flashing (2+1) used on modified Lateral marks indicating a preferred channel. Examples are:

	Red light			Green light	
Q.R		Continuous-quick light			Q.G
Fl.R		Single-flashing light			Fl.G
LFl.R		Long-flashing light			LFl.G
Fl(2)R		Group-flashing light			Fl(2)G

The lateral colours of red or green are frequently used for minor shore lights, such as those marking pierheads and the extremities of jetties.

PREFERRED CHANNELS

At the point where a channel divides, when proceeding in the conventional direction of buoyage, a preferred channel is indicated by

Preferred channel to starboard	Preferred channel to port
Colour: Red with one broad green band.	Colour: Green with one broad red band.
Shape: Can, pillar or spar.	Shape: Conical, pillar or spar.
Topmark (when fitted): Single red can.	Topmark (when fitted): Single green cone point upward.
Retroreflector: Red band or square.	Retroreflector: Green band or triangle.

DIRECTION OF BUOYAGE

Red light		Green light
Fl(2+1)R	Composite group flashing (2+1) light	Fl(2+1)G

NOTES

Where port or starboard marks do not rely on can or conical buoy shapes for identification, they carry the appropriate topmark where practicable.

Even numbers are to port, odd to starboard, increasing from seaward.

LATERAL MARKS — REGION B

This diagram is schematic and in the case of pillar buoys in particular, their features will vary with the individual design of the buoys in use.

PORT HAND

Colour: Green.

Shape: Can, pillar or spar.

Topmark (when fitted): Single green can.

Retroreflector: Green band or square.

DIRECTION OF BUOYAGE

STARBOARD HAND

Colour: Red.

Shape: Conical, pillar or spar.

Topmark (when fitted): Single red cone, point upward.

Retroreflector: Red band or triangle.

LIGHTS, when fitted, may have any rhythm other than composite group flashing (2+1) used on modified Lateral marks indicating a preferred channel. Examples are:

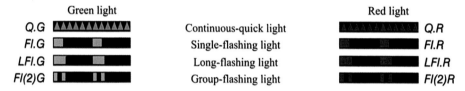

Green light		Red light
Q.G	Continuous-quick light	Q.R
Fl.G	Single-flashing light	Fl.R
LFl.G	Long-flashing light	LFl.R
Fl(2)G	Group-flashing light	Fl(2)R

The lateral colours of red or green are frequently used for minor shore lights, such as those marking pierheads and the extremities of jetties.

PREFERRED CHANNELS

At the point where a channel divides, when proceeding in the conventional direction of buoyage, a preferred channel is indicated by

Preferred channel to starboard

Colour: Green with one broad red band.

Shape: Can, pillar or spar.

Topmark (when fitted): Single green can.

Retroreflector: Green band or square.

DIRECTION OF BUOYAGE

Preferred channel to port

Colour: Red with one broad green band.

Shape: Conical, pillar or spar.

Topmark (when fitted): Single red cone point upward.

Retroreflector: Red band or triangle.

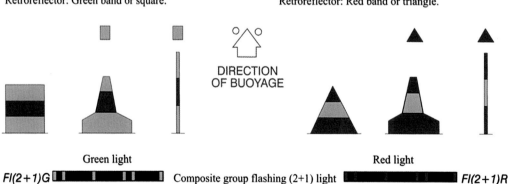

Green light   Fl(2+1)G   Composite group flashing (2+1) light   Fl(2+1)R   Red light

NOTES

Where port or starboard marks do not rely on can or conical buoy shapes for identification, they carry the appropriate topmark where practicable.

Even numbers are to port, odd to starboard, increasing from seaward.

REGION A

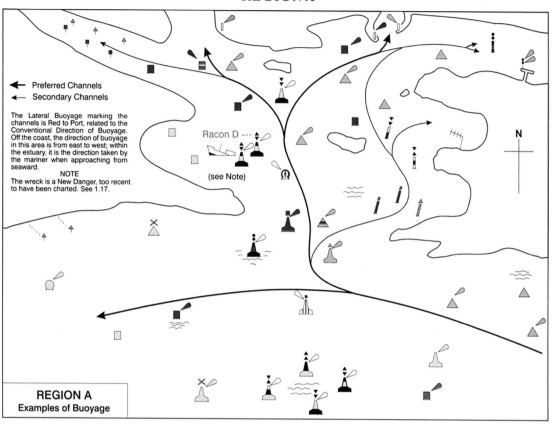

REGION A
Examples of Buoyage

Preferred Channels

Secondary Channels

The Lateral Buoyage marking the channels is Red to Port, related to the Conventional Direction of Buoyage. Off the coast, the direction of buoyage in this area is from east to west; within the estuary, it is the direction taken by the mariner when approaching from seaward.

NOTE
The wreck is a New Danger, too recent to have been charted. See 1.17.

Racon D

(see Note)

N

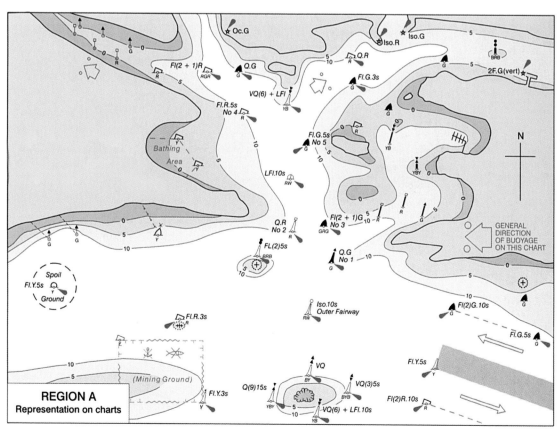

REGION A
Representation on charts

REGION B

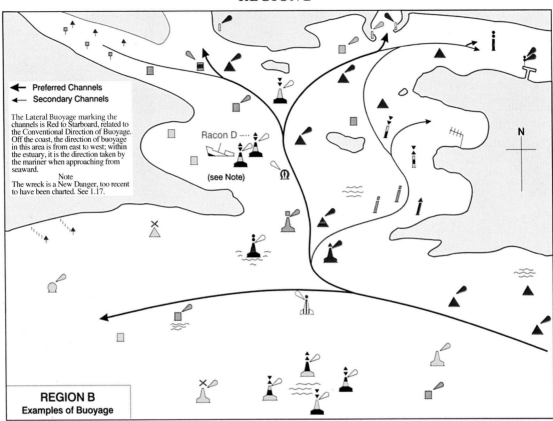

Preferred Channels

Secondary Channels

The Lateral Buoyage marking the channels is Red to Starboard, related to the Conventional Direction of Buoyage. Off the coast, the direction of buoyage in this area is from east to west; within the estuary, it is the direction taken by the mariner when approaching from seaward.

Note
The wreck is a New Danger, too recent to have been charted. See 1.17.

Racon D

(see Note)

N

REGION B
Examples of Buoyage

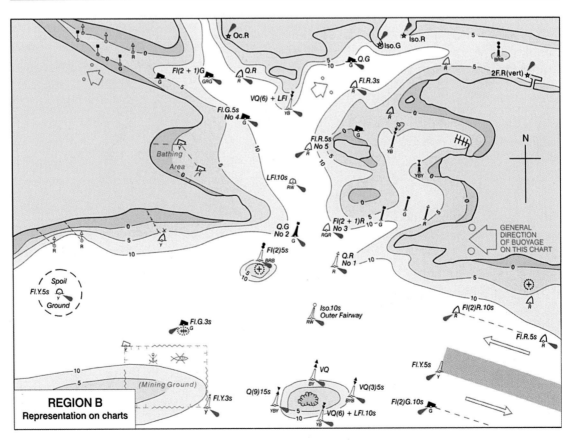

REGION B
Representation on charts

no indication of which side of the channel they guard. There's no problem at night, of course, when they flash the appropriate red or green color. But during the day there's no telling from their shape alone what they might be; you have to wait until you can see a color or a number.

Red-and-green horizontally banded buoys mark junctions in a channel or isolated dangers that you may pass on either side. If the topmost band is green, the buoy acts as an all-green buoy; that is, it should be on your port side, and the preferred channel is to starboard of it. If the topmost band is red, treat it as an all-red buoy and leave it on your port side.

A red-and-white buoy with vertical stripes marks the middle of a channel or fairway, and you may go on either side of it.

The lateral system is uniformly used in all U.S. waters under federal jurisdiction and in inland lakes and rivers where it can be applied. However, because channels don't always conveniently lead from seaward to a harbor, there has to be some arbitrary way to apply the lateral system to offshore buoys along the coast. This is how it works: *Proceeding in a clockwise direction around the U.S. coast is considered the equivalent of returning from sea.* That means if you're traveling south off the East Coast, west off the Gulf Coast, and north along the Pacific Coast, you are regarded as returning from sea.

On the Great Lakes, the equivalent direction is from the outlet end of each lake toward its upper end, which will normally be toward the north and west.

The exception is Lake Michigan, where the upper end is southward. Channels leading into ports are marked in the usual manner, just as coastal channels are.

On the Mississippi and Ohio Rivers and their tributaries, buoys and other aids to navigation are marked as if *returning from sea* were upstream, proceeding toward the head of navigation.

See also **Piloting**.

Buys Ballot's Law

Determining the center of an oncoming low-pressure center

This is the law that helps you determine where the center of an approaching depression lies, so that you can take action at sea to avoid it.

Christoph Hendrik Diederik Buys Ballot (1817–1890) was a Dutch scientist who founded the Royal Netherlands Meteorological Institute. He realized that if you face directly into the wind in the Northern Hemisphere, the center of the low atmospheric pressure is between 90 and 110 degrees on your right hand. Higher pressure lies to your left, of course.

South of the equator, low pressure is on your left hand when you face the wind, and barometric pressure increases on your right hand.

If the approaching storm system is still some distance away while you're at sea, you might be able to place yourself to the north or south of it before it arrives, thereby missing the worst winds and waves.

See also **Air Masses**.

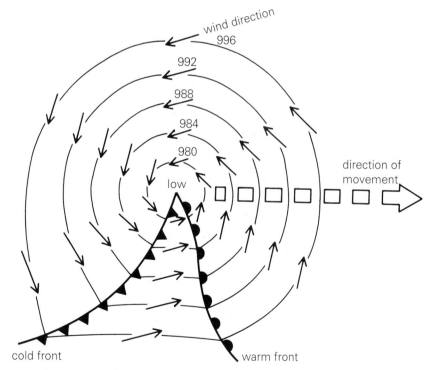

Notice the wind-direction arrows in this Northern Hemisphere low-pressure system. Buys Ballot's Law says that if you face directly into the wind, the center of the low is between 90 and 110 degrees on your right.

C

Calling for Help

The many ways to attract assistance in an emergency

Although the U.S. Coast Guard requires you to carry certain distress signals, they aren't the only way to attract help in an emergency. Here is the list of approved signals from the International Regulations for Preventing Collisions at Sea (COLREGs), which are the nautical rules of the road. Used or exhibited either together or singly, they indicate distress and need of assistance:

- a gun or other explosive signal fired at intervals of about a minute
- a continuous sounding with any fog-signaling apparatus
- rockets or shells, throwing red stars, fired one at a time at short intervals
- a signal made by radiotelegraphy or by any other signaling method consisting of the group SOS in Morse code
- a signal sent by radiotelephony consisting of the spoken word "Mayday"
- the International Code Signal of distress indicated by flags N and C

- a signal consisting of a square flag, having above or below it a ball or anything resembling a ball
- flames on the vessel (e.g., from a burning tar or oil barrel)
- a rocket parachute flare or a hand flare showing a red light
- a smoke signal giving off orange-colored smoke
- slowly and repeatedly raising and lowering arms outstretched to each side

 Gun or other explosive signals fired at intervals of about a minute.

 Rockets or shells throwing red stars (not white stars) one at a time at short intervals.

"MAYDAY" Spoken word *Mayday* sent by radio.

 International code flags N and C in vertical line, with N close on top.

 Open flames, as from a burning bucket of oil or tar.

 Handheld flare showing a red light.

 Raising and lowering outstretched arms slowly and repeatedly.

 Continuous sounding with any fog signaling apparatus.

 SOS signals in Morse code by any method, including radio, sound, or light.

 The letters N and C in Morse code.

 A rectangular flag or shape with a ball, or anything resembling a ball, below it.

 Rocket parachute flare showing a red light.

Smoke signal giving off orange smoke.

 Alarm signals from an EPIRB, or radiotelephone.

Approved distress signals from the International Regulations for Preventing Collisions at Sea, or COLREGs.

- the radiotelegraph alarm signal
- the radiotelephone alarm signal
- signals transmitted by an emergency position-indicating radio beacon (EPIRB)

It's illegal to use any of the signals or any that may be confused with them if you are not in need of assistance.

The following two signals are also officially recognized and are useful to air search-and-rescue teams:

- a piece of orange-colored cloth with either a black square and circle or another appropriate symbol
- a dye marker

If you're expecting help from the air, place the orange flag flat on the deck or cabintop.

See also **Distress Signals**.

Capsize

Breaking waves and their effect; contributing factors

Seaworthy powerboats are designed to resist capsize by careful calculation of their centers of gravity and buoyancy. As long as they maintain power and are correctly handled, they are relatively immune to capsize in anything less than full gale-force winds. Planing hulls gain stability at speed; displacement hulls often have passive or active stabilizers that reduce rolling as long as the boat is moving.

But a powerboat that loses power in heavy weather is vulnerable to capsize. Unless a sea anchor is deployed to keep her head-on to the seas, she will tend to lie beam-on to wind and waves. In this position, she is likely to sustain structural damage and flooding from damaged ports, which, if severe, will cause her to roll over with no chance of recovery.

Even sailboats with heavy ballast keels can capsize because the usual cause of a 180-degree capsize is wave action, not wind action. Correctly ballasted keelboats will, however, right themselves from an upside-down position if they are correctly proportioned and watertight.

According to tests conducted at Southampton University in England, any monohull sailboat can be "turned turtle" by a breaking wave with a height equal to 55 percent of her overall length. Thus, a 35-foot (10.7 m) boat would be capsized through 180 degrees by a 20-foot (6 m) wave—which could result from a 40-knot wind blowing for 40 hours. Even a breaking wave with a height equaling only 35 percent of the boat's length (12 ft. or 3.7 m for a 35-footer) would roll her 130 degrees, from which position she could either turn turtle or recover.

A yacht at sea is a dynamic system that receives energy from waves—energy of which it must rid itself. A "traditional" keel and hull shape are effective at dissipating this energy gradually to the water beneath. A fin-keeled boat has less area in contact with the sea and is more

The traditional hull and keel of the Southern Cross is very resistant to capsize and will recover quickly if she turns turtle.

vulnerable to capsize if she's lying still in the water. Therefore, she should be kept moving—the better to dissipate the incoming wave energy into a greater area of water.

The traditional hull—the old-fashioned fishing-boat type of hull with a long keel and short overhangs—is better at slowing down rolling, and so can look after herself better when she's lying almost still in the water, ahull or hove-to.

Nevertheless, no hull is absolutely safe from capsize, and if a boat continues to turn upside down, the efficiency of the ballast keel keeps tapering off until it is sticking straight up in the air—at which stage it has no righting effect whatsoever.

But if your boat's beam is reasonably narrow and her keel is quite deep, any approaching wave will tend to heel her over, so that the weight of the keel falls to one side and starts to gain some righting momentum again.

If your boat has excessively wide beam, it will be much more difficult for the waves to tilt her sufficiently for the keel to exert any righting pressure. You may recall that capsized 60-foot boats taking part in the Vendée Globe race have spent many *days* upside down in the Southern Ocean with their keels sticking up in the air.

Many racing boats have this excessive beam because it provides initial stability and enables them to carry more sail and plane faster. They pay for it, however, when they are capsized by a breaking wave. Modern coastal cruisers often carry excessive beam, too—not only because they tend to mimic the racers, but also because it provides more accommodation and stowage space below.

See also **Capsize Screening; Center of Buoyancy; Center of Gravity; Length-to-Beam Ratio; Pitchpoling; Plunging Breakers; Stability; Stability Limits.**

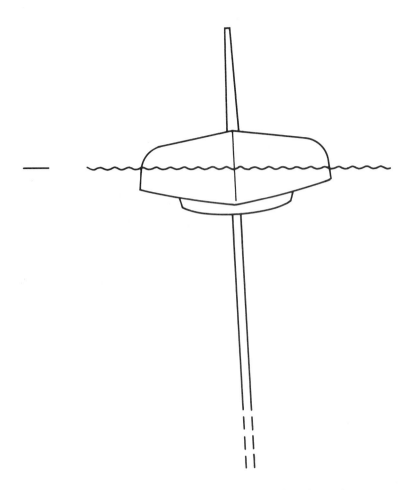

Above: A boat with a wide shallow hull will take a long time to recover from a capsize and may ship enough water while inverted to sink her. *Right:* Capsize screening values for production sailboats. Anything below 2.0 should be safe offshore.

Capsize Screening

Estimating a sailboat's chances of capsizing at sea

You can estimate your sailboat's chances of capsizing at sea with a simple formula devised by the U.S. Yacht Racing Union (now U.S. Sailing Association) after the disastrous 1979 Fastnet Race in Great Britain, when about half the fleet of oceangoing racers suffered knockdowns or capsizes.

The formula is based purely on beam and displacement—two factors regarded as most important in preventing capsize. Wide boats give the waves more leverage to initiate a roll, and wide beam in shallow boats makes it difficult for them to recover from a 180-degree capsize, as demonstrated so graphically among the 60-footers sailed by single-handed around-the-world racers. On the other hand, comparatively narrow boats demonstrate more inertia; that is, they are less susceptible to *sudden* rolling motions.

Light-displacement boats demonstrate violent responses to large waves and are more easily rolled over in the first place.

You can work out your own boat's capsize resistance this way: Take the boat's half-load displacement in pounds and divide by 64 to get its volume displacement in cubic feet. Now find the cube root of the resulting number. Next, take the boat's beam in feet and tenths of a foot, and divide it by the cube root just obtained. Normal resistance to capsize is indi-

Boat	Capsize Factor*	Boat	Capsize Factor*	Boat	Capsize Factor*
Alerion Express 28	1.99	Compac 25	1.90	Pacific Seacraft 40V	1.71
Alerion Express 38	1.88	Compac 27/2	2.09	Pacific Seacraft 44V	1.70
Baltic 35	2.14	Compac 35	2.06	Sabre 362	2.00
Baltic 40	2.07	Freedom 24	2.23	Sabre 402	2.00
Baltic 43	2.04	Freedom 35	1.97	Sabre 452	1.90
Baltic 47	1.98	Freedom 40	1.88	Santa Cruz 52	2.03
Baltic 52	1.94	Freedom 45	1.79	Shannon 39	1.81
Baltic 58	1.92	Gozzard 31	2.01	Sundeer	1.64
Baltic 60	1.89	Gozzard 37	1.80	Sweden Yachts 340	1.98
Baltic 64	1.81	Gozzard 44 & CC	1.80	Sweden Yachts 370	1.96
Baltic 67	2.06	Hunter 240	2.50	Sweden Yachts 390	1.99
Baltic 70	1.89	Hunter 260	2.10	Sweden Yachts 41	1.96
Beneteau 25	2.43	Hunter 280	3.03	Sweden Yachts 45	1.90
Beneteau First 33.7	2.03	Hunter 31	2.14	Sweden Yachts 50	1.80
Beneteau First 40.7	1.98	Hunter 34	2.10	Sweden Yachts 52	1.77
Beneteau Oceanis 36cc	2.11	Hunter 376	2.04	Sweden Yachts 70	1.67
Beneteau Oceanis 40cc	1.92	Hunter 410	2.06	Tartan 3500	2.09
Beneteau Oceanis 411	2.02	Hunter 42	1.95	Tartan 3800	1.98
Beneteau Oceanis 44cc	2.04	Hunter 430	1.95	Tartan 4100	2.03
Beneteau First 42s7	2.06	Hunter 450	1.89	Tartan 4600	1.99
Cabo Rico 36	1.77	Island Packet 320	1.98	Trintella 42	1.78
Cabo Rico 38	1.67	Island Packet 350	1.91	Trintella 47	1.80
Cabo Rico 40	1.70	Island Packet 37	1.84	Valiant 39	1.74
Cabo Rico 45	1.60	Island Packet 40	1.83	Valiant 42	1.70
Caliber 35LRC	1.93	Island Packet 45	1.75	Valiant 50	1.69
Caliber 40LRC	1.82	J/120	2.00	Westerly Ocean 33	2.08
Caliber 47LRC	1.64	J/130	2.08	Westerly Oceanquest 35	2.03
Cambria 40	1.75	J/160	1.85	Westerly Oceanranger 38	2.02
Cambria 44/46	1.77	J/32	2.05	Westerly Oceanlord 41	1.96
Catalina 22 MkII	2.53	J/42	1.81	Westerly Ocean 43	1.80
Catalina 250	2.25	Jeanneau 34.2	1.99	Westerly Ocean 49	1.98
Catalina 270	2.14	Jeanneau 36.2	2.15	X-Yachts X-99	1.91
Catalina C28 MkII	1.74	Jeanneau 40	2.05	X-Yachts IMX38	2.13
Catalina C30 MkII	2.00	Jeanneau 42.2	2.04	X-Yachts X-302	1.97
Catalina 320	2.10	Jeanneau 42cc	2.02	X-Yachts X-332	2.04
Catalina 34 MkII	2.06	Jeanneau 45.2	2.14	X-Yachts X-362	2.03
Catalina 36 MkII	2.01	Jeanneau 47cc	1.93	X-Yachts X-382	2.01
Catalina C380	1.85	Jeanneau 52.2	1.89	X-Yachts X-412	2.02
Catalina 400	2.00	Morgan 38	1.85	X-Yachts X-442	1.97
Catalina 42 MkII	2.03	Morgan 45	1.90	X-Yachts X-482	1.90
Catalina 470	1.87	Pacific Seacraft 34V	1.68	X-Yachts X-612	1.85
Compac 23/3	2.18	Pacific Seacraft 37V	1.72	* See calculation for capsize factor in text.	

C

cated by an answer of 2. Anything less than 2 is regarded as better; anything more than 2 indicates a boat that should not compete in ocean races.

Incidentally, although this formula provides a good indication of a boat's resistance to sudden capsize and her ability to recover from complete inversion, several other factors also come into play in dynamic situations. Interestingly, the study that came up with the screening formula concluded that a boat's static stability—that is, her resistance to being heeled while at rest in calm water—was not a good predictor of dynamic capsize, which occurs when a moving boat is exposed to the energy of moving waves.

Don't forget that ultimate stability is a boat's ability to right herself from the upside-down position. Excessive beam is obviously detrimental to ultimate stability.

See also **Displacement; Gales at Sea; Inertia; Length-to-Beam Ratio; Stability; Stability Limits.**

Castaways

Learning to beat panic and black despair on the open sea

Statistics gathered by the French scientist and adventurer Dr. Alain Bombard indicate that nine out of ten castaways adrift at sea die within three days. This is an extraordinary finding, considering that it takes longer than that to perish of hunger and thirst. It appears that the onset of death is greatly hastened by panic and loss of morale.

You can get over panic after a while; it subsides naturally. But the blackness of despair that accompanies loss of morale is harder to fight, and it's particularly deadly when you find yourself adrift with no plans and no ability to make progress toward land or a shipping lane—in short, no hope.

Most castaways who survive long periods adrift at sea have been able to guide their boat or raft under makeshift sail on a logical course of their choosing. The length of time they spend on board is not as important as the fact that they are in control of their own destiny. As long as they can catch fish or gather plankton and make progress toward civilization, no matter how slowly, the will to live is very strong. Those who merely sit and wait to be rescued, knowing that rescue is unlikely, soon lose all hope.

If you intend to cross an ocean, spend some time preparing for possible shipwreck. Think about the type of life raft or dinghy you need and how it might be sailed many hundreds of miles on the open sea, if necessary.

Make up an emergency grab bag to take with you when your yacht sinks, and leave air space in some spare jugs of water so they'll float when you throw them overboard. Check the batteries in your EPIRB if you choose to carry one. Don't forget charts and a small compass, a flashlight, food and clothing, a handheld VHF radio, a first-aid kit, sunscreen, a knife, a signal mirror, flares, matches, a pot, and all the other items you'll need for camping on the water. And make sure you have plenty of

fishhooks and line—don't ever rely on the contents of your life raft to keep you alive.

See also **Abandoning Ship; Eating Plankton; Emergency Navigation; Watermakers.**

Catching Water

Figuring out ways to augment your fresh water from rain showers

Most serious ocean voyagers have concocted some method or another to catch rainwater to top off their freshwater tanks. During a rain shower at sea, with the mainsail raised, you can catch water in buckets placed beneath the boom gooseneck. It's better if the boom is lifted slightly by the topping lift. A surprising amount of water comes off the sail that way, but wait a few minutes until the salt and grime has washed off the sail before you start collecting.

On some boats with deep toerails or bulwarks, it's possible to stop the scuppers with rags, and siphon water from the lowest point of the side decks into containers in the cockpit. Some cockpit awnings can be adjusted so they hang downward in a deep V, from the middle of which rainwater is led to containers by a hose attached to a plastic through-hull fitting that pierces the awning.

The cockpit will gather many gallons of water in a heavy rainstorm, so you need good plugs to stop up the drains temporarily. A dinghy left upright on the deck makes a good collector too.

If you find yourself in a dead calm at sea with heavy rain beating the sea flat, you can scoop many gallons of near-fresh water off the surface of the sea because the fresh water floats on top. Don't dip deeper than an inch or so. It won't be entirely fresh, but it will keep you alive and it's much safer than drinking seawater.

See also **Watermakers**.

Cavitation

Selecting a propeller with enough blade area for the job

When air gets sucked into a propeller or when a partial vacuum forms around the blades, the ef-fect is for the propeller to lose its grip on solid water and to race in-effectively.

Air can be sucked down when a boat makes a sharp turn or when wave action brings the pro-peller out of the water, but cavita-tion is also experienced when too much power is applied to too small a propeller, which then forms bubbles of partial vacuum.

As water rushes in to fill the vacuum, it is vaporized. It im-plodes against the propeller with enough force to cause pitting. This, in turn, leads to poor bal-ance, vibration, and further pit-ting, so that the metal of the blades is greatly weakened.

To prevent this permanent form of cavitation, the load on the propeller blades must be kept fairly low, which means increas-ing the size of the propeller or re-ducing the power of the engine. A good safe level of loading for the propeller blades is about 6.4 pounds per square inch (450 g/cm^2).

If cavitation occurs with a two-bladed propeller, the answer is to change to a three-bladed prop with more area. If the culprit is a three-bladed prop, the answer is to increase diameter, select wider blades, or fit a four-bladed prop.

See also **Propeller Advances**.

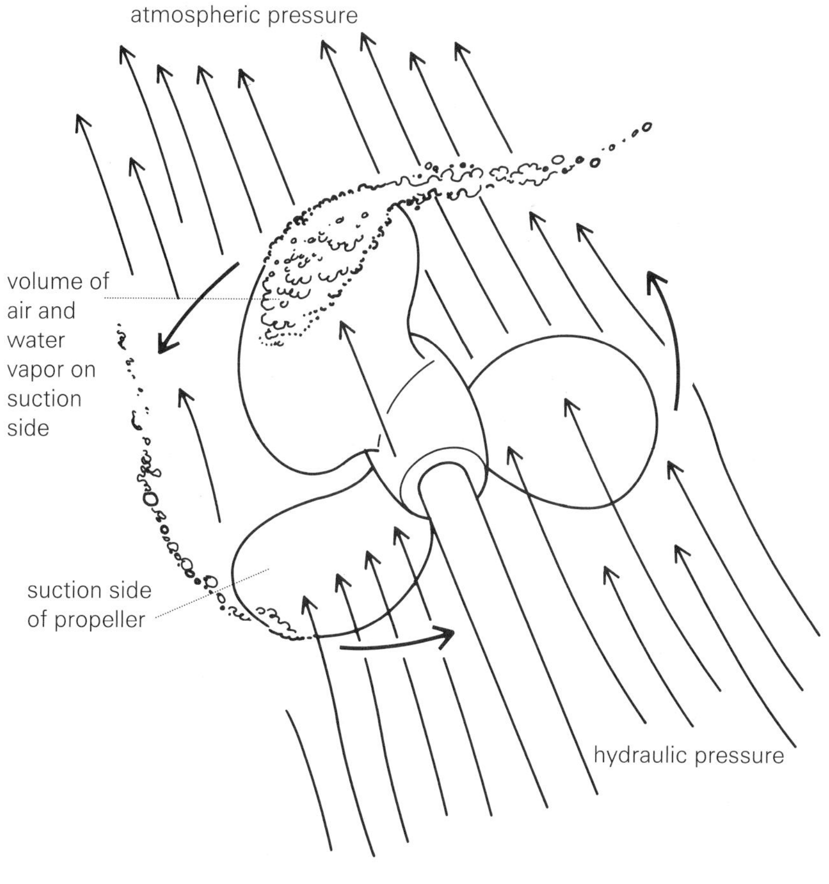

C

atmospheric pressure

volume of air and water vapor on suction side

suction side of propeller

hydraulic pressure

Cavitation results when air is sucked into a propeller or when too much power causes bubbles of partial vacuum. The effect is for the propeller to race and lose its grip on the water.

Centerboards

Stopping that sideways move-ment through the water

A centerboard is a pivoting plate of wood or metal that is lowered into the water through a slot along the centerline of a sailboat. Its main purpose is to prevent the boat from being blown sideways, but you can also use a center-board to balance the helm by par-tially lowering or raising it, which moves the hull's center of lateral resistance (CLR) forward or aft. If the centerboard is made of thick, heavy metal, it may also con-tribute to the boat's stability.

The centerboard is housed in a narrow case, or trunk, that nec-essarily protrudes into the footwell of a dinghy or the ac-commodation of a yacht. It is of-ten used in place of a fixed keel on small sailboats to allow them easier access to a road trailer. De-

C

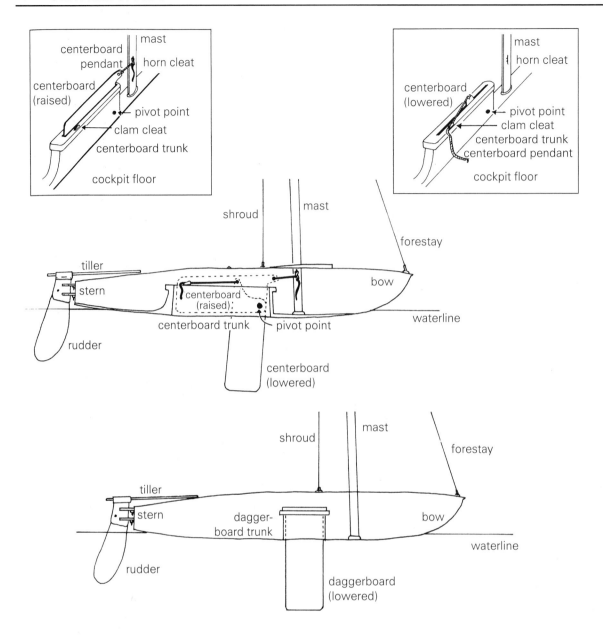

Centerboards (pivoted) and daggerboards (sliding) stop sailboats from being pushed sideways by the wind. Weighted boards also act as ballast to aid stability.

signers also use the centerboard on craft used to explore shallow waters, where a deep fixed keel would make navigation impossible, or on boats used for sail-camping that are drawn up on a beach at night. There are also hybrid keel-centerboard designs in which a centerboard is housed entirely within a comparatively shallow keel and lowered when

additional sailing efficiency is needed.

On sailing dinghies, the pivoting centerboard is usually raised and lowered by hand, although a steel plate may require the use of a small tackle. Invariably, on larger boats, some form of block and tackle or mechanical device is used.

Very small boats, say those 10

feet in length or less, mostly use daggerboards in place of centerboards. A daggerboard has no pivot and simply slides up and down in a close-fitting case, or trunk.

See also **Block and Tackle; Leeboards**.

Center of Buoyancy

Its relationship to stability; where it's normally located

A boat's center of buoyancy (CB) is an important indicator of its stability. I always imagine the hull's center of buoyancy as having two axes around which the hull rolls. The first axis is the fore-and-aft line, and determines the rolling motion from port to starboard and back; the second axis is perpendicular to the first, and determines the pitching of the bow and the plunging of the stern. This is purely imaginative stuff, of course, but it satisfies my simple mind.

In technical terms, the CB, also known as the center of immersion, is the center of gravity (CG) of the volume of water displaced by a floating object. In other words, it's the center of the total force that is pushing upward on the hull. Together with the boat's CG, it determines how stable the vessel will be.

If the CG is a long way beneath the CB, the boat will be relatively stable; that is, if she's tipped sideways by wind or waves, she will tend to return to the normal upright position. But if the CB is close to the CG, the boat will be relatively tender and will readily list to one side or the other. That's why it's important to stow all heavy objects, including spare anchors, canned goods, and libraries of books, as low as possible inside the hull. It keeps the CG low and helps right the boat when she heels over or even capsizes.

Displacement hulls in powerboats and sailboats usually have their CBs about 55 percent of the waterline aft of the bow. In most other powerboats, it's a little farther back—about 60 percent of the waterline aft of the bow.

See also **Center of Gravity**.

Center of Effort

Balancing the sail plan with the underwater pivot point

The center of effort (CE) is the theoretical middle of a boat's sail area. It's a handy concept that designers use in combination with the boat's center of lateral resistance (CLR) to try to create a boat with a balanced helm. The CLR is the theoretical underwater pivot point around which the hull swings from side to side.

Simply put, if there is an excess of sail area forward of the pivot point, the bow of the boat will tend to be blown away from the wind consistently, causing what is called lee helm. If there is too much sail area aft of the CLR, the bow will try to round up into the wind all the time, causing weather helm.

Naval architects aim to balance the CE and the CLR so that the boat normally carries a slight amount of weather helm—that is,

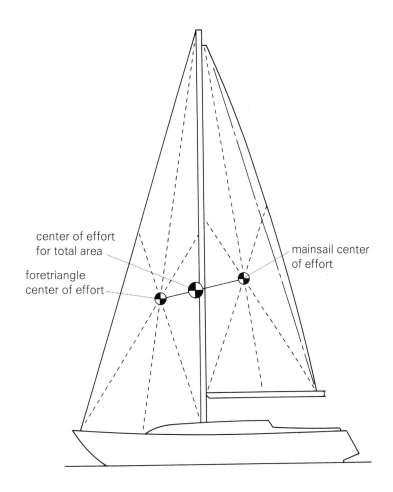

center of effort for total area

foretriangle center of effort

mainsail center of effort

The center of effort of the sailplan is the theoretical middle of a boat's sail area. Together with the boat's center of lateral resistance, it accounts for weather helm or lee helm.

the rudder (not the tiller) has to be held to leeward between 1 and 4 degrees. There is no precise method of doing this, however. There are so many complicating factors involving hydrodynamics and aerodynamics that designers must, to a large extent, rely on their instinct and experience. Sometimes excessive weather helm can be cured by adding a bowsprit to move the sail area (and, consequently, the CE) farther forward. Lee helm can be alleviated by moving the sail area aft; raking the mast aft is one way of doing that.

Moving the CLR forward or aft would have the same effect, of course. This cannot be done if the boat has a fixed keel, but a pivoting centerboard can be used to good effect in this way. Some specialized boats carry additional daggerboards that can be lowered or raised to alter the CLR.

You can find a boat's theoretical CLR by cutting out a paper silhouette of her underwater body and balancing it on a knife blade.

On most boats, both the CE and the CLR change constantly with boat speed, heel angle, and wind speed. Other factors affecting helm balance include the amount of fullness or flatness in the sails and the amount of twist.

See also **Balanced Helm; Lead Percentage; Lee Helm; Sail Area; Weather Helm.**

Center of Gravity

*Keeping weights low
contributes to stability*

For purposes of discussion and calculation, all the weights in a boat are imagined to be a single force acting vertically downward through the center of gravity (CG).

The CG is important because it interacts with the center of buoyancy (CB) to make a boat stable. When a boat heels, the underwater hull shape changes and the CB moves out toward one side or another, thereby creating a righting moment that tends to bring the boat back to an upright position.

The CG does not shift position as the boat heels, except when crew members in racing boats line the rail, or water ballast is pumped from tank to tank, or a canting keel is shifted to a new position.

To a large extent, a boat's stability depends on the location of the CG relative to waterline level. The lower the CG, the greater the righting moment. That's why all heavy weights in boats, such as ballast, engines, and tanks of fluid, are kept as low as possible. Spare anchors, chain, batteries, stores, and even books will improve a boat's stability if they are stowed low. However, outboard motors stowed on the aft pulpit, dinghies on deck, and jib poles

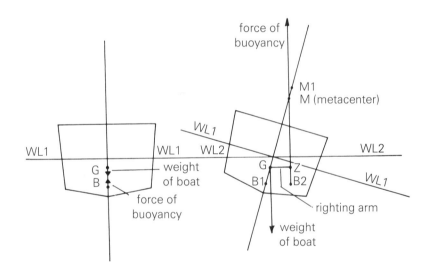

Naval architects use the term "center of gravity" ("G" in the diagrams) to mean the sum of all weights in a boat, acting vertically downward in a single force. This diagram shows a boat on an even keel and at an angle of starboard heel. The center of gravity (G) does not move as the boat heels to 10 degrees, but the center of buoyancy (B) shifts to starboard (B2). If we were to draw a vertical line straight up from B2, it would intersect another line drawn up from the hull's centerline (like a mast) at a point called the metacenter (M). The amount of force available to return the boat to an even keel (the righting moment) is determined by the boat's weight and by the distance from G to Z, which is a point above B2 and level with G. Through the first few degrees of heel, M (an indicator of initial stability) falls in about the same place as B moves outboard. But as the boat heels beyond about 10 degrees, M ceases to be an indicator of stability since it no longer focuses about a single point above centerline. In other words, M1 migrates substantially from its consistent low-heel-angle position (M).

stowed up the mast all *detract* from a boat's stability.

See also **Center of Buoyancy**.

Chafe

Learning to deal with chafe before it causes danger

All boats have gear that is subject to chafe, but it is particularly a factor aboard a sailboat on a long passage. Not only sails, but also running rigging and even electrical cables can fail because of chafe.

Wherever a soft line or piece of sail cloth can rub against a harder object such as a shroud or a coaming, chafe will result. Sometimes the results can be dangerous; almost always, they are inconvenient.

Headsail sheets often rub against the shrouds, and they're particularly prone to chafe when you're hove-to and the headsail is aback. Protect them by fitting plastic tubing or split wooden rollers over the lower parts of the shrouds.

Check that the topping lift doesn't contact the leech of the mainsail; it can do a lot of damage to the sail in quick order. Similarly, make sure the genoa doesn't rub on the spreader when you're beating. In a choppy head sea, you can poke a hole through the sail that way.

When you're running before the wind and the boom is squared off, watch the mainsail for chafe against the rigging. In particular, be certain the sail isn't rubbing up and down against a shroud as the boom rises and falls. If it is, pin the boom down tightly with its

own vang, or else attach a preventer guy to the boom end and make it fast at deck level up forward. If you want that old-fashioned look (along with added windage), use baggywrinkle—fluffed up ends of small line made tightly fast around the shrouds—to help prevent the mainsail from chafing.

Hose down your sails with fresh water, or let the rain do the job, after they get sprayed with salt water. Dried salt crystals are abrasive and will gnaw away at Dacron or nylon fibers.

The mainsheet can chafe on the lifelines, the dinghy painter can chafe on the transom, and an anchor cable can chafe on a bowsprit bobstay or on the sharp edges of a bow-roller fitting. Mooring lines chafe on toerails and in roughly finished chocks. Electrical cables in a mast or down below that are not fixed in place every foot or so can joggle around, snag on obstructions, and chafe through their insulation where they pass through bulkheads. If they touch other bare wires or metal, they can short out and cause a dangerous fire.

Beware of chafe all the time you're on a boat, even where you can't see it. It's everywhere.

See also **Booms; Headsails; Lifelines; Preventers; Sail Cloth; Shrouds and Stays; Spreaders**.

Chain

Choosing the right kind for your type of boat

An all-chain anchor rode is comforting when it's down and doing its work. But raising it, even with

proof coil

BBB chain

high-test chain

Three kinds of anchor chain.

mechanical help, can be very hard work. Nevertheless, it has so many advantages over a rope rode that most long-distance cruisers use nothing but chain with their working anchors.

Proof-coil chain is made of low-carbon steel and has relatively long links. Its breaking strength is three and a half to four times its working load limit. But the chain most commonly used in cruising yachts is BBB chain. It's made from the same material as proof-coil chain, but it has shorter links that fit better in windlasses. It has the same breaking strength as proof-coil.

High-test chain is stronger than the other two types, for the same weight, because it has a higher carbon content. But it is more prone to rust and its breaking strength is about three times the working load limit. It may part without warning when its limits are reached, whereas the softer proof-coil and BBB chains will first elongate to warn you. High-test chain is often used aboard performance cruisers where weight is considered detrimental. All three types are supplied with a galvanized-zinc coating.

Whatever kind of chain you use, make sure the bitter end is firmly secured to the inside of the chain locker. Use strong nylon line for this, so that it will absorb some of the shock if the chain ever runs away from you and fetches up sharply at the bitter end. And make the nylon line long enough to reach the deck, so you can cut the cable quickly and dump the anchor and chain in an emergency (mariners call it "slipping the cable").

See also **Chain Stoppers; Rodes**.

Chain Locker

Keeping heavy chain low and inboard presents problems

Stowage of chain presents a problem on a small boat. On sailboats and powerboats, chain lockers—compartments in which the anchor chain is stored—need to be underneath a windlass or a deck chain pipe situated at the bow or stern. But weight in the ends of a small boat is detrimental to its performance, especially when sailing to windward or powering into a head sea, when it can cause hobbyhorsing. That's when a boat trying to make way against waves tends to plug away in the same hole instead of surging buoyantly ahead over the waves. Hobbyhorsing is less common in powerboats because their power-to-weight ratio is high enough to force the bows through oncoming waves, but sailboats try to concentrate weight low down in the center of the boat to avoid hobbyhorsing.

To mitigate the hobbyhorsing problem, some anchor windlasses are set well back from the bow—sometimes near the foot of a sailboat's mast—but this can present problems down below, where the chain locker will intrude on the accommodations. On boats of 35 feet (11 m) and more, the problem is not so acute; the chain locker can be located in the forepeak several feet aft of the bow roller. The chain can feed into the locker via a large-diameter pipe sloping down and aft.

There's not much that can be done about a stern chain locker, except to locate it right near the transom; fortunately, most boats use only a small length of chain on a stern line, at the end of a nylon line.

Most modern boats have a covered anchor well set into the foredeck, but this is not a particularly good place in which to store chain. Not only is the weight held comparatively high, which will make the boat less stable, but also in the case of a 180-degree capsize, the chain could burst open the cover and escape. Stow the anchors there by all means, but send the chain lower down into a proper locker.

You can estimate the size of a self-stowing chain locker using the following formula:

$$\text{volume in cubic feet} = (\text{fathoms chain x diameter in inches}^2) \times 0.85$$

Incidentally, nylon line of the same strength usually requires at least 25 percent more space than chain does because it doesn't compact itself like chain.

See also **Chain; Hobbyhorsing; Windlasses**.

Chain Stoppers

Simple but little-used devices to help raise anchor

A chain stopper is a simple pawl set in a bow roller or on deck. It lifts and clicks lightly over the links of an incoming chain, but jams down hard when the chain tries to run back.

It is such a great aid to raising anchor, by hand or by powered windlass, that it's a mystery to me why it's so little used.

The well-known British circumnavigator, Eric Hiscock, maintained that a chain pawl will make it feasible to do away with a windlass altogether when you're using a 35-pound (16 kg) anchor and $^5/_{16}$-inch (8 mm) chain, particularly if you can jiggle up to the anchor under power or sail. He's right. I have weighed a 35-pound C.Q.R. on $^5/_{16}$th chain by hand many times in water up to 90 feet (27 m) deep. But I was young and

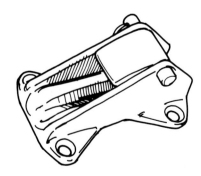

Chain stoppers prevent chain from being stripped off the anchor winch when a rising bow exerts excessive force on the chain.

silly then; I wouldn't want to do it now. If your boat exceeds 5 or 6 tons displacement, I would recommend some form of mechanical assistance.

Even a power windlass will benefit from a chain stopper, which prevents the chain being stripped off the gypsy as the boat rises in big swells and exerts an abnormally strong pull on the rode. You can buy a chain stopper at a marine store, but it's also possible to have a simple pawl fabricated to your own design, if necessary.

Incidentally, the pawl will work with nylon line, too, but don't use it that way except in an emergency because it will compress the fibers and eventually damage the line.

See also **Anchors, Anchoring; Windlasses**.

Chart Datums

Using fixed datums to establish depths, heights, and distances

A datum is a fixed level or a plane of reference from which certain distances are measured. Mariners' charts use two datums: vertical and horizontal.

Vertical datums are needed to indicate the depth of water and the height of objects and land masses above sea level. The five most common vertical datums are mean sea level, mean low water, mean lower low water, low-water ordinary springs, and lowest astronomical tide.

American charts make extensive use of the mean lower low-

water datum to indicate depths from which tidal heights may be calculated. British and many other foreign charts mostly use the lowest astronomical tide as their datum. Thus, low tides frequently fall below the lowest depths depicted on American charts, resulting in so-called minus tides, whereas the water level is almost never less than that shown on British charts.

Horizontal datums, which establish your position on the Earth's surface in terms of latitude and longitude, are more difficult to establish because the world is not uniformly round or even perfectly ellipsoid. So if you were to enclose the Earth in a geometrically perfect "cage" consisting of latitude and longitude grids, many areas would not touch the inside of the cage.

Consequently, various geographers developed ellipsoids that fit their part of the world almost perfectly, but which would not be as accurate elsewhere. Such ellipsoids, combined with an astronomically determined starting point and a measured baseline, are known as geodetic datums.

There are more than 100 geodetic datums now in use. The standard used by GPS receivers is called World Geodetic System 84 (WGS 84). This ellipsoid cannot give absolutely precise latitudes and longitudes for every spot on Earth, but most GPS receivers can be switched to the local geodetic datum specified on the chart itself for increased accuracy. North American charts are being converted to a datum known as North American Datum of 1983 (NAD 83), but there is no need to

switch from WGS 84 in this case because for all intents and purposes the two are the same.

Users of GPS and electronic charts should be sure to check the geodetic datum of the chart in use and to switch the GPS to that datum if necessary. In some parts of the world, the GPS standard ellipsoid (WGS 84) will give latitude and longitude positions that differ by as much as half a mile from the local ellipsoid used to create the chart.

See also **Charts**; **Electronic Charts**; **GPS**.

Charts

Understanding chartwork is the basis of good seamanship

Most of the work of charting the world's oceans and coasts was done in the days of sail, and involved great feats of seamanship and endurance. Charts provided predatory nations with the invaluable knowledge they needed to trade and conquer, so the chartmakers were equipped at great expense with what was then regarded as the latest technology. They had no GPS, of course, and only lead lines in place of electronic depth-sounders; no radio to check the chronometers for longitude; no enclosed power launches to do the inshore work—only sailing ships and open longboats rowed by 4 to 10 men. By today's standards, they performed miracles with the rudimentary equipment available to them.

The main difficulty with drawing a chart is that the paper

is flat but the Earth is round. Claudius Ptolemy, the Egyptian astronomer, produced a conic projection of the world in about 230 B.C. However, the projection most useful to sailors up to this very day was the work of the Dutch mathematician, Gerard Mercator, and it didn't come until the sixteenth century.

Mercator's projection treats the globe as a cylinder, which means that the outlines of land masses become increasingly large

and distorted as the poles are approached. Its major contribution to navigation is that it results in a chart on which a straight line drawn between two points represents the constant compass course to be steered all the way. Although this results in a slightly longer course over the curved Earth's surface, it has the overwhelming advantage of simplicity.

Furthermore, a Mercator chart provides an easy way to measure distances. The parallels of the grid are spaced so that 1 minute of latitude always equals 1 nautical mile, and the parallels are conveniently measured on either side of the chart.

The chart projection that provides the shortest route between two points is the great-circle, or gnomonic, projection, where one point on the Earth's surface is used as a center from which land and water are increasingly dis-

torted outward. A straight line drawn on a great-circle chart crosses each meridian at a slightly different angle, theoretically resulting in slight but continuous course changes for any vessel following it. In practice, vessels change course more substantially at every 10-degree meridian, with little loss.

Only seldom can a sailboat follow a great-circle course exactly, but she should follow it as closely as circumstances allow, especially in higher latitudes because the savings in distance are greater the nearer she approaches the poles. The most favorable tack for a boat beating to windward is the one that takes her closest to the great-circle course.

The amount of information contained in a nautical chart—from bottom depths and types to navigational aids and dangers—is extraordinary. There is so much detail, often presented in a special shorthand form, that it takes study and practice to extract the most benefit from a chart. Efficient chartwork, in fact, is the basis of good seamanship.

See also **Chart Datums; Chart Scales; Chart Stowage; Depth-Sounders; Electronic Charts; Rhumb Lines.**

Mercator's charts result from the round surface of the Earth being projected onto a cylinder having the same diameter as the projected globe but touching it only at the equator.

Chart Scales

Sorting out the confusion over large and small scales

The scale of a chart is always noted on its face. It represents a ratio; for instance, a ratio of 1:50,000 indicates that any one unit of measurement on the chart (an inch, a centimeter, or anything else) represents 50,000 of those same units on the Earth's surface.

There is often confusion about large and small scales. An easy way to sort it out is to remember that large-scale equals large (much) detail; conversely, small-scale equals small (scant) detail. The following are commonly found scales, with their uses:

Harbor charts, 1:10,000 to 1:50,000: Used for navigating in harbors. They give magnified detail of channels, wharves, buoys, lights, and anchorages.

Coastal charts, 1:50,000 to 1:150,000: Used for coastal pilotage. They give much detail of harbor entrances, the sea bottom, buoys, lights, and offshore hazards.

General charts, 1:150,000 to 1:600,000: Used for offshore coastal cruising. They show only major navigational marks and depths, but cover a large area.

Sailing charts, 1:1,200,000 to 1:8,000,000: These are for long-distance voyaging and planning routes for ocean crossings. The navigational detail is scant.

Pilot charts, 1:15,000,000: Used for ocean-route planning. Monthly charts show average ocean wind and weather conditions.

See also **Charts**.

Chart Stowage

Rolling leads to madness; stow them flat for sanity

Although charts don't occupy a great volume of space, their stow-age presents problems on small boats because they need to be kept clean, dry, and readily accessible. And if you're to stay sane, they should also be stowed flat, which presents another problem.

Some sailors roll them tightly inside each other and store them in tubes like the layers of an onion. It's convenient storage and can be made perfectly waterproof, but when you extract a chart that has been rolled for some time and try to spread it out on the chart table, it snaps shut and rolls away out of sight. Even if you pin the edges down with masking tape, it will assume a concave shape that makes work with parallel rules difficult if not impossible. In short, rolled charts lead to madness, especially in violent motion at sea.

So fold your charts to the size of your chart table and stow them flat. If you don't have a dedicated chart drawer, stow them under bunk mattresses in large plastic envelopes, if necessary.

Even in the smallest of vessels, the minimum size for a chart table is 21 by 28 inches (530 by 710 mm). If you have the space, a slightly bigger table will be more convenient to work on—one 22 by 36 inches (560 by 915 mm) will accept most charts folded just once. Best of all is a chart table 28 by 42 inches (530 mm by 1.1 m), but navigators are not often provided with such a luxury.

Incidentally, about 100 charts folded once will take up a depth of about 2 inches (50 mm) in a drawer. The best pencil for most chartwork is one with a medium lead—a No. 2 or an HB. Softer pencils make bolder lines, but they tend to smudge and spread. Lines drawn with harder leads are difficult to see and harder to erase. They also dig into the paper quite deeply and shorten the chart's life.

See also **Charts**; **Chart Scales**.

Checking a Battery

C

Two ways to see if your batteries are in good health

The only practical way to check the health of a sealed battery is to take a voltmeter reading. You'll need a really accurate voltmeter for that because the difference between a fully charged and a fully discharged battery is little more than 1 volt.

But you can get a good idea of the condition of a vented lead-acid battery with a hydrometer, which will show you the state of

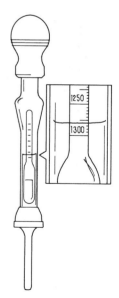

Hydrometers use a weighted float in a tube to give a direct reading of the specific gravity of the electrolyte in a flooded battery—and thus the battery's state of charge.

charge in each cell and alert you to possible problems.

A hydrometer is a simple glass tube topped with a rubber bulb that draws electrolyte up into the tube. A weighted float in the tube gives you a direct reading of the specific gravity of the electrolyte, which varies with the state of charge.

Most manufacturers rate the specific gravity (SG) of a fully charged cell at about 1.278. That's valid when the temperature of the electrolyte is 77°F and it's just covering the top of the plates. A half-charged cell would show about 1.198, a fully discharged cell about 1.108.

For different temperatures and electrolyte levels, apply the following corrections:

- Add 1 point of SG (0.001) for every 3°F above 77°F. Subtract 1 gravity point for each 3°F below 77°F.
- Add 15 points (0.015) for each half inch that the electrolyte level is above normal. Subtract 15 points for each half inch that the electrolyte level is below normal.

Any cell that reads 50 points (0.050) lower than the average of the other cells indicates trouble, and the battery should be replaced as soon as possible.

Incidentally, you can buy a hydrometer at a marine hardware store, but it's likely to be less expensive at an auto-parts store.

A final warning: Don't test for SG immediately after you've topped off the cells with distilled or demineralized water because the fresh water on top of the cells will make the reading too low. Give the electrolyte a chance to mix thoroughly.

See also **Amp-Hour Ratings; Battery Choices; Battery Needs; Cranking Ratings; Locating Batteries**.

Chines

Defining the angle where the bottom meets the sides

When the side of a boat meets the bottom at a well-defined angle, rather than a rounded section, the

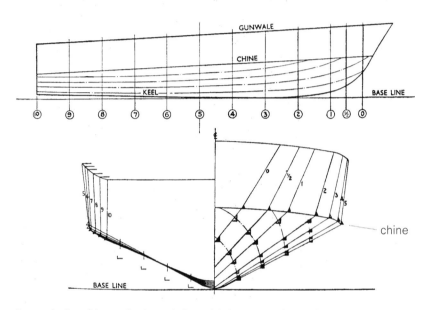

An early Ray Hunt–designed deep-V, the smoothest-riding planing boat of its day. Modern refinements missing here include chine flats and a padded keel, which would add form stability and planing efficiency. This hull became an early Bertram and is the paradigm for all modern planing hulls.

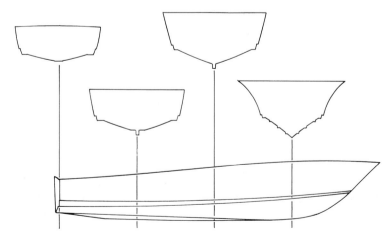

A Viking 52 profile with selected stations showing the change in shape from bow to stern. Viking uses double chines, which, when on plane at high speeds, reduce wetted surface by effectively narrowing the beam.

resultant "corner" is known as the chine. The more abrupt the angle, the harder is the chine.

In a boat with a flat or V-bottom, the chine coincides with the turn of the bilge. Instead of one hard chine, a boat may have two or more softer chines, in which case it is known as a multichine hull.

Chine construction is particularly suitable for building with metal or plywood, resulting in perfectly seaworthy craft, although to some they are not as pleasing to the eye as traditional round-bilged boats. Many small pram dinghies are also of hard-chine design, not only for ease of construction, but also because hard chines add greatly to stability. Some modern powerboats have deep-V designs featuring rows of thin longitudinal chines to give them a softer ride at high speed in choppy seas.

See also **Bilge**.

Choosing a Boat

Deciding what's right for you; taking the first steps

No boat can do everything for all people. It's a simple truth that the amount of pleasure you get from your boat will depend on how suitable it is for your needs. Boats are deliberately designed for specific purposes, and the first step in choosing a boat is to decide why you need it. Strangely enough, that's not always an easy thing to analyze.

If you've been bitten by the bug but are new to boats, you may need to do a little homework and get a little experience on other people's boats before you decide on one of your own.

The first decision is whether you want power or sail. Powerboats are designed for deep-sea fishing, coastal fishing, and river or lake fishing. There are racing boats for use on the ocean or inland waters. Other special powerboat designs are for crossing oceans, coastal cruising, extended exploring in wilderness areas, fast commuting, and living aboard.

Sailboats fall basically into two categories: racers and cruisers. Among the latter, the faster, lighter ones may be hybrid racer-cruisers, but the slower, heavier ones are just plain cruisers. Racers, in turn, are especially designed for use offshore, on rivers and lakes, or for semiserious club racing in protected waters. Cruisers are designed for ocean or coastal work, exploration in shallow waters, and permanent living aboard. There is also a choice between monohulls and multihulls.

Each specific design has features that may or may not suit your purposes. The right one for you is the one that makes your favorite on-the-water activity easy. You can swim or dive or fish from most boats, but some boats are better suited to these activities than others. A boat designed to take you safely across an ocean might seem slow and unglamorous to the weekend crowd, but if you're planning to sail around the world, it's the right boat for you.

All boats are compromises, of course. The best you can hope for is an honest boat that suits most of your needs most of the time. While you're searching for yours,

read the (supposedly unbiased) editorial reviews in boating magazines and make due allowance for advertisers' hyperbole. Before you buy, try to get afloat on the type of boat you've chosen. Swallow your pride: go down to the marina and ask for rides (most owners will be flattered if you tell them you're considering buying the same model) or charter a boat if you must. Don't begrudge the money; buying the wrong boat can be a very expensive mistake.

Circles of Position

Navigating with the help of circles drawn on the chart

Although every competent navigator makes use of straight lines of position to plot angles on a chart, circles of position are less well known. If you know your exact distance from some landmark, you can draw on the chart a circle with that radius. You then know with certainty that you are on that circle somewhere, and if you can get another circle or line to intersect it, you'll have a position fix.

There is another fascinating thing about small-angle circles of position. Let's first imagine we have two leading marks in line in front of us. If we keep the marks in line, we'll go straight toward them. But if we go to one side or the other, opening up a small angle between them *and keeping that angle constant*, our course will form an arc of a circle.

You can actually preplot such a circle on a chart and place yourself accurately on it by keeping constant the chosen angle be-

C

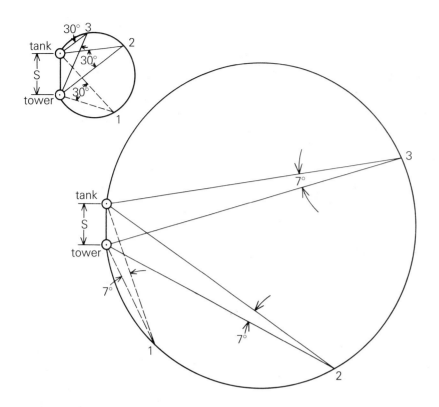

If you can measure the horizontal angle between two charted objects on shore, you must be somewhere on a circle that passes through the two objects.

tween your leading marks. You don't necessarily have to use leading marks, of course. Two off-lying islands will keep you clear of hazards while you round a point, for instance, holding up a finger or two at arm's length to judge the angle between the islands.

See also **Lines of Position**.

Circumnavigation

Defining more strictly a voyage around the world

There was a time when it was possible to sail around the world any way you chose, and then claim that you had completed a circumnavigation. Perhaps it's the fact that more people are doing it

these days, or perhaps it's because of the insatiable need to keep breaking records; but, for whatever reason, a circumnavigation is now more strictly defined.

The rule of thumb is that the route of a "true" circumnavigation must encompass two antipodes—points opposite each other on the surface of the globe. These are points that would be joined by a straight line passing through the center of the Earth.

Furthermore, because by definition the word *circumnavigation* means a journey "around" the Earth, you can't claim one for a voyage whose course merely runs from one point to the other and straight back along a reciprocal course; you have to make the round trip.

Cleats

Even these simple fittings need to be properly installed

A standard cleat seems to be a simple, almost foolproof fitting but, like many things on a boat, it needs to be installed properly. It's simply a wooden or metal projection with two arms, or horns, around which you wrap a line to make it fast. Cleats must have been among the first boat fittings man ever invented.

The length of a cleat—that is, the total length of the two horns combined—should be at least 12 times the diameter of the rope used with it. Preferably, it should be 16 times the diameter. This old formula provides the rope with lots of breathing room and avoids the frustration associated with cleats that are too small to accept a couple of decent figure-eight turns plus a finishing half hitch on top.

Wherever possible, the cleat should be fastened (always with bolts, never with screws) at an angle of about 15 degrees to the direction of pull on the line; otherwise, the line tends to ride over itself and jam.

Finally—and this might seem obvious, but I've seen it done incorrectly many times—be sure to wind the bitter end of the line around the cleat; that is, the end farthest away from the load. You should end up with the bitter end on top of the cleat. Don't lay the bitter end of the line down alongside the cleat and then start winding the line leading to the load around the cleat. If you do, the bitter end will be buried and the

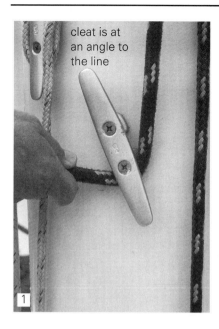
cleat is at an angle to the line

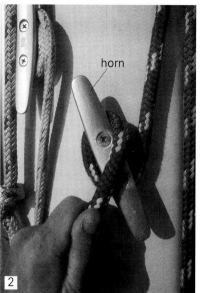
horn

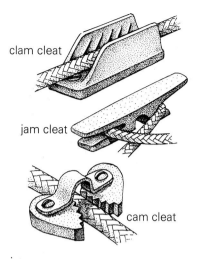
clam cleat

jam cleat

cam cleat

Three types of cleats. From top: a clam cleat, a jam cleat, and a cam cleat.

To make a line fast to a cleat: (1) bring the line under the farther horn; (2) take a turn around the cleat, under the nearer horn and diagonally across the top; (3) tuck the line under the first horn and diagonally across the top the other way; (4) go around beneath the first horn once more and tuck the line under itself to finish.

loaded line will be leading off the top of the cleat. When the full strain comes on the line, you will not be able to release it unless you cut it free.

Special types of cleats and line clutches have been developed for situations where you need to hold or release sheets in a hurry. Among them are various forms of jam cleats that squeeze a line until it holds fast, but will release it quickly and easily under a reasonable load, usually by merely flicking it out of the fitting. Cam-action cleats are popular and consist of two cams mounted on a base. Spring action forces the cams to bear against the line, and ridges on the cams prevent the line from slipping as the cams are drawn tighter together. A quick tug will pull the line out from between the cams and release the line. Rope clutches work in a similar fashion but are controlled by an upright lever attached to the cam, which squeezes the line between itself and a fixed base. Lifting the lever immediately releases the line.

Clouds

Nature's weather indicators are invaluable to sailors

A cloud, as the venerable Mr. Webster so succinctly informs us, is nothing more than "a visible mass of condensed water vapor suspended in the atmosphere, consisting of minute droplets or ice crystals." It's not the most romantic description, but it's accurate.

Water vapor is present in most air masses, but it's invisible in its natural form. It's forced to come out of hiding, and condense, when the ambient temperature falls.

Air that flows into a stormy, low-pressure system is forced skyward into the cooler upper reaches of the atmosphere, where the water vapor must condense and form clouds. In this way, nature gives us a visible warning that a storm is on the way.

Not all clouds are associated with bad weather, of course. Those little cotton-puff trade-wind clouds seem to ride along merrily overhead without ever obscuring the sun and those high, streaked clouds that glow red at sunset are harbingers of fine settled weather. But there's no mistaking the ever-thickening, ever-lowering layers of dark gray cloud in the vanguard of a storm.

Clouds are commonly divided into the following four groups:

- high clouds at and above 20,000 feet, including cirrus, cirrostratus, and cirrocumulus
- intermediate clouds between 6,500 and 20,000 feet, including altostratus and altocumulus
- low clouds, below 6,500 feet, including stratus, stratocumulus, and nimbostratus
- tall vertical clouds, such as cumulus and cumulonimbus

Clouds are named according to the way they look and how

Cumulus with little vertical extent

Cumulus with moderate vertical extent

high they float. They are often combinations of two or more types. The Latin prefix *alto*, for example, means high; *stratus* is the word for a layer. Cumulus means heaped, or fluffy. Cirrus refers to wispy tendrils or feathery tufts. Nimbus is the turbulent black rain cloud. Cumulonimbus is, therefore, the imposing thunderstorm cloud with the cauli-

flower-shaped top and the black menacing base. You'll often see the top being blown away by high-speed upper-atmosphere winds into the shape of an anvil.

Clouds are important weather indicators for mariners, especially on the open ocean or in areas where meteorological forecasts are not available. The cloud types, together with wind speed and direc-

Cumulonimbus with no anvil

Stratus in sheet or layer

Stratus fractus/cumulus fractus of bad weather

Stratocumulus from spreading cumulus

Cumulus and stratocumulus at different levels

Stratocumulus not from spreading cumulus

Cumulonimbus

C

Altostratus, translucent, sun or moon visible

Altocumulus, semitransparent, multilevel

Altostratus, opaque, sun or moon hidden

Altocumulus in layers

Altocumulus, semitransparent

Altocumulus from spreading cumulus

C

Cirrus filaments, strands or hooks, not expanding

Cirrus hooks or filaments, increasing

Dense cirrus in patches

Cirrostratus covering whole sky

Cirrus, anvil remaining from cumulonimbus

Anvil Clouds. When a mature cumulonimbus cloud rises to the tropopause inversion boundary, the top spreads out in an anvil. This nasty-looking cloud can bring heavy rain, hail, and thunderstorms, perhaps with downbursts.

C

Puffy Clouds (cumulus mammatus). Spawned from cumulonimbus, mammatus clouds indicate thunderstorm activity somewhere in the vicinity. If the clouds are large and headed your way, you may be in for some severe weather.

Wave Cloud. Formed by a wavelike transport of air into and out of an atmospheric layer wherein condensation occurs, these clouds, unlike roll clouds, do not augur squalls.

Roll Cloud. A roll cloud precedes a squall line, which in turn may precede a cold front by a hundred miles or more.

and acquire the appearance of vertical stacks.

See also **Air Masses; Weather Fronts; Downbursts.**

Coast Guard

Battling the budget blues is the order of the day

The U.S. Coast Guard is at once the boater's best friend and worst enemy: best friend in times of emergency, when its personnel risk their lives to rescue boaters in trouble at sea; worst enemy when it must enforce Congress's Draconian laws relating to the boarding and searching of pleasure craft without search warrants.

The U.S. Coast Guard, which can trace its history back to 1789, is a strange hybrid of military and law-enforcement agencies. It has evolved from five separate federal agencies: the Revenue Cutter Service, Lighthouse Service, Steamboat Inspection Service, Bureau of Navigation, and Life-Saving

tion, and a record of the barometer's movements will provide a reliable picture of the weather to come for at least 12 hours.

At sea in the tropics, it's common for walls of cloud to pile up menacingly on the windward horizon, but more often than not they are harmless puffs of white cumulus clouds. The key to this illusion is that we have no way of knowing their true size or their distance from us, so our brains place them at equal distances along the curved "dome" overhead. However, our straight line of sight makes them crowd together at the horizon

Service. Formerly an agency of the Department of Transportation, it is now part of the federal Department of Homeland Security, created in March 2003 to combat terrorism.

The U.S. Coast Guard sometimes makes use of large U.S. Navy vessels to patrol international waters in search of smugglers. Historically, in time of war or national emergency, it has become an arm of the navy. U.S. Coast Guard vessels and aircraft are identified by a large red-and-blue slanted stripe near the bow.

In addition to its law-enforcement and safety-afloat duties, the coast guard operates many thousands of aids to navigation, ranging from day beacons to lighthouses. In keeping with its maverick makeup, it even ran a network of differential global positioning system (DGPS) radio stations that deliberately thwarted the efforts of the Pentagon to blur the accuracy of GPS signals, thus curtailing their usefulness to an enemy. The coast guard broadcast signals that restored accuracy to the GPS signals available to the public (and to America's enemies, of course). The Pentagon finally surrendered and stopped "dithering" the GPS signals, but there was no assurance that this was to be a permanent arrangement. The now-improved GPS service is already being augmented by satellite-based corrections feeding directly into GPS sets, which ensure accuracy to within a few feet.

At one time, the U.S. Coast Guard would offer free "courtesy" tows to boats that had run out of fuel, suffered engine failure, or gone aground; however, budget constraints have put an end to this friendly service. As long as you're not involved in a life-threatening situation, the coast guard will pass you off to a commercial towing operation.

In view of all the duties and responsibilities thrust upon it, the U.S. Coast Guard is understaffed, underfinanced, and probably underappreciated; but, like all good sailors, it does its best in difficult circumstances.

Cockpit Drains

Addressing the need for fast removal of boarding waves

Even if it is self-bailing, a cockpit filled with water by a breaking wave takes a long time to empty itself. Although it is true that much of the water will be spilled out as the boat rolls, what remains is heavy enough to depress the stern and make the boat vulnerable to the next wave rolling up astern. Fast drainage is important.

The cockpit that empties itself quickest is the racing-style type that has no transom. The next fastest is the aft-draining type that has large ports opening through the transom. But most boats have drains that empty downward through the hull, and they're usually located at the forward end of the cockpit, against the bridge deck. They should be at least 1¼ inches (30 mm) in diameter (preferably 1½ in. or 40 mm) and they should be fitted with bronze through-hulls and proper seacocks.

The hoses connecting the cockpit floor to the seacocks are the only things keeping the sea out of the boat when the seacocks are in their normal open position. The hoses deteriorate with age, so check them frequently by squeezing them. Replace them if they

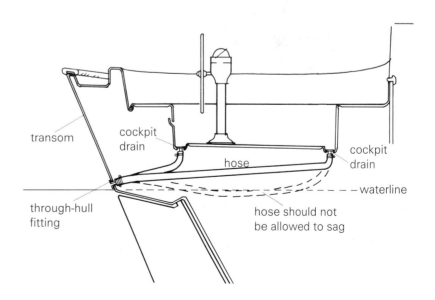

You won't need seacocks if you plumb your cockpit drains this way—but they'll need to be extra big to discharge quickly.

feel sticky or suspiciously soft and rubbery.

See also **Cockpits**; **Seacocks**; **Through-Hulls**.

Cockpits

Self-draining enclosures add safety and convenience

A cockpit used to be a small enclosure in which cockfighting took place, so it's probably not difficult to see how it also came to be the name for the sunken area where the crew fights to control the boat.

Most boats have cockpit floors that, although lower than the decks, are higher than the waterline in order to be self-draining—that is, any water that enters the cockpit will run out through floor drains.

The cockpit provides a modicum of comfort and protection for crew members who are steering, navigating, trimming sails, or keeping watch. It may have seats along the sides, across its aft end, or both, and it's usually protected from splashes by a coaming, or surrounding rail.

In oceangoing sailboats, the forward end of the cockpit should terminate in a bridge deck, which ties together the two side decks (in fact, it's part of the one-piece deck molding in a fiberglass boat) and provides a deck-level barrier between the cockpit and the companionway to stop water flowing down below in case the cockpit is flooded by a large wave.

See also **Cockpit Drains**.

Code Flags

Flying single flags to communicate special messages

Flags of the international single-letter code have meanings that are understood all over the world. Each letter of the alphabet is a complete signal, not only when

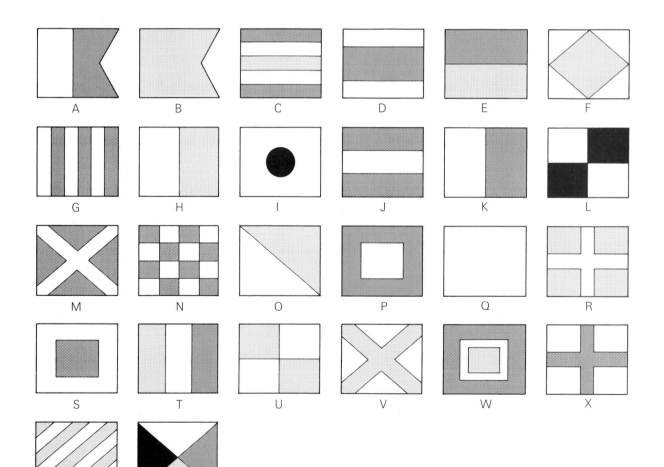

International code flags. Their meanings are the same in any language.

flown as a flag, but also when transmitted by Morse code with a signaling lamp, radio, or any other means. Following are the 26 messages of the single-letter code:

A I have a diver down; keep well clear at low speed.

B I am carrying dangerous cargo.

C Affirmative. Yes.

D Keep clear of me. I am maneuvering with difficulty.

E I am altering my course to starboard.

F I am disabled. Communicate with me.

G I require a pilot.

H I have a pilot on board.

I I am altering my course to port.

J I am on fire and have dangerous cargo on board. Keep well clear.

K I wish to communicate with you.

L You should stop your vessel instantly.

M I am stopped and making no way through the water.

N Negative. No.

O Person overboard.

P In harbor: All persons should report on board as the vessel is about to proceed to sea. At sea, on fishing vessels: My nets have come fast upon an obstruction.

Q My vessel is healthy and I request free pratique (permission to do business in port, or make use of its amenities).

R (Spare: no meaning has been assigned to this flag.)

S I am operating astern propulsion.

T Keep clear of me. I am engaged in pair-trawling.

U You are running into danger.

V I require assistance.

W I require medical assistance.

X Stop carrying out your intentions and watch for my signals.

Y I am dragging my anchor.

Z I require a tow. (Or, when flown by fishing vessels operating close to each other: I am shooting nets.)

In addition, code flag B is worn by a racing yacht as a protest flag, of course.

See also **Flags**.

Coiling Line

Building in twists to make your halyards run more easily

The trick to making a neat coil of a halyard after you've raised the sail is to put a half twist into each loop with your thumb and fingers as you make it. However, that assumes the bitter end is free to revolve, which it mostly isn't because you've wisely made it fast to something to prevent it from disappearing up the mast when you're not looking.

The braided lines used for halyards and sheets seem to give more trouble than three-strand laid rope, so the experts advise you to coil it with what they call alternate-hitch coiling. Brion Toss, a professional rigger, explains in his book *The Complete Rigger's Apprentice* that this means you alternate regular loops with backhanded loops that impart twists in the other direction. The twists cancel each other out and result in a coil that runs free without kinks.

Unless you've practiced and become accustomed to alternate-coil hitching, you may find this an unnatural way to proceed. I compromise by building in as much twist as I can in the ordinary way, and then hitching the coil to the cleat in a less-than-immaculate bunch. Despite its untidiness, the coil always seems to render easily through the masthead sheave after I have dumped it on deck to indulge in a little freestyle writhing.

If you have a long line that must run clear at high speed without snarls, such as a heaving line or a sounding line, lay it down on deck in the shape of figure eights, one on top of another. Just keep your feet out of the coil when it starts to pay out.

Coin Under Mast

How it all got started, and why you still need one there

Sailors have long believed a coin under the mast brings luck. This ritual is believed to have started with the Romans, whose custom it was to place a coin in the mouth of a dead person to pay Charon, the boatman who ferried the souls of the dead across the River Styx to Hades. Hades in those days was simply the home of the dead, not the specific domain of Satan in the modern colloquial sense.

Of course, there may be some of you who are convinced that you are headed for hell anyway, no matter what happens. So you might want to forgo the coin-placing ritual and spend the money instead on wild women, liquor, poker, new gear for the boat, and other sinful pleasures. What's to lose?

More cautious boaters will realize that placing a coin under the mast is another way to earn points for the black box in which your boat's luck is stored. It's a cheap price to pay.

Skeptics should note that even the U.S. Navy takes this ritual seriously. Officers of the USS *New Orleans*, launched in 1933, placed 33 coins—pennies, nickels, and dimes—under her foremast and mainmast. All were carefully placed heads up. And the destroyer USS *Higgins*, commissioned in April 1999, had 11 coins specially selected for her mast stepping, some of them very rare and going back to Roman times.

But you don't need to use rare or expensive coins. In fact, in the days of wooden ships, when even skilled artisans earned comparatively little, it was regarded as imprudent to use gold. Besides, there wasn't much point in paying Charon more than he could find change for. Rather, select a coin that means something to you, one that was minted in the year the boat was launched perhaps, or one from the year you were born.

Incidentally, most people glue the coin in place with epoxy or 3M 5200 these days, but it does worry me; I hope Charon can get it if the need arises.

See also **Black Box Theory**.

Collision Bearings

What they are, and how they can prevent accidents at sea

When another vessel is heading toward yours or overtaking you from an aft quarter, it's often difficult to tell if you're on a collision course. If you know with certainty that your respective courses and speeds will result in a collision, it's easy and convenient for you to make an early change in your speed or direction that will correct the situation, but not knowing can result in a lengthy period of anxiety and a growing likelihood of drama.

Adding to the uncertainty is the unwritten law that a small boat gets out of the way of a big ship, especially at night. Although you may have the right of way, you might want to cede it to the ship, just in case she hasn't seen you or because you don't want to bother the professionals—you know how much more difficult it is for a large ship to maneuver in close quarters than it is for you.

To let the ship know that she may maintain her course and speed without hindrance, you have to make a change in your own course or speed, and you

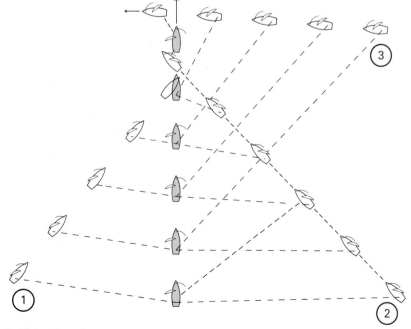

Collision bearings.

1 When the relative bearings of the black and white boats remain the same as they approach, a collision occurs.
2 When the relative bearing of the white boat moves aft, *it will pass astern of the black boat.*
3 When the relative bearing of the white boat moves forward, *it will pass in front.*

Notice how slowly the relative bearings change until the boats get quite close—this can be very disconcerting in real life!

have to make it early and obvious. So it becomes imperative, right from the beginning, that you should be able to tell if you're going to collide.

Luckily, it's very simple. Take a compass bearing of the ship as soon as you sight her on the horizon. A hand bearing compass will do just fine. If you're going to miss each other, the bearing will change substantially—that is, by 5 degrees or more—within a few minutes. The quicker it changes, the greater the distance there will be between you.

If, however, the bearing remains substantially the same or changes very slowly, you're probably on a collision course. You must make a substantial change of course—60 degrees or more—and hold it until you judge the danger is past. That amount of change will also spell out your intentions clearly to the other ship if she's watching you on radar, whereas miserly changes of 10 or even 20 degrees won't.

The best way to take the bearing is with a small hand bearing compass, one of the hockey-puck type that you can keep hung around your neck so it's always ready for action. If need be, though, you can take a relative bearing by sighting over a stanchion or some convenient marker on deck—but there are two caveats here: the boat must be kept on a steady compass course, and you must not move your head around. If the boat wanders around or if you shift your position, the relative bearing will not give you a true reading, and you might find yourself in trouble in the few minutes it takes a fast

ship to reach you from the horizon.

Incidentally, if you're as forgetful as I am, it pays to write down the original bearing as soon as you've taken it. Use a wax pencil on the cockpit seat or bulkhead; you can wipe the wax off later with paper or a rag dampened with alcohol, paint thinner, or WD-40.

See also **Compass Bearings**; **Compass Types**; **Rules of the Road**.

Collision Regulations

See Rules of the Road.

Color at Sea

Estimating distance and preserving night vision

It's a little-known fact that some colors appear closer than others at sea in daylight. For instance, if you're trying to judge your distance from an object, red colors generally appear closer than blue and green colors. So you may not be as near to that red buoy as you think.

Even more fascinating is the fact that this effect is reversed at twilight. As your eyes become accustomed to growing darkness, they are more sensitive to blue light than to red, so blue seems to be closer. And, as night falls, red objects grow correspondingly dimmer and blacker. That's also why chart lights and compass lights are

red—they don't destroy your night vision as white lights do.

If you're on watch in the cockpit at night and have to go down below temporarily into a lighted cabin, there are two good ways to preserve your night vision. The first is to put on a pair of red ski goggles, which filter out all except red light. The second is to keep one eye tightly closed—or to slip an eye patch over it. In the latter case, you'll only be preserving your night vision in one eye, but considering that it takes up to 20 minutes to regain full night vision, you'll be a lot better off with one good eye than with none.

See also **Nighttime Boating**.

Color Blindness

Checking your crew for a possibly dangerous disability

It's a sure bet that there are many pleasure-boat crew members who can't tell a red buoy from a green one at night, and who can't distinguish between the port and starboard lights of an approaching steamer. One in every 10 men is color blind, but few amateur skippers ever think to ask.

Part of the problem is the fact that most color-blind people are good at hiding their disability, and another part is that not all are affected to the same degree. Nevertheless, it's not a good idea to leave a color-blind person in sole charge of the watch at night if you can possibly help it. If there's no alternative, make it a rule that someone with good color vision is called every time an unidentified light is spotted.

Incidentally, although women are the ones who pass on color blindness from generation to generation, few of them suffer from it themselves.

Commissioning

Facing up to the fact that only you can make the list

The process of commissioning, or fitting out, is simply one of getting the boat ready for sea after she has been laid up on shore for the winter or left idle at a slip or mooring for a long time.

Every year, just in time for spring, the yachting magazines print commissioning lists. But every boat needs a different fitting-out list, and the list of things that need to be done to *your* boat depends entirely on how much you did or didn't do before you laid her up. What you need is your very own "boat book"—an 8½-by-7-inch school composition book with ruled lines—and the determination to keep it up to date. It should be divided into two sections—reference and running repairs. In the reference section, make notes about the kind of varnish you used on the cockpit coaming, the make of filters you need for the engine, the height of the mast above the water, the amount of water in the starboard tank, and so on. In the running repairs section, write down what has been done, when it was done, and what needs to be done in future.

The fitting-out process for most small boats can be divided into seven convenient sections:

- exterior painting and varnishing
- interior painting and refinishing
- engine and mechanical gear
- spars, rigging, and sails
- anchors and mooring lines
- safety and navigation equipment
- galley and head

You surely knew that already. And it still doesn't tell you what needs to be done—you're on your own here. There's not a magazine editor in the world who can tell whether you need more toilet paper for the head or rum for the liquor cabinet.

Companionway Formula

Kinney's design for a safe and comfortable staircase

Companion is an old term for a doghouse or raised skylight on the upper deck, often featuring seats on its sides and opening windows. It's also the term for the companionway, a stairway leading from the deck or cockpit to the main saloon below.

On small boats, of course, the stairway is unavoidably steep and more likely to resemble a ladder than a staircase, with steps about 12 inches apart. It's a great luxury on a larger boat to be able to descend gently sloping companionway steps with an armful of sails or other gear.

There's a formula for such steps. They should be between 9 and 11 inches apart, and they must all be equally spaced. They can be as narrow as 15 inches, but 18 inches is better, and even more width will allow you to make an entrance into the saloon with great elegance.

Here is Francis S. Kinney's method of designing safe and comfortable steps, taken from Skene's *Elements of Yacht Design:*

1. Divide the vertical distance between the deck and cabin sole

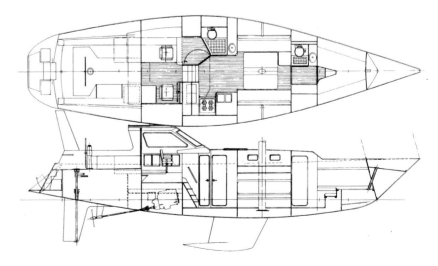

This arrangement plan for a voyaging sailboat designed by Roger Marshall shows the companionway stairs from pilothouse to saloon in profile and plan views.

into equal spaces of between 9 and 11 inches each.

2. Lay out the horizontal distance by allowing a projection forward of 9 inches for the top step, and successive projections of 5 inches forward for each following step.

3. Let each step measure 6 inches from fore to aft, allowing an overlap of 1 inch.

For safety reasons, companionway stairs should never be varnished unless they are provided with nonskid strips on top of the varnish. Sometimes fancy stairs have individual arc-shaped steps that curve upward at the outboard ends. The theory is that you can find an upright landing for your feet no matter how much the boat is heeled over; but, frankly, most of us seem to manage quite nicely with normal steps.

One final note about companionway steps: sitting on the top step is a favorite habit of guests and off-duty crew members. Make it illegal. Post notices forbidding it. Punish transgressors. It is very annoying to have to keep asking someone to move out of the way every time you want to go below or come on deck.

Compass Bearings

Be absolutely sure you know how to describe your position

A bearing is the horizontal direction of an object as measured *from the observer* in degrees. This may seem elementary, but for some

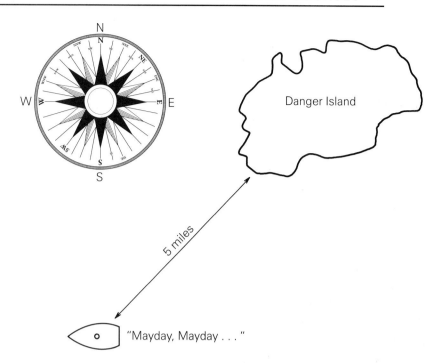

In the stress of an emergency it's easy to confuse bearings and directions. Here, your position is 5 miles southwest of Danger Island. Or, you can say "Danger Island bears 5 miles northeast."

reason, too many people sinking in a position 5 miles southwest of Danger Island are just as likely to incorrectly report their position as "Danger Island is bearing 5 miles southwest." In fact, it's bearing 5 miles northeast.

It doesn't matter to the U.S. Coast Guard how you report your position, but you must get it right in your own head, so it pays to practice. Choose one method and stick to it. Either say: "We're 5 miles southwest of Danger Island," or "Danger Island is bearing northeast, 5 miles." If you're using 045 or 225 degrees instead of northeast and southwest, make sure you add "true" or "magnetic." Then you can be certain the Coasties will find you.

The compass bearing is the fundamental building block of eyeball navigation, or piloting.

See also **Compass Courses;**

Course Corrections; Danger Bearings; Fixes; Lines of Position; Piloting; Reciprocal Bearings.

Compass Courses

Why you must adjust for variation and deviation

If your steering compass is out by only 5 degrees, you will be 1 full mile off course for every 11.5 miles run. This illustrates the importance of having your compass swung, to test its accuracy. You can have it swung by a professional, who can also correct it so that it always shows the correct magnetic course. Or you can swing it yourself and make a simple correction chart that provides the correct allowance to make for deviation. It's a relatively easy process that's described in detail in several boating books.

There are two effects that prevent a magnetic compass from pointing to true north. The first is the fact that the Earth's magnetic poles, to which the ends of a compass needle are drawn, are not in the same spot as the geographic poles. The difference, in degrees, is known as magnetic variation. And vary it does, from place to place on the globe. Depending on your location, the magnetic north pole might lie to the west or east of the true north pole by 20 degrees or more. Luckily, magnetic variation is well recorded and shown on all charts. It changes slowly over time, however, so if you're using an old chart (which you shouldn't be), you may need to allow for this. The rate of change is usually given in the compass roses printed on the chart.

The second effect is known as magnetic deviation. It's generated by metal and magnetic currents present on your own boat, to which the compass needle may be attracted or repelled. The mass of a steel engine near the compass will affect its accuracy, as will strong magnets in a radio or speaker box or even a knife in the pocket of a crew member.

Every boat is individual in this respect and, to complicate matters, the amount of deviation varies with the heading of the boat. It is usually greater on some courses than others. Deviation up to about 5 degrees is common and does not require correction. Simply consult your deviation card and steer a little left or right of the correct course to compensate. But

if your deviation is more than 5 degrees, as it probably will be on a steel boat, the compass should be corrected.

Some compasses have built-in corrector magnets that you can set with a small screwdriver so that the compass points to magnetic north on all courses. Then all you have to worry about is the variation mentioned previously. If you don't trust yourself to do this important work, a professional can set the corrector magnets for you or cure the deviation with external magnets and/or iron masses.

If your steering compass is behaving suspiciously, you can quickly check it with a hand bearing compass. Stand exactly on the centerline of the boat and sight with your hand bearing compass directly forward over the middle of the bow, making sure you are 5 feet or more away from any magnets or magnetic metal. This small compass should then be free of variation. Note its heading and read the steering compass at the same time. The difference gives you the deviation of the steering compass and will alert you if something is seriously wrong. By the way, if you wear glasses with steel parts, take them off when you use the hand bearing compass; even the tiny steel hinge screws can affect the compass at close range.

Wires carrying electrical current create magnetic fields that can affect the compass, so be sure that the wires leading to your red compass light are twisted around each other, canceling out the magnetism. Look out for portable radios, headphone sets, or other

electronic devices left near the compass—they have powerful magnets. Make sure there's nothing within at least 3 feet (preferably 5 feet) of the compass that could affect its accuracy, including tools, cans, and engines. It's difficult to achieve this on a small boat, of course, but do your best and expect the worst.

See also **Compass Bearings**; **Course Corrections**; **Compass Types**; **Deviation Cards**.

Compass Tests

Checking compasses for friction and proper damping

After the human brain, the most important navigation instrument on a boat is the fixed steering compass. It's an extremely low-tech piece of equipment that has been around for centuries, if not millennia, but the quality and accuracy of compasses can vary widely.

As usual, the old rule applies: You get what you pay for. If you're buying a new compass or checking one that's already installed, here are two simple tests that will give you a good idea of its quality.

Pivot friction: Using a small magnet or a piece of ferrous metal, deflect the compass about 5 degrees to one side, and then quickly move the magnet well away. The compass should return to its previous position *exactly*. Do a similar test from the other side.

Proper damping: Deflect the compass card again, but this time let it turn 30 degrees or so. When it returns, see how far it shoots past the original mark. A quality compass with proper damping has very little overshoot, and will return to its original position without excessive "hunting" back and forth. An inexpensive compass will hunt endlessly and drive you to despair in a seaway.

If you're buying a hand bearing compass, test it by moving it swiftly upward to one side, then to the other, to simulate the rhythmic movement of a bouncy boat, and observe how much it sways and swings. A little swinging seems to be the inevitable result of centrifugal force, and navigators soon learn to take bearings with a mean average reading; however, the better the compass, the less it will suffer from this drawback.

By the way, a new compass will not eliminate the bad case of deviation from which the old one suffered; deviation is caused by forces outside the compass.

Finally, see how much the card is tilted toward the north or south. The closer you approach the north or south pole, the more the north or south end of the compass is pulled downward out of horizontal. Some magnetic compasses and many hand bearing compasses need to be professionally rebalanced if they're to be used in latitudes greater than 40 degrees in the hemisphere for which they're *not* compensated.

In a dome-type compass, where the card is free to tilt without dragging against the glass, the angle of dip is of less consequence, although its directional stability will improve with proper compensation and it will certainly be easier to read.

See also **Compass Types**; **Lubber Line**.

Compass Types

Finding the compass that's just right for your boat

Compasses fall mainly into two categories: fixed steering compasses and portable hand bearing compasses. There is a third type, called the telltale compass, that is built upside down and fastened to the deckhead so that a person lying in a bunk can see the ship's course displayed overhead, but it's now fairly rare. A small hand bearing compass on a nearby bulkhead fulfills much the same function.

Steering compasses are specially made for the differing needs of powerboats and sailboats, and there is a wide choice of mounting methods. Sailboats are most often fit with binnacle-mounted compasses if they have wheel steering or bulkhead compasses if they have tillers. Powerboats often use flush-mount compasses recessed into a countertop, but small powerboats also have bracket- and surface-mounted compasses that can easily be removed.

Most compasses are magnetic for the simple reason that they are reasonably priced and seldom go wrong, but there is a growing number of electronic fluxgate compasses available in all types. They work by electronically sensing the Earth's magnetic field and displaying a digital heading; however, they are more expensive and they require DC power. Hand

Magnetic steering compasses (top to bottom): *An* indirect-reading compass, *as seen on a sailboat's binnacle or in a pilothouse. The course is read from the far side of the card, beneath the lubber line, and the card remains oriented to magnetic north as the boat turns. A* direct-reading compass *may be chosen for a bulkhead-mounted installation. It reads from the side nearest the observer, and is less intuitive to steer by than an indirect-reading compass. A* combination compass *can be read either directly or indirectly. This bulkhead-mounted model includes an inclinometer for measuring angle of heel, which can affect compass readings.*

A hand bearing compass.

C

bearing fluxgate compasses have the great advantage of being able to record and recall a number of bearings taken in succession.

GPS receivers also act as compasses, of course, but only when your boat is in motion, when they provide an average of the course you have recently followed.

Most magnetic compasses are internally gimballed these days, but older models with external gimbals work just as well.

As a rule of thumb, the bigger the compass, the better, because it will be better damped and easier to read. The easiest compass I ever had to work with was an old-fashioned grid-steering type, which had a movable ring by which to set the course. Then all you had to do was keep the long north-south needle centered between two parallel lines. There was no parallax error, so you could sight it from almost anywhere. Sadly, grid compasses seem to have gone out of fashion in the United States, although they are still made in Europe.

The worst enemies of compasses are vibration, heat, and strong sunlight. When you're not using your steering compass, keep it shaded and cool.

Some decades ago, all compasses were damped with a fluid that was primarily alcohol. The U.S. Navy's standard type, for example, was a damping fluid that was 45 percent grain alcohol and 55 percent distilled water. When those compasses developed bubbles, you could top them off with gin. Alternatively, if you ran out of gin, you could drink the compass fluid. Don't try that now; they've changed to mineral oil. Now, in a pinch, you can top off with mineral spirits or clear kerosene. And, if you run out of diesel fuel, you can make it home on the compass fluid.

Compass cards for small boats don't need gradations of less than 5 degrees. Experience has shown the human eye to be very efficient at estimating positions of single degrees on markers 5 de-grees apart; anything more ambitious simply clutters the card.

See also **Compass Bearings**; **Compass Tests**; **Course Corrections**; **Deviation Cards**; **Lubber Line**.

Complex Lights

Get close before you trust these multicolored lights

Some navigation lights show different colors over different sectors, but what's not usually shown on the chart is how far you can see those individual colors. So, if you're new to these so-called complex lights, beware. Don't trust them until you are well within the range of all the lights.

The problem is that you may misidentify a complex light, which should be showing, say, red, white, and green, because

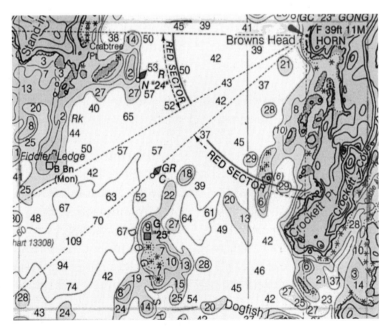

Browns Head in Penobscot Bay, Maine, has a complex fixed light showing white in the center, flanked by red sectors on either side.

only one white light is visible. That's because colored lights aren't visible for the same distance as white lights. The rule of thumb is that the nominal range of a red or green light is between 15 and 30 percent less than that of a white light. Thus, at extreme range, when you first sight the navigational aid, you may see white only, not a hint of red or green.

Even when you've closed with the lights and are well within the range of the red and green, you should still be cautious if you're trying to position yourself by the way the colors change. Lights don't simply change from red to green in a flash when you cross a sector, as a look at the chart might suggest. They shade gradually from one to another while you cover a fair amount of ground, and the speed with which they do so depends on your distance from the lights. Sometimes, when you're right on the dividing line between red and green, they'll even appear white, because red and green light together make white light.

See also **Faint Lights**.

Computers

Like all boat electronics, they're useful but vulnerable

There are many areas in which computers are either useful or entertaining on a boat, but they should never be regarded as essential. Small boats were successfully sailing around the world centuries before computers were invented.

So much electronic equipment incorporates some form of computer chip these days that it's difficult to define exactly what a computer is, but if a GPS receiver falls into that category, it's the greatest boon that the science of computing has ever offered boaters. It has changed the art of navigation forever, and it will keep many small boats out of trouble.

Nevertheless, don't ever forget that electronic equipment requires electrical power; boats and electricity have always had an uneasy relationship. If the power isn't there when you need it, electronics are useless—or worse than useless if they've deceived you into relying on them.

Ever since French Admiral Marcq St. Hilaire discovered a simpler way to plot and process sextant sights in 1885, astronavigation has involved nothing more than simple addition and subtraction after consulting the sight-reduction tables, so there's little excuse for not learning it. It's also a very satisfying art once you get the swing of it. Mary Blewitt's book, *Celestial Navigation for Yachtsmen*, explains it all simply and succinctly.

Desk or laptop computers are useful navigation aids that can display charts and weather information, as well as send text messages by radio or satellite, but they really need more power and pampering than a small boat can easily provide. The larger the boat, the more protected and more useful they will be, and a laptop computer interfaced with a GPS to display an electronic chart showing your boat's position and track is an extremely useful setup.

More and more computers will find their way onto boats as the years progress. More engine functions will be controlled by them, and we can expect to find them in greater numbers with more muscle power in communications and safety equipment. Let's hope their vulnerability to salt air and loss of power decreases as much as their computational ability increases.

Until computers can truly be regarded as invulnerable, it will always pay to have a simple, reliable backup. A depth-sounder, which computes the distance to the ocean floor, is probably the most reliable piece of electronic equipment yet invented for boats, but if it goes on the blink, it's good to know that a lead line will still work. Gravity never runs out of power and it's truly invulnerable to salt air.

See also **Depth-Sounders**.

Cooking Afloat

Turning out meals at sea is a difficult, exhausting business

Unless you have been to sea for an extended period on a small boat, you have no conception of how difficult it is to cook even the simplest of meals in a wildly erratic galley that never stops lurching.

Food preparation takes far more planning underway than it does on shore. First, get out in advance all the implements and ingredients you need because once you start the mixing and cooking, interruptions are awkward, particularly when the lids of the icebox and the dry-stores locker form your working surfaces. Once you start stirring things up, it's a major job to get into either one.

When everything is out, you need a place in which to stow it all—perhaps a square plastic basin that you can wedge into a corner. Of course, if the corner is in front of the pan locker, be sure to first get out all the pans you need.

Once you start mixing and cooking, have a plan for putting down the things you've finished with. Your sink will quickly fill up, so you might need a plastic bucket somewhere, as long as it's fastened down.

Think about where you will put hot pans if the sink is full. There's nothing worse than holding a hot, heavy pan in a rough sea with nowhere to put it down, while the potatoes are boiling over on the stove.

If your mugs and dishes haven't been painted with rubber cement on the bottom to stop them from skidding, place them on damp cloths or the soft, rubber, antiskid material made specially for the purpose.

Never put a newly opened can down on an ungimballed surface.

Always pour from a kettle with the spout facing fore and aft, never athwartships. Never try to pour into a stationary mug or other container. Keep the kettle in one hand and the mug in the other, so they move together.

Sit down to work, if you can, or wedge yourself into as secure a position as possible so you can use two hands. Some cooks prefer waist straps to keep them in place, but others are afraid of not being able to escape hot spills. Burns are serious at sea, so many cooks wear long plastic aprons, even when it's sweltering.

Use a mug or ladle to dish up hot food. Don't try to pour from the pan.

Learn to serve one-dish meals as often as possible and try to avoid anything that has to cook for longer than 20 or 30 minutes unless you are becalmed.

Preparing a meal can be exhausting on a small boat in bad weather, so opt for convenience foods when the going gets really rough, saving your culinary skills for entertainment in port.

See also **Galley Placement**.

Coral Reefs

Estimating depths by eye; preventing anchor snubbing

Coral reefs are the stuff of which many dreams are made. They conjure up images of white beaches fringed with palm trees, crystal-clear water, and hot sunshine. But there's not much romantic about a coral reef if your boat is near one—it's just another bunch of rocks waiting to put a hole in your boat. In areas where coral reefs abound, navigation is done by eye. The rule is to wait until the sun is high and behind you, from about 10 A.M. to 4 P.M. Simply send someone up to the spreaders (because height is an advantage) to guide you slowly through the reefs.

Sometimes it's difficult to see anything underwater, especially on calm gray days. Polarized sunglasses can help, but they don't always work. Caution is your friend, particularly if you don't have anyone to send up the mast.

When the sun is shining, the color of the water and the underwater obstructions help you estimate the depth available:

- Dark blue tones indicate deep water, 20 fathoms or more.
- Lighter blue means decreasing depth.
- Turquoise (vivid green-blue) is a warning of shoaling. It's the color of coral sand in water less than 30 feet deep. Again, the lighter the hue, the shallower the water.
- Brown or yellow patches underwater indicate reefs with a depth of 3 to 4 feet over them.
- Dark brown indicates coral heads—well below the surface if they're indistinct, but dangerously shallow if they're detailed.
- Green-brown means a grassy bottom.
- A shade of white ahead means you're probably going aground any second in 18 inches of water.

If you have to anchor where coral heads are prevalent, beware of fouling an all-chain rode. The chain can wrap around the heads, dangerously shortening the scope and causing the anchor chain to snub badly if the wind picks up. Buoy the chain so the main part of the rode can't foul the coral. You'll probably need several buoys if the water is deep. A rope rode is less likely to foul coral heads because less of it will be on the bottom. If it does foul, however, it can abrade rapidly.

Experienced cruisers often prefer to anchor in water 90 to 120 feet deep because there aren't many coral heads at that depth. But doing so requires a lot of anchor rode and hard work to raise the anchor.

See also **Anchors, Anchoring.**

Coriolis Force

Rotating Earth causes moving bodies to deflect

Sooner or later, if you read about ocean currents and the weather that causes them, you'll come across mention of the Coriolis force, which was discovered by G. G. de Coriolis, a nineteenth-century French mathematician.

It's an inertial force caused by the Earth's rotation, and its practical effect is to deflect a moving body to the right in the Northern Hemisphere and to the left in the Southern Hemisphere. Thus, the trade winds blowing from north to south in the Northern Hemisphere get deflected to the west, and are felt as northeasterlies. Monsieur de Coriolis's force is felt by ocean currents, too, so that they make a stately circle to the right in the Northern Hemisphere in the absence of more powerful influences.

Don't worry about the Coriolis force affecting the course of your boat; scientists emphasize that it affects only very large bodies of air or water. They maintain that it has no effect on smaller tidal streams or local winds, and it certainly doesn't affect the way water swirls out of the plughole, no matter what laymen think. I suspect, however, that it explains why people tend to move in a clockwise circle in fog.

See also **Accidental Circling; Ocean Currents.**

Counting Seconds

Learning to estimate short time intervals for navigation

When navigating at night in areas where there are several flashing lights that you need to identify positively on the chart, there's no doubt about it: you need a stopwatch to time the different intervals between the flashes of light-buoys, lighthouses, and other navigational aids.

But where there are only one or two lights, and their periods are reasonably far apart, you can judge the time fairly accurately after a little practice. If you haven't practiced the art of estimating short intervals of time—up to 30 seconds—you are likely to be wrong by about 16 percent, according to scientific studies. That's nearly 1 second in 5.

You can improve your judgment of time by practicing with a watch or stopwatch as a control. Most people find it easier to count two distinct beats to a second. The old standby is "one Mississippi, two Mississippi . . . " and so on, which is quite a fast mouthful, but some sailors prefer to count the slower "oh one, oh two . . . oh nine, one oh, one one . . . " Whichever method you choose, with practice you should be able to achieve 90 percent accuracy on counts of up to 30 seconds.

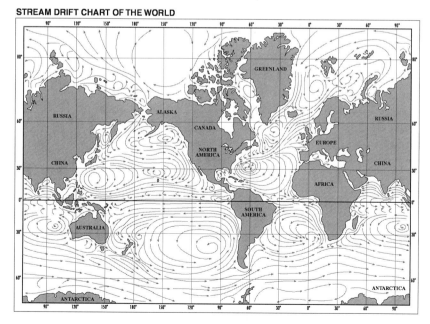

STREAM DRIFT CHART OF THE WORLD

Principal ocean currents of the world demonstrate how the Coriolis force deflects them to the right in the Northern Hemisphere and to the left in the Southern Hemisphere.

Course Corrections

How to make corrections for variation and deviation

There are well-known memory aids that say "variation west, com-

T	V	M	D	C	(+W)
045	20E	025	5W	030	
090	20E	070	4W	074	
135	20E	115	2W	117	

Here's a convenient way to make corrections for variation and deviation. You can draw this little table on any convenient part of a chart. See text for instructions.

C

pass best" and "variation east, compass least." They indicate that, if magnetic variation in your area is west, your compass course will be greater than the true course, and vice versa. For example, if your true course according to the chart is 180 degrees and magnetic variation is 20 degrees west, the magnetic course to steer is 200 degrees. The same principle applies to compass deviation.

The problem is that by early spring, just in time for the boating season, the only thing that remains with most of us is "east is least" and "west is best." That isn't a lot of help, so we have to go back to the textbooks.

One of the simplest ways to remember the rules is to apply the old mnemonic: Timid Virgins Make Dull Companions—Add Whisky. On a blank space on your chart, write the six headings, T, V, M, D, C, +W. They stand for True (course), (magnetic) Variation, Magnetic (course), (compass) Deviation, and Compass (course). The +W is simply a reminder to *add westerly variation and deviation when moving from left to right* (+W) through this little table and, by implication, to *subtract easterly variation and deviation (–E).*

If you move backward through the list—that is, from right to left or from Compass to True—you must reverse the +W and –E signs, so that you subtract westerly variation and deviation (–W) and add easterly variation and deviation (+E).

Have I lost you? Don't despair. It honestly is much easier if you write it down. Here's an example:

Left to right, +W, –E
Right to left, –W, +E

T	V	M	D	C
045	20E	025	5W	030

So, when you want to steer a true course of 045 degrees, and the variation is 20 degrees east, the magnetic course is 025, because you're moving from left to right through the table and you have to subtract easterly variation. When your compass deviation on a magnetic course of 025 is 5 degrees west, the compass course is 030, because you have to add westerly deviation.

Work from left to right through this exercise, and from right to left. Draw horizontal arrows over the table instead of "left to right" and "right to left" if it helps you.

One of the advantages of writing down these corrections on the chart is that if you occasionally become wracked with doubt about the correctness of your course, as navigators sometimes are, you can go back and check your calculations.

Finally, let me state the obvious: the magnetic course and the compass course are not the same thing. The difference is the compass deviation.

See also **Compass Courses; Deviation Cards.**

Cranking Ratings

How to tell if a battery will start your engine in the cold

A battery's ability to start an engine is often marked on the casing in cold-cranking amps (CCA) or marine-cranking amps (MCA). CCA defines the useful number of amps delivered for 30 seconds at 0°F (–18°C). This is important information because a battery's ability to deliver current drops drastically with the temperature. Obviously, the larger the CCA figure, the bigger the engine the battery will crank in those arctic conditions.

MCA is the same thing, but measured at a temperature of 32°F (0°C), presumably because the engine of a boat working in water will rarely get that cold. The MCA figure should be about 20 percent greater than the CCA figure for the same battery because of its increased efficiency at the higher temperature.

For diesel engines, you should allow 2 CCAs for each cubic inch (about 16 cc) of total piston displacement. For gasoline engines, which have much lower compression ratios, about half that amount will do.

See also **Amp-Hour Ratings; Battery Choices.**

Crew Overboard

Recovering someone from the sea needs thought, practice

Each boat should have an emergency drill for crew overboard and it should be practiced regularly. It's not something that can be looked up in a book at the last moment.

The essential first move is to throw flotation overboard for the victim to cling to—cockpit cushions, a lifebuoy attached to a dan buoy, anything buoyant. Make a mental note of the compass course. Start a stopwatch, or begin counting seconds out loud. If possible, designate someone to do nothing but keep an eye on the victim and to keep pointing to the victim with an outstretched arm. Push the "MOB" (man overboard) button on your GPS.

Turn the boat around quickly onto the reciprocal compass course, note the number of seconds, and then start counting again until you reach the same number. You should now be at or very near the spot where the crew went overboard. Your GPS will guide you back with great accuracy. The quicker you turn back, the better. Once the victim drifts out of sight, chances of recovery are drastically reduced.

There are several ways to make the turn, but no perfect way. On a sailboat, I prefer to change course to a beam reach immediately, no matter what course I'm sailing at the time. Then I come about and close-reach back to the victim, keeping him or her to leeward of the bow, and freeing the foresail at the last moment so the victim has a chance to grab a flogging sheet.

On a powerboat, I would immediately turn roughly 60 degrees to port or starboard and then turn to go straight back down the reciprocal course (the U.S. Coast Guard calls this a Williamson turn).

If you have a Lifesling buoy on a long tether, throw it overboard and circle until the victim can grab the buoy and fasten it on. Then drop the sails or put your engines in neutral, and slowly haul the victim toward the boat. Stop the engines completely when the victim is within range of the propellers.

Hauling a person from the water is usually very difficult, even if you have steps at the stern. You may need to arrange a four-part block and tackle attached to a halyard hauled about 10 feet above deck to winch the victim in over the lifelines. Lacking other alternatives, drop a bight of line into the water—made fast to a cleat at one end and to a winch at the other—so that the victim can stand in the bight and be winched up slowly.

There are many ways to get someone back on board, but they are specific to each boat and need to be thought about, worked out, and practiced in advance. And don't overlook the role a dinghy can play, especially an inflatable.

See also **Block and Tackle.**

Cruising Anchors

The tried and tested few; how many you need, and why

For serious cruising, you need at least three anchors. The most popular working anchors used by long-term cruisers are the C.Q.R., the Delta, and the Bruce. All three stow easily in a bow roller, and all are adequate in most bottoms. Choose one for your first working anchor.

For your second working anchor, choose a lightweight pivoting-fluke anchor, preferably a high-tensile Danforth or a Performance. They hold better in mud

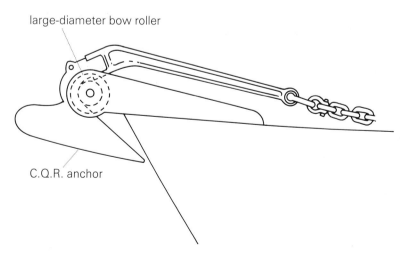

large-diameter bow roller

C.Q.R. anchor

C.Q.R. anchors are popular among long-distance cruisers. They are rugged and stow easily on a bow roller.

and sand than the plow anchors mentioned previously, provided they are not prevented from setting by grass or weed.

Your third anchor should be a hefty storm anchor. Choose a fisherman type, such as a Herreshoff (if you can find one) or a Luke. But make it big—an everyday working fisherman should weigh 2 pounds for every foot of boat length (3 kg per m), but a storm anchor should be two sizes bigger. Stow it in pieces down below, well secured.

See also **Anchors, Anchoring; Anchor Types**.

Cruising Boat Size

Calculating the smallest size for comfortable cruising

Cruising boats come in all sizes, of course, and the size you choose often depends on how big a boat you can afford and how many crew members you have to handle her. But a question that naval architects frequently have to deal with is this: How *small* a boat will be seaworthy and still provide reasonably comfortable living space and amenities?

The answer depends on two factors: the number of crew to be carried, and the weight of the stores. As a general rule, you can find the minimum displacement for a cruising sailboat by multiplying the combined weight of her crew, stores, safety reserve, and personal gear by 7. The answer will give you 10 percent leeway either side. Note that the size of the boat will vary according to the weight of the stores you need

to carry, according to the number of days in your longest ocean passage.

For the purposes of this rule, use the following guidelines:

- crew: multiply the number of crew by 160 pounds (72 kg)
- stores: allow 6 pounds (2.8 kg) per person per day
- water: allow 8.5 pounds (3.8 kg) per person per day
- safety reserve: multiply the total of stores and water by 1.5
- personal gear: allow 5 pounds (2.3 kg) per day, or a maximum of 120 pounds (55 kg) per person; for permanent liveaboards, a maximum of 500 to 1,000 pounds (225 to 450 kg) is more appropriate

For example:

1. find the minimum boat displacement for two people with water, provisions, and gear for 42 days

2. displacement = (weight of crew, stores, water, safety reserve, and personal gear) x 7

3. longest time between provisionings = 42 days

4. number of crew = 2. Crew weight = 2 x 160 = 320 pounds

5. daily stores = 6 pounds x 2 crew x 42 days = 504 pounds

6. water = 8.5 pounds x 2 crew x 42 days = 714 pounds

7. safety reserve = 504 (stores) + 714 (water) = 1,218 x 1.5 = 1,827

8. personal gear = 120 pounds x 2 = 240 pounds

9. total weight of crew, stores, water, safety reserve, and personal gear = 320 + 1,827 + 240 = 2,387 pounds

10. displacement = 2,387 x 7 = 16,709 pounds, or 7.5 tons

11. displacement range (within 10 percent) = 15,000 to 18,000 pounds (7 to 8 tons)

This suggests a cruiser of between 30 and 40 feet. A Westsail 32 displaces about 19,500 pounds, a Nicholson 39 about 18,000 pounds. Of course, many couples cruise in smaller boats, from about 25 feet and upward in length, but they will sacrifice the "reasonable comfort" this formula provides.

There are few small powerboats that can carry sufficient fuel to cross oceans, but those specially designed for the purpose will usually conform to the guidelines listed previously for sailboats. The Nordhavn 40, for example, a long-distance trawler, carries 920 gallons of fuel and has a range of 1,703 nautical miles at 8 knots. For ocean-voyaging powerboats, 40 feet is about the practical minimum, but an extra 10 feet would provide a welcome increase in seaworthiness and comfort.

For open-water cruising across smaller bodies of water, the practical minimum is also about 40 feet. Mainship's 390 trawler, a semidisplacement boat with a hull speed of about 8 knots, is a good example. A boat of this size will provide a safe fuel reserve and reasonable living space and storage for a couple and their occasional guests.

For coastal cruising in protected waters, the smallest power cruiser adequate for the sea conditions is likely to be one of about 35 feet in length. The Grand Banks 36 Classic, a wholesome diesel trawler, fills the bill nicely.

Cruising Lifestyle

For many, it's a dream that doesn't last very long

Only 35 to 40 percent of people who set sail on planned cruises of 6 to 18 months complete them successfully; 60 percent or more drop out before the allotted time. As for those who say it's their intention to sail around the world or to go cruising "indefinitely," only 10 to 20 percent achieve their goals.

These are not precise statistics, of course. But they are highly informed guesses by Lin and Larry Pardey, the well-known cruising authors who are two of the world's most experienced voyagers. The Pardeys' definition of cruising "success" is this: "Finding satisfaction or enjoyment from what you are doing; having a sense of harmony on board; feeling glad you had the experience; being eager to continue, or go off again."

The Pardeys also invented the following rule of thumb concerning the cost of cruising:

Take your everyday, onshore living expenses. Subtract all of your automobile costs, your home rent or mortgage payments, your mooring costs, and two thirds of your clothing expenses. Add one third of your food costs. The result is close to what it will cost you to cruise for an extended period. The legendary French single-hander, Bernard Moitessier, was totally pragmatic when he told a San Francisco lecture audience that long-term cruising costs you "just as much as you have."

Sometimes the best bargains in cruising yachts are those that have just returned from a long cruise, because most of the equipment you'll need has already been installed. If you opt for a new production boat, you'll find that it will cost you an additional 25 percent or so of the purchase price to prepare her for serious cruising.

See also **Cruising Boat Size**.

Currents

*See **Fighting Currents**.*

D

Dacron

One of the best synthetic fibers for rope and sails

Modern sails and lines for boats are mostly made of a plastic called polyester. In resin form, it's combined with glass fibers to build the hulls and decks of boats. In fiber form, it's woven into sailcloth and rope.

In the United States, the trade name for this synthetic fiber is Dacron. In Britain and most of the British Commonwealth, it's known as Terylene. In France, it's Tergal; in Japan, Tetoron; in Russia, Lavsan.

Dacron is very strong and rot-resistant. A conservative breaking strength for half-inch, three-stranded Dacron is 4,500 pounds (about 2,000 kg). That's about 500 pounds (about 225 kg) less than equivalent-sized nylon line, but whereas nylon is stretchy—about 14 percent of its length at 30 percent of the breaking load—Dacron is very stretch-resistant. Braided Dacron line elongates only 5 percent under the same load. Consequently, Dacron is widely used for halyards and sheets on sailboats.

See also **Plastics; Rope Strength; Rope Stretch; Sail Cloth; Synthetic Fibers**.

Danger Angles

Useful navigational aid with limited applications

Horizontal danger angles will keep you out of trouble if you can identify two objects on shore near the hazard you're trying to miss. They work on a simple principle that you probably dozed through in geometry class, which is: As you move closer to two objects, the angle between them will become larger.

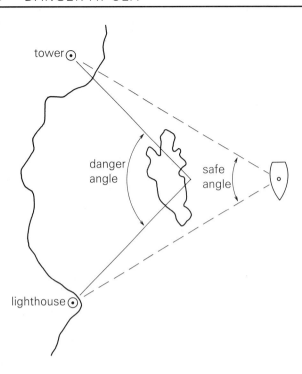

A horizontal danger angle—the angle between two objects on shore— will keep you clear of off-lying dangers, but you'll need a sextant for accuracy.

So, if you draw two lines— one from each of the two shore objects—that meet near the hazard, you can measure the angle at the hazard. Then, as you approach, you know that if the angle between the shore objects is smaller than the measured angle, you're farther away from the hazard. If it's larger, you'll be closer in and probably in a lot of trouble.

There are two areas in which this much-vaunted navigational aid falls short. The first is the difficulty in positively identifying two objects on the chart in the right position relative to the danger. The second is the difficulty in measuring the angle between the two shore objects. The navigation books tell you that a horizontal sextant sight is the most accurate way to measure the latter, but how many of us carry sextants these days? And, of those who do,

how many practice horizontal sights?

It's possible to measure the angle by noting the difference between two compass bearings of the shore objects, but such bearings are far less accurate, and you would need to leave a lot of room for error. In fact, if you took a simple four-point bearing on one shore object a little way on your side of the danger, you would have an equally good idea of how far from it you were.

See also **Danger Bearings; Four-Point Bearings**.

Danger at Sea

Risking drowning, discomfort, exposure, fright—for what?

Why do amateur mariners insist on risking danger at sea, time

and time again? That's the question Michael Stadler poses in his book, *The Psychology of Sailing*. Stadler, professor of experimental psychology at Bremen University in Germany, says: "Fully aware of the dangers that may be in store, they surrender themselves to being tossed about in a small boat between mountainous waves several times the height of the freeboard, exposed to cold and wind and spray; to being packed together with others in the most cramped conditions; to trying to determine their position with numbed fingers and great mental effort; to living out of cans—and all in the name of pleasure."

Are boaters really as demented as they appear? Is it crazy to pay a small fortune to indulge in an activity for which a professional would be paid danger money?

Stadler argues that the craving for the dangers of the sea is often a reaction against a monotonous urban lifestyle. "These people enjoy dangerous activities precisely because of the risk involved. Little do they realize that, from an insurance company's point of view, there is a much greater statistical risk involved in taking a car on vacation on overcrowded freeways than in cruising at sea."

There is a reward for taking risks, however. According to psychologists, overcoming dangers— even small ones—breeds self-confidence, and when the cruise is over, the boater carries this new confidence into the everyday world.

See also **Fear**.

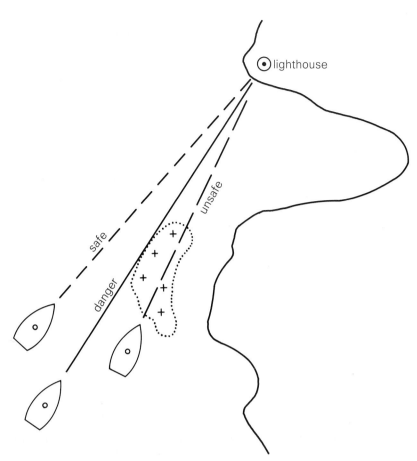

If you draw a line on the chart from a prominent object back past a danger, you can safely approach by taking bearings of the object. In this case, if the danger bearing is 035°, then a safe bearing will be 036° or (preferably) more. An unsafe bearing will be less than 035°.

Danger Bearings

Drawing a line on the chart to keep you clear of danger

You can draw a bearing line on the chart that will leave unmarked navigational dangers on one side and safe water on the other. It's called a danger bearing, although it might equally be known as a safety bearing.

Draw a line on your chart from some prominent object on shore that you can positively identify, back past the unmarked offshore shoal or rock toward your position. As you note the bearing of the line on your approach, you will see that if your course by compass is greater than the bearing, you will run into trouble; if it's less, you'll be safe (or vice versa, if the danger is on the other side).

It's basic pilotage, and a very neat exercise in the classroom, but in practice it's much harder because of the difficulty of identifying some shore feature beyond the danger area. Consequently, most small-boat navigators tend not to make use of danger bearings unless a prominent cape or lighthouse happens to lie in the right place just beyond the danger. In most cases, they simply rely on

GPS or loran positions, or they give the rock or shoal a really wide berth and hope for the best. In fact, you can substitute a GPS waypoint for that prominent shore feature and practice the same technique. This has the added benefit of drawing part of your attention from the GPS display to the chart—always a good thing.

See also **Danger Angles**.

Dead Reckoning

Educated guesswork fuels this basic navigation method

Dead reckoning (DR) is a way of keeping track of a boat's position without any help from external features. It consists of nothing more than charting the course steered and the distance run, and yet it's the very basis of safe pilotage.

Most authorities believe the term to have originated as deduced reckoning, the abbreviation for which was *ded. reckoning*. That, in turn may have been corrupted to *dead reckoning*.

But another possibility, mentioned in *The Complete Boating Encyclopedia*, is that the phrase may have come from the nautical use of *dead* to mean *directly*; for example, in *dead ahead*. In that case, dead reckoning could mean direct reckoning, which fairly well sums it up.

How does it work? From your last known position, plot (draw) on the chart the course(s) traveled and the estimated distance(s) covered. Let's say, for example, that from a charted navigation buoy, you steam along a course of

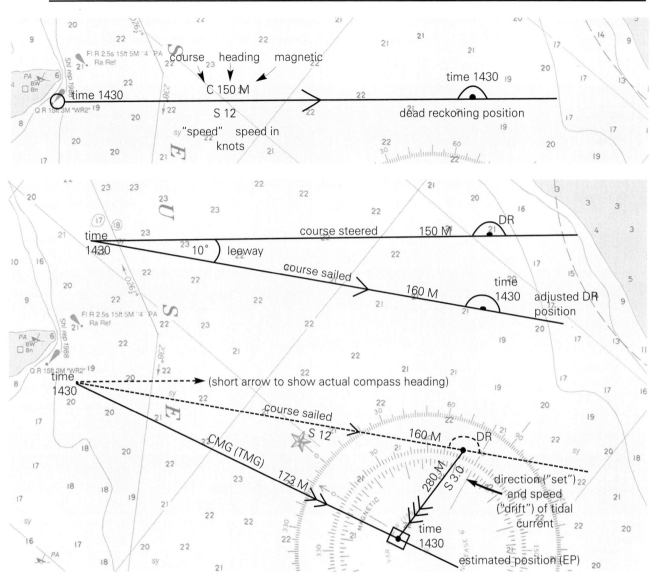

Simple dead reckoning (top) *with adjustments for leeway* (center) *and both leeway and current* (bottom).

150° magnetic at an estimated speed of 12 knots for 20 minutes. Ignoring the effects of current, wind, and waves for the moment, your dead-reckoned position is 4 nautical miles along the 150° course line on your chart.

In real life, of course, it would be foolish to ignore the effects of a strong tidal current. Suppose the tide-current tables alert you to a tidal current with a set (direction of travel) of 280°

and a drift (speed) of 3 knots. In 20 minutes, it would displace you 1 nautical mile in its direction of travel. Plot an equivalent vector from your initial DR position to obtain a more realistic DR. If that new DR puts you atop a ledge, you would have been better off to do the plotting *before* you charged off into the fog at 12 knots!

Leeway and current that affect the boat's course must be allowed for in the best way possible—ed-

ucated guesswork—but there is, of course, no way to check the accuracy of a DR position without resorting to other means. These include bearings from charted objects, astronomical sights, radio signals, and GPS or radar readings. Confirm your position by these means as often as possible. DR is fallible, but it is a fundamental navigational process that is as old as boats themselves—and, unlike a GPS, it will never *not* work.

See also **Course Corrections; Fixes; Speed of Boats; Tidal Streams**.

Deadrise

Why some boat bottoms are V-shaped and others are flat

The amount of V shape in the bottom of a hull is known as deadrise. Technically, deadrise is an angle measured upward from a horizontal plane at keel level. If you stand in front of or behind a hard-chined boat and look along the hull, you will be able to judge the amount of deadrise.

A flat-bottomed boat has a deadrise angle of 0 degrees; a deep-V hull has about 24 degrees of deadrise. The amount of deadrise varies with the intended use of the boat. A flat-bottomed boat rises onto a plane quickly and provides a comfortable, stable ride in calm water—but it will pound heavily in rough water. A deep-V hull provides a softer ride in those conditions, but

will be more reluctant to rise onto a plane. An all-purpose hull—a common compromise—has a deadrise angle of about 15 degrees.

Deadrise angles are not always constant along the length of the hull; they often vary progressively from midhull to stern. The deeper V at the bow allows the hull to cut through waves more smoothly, while the flatter sections aft make for more efficient planing.

See also **Bilge; Chines, Hull Shapes**.

Delivery Trips

The essential documents you need to prove your authority

If you're doing a friend a favor by moving his or her boat from one port to another, you're technically a delivery skipper, whether or not you're being paid. As such, you must carry a document to prove you have the legal right to move the boat. This is especially impor-

tant if you're traveling from one country to another.

The usual procedure is for the legal owner to write a letter headed "To Whom It May Concern" stating the skipper's name, the extent of the delivery voyage (naming the ports of departure and arrival), and the planned duration of the voyage. The letter should state specifically that the skipper is empowered to act on the owner's behalf in all matters pertaining to the safety and operation of the vessel during the delivery trip.

Have the letter legally notarized and dated, and make notarized copies to hand to the authorities if necessary. Also have notarized copies of the boat's registration or documentation papers and any other documents you think might apply to your delivery trip.

Depth-Finders

See Depth-Sounders.

Depth-Sounders

Measuring the water's depth by means of sound signals

Of all the electronic equipment used on boats, the depth-sounder (also known as a depth-finder or fathometer) is probably the most reliable. It works by beaming sound signals toward the bottom of the sea through a transducer, which may be located inside or outside the hull. It measures the time the signals take to travel

Deadrise is the amount of V shape in the bottom of a hull. The angle can change from midhull to stern. Here, a 65-foot Viking Sport Cruiser shows her deadrise at station 4, or about 40 percent of the hull length aft of the bow.

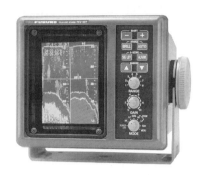

This Furuno depth-sounder (top) *has a color graphic display and operates on two frequencies, 50 and 200 kHz. The Datamarine model* (bottom) *shows the depth digitally in large, easily visible numbers.*

from the bottom of the boat to the seabed and back again, and—because the speed of sound in water is known—it can measure the depth of the water.

Transducers for pleasure craft usually work with a signal frequency of 50 or 200 kHz—either being much too high a frequency for humans to hear—although 75 kHz transducers are becoming more popular.

Lower frequencies penetrate water better, so a 50 kHz transducer will give readings in deeper water. The higher-frequency 200 kHz transducers provide greater detail, so sportfishers usually choose them for sharper pictures of the bottom and fish.

The accuracy of most units is within about 5 percent either way, but you can expect maximum depth readings in salt water to be 25 to 50 percent less than the manufacturers' claims, which are usually based on freshwater readings.

For the greatest efficiency, transducers should be placed on the outside of the hull in faired mountings, but they may also be fixed inside wooden or fiberglass hulls. In penetrating the hull, however, they lose a substantial amount of power, thus reducing the depth-sounder's ability to record the greatest depths.

Deviation Cards

Compensating for the inaccuracy of the compass

If you wish to steer accurate courses by compass, you must know the compass's deviation, or the amount by which it deviates from the magnetic course. Deviation is complicated—it changes as you swing the boat around and varies for every course, so it's convenient to make up a graph or a table that can be displayed on a deviation card for quick reference.

The process of calculating deviation is known as "swinging the ship." All it involves is measuring the difference between a known magnetic bearing and what your steering compass says the bearing is. These differences are measured every 15 to 45 degrees while the boat is swung around the clock in a tight circle.

The results are displayed on a deviation card, and tell you at a glance what compass course to steer for any given magnetic course, which you can either read straight off a magnetic compass rose on the chart or calculate for yourself from a true course.

It's not difficult to make your own deviation card, and it's a good skill to learn because deviation usually changes with time. All you need is an inexpensive pelorus from a marine hardware store and a modicum of patience while you swing the ship. There is no great mathematical skill involved, just simple addition and subtraction.

There are several other ways to check for deviation and many good books that describe the methods, but *Chapman Piloting: Seamanship and Small Boat Handling* is the old standby, providing as much detail as you're ever likely to need.

Some small-boat compasses will introduce a surprising degree of error into courses steered if they are not checked for deviation—as much as 20 degrees is quite common. They must, therefore, be compensated, or adjusted, so that deviation is reduced as much as possible—that is, within about 5 or 6 degrees.

There are professional compass adjusters who can do this for you, but you can also do it yourself by means of the adjustable external magnets found on most marine compasses. It's not black magic, and you can hardly do any permanent damage to the compass during your experimentation. If you're planning to cross an ocean, however, it might be wise to call in an expert, just for peace of mind. Once your compass is corrected, keep it free of nearby magnetic influences such as anchors, binoculars, and steel beer cans.

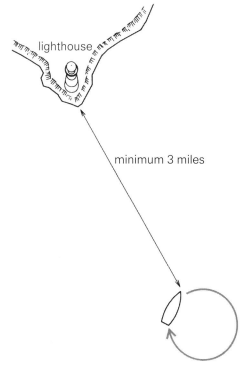

lighthouse

minimum 3 miles

Deviation

Magnetic Heading	7°W	6°W	5°W	4°W	3°W	2°W	1°W	0°	1°E	2°E	3°E	4°E	5°E	6°E	7°E
000°										X					
045°								X							
090°							X								
135°								X							
180°										X					
225°										X					
270°										X					
315°								X							

Simple Deviation Table

MAGNETIC HEADING	BOAT'S COMPASS	DEVIATION
000	358	2°E
045	045	0
090	091	1°W
135	135	0
180	178	2°E
225	223	2°E
270	268	2°E
315	315	0

The boat is motored around in a tight circle while measuring the bearing to the lighthouse with a hand bearing compass. The bearing should remain constant. If so, the boat is steered *by the hand bearing compass* on headings of 000 M, 045 M, 080 M, etc., noting the boat's compass heading on each heading. The difference between the magnetic and compass headings is the deviation on that particular heading.

To check your main steering compass's deviation, motor around in a tight circle three miles or more from a prominent landmark while measuring the bearing to the object with a hand bearing compass. Note the difference in degrees between the bearing compass and the heading shown by the steering compass, which indicates its deviation. Tabulate the results in a simple deviation table as shown with headings "Magnetic Course" (or "Magnetic Course Desired"), "Boat's Compass" (or "Compass Course to Steer"), and "Deviation." If deviation is more than 5 degrees on any course, consult a professional compass adjuster.

See also **Compass Courses; Course Corrections**.

Diesel Engines

The reasons they are so popular in today's boats

Although diesel engines cost more than gasoline engines and are usually heavier, they have become the power plants of choice for most auxiliary sailboats and the majority of inboard powerboats.

One major reason for this is safety: diesel fuel is not explosive as gasoline is, although it will burn fiercely if it is first heated. It takes only about half a cup of gasoline mixed with air to create an explosion powerful enough to blow most boats to pieces. The other virtues of diesel engines are long life, economy, and reliability.

The defining difference between diesel and gasoline engines is the method of igniting the fuel. Whereas a gasoline engine depends on an electrical spark to set off combustion, a diesel's power stroke is started when fuel is injected into a cylinder of air hot enough to make it ignite. The air is heated by compression as the piston travels up the cylinder. To achieve an ignition heat of between 500°F and 1,000°F (260°C to 538°C), compression ratios of as high as 20 to 1 are used, together with finely machined, close-fitting pistons and rings.

The engine was named after Rudolf Christian Karl Diesel (1858–1913), a German engineer. He studied in England and then attended the Polytechnic School in Munich, Germany. He patented a machine using hot-air ignition in 1892. His first experiments were as exciting as they were instructive—at least one early model blew itself to bits at first try. Others ran more successfully, using finely ground coal dust as fuel. Eventually, the ideal fuel turned out to be a petroleum distillate similar to furnace oil—what we now know as diesel fuel. In 1913, while he was on a voyage to England, Diesel drowned in the English Channel.

It took many years to perfect a foolproof system of delivering the fuel by means of forcing it directly into the cylinder through small nozzles, or injectors, that turn it into an easily ignited fine mist.

Diesels are not without vices. They suffer greatly from vibration, especially the single-cylinder models, and they are noisier than gasoline engines. They cost more, are harder to start in cold weather—that is, as soon as the ambient temperature falls to 50°F (10°C) or below—and are slower to accelerate. They are also heavier and more expensive to over-

haul and repair when something goes wrong. For these reasons, gasoline is still the fuel of choice for outboard and stern-drive engines.

See also **Diesel Fuel; Diesel Smoke; Engine Life**.

Diesel Fuel

Dealing with dirt, water, and algae is the main problem

Most problems with diesel engines spring from trouble with the fuel. This is something to bear in mind if you think your twin-engine sportfisher gives you full engine redundancy. If both engines are sharing the same fuel, think again. Keeping fuel tanks completely free of dirt, water, and bio-organisms is almost impossible on a boat, but luckily there are ways to get rid of these pollutants before they enter the engine.

Water condenses in the fuel tank even if it doesn't seep in through the filler pipe or breather tube. Dirt particles either find their way into the tank with the fuel or form inside the tank through chemical reaction. Certain types of algae—microscopic organisms from the vegetable kingdom—thrive on a mixture of water and diesel fuel, forming a sludge that quickly blocks filters.

So the first thing to do is to add a biocide to your fuel to kill existing organisms and prevent future growth. Several brands are available at marine stores. From then on, your fuel must pass through a primary filter, preferably one incorporating a water separator, and a secondary filter

Clean fuel is vital for diesel engines. These dual Racor filters may be cleaned one at a time while the engine is running.

on the engine itself. The importance of water separators and fuel filters can hardly be exaggerated. Frequent inspections and changes of filters do more than anything else to stave off engine failure.

Never let air enter the fuel lines; otherwise, your engine will stall and it won't start again until you have bled the system or purged all the air from the fuel lines. Therefore, never start the engine if the fuel tank stopcock is turned off. Never let the fuel tank run dry. And beware of heeling over so far that the fuel runs to one side of the tank and exposes the fuel pick-up line to fresh air.

Given that fuel problems are the major cause of diesel breakdowns, it will pay great dividends to learn to bleed your engine if it's not self-bleeding. It's very simple once you know how. You'll find instructions in your engine's manual.

Diesel fuel tends to deteriorate as it ages, so try not to let any remain in your fuel tanks for more than six months. It will experience a drop in cetane value, which is its ability to ignite easily. A good grade of diesel fuel has a cetane value of about 50. When the cetane value drops, the engine becomes difficult to start, and the combustion process becomes an explosion rather than a controlled burn. This produces undue stress on engine parts and creates more noise than normal, particularly the trademark diesel clatter. Either pump old diesel fuel out of the tank and replace it with fresh or treat it with a cetane booster and conditioner.

See also **Diesel Engines; Diesel Smoke**.

Diesel Maintenance

Changing oil and filters; replacing sacrificial zincs

Diesel engines require much less routine maintenance than gasoline engines. Exactly what you need to do, and how often, depends on the kind of engine you have. Your owner's manual will tell you what's needed.

Nigel Calder, author of the definitive *Marine Diesel Engines*, stresses that two things are absolutely critical to the long life of a diesel engine: clean fuel and clean oil. "If you keep the fuel uncontaminated and properly filtered, and you change the oil and filter at the prescribed intervals (generally every 100 to 150 running hours), most diesels will run for years without giving trouble," he says.

There are certain maintenance principles that are common to all diesels, of course. Because diesels depend so greatly on good clean

fuel, you should check the primary and secondary filters frequently and replace them as necessary. Changing filters sometimes introduces air into the fuel lines, so you must also learn to bleed the fuel system—otherwise, the engine will never start, no matter how long you wind the starter.

Before you start the engine, check the oil level. If it's higher or lower than it should be, that could spell trouble. Change the oil at the engine-hour intervals given in your owner's manual, or at least once every six months if you don't use the engine much.

Don't forget to check the oil level in the transmission, or gearbox, at regular intervals. A low level could indicate a leaking seal with potential for ruining the transmission.

Another thing to check before you start the engine is that the seawater intake cock is open; it's easy to forget. If you start the engine with the seacock closed, the impeller in the water pump will probably melt from friction. Some owners keep the engine keys attached to the seacock handle so they can't forget to open it before starting the engine.

To be sure that cooling water is being pumped through, check the exhaust as soon as the engine starts to run. It's a good idea to change the impeller once a year, no matter how much use it sees.

Check your engine's sacrificial zinc regularly, and replace it when it's half eaten away.

Once a month or so, take a set of wrenches and test every nut you can see for tightness, including the engine mounts. Nuts have a habit of loosening under vibra-

tion. If necessary, add some thread locker to prevent them from unwinding themselves.

Finally, inspect the engine all over as often as possible for oil and water leaks. Use your eyes to see them and your hands to feel them; then use your brain to cure them.

See also **Diesel Engines; Seacocks**.

Diesel Smoke

Learning what the exhaust smoke signals really mean

Exhaust gases from a diesel engine should be colorless. Smoke of any color is a clue that it's not running properly. Here's what exhaust smoke tells you:

- Black smoke is a sign of engine overload, a restricted air supply, or a malfunctioning injector. For some reason, excess unburned fuel is being blown out of the exhaust.
- Blue smoke forms when the engine's own lubricating oil is being burned. This can indicate worn piston rings, valve guides, or seals. The oil can also come from an air filter overfilled with oil or an excess of oil in the crankcase.
- White smoke is a sign of water vapor or fuel that has been atomized but not burned. The water vapor may be present in the fuel or water may be leaking into the cylinder from the cooling system. Air in the fuel can also cause white smoke.

Don't confuse white smoke with the steam of warm engine-cooling water on a cold day, which is normal. The steam is thin and wispy, and reevaporates quickly. White smoke is slightly denser and oilier, and takes longer to disperse.

See also **Diesel Fuel**.

Dinghies

Choosing a tender involves making many difficult choices

There is no such thing as a perfect dinghy for a yacht. There are simply too many conflicting requirements, and your choice of a tender depends on what sacrifices you're prepared to make.

There are two major types of dinghies: those with hard hulls of plastic or wood, and those with inflatable hulls of fabric-reinforced vinyl or Hypalon. Some dinghies, mostly larger ones, are a

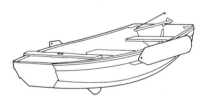

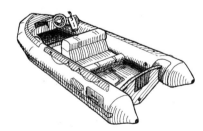

Choosing a dinghy for a tender involves many compromises. Two major types are dinghies with hard hulls of plastic or wood (top) *and those of inflatable fabric such as the rigid inflatable boat* (bottom), *which has a hard fiberglass bottom.*

sort of hybrid, with rigid plastic bottoms and inflatable topsides. These are called rigid inflatable boats, or RIBs.

Hard dinghies are easier to row and sail and make better sea boats. They tow with less resistance and are more resistant to abrasion from rocks and shells on shore. But they are bulkier, heavier, and less stable.

Inflatable dinghies are compact when deflated and attain planing speeds with small outboards. They have a greater load-carrying capacity, are more stable, and are easier for swimmers to enter from the water. But they are vulnerable to punctures, difficult to row in strong winds, and have much shorter lives.

If you intend to cross large open stretches of water where towing a dinghy would be inadvisable, you must carry your dinghy on board. An inflatable of almost any size can be deflated and stowed in a locker, but it is always difficult to find deck space for a hard dinghy. Some hard dinghies are designed to break down into two or more sections that nest inside each other, allowing, for example, an 11-foot (3.3 m) tender to stow in a space only 5 feet, 10 inches (1.78 m) long.

The smallest practical hard dinghy for two adults is a 7-foot (2 m) pram weighing about 70 pounds (32 kg).

The famous American naval architect, L. Francis Herreshoff, listed these requirements for the "ideal" tender. It would:

- row easily, light or loaded
- be light enough to be hoisted aboard easily

- be stable enough to get into and out of easily
- be constructed strongly, so it will not leak, and will take some abuse
- tow easily, always holding back on its painter and never yawing around

See also **Dinghy Capacities**; **Dinghy Life**.

Dinghy Capacities

Assessing a small craft's ability to transport people

Yacht's dinghies tend to be as small as possible, so there's always a temptation to overload them with people or stores. In fact, capsized dinghies are a major cause of boating deaths, especially in cold water.

If your tender is fairly new and factory-made, it will have a label that states the maximum number of people it can legally carry. You'll usually find the label, headed "U.S. Coast Guard Maximum Capacities," on the inboard face of the transom.

Where there is no label, use this U.S. Coast Guard–approved formula:

$$\text{number of people} = \frac{\text{overall length x beam, in feet}}{15}$$

Or

$$\text{number of people} = \frac{\text{overall length x beam, in meters,}}{1.4}$$

This is the number of people of average weight an open boat less than 20 feet (6 m) will safely carry in calm water. Weight for this formula is usually understood to be 160 pounds (72 kg) per person. The answer should be rounded up or down to the nearest whole number.

The label doesn't absolve you from using common sense, of course. All dinghies behave differently and some people are bigger than others, so if the water is rough, keep your load light and use extra care. Don't forget that it's now mandatory to have lifejackets *available* for every person on board a dinghy. Better still, *wear* them.

Incidentally, inflatable dinghies are usually rated for higher capacities than are hard open dinghies of the same length. You can safely add one person to the

numbers you obtain from the formula given previously for hard dinghies of the same length.

See also **Dinghies**; **Dinghy Life**; **Overloading**.

Dinghy Life

Inflatable dinghies call for lots of tender loving care

A plastic or fiberglass dinghy is extremely durable and requires little maintenance. It should last the life of your boat. A wooden dinghy also is durable, but it's more dependent on maintenance.

An inflatable dinghy, being vulnerable to damage from puncture, abrasion, and deterioration

by sunlight, is greatly dependent on tender loving care.

There's no reason why an inflatable shouldn't last 20 years or more if you deflate it after each use, dry it, pack it neatly, and stow it in a cool dry place. Unfortunately, few of us ever bother to lavish such care on a dinghy.

Liveaboard cruisers on extended voyages usually reckon on a life of about four years for an inflatable dinghy because they're subjected to abnormal wear year-round. Boaters who use inflatables only during weekends and vacations should get 10 to 15 years of good service.

DuPont's Hypalon skin, which is recommended for the tropics, is usually guaranteed for 10 years. Polyvinyl chloride (PVC) inflatables, which are excellent in temperate climates, are usually guaranteed for five years.

See also **Dinghies**.

Dinghy Oars

Choosing the right length of oar for your dinghy or tender

Good dinghy oars are made from ash or spruce, but many are also made from so-called southern hardwoods or aluminum these days. Ash is hard and durable, but heavy. Spruce is 35 percent lighter and doesn't rot easily, but it's soft and will wear quickly without protection.

If you paint or varnish your oars, leave the handgrips bare; otherwise, they'll be too slippery when they're wet. All dinghy oars benefit from strips of copper or fiberglass around the end of the

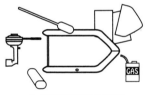
1. DISASSEMBLE BOAT

2. VACUUM BOAT

3. DEFLATE BOAT

4. DRAIN WATER

5. SPRINKLE WITH TALCUM POWDER

6. WITH SOFT TAILS, FOLD IN THIRDS OR ROLL UP

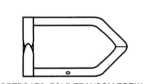
7. SPORTBOATS: FOLD TRANSOM FORWARD AND COLLAPSE TUBES ONTO TRANSOM

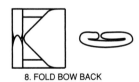
8. FOLD BOW BACK

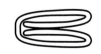
9. FOLD TRANSOM ONTO BOW

10. TIE BOAT WITH NYLON STRAPS

There's no reason why an inflatable dinghy shouldn't last twenty years if you deflate it after every use and give it some tender loving care.

blades to prevent splitting and lessen damage from sand and rocks.

Oars are sized according to the size of the dinghy; for the typical yacht tender of 7 to 9 feet (2.1 to 2.7 m), they should be about 6 feet (1.8 m) long. For a standard rowboat of 10 to 12 feet (3 to 3.6 m), 7-foot (2.1 m) oars are about right. Larger rowboats up to about 16 feet (4.8 m) will need oars 8 feet (2.4 m) long, but not many yachts will have rowing tenders that big. Boats with narrow beam or low freeboard may need shorter oars, and many cruisers choose short oars for heavy windward work, such as carrying out an anchor in bad weather, when the "low gear" is advantageous over short distances.

On boats designed for serious rowing, the oar length is governed by the distance between the rowlocks, or oarlocks. You can work out the correct length by finding the inboard length first. It's one half the rowlock span plus 2 inches (50 mm). The total length of the oar is $^1/_7$ that total figure, times 25.

Thus, the formula for a boat that measures 4.5 feet between rowlocks is 4.5 ÷ 2 = 2.25 + 0.167 = 2.417 ÷ 7 = 0.345 x 25 = 8.632 (say 8$^1/_2$ feet for comfort).

Dipping Lights

Using a disappearing light to fix your position at sea

One of the magical moments when you're returning from sea at night is when you first raise a lighthouse on the horizon. As you rise and fall on the swell, you see the light, then lose it briefly. It will appear and disappear steadily for a minute or two.

At that time, you have the opportunity to fix your position with a fair amount of accuracy and with great simplicity, because you can find your bearing and distance from the lighthouse without any plotting on the chart. All you need is the table known as the Distance of Sea Horizon, which is included in all nautical almanacs and many other publications.

For a full position fix, take these simple steps:

1. Take a bearing of the light with a hand bearing compass.

2. Use the Distance of Sea Horizon table to find the distance from your eye to the horizon. (Simply enter your height of eye above water and the table will give you the answer. The formula is: Distance to horizon [in nautical miles] = 1.17 x square root of height of eye [in feet].)

3. Similarly, check the height of the lighthouse on the chart, and then find from the table the distance from the lighthouse to the horizon. (Or use the same formula, substituting height of light for height of eye.)

4. Add the two distances.

5. Now you have a distance and a bearing from the light, which you can plot as a fix on your chart.

You may also come across a handy table known as the Geographic Range (Dipping Range) of Lights, which combines these two calculations for you. All you need to use the table is the height of the light and the height of your eye above sea level.

Using the table and interpolating for the nearest numbers, we have

1. the visible range with 10-foot height of eye = 3.7 nm

2. the range of a 60-foot light is 9.1 nm

Total = 3.7 + 9.1 = 12.8 nm

This is a little on the high side because we have rounded up both the height of eye and the height of the light.

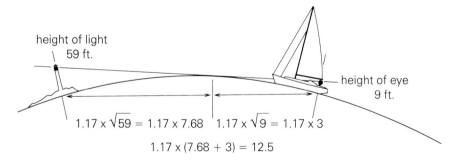

Dipping a light. In this example, when the light first appears on the horizon it is about 12.5 miles away. Use a Geographic Range (or Distance of Sea Horizon) Table like the one shown opposite to make your computations.

You can also use this technique in reverse, of course, when you're heading away from land. Keep watching the light until it just starts to dip and rise on the horizon, and then follow the steps given.

See also **Lighthouses**.

Geographic Range Table

HEIGHT Feet	Meters	DISTANCE, nm
5	1.5	2.6
10	3.0	3.7
15	4.6	4.5
20	6.1	5.2
25	7.6	5.9
30	9.1	6.4
35	10.7	6.9
40	12.2	7.4
45	13.7	7.8
50	15.2	8.3
55	16.8	8.7
60	18.3	9.1
65	19.8	9.4
70	21.3	9.8
75	22.9	10.1
80	24.4	10.5
85	25.9	10.8
90	27.4	11.1
95	29.0	11.4
100	30.5	11.7
110	33.5	12.3
120	36.6	12.8
130	39.6	13.3
140	42.7	13.8
150	45.7	14.3
200	61.0	16.5
250	76.2	18.5
300	91.4	20.3
350	106.7	21.9
400	121.9	23.4
450	137.2	24.8
500	152.4	26.2
550	167.6	27.4
600	182.9	28.7
650	198.1	29.8
700	213.4	31
800	243.8	33.1
900	274.3	35.1
1,000	304.8	37

Note: nm = nautical miles.

Direction

Boxing the compass is (thankfully) a lost art

The direction of a compass bearing or a boat's course is referred to in terms of the 360 degrees in a circle, with 360 and 0 degrees representing true north and 180 degrees true south.

This simple method is of fairly modern origin. In the days of sailing ships, the compass was divided into points. The cardinal, or principal, points were north, east, south, and west, but they were divided into 32 points of 11¼ degrees each, and portions of points. Seamen had to be able to box the compass; that is, name the 32 points in the correct sequence thus: north,

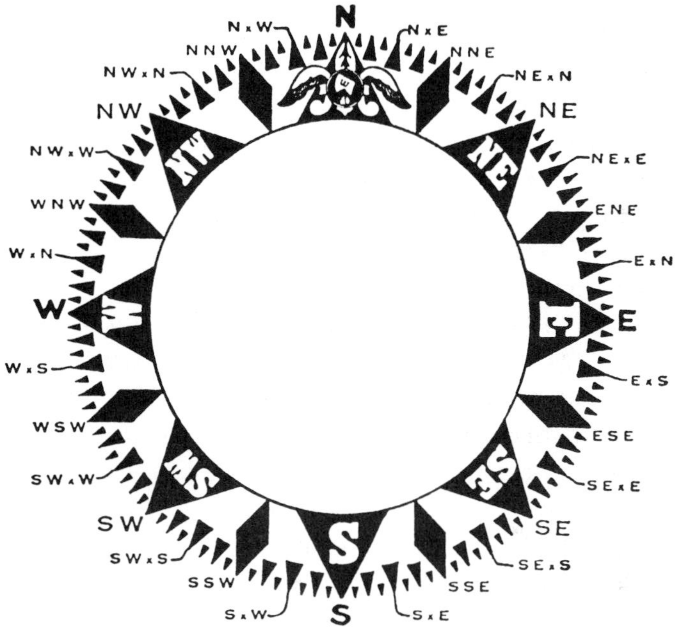

NORTH	0	EAST	90	SOUTH	180	WEST	270
N. ¼ E.	2¾	E. ¼ S.	93	S. ¼ W.	182¾	W. ¼ N.	272¾
N. ½ E.	5½	E. ½ S.	95½	S. ½ W.	185½	W. ½ N.	275½
N. ¾ E.	8¼	E. ¾ S.	98½	S. ¾ W.	188½	W. ¾ N.	278½
N. by E.	11¼	E. by S.	101¼	S. by W.	191¼	W. by N.	281¼
N. by E. ¼ E. .	14	E. by S. ¼ S. ..	104	S. by W. ¼ W.	194	W. by N. ¼ N.	284
N. by E. ½ E. .	17	E. by S. ½ S. ..	107	S. by W. ½ W.	197	W. by N. ½ N.	287
N. by E. ¾ E. .	20	E. by S. ¾ S. ..	109¾	S. by W. ¾ W.	199¾	W. by N. ¾ N.	290
N. N. E.	22½	E. S. E.	112½	S. S. W.	202½	W. N. W.	292½
N. E. by N. ¾ N.	25	S. E. by E. ¾ E.	115¼	S. W. by S. ¾ S.	205¼	N. W. by W. ¾ W.	295¼
N. E. by N. ½ N.	28	S. E. by E. ½ E.	118	S. W. by S. ½ S.	208	N. W. by W. ½ W.	298
N. E. by N. ¼ N.	31	S. E. by E. ¼ E.	121	S. W. by S. ¼ S.	211	N. W. by W. ¼ W.	301
N. E. by N.	33¾	S. E. by E.	123¾	S. W. by S.	213¾	N. W. by W. ..	303¾
N. E. ¾ N.	36½	S. E. ¾ E.	126½	S. W. ¾ S.	216½	N. W. ¾ W. ...	306½
N. E. ½ N.	39½	S. E. ½ E.	129½	S. W. ½ S.	219½	N. W. ½ W. ...	309½
N. E. ¼ N.	42	S. E. ¼ E.	132¼	S. W. ¼ S.	222¼	N. W. ¼ W. ...	312¼
N. E.	45	S. E.	135	S. W.	225	N. W.	315
N. E. ¼ E.	47¾	S. E. ¼ S.	137¾	S. W. ¼ W. ...	227¾	N. W. ¼ N. ...	317¾
N. E. ½ E.	50½	S. E. ½ S.	140½	S. W. ½ W. ...	230½	N. W. ½ N. ...	320½
N. E. ¾ E.	53½	S. E. ¾ S.	143½	S. W. ¾ W. ...	233½	N. W. ¾ N. ...	323½
N. E. by E.	56¼	S. E. by S.	146¼	S. W. by W. ...	236¼	N. W. by N. ...	326¼
N. E. by E. ¼ E.	59	S. E. by S. ¼ S.	149	S. W. by W. ¼ W.	239	N. W. by N. ¼ N.	329
N. E. by E. ½ E.	62	S. E. by S. ½ S.	152	S. W. by W. ½ W.	242	N. W. by N. ½ N.	332
N. E. by E. ¾ E.	64¾	S. E. by S. ¾ S.	154¾	S. W. by W. ¾ W.	244¾	N. W. by N. ¾ N.	334¾
E. N. E.	67½	S. S. E.	157½	W. S. W.	247½	N. N. W.	337½
E. by N. ¾ N...	70¼	S. by E. ¾ E...	160¼	W. by S. ¾ S. .	250¼	N. by W. ¾ W.	340¼
E. by N. ½ N. .	73	S. by E. ½ E...	163	W. by S. ½ S. .	253	N. by W. ½ W.	343
E. by N. ¼ N. .	75	S. by E. ¼ E...	166	W. by S. ¼ S. .	256	N. by W. ¼ W.	346
E. by N.	78¾	S. by E.	168¾	W. by S.	258¾	N. by W.	348¾
E. ¾ N.	81½	S. ¾ E.	171½	W. ¾ S.	261½	N. ¾ W.	351½
E. ½ N.	84½	S. ½ E.	174½	W. ½ S.	264½	N. ½ W.	854½
E. ¼ N.	87	S. ¼ E.	177¼	W. ¼ S.	267¼	N. ¼ W.	357¼
East	90	South	180	West	270	North	360

Converting compass points to degrees and vice versa.

north by east, nor'northeast, northeast by north, northeast, and so on.

To complicate matters, the compass card was further divided into half and quarter points (of 5.625 degrees and 2.8125 degrees, respectively) so the transition from north to nor'northeast went this way: N, N $\frac{1}{4}$ E, N $\frac{1}{2}$ E, N $\frac{3}{4}$ E, N by E, N by E $\frac{1}{4}$ E, N by E $\frac{1}{2}$ E, N by E $\frac{3}{4}$ E, NNE. It became even more cumbersome when you got down to NE by E $\frac{1}{4}$ E, and so on. Thankfully, we don't have to worry about that any longer.

See also **Compass Types**.

Displacement

How to describe the true weight of a boat correctly

It's important to understand the word *displacement* because it is a vital part of the description of any boat. To many people, displacement is simply the "weight" of a boat—but the weight of boats changes as crew, water, fuel, stores, and gear come aboard, so there is a need for a better definition.

At any given moment, the true displacement of a boat is equal to the volume or weight of the fluid she displaces while she's floating free. To a naval architect, however, displacement is the total weight of a vessel and her full crew, with all tanks two-thirds full and two-thirds of her stores aboard.

Because a boat's displacement literally equals the weight of the water displaced, it's also a measure of her underwater volume; that is, the volume from the waterline downward. Salt water weighs 64 pounds per cubic foot,

so you can calculate underwater volume by simply dividing displacement in pounds by 64.

Unfortunately, displacement is still ill-defined in many circles, and is often used too loosely by boatbuilders and sales agents for their own benefit. The displacement figures you see in sales brochures are often "light displacements": no fuel, no stores, no gear, no passengers.

See also **Displacement Ratio; Tonnages**.

Displacement Ratio

Length and displacement together tell a hidden story

By comparing a boat's displacement with her waterline length, you get a good idea of how "heavy" or "light" she is without being able to see her underwater body.

The displacement-to-length ratio (DLR) is simply the boat's displacement in long tons (2,240 pounds) divided by $\frac{1}{100}$ of the waterline in feet cubed.

The accompanying table shows how to interpret the result.

DLR	Displacement
380:1 or more	very heavy
320:1 to 380:1	heavy
250:1 to 320:1	medium
120:1 to 250:1	light
50:1 to 120:1	very light
less than 50:1	ultralight

Heavy displacement is not an infallible indicator of strength or seakindliness, any more than light displacement is an indication of

speed and cramped accommodations, but it's a general principle that spreading displacement over a longer waterline makes a boat faster and livelier.

Racing boats, sail or power, are usually light to ultralight, of course, whereas cruisers are of medium to heavy displacement. But on transoceanic voyages, the amount of fuel, water, and stores required by light-displacement boats affects performance so adversely that heavy-displacement boats, with their ability to carry extra weight with little penalty, are often keenly competitive.

See also **Displacement; Planing**.

Distance Logs

Reckoning your distance run with paddle wheels and props

The latest speed and distance logs are a far cry from the log old Vitruvius wrote about in the year 20 B.C. in his magnum opus, *De Architectura*. Vitruvius's log consisted of an axle carried through the side of the vessel, with a 4-foot-diameter paddle wheel striking the water. The inboard end was attached to three drums, hundreds of cogs, and a store of small round pebbles.

"Thus, when a ship is moving," quoth Vitruvius, "whether under oars or sail, the paddles on the wheel will strike the resisting water, and being driven forcibly backward will revolve the wheel, and the wheel as it revolves will turn the axle and the axle will turn the drum.

"The tooth of the first drum

in every revolution strikes and moves one of the teeth in the second drum. And so when, by the action of the paddles, the wheel has revolved four hundred times, it will, by the pressure of the cog at the side of the vertical drum, move the horizontal drum on one point.

"As often, therefore, as the horizontal drum in its course brings a pebble to an opening, it will let it drop through the pipe. Thus by sounding and by the number (of pebbles that have dropped) the length of the voyage in miles will be shown."

Distance logs have shrunk in size remarkably since Vitruvius's time, but modern knotmeters still use the same principle. However, now a paddle wheel the size of your thumb sticks halfway out of the hull under the water, and its impulses are recorded electronically and displayed as speed and distance on a small screen. Other electronic knotmeters dispense with the impeller and instead sense passing water flow by means of pressure.

Older patent logs, like the Walker taffrail log, work by dragging a propeller through the water on the end of a thin line. The revolutions of the propeller and its line turn a series of cogs and pointers that give a remarkably accurate record of the distance run. If you want average speed, you must divide distance by time.

Taffrail logs are intriguing pieces of machinery, and the quiet whirring of their works is very companionable on a long night watch; however, they have been made obsolete by GPS receivers that cost less than half the price

and provide an exact distance run and/or average speed at the push of a button. Unlike all the methods described previously, GPS gives you speed over ground or speed made good—not speed through the water, which must be corrected for the effects of current to estimate how far you've really traveled. Yes, GPS is very practical—but it's not very companionable.

Distance Off

How to judge distances without using instruments

Every navigator worthy of the name ought to be able to estimate by eye distances up to about 5 nautical miles, and often more. You can train yourself to do this quite easily with the help of these guidelines:

- the *shapes* of prominent lighthouses, trees, and houses become distinguishable from seaward at about 8 miles
- you can make out a light-colored beach at about 4 miles—although you may need to stand on deck to see it
- individual windows in a building are discernible by day or night at 2 miles
- a large buoy is visible at 2 miles
- a small buoy is visible at $1\frac{1}{2}$ miles, but you can't tell its shape or color
- the shape of a small buoy is discernible at 1 mile
- the color of a large buoy is discernible at 1 mile

- you can see a person as a moving black dot without limbs at 1 mile
- you can see a person's legs or a rower's arms at about 400 yards (400 m)
- faces are discernible (but not recognizable) at about 250 to 300 yards (250 to 300 m)

The distance to the horizon from a small boat is often over-estimated—it's mostly surprisingly small. For instance, if your eye is 5 feet (1.52 m) above water level, the horizon is only about $2\frac{1}{2}$ miles away. The rule of thumb is that the distance to the horizon in miles is $8/7$ of the square root of your height of eye in feet.

Distress Signals

What the U.S. Coast Guard says you must carry on board

The U.S. Coast Guard requires all vessels used on coastal waters, the Great Lakes, territorial seas, and those waters connected directly to them (up to a point where a body of water is less than 2 miles wide) to be equipped with U.S. Coast Guard–approved visual distress signals. The same applies to U.S. vessels operating on the high seas.

The following vessels need not carry day signals, but must carry night signals when operating from sunset to sunrise:

- recreational boats less than 16 feet (4.88 m) long
- boats in organized events such as races, regattas, or parades

Distress signals.

50 to 70 times a minute is considered a distress signal.

The U.S. Coast Guard offers the following illustration of the variety and combination of devices that can be carried to meet its requirements:

- three handheld red flares (good for both day and night signals) OR
- one handheld red flare and two parachute flares (also good for day and night) OR
- one handheld orange smoke signal, two floating orange smoke signals, and one electric distress signal (the orange smoke signals are approved for daytime only and, because pyrotechnics were chosen, there must be three of them; the distress light is approved for night use only)

Aerial red meteors launched from pistols must be handled with great caution. In some states, flare pistols are considered firearms and you may not be legally allowed to use them.

Note, too, that a VHF radio telephone, probably the most effective and most-used distress device, is not *required* by the U.S. Coast Guard on small recreational boats.

See also **Calling for Help; Pan-Pan Calls.**

Dockage Costs

While the cost of berths rises, boat values fall

Generally speaking, a slip in a marina will cost three or four times as much as the hire of a mooring. A

- open sailboats less than 26 feet (7.9 m) long that do not have engines
- manually propelled boats

In any other boat, you must carry at least one approved day signal and one approved night signal—however (and this is important), if you choose a pyrotechnic device of any kind, such as a rocket or flare, you must have at least three of them. Some pyrotechnics are accepted as both day and night signals, in which case you need only three in total.

Approved day-only signals include orange smoke and a distress flag that is at least 3 feet square and that has a black square and a black ball on a bright orange background.

An electric distress light that automatically flashes the international distress signal SOS is acceptable for night use only.

Signals suitable for day and night use include handheld red flares, red parachute flares, and aerial red meteors. Note that white flares are not distress signals, and may be used legally simply to draw another ship's attention to your presence. But, *under Inland Navigation Rules only,* a white strobe light flashing marina berth on a floating pier is most convenient, and many such berths have telephone and cable television lines laid on, as well as the usual water and electricity supplies. But whereas slip fees tend to rise year after year, the value of your boat goes down.

Most boaters who leave their vessels in the water year-round spend 6 percent or more of their boats' value in marina fees every year. Therefore, in 15 years (often much sooner), they will have spent as much on dockage as the boat is now worth.

In many marinas where the basis for moorage fees is a fixed sum for every foot of boat length, big boats get a better deal than small boats because the displacement, accommodation, and value of boats rise by the cube of their length or more. For example, whereas a 22-foot (6.5 m) Catalina 22 displaces 2,490 pounds (1,129 kg), a 40-foot (12 m) Islander P-40 displaces 17,000 pounds (7,709 kg). In other words, the Islander is nearly seven times bigger than the Catalina and is worth seven times as much, but pays only twice as much.

Docking

Excitement and uncertainty mark the end of each voyage

If landlubbers think parking is such "street sorrow," then docking must be the mariner's main misery. Docking is the cause of more minor accidents and major screaming matches than all other boat maneuvers put together.

Bringing a boat into a slip in a crowded marina so that it comes to a halt 6 inches away from the walkway on one side and 6 inches from the main pier at the bow is a major feat of seamanship, and one that is clouded with uncertainties.

Three factors affect the accuracy of your approach: the wind, the current, and the vessel's speed and handling. Ironically, the more slowly you approach, the less control you have of the vessel's direction. Conversely, the faster you approach, the harder you'll hit the pier.

If all three factors were unchanging, you would soon learn to compensate; however, they're never the same twice. In particular, the wind and the current vary in both speed and direction. Your boat speed depends on how long it's been since the bottom was scrubbed and whether you remembered to put the engine in neutral, but this at least is within your control. Judging your boat's handling characteristics is a matter of practice. Twin engines give you more control, and so does an outboard engine that can be swiveled. On a big boat, a bow thruster is a great comfort. Especially if you drive a single-engined inboard, learn its quirks in reverse, when the propeller wash will not be directed over the rudder to give you added control. You might get "propeller walk" in reverse, too—a tendency to turn one way or the other even when the rudder is amidships. Get to know your boat and learn which combinations of forward and reverse thrusts—and at what throttle—are most likely to produce a desired effect. Then add in wind and current, and try to get them

to cancel rather than add to your boat's natural tendencies.

Quite often there's a fourth factor that affects the precision of your docking: the amount of space you have in which to line the boat up for final approach. In many marinas, conditions are so crowded that you have no option but to start to turn into your slip before you're fully lined up, with all the blind uncertainty that doing so involves. At those times, a spring line can be a great help. Say you're trying to dock starboard-side to against an annoying wind or current. Secure an after-bow spring to a bow cleat and get a dockhand or a leaping crew member to take some turns with the other end around a dock cleat or piling aft of amidships. Put your rudder hard to port and your engine in forward. The bow will want to turn to port but the after-bow spring prevents that; instead, the boat should "walk" right into the dock. With twin engines, you can make this work even better. It's "the poor man's bow thruster."

There is comfort in the knowledge that even the most experienced boaters have docking accidents occasionally. It's uncanny how often they only discover too late that their engines won't go into reverse gear—that is, when they're approaching a slip at a good lick.

It's a good idea to have at least three fenders out on each side before you try to dock, and it's just as important to line the dock with rubber or plastic fendering. Ignore the scoffing of the macho mariners—better to bounce off than to be stove in.

Oh, and never moor your

D

dinghy across the head of the slip, because if you lose reverse gear as you approach, the dinghy makes a nasty crunching noise when you T-bone it at 4 knots. Trust me.

See also **Dock Lines**.

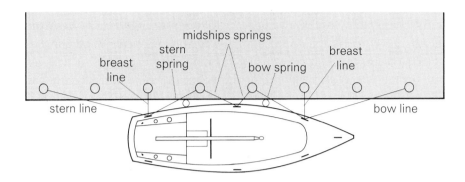

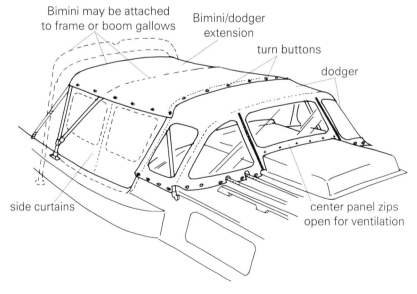

Dock Lines

Naming the various lines and learning what their uses are

In general terms, spring lines run fore and aft, whereas bow lines, stern lines, and breast lines run mostly athwartships. Thus, springs prevent a boat from moving forward or backward; the other lines keep her from moving sideways. All docking lines should be of nylon, which is stretchier than Dacron; it will, therefore, absorb the shock of sudden movements due to wave or wind action.

You should carry at least two spring lines that are a quarter longer than your boat. That might seem an excessive length, but if you ever have to make fast alongside a wall or wooden jetty in an area with a large tidal range, you'll find them very useful. The longer the springs, the better your boat will maintain her position and the less attention the lines will need as she rises and falls with the tide.

Bow and stern lines are usually about two-thirds the length of the boat. Spring lines are named for the direction in which they lead. For example, the after-bow spring leads from the bow backward toward the stern, and the forward-quarter spring leads from the quarter toward the bow.

Dock line terminology. In common practice the bow and stern lines do not lead as far forward and aft, respectively, on the dock as what's shown here. Note that the after-bow spring and forward-quarter spring may be called simply bow spring and stern spring.

Bow and stern lines usually lead a little forward and aft, respectively, as well as sideways. This is not to prevent fore-and-aft movement—the springs take care of that—but rather to gain a little length—and thus more elasticity—to prevent snubbing.

The diameter of an eye splice in a dock line should be at least three times (and preferably four or five times) the diameter of the piling or bollard it fits over, so that it will not tend to pull apart at the throat when tension is applied, as a short eye splice might.

The rule of thumb for dock lines is that they should be $1/8$ inch (3 mm) in diameter for every 9 feet (2.7 m) of overall boat length. Small lines are hard to handle, however, so on a small boat you might want your lines at least $3/8$-inch (9.5 mm) diameter.

A dodger over the companionway and forward end of the cockpit provides shelter from the elements and acts as a transition from "down below" to "on deck."

Dodger

Check the height of yours and its ability to fold down

A spray dodger is a canopy, usually made of acrylic canvas stretched over a framework of stainless steel tubing, that provides shelter for the crew in the cockpit and prevents rain and spray from entering the main cabin.

Acrylic plastic windows provide views forward and to the sides, but if they become misted over from fog or spray, you should be able to stand in the cockpit or at the helm and see over the top of the dodger without strain.

To reduce windage during storms at sea, and even in exposed anchorages, the dodger should easily fold down flat against the cabintop where it can be lashed securely in place. A dodger that is unable to fold down because it has a hard top and/or sides is vulnerable to big seas.

Doldrums

Equatorial region with a bad reputation for thunderstorms

The region of low pressure over the oceans at the equator is named the Intratropical Convergence Zone (ITCZ) or doldrums and is known mostly for its dead calms and light, fluctuating winds. But it is also capable of producing heavy rains and thunderstorms.

The trade winds blow toward the equator from either side and diminish there to form a doldrum belt with an average width of be-

tween 200 and 300 miles. This belt is biased toward the Northern Hemisphere, being located between the equator and 7°N in February and between 5°N and 12°N in July at its greatest breadth. That breadth varies considerably, being widest on the eastern shores of the Atlantic and Pacific Oceans.

If you're lucky, and especially if you're near the western edge of the doldrums, your sailboat might pass through the region from one trade-wind belt to the other without a hitch. But it's more likely that you'll have to take advantage of every squall and fitful breeze to get through, under sail alone, in a week at best.

This is what the famous British yachtsman, Eric Hiscock, has to say about the doldrums in *Voyaging Under Sail*: "I am glad to

have had the opportunity of making a passage through the doldrums under sail, for I feel that is an experience which every sailorman ought to have once in his lifetime, so that he may learn to be patient and appreciate some of the difficulties with which his forefathers had to contend. But once is enough, and if I ever have to pass through that area of calms, squalls, heat, and rain again, I hope to have an engine of useful power and a plentiful supply of fuel for it."

See also **Trade Winds**.

Downburst

Beware of dangerous jets of wind from thunderstorms

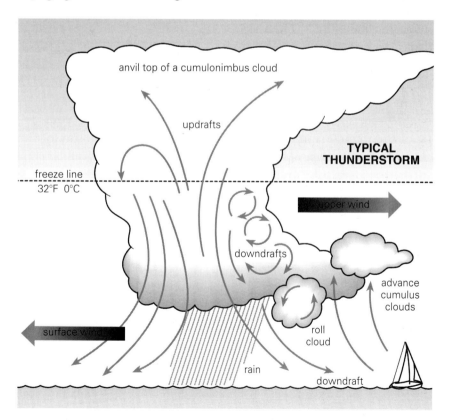

Section through a thunderstorm cell. This is a young storm. As it matures, the downdrafts could turn into more dangerous downbursts.

A downburst, or microburst, is a dangerous mass of cool air that shoots downward out of a thunderstorm. Downbursts with the energy of small tornadoes achieve speeds of 100 knots or more, and shift direction rapidly.

Some are bigger than others, but all are capable of capsizing sailboats whose crews are unprepared. There is no way of forecasting downbursts; therefore, if you find yourself stuck in the path of an approaching thunderstorm, the safest action is to douse the sails and make everything fast on deck.

The telltale sign of a thunderstorm large enough to create downbursts is a cumulus cloud that appears to be growing larger as you watch it. Cumulonimbus is tall and imposing, with a cauliflower-shaped top and a black, menacing base. You'll often see the top being blown away into the shape of an anvil by high-speed upper-atmosphere winds.

As the cloud approaches, you might notice another characteristic of the thunderstorm: an area along the leading edge of the base where the clouds seem to roll vertically.

The winds ahead of the thunderstorm will weaken as the roll cloud draws near and, as it passes overhead, you can expect violent winds from many different directions, including downdrafts and more violent downbursts. Even in a normal summer afternoon storm, these winds can exceed 60 knots. Behind the roll cloud, heavy rain (and possibly hail) begins to fall as the dark area of the cloud passes overhead.

On inland and coastal waters, thunderstorms are more common in summer, and usually develop in the late afternoon when the ambient air has been heated for many hours. In midocean, away from the influence of land, they mostly occur between midnight and sunrise.

Always take thunderstorms seriously—most are accompanied by dangerous lightning, if not downbursts. An inexpensive AM radio receiver will provide advance warning of approaching thunderstorms, announcing their arrival with loud crashes of static noise. If possible, plot the course of any thunderstorm you spot, and take early action to get out of its direct path.

See also **Clouds**.

Dragging Anchor

A dangerous situation that demands prompt action

It happens to every boater sooner or later. The wind in your anchorage rises, the motion of the boat increases, and your anchor starts to drag. Sometimes the rumbling of an all-chain rode warns you. At other times, your first indication may be when other boats firmly anchored to leeward appear to be moving slowly upwind toward your stern. That's an astonishing sight the first time you experience it.

The first sign of dragging in a crowded anchorage calls for immediate action. If you have just lowered the anchor, pull it up and try again, perhaps in a different spot. If you've been swinging comfortably on the "hook" for a while, however, a solution other than weighing anchor and re-anchoring may be in order. First, let out more anchor line, as much as you can without fouling another boat. That will give your rode a more efficient angle of pull so that the anchor should dig into the ground instead of being pulled upward out of it.

If that doesn't solve the problem, you can start the engine and run it ahead slow to take some strain off the anchor while you think things through or wait for the squall to blow over.

But what if your engine won't run because, in all the excitement, your dinghy painter has fouled the prop? Or what if the storm is settling in for a while and you need a longer-term solution? Next, load the kedge, or secondary, anchor into the dinghy and flake its line down on top of it. Make the bitter end fast to the boat and take the dinghy to windward, paying out the anchor line as you go. When you reach the end of the line, drop the anchor a couple of boat lengths to one side of the anchor already down there so that the two lines together form a shallow V from the bow of the boat.

Back on the boat, haul away on the new anchor line until you feel it dig in, and make it fast at the bow. Adjust the lines so that both anchors are now taking the strain fairly.

If your primary anchor has still not reset itself or if it was fouled in the first place, allow the newly set kedge to take all the strain while you weigh the first anchor and reset it from the dinghy, just as you did with the kedge.

If necessary—if you have a reef close astern, or the engine isn't working, or other boats are too near for comfort—you can set and weigh anchors alternately to gain ground to windward, but it's a lot of work and may be dangerous in a rising wind at night. So, having recovered your main anchor, you might want to consider making a buoy or fender fast to the kedge line, casting off, and finding a safer spot in which to anchor from scratch. You can recover the kedge when conditions improve.

If the wind is onshore and the holding quality of the anchorage is uncertain, prudent seamanship might even dictate your putting to sea. That's something you should consider every time you arrive in a new anchorage. Cautious sailors will tuck a reef or two into the mainsail before stowing it on the boom for the night because they know that if the anchor drags, it's likely to be blowing a gale. And they will make a note of a bearing that will take them safely out of the anchorage in the pitch dark. You will probably find that if you go to this much trouble, your anchor will never drag. But do it anyway; it's cheap insurance.

See also **Anchors, Anchoring; Anchor Types; Cruising Anchors.**

Drinking Seawater

Don't do it unless you're drinking fresh water as well

Doctors who have examined castaways say you shouldn't drink seawater unless you also drink an ample supply of fresh water. Sea-

water alone is likely to do more harm than good.

Well-known circumnavigators such as John Voss and Francis Chichester regularly drank seawater. Voss drank a glass a day for his health, and Chichester found that an occasional drink of salt water relieved leg cramps caused by excessive sweating in the tropics. But both of them were drinking plenty of fresh water as well.

Prolonged seasickness can cause a serious chemical imbalance in the human body, but small quantities of seawater will provide all the sodium and other chemicals needed to restore that balance—with the exception of calcium, which may be taken in tablet form. As befits creatures who came from the sea, humans have blood that is similar in chemical composition to seawater.

A physician who was also a small-boat sailor once advised me to drink half a cup of seawater once or twice a day during prolonged bouts of seasickness. Although it was not likely to remain in the stomach long, he said, the tissue would swiftly absorb the minerals needed.

See also **Ocean Water; Seasickness.**

Drogue

Slowing a boat down to help her ride out stormy weather

Most dictionaries will tell you that a drogue is the same thing as a sea anchor, but they are behind the times. In modern yachting terms, a drogue is anything deployed from the stern and dragged behind a boat to reduce her speed by a few knots, particularly in bad

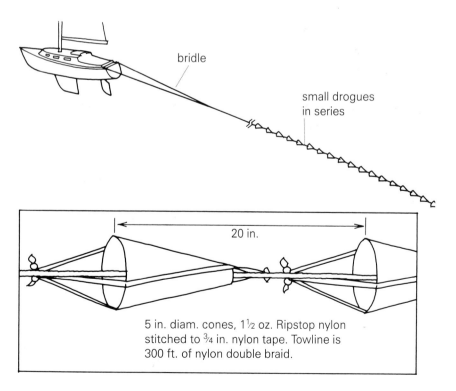

bridle

small drogues
in series

20 in.

5 in. diam. cones, 1½ oz. Ripstop nylon stitched to ¾ in. nylon tape. Towline is 300 ft. of nylon double braid.

The Jordan series drogue.

weather. A sea anchor, on the other hand, is a large underwater parachute designed to be deployed from the bow and stop a boat almost dead in the water.

The principle of the drogue is explained in this passage from *A Manual for Small Yachts*, by Commander R. D. Graham and J. E. H. Tew: "When you no longer dare lie a-hull, that is, without any sail set, either because too much water is coming in aft, or because you fear that the breaking crest will stave in the hull, you must put her before it. Get out two warps, tie bundles of old rope, motor tires, or cushions on the ends, and pay out on each quarter. Tie up the clew of the foresail in a bunch and hoist the head a few feet. With the aid of the helm, the ship will pay off and forge slowly ahead before the wind. Lash the helm amidships or as seems best. The ship will yaw six points on either side but will ride the seas with surprising security. A breaking crest will occasionally strike her, perhaps once or twice in an hour. Her stern offers less resistance than her side, and being struck end-on, she can recoil more easily."

Modern drogues come in many forms, saving you the trouble of tying your bundles of dirty laundry to the warps. Some are planks of wood bolted to metal frames; others consist of a series of small fabric cones strung along an anchor line. Developed by Donald Jordan, the Jordan series drogue deploys a hundred or more such cones, depending on the size of the boat. The effect is to dampen sudden accelerations and decelerations and avoid the wave-skipping and erratic behavior of a single drogue.

Some drogues have trip lines, so you can recover them more easily. Auto tires have always been popular drogues because they are easy to fasten to a line and because they create a good amount of drag, but they are difficult to stow on small boats.

There is much less heavy-weather experience to learn from in powerboats than sailboats. Most recreational powerboats are unsuitable for drogue deployment, however. With their wide sterns and much narrower bows, they are prone to broaching in a following sea. Any drag device sufficient to prevent this is likely to render them susceptible to pooping, and few powerboats—with their broad sterns, huge cockpits, and vulnerable cabin doors—could shrug off a boarding sea without serious damage or even foundering. A powerboater can try taking the seas on the stern quarter, playing the throttle to prevent being pooped or digging into the back of the wave ahead. This takes a lot of skill.

When the seas feel too big for that, you can turn to face them. Use just enough throttle to maintain headway, with your bow into the seas or just a few points off. Fishermen call it "jogging" and others call it "heaving-to." Particularly in a single-screw boat with high topsides forward, you may find it hard or impossible to keep the bow from falling off, exposing your beam to dangerous seas. In that situation, deploying a sea anchor from the bow might help. Better, though, to watch the weather and make shelter before the storm.

See also **Pooping Seas**; **Sea Anchors**; **Towing Drogues**.

Drowned Outboard Motors

First aid for motors that have taken the watery plunge

Surprisingly few dinghy motors seem to end up in the drink, considering the large number of opportunities for dropping them overboard, but every now and then one does take the suicidal dive. If it should happen to yours, try to render first aid immediately, for fatal corrosion sets in within a matter of hours.

First turn the flywheel, if you can, and listen for the grating and grinding that indicates sand was drawn into the cylinder. In that case, you have two choices: disassemble the engine yourself, or call for expert help after hosing everything down with fresh water. If there isn't any grating, proceed as follows:

1. Wash away all traces of salt water with fresh water. Douse everything, including the electrics.

2. Unscrew the spark plugs and dry them.

3. Remove the carburetor (assuming a small motor without electronic fuel injection). Empty it, clean it, and dry it.

4. Turn the engine so the spark-plug holes face down, and spin the flywheel several times to drain out all water.

5. Squirt light engine oil into the cylinders.

6. Replace the carburetor and plugs.

7. Start the engine.

If the engine won't start after several attempts, remove the plugs and dry them again. Check to see if there's any water in the carburetor or its jets. Keep trying to start the engine, and be persistent.

When it runs, let it get good and warm so that everything dries out properly. If it absolutely refuses to start, try to submerge it in fresh water until a professional can deal with it.

See also **Outboard Motors**.

Dry Rot

Finding the fatal fungus, repairing the worst damage

In the days of wooden boats, a diagnosis of dry rot was the news a sailor most dreaded to hear. Dry rot is an invasive fungus that literally eats wooden boats for breakfast—and every other meal, too. It feeds on the fibers of moist wood, turning it into a soft, spongy mass with a telltale musty smell. It spreads persistently in the right conditions, affecting more and more wood until the strength of stress-bearing timbers is totally destroyed. Worse yet, it spreads under a concealing coat of paint, giving little hint of its presence until it's too late.

The name is a misnomer, of course. Dry rot flourishes only in wood with a moisture content of 20 percent or more. It prefers temperatures between 75°F and 85°F (24°C to 30°C) and it needs air, so it will not attack submerged or waterlogged wood.

Fresh water is conducive to dry rot, whereas the salt in seawater inhibits it. Fishing boats and other working vessels frequently had rock salt strewn among their timbers for this reason.

If you're buying an old wooden boat, check for dry rot by probing everywhere with a small ice pick or a penknife blade; areas of dry rot offer no resistance. If you're buying an old fiberglass runabout with a wooden transom or a transom made of wood covered with fiberglass, be wary—this is a notorious place for dry rot.

The old way of preventing dry rot was to soak the wood in a good preservative, usually based on copper. Modern methods include sealing the wood all around with a deep-penetrating epoxy resin. The only positive cure is to cut out the affected area and a generous portion of the good wood surrounding it. Less radical measures, such as letting the rot dry and then injecting it with epoxy resin, leave the surrounding wood vulnerable to attack from huge quantities of microscopic spores.

Probably the best preventive measure is a good supply of clean fresh air, because air circulation discourages the growth of fungi. Sunlight is an effective deterrent too.

Eating Plankton

Catching minute organisms that could save your life

The renowned ocean scientist, William Beebe, said in 1927 that "shipwrecked men in an open boat, if their lot is cast on waters rich in plankton, need never starve to death."

Plankton is the collective name for minute animal and vegetable organisms that live in the sea near the surface. It is a rich source of nutrition—thousands of different kinds of fish and sea mammals live almost exclusively on plankton.

If you ever venture across an ocean, you should at least be aware of the possibility of catching plankton. Under survival conditions in a life raft or dinghy, you can drag an old shirt like a net through the water to scoop up plankton. It will look like gray scum and have the consistency of jelly. You'll probably end up with a great percentage of minute crustaceans, which make plankton a rich, nourishing food, even raw. Do your trawling at night, because although phytoplankton need sunlight for photosynthesis, most zooplankton dive to avoid sunlight and even bright moonlight. A towing speed of 2 knots is about right.

In 1952, Alain Bombard, a French doctor and adventurer, drifted across the Atlantic from Casablanca in a rubber life raft called *L'Heretique* to prove Beebe's point. He lived exclusively on fish he caught and plankton "soup" he trawled with a fine-mesh net.

Do not eat plankton if the red tide is prevalent. This is a discoloration of the sea caused by red dynoflagellates—minute organisms that contain toxins. If you're dragging for plankton at night when such activity is more productive, examine your catch under a strong light for signs of the telltale red color before eating it—or else wait for daylight.

See also **Castaways; Plankton**.

Echo Pilotage

Making noise can be a useful navigation trick in thick fog

You can use echoes to gauge your approximate distance from shore, and maintain it safely, when you're running along a coast with cliffs. Simply make a loud, sharp noise with a whistle or other signal and then note the time it takes for the echo to return to you.

Every second's delay indicates a distance off of one cable, or 200 yards. Every 10 seconds' delay indicates a distance of 1 mile. (The rule of thumb is that sound in air travels about 1 mile in 5 seconds, but your sound has to travel twice the distance from you to shore.)

Echo pilotage can be very useful in fog or at night, although you should never discount the possibility that your echo is being returned by the topsides of a passing freighter, or even an iceberg if you're in high latitudes.

A pistol firing blanks produces a nice sharp retort, but the ship's bell or horn will produce good results. Even a loud shout works at close quarters.

Electrical Bonding

Reducing the potential for corrosive electrical currents

There are two schools of thought about electrical bonding: one says that all underwater fittings should be bonded, and the other says that none should be (i.e., they should all be electrically isolated).

The aim of bonding, where underwater fittings and hardware are concerned, is to even out differing electrical potentials that could cause stray currents and electrolytic corrosion, but it is a subject complicated by many factors, including the variety of electrical equipment you have on board. Therefore, the only safe way to establish what's best for your boat is to consult a marine electronics expert.

A good bonding system consists of a heavy copper bus bar running the length of the boat (but not in the bilgewater), from which heavy stranded copper wires (at least #8 AWG) branch out to the various exposed, metallic, non-current-carrying components that are to be protected. The bus bar is connected

to the boat's common ground point, which is in turn connected through underwater hardware to Earth's ground. Any stray AC or DC currents leaking from faulty electrical equipment or connections will thus be conducted overboard without attacking the boat's metallic components.

But it's not quite that simple. Although protecting the boat from electrolytic corrosion due to stray currents originating within the boat, a bonding system might have the opposite effect in the presence of an electrical field in the surrounding water—as when a nearby boat in a crowded marina has malfunctioning AC equipment. In this case, the bonding circuit could conduct a current aboard, corroding a prop or through-hull. Furthermore, by electrically connecting dissimilar metals (e.g., a cast-iron engine block, stainless steel propeller shaft, and bronze prop and through-hulls) that sit in a common electrolyte—seawater—we've created all the right conditions for galvanic corrosion to occur. The effects of galvanic corrosion are not as rapid and immediately destructive as electrolytic corrosion, but over the course of a season or two, it can waste away a through-hull and sink a boat.

To prevent these occurrences, the bonding system must be connected to one or more sacrificial zinc anodes, which—being less noble than any associated metal—are "eaten up" in preference to the fittings and gear you want to protect. Zincs must be checked periodically and replaced in timely fashion.

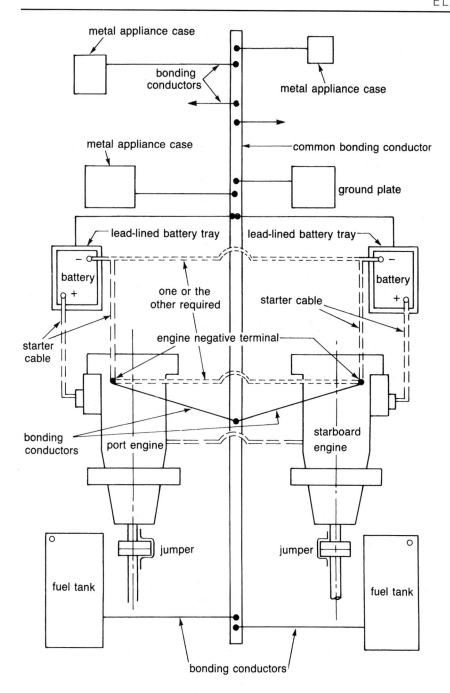

Schematic diagram of the American Boat and Yacht Council's (ABYC) recommended bonding practice.

rosion control, only those metal components in contact with bilge-water or surrounding seawater—engines, transmissions, propellers and shafts, through-hulls—need to be bonded. But when the mission expands to include safety and radio-interference suppression, so do the components included. If you want your bonding system to bleed off potentially harmful charges from malfunctioning AC and DC appliances, you'll also tie in the metal cases of all electronic and electrical equipment, as well as motors, generators and pumps, metal battery boxes, and the like. If your boat is gasoline-powered, the American Boat and Yacht Council (ABYC) says that a metal fuel tank(s) and fuel-fill fittings *must* be bonded; with diesel engines, it is optional. For lightning protection, you'll want to tie in rigging chainplates, metal cabinets, water tanks, and other large nonelectrical metal objects.

Incidentally, the bonding system isn't meant to carry everyday loads. It's purely a backup system that connects with your boat's grounded conductor at one point only—the common ground point—and it's entirely separate from your DC and AC systems.

The ABYC doesn't require individual through-hull fittings to be joined to the bonding system if they are electrically isolated—unless you use a zinc block for protection against galvanic action, as in the majority of boats. In fact, you'll find that most through-hulls *are* joined to the bonding conductor.

See also **Electrical Wiring; Galvanic Corrosion.**

Protection from corrosion is not the only reason for bonding a nonmetallic boat. Here are others:

- bonding prevents high voltages in exposed metal cases and electrical equipment that develop a fault

- bonding provides a low-resistance path to ground for lightning strikes
- bonding may also reduce interference with radio signals, depending on your setup

When the sole purpose is cor-

Electrical Wiring

Poor working conditions call for special high-quality wire

Although most electrical system in yachts run at low voltage, the batteries store sufficient energy to start a fire very quickly if the wiring ever short-circuits. Current-carrying wires for boats must, therefore, be of especially high quality because they often work in conditions of excessive vibration, humidity, and damaging salt spray.

In general, wiring for boats should have at least 20 strands in each wire to absorb flexing and vibration. The insulation should contain no paper or fabric that could be attacked by a damp atmosphere. Copper is the preferred conductor, preferably tinned to reduce corrosion.

Wire that is too thin resists the flow of electricity, leading to a voltage drop at the end of its run.

It can heat up and pose a fire risk, even in the absence of a short-circuiting.

A voltage drop of 10 percent is permissible for cabin-light circuits and other applications where voltage is not critical, but a drop of more than 3 percent should not be tolerated for electronic gear or navigation lights. Voltage drop is proportional to the length of the wire so, the longer the run, the thicker the wire needed.

The ABYC publishes tables nominating wire thicknesses for various applications along with recommendations for color-coding DC systems under 50 volts.

See also **Electrical Bonding**.

American Wire Gauge
(actual size)

- 18
- 16
- 14
- 12
- 10
- 8
- 6
- 4
- 2
- 1
- 0 (1/0)
- 00 (2/0)
- 000 (3/0)
- 0000 (4/0)

Standard American wire diameters, or gauges, shown actual size.

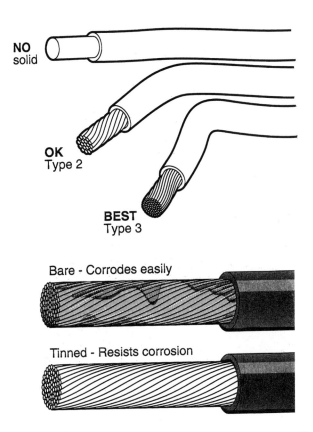

Solid wire is fine for the home but has no place on a boat. Finely stranded type 3 wire has the flexibility you want in wire on your boat. The wire should be copper, and it should be tinned to reduce corrosion.

ALLOWABLE AMPERAGE

Wire Type	TW	THW, HWN, THWN	MTW, XHHW	AWM, BC5W2, UL1426 Boat Cable
Temperature Rating	60°C (140°F)	75°C (167°F)	90°C (194°F)	105°C (221°F)
Wire Gauge (AWG)	Outside/Inside Engine Space	Outside/Inside Engine Space	Outside/Inside Engine Space	Outside/Inside Engine Space
18	10 / 5.8	10 / 7.5	20 / 16.4	20 / 17.0
16	15 / 8.7	15 / 11.3	25 / 20.5	25 / 21.3
14	20 / 11.6	20 / 15.0	30 / 24.6	35 / 29.8
12	25 / 14.5	25 / 18.8	40 / 32.8	45 / 38.3
10	40 / 23.2	40 / 30.0	55 / 45.1	60 / 51.0
8	55 / 31.9	65 / 48.8	70 / 57.4	80 / 68.0
6	80 / 46.4	95 / 71.3	100 / 82.0	120 / 102
4	105 / 60.9	125 / 93.8	135 / 110	160 / 136
2	140 / 81.2	170 / 127	180 / 147	210 / 178
1	165 / 95.7	195 / 146	210 / 172	245 / 208
0	195 / 113	230 / 172	245 / 200	285 / 242
00	225 / 130	265 / 198	285 / 233	330 / 280
000	260 / 150	310 / 232	330 / 270	385 / 327
0000	300 / 174	380 / 270	385 / 315	445 / 378

WIRE SIZE FORMULA

$$CM = \frac{I \times L \times 10.75}{E}$$

CM	=	Wire size in circular mils
I	=	Current
L	=	Length of wire (round trip)
E	=	Allowable voltage drop—generally 0.36

WIRE RESISTANCE

Circular Mils (CM)	Wire Gauge (AWG)	Ohms per 100 Feet (@ 77°F)
1,620	18	.654
2,580	16	.409
4,110	14	.258
6,530	12	.162
10,380	10	.102
16,510	8	.064
26,240	6	.040
41,740	4	.025
66,360	2	.016
83,690	1	.013
105,600	0	.010
133,100	00	.008
167,800	000	.006
211,600	0000	.005

Note: Circular mils are calculated by squaring the wire diameter in mils (thousandths of an inch)

KEY TO WIRE CODES

BC	=	Boat cable
H	=	Heat resistant (75°C rating)
HH	=	High heat resistant (90°C rating)
N	=	Nylon jacket
M	=	Oil resistant
T	=	Thermoplastic
W	=	Moisture resistant
X	=	Cross-linked polymer

Electrical wire selection. To run a 10-amp current through a 40-foot wire (round trip to the load and back again), the formula says you will need a wire size of 11,944 circular mils, which is between 10 and 8 AWG. Better to be safe and go with the larger size—8 gauge.

E

Electronic Charts

*They may not be as accurate
as they appear to be*

The two basic types of electronic charts are raster charts and vector charts. Both are displayed on computer screens or other electronic devices to which they may be connected, such as GPS receivers.

The differences between raster and vector charts become increasingly blurred as technology advances, but in the simplest of terms raster charts are scanned copies of paper charts. Vector charts, on the other hand, assign a latitude and longitude to every relevant feature of a paper chart. For example, on a coastline they plot the salient points on the screen. They then connect those features with lines.

Combined with readings from a GPS receiver, electronic charts indicate the position of your vessel on the chart.

All electronic charts combined with GPS must be used with caution, however. The display looks very authoritative, but it may be several hundred yards out.

As far as accuracy is concerned, you should presume an error of 1.5 mm at the original scale at which the chart was published. For example, for a chart of a scale of 1:40,000, the minimum presumed error is 40,000 times 1.5 mm, which equals 60 meters (60 yd.). It may be much more, depending on the accuracy of the data from the GPS receiver, the accuracy of the original survey, and the compatibility between the geodetic ellipsoids used by the GPS and the original chart.

An advantage of electronic charts is that they may be enlarged for easier reading. But too much enlargement can be dangerous, especially with vector charts. If you overzoom a raster chart it is immediately obvious because figures, letters, and symbols become increasingly distorted. On a vector chart, however, the lettering remains the same size no matter how much you zoom the chart. Consequently, an overzoomed channel among rocks might tempt you to take what appears to be a wide and safe route that is actually dangerously narrow and probably not densely surveyed.

See also **Charts**; **Chart Datums**.

Emergency Navigation

*Finding your way to land after
an emergency at sea*

Statistically, you're never likely to have to use emergency navigation. It's needed only by sailors who survive shipwrecks and find themselves cast away at sea with little or nothing in the way of navigational equipment.

Nevertheless, if you know anything at all about navigation, you will find the theory of emergency navigation quite fascinating. Entire books have been written on the subject, so probably the best advice is: read about it now; worry about it when it happens.

Much of the theory of finding your way to land without instruments, or with few instruments, is common sense based on natural phenomena every sailor experiences and understands; some of it depends entirely on luck (which instruments and tables are available to you); and the rest is deeply rooted in mathematical and celestial esoterica so profound that only a professional navigator could love it.

Deep-sea voyaging involves so many different disciplines, from aerodynamics through culinary arts to mechanical engineering, that there just isn't time in one human lifespan to plunge into all of it to any great depth. Emergency navigation is not near the top of most sailors' priorities. Even David Burch, author of the well-respected *Emergency Navigation*, admits: "This book does cover the best possible ways to find your position from scratch, but, realistically, this is not a challenge we are likely to face."

If you've done a reasonable amount of reading, have a broad-based education in the arts and sciences, and have enough experience to attempt an ocean crossing, you should be able to find your way back to land. It might not be the nearest land if it's a tiny coral island, but as long as you can keep going, you can hardly miss the continents.

Given the options, most sailors would rather devote their time to studying deep-sea survival techniques than emergency navigation. The ability to catch fish and plankton and gather fresh water is probably at least as important as knowing your position, if not more so.

This in no way diminishes the

Using a kamal. The rectangular piece of wood subtends a known vertical angle (determined empirically) when held a given distance from your eye. A knotted string from the wood to your cheekbone establishes that distance; increase the distance and you decrease the vertical angle measured. With the base of the wood aligned to the horizon, you can measure the vertical angle, or declination, of the sun or a star.

value of reading books on emergency navigation, nor the additional interest and satisfaction they can bring to a voyage. Navigation is a pleasing art when you have mastered it, and familiarity with such fundamental instruments as a sextant and a pair of parallel rules gives you a wonderfully intimate sense of connection to close-knit generations of mariners stretching back through the centuries.

So, in anticipation of the day when you have to abandon ship or the day when a computer glitch deactivates all the GPS satellites, buy a book on emergency navigation, read it carefully, and tuck it away in your abandon-ship bag together with a small compass and a plastic sextant.

If you find yourself in dire straits, you can rig a makeshift sextant from a printed compass rose from a chart and a piece of plastic or plywood. Or you can make a kamal, an astonishingly simple device of wood and string that is very efficient at measuring small angles. Arab navigators were using kamals to navigate the Indian Ocean 500 years before Vasco da Gama rounded the Cape of Good Hope, and still use them on dhows to this day.

See also **Abandoning Ship; Castaways; Danger Angles; Danger Bearings; Dead Reckoning; Echo Pilotage; Estimating Angles.**

Emergency Position-Indicating Radio Beacon

See EPIRBs.

Engine Life

Poor working conditions lead to earlier overhauls

Most boat engines (and particularly those on auxiliary sailboats) work under adverse conditions, so you shouldn't expect them to run as long as automobile engines do without a major overhaul.

The average gasoline engine on a boat runs 1,500 hours before needing an overhaul, and the average diesel engine on a boat runs 5,000 hours under the same conditions—that is, more than three times as long. These are general rules of thumb, of course, because the life of an engine depends on how it's used and maintained, but they are well accepted in the industry.

The gasoline engine mostly runs trouble-free for 1,000 hours. During the next 500 hours, minor troubles become increasingly likely, turning into major problems with the approach of the 1,500-hour mark.

By way of comparison, the average car engine runs an average of 2,900 hours before requiring an overhaul at 100,000 miles—about double the life of a boat engine. But car engines run at no more than 30 percent of their capacity most of the time, whereas boat engines work steadily at 75 to 90 percent of their maximum output.

A well-maintained gasoline boat engine might run well for more than 1,500 hours before a major overhaul if it's given the best working conditions. However, those that operate in damp bilges surrounded by salt air will certainly last fewer hours, especially if they are used only inter-mittently and maintenance is neg-lected.

Diesel engines last longer be-cause they're more heavily built and have closer tolerances. They can withstand more abuse than gasoline engines can and often deliver 8,000 hours before need-ing major surgery. In fact, there's no reason why a well-maintained diesel sailboat auxiliary shouldn't last the life of a boat. After all, the average pleasure boat logs 200 en-gine hours a year, so it would take 40 years to reach 8,000 operating hours.

The trouble is that few marine diesels are run under ideal condi-tions. Diesels like to run long and steady. Curtailed running times and infrequent use doom them to shorter lives, particularly when (as so often happens on sailboats) basic maintenance is neglected because of poor accessibility.

See also **Diesel Engines; Diesel Maintenance**.

Engine Oil

Simple checking of the oil level warns of engine trouble

If you know nothing else about your engine, you should at least know where the oil dipstick is. Checking the oil level is one of those simple tasks that brings great satisfaction. It makes you feel like a professional, even if you don't know the injector from the alternator, and it seems to be one of the little engine rituals (like polishing the gear-lever knob) that wards off bad luck and breakdowns.

The experts say you should check the oil level *every time* be-fore you start the engine, but most of us think that's taking cau-tion to excess. Once a day should be enough if the engine's running normally.

First, look at the level of oil on the dipstick to check that it's within the limits. If it's low, add oil as necessary. If it seems to be getting low more often, check your exhaust for *blue* smoke. A lot of blue smoke indicates that your engine is burning oil, probably because the piston rings have broken or become stuck. Worn valve guides will also let oil into the cylinder.

If the oil level is higher than it was the last time you checked, you've got trouble. When oil in the crankcase starts to rise, the most likely culprit is a leaking cooling system. In a diesel engine, it could also be fuel finding its way in from a leak in an internal fuel line or from a blown trans-mission seal. Wherever it's com-ing from, the extra fluid is going to cause trouble and no amount of gear-knob polishing is going to cure it, so call in professional help.

Next, look at the color of the oil on your dipstick. When you first put it in, the oil is an attrac-tive golden brown, but marine en-gineers say there is only one color for engine oil that's been used for a few hours—jet black. If it later turns brown or milky, it's another indication that the oil is being contaminated with water or diesel fuel. A soft white goo on the dip-stick betrays water in the oil of ei-ther a gasoline or diesel engine. Do not run the engine. A me-chanic's diagnosis is needed im-mediately.

See also **Diesel Engines; Powerboat Engines**.

Enlarging Plans

Increasing a boat's size brings interesting results

It frequently happens that prospective amateur boatbuilders have trouble finding plans that suit their needs exactly. The temptation then is to buy stock plans that a designer has drawn up for a smaller boat and enlarge them on a photocopier. However, that way leads to disaster, as many homebuilders have found to their cost.

Interesting things start to happen when you alter the size of a boat. Following is the law of me-chanical similitude for boats of similar shape.

If you double the size of a ves-sel evenly all around, then:

- length, beam, and draft all in-crease by 2 times
- wetted surface area increases by 4 times
- interior volume increases by 8 times
- weight increases by 8 times
- stability increases by 16 times

The new boat would be 41 percent faster and could carry four times as much sail. The great increase in stability that accom-panies an increase in length means that a longer boat needs proportionally less beam than a smaller boat. Thus, there is no one master plan that fits all needs;

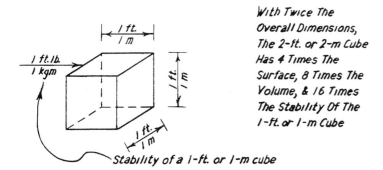

With Twice The
Overall Dimensions,
The 2-ft. or 2-m Cube
Has 4 Times The
Surface, 8 Times The
Volume, & 16 Times
The Stability Of The
1-ft. or 1-m Cube

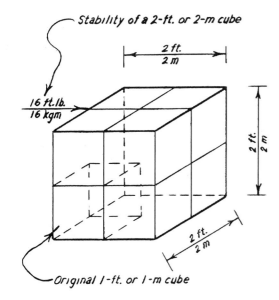

When you double the length of a cube, you multiply its volume eight-fold. It's the same with boats.

each boat must be individually designed to the size required.

EPIRBs

Satellite safety equipment for emergency rescue at sea

Emergency position-indicating radio beacons (EPIRBs) are carried voluntarily on many pleasure boats as safety equipment. They transmit radio Mayday signals via satellites.

Classes A and B EPIRBs broadcast on a frequency of 243 MHz and are effective only when a re-

ceiving satellite is also in line of sight with a ground receiving station, most of which are in the Northern Hemisphere. This means that emergency signals may not be immediately picked up from boats in trouble south of the equator.

Categories 1 and 2 EPIRBs, on the other hand, transmit on 406 MHz. Their signals are recorded by satellites that retransmit them when they are within range of a ground station, thus ensuring worldwide coverage. The signals are also coded to identify your boat and provide helpful details to rescuers.

More accurate positions are

provided by 406 MHz EPIRBs than by 243 MHz models—often to within a 2-mile radius, compared with a 10- to 15-mile radius. Both have a simultaneous 121.5 MHz transmission that allows rescuers to home in on your vessel. The most accurate positions are from EPIRBs with built-in GPS systems—so-called GPIRBs.

The only difference between class A and class B is that the former automatically floats free of its mount and turns itself on; the latter must be turned on by hand. The same applies to categories 1 and 2.

EPIRBs operating at 243 MHz sell for about a third the price of a 406 MHz model, but the international Cospas-Sarsat Program has announced that it will stop satellite processing of distress signals from 121.5 and 243 MHz distress beacons in the future. Presumably, your signal would still have a chance of being picked up on 121.5 and 243 MHz by airplanes if they happened to be overhead and listening to those frequencies, but the message is very plain—the trend is toward 406 MHz if you want to be certain of rescue with the help of satellites. The promise is that the phase-out will take place over a number of years—but, if you're thinking of investing in a distress beacon, think 406 MHz.

The availability of EPIRBs raises for boaters the same type of ethical questions facing wilderness hikers and mountain climbers, who can now call for help with the aid of cellular phones. In fact, some long-distance voyagers choose not to carry distress beacons because they believe that amateur sailors have no right to take advantage of expensive search-and-rescue operations mounted by foreign countries. Indeed, it has become too easy to call for help and spend taxpayers' money, even when the safety of the ship or crew is not really at stake.

A recent case in point concerns a Tayana 52 on a delivery trip from California to Honolulu with a crew of two. When the steering failed, the sleep-deprived crew set off the EPIRB "to let someone know where we were and what the situation was."

After a U.S. Coast Guard Hercules HC-130 aircraft located them hundreds of miles out to sea, but in no immediate danger, the crew inspected the steering gear and found they could easily fix it themselves.

Some famous long-distance voyagers have even refused to carry shortwave radio transceivers capable of issuing distress calls because they felt that, whereas professional mariners earned the right to rescue at whatever cost, they were participating in an amateur sport in which everybody should be self-sufficient.

As the price of EPIRBs and other satellite communication equipment falls, there undoubtedly will be a steep increase in the number of distress calls, which presages much future international discussion about who should pay for expensive search-and-rescue operations involving amateurs who voluntarily roam the high seas for their own pleasure.

See also **Mayday Calls; Radio Transmitters**.

Epoxy

Synthetic resin with great strength and adhesive power

Epoxy resin is widely used in the boatbuilding and repair business as a tough gap-filling adhesive. It also forms high-grade laminates with glass fibers and other materials.

Clear epoxy in thin consistency is used to seal wood and protect it from water penetration. It's also used extensively in paints as a sanding filler and a barrier coat to help prevent osmosis in fiberglass hulls.

For amateur use, epoxy is supplied as a liquid resin and a separate liquid catalyst, which must be mixed together to start a chemical cure. It's particularly effective in repairs to fiberglass hulls, which are typically made from polyester resin, but when it's properly applied, it forms an extremely strong bond that clings tenaciously to almost any surface. And while it is very strong, it stays flexible.

Epoxy resin has revived interest in wooden boatbuilding because of its promise to reduce maintenance and extend the life of wooden hulls. The theory is that wood saturated in epoxy is immune to attack by dry rot and even by the various kinds of wood-boring mollusks that have always been attracted to wooden boats.

The resin can be thickened and strengthened with various fillers that make gap-filling easier and compensate for lack of woodworking skill in amateur builders —a fact many traditionalists de-

cry. Some critics believe epoxy has no place in wooden boatbuilding because it is sensitive to heat and starts to deform at temperatures commonly found on deck in hot climates. Most epoxy is not totally waterproof, either, and is rated only as water-resistant. It is particularly vulnerable to degradation by the sun's ultraviolet rays and, therefore, must be protected by coats of paint or varnish loaded with ultraviolet filters.

However, *epoxy* is a generic term for a whole group of resins, any of which might be formulated for special purposes such as better resisting heat or moisture penetration. The adhesive most commonly recommended for wood-to-wood applications is resorcinol, which is used extensively in outdoor- and marine-grade plywood.

See also **Adhesives**.

Estimated Position

See **Fixes**.

Estimating Angles

A handy way to gauge angles without instruments

When you're at the helm and the navigator tells you to head up 3 degrees, it's handy to be able to respond quickly and accurately without referring to a compass. In fact, there are many occasions on a boat when it's useful to be able to gauge a horizontal angle.

Here's how you can do it.

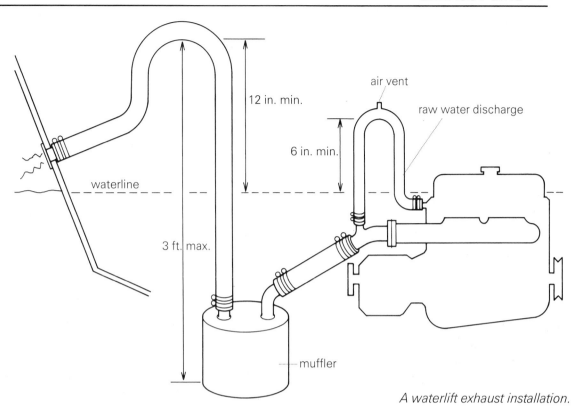

12 in. min.

air vent

raw water discharge

6 in. min.

waterline

3 ft. max.

muffler

A waterlift exhaust installation.

E

With your hand held up at arm's length to the horizon, the following are the approximate angles covered:

- 20 degrees: full hand span, from your thumb tip to the tip of your little finger
- 15 degrees: closed fist with extended thumb
- 10 degrees: closed fist
- 3 degrees: one thumb width
- 2 degrees: little finger width

Exhaust Line

What goes up must not come back down to your engine

A marine engine's exhaust line is an interesting problem in design,

considering that many engines are below the waterline. The engine cooling water that exits with the exhaust gases naturally flows downward, but it must pass through the boat's hull above the waterline.

The answer in many sailboats is to pipe the water and gases from the engine downward to a waterlift muffler, a type of pressurized sump. From there, the water is forced up in spurts, then down and out, by the pressure of the incoming exhaust gases.

Alternatively, an exhaust-gas riser may be used to gain the initial height needed. The cooling water is then pumped up separately and enters the riser in its downward leg. From there, through the muffler to the ves-

sel's hull, the exhaust line should have a continuous drop of at least 1 inch (25 mm) for every 2 feet (60 cm) of run. This is the approach used in most wet-exhaust inboard powerboats, both gasoline and diesel. Many fishing boats and some trawler yachts use dry exhaust systems in which the hot gases are exhausted through a metal pipe high above deck, and the cooling water is pumped directly overboard.

There must be no possibility in a wet-exhaust system of seawater or engine cooling water finding its way back up the line to the exhaust manifold, whence it could make its way to the cylinders and pistons with disastrous results.

F

Faint Lights

Looking askew is sometimes the cleverest thing to do

There are many times at sea at night when you find yourself looking for the first sign of a faint light. It might be a lighthouse you're anticipating to see on the horizon, an anchor light, or a minor star in a dark sky.

Nine times out of ten, you'll find it sooner if you don't look where it should be, but rather a little to one side instead. Eye specialists explain what sailors have always known—when you look directly at an object, the light rays focused by your eye fall on an area of the eye that is not as sensitive as the surrounding areas.

So if you look off to one side, the faint light will impinge on a more sensitive area of your eye. That's why you so often see a light in the corner of your eye first. After having located it thus, you can then gaze straight at it. Sometimes, however, when you do, the very faintest lights will disappear again and won't reappear until you look slightly away.

See also **Complex Lights**.

Fathometers

See Depth-Sounders.

Fathoms

Embracing a misconception: an illogical, regressive move

The fathom is gradually being ousted on new charts by the meter, so it will pay you handsomely to inspect the notes on your charts to see how water depths are measured. It can come as a nasty shock to find yourself in 2 meters where you thought there were 2 fathoms.

The change to meters—although inexorable—is hardly logical because the meter itself was a miscalculation. The French believed there were exactly 10,000 kilometers between the equator and the poles. However, they did not do their sums properly, and the length of the meter later had to be redefined (incredibly) as 1,650,763.73 wavelengths of the orange-red radiation of an isotope of krypton (Kr^{86}).

You probably won't have an isotope of krypton handy when next you're sounding the depth of your anchorage with a lead line, but you do have two arms, from which spring the far more natural measurement called a fathom. It comes from the Old English *fæthm*, meaning outstretched

arms, or an embrace. Different sailors had different-sized embraces, of course, so the unit known as the fathom was eventually standardized at 6 feet.

Now 6 feet is a good, enthusiastic embrace, but it's also a subdivision of the cable, which is 100 fathoms (600 ft.). The cable, in turn, is a subdivision of the nautical mile, which—for practical boating purposes—is understood to be 6,000 feet, or 10 cables.

The nautical mile equals exactly 1 minute of latitude and may be measured directly off the side of a Mercator chart, which is why France and other metric countries still navigate with trusty nautical miles rather than tainted kilometers. The change to meters on nautical charts is surely a regressive move, a triumph of uniformity over logic.

See also **Miles**.

Fear

A natural, helpful reaction that sharpens your senses

There is an element of danger in boating that cannot be eradicated. Consequently, there is always something for boaters to fear—which happens to be a good thing.

If you spend sufficient time afloat, sooner or later you will experience fear; but, if you understand that fact and accept it before you set out, you will deal with the fear-provoking situation more easily when it arises.

Fear is often greater when you're alone and forced to fall back on your own resources. It seems to be a perfectly natural part of single-handed sailing, no matter how macho you might feel before or afterward. According to research done by solo sailor, Dr. David Lewis, in collaboration with the Medical Research Council in Great Britain, four out of five contestants in the first single-handed transatlantic race experienced not only fear, but acute fear.

Lewis discovered, however, that they did not afterward recall the *extent* of their fear. They remembered that they were scared but couldn't say how badly. Lewis deduced that "observations noted *at the time* are the only valid ones. I honestly forgot that I had been frightened at all during one gale until I looked up my notes."

In general, there are two types of fear. The first includes those generalized tensions and anxieties familiar to everyone when we move to a new house, change jobs, get married, or take an exam. Fortunately, this kind of fear mostly disappears after a few days: once we adapt to the new circumstances, they become less frightening.

The second type of fear is more specific: an approaching storm, a risky feat of navigation, a collision with a balk of timber, and so on.

"As long as fear is the response to actual danger, it is a natural and even useful phenomenon," says Dr. Michael Stadler in *The Psychology of Sailing*. He adds

that fear in an ample (but not excessive) degree can sharpen your senses and improve your capacity to anticipate and assess the risks inherent in certain situations.

Seasoned sailors, therefore, experience anxiety before the danger arrives and are in a better position to deal with or even avoid it. Inexperienced sailors may wander blindly into danger and then become incapacitated with fear when it's too late.

Richard Henderson, the well-known American sailor and author, believes the best weapon against fear is self-confidence, built up by "careful preparation, attention to one's health, seeing that the boat is sound and well equipped, learning all one can about the proposed route and weather conditions, preparing for all possible emergencies, and gradually building experience."

See also **Single-Handed Sailing**.

Fensers

Keeping boat hulls away from damaging scrapes

A fender is a piece of soft padding placed between a boat's hull and a pier or another boat. Fenders are usually made of vinyl plastic, shaped like fat sausages, and filled with air. Some are shaped more like large round balloons, and are favored where there is constant motion in all directions between a boat and another object.

The typical color for a fender is white, to match the boat's hull, but high fashion appears to have mounted a determined invasion

A fender with an eye at both ends gives you the option of hanging it horizontally.

on fenders, for even the more respectable boating catalogs now offer them in such unlikely colors as hunter green, teal, gray, and cranberry.

There is also a wide variety of fender accessories, such as fabric socks to keep them out of the sun and further protect topsides from scuffing, lanyards on height-adjustable clips that do away with "hard-to-untie knots," and stainless steel storage containers.

The larger the fender, the better. The limiting factor for most boats is stowage space, because you need at least three and should probably carry four or five. Fenders make good anchor buoys in emergencies.

The minimum diameter of fenders should be about 1 inch for every 5 feet of boat length (about 15 mm for every m).

Fetch

Defining a word with many useful nautical meanings

The term *fetch* is often misused by boaters. It seems to have acquired the meaning of *popple*, or choppy seas, whereas in fact it is the distance a wind can blow over the sea without appreciable interference from land. For example, you could say, "For a wave to reach its maximum height requires a fetch of at least 600 miles." Or, "There was a 5-mile fetch in the anchorage, so the wind was able to create large seas."

There are several other nautical meanings of the word, of course. In old writings you will see it used for "arrive at" ("we fetched the harbor in good time"). To "fetch the mark" in a racing boat is to round it without having to make another tack, and to "fetch up all standing" once meant to come to a sudden unexpected halt.

In many English-speaking countries, the word *fetch* is used to describe a point of sailing between close-hauled and reaching; thus, a boat sailing on a fetch (or fetching) is close-reaching.

See also **Wave Height**.

Fiberglass

Laminating layers of glass and resin to make a boat hull

The most popular boatbuilding material is a mixture of fine glass strands and cured polyester resin known as fiberglass, glass-reinforced plastic (GRP), or fiber-

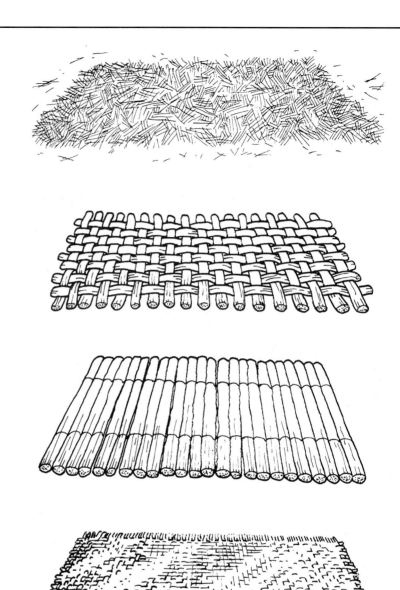

Common fiberglass materials include the following (top to bottom)*: Chopped-strand mat, in which randomly oriented glass strands of irregular length are either glued to a scrim backing or loaded into a chopper gun for professional application. Woven roving comprises bundles of continuous glass strands assembled into a coarse weave. In **unwoven roving** the bundles are stitched together parallel to one another to give great strength along the axis of the bundles. If the unwoven roving shown here were cross-stitched to a second layer oriented 90 degrees to this one, the result would be a biaxial roving with greater strength in two directions than even a woven roving of the same weight provides. The **fiberglass cloth** at bottom has a finer weave and a lighter weight than woven roving. Professional builders use it in specialized applications but rarely in hull construction. For do-it-yourself repairs, however, you'll have an easier time and get better results if you use mat and cloth rather than mat and roving.*

reinforced plastic (FRP). Its success stems from the fact that one set of molds can produce hundreds of identical hulls, decks, cockpits, and cabintops.

Most boatbuilders use the same laminate—alternating layers of chopped strand or mat ($1\frac{1}{2}$ to 3 oz. per square yard) and woven roving (24 oz. per square yard) wetted out with standard polyester resin. Vinylester resin is more expensive than polyester but less permeable to moisture and more resistant to osmotic blistering or "boat pox." Some expensive boats use vinylester throughout the layup; in other boats, it's used only in the surface layer of the laminate, where it bonds very well to the polyester resin beneath it. A skin coat (just beneath the gelcoat) consisting of 3 ounces of chopped strand or mat wet out with vinylester resin greatly reduces the odds of blistering. A skin coat is always a good idea no matter the resin because it prevents "print-through" of the coarse woven-roving pattern onto the gelcoat.

Epoxy resin, which is stronger and more flexible than polyester, is not normally used for production hulls because it is more expensive, but it's widely used for repair work and special projects. Epoxy adheres well to the old polyester resin in boat hulls and gelcoats, but polyester does not fare so well when applied to old epoxy.

The two layers mentioned previously (mat and roving) constitute one ply and measure about $\frac{3}{32}$ inch (2.4 mm) in thickness. Such a laminate weighs about 94 pounds per cubic foot (1,506 kg per cu m). The glass fibers should comprise about 35 percent of that weight.

The thickness of a fiberglass hull in inches should roughly equal the waterline length in feet divided by 150, plus 0.07. The topsides are usually 15 percent thinner than average, whereas the hull at the waterline and below is 15 percent thicker. Powerboats need hulls that are thicker than normal by 1 percent for every knot in speed over 10 knots.

Despite its popularity, GRP has some major drawbacks. It lacks the warmth and personality of wood and weighs about three times as much for the same volume of material. It is the floppiest of all boatbuilding materials; therefore, to provide the stiffness a boat requires, most solid fiberglass hulls should have five or more longitudinal stringers on each side of the inside of the hull. Bulkheads also provide stiffness, as do the molded, ribbed fiberglass grids often placed under the cabin sole in fiberglass construction.

Early fiberglass boats of the 1960s and 1970s were often overbuilt by manufacturers who were just making the transition from wood and still unsure of fiberglass's strength. Most of those early boats are still around, and when they are well maintained and updated, they can make great bargains on the used-boat market. Recent boats—especially at the high end—are not just built but also engineered. Most now have foam or balsa cores sandwiched within inner and outer laminates of fiberglass for stiffness and lightness. High-performance boats may have super-lightweight honeycomb cores encased in laminates of vinylester or epoxy resin in which the fiberglass reinforcement is replaced in high-stress areas with Kevlar or carbon fiber. Such hulls are usually laminated with vacuum bagging to remove all excess resin for the very lightest weight.

Fiberglass decks are almost always cored construction these days because stiffness in that location is at a premium and cannot be gained from convex curvature in a relatively flat expanse. A "squishy" deck that yields underfoot is often an indication that moisture has invaded and rotted a balsa core—often through fastener holes. Spider-web crazing or local swelling in the deck gelcoat may indicate the same thing. Beware: the repair can be expensive.

Fiberglass is long-lasting but not maintenance-free. The gelcoat surface eventually chalks, degrades, and requires painting. Water vapor passing through the outer layers of the underwater hull can cause blistering (osmosis) and delamination—expensive repairs.

See also **Blisters in GRP; Gelcoat; Plastics.**

Fiddles

Keeping things in place when the boat is heeling over

Coastal and ocean cruisers need fiddles, or raised edges, on all tables and counters to stop things from sliding off when the boat heel or rolls. Surprisingly, even professional builders often forget

F

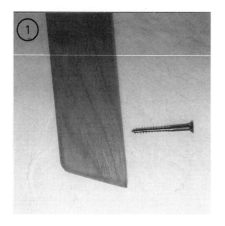

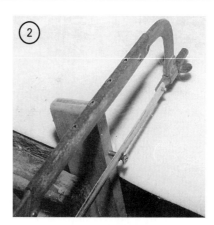

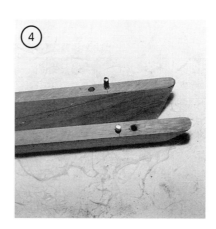

Making removable fiddles. 1. Drill teak fiddle and install screw. 2. Cut off screw head. 3. File cut edge smooth. 4. Extra holes allow fiddles to fit into each other for compact storage. 5. This cockpit table has two sets of holes, one inboard (shown) and another set farther out at the table edges.

to supply them (or deliberately omit them for cost reasons) or else fit them incorrectly. A Dutch builder supplied fiddles on Eric Hiscock's famous *Wanderer IV* that were wedge shaped in profile so that a glass or plate sliding into contact with them was neatly lifted over the edge.

Some deep-sea boats have dining tables with a grid of carefully sized fiddles that will keep bowls from sliding around at a fairly steep angle of heel.

The best (and most expensive) fiddles fold down or are removable in port, allowing the table to be used for other work. The old rule of thumb was that a yacht's saloon table should have fiddles 1¹⁄₂ inches (say, 40 mm) high.

Fighting Currents

A time when normally sensible sailors tend to lose patience

Many otherwise sensible sailors lose both their patience and their logic when they are motoring against a current. Sailboat skippers normally content with the speed their boats make under auxiliary power suddenly complain that their engines are "not strong enough to push against a current" and start making earnest inquiries about installing a bigger engine.

There's something about a contrary current that makes people irrational, particularly in narrow channels where they can see the land going past much more slowly than they think it should. Perhaps they equate it with going uphill in a car—but that's really not a valid comparison as far as a boat is concerned.

The simple truth is that a boat goes the same speed through the water whether or not she's in a current. When she's battling a contrary current, she doesn't go as fast *over the ground*, that's all. Her speed over the ground is her forward speed through the water minus the speed of the current.

To go faster against a current (and, therefore, faster over the ground), you have to first make your boat go faster through the water. But modern boats, even auxiliary sailboats, almost always have sufficient power to give them full hull speed, and it's almost impossible to make a displacement hull exceed her hull speed without a disproportionate increase in engine size. In other words, the boat is already going as fast as she reasonably can, and

putting in a bigger engine is not going to make much difference running against a current.

In many cases, the agony of inching along against a current can be alleviated by consulting the tide and current tables, and timing your trip to catch a favorable current instead of a contrary one. It might require an injection of patience, but patience has long been a boater's best friend. For example, if you were doing 6 knots against a 3-knot current, the land would crawl by at 3 knots. But if that current were flowing with you at 3 knots, the land would be flashing by at 9 knots. The vast difference between 3 and 9 knots is just a matter of timing.

It's not always possible to plan trips this way, of course. Not all currents reverse, and sometimes it's not feasible to wait for slack water or a favorable current. The

answer then is to cultivate patience and serenity. If the laws of nature aren't working the way you want them to and the land wants to go by slowly, let it.

See also **Speed Limits**.

Figure-Eight Method

Recovering crew who have fallen overboard at sea

The method of crew-overboard recovery under sail promoted by the American Sailing Association is known as the figure-eight method. It avoids jibing (a feature of the rival "quick-stop" method), which can be a dangerous and disorienting maneuver in the stressful moments following a crew-overboard accident. However, it involves sailing away from

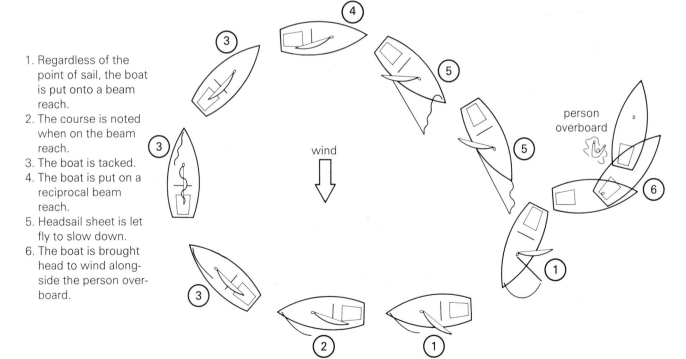

1. Regardless of the point of sail, the boat is put onto a beam reach.
2. The course is noted when on the beam reach.
3. The boat is tacked.
4. The boat is put on a reciprocal beam reach.
5. Headsail sheet is let fly to slow down.
6. The boat is brought head to wind alongside the person overboard.

wind

person overboard

The figure-eight method for recovering a crew member from the water.

the victim for up to 10 boat lengths, which might make it more difficult to keep the person in sight. The figure-eight method does have another advantage, though: the extra seconds taken to return to the person in the water allow you to shape a course that has a better chance of recovering your victim on the first pass—an important consideration if the water is cold or the victim is semiconscious.

When the crew-overboard alarm is sounded, immediately bring the boat onto a beam reach, regardless of what point of sail you were on before. In other words, start sailing at right angles to the wind. At the same time, your crew should throw overboard flotation cushions, a horseshoe buoy, and a marker pole. One crew member should do nothing but keep a close watch on the victim in the water, pointing at the victim with an outstretched hand. If possible, prepare a line with a loop in the end of it for the victim to grasp.

After no more than 10 boat lengths, come about and bear off onto a broad reach. Aim at a spot about four or five boat lengths from the victim and slightly downwind so that you can make the final approach to the victim on a close reach with the jib flapping and the mainsail doing all the work. Adjust your speed by trimming or easing the mainsheet.

Stop beside the victim, preferably to windward, but to leeward if it appears better in your judgment of the conditions prevailing. A windward approach provides some shelter from wind and wave,

and allows the person in the water to grab a trailing jib sheet or a line thrown from the boat. However, you must beware of drifting down onto a victim and causing the boat to drop on top of him or her in really heavy weather.

Don't start the engine unless it's dead calm, and then stop it as soon as you're alongside the victim. Don't start it again until the victim is safely on board and you have checked for lines trailing overboard. For crew-overboard recovery in a powerboat, see Crew Overboard.

See also **Crew Overboard; Lifesling System; Quick-Stop Method**.

Figureheads

Pleasing embellishments with ancient but gruesome origins

A figurehead is a carving of a bust or a full-length figure placed under the bowsprit at the boat's bow. Some are of famous admirals looking stern and displaying the sterling qualities of leadership; others are of long-haired, barebreasted women whose contribution to sailors' morale and contentment was probably equally appreciated.

Figureheads are a rarity these days, and more's the pity, because they not only add interest and colorful detail to a boat, they also bring a touch of mystery that goes back to the origins of boating. They are, in fact, believed to represent the sacrifices that sailors made to the gods of the wind and sea—which is why they should always be carvings of human beings, never any other creature of land or sea.

It has been suggested that in ancient times real human heads were placed on the bow of an important vessel starting her first voyage—more often than not, the heads were those of beautiful maidens. These were major sacrifices, of course, intended to ensure the safe passage of the vessel and her crew across stormy waters ruled by a few powerful gods and a host of minor ones.

Representative figureheads from the clipper ships Donald McKay, Morning Light, *and* Galatea.

The sacrifices also were supposed to provide the ships with their own soul because it was believed that every ship needed one. When the human head fell off the bow, it was a sign that the gods had accepted the sacrifice and the maiden's pure soul had entered the ship.

There is no actual proof that such practices ever prevailed, so we will probably never know the truth. Not that it matters much because mariners no longer dare sacrifice virgins for figureheads anyway, and maiden voyages are maiden in name only.

See also **Renaming a Boat**; **Unlucky Colors**.

Fire on Board

It's wise to carry more extinguishers than required

Donald Street, well-known sailor and author, got it right when he wrote: "Since earliest times, fire at sea has been the seaman's greatest fear. Even on today's boats of steel or aluminum, fire at sea can be disastrous, for there is still so much wood in the interior of the vessel that a fire allowed to get out of hand can cause complete destruction."

Fiberglass hulls also burn hot and nasty, spitting out fiery globules of molten plastic.

U.S. Coast Guard regulations require that you have fire extinguishers on board, but it stipulates only a bare minimum, according to the size of the boat; it is advisable to carry more. Remember that most extinguishers sold for small-boat use have a discharge time of between 8 and 20 seconds only, so use them effectively from the start: don't delay, get close, and aim low.

You need an extinguisher in each compartment in the boat, but try not to place them right where a fire is likely to break out; position them *nearby* and on escape routes. There should definitely be one near the galley and the engine because these locations are where most fires start. It's also a good idea to have one available in the cockpit.

There are three basic ways to fight a fire: starve it of oxygen, remove the material it's feeding on, or cool the burning material below combustion point.

A well-aimed bucket of water will put out most small fires on a boat, but for burning grease or fuel you'll need an extinguisher that uses dry powder, foam, or chemical gas. Don't ever use water on fires involving high-voltage electricity, of course, or you'll risk being shocked.

Portable extinguishers must be marked with a U.S. Coast Guard approval number and must be mounted in the special plastic bracket provided. You can choose among extinguishers that use dry chemicals (which make a mess of

F

Fire Classes and Extinguishing Agents

Class	Fuel Sources	Primary Extinguishing Agent	Primary Effect
A	Common combustible materials such as wood and wood based materials, cloth, paper, rubber, and certain plastics.	• Water • ABC Dry Chemical	Removes the heat element.
B	Involves flammable or combustible liquids, flammable gasses, greases, petroleum products, and similar products.	• Foam AFFF (Aqueous Film Forming Foam) • CO_2 • PKP (dry chemical)	Removes the oxygen element.
C	Involves energized electrical equipment, conductors, or appliances.	• CO_2 (Carbon Dioxide) • PKP (dry chemical)	Removes the oxygen element, and temporarily removes elements of oxygen and heat.
D	Involves combustible metals, such as sodium, potassium, magnesium, and titanium.	• Water (high velocity fog) • Sand (placed underneath the metal)	Removes the heat and oxygen elements.

everything), carbon dioxide gas, and gases designated FE-241 or FM-200 (the successors to Halon 1211 and 1301, which are no longer manufactured). FE-241, which is toxic, is used for engine compartments and unoccupied areas. The table on page 121 lists classes of fire extinguishers and the types of fires for each.

A fire in the engine compartment might not be discovered until it is out of control, so automatic fire-extinguishing equipment has a place there. It's expensive, but it could save your boat and your life.

See also **Gasoline Dangers**.

First Aid

Planning for medical emergencies when you're far from help

Most pleasure boats carry more information about repairing their engines than repairing the human body. Perhaps that's because of a misapprehension that a quick radio call to the U.S. Coast Guard will take care of all medical emergencies. Not so—it's very unlikely that a helicopter will appear on the scene within minutes to convey a victim to the hospital. Most coast guard rescues are done by boat, and boats can take many hours to reach you.

If you're a day-tripper and weekender, rarely venturing far from the madding crowd, a basic first-aid kit from your local marine store will suffice. If the kit doesn't contain a first-aid book, get one and read it.

If you like to gunkhole, visiting more secluded places, and plan to be aboard for several days at a time, consider supplementing the basic first-aid kit and book with the following: antidiarrheal medicine, adhesive bandages of various sizes, aspirin, bandage compresses (2 and 4 in. or 50 and 100 mm), ammonia inhalants, burn treatments, eye dressing and cup, Furacin ointment, iodine swabs, hexachlorophene ointment, a splint, and sunscreen.

First aid is largely a matter of forethought and common sense. If you plan to be away from civilization for extended periods, I suggest that you buy a good first-aid book, make a preliminary list of your requirements for a comprehensive kit, and then ask your doctor for advice about supplementing it. Also request a quick lesson in closing gaping flesh wounds with stitching, clamping, or surgical staples, and some effective painkillers. If you are able to obtain morphine or any scheduled drug, keep it under lock and key with a copy of the doctor's prescription to show the U.S. Coast Guard and port authorities if they board your boat.

See also **Hypothermia**; **Seasickness**.

Fisherman Anchor

These old-fashioned anchors still have specialized uses

The fisherman anchor, also sometimes known as the yachtsman's anchor, is the old-fashioned anchor seen in coats of arms and old paintings. Made of galvanized steel, it has a long straight shank

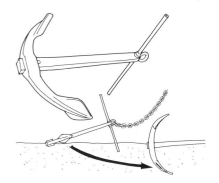

Fisherman anchor.

with a ring at one end to which the anchor line is fastened, and two curved arms at the other end to hook into the ground. Each arm terminates in a broad fluke with a sharp bill, or pea, as it used to be called.

At the ring end of the shank, there is a broad stock, or transverse rod, whose purpose is to capsize the anchor so that the two curved hooks forming the crown lie vertically, better to bite into the seabed. The stock of the fisherman is usually removable so that the anchor may be stowed flat.

Few small boats now carry fisherman anchors as working anchors because they are very heavy compared with more modern anchors, and they are awkward to handle. But they are still useful as storm anchors and will hold fast in rock or foul ground where no other anchor will grip.

Claud Worth, British sailor and author of the classic *Yacht Cruising*, gave this advice for the selection of a fisherman anchor: "The arms and shank should be oval or flat in section. The flukes should be sharp and long to bite into hard ground. They should make an angle of about 40 degrees with the shank. The measurement from the crown to the hole for the stock should be not less than $1\frac{1}{2}$ times, nor more than $1\frac{2}{3}$ times, the length of the chord—the chord being the distance between the tips of the two flukes. The stock should be the same length as the shank."

See also **Anchors, Anchoring; Anchor Types; Cruising Anchors**.

Fishing Boats

Knowing your rights doesn't always mean you'll get them

Sailboats and powerboats are obliged by law to keep clear of "a vessel engaged in fishing." Because fishermen know this full well, they sometimes stretch the rules in narrow waterways to the extent that they hinder your passage.

But the fact is that you don't have to give way to any old boat with a fishing line hanging overboard. The inland and international navigation rules both define "a vessel engaged in fishing" as "any vessel fishing with nets, line trawls or other fishing apparatus which restricts maneuverability." That's the defining feature—lack of maneuverability. The rules specifically *exclude* a "vessel fishing with trolling lines or other fishing apparatus which does not restrict maneuverability."

Unfortunately, knowing the rules doesn't always mean you will be afforded your rights under them; therefore, most sensible boaters try to steer well clear of fishing boats. If that's not possible, proceed warily and try to call

them on VHF channel 16. If they're busy fishing, you may not get an answer, but it's worth a try. If they have nets out, ask which way you should steer to avoid them. And keep your fingers crossed.

See also **Rules of the Road**.

Fixes

Clearing up confusion about fixing your boat's position

A fix is the name given to the charted position of your boat as determined from the bearings of two or more points positively identified on the chart. It is, in the words of an old encyclopedia, "the establishment of a ship's position beyond a reasonable doubt by any of several methods." Those

methods include celestial navigation, loran, radar, radio cross-bearings, GPS, and visual bearings.

All amateur navigators should be aware of the difference between a dead-reckoning position, sometimes erroneously referred to as a "DR fix," and a true fix. A DR position is, at best, a guess; it's not "beyond a reasonable doubt." Even though it's plotted on the chart, it simply shows your vessel's movements according to compass direction and distance, with allowances for current and leeway. But all these factors are variables—they're only estimates, albeit fairly accurate ones at times, so they can't be relied upon to navigate a narrow passage between rocks, for example.

If you are near land with easily identified charted objects, it's

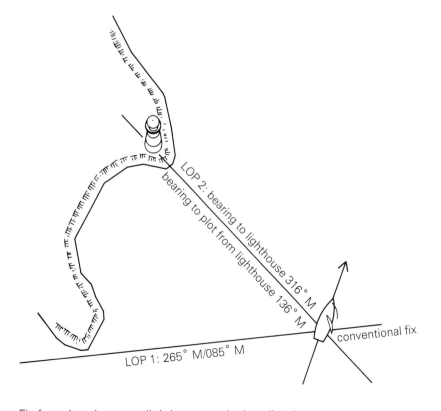

Fix from bearings to a lighthouse and a headland.

easy to take two or three bearings to get a fix. But unless conditions are calm and your sights are super-accurate, three bearings will not all pass through the dot indicating your charted position. They usually form a small triangle of uncertainty, and you should plot your position within this triangle as that nearest to possible danger.

Having established your position with a fix, you can now compare it with your plotted DR position and deduce how your course over the land has been affected by current or leeway—facts that might enable you to steer a more accurate course on the next leg of your trip.

One other fact is important to note: an estimated position is not the same as a fix or a DR position. Some authorities hold that an estimated position is a dead-reckoned position adjusted for presumed effects of current and leeway. However, more properly, estimated positions are used in celestial navigation, not piloting, to round off numbers and make the calculations easier. When you reduce a sextant sight, an estimated position is derived from your DR position—which is usu-ally not an easy whole number to work with—and is the closest convenient position to it.

See also **Danger Angles; Danger Bearings; Dead Reckoning; GPS; Lines of Position.**

Flags

Conveying information and bringing life, color to boats

Flags bring color and movement to a boat. It's fascinating how even a small burgee flapping at the masthead can add life and interest to a boat. But flags also communicate information on several levels, of course, and are used singly or together to convey code messages—many of which are internationally recognized.

Centuries of maritime use have resulted in a flag etiquette governing the position in which flags should be flown and the times of their use. This etiquette is not universally known or adhered to, but for those who care, here are some pointers:

Old Glory and other national ensigns should be worn at the stern staff or from a position two-thirds up the mainsail leech. Gaff-rigged sailboats may also wear it from the afterpeak while they are underway.

However, boats that are racing should wear neither the ensign nor a triangular burgee—only a rectangular racing flag.

Boats outside U.S. territorial waters should fly only the Stars and Stripes, not the U.S. Yacht Ensign, which is the Betsy Ross flag with a ring of 13 stars surrounding a fouled anchor. The use of the

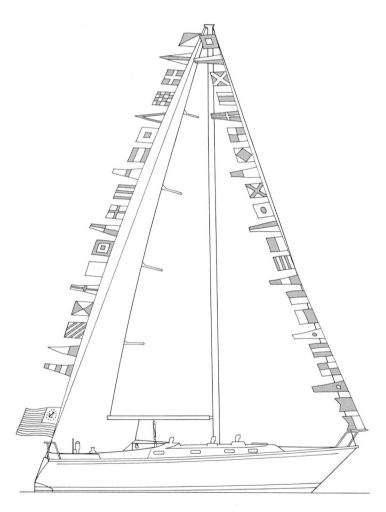

*A yacht "dressed" with flags in the prescribed sequence, bow to stern. See **Code Flags** for explanation of the rectangular (letter) flags; the truncated triangular flags are numeral pennants.*

latter ensign within U.S. territorial waters was originally restricted to the elite on documented yachts, but it's now flown on all sizes and makes of boats, seemingly without penalty.

A club burgee should be worn at the masthead or from the starboard spreader beneath the courtesy flag of any country you're visiting.

Fun flags should be worn at the port spreader.

Racing-yacht battle flags are worn halfway up the forestay.

Racing-yacht-class pennants are worn on the backstay.

And if you're a stickler for etiquette, you'll know that flags are *worn* by a yacht and flown by the *owner*.

On July 4 and other days designated by the authorities, you can dress ship with flags of the International Code from bow to stern. Use only code flags to outline the silhouette of your boat—the ensign, burgee, and other flags are worn in their usual places. Following is a recommended sequence for a balanced display of color, from the bow. The flags are grouped in threes here only for easier reading: AB2, UJ1, KE3, GH6, IV5, FL4, DM7, PO third substitute, RN first substitute, ST zero, CX9, WQ8, ZY second substitute.

The times at which flags are raised and lowered are as follows:

- The national ensign is hoisted at 0800 and lowered at sunset. It may be hoisted earlier, however, if you're leaving port in daylight.
- The burgee should be hoisted and lowered at the same time

as the ensign, but many owners prefer to leave the burgee flying day and night, as long as they are on board.

As far as dimensions go, the hoist of an ensign—that is, its size from top to bottom—should be about two thirds the size of its fly, which is its horizontal length.

Choose the correct size of ensign for your boat by applying the formula of 1 inch on the fly for every 1 foot of boat length overall (about 75 mm per 1 m of boat length). Err on the side of generosity because, whereas a large ensign adds a certain grace, one that's too small appears curiously inelegant, like a cat with a chopped-off tail.

The length of the stern staff from which the ensign is flown should be about twice that of the flag's hoist.

The size of foreign courtesy flags, which are flown in the premier position at the starboard spreader, should be about $5/8$ inch on the fly for every 1 foot of boat length (about 50 mm/m).

See also **Code Flags**.

Flare

Defining two words to dazzle your boating friends

If you want to impress fellow boaters with your nautical knowledge, arrange to drop two words into your casual conversation sometime: flare and flam. Comparatively few boaters know what flare is; even fewer have any idea what flam is.

Flare is the outward, upward curve or slant of a vessel's sides, from the waterline to the deck

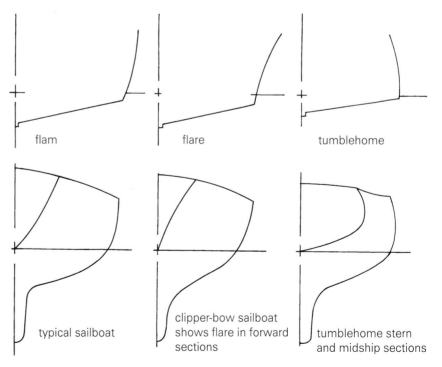

Naval architect Ted Brewer's graphic explanation of flam, flare, and tumblehome.

line. It's usually referred to in connection with the bow of a boat. You could mention, for example, that your boat was designed with a good deal of flare to gradually increase buoyancy as she plunges into head seas.

The reason flam is so little understood is partly because authorities are not always in agreement about its definition. Some define it as a part of flare. Flam, they say, is the exaggerated outward curve right at the top of the flare. It's often incorporated into a boat's hull to repel spray and keep her foredeck dry in head seas. So you could say, for example, the flam on your boat was ideal for yesterday's choppy conditions on the bay.

In addition, a designer will sometimes give a boat flam to increase the width of the foredeck for some reason.

However, naval architects such as Ted Brewer and Howard I. Chapelle, former Historian Emeritus in the Department of Industries of the U.S. Museum of History and Technology, Smithsonian Institute, hold that flam is the convex shape of the hull above the waterline, particularly noticeable in the forebody, where it imparts buoyancy when the vessel is heeled.

That interesting word *tumblehome*, which is the inward, upward curve of a hull from the waterline up to deck level, is the exact opposite of flare, of course, but seems to be far better known and understood.

Flotation

Keeping that sinking feeling at bay with buoyancy aids

Most boatowners have wished at some time or other that their boats were unsinkable. That feeling is remarkably strong in gales or when one finds oneself unexpectedly among unmarked underwater rocks.

The fact is that most boats will sink rapidly if they're badly holed. Few ordinary bilge pumps can keep up with the inflow of water through a hole the size of a man's fist.

The answer would seem to be flotation, either in the form of waterproof compartments, slabs of plastic foam, air bags, or some other buoyant devices, but the problem is their bulk. You can have all the flotation you want—yes, your boat will certainly be unsinkable—but you'll pay in the form of reduced accommodation.

There's nothing new about the idea of flotation. That intrepid French sportsman and explorer, Marcel Bardiaux, built some into his 31-foot sloop, *Les Quatre Vents*, when he single-handed her around Cape Horn from east to west in the 1950s. He fastened empty cans under the side decks in his small cabin and was glad to have them when he went aground on a reef in the South Pacific. The boat was flooded but he managed to float her off, and—with the help of a large rubber life raft that he inflated below—he sailed her to Nouméa, New Caledonia, with the decks awash.

To keep afloat a sailboat with a fiberglass hull and a ballast ratio of 35 percent requires at least 1 pound of added buoyancy for every 1.6 pounds of displacement. An additional safety margin of 25 percent is recommended. Wooden hulls need buoyancy equivalent to the weight of the ballast and engine, plus 25 percent.

For example, to keep afloat a fiberglass 35-footer displacing 12,500 pounds, you would need 7,812 pounds of buoyancy, plus 25 percent, which equals 9,766 pounds. Air bags and foam provide about 62 or 63 pounds of lift per cubic foot, so you would need about 157 cubic feet of buoyancy. The standard kitchen refrigerator has a volume of 18 cubic feet, so you would need to find space for nearly nine of them on your 35-footer.

Small powerboats, rowboats, and sailboats are made unsinkable by means of buoyancy bags or tanks containing air or, in the case of boats such as the Boston Whaler, with enclosed foam.

If you're contemplating adding buoyancy to your boat, seek professional advice. The fastening and positioning of post-construction flotation material is a complicated subject, and one best tackled by a naval architect.

See also **Watertight Bulkheads**.

Flotsam and Jetsam

Learning the subtle differences between the two

The words *flotsam* and *jetsam* are often incorrectly used interchangeably. They are not one and the same thing.

Occasionally, ships have to jettison cargo or other material to lighten them when they're in danger. If the cargo floats after it's been thrown overboard, it's called flotsam; if it sinks, it's called jetsam. And if it's buoyed so it can be recovered later, it's called lagan.

The British have a slightly different terminology. They regard flotsam as all that remains floating on the water after a boat has accidentally sunk, and jetsam as everything deliberately jettisoned, even if it floats.

Fog Prediction

Aching bones, white breath, strange noises: fog coming?

Fog is not easy to predict with any accuracy because the requirements for its formation vary so widely with humidity and temperature.

The basic rule about fog is simple: Warm air can hold more moisture (water vapor) than cold air can. So, if you take warm, humid air and chill it, the moisture will condense and form fog.

But before you can forecast fog, you need to know how much moisture the air contains. The more moisture, the less chilling it needs. The temperature at which condensation occurs in any air mass is known as the dew point.

To find out how much moisture is in the surrounding air, you need one of two instruments: a hygrometer with wet- and dry-bulb readings, or a fascinating piece of equipment called a psychrometer, which you whirl

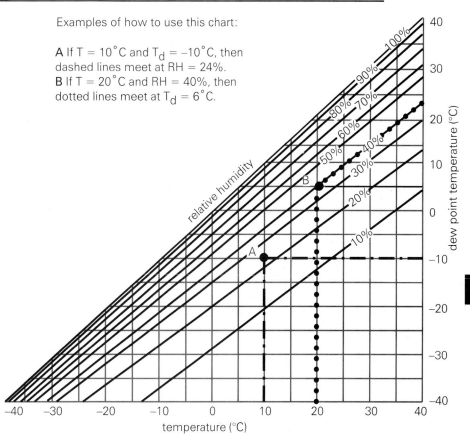

Examples of how to use this chart:

A If T = 10°C and T$_d$ = –10°C, then dashed lines meet at RH = 24%.
B If T = 20°C and RH = 40%, then dotted lines meet at T$_d$ = 6°C.

Predicting fog. If the outside temperature is 20°C (68°F) and your hygrometer or psychrometer registers a relative humidity of 40 percent, the dew point is 6°C (43°F). If the temperature should fall to that point, fog will form.

around your head on the end of a lanyard. It's basically the same as a hygrometer, but faster acting. Once you know how wet or dry the air is, you can find the dew point from tables.

Some people say they know when fog is coming by the way their breath condenses or the way their bones ache. Others claim to be able to tell by the particular noise certain distant sounds make. A prudent skipper in San Francisco Bay, the Gulf of Maine, and other waters known for fog simply assumes fog can happen at any time and plans all navigation accordingly.

See also **Fog Types; Noises in Fog**.

Fog Types

Differing ways in which fog is formed; areas affected

Fog is condensed water vapor, a cloud at sea level. Because it reduces visibility so greatly, it makes navigation dangerous.

If you're caught out in fog on a coastal passage, the standard advice is to get into water shallow enough for anchoring and wait there until the fog clears. That way, you'll be in no danger of being run down by a large ship.

But it's not always possible to follow that advice. Lively seas may make anchoring impractical and, if you're not sure of your position, it may be foolhardy to close with the shore. If you choose to hold your course, slow down, keep a sharp watch, sound the correct signal at the correct intervals, and listen for signals from others.

Rig a radar reflector if one isn't permanently installed and, if you have active radar, switch it on and monitor it. A GPS receiver reduces much of the anxiety of navigating in fog because it continuously provides your position and enables you to steer an exact course between waypoints. GPS has its dangers, too, because it is accurate enough to tempt you into a harbor where you may meet several other vessels blundering through the fog.

Of course, you need a reliable compass; without one (or a GPS), you won't know which way you're heading and your only option will be to stop until the fog clears.

In U.S. waters, the frequency of fog diminishes from north to south, but the transition is quicker on the Atlantic Coast than on the Pacific Coast. Southern California, from Los Angeles to San Francisco, has about three times as much fog as the same latitudes on the Atlantic Coast. On the West Coast, the foggiest stretch (10 percent of the time) is from the Strait of Juan de Fuca to Point Arguello, California; it is particularly prevalent in the summer months. On the East Coast, there is a similar incidence of fog from the Bay of Fundy to Montauk Point, New York.

The coast of Northern California and the coast of Maine are the foggiest—about 20 percent of the year.

Following are the types of fog usually experienced by boaters:

Advection fog. This is probably the most common type of fog, which forms when warm, moist air flows over colder water. Given the right conditions—such as warm air from a stationary Bermuda High flowing over the cold waters of the Labrador Current, the Grand Banks, and the Gulf of Maine—this fog can persist for days. Wind does not blow this kind of fog away—it creates more. The fog will not clear until there is a change of wind direction and its moisture content, or a general heating of the ambient atmosphere.

Radiation fog. This kind of fog forms in near calms on clear nights when the ground radiates its heat into space and cools down. Moisture in warmer air passing over the cool land may condense as fog and drift out over water. Radiation fog normally disappears in the morning when the sun heats the air.

Steam fog. Also known as sea smoke, steam fog forms when cold air flows across warmer water. It's usually short-lived and patchy.

Precipitation fog. This kind of fog forms when warm rain falls through a lower layer of cold air. It, too, is usually short-lived.

See also **Accidental Circling; Air Masses; Fog Prediction**.

Fouling Sheets

Dealing with wayward jib and forestaysail sheets

It's extraordinary how many things there are on the foredeck of a sailboat on which the jib and foresail sheets can snag. This only happens at the worst of times, of course, in the middle of coming about, when the flogging sheets are most attracted to the siren lure of mast cleats, hatch corners, and so forth.

But there is a simple cure for fouling sheets. It's an ancient and little-known wrinkle that keeps blood pressure at a safe level in the cockpit during tacking matches. The idea is to bend a line to the mast at about gooseneck level, or a little above if you can, and to make the other end fast to the stemhead or samson post. Tighten it up, and you'll find that the sheets ride up and over it, out of the reach of the many temptations on the mast and the deck below.

On old sailing ships, a handy line like this was called a timenoguy (pronounced *tim-EN-oh-guy*), but it's not a word in use any longer.

Foul-Weather Gear

Selecting the right gear depends on where you sail

Warm clothing is a necessity if you're planning anything longer than day trips in your boat, and waterproof foul-weather gear is especially necessary on sailboats whose open cockpits expose the

F

deck crew to spray and rain for hours on end. Even in the tropics, a midnight rainstorm can be surprisingly cold and miserable.

Most deep-sea cruisers prefer the kind of suit that has a jacket with a hood, and separate pants with suspenders and a high-cut bib. For warmth beneath, you should wear loose-fitting layers, starting with a T-shirt and a long-sleeved shirt, topped with a woolen or polyester-fleece sweater if necessary.

Foul-weather gear is designed to keep you warm and dry in stormy conditions and must be comfortable without being bulky. It's divided into four major categories for dinghy sailing, inshore work, coastal work, and ocean sailing.

Different fabrics and standards of finish and detail are used in each category; the price escalates dramatically as you advance from dinghy to offshore. Your choice should depend on the kind of sailing you do. For example, the considerable outlay for the best jacket and pants for ocean work may not be justified if you do most of your sailing on inshore waters.

The best (and most expensive) fabrics, such as Gore-Tex, work on the principle that a molecule of water vapor is smaller than a drop of water. Thus, your body sweat, in the form of vapor, can escape through minute holes in the fabric, but the rain and salt spray can't penetrate. Such materials provide excellent water-proofing with good ventilation and breathability. They are not only supple enough to allow free movement, but also durable enough to withstand the considerable abrasion that active boating entails.

In use, sweat still seems to condense inside the fabric, even if the quantities are smaller, so the best defense is to wear all wool under your jacket—it will keep you warm even if it's wet.

Hook-and-loop closures such as Velcro are excellent for making snug-fitting closures at the neck, wrists, and ankles.

If you choose less expensive gear lined with PVC or urethane, be sure it has an adequate number of vents to help remove the water vapor from your body.

F

Four-Point Bearings

A fix from two relative bearings of one charted object ashore

A four-point bearing (also known as a bow-and-beam bearing) tells you how far away you are from a single object on shore at the time when it's abeam. If you can identify the object on the chart, two simple sights will result in a position fix.

While you're maintaining a straight course, note the bearing of the object when it is exactly 45 degrees (four points) to port or starboard of the bow. Then note when the bearing is exactly 90 degrees to port or starboard. The distance you have run between taking the two bearings equals the distance you are abeam of the object. Now you have a bearing and a distance from a charted object on shore, which gives you a positive position fix.

To measure the distance between the two bearings where they cut your course line, you can either multiply your speed by the

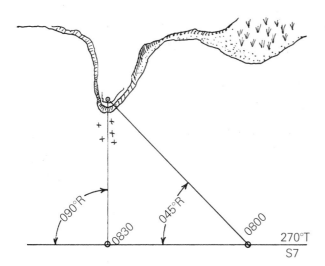

A typical use of a bow-and-beam bearing. A vessel making 7 knots takes a bearing at 0800 on a light at 45 degrees relative (315 degrees true). A half hour later the light bears 90 degrees (360 degrees true). Since the boat had traveled 3.5 miles in the 30 minutes between bearings, its position at the time of the second bearing must be 3.5 miles from the light or the reciprocal bearing of 180° true. In practice it usually proves more convenient to work with magnetic rather than true courses and bearings.

time it took or take direct readings off a calibrated distance log.

It's often more useful to know how far offshore you are *before* you reach a headland, of course—in that case, you can use the same technique as the four-point bearing except with smaller angles on the bow. Use any relative angle you like for the first bearing, and double it for the second bearing. This is known, logically enough, as "doubling the angle on the bow."

Small angles are difficult to work with, however, and lead to bigger errors, so your first relative bearing should be about 20 or 30 degrees, and the second, 40 or 60 degrees. That will leave you space to make an offing if you find yourself too close inshore.

See also **Danger Angles; Danger Bearings; Fixes.**

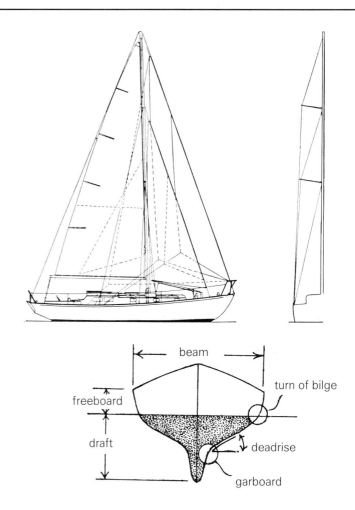

Top: The modest freeboard of a traditional cruising sailboat contributes to its overall beauty. *Above:* In sectional view, such a boat looks something like this. The full keel and resultant depth of hull body permit standing headroom below without a lot of freeboard.

Freak Waves

Assessing your chances of being caught by a giant wave

There is more truth than you might think in the old adage that every seventh wave is bigger than the rest. At random intervals, wave trains coming from different directions can fall in step with one another, literally riding on each other's backs to form an exceptionally high wave—or an exceptionally low trough.

It doesn't need to be blowing a gale for this to happen, but if the weather is indeed stormy—and particularly if there is a contrary current to steepen the face of a giant wave—it will topple over and release its energy in the form of a

plunging breaker large enough to overwhelm any small sailboat.

Scientists maintain that the probability of such waves can be predicted. According to Laurence Draper, of the National Institute of Oceanography, 1 wave in about 23 is more than twice the height of the average wave, 1 in 1,175 is more than three times the average height, and 1 in 300,000 exceeds four times the average. There is an equal chance, Draper says, of an unusually deep trough occurring.

See also **Waves in Gales.**

Freeboard

Putting the best face on a controversial design feature

Until the 1960s and 1970s, freeboard—the height of a boat's deck edge above the waterline—was comparatively low on sailing yachts but often substantially higher on powerboats. Low freeboard didn't help a sailboat's accommodation space, which was already constricted by narrow beam, but it certainly added to a boat's looks. Sailboats from that

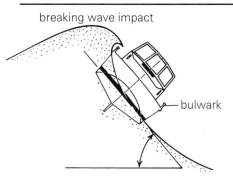

breaking wave impact

bulwark

The higher the freeboard, the greater the topside surface area exposed to the force of a breaking wave. High freeboard is an advantage on the down-wave side of a boat, however, making the deck edge less likely to submerge and contribute to a danger of capsize.

era are still greatly admired for their pretty sheerlines and graceful overhangs.

Today's boats have far more beam and freeboard. Among sailboats, racers started the fashion for beam because it helps them carry more sail. Production cruising sailboats added freeboard to help reduce the height of ugly deckhouses needed to satisfy the new demand for standing headroom in small boats. Because most production sailboats today are fin-keeled and flat-bilged, their cabin soles are not as deep as in a traditional sailboat. In the search for headroom, the only place to go is up.

The average height of freeboard in a classic cruising sailboat was $2^{1}/_{2}$ inches per foot of beam (about 190 mm/m) and, considering how narrow those boats were, it didn't result in much freeboard.

Freeboard creates windage, so the more freeboard you have, the poorer your performance to windward. In a storm, high freeboard

also gives a breaking wave a bigger target. Today's boats have plenty of freeboard and—because high freeboard is said to provide a greater range of stability—suddenly it's not being rued as detrimental, but rather touted as one of the most important features contributing to safety.

It is difficult to know the truth. Freeboard is far from the only factor contributing to a large range of stability; it may not even be the major factor. And there were no protests in the old days about lower freeboard making boats less safe. So it seems quite possible that modern designers are putting the best face on a feature that exists primarily for creature comfort and has little to do with seaworthiness.

In a powerboat, too, high freeboard is a mixed blessing where seaworthiness is concerned. A hull with higher freeboard forward ships less solid water on deck and gives a drier ride. This is why sportfishing boats combine high freeboard forward with low freeboard aft (for handling fish). High freeboard aft might make it possible to run down-sea in steep waves without being pooped—a point at which sportfishing boats, for one, are vulnerable. A high-freeboard boat will also remain stable through greater roll angles and is less likely to trip over a submerged deck edge while sliding sideways down a wave face. On the other hand, high topsides expose a larger surface to the energy of a breaking wave and also move a boat's center of gravity higher, especially when combined with a high superstructure (e.g., flying

bridge, tuna tower). In heavy weather, a high center of gravity is the last thing you want. Consider, too, the windage of high topsides and superstructures, which will make a boat harder to handle in high wind.

Freeing Anchors

Here's how to save the day if an anchor jams in the ground

Sooner or later, you'll discover that the anchor won't come up when you want it to. It may have dug itself deeply into the ground, become jammed in rock, or snagged a cable or line.

First, shorten the anchor line as much as you can, until the rode is nearly straight up and down. Then go away for a few minutes and think about things. As the boat rises and falls on the waves or an incoming tide, the increased strain will gradually free a deeply buried anchor, and you'll start drifting.

Alternatively, let out a little slack on the rode and start the engine. Power forward at full speed until the anchor line brings you to a sudden halt. Repeat the action from several different directions.

If nothing has happened after 15 minutes of waiting or 5 minutes of powering, try to ascertain whether the anchor is jammed in rock or fouled on a cable. If a cable is the problem, you'll feel a little give and take as you lift both anchor and cable together. If the anchor is jammed in rock, you won't feel any "give" at all.

You might be able to hook a cable with a grapnel on a line, and

F

lift it enough to allow your anchor to fall clear. Another trick is to shackle a loop of chain around your anchor rode and attach it to a line. Let the chain loop drop down to the anchor, get in the dinghy, and take the end of the line forward. You may be able to drag the anchor forward, clear of the cable.

If you're stuck in rock, a loop of chain might help, but a pull from a different direction is a better bet. First try pulling it back the way it went in. Be careful not to put an unfair strain on anchors with long shanks; otherwise, they will bend.

If you are forced to anchor on rock or foul ground, it's safer to set a trip line and buoy with the anchor. To the crown of the anchor, secure a fairly light line that's a little longer than the maximum depth of water. Buoy the end of the line and ease the line overboard with the anchor and rode. In theory, you should be able to pull the anchor straight up with the trip line. In practice, nothing about anchors is altogether certain.

See also **Anchors, Anchoring**.

Fuel Capacity

Working out how much fuel a boat needs to carry

The designer of your boat had to do a lot of thinking about how much fuel she needs to carry. Naval architects typically build in the minimum of tankage, taking into account the nature of the boat, reasonable usage, and the distance between fuel docks in your normal area of operation.

For instance, a 50-gallon (190 L) tank of diesel feeding a 25-horsepower (hp) auxiliary engine cruising at 80 percent of top speed is sufficient to take a 33-foot (10 m) sailboat 300 nautical miles at 7 knots in calm weather. But that same amount of fuel would take a twin-engine 40-foot (12 m) sportfisher only about 33 miles at 40 knots. In fact, this boat would need about 450 gallons (1,710 L) to cover 300 miles at that speed.

Planing hulls need more power than slower-moving displacement hulls, and thus use more fuel per mile. Therefore, they also need more tankage, but there's a limit to how much fuel they can carry because they have to be reasonably light to plane.

See also **Fuel Weight**.

Fuel Consumption

For safety reasons, learn how far a tank will take you

The only way you can estimate how far a tank of fuel will take you is if you know the fuel-consumption figures for your engine. Following are some general rules:

A marine diesel engine consumes about 1 gallon per hour (GPH) for every 18 hp generated (a 27 hp engine running at two-thirds capacity will generate 18 hp).

Another way to calculate the amount of diesel fuel used in 1 hour is to multiply the horsepower being used by 0.055.

Four-stroke inboard gasoline engines need about 1 GPH for every 10 hp generated. Alterna-tively, you can estimate the number of gallons consumed in 1 hour by multiplying horsepower used by 0.1.

Gasoline outboard motors vary so much in the duties they are required to perform that no one formula is accurate for all; however, all outboards use more gasoline per mile than inboards. Furthermore, two-stroke outboards have a much greater thirst than four-strokes. Individual fuel-consumption figures must be arrived at by careful measurement of fuel used over a measured distance, preferably on a "there-and-back" run to cancel out the effects of current.

It is fairly safe to assume, however, that an older two-stroke gasoline outboard will be 10 to 50 percent thirstier than an inboard gasoline engine of the same horsepower. Newer fuel-injected two-stroke outboards show a considerable improvement in fuel-consumption figures, however.

The few diesel outboard engines available are mainly used by professional inshore fishermen. Amateur sailors tend to avoid them because of their weight, vibration, and high initial expense, but their miserly fuel consumption gives small boats a long range and their heavy engineering ensures long life and reliability.

Most marine engines, gasoline or diesel, are designed to run continuously at about 70 to 80 percent of their maximum output. Diesels, in particular, thrive on hard work and tend more toward the top of the range.

The rule of thumb about fuel reserves is that you should plan on using one third of your total capacity to get where you're going and one third to get back; the other third is your emergency reserve.

See also **Fuel Economy; Fuel Capacity; Fuel Weight; Wasted Fuel.**

Fuel Economy

Understanding the difference between displacement and planing

You can save a lot of fuel if you understand the basic difference between displacement hulls and planing hulls. Displacement hulls are those designed to force their way slowly through the water as they go—displacing the water with their own hull shapes. Planing hulls are designed to rise up over their own waves and skim over the surface of the water at high speed.

Displacement hulls—power and sail—have a theoretical top speed that they cannot exceed without vastly increasing their power, with correspondingly vast penalties in fuel consumption. Planing hulls, in theory, are limited in speed only by the amount of power available, but they, too, show greatly increased fuel consumption for every extra knot they make while on the plane.

For displacement hulls, which include those of most sailboats and power trawlers, the theoretical maximum speed is the square root of the waterline length in feet times 1.34. (In metric terms, maximum speed is the square root of the waterline length in meters times 2.43.)

Krogen 39 Trawler Performance Results

RPM	Speed, knots	Fuel Usage, gph	Nautical mpg	Range, nm
1,000	5.3	0.85	6.2	3,928
1,200	5.6	1.08	5.2	3,267
1,400	6.3	1.34	4.7	2,962
1,600	7	1.79	3.9	2,464
1,800	7.3	2.33	3.1	1,974
2,000	7.7	2.94	2.6	1,650
2,200	7.9	3.88	2.0	1,283
2,400	8.3	4.83	1.7	1,083
2,600	8.6	6.3	1.4	860

Tests are with a single, 115 hp John Deere diesel engine.

The Krogen 39 trawler yacht, a displacement boat, is exceeding theoretical hull speed at 8.6 knots. At that speed it gets less than half the mileage per gallon of diesel it would at 7.3 knots. Put another way, since a diesel engine develops about 20 hp for every gallon burned per hour, it requires only 47 hp to push the boat at 7.3 knots, compared with 97 hp at 8.3 knots.

Krogen 49 Performance Results

RPM	Speed, knots	Fuel Usage, gph	Nautical mpg	Range, nm
800	5.7	1.6	3.6	1,924
1,000	7.6	2.5	3.0	1,642
1,400	9.0	5.1	1.8	953
1,600	9.8	8.0	1.2	661
1,800	10.3	11.9	0.86	467
2,000	12.4	15.7	0.79	426
2,200	14.2	19.9	0.71	385
2,400	16.6	25.5	0.65	351
2,600	18.4	30.3	0.61	328
2,780	19.7	35.5	0.55	300

Tested with twin 350 hp Caterpillar 3116 engines.

The Krogen 49 is a semidisplacement trawler yacht capable of speeds close to 20 knots—but at a substantial cost in fuel usage. Its range at top-end speeds is 20 percent or less of the range at slower cruising speeds, but the speed reserve is there when you want it.

Thus, a boat with a waterline length of 25 feet has a maximum speed in still water of 6.7 knots. Any attempt to go faster will result in drastically increased fuel consumption with little or no increase in speed. Basically, the slower you go in a displacement hull, the farther you'll travel on a gallon fuel.

Take the Krogen 39 trawler yacht as an example. With a waterline length of 36 feet, 8 inches, its theoretical hull speed is 8.1 knots. It will reach 7.9 knots with a fuel economy of 2.0 nautical

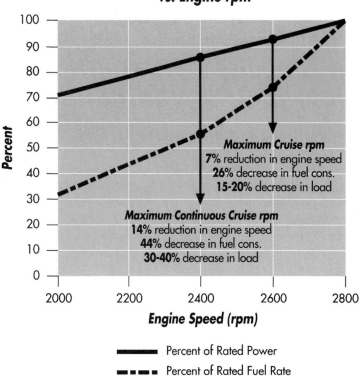

Engine Power and Fuel Consumption vs. Engine rpm

Maximum Cruise rpm
7% reduction in engine speed
26% decrease in fuel cons.
15-20% decrease in load

Maximum Continuous Cruise rpm
14% reduction in engine speed
44% decrease in fuel cons.
30-40% decrease in load

Percent (y-axis)
Engine Speed (rpm) (x-axis)

——— Percent of Rated Power
■■■■ Percent of Rated Fuel Rate

This graph from Caterpillar shows how much fuel can be saved with a modest decrease in engine throttle.

miles per gallon, but when you push it beyond its theoretical hull speed to 8.6 knots, it gets only 1.4 nautical miles per gallon—a heavy penalty.

Of course, 6 to 8 knots is somewhat slow for some powerboaters, so designers often come up with a hybrid called a semidisplacement or semiplaning hull. This is simply a displacement hull with enough bearing surface in its underbody (especially aft) and a high enough power-to-weight ratio to develop a little more hydrodynamic lift. Thus, a semidisplacement hull will climb partway out of the water and reduce wave-making resistance and drag. It will not plane in the proper sense, but it

will go a few knots faster than a pure displacement hull. It will also create an enormous wake and pay a heavy price in fuel consumption and carrying capacity, but those reserves of speed may increase your cruising range along with your fuel costs—and might even get you to port ahead of bad weather.

The semidisplacement Krogen 49 is a good example. With a 48-foot waterline, its hull speed is about 9.3 knots, but it will do close to 20. At 9 knots, it gets 1.8 nautical miles per gallon, whereas at 18.4 knots, its fuel economy drops by two thirds—but when you want the speed, it's there. At displacement speeds, a semidisplacement hull is less effi-

cient than a pure displacement boat but more so than a planing boat.

True planing hulls will achieve speeds of about 25 knots if they weigh about 40 pounds for every 1 hp delivered to the propeller. That weight includes everything on board. To increase that speed to 50 knots, you would have to reduce the ratio to about 10 pounds for every 1 hp.

These are maximum speeds, not economical speeds. The best fuel economy on a planing boat occurs just after it has popped up onto the plane. The minimum resistance and best economy are ensured by trimming the stern by 2 to 4 degrees from the horizontal. A planing hull traveling at slightly *less* than planing speed creates great resistance and throws up a large disturbed wake. At this stage, fuel economy is at its worst. In fact, a planing hull, with its broad transom and flat underbody sections aft, is inefficient at any displacement speed.

Incidentally, twin-screw installations are about 20 percent more wasteful of fuel than are single engines of the same horsepower.

See also **Fuel Consumption; Fuel Capacity; Hull Shapes; Twin Screws.**

Fuel Weight

Allowing for the effect of fuel weight on performance

The weight of fuel can affect your boat's trim and stability, so—ideally—it should be stored in tall narrow tanks low down near the center of the boat.

These ideal conditions are seldom achieved in practice—many boats with fuel tanks placed too far aft will be down by the stern when they start a trip and possibly down by the bow when they return. Powerboat builders sometimes seek to alleviate this problem by installing forward and aft fuel tanks, between which fuel can be pumped back and forth to compensate for changing trim.

Although fuel weighs less than water, it still amounts to a substantial mass. Gasoline weighs about 6.1 pounds per gallon (lb./gal.) (728 g/L). Diesel fuel weighs about 7.1 lb./gal. (840 g/L).

Therefore, 300 gallons is a ton of fuel sloshing around and, in a wide fuel tank, the resultant free-surface effect could dramatically decrease a boat's stability. For this reason, large fuel tanks should be internally baffled.

By and large, gasoline inboard engines use about 0.6 pound (272 g) of fuel per horsepower *generated* per hour, and diesel engines need about 0.4 pound (181 g) per horsepower *generated* per hour.

On average, diesel fuel contains about 140,000 Btu per gallon (3.8 L), or 10 percent more energy than the same *volume* of gasoline.

See also **Fuel Capacity**; **Fuel Consumption**.

G

Gaff Mainsails

Still many advantages to an old-fashioned seagoing rig

Although the tall narrow sails of the Bermuda rig rule the roost now, a heavy-displacement cruising sailboat might still find advantages in the old-fashioned gaff rig, with its four-sided mainsail and heavy gaff.

It's powerful off the wind, for a start—and most long-distance voyaging is done downwind. The mast is shorter, which not only enables it to pass under lower bridges, but (more importantly) also means that it can be stayed more securely without the need for spreaders. If a gaff-rigged yacht is rolled over or pitchpoled, she is less likely than a Bermuda-rigged yacht to lose her mast.

A gaff mainsail also comes down when you want it to, even

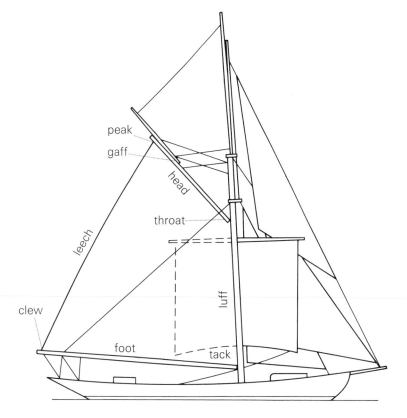

Though it can't match a taller Bermuda rig in upwind performance, a gaff mainsail lowers the sail plan's center of effort, requires no battens, pulls like an elephant off the wind, and just plain looks good. This boat can also set a topsail and flying jib on the topmast, plus a squaresail for off-the-wind sailing.

on the run. The heavy spar aloft sees to that, and the sail has no battens to get hung up on the lee rigging. In light weather, you can set a topsail to take advantage of every little breeze aloft.

A little-realized benefit of the gaff rig, especially on a boat with a bowsprit, is that the sail area is spread out more in a fore-and-aft direction. This lowers the sails' center of effort, which helps reduce heeling and weather helm, producing a well-balanced boat.

And not the least of the gaff rig's attractions is the way its purposeful curves please the eye. It is a very handsome rig.

Following are the traditional proportions for a gaff mainsail:

- the length of the luff should be between $2/3$ and $4/5$ the length of the foot
- the length of the head should be between $3/5$ and $2/3$ of the length of the foot
- the gaff should stand about 35 degrees from the vertical, except that a gaff on a narrow sail needs to be more horizontal or it will sag to leeward—hence, the shape of a schooner's foresail, which is also circumscribed by the spring stay, of course
- the height of the mainsail clew above water level should be about 1.4 times the height of the tack above water level

Gales at Sea

Planning carefully will keep you out of the worst trouble

"The fear of bad weather is no longer such a bogy as it used to be," declared the British voyager Eric Hiscock in *Voyaging Under Sail*. "This is probably due to the fact that in recent years the numbers of small yachts have increased enormously, they make more ambitious voyages, and, as few of

them get into serious trouble, it is reasonable to assume that the dangers of bad weather have at times in the past been over-stressed, and that a small sailing yacht can be just as safe, though not so comfortable, as a larger one."

With all due respect to Hiscock, the dangers of really bad weather cannot be overstressed. Although it's true that comparatively few small boats get into serious trouble, it's also a fact that the occasional bad gale causes tremendous damage and often loss of life. Fifteen people died in the Fastnet Storm that hit a racing fleet in Britain in 1979, and three died during the Queen's Birthday Storm off New Zealand in 1994, to mention only two. In storms like those, good big boats are, without a doubt, safer than good little boats, everything else being equal.

The trouble is that everything else is never equal; nevertheless, two things can be stated with confidence. First, size alone does not ensure seaworthiness. Many small boats are better designed and equipped to weather gales than some of their bigger cousins. Second, your chances of running into really bad weather are slim if you plan your voyage so that you're in the right places at the right times. The various pilot books are full of good advice in this respect.

The frequency of gales naturally varies with location and season, but round-the-world yachts making the popular westward circumnavigations through the trade-wind belts in the most favorable seasons and rounding the Cape of Good Hope report an average of 2 sailing days in 100 in which they experience ocean

gales of force 8 (34 knots) or more.

See also **Capsize; Heavy Weather**.

Galley Placement

Cooking is easier, safer, on a stove down to leeward

The galley of a sailboat is traditionally placed on the port side, although not all boat designers adhere to that old rule.

The idea was that you could still cook if the boat were hove to on the starboard tack in bad weather. It's easier and safer to cook when the galley is down to leeward; when you heave to on the starboard tack, you have the right of way over most other vessels, so it's unlikely that you'll have to go about to avoid them.

Some designers place the galley fairly far forward in the saloon, where the cook is out of the way of crew members passing to and from the cockpit and where the stove is more protected. This position is fine on bigger boats—say, 45 feet long or more—where the motion is reasonable.

But mostly the cook's area is situated near the main companionway, where the motion is easier and there is a copious amount of fresh air to dissipate smoke and fumes. Cooks seem to prefer to work there, despite the occasional dollops of spray, the puffs of wind that blow out the stove burners, and the to and fro of the various watches. The most popular location for the galley in a powerboat is in the saloon (which most powerboaters prefer to call the salon).

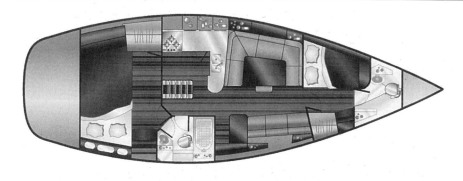

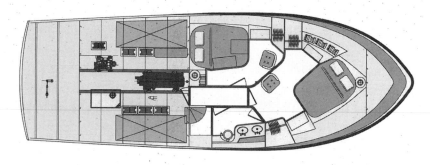

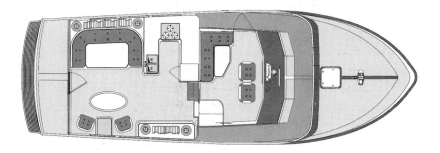

The Hunter 410 (top) *and Voyager 43* (above three) *typify galley locations in a midsize cruising sailboat and trawler yacht, respectively. Note the Voyager 43's full-width saloon.*

See also **Cooking Afloat; Gimballed Stoves; Stove Fuels**.

Galvanic Corrosion

Using sacrificial zinc to prevent underwater corrosion

Dissimilar metals in an electrolyte such as seawater form an electric cell when a conductor connects them. Galvanic corrosion eats away the anode—the active electrode—which is the less "noble" metal.

This phenomenon is named after Professor Luigi Galvani (1737–1798), the Italian physicist who discovered dynamical or current electricity. It is also widely known as electrolysis, which is a misnomer because electrolysis is the breakdown of the electrolyte, the fluid conductor. Galvanic corrosion proceeds more rapidly than electrochemical corrosion (corrosion involving a single piece of metal) and can be severe and even catastrophic.

To protect important metal fittings such as the propeller and the through-hulls from galvanic corrosion, bond all such fittings together and join them to a sacrificial block of an "unnoble" metal such as zinc.

Bonding is a traditional method of preventing corrosion. It consists of joining all the large metal fittings—such as chainplates, engine, keel bolts, mast, stem fittings, and seacocks—with a heavy copper wire or solid strip, which is then grounded at the potential of the surrounding water and linked to a zinc. The hope is to protect not just from galvanic

G

137

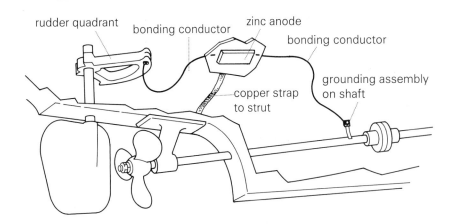

Components of a bonding system.

corrosion, but also from the even more fast-acting and insidious electrolytic corrosion, which requires a stray current from faulty electrical equipment in addition to two separate metals immersed in an electrolyte; it's often called stray-current corrosion. Sacrificial anodes will prevent galvanic corrosion but not always electrolytic corrosion, and there is still a lot that is unexplained about electrical action between metals. If your boat is bonded and you still have bad corrosion problems, one option is to sever all connections and go immediately to the alternate method of preventing corrosion, which is to keep all metal fittings entirely separate from each other. You should first get professional advice, however.

Important fittings such as the propeller, rudder straps, and through-hull fittings are furnished with zinc blocks, which will be eaten away in preference to the more noble metal as long as they last. It is important to join the zinc directly to the metal to be protected. It should be clamped to the propeller shaft or fit against the aft end of the propeller hub as

a streamlined nut. Through-hull fittings and rudder straps must be joined to the zinc with copper strap. There must be metal-to-metal contact underwater; otherwise, the zinc cannot do its work properly.

Following are the metals most commonly found on boats, listed in their order on the Galvanic Scale. The farther apart two metals are on this list, the greater the rate of corrosion; the closer together, the less chance of corrosion. The least noble metals, which are listed first, will be eaten away; the metals listed last are the most resistant to galvanic action: magnesium, zinc, aluminum, mild steel, cast iron, stainless steel (type 410, active), lead, Monel, Muntzmetal, manganese bronze, naval brass, yellow brass, aluminum bronze, copper, silicon bronze, nickel, and stainless steel (types 304, 316, and 410, passive).

Stainless steel appears twice on the scale. When it's freely supplied with oxygen, in air or water, it forms a thin corrosion-proof layer and is in a passive state, which makes it very noble. But when it's deprived of oxygen for

some time in a damp area—such as in a keel bolt, a rudder shaft, or a propeller shaft—it's hardly more resistant to corrosion than mild steel, and can suffer badly from what's called pitting corrosion. In this state, it's called active, and it becomes much less noble on the Galvanic Scale.

Corrosion occurs out of water also, such as between stainless steel fastenings and an aluminum mast, but more slowly.

See also **Electrical Bonding**; **Zinc Anodes**.

Gasoline Dangers

Sniffing out the great peril lurking quietly in the bilges

The dangers of using gasoline engines are often greatly exaggerated, but you do need to respect a fuel so explosive that half a cup of it mixed with air in the correct proportions is sufficient to blow most yachts to pieces.

Most pleasure boats carry gasoline—if not for the main engine, then for the dinghy's outboard. Many thousands, if not millions, of powerboats and sailboats are propelled by gasoline engines, and few ever get in trouble.

Gasoline fumes are heavier than air, so when there is a gasoline leak in the engine of your car, the fumes drift down and out and dissipate in the wind. In a boat, however, the fumes collect and lurk in the bilges unless they are deliberately blown clear.

You can buy an alarm that warns you if there is gasoline in the air, but the best alarm is your nose, which is sensitive to gasoline fumes in even the smallest proportion. The best advice, therefore, is to sniff the bilges before you do anything that might cause a spark, including starting the engine.

The engine compartment should also have a blower—a fan designed to exhaust air, not blow it in—and it should be run for at least 5 minutes before you start the engine. That's a long time when you're anxious to get going on a trip, but it is the safe thing to do because it takes surprisingly little gasoline to form an explosive mixture. The engine should also have an approved flame arrester attached to the air intake in case of backfires.

The safest place to keep jerricans of gasoline is on deck, where fumes easily dissipate with the breeze. However, this is impractical on many small boats, so spare fuel often ends up crammed into cockpit lockers, where escaping fumes might be trapped for some time.

Steel jerricans are considered safer than plastic ones because they are stronger and won't melt in a fire, but they are unpopular on boats because they eventually rust in a salt-air atmosphere. Plastic cans are more prone to create static electricity by rubbing against each other as a result of engine vibration. They should not be moved if you smell gasoline fumes nearby—they could spark and cause an explosion.

Be sure to keep fire extinguishers near any gasoline storage site, and be sure they are type B extinguishers suitable for tackling gasoline fires. Be aware, also, that

gasoline will burn fiercely in the presence of oxygen, but it will not explode unless the proportions of gasoline to air are within certain limits.

At the fuel dock, stop all engines, turn off all electrical devices, and eliminate all flames (including burner flames and cigarettes) before pumping gasoline. Fill portable gas tanks ashore. Keep the hose nozzle in contact with the fill fitting to avoid any buildup of static electricity. Avoid overfilling, and wipe up any spillage. And take note: there have been reports of self-service gas pump explosions caused by the ringing of a cell phone in a motorist's pocket while he was pumping gas.

Careful attention to safety rules, combined with common sense and a lot of sniffing, will almost eliminate any chance of accidental explosion on a gasoline-powered boat.

See also **Fire on Board**.

Gelcoat

Repairing nicks, scratches, cracks, and surface crazing

Gelcoat is made of polyester resin, the same stuff used to build the hull of your boat, except that it has none of the fiberglass embedded in it. Your gelcoat may be pigmented and it may also have additives to protect it against destructive ultraviolet rays. It may even be formulated to be more waterproof than normal, and to be more resistant to abrasion. But basically it's just plain old polyester resin.

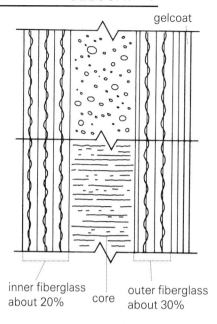

Cross-section through a fiberglass hull showing typical sandwich construction with a closed-cell foam (top) or balsa (bottom) core. The fiberglass laminate commonly comprises alternating layers of mat and woven roving. Often there are two layers of mat immediately beneath the thin gelcoat to prevent "print-through" of the coarse weave of the underlying roving.

It is normally applied in a very thin layer—about 20 mils (0.02 in. or 0.5 mm)—and when it is accidentally applied in thicker layers during construction, its brittleness causes it to crack. For these cracks and others caused by impacts or excessive strain, matching gelcoat repair kits are available at marine hardware stores. They are also good for fixing crazing, scratches, and minor gouges.

Cracks should be opened up into a deep V by drawing the corner of a screwdriver or a can punch along them. That way, the repair gelcoat can penetrate properly and not merely bridge the gap.

Most repair gelcoat needs to be protected from the air after it has been smoothed into place; otherwise, it will not cure hard. Seal it with plastic wrap and tape or spray it with a PVA (polyvinyl acetate) curing agent.

If you plan to paint over the repair afterward, you can use epoxy resin or epoxy putty instead of repair gelcoat. The epoxy has the advantage of remaining flexible when cured. Epoxy paints designed as surface finishers do a good job of repairing crazing on old gelcoat. Remember, though, that you cannot then finish off with gelcoat because, whereas epoxy will cling tenaciously to matured polyester, the polyester gelcoat will not bond to an under layer of epoxy. You must paint over epoxy.

New gelcoat eventually oxidizes and becomes dull and chalky, which is especially noticeable in dark colors. You can renew the surface gloss by buffing or rubbing with a fine compound. It is not necessary to wax the gelcoat, but many boatowners do so anyway—not only for the brilliant sheen, but also because they believe it protects the gelcoat from oxidation. If you're planning to paint the topsides or deck in the future, however, don't use a silicone wax—it is extremely difficult to remove and every tiny bit must go before you can paint. Use a good carnauba-based wax, which is easily and thoroughly removed with the solvent toluene.

See also **Epoxy; Fiberglass; Paints**.

Gimballed Stoves

Keeping the pots and pans on the galley burners

Almost all galley stoves are gimballed in a fore-and-aft axis. Some sailors insist that the correct way to gimbal the stove is athwartships, but they probably also believe the Earth is flat.

Unlike a compass, the stove is usually gimballed in one plane only; therefore, if you install it with the axis running from port to starboard, it will tilt as the boat heels and send everything sliding downhill. If the axis lies fore and aft, the stove will remain upright as the boat heels. The pitching motion of a boat bucking a bad head sea may put a stop to cooking, but in ordinary weather, adjustable potholders will keep the pots from sliding.

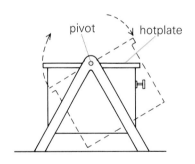

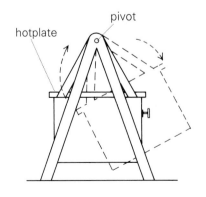

Correct (top) and incorrect (above) stove gimbal configurations.

To prevent oscillation, the pivots for a swinging galley stove should be level with the hotplate so that the motion mimics that of a seesaw. If the pivot point is higher than the hotplate, the stove will swing like a pendulum and tend to spill the contents of the pots.

See also **Galley Placement; Stove Fuels**.

GPS

Satellite system introduces great accuracy to navigation

The Global Positioning System (GPS) operated by the U.S. Department of Defense (DoD) has brought about history's biggest revolution in navigation. It is the first system to provide accurate fixes anywhere in the world at all times and in any weather, and it is available free to anyone with a modestly priced, fixed or handheld receiver. No knowledge whatsoever of navigation is needed to work the system.

Orbiting high-altitude satellites transmit signals that provide instant position fixes with a minimum accuracy of about 45 feet, or 15 meters. Often, the accuracy is 30 feet (10 m) or better.

Differential GPS (DGPS), a shore-based radio system designed to make GPS more accurate, has been overtaken by the satellite-based system known as the Wide Area Augmentation System (WAAS). Satellite signals are processed in the GPS unit itself, so no extra equipment is required, and the accuracy of WAAS is designed to be 10 feet (3 m) or better.

GPS offers such ease of use and safety that it has become the primary means of navigation for most boaters, but it still has limitations. The entire system can be switched off at will by the DoD and, indeed, has been. It could also be the target of computer hackers. Because no prudent navigator relies solely on any one aid, you should be familiar with the ordinary instruments of piloting and dead reckoning for nearshore work and the sextant for offshore work. It's not necessary to carry an expensive metal sextant; a plastic one will give your position to within about 5 miles, and that's good enough for most emergency navigation.

See also **Dead Reckoning; Fixes; Sextant**.

Green Flash

Where to look for a rare atmospheric phenomenon

The legendary green flash of the sun is rarely seen, but it certainly exists. If you're lucky you'll see it, when atmospheric conditions are right, in the last rays of the sun as it sinks into the sea. Several well-known ocean voyagers have noted it, and I have seen it myself on a calm evening in the southeast trades.

It is very short-lived, lasting only a fraction of a second to (at most) a few seconds. It is a misnomer because there is no flash—just a green glow at the top edge of the sun. You may prolong it slightly by standing up as it occurs.

It's caused by refraction of the sun's light through the Earth's at-mosphere, which separates the light into different colors. Blue light is bent more strongly than red light and the separation is exaggerated vertically, so the blue light is the last to be seen. But contamination in the atmosphere scatters blue light and removes it from our line of sight, leaving mainly green light to be observed.

According to experts at the Mount Wilson Observatory, near Los Angeles, where the green flash is frequently observed, it is also possible to see a blue flash in extraordinary conditions.

You're most likely to see the green flash in a calm and stratified atmosphere. As the sun gets closer to the horizon, it distorts and flattens in the vertical direction, and soon its edge becomes "notched" on both sides. The notches seem to be riding up the sides of the sun, but it's actually the sun that's moving down while they stay still.

When the notches get to the top of the sun, they meet and pinch off the edge of the disk so that it looks like a floating cloud—this is the part that suddenly turns green.

Groundings

Hauling yourself off with the help of a kedge anchor

If there are any boatowners who have not accidentally grounded their craft, they must be very new to the game. Sooner it later, it happens to almost everyone.

The first thing you need to know when you go aground is the state of the tide. If it's rising, you have little to worry about, because you will float off again shortly. If it's falling, you need to act quickly or you will be stuck fast for hours.

Grounding on rock or coral is likely to be serious, especially if there is a sea running that will lift the boat's hull and let it pound hard on the rock. If the boat is

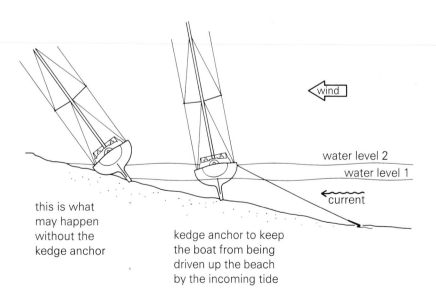

this is what may happen without the kedge anchor

kedge anchor to keep the boat from being driven up the beach by the incoming tide

wind

water level 2
water level 1

current

Use of a kedge anchor to keep a grounded boat from being driven farther ashore as the tide rises.

G

holed immediately and would sink in deep water, stay put or get the boat into shallower water where she might be salvaged. If she's a sailboat, try to keep her upright with anchors on either side and their lines taken to the masthead by the halyards.

If she's not holed, try to back her off under power. On a sailboat, get the sails down immediately, start the auxiliary, and heel her over to reduce draft. If that doesn't move her, launch the tender and take a kedge anchor out the way you came in. Set it firmly and then try to haul her off with the anchor winch, cockpit winches, or a handy-billy tackle. If the tide is falling, you may have to wait it out and arrange for a tow when the water level rises again.

If you feel yourself touching a soft bottom, try immediately to reverse your course while you still have way on. On a sailboat, tack or jibe, whichever seems appropriate. If that doesn't work, try backing off under power, but beware of fouling the engine's water intake with abrasive sand or grit from the bottom.

The next step is to take a kedge anchor out in the direction of deep water and to keep a good strain on it. Rock a powerboat to break suction on the bottom; heel a sailboat with the mainsail (as long as it will not blow you farther on shore) or a crew member on the swung-out boom.

If your efforts are fruitless and the boat is firmly aground, prepare her as best you can against waves splashing into the cockpit with the incoming tide. A sailboat should be heeled away from deep water if possible; if not—that is, if the cockpit is heeled over toward the rising water—you must cover the cockpit with tarpaulins to keep out the spray and heavy water that could be dangerous.

A kedge anchor and a means of setting it are the two most important factors in self-rescue after going aground. Except in the mildest weather, a hard dinghy that can be rowed is usually more helpful in transporting the kedge than an inflatable that has to be powered by an outboard. Lower the kedge into the dinghy first—or make it fast temporarily in the water outside the transom—and then pile its warp into the dinghy until you reach the bitter end, which should be made fast to the yacht. Then you can row the dinghy out without the heavy drag of pulling the line through the water.

See also **Anchors, Anchoring**.

H

Hallucinations

When the mind harnesses a parade of "waking dreams"

Dreams are important for mental health, and if you are denied dreams through lack of sleep—as you might be in a gale at sea on a small boat—your mind will present an alternative: a sort of parade of waking dreams known as a hallucination.

Hallucinations caused by fatigue are common among sailors undertaking long voyages. Dr. Gilin Bennet, a psychologist, reported that 50 percent of the competitors in the 1972 single-handed race across the North Atlantic experienced one or more illusions or hallucinations.

You may recall the famous hallucination that affected Joshua Slocum, the first man to circumnavigate alone. In his classic book, *Sailing Alone Around the World*, Slocum mentions that he looked out of the companionway and, to his amazement, saw a man at the helm of the *Spray*. "I am the pilot of the *Pinta* come to aid you," the man said. "Lie quiet, señor captain, and I will guide your ship tonight."

Slocum's hallucination came after he had passed out on the cabin floor, delirious with stomach cramps, so it may have resulted more from toxic reaction than from fatigue, but it typifies the kind of hallucination commonly experienced.

Frank Robb, a South African author and sailor, told me the story of a single-hander who ran into days of rough weather in the Caribbean, when he got little sleep. When the storm subsided, he wasn't sure of his position, but he soon came upon a fishing boat and, near it, an island with a protected harbor. He sailed in, passing a launch full of sightseers, and found a good anchorage, where he doused sail and dropped the hook before going below to pass out on the cabin floor.

He woke up 12 hours later and went on deck to find there was no land in sight, no boats—nothing but sea. The anchor was 8 fathoms down, but it wasn't touching bottom. His mind had invented the island and the harbor to relieve him of the anxiety that was stopping him from getting sleep, and his physical actions had been controlled by powerful fatigue hallucinations.

Experts say such hallucinations are usually harmless and leave no lasting scars.

See also **Voices in the Night**; **Watchkeeping**.

Halyards

Avoiding stretch to keep the most efficient sail shape

The word *halyard* comes from the Middle English *hallyer*, a hauler or puller. A halyard is a steel wire or fiber line used to haul up a yard or a sail. It can be all wire, all rope, or a combination of both. Halyards need to be set taut, especially on headsails, to maintain the shape of the sail in a good breeze.

Halyard stretch is avoided on many sailboats by using 7x19 stainless steel wire halyards with rope tails. When the sail is raised, the wire should end a few inches above the halyard winch so that the winch barrel accommodates rope, not wire, and can be cleated off nearby. The small length of rope between the winch and the start of the wire won't stretch significantly.

Don't be tempted to take the wire around an ordinary winch. The wire-to-rope splice is designed to take the full strain applied to the halyard, and will do so when the sail is reefed.

Instead of wire-to-rope halyards, many racing boats of twenty years ago used all-wire halyards brought home to special reel winches that needed special care in handling because of the enormous strains imposed on them.

Wire halyards need special masthead sheaves with a small groove of the correct diameter.

Cruising yachts and small sailboats find all-rope halyards perfectly acceptable and much kinder to use. Double-braid polyester (Dacron) line—with a braided cover surrounding a braided core—stretches very little; parallel-core polyester line—with a core of parallel fibers surrounded by a braided cover—stretches even less, although it is somewhat stiffer. On racing yachts, all-rope halyards are increasingly constructed of high-modulus low-stretch exotic fibers such as Spectra, Technora, Vectran, and Kevlar. Spectra, an extremely strong and light fiber from the polypropylene family, has about the same stretch as wire. One popular construction surrounds a Spectra core with a braided Dacron cover to combine low stretch and high strength with ease of handling and resistance to the elements.

Whatever construction you use, be sure to capture permanently the bitter end of your halyards. Make them fast to a deadeye on the mast, or some similar arrangement, so they cannot dis-

appear aloft of their own accord and run out of the sheave.

A rope topping lift for the main boom, rove through a separate block at the masthead, makes an excellent emergency mainsail halyard and could spare you the dangerous task of going aloft at sea.

See also **Rope Strength**; **Rope Stretch**; **Sheet Sizes**.

Handy-Billies

Here's the simple tool you need for a good hefty pull

Most sailboats and many powerboats have at least one handy-billy on board, although that's not usually what their owners will know them as. In fact, a handy-

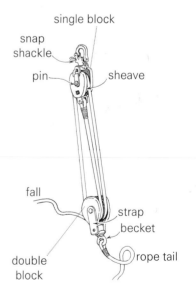

Attach the snap shackle of this handy-billy to a deck padeye and the rope tail to the load—say the clew of a sail or a dinghy you want to move—and you get a 4:1 mechanical advantage. Cleat the rope tail and fasten the snap shackle to the load, and your advantage is 3:1.

H

billy is any small block and tackle, often portable, set up to give a purchase, or mechanical advantage, of three or four.

Small tenders are often raised in their davits by handy-billies; booms on sailboats are often hauled down with handy-billies; and crew-overboard rescue systems often rely on handy-billies to recover victims. A handy-billy attached to a sailboat's boom will lift an auxiliary engine from its bed to deck level. A sailboat's mainsheet is often rigged as a handy-billy.

Create a handy-billy with a suitable line and two double blocks, or a double and a single, to perform a variety of tasks on board, including lifting loads and tightening halyards. Anywhere that a good hefty pull is needed, a handy-billy will do the job. When his steel bowsprit was bent in a collision with a steamer during the first single-handed nonstop race around the world, Bernard Moitessier straightened it with the help of a handy-billy.

Whenever possible, rig your handy-billy so the hauling part comes from the moving block, not the standing block, to gain an extra purchase. The standing blocks add no mechanical advantage—they merely change the angle of pull.

If you attach the moving block of a handy-billy to another purchase, the mechanical advantage gained is one multiplied by the other, not one plus the other. In other words, a four-part handy-billy combined with a two-part purchase results in an advantage of eight, not six.

See also **Block and Tackle; Block Sizes; Purchases.**

Harnesses

Better not to go over the side in the first place

A harness is a webbed Dacron belt that fits closely around your chest and over your shoulders. It clips to a tether attached to the boat in such a way that if you fall overboard, you'll be dragged with your head clear of the water.

A better use for a harness is to prevent your going over the side in the first place. This could be managed with a short tether attached to a jackline or separate fittings on the fore-and-aft centerline of the boat, but there is usually gear and equipment that gets in the way.

If you choose to use jacklines running along the port and starboard decks, close to the cabintop (as most people do), be sure to end them 5 or 6 feet forward of the transom. Then, if you fall in the water, you will be towed alongside, not clear astern—that makes it much easier to get back on board.

Harnesses should be worn at the first sign of bad weather but usually are not; too often, the dangerous business of shortening sail in a sudden squall is accomplished without the security of a harness.

In bad weather at sea, especially at night, clip your harness to a strong fitting in the cockpit before you emerge totally from the companionway; that way, a boarding sea cannot wash you overboard before you have found your bearings.

Never clip your harness to the lifelines—they are not designed to take the sudden strain.

*Top: Clipping a tether to a jackline. The other end of the tether is clipped to the harness with a carabiner. **Above:** An inflatable life vest with built-in harness.*

It's important to be able to release your tether at the snap shackle on your chest; otherwise, you can become trapped underwater in the cockpit if the boat capsizes and stays inverted for any length of time. Test your snap shackles under tension to be sure you can open them; a short lanyard on the snap shackle's release ring will help. A carabiner hook is *not* an acceptable means of attaching your tether to your harness because it cannot be released under tension.

The chest strap of the harness should fit about 1 to 2 inches (25 to 50 mm) below the armpits. Women should choose harnesses carefully, and not wear those with chest straps below the bust. If you fall overboard, the harness pulls upward with a tremendous jerk as you reach the end of your tether.

Some inflatable life preservers have integral harnesses, as do some foul-weather jackets, which is an excellent idea because it ensures that the harness is available at the approach of bad weather.

See also **Accidents on Board; Foul-Weather Gear; Jacklines**.

Hatches

Minimum sizes of deck openings for sails and people

Hatches are openings in a deck or bulkhead furnished with watertight lids, either hinged or sliding.

The absolute minimum size for a person to get through is 22 by 22 inches (560 by 560 mm). The typical size for an access hatch is 24 by 24 inches (610 by 610 mm).

The minimum size to pass a sail through depends on whether you're racing or cruising. For a racing boat, the formula is

sail area ÷ 160 = hatch area in square feet or square meters

For a cruising boat, the formula is

sail area ÷ 200 = hatch area in square feet or meters

Although many racing boats have foredeck hatches with lids hinged along their after ends so that they open forward for easier sail handling, it's safer to have the lids hinged along their forward ends so they slam shut if a big wave comes on board.

A forehatch that opens aft also acts as an exhaust when you're at anchor. It accentuates the natural airflow from aft forward, and also protects the interior from rain.

On seagoing boats, the main-companionway sliding hatch should be covered by a sea hood, or turtle, to prevent water from being driven under its edges into the saloon.

See also **Passages, Gangways**.

Hauling Out

Preparing for repairs or maintenance on dry land

Boats are hauled out of the water for maintenance and repair by several different methods.

Marine ways, or railways, allow a wheeled cradle to submerge in the water on an inclined ramp. The boat is floated over the cradle, secured, and then hauled up the ways to dry land.

Cranes with wide slings are also used to lift boats directly out of the water and deposit them on land, where they are propped upright with poppets, or adjustable stands. Travelifts are mobile cranes with two slings; they can not only lift a boat, but also transport her for short distances overland and deposit her anywhere in a boatyard.

Some marinas, boatyards, and yacht clubs have cranes running along overhead beams. These gantry cranes use slings to lift boats weighing many thousands of pounds and place them on road trailers.

It's a good idea to label the gunwales fore and aft where the lifting slings should be situated; otherwise, improperly placed slings might damage the rudder, propeller, or underwater transducers.

If you're having your boat hauled for a new coat of antifouling paint, make sure the hull is pressure-washed as she comes out of the water. Failing that, keep the bottom wet with fresh or salt water until you can start scraping off the weed and barnacles. If you let them dry on the hull, they're very difficult to remove without damaging the gelcoat. Sometimes barnacles will drop off of their own accord if you spray them with lemon juice or another mild acid.

None of these haulout methods need concern you, of course, if you're one of the many fortunate boatowners whose vessel is trailerable. Just find the nearest launch ramp and practice backing that trailer!

See also **Trailerboats; Winterizing**.

Headroom

Minimum heights for standing and sitting below deck

It's unfortunate, from a yacht designer's point of view, that humans are vertically oriented, whereas boats are horizontally oriented. If we were designed to carry ourselves more like the snake or the centipede, we would fit much more conveniently into the long, low shape of an efficient boat.

It's not until a boat approaches 27 feet (8.2 m) in length that it becomes possible to offer full standing headroom below without spoiling her looks and efficiency with a large and ugly deckhouse.

The generally accepted definition of full standing headroom is 6 feet, 1 inch (1.85 m) clear beneath the deck beams or headliner. Clear sitting headroom on small boats is usually understood to be between 4 feet, 0 inch (1.22 m) and 4 feet, 9 inches (1.45 m). Anything more, but lacking full standing headroom, is an irritant because it constantly invites you to stand and hit your head.

Standing headroom is not an important component of seaworthiness or sailing ability; rather, it's the opposite. In any case, on an ocean passage, most of your time down below is spent sitting or lying down. Scores of small boats without standing headroom have crossed oceans, and many have even circumnavigated. As

the British yacht designer, Uffa Fox, pointed out, if you want standing headroom, there's plenty on deck.

Heads

Dealing with the problem of pollution and onboard sewage

The head is a boat's toilet. It was named after the beak-head, an old term for the upper part of the hull at the stem. It was there that a small platform was built to contain latrines for the crew.

The head on a modern yacht has been a source of many problems and much agonizing since the introduction of strict antipollution regulations that forbid overboard discharge of untreated sewage within the 3-mile limit. There are even special areas—and increasing numbers of them in crowded cities and waterways—where no discharge at all is permitted, even of sewage treated on board to federal standards.

The effect is that boaters must carry their sewage around with them in the close confines of their vessels—sleeping, cooking, and eating with it under their nose until they can either get to seaward of the 3-mile limit or dispose of it at one of a limited number of pumpout stations in harbor.

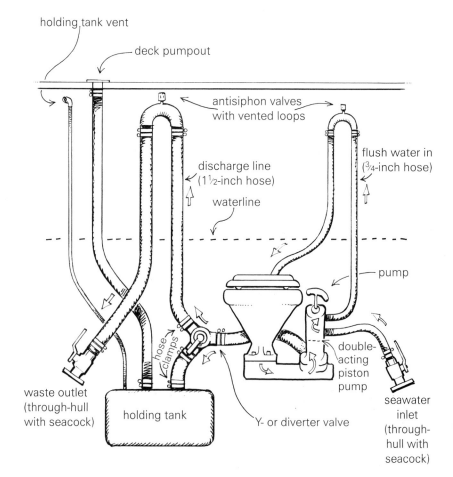

Typical toilet plumbing.

Although almost all boaters agree with the need to avoid polluting pristine bays, estuaries, anchorages, and marinas where there is little movement of water, many continue to discharge relatively small amounts of raw sewage illegally in uncrowded areas where tidal currents provide a flushing effect. They argue that there is no direct evidence that the amount of sewage they produce affects sea life adversely. Even ocean scientists studying the effects of partially treated city sewage discharged from underwater pipelines, such as San Diego's, have been unable to agree. Some even argue that it provides beneficial nutrients for the plankton from which all sea life springs.

Boaters also point to the fact that big cities, such as Victoria, British Columbia, send millions of gallons of raw or partially treated sewage out to sea only a few miles across the border from where U.S. boaters are forbidden to dump even a teaspoonful.

Be that as it may, U.S. law mandates zero discharge inside the 3-mile limit unless you use a type 1 or type 2 marine sanitation device (MSD), which uses heat or chemicals to break down the waste and reduce the bacteria count below specific levels. Once again, it seems illogical and insupportable to many that mixing effluent with chemicals will do less harm than effluent alone.

Most boaters use type 3 MSDs, or holding tanks, which they discharge into the sea beyond the 3-mile limit or into the tanks of pumpout stations ashore. It is illegal for an installed marine toilet to be connected directly to an overboard through-hull fitting. The U.S. Coast Guard will check your system if you are boarded for inspection, and it may issue a citation if it is deemed illegal.

Portable toilets not connected to the ship's plumbing are legal, as is the traditional cedar bucket. The only trouble with the bucket is that you'll need a tight-fitting lid until you can legally dump its contents on the other side of the 3-mile limit. (Although there is nothing in current federal marine sanitation law to stop you using a bucket and throwing the contents overboard, the Marpol Treaty prohibits the dumping of raw sewage from any source into U.S. territorial waters.) Some owners of racing sailboats have ripped out their heavy fixed toilets and replaced them with plastic buckets lined with strong plastic bags. After use, the bags are tied firmly and stored until they can be disposed of ashore.

One good result of the antipollution laws is that insurance companies report fewer males being lost overboard while following the traditional (but now illegal) practice of urinating from the leeward shrouds.

See also **Holding Tanks**.

Headsails

Knowing what to call them proves you know the ropes

Sailors in the age of sailing ships were careful in their use of words and for good reason. The correct terminology was of paramount importance when a vessel had a score or more of sails with literally hundreds of lines controlling them.

Unfortunately, many modern amateur sailors don't feel the same need for precise semantics, a tendency that reveals itself particularly in regard to the naming of the sails in front of the mast. Admittedly, a forestaysail by any other name would pull as sweet, but you can tell a sailor who really knows the ropes by the way he or she names the headsails.

In most fore-and-aft rigged sailboats, a forestaysail is a sail set on the forestay, which extends from the stemhead to a point at or near the top of the mast. It can vary in size and shape from a low-cut genoa to a high-cut Yankee, or even to a tiny storm staysail. The word *forestaysail* is usually abbreviated to *foresail*, which does nothing to clear up the confusion.(In a schooner, the foresail is the sail that extends aft from the foremast, so the sails in front of it are called jibs; starting from forward: the flying jib, the inner jib, and the staysail, or jumbo jib. My advice is to stay well away from schooners while you're learning headsail terms.)

A headsail is any sail set forward of the mainmast of a ketch, yawl, sloop, or cutter. Confusion arises when people use the word *foresail* interchangeably with *headsail*. Headsail is a generic catch-all term for genoas, jibs, spinnakers, gennakers, bloopers, reachers, drifters, screechers, and the like, although its usage is usually restricted to forestaysails and jibs.

Properly speaking, a jib is a foresail set forward of the forestay, whether hanked to a topmast stay

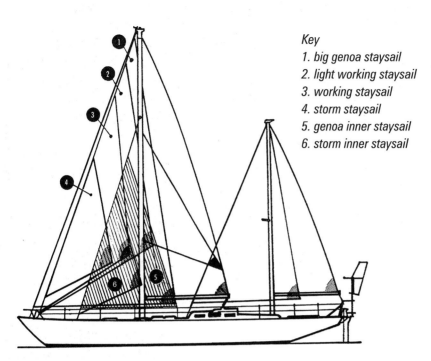

Key
1. big genoa staysail
2. light working staysail
3. working staysail
4. storm staysail
5. genoa inner staysail
6. storm inner staysail

In 1967, Francis Chichester, age 65, completed a solitary nine-month journey around the planet in his 53-foot ketch Gipsy Moth IV, *stopping only once and establishing a new solo speed record.* Gipsy Moth's *sail plan included six headsails.*

of its own or (more properly) set flying from its own halyard. The jib is sometimes defined as the foremost headsail.

This can all be simplified by the following:

- headsails are any sails set ahead of the mainmast
- forestaysails are hanked or rolled onto the forestay, which is the stay that ends at the stemhead
- jibs are sails set forward of the forestay. In common parlance, however, any sail flown from the forestay of a single-head-stay boat is referred to as a jib if it is entirely confined to the foretriangle, and an overlapping jib or genoa if it is large enough to overlap the foretriangle.

The names of a cutter's headsails depend on whether there is a bowsprit or not. If so, the sail set from the bowsprit is the jib and the sail set from the forestay is the forestaysail. In the absence of a bowsprit, the foremost sail is the forestaysail, the other the inner staysail. A double-headsail sloop is a sloop rig to which another foresail has been added. A cutter's mast lies farther aft than a sloop's, but sometimes it is thought advantageous to split a sloop's foresail area into two units; it then becomes a double-headsail sloop. Reachers, drifters, screechers, and the like are names for specialized sails used to increase sail area or improve performance under differing circumstances, such as light winds or winds coming from certain directions.

See also **Jib Numbers; Roller Furling.**

Heaters

Keeping the cold at bay when you cruise in cold climates

If you cruise in the higher latitudes, one of the greatest comforts on your boat will be a cabin heater. There can be nothing more heartening than leaving a wet, freezing cockpit for the dry warmth of a cheerful stove down below.

Not so many years ago, when boating was a more Spartan sport, the purists would have regarded a heater as a sign of weakness and moral turpitude. Sailors, like mountain climbers, backpackers, and other outdoor enthusiasts, were *expected* to suffer in order that they might better appreciate, by comparison, the subtle highlights of their experiences: the glorious sunsets and the panoramic vistas.

The advantage of boating, compared with most other outdoor sports, is that you *can* have a heater. The size and type of heater you need depends, as always, on the size and type of your boat and where you do your boating. I have cruised on a Santana 22 in which a Coleman pressure kerosene lamp provided not only brilliant light, but also sufficient heat to warm up the cabin and dry out my soaked underwear.

Most cruising boats, however, are better served by a compact heater permanently mounted on a bulkhead or—if you want to get a little fancier—an oil-burning furnace in a locker, with electric fans and ducts to distribute the warm air throughout the boat.

Bulkhead heaters burn almost anything, including flotsam and driftwood from the beach. The marine catalogs list heaters that burn propane gas, diesel fuel, kerosene, charcoal, cardboard, coal, wood, and pellets.

If you already carry diesel fuel for your engine, a diesel heater makes sense—except on a very small boat because they run exceptionally hot. Like a kerosene heater, a diesel heater can be fed by a pressure tank or, if the source of supply is raised, it can function as a drip-feed.

Many heaters have glass fire doors to create a cozy fireplace atmosphere and have a comforting "shippy" look about them. They should be vented through the cabintop via a stainless steel flue and deck-pipe cap, or Charley Noble.

Don't be tempted to buy a household kerosene heater from your local hardware store: they tip over easily and create a dangerous fire hazard.

Alcohol heaters are small and cheap, but they put out comparatively little heat and are expensive to run for long periods. If they're not vented to the outside atmosphere, they also produce a lot of moisture, which will condense in the cabin as soon as the temperature drops.

All unvented heaters give off copious quantities of the killer gas, carbon dioxide, so make sure your cabin is well ventilated. In fact, even vented heaters, if they are not completely airtight, will introduce some carbon monox-ide into the cabin. One of the great dangers of this gas is the speed with which it can travel upstream against a flow of air. If you have a heater, place a carbon monoxide detector in each sleeping area.

See also **Accidents on Board**.

Heaving Lines

More than meets the eye to throwing a line any distance

Occasionally, when you might need to get a line ashore or across to another boat, you'll feel the need for an efficient heaving line—and you probably won't have one. Even if you do, you probably won't be able to find it on the spur of the moment. If you're like most boaters, you'll just cast about for any old piece of line that seems to be unemployed, and hurl it roughly in the right direction as best you can.

You had better hope that your target is fairly close because it's impossible to heave a line any distance unless it's properly prepared and thrown.

A heaving line—also called a messenger—doesn't have to be thick and strong. It is merely a leader to which a stronger line may be attached and swiftly drawn in. For most yachts, there's no need for a heaving line to be more than a $\frac{1}{4}$ inch (6 mm) in diameter. If it's Dacron, it will have

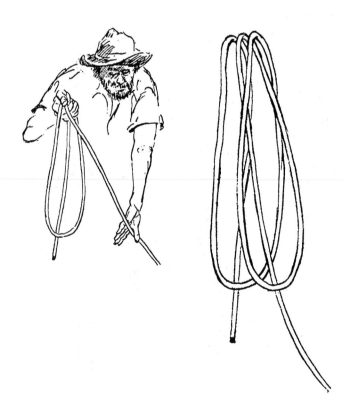

The best way to prepare a heaving line is with alternate-hitch coiling, in which regular turns are alternated with turns made, as shown here, by grasping the rope with the back of your hand turned toward you, then turning the palm toward you as you bring your hands together.

a breaking strength of more than 1,000 pounds (454 kg).

Traditionally, heaving lines have had special hollow knots on the end, such as monkey's fists or capsized Turk's heads. These knots conceal a variety of weights ranging from golf balls to hunks of lead capable of felling an elephant. If you make your own traditional heaving line, don't go overboard with the weight. A few ounces is enough, especially if you are the target.

To avoid snarls, expert heavers coil their lines by alternating regular clockwise turns with half hitches, and then hold half the coil in one hand while they throw the weighted half with the other. (This, by the way, is also the best way to heave a dockline ashore: split it into two coils, then heave one with one hand while feeding line from the other.) You can avoid birds' nests by laying the line down on deck in overlapping figure eights that will run out smoothly without twists.

Perhaps the best solution for the amateur boater is what the marine catalogs call a throw rope, which is a line in a buoyant bag. You simply hold the end of the line and throw the entire bagful of rope, allowing the line to feed itself out of a hole on top as it goes. You won't be able to throw the rope as far as a traditional lineheaver can, but you're not half as likely to make a fool of yourself.

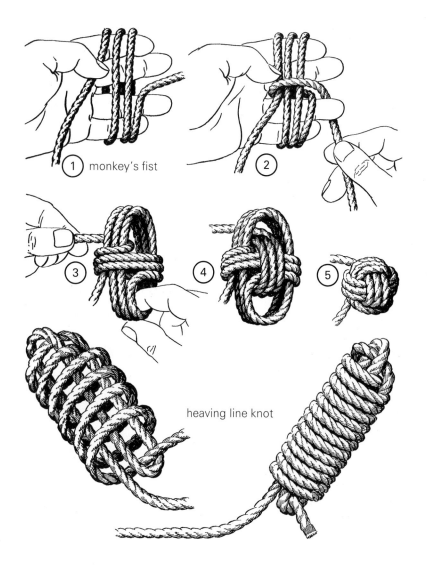

1. monkey's fist
2.
3.
4.
5.
heaving line knot

You can terminate a heaving line with a monkey's fist or heaving line knot for throwing distance.

Heaving To

Tucking her head under her wing for safety in a storm

In a moderate gale of 28 to 33 knots, a sailboat will usually lie quite safely if she's hove to with her head tucked under her wing, 50 to 60 degrees off the wind.

To heave to, simply pull the sheet of the storm jib to weather until the sail is backed. Because all boats are different, you may need to experiment to see how far the jib should be brought to weather of the mast. The farther it comes to weather, the more it tends to push the bow away from the wind.

At the same time, give the mainsheet some slack so that the double- or triple-reefed mainsail is almost feathering. Once again, you may have to experiment with it to see where she likes it best. The more you pull the mainsail in, the more the boat will point up into the wind—but she'll heel excessively if it's pinned in too far.

You will need to lash the tiller down to leeward so that if the boat gathers way, the rudder will head her into the wind and waves, and slow her down again.

Heave to on the starboard tack if possible, so you have right of way over most other vessels.

You may be astonished at the difference in your boat's behavior when you heave to. If you were bashing and crashing to windward before, shipping seas green and heeling the side decks under, now you'll lie quietly and much more upright, drifting sideways at about 1 knot and making a course of about 90 degrees to the wind—but crabbing slightly forward over the ground.

Some ultralight sailboats with fin keels won't heave to no matter what you try. The rest of us, however, can heave to for reefing, to snatch some sleep, to cook a meal, to do some navigating, or simply to wait out a contrary gale. With rising wind and seas, however, the boat's head will be thrown about mercilessly. Then it will be time to try something else instead: possibly heaving to with a sea anchor, or running off before the gale while trailing a drogue, or, on some boats, lying ahull.

Heaving to in a powerboat means pointing your bow into the seas or just a few points off and applying just enough throttle to maintain headway. When the boat feels unsafe running down sea in a gale (and most powerboats are vulnerable to broaching and boarding seas on this course), heaving to may be the only tactic left to try. If windage forward is forcing the bow too far off, a sea anchor might help.

See also **Drogue; Heavy Weather; Lying Ahull; Running Off; Sea Anchors; Scudding; Trysails**.

Heavy Weather

Knowing what options you have for fighting storms at sea

The Australian novelist and yachtsman, Nevil Shute, wrote: "When I began yacht cruising after the First World War it was regarded as axiomatic amongst yachtsmen that a small sailing vessel, properly handled, is safe in any deep-water sea.

"I think that Claude Worth, the father of modern yachting, may have been partly responsible for this idea, and it may well be true for the waters in which he sailed. A small yacht, we said, will ride easily over and among great waves if she is hove to or allowed to drift broadside under bare poles; you have only to watch a seagull riding out the storm upon the water, we said. . . . We now know with certainty that the seagull parallel was wrong. A small yacht, well found, well equipped, and beautifully handled, can be overwhelmed by the sea when running under bare poles dragging a warp, or when lying sideways to the sea, hove to under bare poles. The Smeetons have proved it twice."

The Smeetons were, of course, Miles and Beryl Smeeton, owners of the 46-foot (14 m) ketch *Tzu Hang*, which twice capsized while trying to round Cape Horn. Miles recounted their dramatic adventures in the cruising classic, *Once Is Enough* (for which

Shute wrote the foreword to the original edition).

If you've already read the Gales at Sea entry, you know that if you avoid Cape Horn and sail around the world following the trade winds, your chances of meeting severe weather are slim, indeed—presuming that you're in the right places at the right times, especially if you're in a fast powerboat that can outrun a storm or beat it to shelter. Nevertheless, you and your boat should be prepared for it, just in case. Furthermore, you should know what your options are when you meet bad weather: heaving to, lying ahull, running off, towing drogues, and scudding. A few boats might find it useful to lie to a sea anchor.

The pros and cons of all these survival tactics are discussed under their own headings in this book.

See also **Broaching To; Capsize; Gales at Sea**.

Height of Eye

Making allowance for your sextant's height above water

When you're taking sights with a sextant, you have to measure the angle between a heavenly body and the horizon from your position at sea level. The trouble is that your eye isn't at sea level, but the calculated altitude worked out from the sight-reduction tables presumes that it is.

Thus, you have to make corrections to all sights except those taken with a bubble sextant or an artificial horizon, neither of which is of much use on a small boat bouncing around at sea.

As you rise and fall on the swells, the height of your eye above sea level changes all the time; however, this doesn't present as much of a problem as you might think. The usual correction for the height of eye in small boats is minus 3 minutes (−3′).

This equates to an actual eye height of about 8 feet (2.4 m) above the water, which is near the average in most cases. If your sighting position is appreciably higher, consult the tables or the nautical almanac for the correction to make because each minute represents a difference of 1 mile on the chart.

See also **Sextants**.

HELP Posture

Adopting certain positions can prolong the survival time

If you fall into the water without protective clothing or a survival suit, it is only a matter of time before your body temperature drops enough to render you unconscious and you become a victim of hypothermia.

You can prolong your survival time. If you're alone, you should adopt the heat-escape-lessening posture (HELP), which involves leaning back against the collar of your life jacket and folding your arms across the front of the jacket to hug it close to your body. You should cross your legs below the knees and draw them up toward your chest as high as you can. In this way, you will trap as much heat as possible within

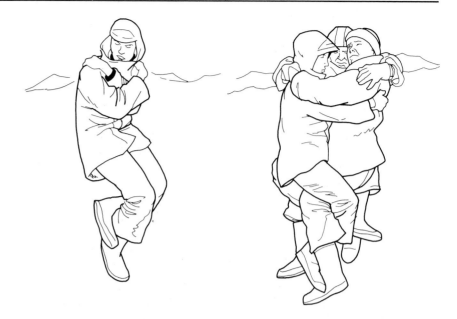

The HELP posture for an individual and a group.

the immediate vicinity of your body.

Unless you are absolutely certain you can swim to land or something floating nearby, you are better off conserving heat and prolonging your survival time. Don't be tempted to exercise your arms or legs to keep warm. It has been well established that you'll lose more heat that way than you can generate from the exercise.

If you are one of two or more people in the water, you should all huddle closely together with your arms around each other's shoulders and your chests in contact. Wrap your legs around each other, too—anything to maintain body contact. This is an especially valuable survival technique for children, who develop hypothermia more quickly than adults. Medical researchers say the huddle position can increase your survival time by 50 percent.

See also **Hypothermia; Life Jackets**.

Hobbyhorsing

Finding the happy medium that drives a boat against waves

A sailboat that hobbyhorses, or pitches, excessively is hopeless to windward, and will exasperate her crew as she plunges up and down "in the same hole" all the time. Similarly, a displacement powerboat that pitches excessively in a seaway will give an uncomfortable ride.

Hobbyhorsing is caused by inertia, the tendency of a moving body to keep moving at the same speed in the same direction. As a boat's bow rises on a swell, the inertia of heavy anchor chain and other gear in the bow wants things to continue that way; even when the swell has receded, the bow still continues to lift. When gravity finally regains control and the bow starts to fall, it continues to fall even when it should be rising to a new swell. The boat rears and plunges ineffectually in the same spot, completely out of step with nature, and wasting most of her energy on fighting inertia instead of driving the boat forward over the waves.

Heavy gear at the stern of the boat contributes to the problem, as does a heavy mast or gear aloft. The size of the swell, too, affects your boat's tendency to hobbyhorse, and conditions are at their worst when the distance between swells is just a little longer than your boat's length on deck.

Certain hull shapes are more prone than others to hobbyhorsing; however, in the absence of any major design flaw, you can cure it—or, at least, eradicate the worst of it. To do so, move the heavy weights toward the center of the boat and trim all excessive weight from the mast of a sailboat.

Instead of plunging into swells, the bow will now ride buoyantly over them and fall with them, making good forward progress. At the same time, the pitching will be appreciably shorter and sharper, possibly to the extent of making the crew uncomfortable and stressing the rigging. The answer is to move some weight back toward the ends of the boat. It will take some experimentation to find the happy medium between excessive pounding and disheartening hobbyhorsing.

To the extent that a powerboat is designed with considerable bearing surface in broad, flat stern sections to support semidisplacement and planing speeds, it is unlikely to hobbyhorse. Pounding is the more usual problem in

this case, and can be alleviated with deep-V sections combined with topside flare forward or by the simple expedient of throttling back. Sometimes a hard-chine powerboat will porpoise at speed: the bow oscillates up and down as the hull's center of dynamic lift shifts forward and aft, even in calm water. Once you learn which combination of speed, weight distribution, and trim-tab and drive positions might cause your boat to porpoise, you'll be able to prevent it.

See also **Inertia**.

Holding Power

Different anchors and how well they perform under test

Because no two sea bottoms are the same and because conditions of wind and wave are always different, it's difficult to judge the performance of one anchor against another. Interested authorities, including the U.S. Navy and the British Royal National Lifeboat Institution, have conducted many tests, but the results often conflict or are inconclusive.

Nevertheless, broad guidelines have been established that are useful to boaters trying to choose an anchor. *Practical Sailor*, a well-respected boating consumer magazine, has plotted and analyzed the results of nine extensive tests of anchors of comparable physical size, but not weight. Here is what the magazine found regarding holding power— an anchor's ability to resist being dragged through or out of the sea bottom. All anchors are compared

with a traditional fisherman's anchor, which is given an arbitrary holding power of 100 percent.

- **Plow anchors:**
  C.Q.R. anchor, 240 percent
  Danforth and Bruce, 250 percent
  Delta, 270 percent
- **Pivoting fluke anchors:**
  Danforth Standard and Danforth Deepset (standard version), 520 percent
  Danforth Deepset (high-tensile version), 540 percent
  Danforth Hi-Tensile, 550 percent
  Fortress, 560 percent

Be aware, however, that holding power is not the only criterion for an anchor. Stowage, handling, and (especially) penetrating power also are important.

See also **Anchors, Anchoring; Anchor Types**.

Holding Tanks

Dealing with the difficult problem of waste disposal

A holding tank holds the boat's sewage until you can legally discharge it overboard or have it removed at a pumpout station.

In an ideal boat sewage system, holding tanks have three hoses: the first, at the top of the tank, comes directly from the toilet; the second, near the bottom of the tank, runs up to the deck or cockpit floor, from where the tank may be vacuumed out at a pumpout station; and the third is a vent that leads up to the deck or exits through the top of the hull.

H

The problem with this system is that you can't empty the tank unless you can get to a pumpout station, which—if you intend to spend a few days at sea—is an obvious disadvantage.

One way to overcome it is to insert a Y-valve into the hose that empties the tank, so you can not only send it to the deck or cockpit discharge point, but you also pump the contents of the holding tank straight overboard via an underwater through-hull fitting. (The second option can only be used when you are outside the 3-mile limit.) You'll need a small hand pump in the line to the through-hull discharge, of course.

If you spend any time outside U.S. coastal waters, where it's legal to discharge directly overboard, it doesn't make much sense to pump your sewage into a tank, only to have to pump it overboard from there. Thus, many sailboat cruisers use an alternative system whereby the discharge line from the toilet has a Y-valve in it; one side goes to the holding tank, the other to the through-hull fitting.

When you're within the U.S. 3-mile limit, you cannot pump your waste directly overboard, of course, so the handle of the Y-valve must be securely fixed in the position that sends sewage from the toilet to the holding tank only. How you do this to the satisfaction of a U.S. Coast Guard boarding officer is not certain. Don Casey, an experienced cruiser and author of *This Old Boat* and many other boating books, maintains that "padlocking the handle, or securing it with a nylon wire tie to an eyebolt, is acceptable, but

wiring or taping it in position is not. If your installation is missing this feature," he adds, "it can cost you up to $2,000."

The handle of the seacock at the waste-discharge through-hull could also be secured in the closed position, of course, which would make overboard discharge impossible and presumably satisfy the law.

See also **Heads**.

Horse Latitudes

Where sailing ships had to jettison their precious cargo

In the vicinity of latitudes 30° N and 30° S, on the outer edges of the trade-wind belt, there are areas of capricious light winds and calms known as the horse latitudes.

The name is more commonly given to the area in the North Atlantic, where the effect is accentuated in summer. This area of comparatively high atmospheric pressure also used to be called the Calms of Cancer, after the nearby Tropic of Cancer.

According to an eighteenth-century authority, the name "horse latitudes" was given to the area because sailing ships often began to run out of provisions and water in the calms. In the days when navies had to transport horses on sailing ships, each horse was allowed 1,350 pounds of stores and water every five days. When the supply ran out, the horses had to be killed

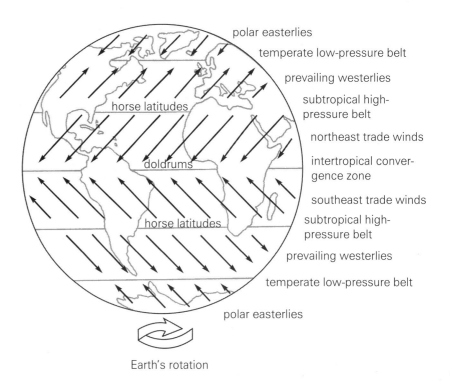

The major planetary wind belts. At roughly 30 degrees North and South there is a region of upper-air subsidence, producing light and baffling surface winds.

and thrown overboard—hence, the name.

See also **Doldrums; Trade Winds; Wind Systems.**

Wind Strength	Wind Speed in Knots	Pressure in Lb./Sq. Ft.	Horsepower per Sq. Ft.	Pressure in kg per Sq. m	Kilowatts
Force 3	7 to 10	0.28	0.015	1.37	0.118
Force 4	11 to 16	0.67	0.020	3.27	0.161
Force 5	17 to 21	1.31	0.040	6.39	0.312
Force 6	22 to 27	2.30	0.070	11.22	0.559

As wind speed doubles, the force on a sail quadruples.

Horsepower

Reckoning the power generated by horses, humans, and sails

Horsepower is a unit of power equal to that required to raise a load of 33,000 pounds by a height of 1 foot in 1 minute. In other words, 1 hp equals 33,000 foot-pounds per minute, or 550 foot-pounds per second. It was regarded as the maximum sustained amount of power the average horse could produce over a short period.

The horsepower produced by a yacht's sails is relatively small at normal wind speeds. In a force 4 breeze (11 to 16 knots), 500 square feet of sail generates roughly 10 hp, which is about 1 hp for every 50 square feet. Similarly, a dinghy sail of 75 square feet generates about 1.5 hp in force 4 winds.

Because energy equals mass times the square of its speed, as Einstein taught us, a wind with a speed of 22 to 27 knots (force 6) does not generate twice the horsepower of wind blowing at 11 to 16 knots (force 4). It generates *four times as much*, or nearly 4 hp for every 50 square feet. This explains why small sailboats need to reef when the wind rises to anything above 15 knots or so.

Horsepower generated by humans is substantially less than that generated by sail, of course.

It is fairly well established in sports medicine that an average man in good condition can produce about $\frac{1}{4}$ hp for about 40 minutes, and between $\frac{1}{6}$ and $\frac{1}{7}$ hp for several hours at a time. Interestingly, rowing a dinghy at a reasonable clip—say 3 to 4 knots in calm water and no wind—takes about $\frac{1}{6}$ hp. The maximum burst of horsepower produced by a trained male athlete seems to be a little less than 2 hp, but it can be maintained only for a few seconds.

See also **Brake and Shaft Horsepower; Fuel Economy; Powerboat Engines; Sailboat Engines.**

Horseshoe Buoys

Keeping a lifesaver ready to throw to a person overboard

Ring buoys are commonly found on shore where the public has access to the water. They are thrown to victims in the water to help them stay afloat until they can be rescued. Small boats often carry them for the same reason, but the most popular type of ring buoy found on pleasure boats is the horseshoe buoy. It's shaped like a horseshoe so that anyone in the water can pull it around his or her

body and wear it under the arms. This design helps to float a person with the head well clear of the water.

Although the ring buoy usually has a light grabline fastened at four points on its circumference, it will not raise you out of the water unless the hole is large enough to accommodate your shoulders. Even then, you have to know the trick of flipping the ring over your head, after which the problem is to get your arms and shoulders through the hole. That's not always possible if you're wearing bulky clothing.

The horseshoe buoy is easier to enter and typically has a strap that can be fastened to keep you inside. The buoy may be made of cork or balsa wood, but most modern ones are made of light plastic foam. The foam is very buoyant, but the lightness of the buoy means it will quickly blow away from the victim if there's any wind. It's recommended, there-

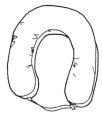

Have at least one horseshoe buoy ready for throwing. Two are better.

fore, that horseshoe and other ring buoys be equipped with small drogues that deploy and slow down the drift of the buoy when it hits the water.

Horseshoe buoys are regarded as type 4 throwable personal flotation devices (PFDs) under U.S. Coast Guard regulations. At least one throwable PFD must be carried on every vessel, mounted so that it is quickly accessible in an emergency.

See also **Life Jackets**.

Hull Colors

You can have any color you like, as long as it is white

Air-sea rescue personnel often complain that there seem to be only two color schemes for pleasure boats: white and blue or blue and white. Imagine the difficulty of spotting a blue-and-white boat in a blue-and-white ocean.

Probably well over 90 percent of hulls are white, which is a practical color for a boat because it hides most defects in the paint or gelcoat finish. Amateurs painting their hulls with twin-pack polyurethane are advised to choose white for this very reason. Dark colors such as red or blue seem to magnify even the slightest imperfections, and the colors tend to fade gradually after a few years in the sun. White is also cool in hot climates, of course, and will help keep the seams of a wooden boat closed in summer.

An old superstition warns against painting a boat in the colors of the sea, lest the gods should think you're usurping their terri-

tory and seek revenge. Although white is a color of the sea, it seems to have been granted immunity.

When it's time to sell your boat, a white hull will be an advantage; brightly colored hulls almost always take longer to sell.

See also **Unlucky Colors**.

Hull Costs

Working out whether or not you'll save on building costs

On boatbuilding sites in many parts of the world, you'll see the hulks of unfinished concrete hulls. Many of them were abandoned after their owners finally realized the tremendous amount of work that lay ahead of them. Others were cast aside for lack of cash, when builders who hadn't done their financial homework came to the accurate conclusion that they'd been misled about the price of a cruising yacht.

The truth is that the hull, deck, and cabin of a normal monohulled yacht comprise only about one third of the total finished cost of the vessel. So, although you may save a few thousand dollars by building a cheap ferroconcrete hull yourself, the other two thirds of the boat—the engine, the masts, the rigging, the ground tackle, sails, winches, and everything else—are going to cost exactly the same as they would on any boat.

After many misguided would-be adventurers had started their concrete hulls, it also became evident that there was a glut of old fiberglass hulls on the market—

because fiberglass was lasting longer than anyone imagined it would. It became cheaper to buy a sound and seaworthy (but no longer fashionable) fiberglass boat than to build a boat of your own.

Even if an old fiberglass hull needed attention, it was almost always cheaper—and certainly much quicker—to reinforce it or repair it than to build a boat from scratch.

See also **Choosing a Boat**.

Hull Shapes

Looking at the character of different types of bottoms

Almost every hull has a bottom built to one of three basic shapes, or a combination of them: flat, V, and round bottoms.

Flat-bottomed boats are the simplest and least expensive to build, but they are mostly restricted to sheltered waters because they are prone to pounding in waves, which creates considerable discomfort for passengers and strains the structure of the boat. Hulls with flat bottoms need flare in their topsides to deflect spray and provide reserve buoyancy when they heel.

The sharpie hull form—a flat bottom with narrow beam and a pointed bow—makes a fast sailer in flat water, though it will pound when sailing to weather in a chop. It requires a big centerboard trunk in its narrow cabin and provides little headroom below, but sharpies can be handsome. As a powerboat, a sharpie needs a deep forefoot to reduce pounding; it should be limited to semidis-

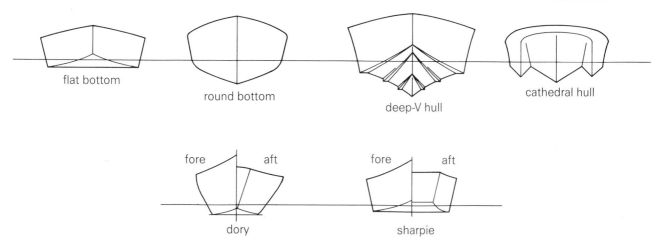

A few representative hull sections.

placement speeds for the same reason. A deep skeg aft allows it to track better in a following sea.

Dories are also flat-bottomed, with narrower bottoms than a sharpie but much more flare in the topsides, giving them greater beam on deck. This hull form makes them initially tippy, but the more they tip, the more they resist further tipping as that flare comes into play. With more rocker than a sharpie, a dory is meant for slow speeds—some of the earliest powerboats were sailing-rowing dories for inshore fisheries in which small engines had been retrofitted.

V-bottomed hulls (also known as deadrise hulls) are more seakindly and far less prone to pounding. Although more often associated with powerboats, they are suitable for a wide range of sailboats, from small plywood dinghies to large seagoing vessels built of steel or aluminum. Fast-planing powerboat hulls often combine a deep V at the bow (i.e., 26 degrees or so of upward slope as seen in section view) to minimize pounding with a much shallower V at the transom (say, 10 to

18 degrees) to facilitate planing. These modified V-bottoms are often called warped-plane or variable-deadrise hulls.

A deep-V or constant-deadrise powerboat carries the steep deadrise of its entry all the way back to the transom. Ever since Dick Bertram's *Moppie* whipped other offshore racing powerboats in 1961, the deep-V hull has been accepted for offshore speed. Without flat after sections, it requires more horsepower to get up on plane and is not as fast in calm water as a modified V, but it can keep flying through seas that require other boats to slow down before they knock your teeth out. Deep-V powerboats are tippy at slow speeds but acquire dynamic stability when planing. They hold course extremely well but may turn with difficulty, and they have a tendency to lay over unpredictably on a side of the bottom—a defect known as chine-walking. Longitudinal running strakes and chine flats (an outward elaboration of the chine, or corner of the bottom and topsides seen in section, into a horizontal shelf) can cure this.

A hull with a V-shaped bottom will naturally have a greater draft than a flat-bottomed hull, as well as greater displacement and, therefore, carrying capacity.

Round bottoms provide the largest interior space for the least area in the water and, therefore, the least hull friction at reasonably slow speeds. They, too, are used for all types of boats, from small dinghies to the biggest ocean cruisers, both power and sail. They are the least prone to pounding of all three types and are often regarded as the most pleasing to the eye. However, they are more difficult to build using some materials, such as steel, and are therefore more expensive to produce, but a round-bottomed hull can be more easily fine-tuned by a designer to the exact performance specifications required.

A round-bottomed hull is ordinarily one meant to operate at displacement speeds because the flat bearing surfaces required by a planing hull are incompatible with a rounded bilge. Nevertheless, some semidisplacement powerboats have rounded hulls; the Maine lobster-boat hull type is

H

one example. The tighter the turn of the bilge, the higher is the hull's potential speed.

See also **Bilge**; **Chines**; **Deadrise**; **Keels**; **Skegs**.

Hull Trim

Adjusting the fore-and-aft angle of a hull in the water

When sailors refer to the trim of a hull, they're talking about the relative heights of the bow and stern above water. A boat floating with her stern lower than her bow (or lower than her waterline shows it should be) is said to be trimmed by the stern, and vice versa.

It can be dangerous to trim a boat by the bow, not only because it reduces her ability to rise to oncoming waves, but also because it makes steering more difficult. The bow tends to take a "set" and veer off to one side, then to the other.

Trimming too much by the stern causes problems, too. An immersed transom creates a great deal of drag and slows a boat down, in addition to making it easier for waves to board and flood the cockpit.

It's often advantageous, however, to trim a powerboat slightly by the stern to help her climb over her own bow wave and start planing. Many planing hulls have trim tabs on the lower edge of the transom to adjust the trim angle while underway. When a powerboat is planing, the most advantageous trim angle—from the point of view of speed and fuel economy—is 2 to 4 degrees down by the stern.

See also **Planing**; **Trim Tabs**.

Hurricane Areas

Where and when to expect tropical revolving storms

Because hurricanes are fueled by large quantities of vapor from warm water, they are restricted to the tropical oceans of the world. Most form when the water is at its warmest, in late summer and fall, but they can and do appear at any time in a six-month period.

In the North Atlantic, they are experienced from May to November and are most frequent in August, September, and October. The period from December to June is usually hurricane-free. In the Far East, where they are known as typhoons, hurricanes can form in any month, but most appear in late summer and early fall.

The sea areas most commonly affected by these tropical revolving storms are as follows:

- the western North Atlantic
- the western North Pacific (Japan to Guam)
- the South Pacific (Marquesas to the Coral Sea)
- the Bay of Bengal
- the southwest Indian Ocean

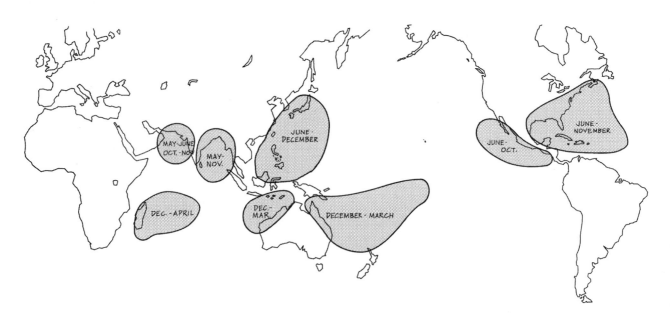

Hurricane areas and seasons worldwide.

Hurricane Tactics

Learning how to navigate your way out of bad trouble

A hurricane is a storm of tropical origin that reaches a wind strength of 64 knots (75 mph) or more. If you find yourself in the vicinity of one at sea, you can expect trouble.

Most storms are roughly circular, often about 300 to 400 miles in diameter, and wind speeds increase toward the eye of the hurricane, which may measure from 5 to 50 miles across.

You first need to know where the center of the storm is relative to your position and the direction in which the entire storm system is moving. You can find the storm center by facing into the wind. In the Northern Hemisphere, the center is on your right side, between 90 and 135 degrees from dead ahead. In the Southern Hemisphere, it's the same distance to your left.

North of the equator, a veering wind—that is, one that's gradually shifting direction clockwise—indicates you're in the path of the dangerous semicircle of the hurricane. In a sailboat, you should sail close-hauled on the starboard tack at right angles to the assumed track of the storm, or (if the center is close to you) heave to on the starboard tack.

If the wind is gradually backing or changing direction counterclockwise, you are in the path of the "safe" or "navigable" semicircle, where wind speeds and wave heights are less. Run with the wind on the starboard quarter, keeping a course at right angles to the storm track and away from its center.

If the wind direction remains steady but the barometer falls rapidly, you are in the direct path of the storm. Run off on the starboard tack, keeping the wind on your starboard quarter, to get away from the dangerous center of the depression and move across to the "safe" semicircle. Remember that "safe" and "navigable" are purely relative; they carry no guarantees.

A hurricane usually moves fairly slowly along its track, at about 10 to 15 knots, but starts to move faster when it curves northward. In the Southern Hemisphere, hurricanes rotate the opposite way, and their dangerous semicircles are on the left of the storm track.

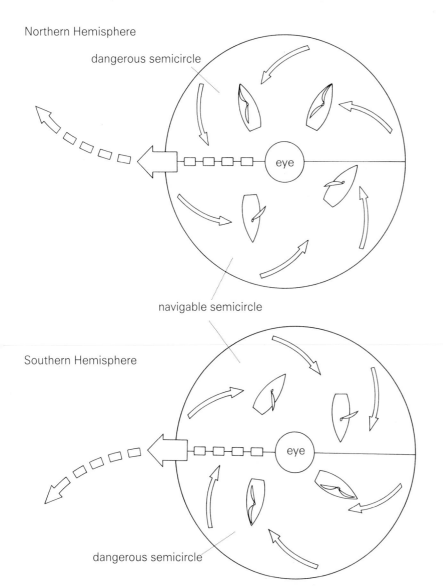

Northern Hemisphere

dangerous semicircle

eye

navigable semicircle

Southern Hemisphere

eye

dangerous semicircle

The boat symbols show suggested courses for the four quadrants of a hurricane in the Northern and Southern Hemispheres.

Hydrofoils

Rising above the waves to improve speed and comfort

The Italian inventor, Enrico Forlanini, is believed to have built the first hydrofoil boat in 1898. It had two sets of submerged foils, one forward and one aft, that behaved much like small airplane wings. At speed, the lift from the foils made the boat rise clear of the water by several inches. Modern versions have two main foils, one on each side forward of amidships, and a third tail foil centered aft.

When she is flying on the foils alone, a boat is capable of greatly increased speed because there is no longer any friction drag on the hull. Alternatively, the reduction in friction means better fuel economy.

When the boat is out of the water and the foils are traveling through the water near the surface, there is no rolling, pitching, or pounding from waves.

Hydrofoil craft present complex problems in design and, therefore, are relatively expensive. The height above water of the raised hull also creates problems with inboard power, which must somehow be transferred to a submerged propeller.

After Alexander Graham Bell saw Forlanini's boat in action, he built a hydrofoil that set a world speed record of 70.85 mph (114.02 km/h) in 1919. Bell's boat suffered from stability problems, however, and was eventually abandoned. Modern hydrofoil designs contend for world speed records under sail at speeds of 40 knots and more.

Hypothermia

Lifesaving treatments for victims of cold water

Hypothermia is a potentially deadly lowering of the body's core temperature. It is a threat to any boater who falls into water colder than 85°F (29°C).

The colder the water, the quicker is the onset of hypothermia. If you fall into water of 65°F (18°C)—a normal summertime temperature over much of the United States—you will lapse into unconsciousness in about two hours if you're not wearing protective clothing.

Your chances of recovery depend on how long you've been in the water. In all cases of hypothermia, the object is to rewarm the body from the inside out, which is a problem on a boat. Signs of mild hypothermia include slurred speech, blue lips, and violent shivering. The victim must be removed from the water and wind and wrapped in warm dry clothes or bedding. Warm, not hot, fluids may be taken, but definitely no alcohol.

A victim of medium hypothermia displays loss of muscle control, incoherent speech, drowsiness, exhaustion, or even aggression—most of the symptoms of drunkenness, in fact. Gentle external warming is required. If too much heat is applied externally, the colder blood will be driven to the body core, doing potentially irreparable damage. Warm wet towels on the head, neck, chest, abdomen, and groin are recommended, but these have to be rewarmed frequently. Sharing a sleeping bag is a practical way to provide gentle heat; both victim and volunteer should be naked, with contact mainly at the chest and back.

If you can time your breathing so the victim inhales your exhaled breath, some valuable heat will be introduced to the lungs. Do not under any circumstances massage the arms or legs.

Severe hypothermia is characterized by collapse and unconsciousness, difficulty in breathing, and heart failure. It is a medical emergency and requiring skilled assistance if possible.

Use cardiopulmonary resuscitation (CPR) as a last resource if there has been no pulse or breathing for 1 to 2 minutes. Although CPR may save a life, it can also precipitate heart arrhythmia or arrest in deeply hypothermic patients.

It's unlikely that you have a bathtub on your boat, but if you do, immersing the patient in warm water may be another practical alternative. The suggested temperature is 105°F to 110°F (40°C to 43°C), or slightly warmer if the victim is clothed. *It is imperative that the legs and arms be kept out of the water.* Adjust the water temperature frequently because the victim will cool it down rapidly.

See also **HELP Posture**.

Iceboxes

*Keeping food and drink cool
on board in hot weather*

Yachting author Donald Street greatly prefers an icebox to a refrigerator or freezer. As a charter skipper and voyager based in the Caribbean, he has had extensive experience keeping food and drinks cold in hot climates, and he has seen too many mechanical refrigeration systems break down.

In his book *The Ocean Sailing Yacht*, Street says he always manages to find ice. "The normal routine in the southern islands is to find a small boy with a dinghy and give him a dollar, along with the money for the ice and a couple of ice bags," he says. "Then one can sit back and relax, have a couple of rums, and in no time the ice arrives."

Street recommends that an icebox for a small boat should hold at least 50 pounds of ice and still have 2 cubic feet of stowage space for food. In a well-insulated box, the ice will last for six to eight days, he maintains. Street is not alone in preferring an icebox to a refrigerator; veteran long-distance voyager and sailing author Hal Roth, after 200,000 sea miles, feels the same way.

On a larger boat, two 50-pound boxes side by side will have sufficient capacity for two or three people. Four people would require two 75-pound boxes.

The minimum thickness for the insulation around the icebox is 2 inches (50 mm); 4 inches (100 mm) is better. Use high-R-factor foam for insulation. A top-opening icebox retains the cold better than a front-opening model.

Melted water must be allowed to drain from the bottom of the icebox through a plastic hose at least $^3/_4$ inch (19 mm) in diameter to avoid blockage. It should not be allowed to drain straight into the bilge because it will promote rot and bad odors. Rather, let it drain into a plastic container in the bilge. The container should be emptied overboard at least twice daily.

It's important for the drain hose to have an S bend in it to trap water; otherwise, it will drain all the cold air from the box.

See also **Refrigeration**.

Ice Damage

*Preparing a boat for freezing
conditions in winter*

Boats kept in areas that experience freezing winters may suffer three causes of ice damage: outside pressure, hull abrasion, and expansion inside the hull.

Outside pressure occurs when the water in which the boat is floating freezes and expands. This is not usually a problem for pleasure boats of normal hull shape.

Hull abrasion is the result of new sheet ice drifting past the boat. It can do considerable damage very quickly. If you have to leave your boat in the water in freezing weather, protect her sides with floating logs moored around her—or anything that would prevent moving ice from making contact. Some boats have special strips of wood or metal sheathing fitted at the waterline, but it's always better to haul the boat out of the water for the winter, if possible.

Inside expansion causes a good deal of damage to through-hull fittings, interior plumbing, and engine-cooling systems. Fresh water will freeze with enough force to crack heavy bronze castings.

Boats should be carefully winterized before hard freezing sets in, and the engine manufacturer's instructions should be followed closely. Pipes that cannot be drained of potable water must be treated with nontoxic antifreeze, and care must be taken to drain any pockets of water from seacocks.

Wooden boats can be damaged by ice forming in plank seams or in the bilge. Any boat that is hauled out for the winter should be covered from the weather. The cockpit, in particular, should be protected because frozen drains can cause significant damage.

See also **Hauling Out**; **Seacocks**; **Winterizing**.

Inertia

Making use of an unusual property to prevent capsize

Inertia is a physical property of boats that is of great importance to seaworthiness. It is one of the principal ways by which a boat resists being capsized by waves.

Inertia manifests itself in two different ways. Matter at rest wants to stay at rest: it resists being moved suddenly. When matter is moving, it wants to keep moving at the same speed in the same direction; again, it will resist any sudden changes.

Thus, a wave breaking against the side of a boat with significant inertia will not immediately throw her over on her beam ends, as it might a boat lacking inertia.

The deeper and heavier a boat, the more inertia she possesses. Heavy-displacement boats have up to five times greater roll moment of inertia than ultralight boats of the same length, according to research scientist and naval architect Tony Marchaj.

A heavy mast on a sailboat or a tall tuna tower on a sportfisher provides considerable inertia and takes a lot of the jerkiness out of rolling, but also tends to lengthen the roll and perhaps exaggerate it. As in everything with yachts, you have to make compromises and find the happy medium.

Inertia also affects hobbyhors-

ing, a boat's tendency to plunge and rear excessively when heading into swells. Inertia makes her press her bows deeper into the water and rise higher than necessary. This detrimental effect can be mitigated by moving heavy weights such as anchor chains away from the ends of the boat and placing them more toward the middle.

See also **Capsize**; **Hobbyhorsing**; **Stability**.

Isobars

Judging the weather with the help of lines on a chart

The word *isobar* is derived from the Greek *isos*, meaning equal,

and *baros*, meaning weight. On a weather chart, isobars are curved lines joining areas of equal barometric pressure.

Isobars on charts are usually spaced at 4-millibar intervals, but the way they spread apart or draw together is a good indication of wind velocity in that area.

Our weather systems are the result of air masses of different temperature and pressure clashing with each other. Air travels from cold regions of high pressure to warm regions of low pressure.

Where the isobars are far apart, there is little change in pressure over any one particular region, so you can expect light winds and good weather. But

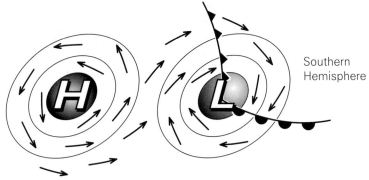

In the Northern Hemisphere winds blow clockwise and outward around areas of high pressure and counterclockwise and inward around areas of low pressure. Low-pressure systems show cold and warm fronts, separating areas of warm and cold air, while highs consist of a single mass of air with no fronts. In the Southern Hemisphere winds blow counterclockwise around areas of high pressure and clockwise around low pressure, just the opposite of the Northern Hemisphere.

WIND SPEED, KNOTS	APPROXIMATE DISTANCE (NAUTICAL MILES) BETWEEN ISOBARS AT 4-MB/HPA INTERVALS			
	30°	40°	50°	60°
10	461	358	301	266
15	307	239	200	177
20	230	179	150	133
25	184	143	120	106
30	154	119	100	89
35	132	102	86	76
40	115	90	75	66
50	92	72	60	53
60	77	60	50	40

Wind speed as a function of distance between isobars at various latitudes. Here the isobar interval is 4 millibars. At a latitude of 30 degrees, an isobar distance of 154 nautical miles produces a wind speed of 30 knots. This geostrophic, or Earth-driven, wind may be modified locally by a host of microclimatic and topographic effects.

where the pressure is changing rapidly because two dissimilar air masses are moving together to form a front, the isobars crowd closely on the chart, and you can expect high winds and stormy weather.

If the Earth were not spinning and there were no surface friction, winds would flow directly from high pressure to low. But the Earth's rotation produces the Coriolis force, which deflects the wind to the right in the Northern Hemisphere and to the left in the Southern Hemisphere.

See also **Air Masses; Coriolis Force; Weather Fronts.**

J

Jacklines

Staying attached to the boat if you are washed overboard

A jackline is a long rope or wire running the length of a boat (usually a sailboat) from the bow to the cockpit. Its sole purpose is to keep you attached to the boat in bad weather.

Clipping the distal end of your harness tether to the jackline allows you to roam the length of the line fore and aft, like a dog in the backyard.

Ideally, a jackline would run along the centerline of the boat—then your tether could be short enough to stop your being washed overboard. But there is a mast in the way, and a boom vang, and possibly a dinghy or life raft, and various other gear and impedimenta on the cabintop, so the usual compromise is to set up two jacklines running along the side decks where they join the deckhouse.

When you clip onto jacklines in that position, the tether will be too long to prevent you from going overboard (unless the boat is extremely beamy) and it will be necessary to stop the jacklines about 5 feet short of the stern.

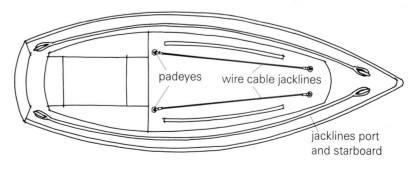

Popular positions for jacklines. The lines on the side decks may be snugged closer into the cabin sides, and they may be made of stainless steel wire, Dacron line, webbing, or tubing.

Then, if you fall in the water, you will be dragged alongside the boat instead of out of reach behind it.

Ideally, you should wear two tethers, one short and one longer—but no more than 6 feet (1.8 m)—so you can move around an obstruction by clipping on the second tether before unclipping the first.

Jacklines must be at least as strong as the safety harness and tethers, and are often made of uncoated stainless steel wire if they can be snugged against the cabin sides. If there is any chance of their rolling underfoot on the side decks, use 1-inch-wide (25 mm) nylon or Dacron webbing instead because it will lie flat. Nylon webbing is more readily available but is not recommended because of its excessive stretch.

If you use Dacron rope instead of webbing, make sure you can distinguish it at a glance from the running rigging. It won't help you much to clip your harness to the spare jibsheet.

See also **Harnesses**.

Jet Drives

Using a powerful jet of water instead of a propeller

Powerboats with jet drives—also known as waterjets—don't have propellers. Instead, an impeller housed in a tube draws water in through a grate in the bottom of the boat and pumps it out at the stern in a powerful jet that provides forward thrust.

Jet-drive boats can operate in shallow water without loss of efficiency, and are safer than propeller boats when there are swimmers in the water. Lacking conventional running gear, they can drive through fields of lobster-pot buoys without fear of entanglement.

One of the distinguishing characteristics of a jet boat is the way it responds immediately to changes in power or direction. For instance, there is no lag when accelerating as there is with a propeller-driven boat, and stopping is so quick that passengers need to be warned in advance.

Steering is a simple matter of turning the water jet; slowing down quickly is done in the same way that big jet airplanes do it: by dropping a deflector over the jet to reverse its direction. In this way, a jet boat can go from full speed ahead to full speed astern without touching the engine. Most jet boats are capable of stopping in their own length. A twin-waterjet boat can almost be walked sideways if the waterjets are far enough apart.

Steering is, of course, less effective the slower you go, although some boats have a rudimentary skeg or rudder to help at slow speeds. A jet drive is inefficient below about 25 knots—that comparatively small impeller just doesn't generate the torque of a larger, free-swinging propeller at lower engine speeds—so it's not appropriate for low-speed hulls. And it gulps air when the hull jumps off waves, drastically reducing its efficiency.

See also **Rudders; Skegs; Torque**.

Jet Streams

Keeping an eye on lofty breeding grounds for storms

Jet streams are found at the borders of the basic north/south air-circulation systems of the atmosphere, where warm air meets cold air. These high-level winds, moving at speeds that average more than 50 knots and often exceed 200 knots from west to east, are too high to affect boaters directly; they are strongest at about 35,000 feet, although they may extend as low as 16,000 feet or more. Knowing their position is important, however, because of the bad weather they portend at sea level.

Three jet streams have so far been identified, of which the polar jet stream is of most consequence to midlatitude sailors. Contrary to its name, it's not located at the north or south pole; it actually snakes back and forth between 40° and 60° in each hemisphere. It moves southward in the winter and intensifies because temperature differences between high latitudes and midlatitudes increase then; it reaches maximum speeds off the east coasts of Asia (near Japan) and North America (near Newfoundland). Most surface lows and large-scale extratropical storms form along the path of the polar jet stream and are steered by it.

The subtropical jet stream generally concentrates around 30° North and South, tending toward higher latitudes in the summer. It's an important factor in the generation of thunderstorms over the southern United States in the summer.

The arctic jet stream is the one most recently discovered. It is generally located at a latitude of around 70° N, at an altitude of between 3 and 5 miles (5 and 8 km), but it's not a permanent feature, nor does it extend all the way around the world.

All three jet streams are about 300 to 500 miles (500 to 800 km) wide, but they vary in strength and position from week to week. The subtropical jet stream may disappear entirely from the North American continent in the winter, while the polar jet moves south and becomes the predominant influence on U.S. weather. With summer, the polar jet retreats to northern Canada.

Meteorologists map jet-stream locations on daily 500-millibar weather maps—the 500 mb constant-pressure level being found near 18,000 feet of altitude in the Earth's atmosphere. This is high enough to locate the bottom of the jet streams, and empirical observations tell us that the upper-level winds mapped at 500 mb reveal the majority of large-scale surface-weather patterns.

Jib Numbers

How to distinguish one headsail from another

It's common to refer to a small sailboat's headsails by numbers according to their size. This includes jibs—which, in the strict definition of the word, should be flying from their own luffs—and forestaysails, which are fastened to a headstay.

Thus, the No. 1 jib could be the biggest light-weather sail, No. 2 a smaller working jib, and No. 3 a storm jib. If you have a greater selection of headsails, they are numbered in a greater range, as their size indicates.

On racing sailboats and modern cruisers, headsails are often referred to by their size as a percentage of the foretriangle—that is, the triangle formed by the mast, the forestay, and the deck. Thus, a 150 percent jib would have an area 50 percent greater than that of the foretriangle.

The word *jib* is used loosely here, of course. Strictly speaking, it refers to a headsail carried forward of the forestay—the stay that joins the stem to the mast. A forestaysail (usually shortened to foresail) is a headsail hanked or rolled on to a forestay.

A Genoa jib is actually a large forestaysail with a low-cut, deck-sweeping foot; a Yankee is another foresail with a high-cut foot ending forward of the mast, usually flown in combination with a working forestaysail on a cutter.

Headsail sheets are usually controlled by winches in the cockpit, sized according to the loads generated by the sails. To find the load on a headsail sheet, multiply the sail area in square feet by the wind speed in knots squared. Dividing the answer by 232 results in the approximate pull on the sheet in pounds. For example, a 150-square-foot jib in 15 knots of wind will create a pull on its sheet of approximately 150 x 225 ÷ 232 = 145 pounds.

See also **Headsails; Sail Area; Winches**.

Jumping Lights

Staring too long at one spot can create this phenomenon

If you've been to sea at night, you've probably experienced the phenomenon known as "jumping lights." It happens when you spot a fixed or flashing light, and it suddenly seems to be jumping around the horizon.

Many small-boat sailors accept it as the inevitable result of slight course changes caused by waves, but psychologists call it the "auto-kinetic illusion." They maintain it comes about through imperceptible eye movements or strain in the eye muscles when we stare fixedly at one point for too long.

The light always reappears some distance to the left or right of where we expect it, and it's sometimes mistaken for two or more lights flashing in sequence. Only experience can teach you what is really what.

See also **Nighttime Boating**.

Junk Rigs

Using ancient technology to power modern cruising yachts

The Chinese junk evolved as a general-purpose working boat in the Orient many hundreds of years ago. It is broad and shallow, with a high stern and a rig consisting of two or three masts with square lugsails. The sails are remarkable for their full-length horizontal battens, any one of which becomes the equivalent of a boom when the sail is reefed. It is a simple rig, but one burdened with many lines.

J

Blondie Hasler's 26-foot Folkboat Jester *with its junk rig.*

Although it is neither as fast nor as close-winded as a Bermuda-rigged sailboat, the simplicity and ease of handling of a junk rig commends itself to some sailing cruisers in the Western Hemisphere, particularly single-handers.

Colonel H. G. "Blondie" Hasler modified a standard 26-foot Folkboat to take a junk rig for the first Single-handed Transatlantic Race in 1960; his boat, *Jester*, crossed the Atlantic many times afterward with the same rig.

Most junks designed as pleasure yachts are between 25 and 40 feet in length—although naval architect Thomas Colvin has drawn them for boats up to 60 feet—and they are fitted with inboard engines rather than the traditional sculling oars, or yulohs, of the traditional working junks.

The bow of a junk is usually high and overhanging, and the sheerline dips to comparatively modest freeboard amidships. To help the shallow hull forge to windward, most junks have a dagger-shaped, retractable centerboard.

Jury Rigs

Using the wreckage of a dismasting to get back home

The word jury used in a nautical sense means makeshift or temporary, although nobody seems to know how this usage came about. A jury rig is one that you construct from the wreckage of a dismasting in order to get you home.

Many remarkable voyages have been completed under jury rig, including two by Miles and Beryl Smeeton, whose 47-foot cutter *Tzu Hang* was twice either pitchpoled or capsized and dismasted in exceptionally heavy weather while trying to round Cape Horn.

On the first occasion, they had help from their crew member, John Guzzwell, a skilled carpenter who built a wooden jury mast from scraps of wood and cupboard doors. On the second occasion, the Smeetons had no crew, but were able to salvage some broken spars and erect a jury rig themselves. In a remarkable display of courage and seamanship, they managed both times to sail the crippled *Tzu Hang* to safety in Chile, many hundreds of miles to the north.

The difficulty of raising a mast at sea on a small boat is enormous because of the violent, jerky motion a vessel experiences when she has lost her spars. Jury masts are, therefore, usually only half as tall as the originals, or even less. This means that headsails, stretched horizontally, are used instead of the mainsail.

Surprisingly little sail is needed to help a boat limp home. Setting about one third of her normal canvas under jury rig, *Tzu Hang* consistently managed to reel off daily runs of as much as 70 miles, or about half her usual distance.

If you're considering crossing an ocean, think about the best way to jury-rig your boat, and carry enough tools, fasteners, glue, rigging wire, and wire-rope clamps to make it feasible.

K

Kayaks as Tenders

Searching for the solution to the small-boat tender problem

A perfect solution has not yet been found for the problem of tenders for small boats. There always has to be a compromise, and it's usually inconvenient or awkward.

Most boats less than 30 feet (9 m) in length simply have no place on deck for a hard dinghy or an inflated rubber dinghy. Similarly, there is rarely space in cockpit lockers or down below for a deflated rubber dinghy. Inflating a dinghy on a small boat is usually an awkward process as well.

Towing a dinghy has its own pitfalls, of course. It slows down your boat, and dinghy painters have an extraordinary affinity for spinning propeller shafts. On the run in any kind of heavy weather, the dinghy becomes a battering ram determined to stove in your transom, and on the beat it will fill with spray and sink within minutes.

Depending on the deck layout of your boat, a sea kayak might be the answer. A kayak is shallow and narrow, and might fit along the side deck on edge, lashed to the lifelines. You can also pur-chase folding kayaks that fit into small containers. All are light and easy to haul aboard and launch.

Kayaks are known for their speed and seaworthiness in the hands of competent paddlers, and they're ideal for exploring quiet new anchorages. They have their disadvantages, too, of course. You won't find it easy to get into a kayak from the deck of your boat, and it won't carry a crate of beer as safely as a conventional dinghy will. But for some of the people, some of the time, a kayak might just be the answer.

See also **Dinghies**.

Keels

Structural members with many and varied purposes on a boat

The keel is the main structural member of a wooden vessel, running fore and aft along the centerline of the bottom. It is the backbone upon which all the other structural members rest.

In modern fiberglass construction, the hull is a monocoque in which the skin, or outer shell, bears most of the stresses. The keel is greatly modified, particularly in sailboats, where it is extended downward from the hull to perform two important functions: to stop the boat being blown sideways by the force of the wind in the sails, and to counterbalance the overturning force of the sails. To accomplish the latter, the keel is either made of, or encapsulates, a mass of iron or lead, and is known as a ballast keel.

A narrow, deep fin keel is more efficient for driving a boat to windward than a wide, shallow keel of the same area. It also makes a boat more maneuverable, but it fails to provide directional stability, so that constant attention is needed at the helm.

A full-length "cruising" keel depends on sheer lateral area rather than hydrodynamic lift to prevent leeway. It acts more like a

K

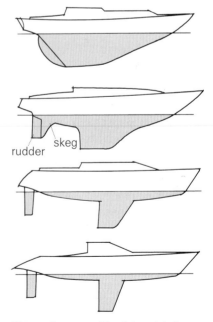

Top to bottom: Traditional full keel, keel with cutaway forefoot and skeg-hung rudder, moderate-aspect fin keel with spade rudder, and high-aspect fin keel and spade rudder.

barn door than an airplane wing. It provides the best directional stability possible, keeping the boat on course for extended periods without attention to the helm.

A fin keel needs to be moving through the water to be effective at stopping leeway, just as an airplane needs to be moving through the air to gain lift from its wings. A traditional cruising keel is almost as effective when it is stopped as when it is moving. With its small wetted surface and, consequently, less drag from friction, a fin keel is favored by racing boats.

Bilge keels, consisting of two heavy plates projecting outward at a slight angle from the bottom near the greatest beam on each side, are favored in some areas where the sailing water is shallow and where boats dry out on mud or sand between tides. Bilge keels enable them to take the ground upright.

Winged keels were originally conceived to improve sail-carrying capacity by getting more ballast down low without increasing draft. They also partly serve the purpose of the wing-end tips on airplanes; that is, to prevent the formation of energy-sapping vortices that occur when a fluid such as air or water encounters sudden large differences in pressure—like those found at the bottom of a fin keel.

Keels with wings have not been proven superior to ordinary fin keels of sufficient depth, and they have the disadvantage that when they run aground, their depth increases as the boat heels over, trapping them even more firmly.

Although most ballast keels are extensions of the basic fiberglass hull with heavy weights well secured inside, some are cast separately and bolted to the outside of the hull. In fact, this method—considered archaic just a few years ago—is now growing in popularity as a way of attaching deep, narrow, high-aspect fin keels to boats with shallow, fairly flat underbodies. The keel bolts should have a cross-sectional area of not less than 1 square inch (645 mm^2) for every 1,500 pounds (681 kg) of outside ballast. This is valid for bronze with a tensile strength of 60,000 pounds per square inch (413,686 kilopascal). Bolts made of stronger material, such as Monel metal, may be correspondingly smaller.

The area of a keel is usually related to a boat's sail area. The following rules of thumb indicate the percentage of lateral plane area compared with sail area:

- full-keel boats: the total lateral plane, including the rudder, should be 12 to 16 percent of the sail area
- fin-keel boats: the area of the fin keel only should be 7 to 10 percent of the sail area

A powerboat doesn't need a keel to resist leeway or to stand up to sails. The functions of a powerboat keel are to give it more course-keeping ability, to confer strength, to protect the hull bottom from groundings, and to dampen rolling. For these purposes, a shallow full-length keel is the best configuration. Keels are most prominent on displacement powerboats, where strength and comfort matter more than the added water resistance of a keel. Trawler yachts sometimes incorporate bilge keels to further reduce rolling, although more active measures such as paravanes are more effective in this regard.

Semidisplacement hulls such as the Maine lobster boat may feature prominent full-length keels; however, on a modified-V planing hull, the keel is likely to be more vestigial—like a shallow skeg. On a deep-V hull, which derives ample strength and course-keeping ability from its hull shape alone, the keel is simply another name for the midline of the underbody.

See also **Hull Shapes; Leeway; Groundings.**

Knots

Joining lines to objects with knots, bends, and hitches

The word *knot* is now a loosely used term for one of the many forms of tying a rope to itself, to another rope, or to an object. In the days of sailing ships, sailors drew greater distinction between knots, bends, and hitches.

Knots were more or less permanent connections made with smaller ropes or interworked strands of the same line. Bends were used to fasten a line to an object, or sometimes to another line. Hitches were connections that could be made and released quickly, but which were not expected to be long-lasting.

There is a lot of talk among boaters about the need for a thor-

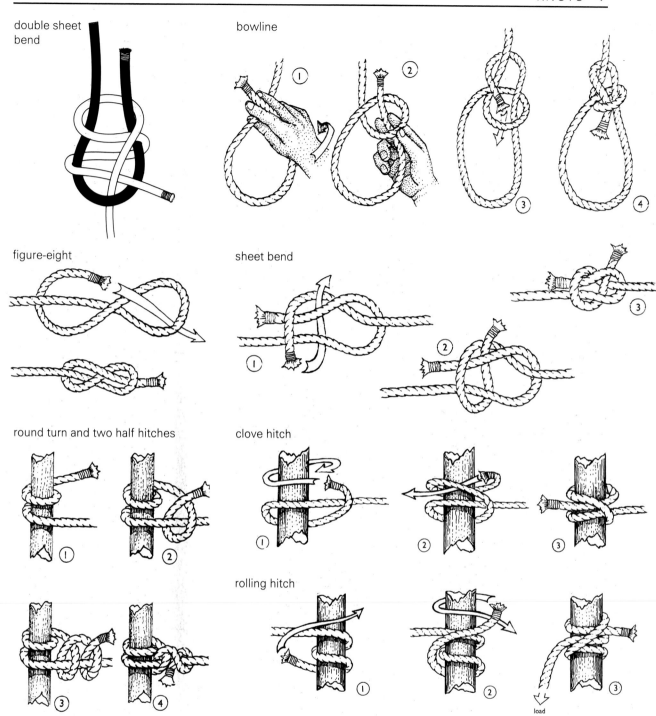

double sheet bend

bowline

figure-eight

sheet bend

round turn and two half hitches

clove hitch

rolling hitch

load

K

ough knowledge of knots and their unique applications—but, in fact, you need very few if you choose them carefully. Following is a list of ten simple knots capable of fulfilling every need aboard a boat: anchor bend (also known as the fisherman's bend), bowline, cleat hitch, clove hitch, figure-eight knot, reef knot, rolling hitch, round turn and two half hitches, trucker's hitch, and sheet bend or double sheet bend. This list is often reduced to three knots, three bends, and three hitches, as follows:

• knots: figure-eight, reef, and bowline

• bends: double sheet, anchor, and sheet

• hitches: round turn and two half hitches, clove, and rolling

In practical terms, it's possible to do everything you need to do on most boats with just two knots, two bends, and one hitch;

reef knot

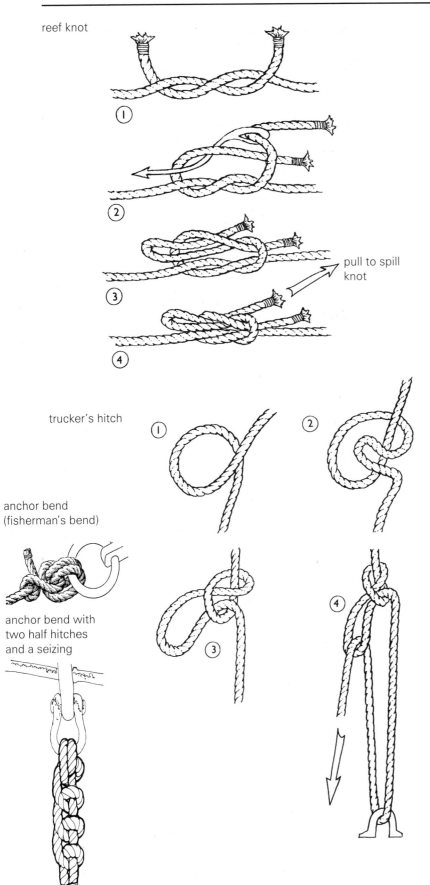

pull to spill
knot

trucker's hitch

anchor bend
(fisherman's bend)

anchor bend with
two half hitches
and a seizing

that is, five in all: anchor bend, bowline, reef knot, rolling hitch, and sheet bend.

A good knot has the following attributes:

- it must hold fast under all conditions
- it must come apart easily when you want it to, even under strain
- you must be able to make it almost automatically—that is, your finger muscles should be able to retain a "memory" of the knot and form it quickly without thought

Any tight kink in a fiber line will weaken it, and there may be many in a knot. Some knots are worse than others in this respect. The following list gives an approximate indication of how much the strength of rope is reduced by various knots:

anchor bend: 24 percent
bowline: 40 percent
clove hitch: 40 percent
reef knot: 55 percent
round turn and two half
    hitches: 30 to 35 percent
timber hitch: 30 to 35
    percent
sheet bend: 45 percent

See also **Cleats**.

L

Lateen Rig

After nine centuries, this ancient sail is still in use

The word *lateen* comes from the Italian and Spanish *vela latina*, the Latin sail. The rig is the forerunner of the gaff rig, which, in turn, gave way to the ubiquitous Bermuda rig on pleasure sailboats. One of the most successful small American sailboat classes of all time, the 13-foot, 10-inch (4.2 m) Sunfish, has a single 75-square-foot (7 m^2) lateen sail, but the rig is now mostly confined to the working vessels of the Nile River, the Red Sea, and the dhows of the Indian Ocean.

The lateen sail is shaped like a right-angled isosceles triangle and has a long spar attached to its head. The spar is slung at an angle from a stumpy mast, and a single sheet from the clew can trim the sail. It is believed that the ancient Arabs invented the rig and, with the possible exception of the Chinese junk rig, it is the oldest still in use. It came into general use in the eastern Mediterranean in the twelfth century, reaching Western Europe in the fifteenth century. The lateen was one of the first rigs that allowed a vessel to sail efficiently against the wind, and all three of Columbus's ships carried lateen sails on their mizzenmasts.

As the science of sailing evolved, the front part of the lateen rig—the triangle forward of the mast—became a separate sail attached to a forestay. The remaining quadrilateral of sail aft of the mast became the gaff mainsail, with its leading edge now attached to the mast.

See also **Junk Rigs**.

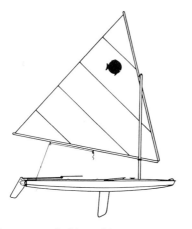

The lateen rig in a dhow of the seventh-century (left) *and in a twenty-first-century Sunfish* (right).

Latitude, Longitude

Measuring and plotting your position on the Earth's surface

Latitude is distance north or south of the equator, and is measured in degrees, minutes, and seconds of arc. Each degree equals 60 nautical miles, and each minute approximately 1 mile.

Actually, because the Earth is not exactly round—being flattened at the poles and bulging at the equator—there is a small difference in the length of a degree at various latitudes. At the poles, for example, a degree equals 60.27 nautical miles; at latitude 45°, it is 59.96 miles; and at the equator, it is 59.66 miles. This is, however, of little consequence to the amateur navigator.

Latitude is shown on charts by lines running east and west. Scales at the left and right (west and east) edges of the chart show degrees, minutes, and (depending on the chart's scale) seconds. Because 1 minute equals 1 nautical mile, you can measure a distance on the chart with a pair of dividers, comparing it with the side scale shown at the same latitude.

Longitude is angular distance east or west of the prime meridian, an imaginary line running from pole to pole through Greenwich, England. The prime meridian is numbered 0°; from it, longitude is reckoned 180° eastward

L

and 180° westward. On the opposite side of the world from Greenwich, the 180th meridian is known as the International Date Line. If you cross the line going west, you must drop a day in your calendar reckoning; if you cross the line going east, you repeat the day.

Meridians, or lines of equal longitude, are marked on charts as lines running north and south, and their scales are given at the top (north) and bottom (south) of charts. Because lines of longitude converge at the poles, the length of a degree of longitude varies according to latitude. At the equator, it is approximately 60 miles; at the poles, it is zero.

Always measure distances from the latitude scale at the east and west edges of the chart, never from the longitude scales at the north and south edges.

See also **Miles**.

Lead Lines

*Finding the depth with
simplicity and reliability*

There is probably no older navigation instrument than the sounding line, or lead line. It's simply a weight on the end of a thin line that measures the depth of the water. In ancient times, a stone would have sufficed for a weight. In modern times, the weight evolved into a lead cylinder weighing about 7 to 15 pounds (3 to 7 kg), with a hollow in the bottom that could be "armed" with tallow or grease to bring up a sample of the sea bottom.

Sounding with the lead was a skilled task in the days of sailing ships, and a good leadsman commanded much respect. An expert could get an accurate sounding with the "blue pigeon," as the lead was called, up to 15 fathoms at a speed of 7 knots. If a ship were feeling her way into shallow waters in bad visibility, however, she would have to heave to or slow down almost to a standstill while more comprehensive soundings were taken.

The line was marked with pieces of leather, linen, flannel, bunting, and cord at various intervals, so the leadsman could tell the depth by feel in the dark. The first 20 fathoms was divided into 9 "marks" at intervals varying between 1 and 3 fathoms; the 11 unmarked depths between them were known as "deeps." Thus, at 2 fathoms, the call would be: "By the mark, twain." At 11 fathoms, it would be: "Deep eleven."

Despite the new technology of electronic sounders and fishfinders, it's still a good idea to carry a ¼-inch line of plaited Dacron about 15 or 20 fathoms long, just in case of a power failure or equipment trouble. The lead line is as reliable an instrument as you could ever wish for, and you don't *have* to use a lead weight—a large shackle or a starter handle will suffice in an emergency.

If you plan to make regular use of a lead line, you might want to use the depth-marking system recommended by British sailors and authors Graham and Tew in *A Manual for Small Yachts*:

Fathoms	Material
1	1 piece of leather bootlace
2	2 pieces of leather bootlace
	red bunting
4	blue serge
5	line with 1 knot
6	tape
8	leather
10	line with 2 knots
15	line with 3 knots
20	2 pieces of line

See also **Depth-Sounders; Soundings**.

Lead Percentage

*Matching theory to practice to
create a balanced boat*

Lead (pronounced *leed*) is the amount by which a sailboat's center of effort (CE) leads her center of lateral resistance (CLR) on the designer's plans.

If the CE is forward of the CLR, the bow tends to fall away from the wind and produce constant lee helm—a most undesirable and sometimes even dangerous condition.

So why would a designer do this? Well, the truth is that like so much in yacht design, the theory doesn't always match the practice. When a boat starts to move through the water, the CLR changes its position. It moves forward a considerable amount relative to the CE, and thus restores helm balance. Therefore, on the designer's board it's customary to show the CE leading the imaginary CLR. The amount of this lead is always expressed as

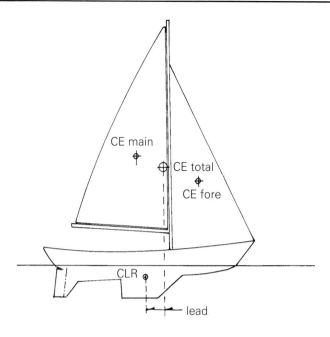

SHORTER LEAD	LONGER LEAD
Fine hull	Beamy hull
Short keel	Long keel
Deep draft	Shoal draft
Fine forward waterlines	Full forward waterlines
Stable vessel	Tender vessel
Low-aspect-ratio rig	High-aspect-ratio rig

Because the center of lateral resistance moves forward when a boat is underway, the designer places the center of effort slightly ahead of the static CLR (top). Amount of lead as a function of hull shape (above).

a percentage of the waterline length. It varies as follows for different rigs:

- cutter: 13 to 17 percent
- ketch: 11 to 14 percent
- schooner: 7 to 12 percent
- sloop: 13 to 17 percent
- yawl: 12 to 15 percent

See also **Balanced Helm; Center of Effort; Lee Helm; Weather Helm.**

Leaks

Dealing with an accident that threatens to sink you

There are two types of leaks of concern to boaters. The first consists of rivulets that find their way through hatches, portlights, and poorly sealed deck fittings, and drip into the accommodations, soaking bunks and turning charts into papier-mâché. Such leaks are an annoyance but do not threaten the short-term well-being of the ship.

The second type of leak results from the sudden puncturing of the hull. It calls for immediate action to prevent the boat from sinking, and your course of action depends mostly on the size of the hole. A hole the size of a man's fist admits more water than most bilge pumps on small boats can handle. A bigger hole certainly means the boat is likely to sink shortly in the absence of outside help.

If your bilge pump is power operated and can keep up with the leak, or at least slow the rising tide below, you might have time to place a collision mat over the hole or rig up a sail to cover it. Then your priority will be to locate the damaged area from inside the hull, repair it as best you can by stuffing a cushion or other material in it, and backing it with a piece of plywood or a cupboard door propped in place with a spar or beam.

Most modern fiberglass boats have an interior fiberglass pan or liner that makes it difficult to locate the leak. You may have to use a heavy ax to chop it away in time to save the boat. On a wooden hull, you might be able to nail a patch of copper or Dacron over the outside of the hole; on a metal or fiberglass hull, you won't have that option.

If you judge from the beginning that the hull is flooding too quickly for any of these options, use what time is left to make a radio Mayday call, set off the EPIRB, fly a distress signal, light a hand or a parachute flare, and prepare to

L

abandon ship. Inflate the life raft or rubber dinghy, and make sure everybody is wearing a life jacket. If you're at sea, don't forget to take your abandon-ship bag when you leave. A handheld VHF radio should be in the bag with a supply of fresh batteries.

See also **Abandoning Ship; Accidents on Board; Bilge Pumps; EPIRBs; Life Jackets; Life Rafts; Mayday Calls.**

Leeboards

Providing resistance to leeway with pivoting boards

Something must be done to provide sufficient lateral plane underwater on very shallow sailboat hulls. Boats meant to be used in shallow water and those that ground frequently cannot have deep conventional keels, of course; their choice is between centerboards and leeboards.

However, centerboards weaken the structure of a boat by cutting the keel in half. They also need heavy housings and are liable to jam with pebbles during groundings.

Leeboards pivot outside the hull, and the one on the leeward side (the side *away* from the wind) is lowered into the water to prevent leeway, whereas the windward one is raised to reduce resistance.

Compared with centerboards, leeboards are more effective because their immersed area starts at the gunwale, whereas centerboards work only from the bottom of the hull downward.

In Northern Europe, where

tidal ranges are significant and many boats take the ground between tides in shallow estuaries, leeboards are far more popular than in North America. The Dutch botters, boeiers, and hoogaars all use leeboards, just as many types of sailing barges and working vessels have in the past.

See also **Centerboards.**

Lee Helm

Test your boat because this condition needs correcting

Slight lee helm is sometimes hard to detect, especially on sailboats with balanced or semibalanced rudders. Test your boat by sailing with the apparent wind on the beam in a fresh breeze under all plain sail. Take your hand away from the tiller or wheel and see what happens. If the boat starts to head away from the wind, she has lee helm—in other words, to make her go straight, you have to hold the helm to leeward.

Lee helm is dangerous and needs to be corrected, not only because it slows a boat down, but also, more importantly, because it encourages uncontrolled jibes.

The causes of lee helm, like those of weather helm, are many and complex, involving both hull design and sail rig. Many boats that have slight lee helm in light weather will lose it when a rising wind makes them heel.

Flat-cut sails can cause lee helm, too, and so can a mast that is positioned too far forward of the underwater center of lateral resistance.

It's not usually easy to cure bad lee helm on a boat with a fixed keel. A fuller cut mainsail helps a little, and raking the mast aft helps a little more, but the real solution would probably involve moving the entire mast aft, with all the complications that can cause. In any case, it's a job for a qualified naval architect.

See also **Balanced Helm; Weather Helm.**

Leeway

Allowing for being blown off course by side winds

Leeway is the sideways drift of a vessel through the water caused by the wind. All boats make leeway to some degree on all courses except two: when the wind is either dead ahead or dead astern.

Powerboats often make more leeway than sailboats because of their greater proportion of topsides presented to the wind compared with the amount of hull underwater, which acts to check leeway. But the *effect* of leeway is mostly less on a powerboat because the sideways component is a smaller percentage of the vessel's forward speed.

To maintain a set course over the ground, you must head your boat toward the wind to offset leeway. It's not always easy to know how much allowance to make for leeway, but there will be occasions when you can look aft in a straight line that is an extension of the boat's centerline, and compare it with the line of the wake. A hand bearing compass will give you the difference in degrees, and

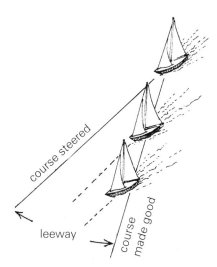

Leeway affects powerboats as well as sailboats.

you can use that knowledge in any similar conditions.

You can assume that a close-hauled sailboat will make between 3 and 5 degrees of leeway in a 7-knot breeze, and up to 8 degrees in a 20-knot breeze.

Length-to-Beam Ratio

How this all-important ratio affects stability and safety

The beam, or width, of a boat is directly related to her waterline length. Beam, together with keel weight, is what gives a hull stability—its resistance to capsize. In sailboats, beam supplies what's known as form stability or initial stability, whereas a ballast keel supplies ultimate stability, which is its ability to regain a level position after having been heeled over. In powerboats, stability derives from beam, from engines or other heavy weights low in the

hull, and from the dynamic stability that results from planing over the surface of water at high speed. A rough rule of thumb handed down from ancient times states that a monohull boat is about three times as long as she is broad.

In reality, it's far more complicated because the longer a boat is, the less beam she needs proportionately. It's one of those strange facts of naval architecture that whereas a boat's resistance to being overturned varies as the fourth power of her waterline length, the heeling moment of the wind pressure on the sails—or, in the case of

Pearson Triton 28. Length-to-beam ratio 2.48 to 1.

Grand Banks 42 Classic. Length-to-beam ratio 3.07 to 1.

Baja 40 Outlaw. Length-to-beam ratio 4.7 to 1.

L

Blackfin 40 Combi. Length-to-beam ratio 2.78 to 1.

a powerboat, the heeling moment of waves and swells—varies as a cube of her length.

In other words, if you double (x2) a sailboat's length, stability increases by a factor of 16 (2 x 2 x 2 x 2), but heeling forces increase only by a factor of 8 (2 x 2 x 2) for the same amount of breeze. This is why a sailboat just a few feet longer than yours can carry more sail with proportionately less beam, and go faster. The same principle applies to powerboats, of course, except that the overturning moment comes mainly from wave conditions, not sails.

Most modern powerboats and sailboats less than 50 feet (15 m) in length have more beam than the old rule requires. For instance, a conservative cruising sailboat design such as the Pearson Triton 28, designed by Carl Alberg, has a length-to-beam ratio of 2.48 to 1. Tom Gillmer's Southern Cross 31 has a ratio of 2.63 to 1, and Bob Perry's Valiant 40 has a ratio of 2.76 to 1. Small sailboats need these wider beams for initial stability in moderate winds.

Beam in powerboats varies considerably. Long, narrow displacement hulls have the ability to reach fast speeds without planing or to travel long distances without refueling. Short, wide hulls offer more interior room, but use more fuel and give a rougher ride in bad weather. Planing powerboats normally have a lot of beam, not only for more accommodations, but also to provide more underwater surface area aft to support the speeding boat. Nevertheless, narrow powerboats can be made to plane, too. In fact, the advantages of long and narrow apply equally to planing hulls and displacement hulls.

The Blackfin 40 Combi, a fast planing sportfisher, has a length-to-beam ratio of about 2.78 to 1, whereas the narrower Grand Banks 42 Classic, a displacement trawler, has a ratio of about 3.07 to 1. The needlelike Baja 40 Outlaw, a 75-knot offshore performance boat, has a ratio of about 4.7 to 1.

Beam that greatly exceeds the accepted ratios

- gives greater initial stability
- provides more interior space
- allows more deck area
- causes a tiresome, jerky movement at sea
- supports more sail area with a shallow draft
- offers a wider, safer base for lateral mast support
- slows the boat by offering more resistance to the water
- makes it more difficult to recover from a 180-degree capsize

Beam that is much less than the accepted ratios

- contributes less initial stability
- offers less resistance to the water
- gives a slower, kinder motion at sea
- cramps the accommodations below deck
- causes more heeling in moderate winds
- makes it difficult to adequately support a mast
- greatly accelerates recovery from a 180-degree capsize

See also **Capsize**.

Life Jackets

Keeping afloat after you've accidentally gone overboard

A life jacket is a buoyant device intended to keep you afloat if you fall into the water. The U.S. Coast Guard knows life jackets as "personal flotation devices" (PFDs) and requires that every recreational boat have them on board.

There are five categories of PFDs required by U.S. Coast

The variety of modern PFDs goes well beyond the old "life jacket." Clockwise from top left: type 5 inflatable collar, compact and inflated; type 5 inflatable pouch, packed and inflated; type 3 bomber jacket; and type 5 immersion suit.

Guard regulations according to the size of your boat, as follows:

- boats less than 16 feet in length must carry one PFD of type 1, 2, 3, or 5 for each person on board
- boats between 16 and 65 feet must carry one type 1, 2, 3, or 5 for each person on board, and must also have at least one type 4 throwable device, such as a horseshoe buoy or foam cushion

The regulations state that types 1, 2, and 3 PFDs must be readily accessible on your boat and wearable by the intended user—not too big or too small. Type 5 recreational hybrid PFDs, those designed for special purposes such as boardsailing or kayaking, must be worn all the time you're afloat and must be approved for the activity for which the boat is being used. An exception to this last rule is the type 5 inflatable vest with a built-in safety harness, which does not have to be worn constantly but must be readily accessible at all times.

Most PFDs use lightweight closed-cell foam for buoyancy.

The type 1 PFD is the so-called offshore life jacket that provides at least 22 pounds of buoyancy and turns the wearer face-up in the water. Type 1 jackets are bulky to wear and hamper movement, but if you ever find yourself in rough water, you'll wish you had one.

Type 2 PFDs are known as near-shore life vests. They are cheap and have less buoyancy. Their performance suffers accordingly, except in calm water. They are bulky to wear.

Type 3 recreational vests are more tailored and provide at least 15 pounds of buoyancy for moderate cost. They will not, however, turn you on your back in the water nor support your head. They are usually recommended for active swimmers in inland waters. Special impact-resistant type 3s are available for water-skiers and personal watercraft drivers whose vests might otherwise be ripped off if they hit the water at high speed.

Type 3 float coats are tailored bomber jackets with built-in buoyancy. They are comfortable in and out of the water and provide good protection against hypothermia.

Type 3 inflatable vests are unobtrusive in normal wear but provide 22 to 35 pounds of buoyancy when inflated. They may be inflated automatically upon hitting the water or by pulling a ripcord. You can also blow into a tube to inflate them if all else fails. They are expensive and they require periodic maintenance, but because they are so compact and wearable, they are more likely to be in place when you need them.

L

Type 4 PFDs are devices—either cushions, life rings, or horseshoe buoys—that can be thrown to a person in the water up to 40 feet away.

Type 5 recreational hybrids are specially designed for various sporting activities, such as offshore fishing, kayaking, canoeing, rowing, and boardsailing.

One type 5 special-use device, an inflatable vest with an integral safety harness, does not have to be worn all the time to satisfy U.S. Coast Guard regulations but should be kept handy for use.

See also **Horseshoe Buoys.**

Lifelines

Putting too much confidence in lifelines may be foolish

Lifelines running around the perimeter of a boat's deck are standard safety equipment, but it isn't wise to place too much reliance on their ability to keep you on board.

Many of the pioneer single-handed circumnavigators back in the 1950s and 1960s had no lifelines on their boats. "It's better to learn to cling like a monkey," Bernard Moitessier once told me.

Moitessier's boats, unlike many modern ones, had deep gunwales against which he could plant his feet when the boat was heeled over steeply, but he may well have had a point because it's doubtful that all lifelines are strong enough to safely stop a heavy crew member from suddenly being flung overboard. The tall stanchions that support the lifelines are subject to great stress

and leverage on a small base, which makes them vulnerable to sideways blows. A better way to stay on board is to wear a harness clipped to a jackstay with a tether short enough to prevent you from falling overboard.

That's not always possible, however, so lifelines are still needed. Even if they only stop you falling overboard when you stumble and lose your balance or get swept off your feet by a wave, they've paid for themselves. Most boats of 25 feet (8 m) or less use ⅛-inch (3 mm) stainless steel wire for lifelines; larger boats use ³⁄₁₆-inch stainless steel wire.

In many cases, the wire is plastic coated to reduce abrasion on sails and running rigging, but that makes it vulnerable to hidden crevice corrosion if salt water penetrates the plastic. Bare wire, 1x19, is preferable in most cases.

The Offshore Racing Council requires double lifelines, with the top line at least 24 inches (610 mm) off the deck—30 inches (760 mm) is better. Anything lower may be worse than no lifeline at all—unusually low lifelines can actually help catapult you overboard. Stanchions should be spaced a maximum of 7 feet (2 m) apart and must be bolted (never screwed) through the deck and backed up with large plates to spread the stress loads.

Many cruising sailors rig extra lifelines of low-stretch Dacron line on each side, from the stern to the bow, rising to chest level at the shrouds, to which the line is seized.

Powerboats do not often use lifelines but should have railings around their foredecks—inexpli-

cably, many don't. Ideally, railings should extend aft to the cockpit on either side, but narrow side decks frequently won't permit this. In such an instance, chest-high grabrails should be provided along the side decks. Although the American Boat and Yacht Council (ABYC) deems 24 inches (610 mm) a sufficient height for railings, 30 inches (762 mm) is better. The 16-inch (406 mm) railings often seen on small powerboats are more hazard than help.

See also **Harnesses; Jacklines; Stanchions.**

Life Rafts

Launching and boarding in bad weather presents problems

There is no guarantee that a life raft will work properly when you need it or that it will stay afloat long enough for you to be rescued.

Well-documented yachting disasters have raised serious questions about the value of life rafts in really bad sea conditions. Seven lives were lost during the storm that hit the Fastnet Race off England in 1979 in incidents "directly attributed to the failure of the life raft," according to the official board of inquiry. In a sobering footnote, the board added: "The yachts these seven people abandoned were subsequently found afloat and towed to harbor." Nineteen years later, when a fierce storm fell on the fleet in the Sydney–Hobart Race of 1998, the life rafts performed no better.

It is obvious that launching and boarding an inflatable life raft

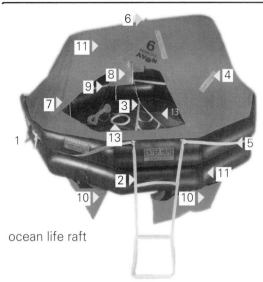

ocean life raft

coastal life raft

Features include:

1. Inflation CO_2 cylinder on the side of the buoyancy tube.
2–3. Boarding system: weighted boarding ladder + webbing bridle inside to ease entry into raft.
4. High-visibility self-erecting canopy with reflective tapes.
5. Outside lifelines.
6. Automatically activated lighting: inside and on canopy arch, with battery-save feature.
7. Entrance flap with ties.
8. Ventilation chute/observation port and rain water collection.
9. Inside bracing lines.
10. Weighted stabilizing pockets.
11. Upper and lower independent neoprene/nylon buoyancy tubes.
12. Inflatable double floor for heat retention.
13. Rescue quoit and line.

Features include:

1. Inflation CO_2 cylinder on the side of the buoyancy tube.
2. High-visibility self-erecting canopy.
3. Outside lifelines.
4. Inside bracing lines.
5. Observation port/water collector.
6. Independent buoyancy chambers.
7. Weighted stabilizing pockets.
8. Rescue quoit and line.

in high winds and heavy seas is no easy matter. In the Fastnet Storm, 12 life rafts were washed overboard and lost before anyone could board them: 8 from their stowage spaces in the cockpit and 4 from deck tie-downs. The inquiry board noted that "life rafts clearly failed to provide the safe refuge which many crews expected."

Most coastal life rafts have just one buoyancy tube, in addition to a canopy and ballast bags underneath to prevent capsizes. Offshore life rafts have two separate tubes, one on top of the other, and self-erecting canopies.

Many rafts have surprisingly little in the way of water, provisions, medical supplies, and safety equipment. Be sure to find out exactly what is inside your raft, and supplement it with an abandon-ship bag—it will be vital to your survival.

Your chances of survival on a raft on the open ocean are greater if you can sail or at least steer it in the right direction. Waiting passively to be rescued in a helplessly drifting life raft is a prime cause of despair and hopelessness.

According to Michael Stadler, a German professor of psychology

and a small-boat sailor, even the most desperate situation is bearable—even for someone on their own—provided they have some sense of controlling their position and environment.

See also **Abandoning Ship**.

Lifesling System

A recognized method of rescuing a person overboard

The Lifesling method of recovering a person from the water was developed by the Sailing Founda-

The Lifesling is designed both to "retrieve" a swimmer and to hoist him or her back aboard.

tion in Seattle, Washington. It is particularly useful on sailboats manned by two people because it enables one person to do all the rescuing.

The Lifesling consists of a buoyant padded sling, or yoke, that goes under a victim's armpits and allows him or her to be hoisted aboard with a tackle. The sling is attached to a long floating line that is made fast to the boat at the stern. Both sling and line are stowed in a semirigid pouch fastened to the stern pulpit.

The Lifesling is quick and easy to use. When someone falls overboard, you simply rip open the Velcro closure on top of the pouch and throw the sling into the water. The line typically feeds itself out of the pouch but may need a little help at first. When all the line has run out, simply sail or motor the boat in tight circles around the victim until he or she can reach the sling. As soon as the victim is safely in the sling, you should halt the boat: stop the motor and drop the sails. Then gently haul the victim in to the side of the boat and cleat the line so that the victim's head is kept clear of the water.

Prepare a halyard and then winch the victim up and over the side; or, if necessary, use a four-part tackle taken to a winch. The tackle should be slung from a halyard set 10 to 15 feet (3 to 4.5 m) above deck, depending on the size of your boat. The sling is designed to support the victim safely while he or she is being hoisted out of the water.

A four-part purchase may be stowed in the Lifesling pouch, ready for an emergency, or you may be able to use your boom vang if it's equipped at either end with quick-release snap shackles.

See also **Crew Overboard; Figure-Eight Method; Quick-Stop Method**.

Lighthouses

Another man-made wonder on the way to extinction

If you've ever experienced the joy and wonder of raising a lighthouse after weeks at sea with only a sextant and your own doubtful mathematical abilities to plot your position, you'll be sorry to hear that lighthouses are doomed to disappear. It won't happen for a long time, of course, but the writing is on the wall.

In an era when GPS satellite signals can provide your exact position in a flash, by day or night, in fog or snow, in rain or hail, there is no longer the same need for lighthouses. Mind you, they had a good long run.

The Pharos of Alexandria was built about 260 B.C., and it was regarded as one of the seven wonders of the ancient world. But

there had been lighthouses long before that, lit by beacons burning wood or coal, and many came afterward.

The first lighthouse in what is now the United States was Boston Light, built in 1716. It was rebuilt in 1859. Now there are hundreds of lighthouses along the nation's seacoasts and the Great Lakes, but only a few are still manned. Most are automatic, and serviced only when necessary.

Over the centuries, lighthouses won a place in the heart of every seafaring nation and were the focus of much glamour and emotion. The buildings were architecturally interesting and often daringly built in hazardous places to defy some of nature's greatest forces. Lighthouses offered primitive shelter to the brave, lonely souls who manned them in windswept seas and faithfully kept the light burning night after night. Although the end of their era is in sight, their aura will endure for many years to come.

Lightning Protection

Taking action to prevent damage from a bad strike

Lightning is a serious hazard in some popular boating areas, and the approach of a thunderstorm should be taken seriously because of the danger of lightning strikes.

A grounded vertical metal conductor 10 feet (3 m) high for every 17 feet (5 m) of boat length will attract and divert lightning flashes, providing a "cone of protection" angled downward 120

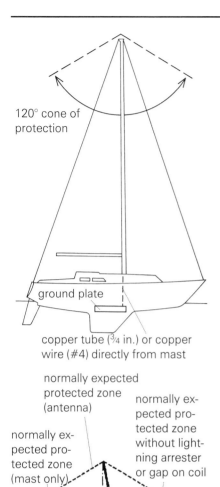

120° cone of protection

ground plate

copper tube (¾ in.) or copper wire (#4) directly from mast

normally expected protected zone (antenna)

normally expected protected zone without lightning arrester or gap on coil

normally expected protected zone (mast only)

A grounded vertical metal conductor 10 feet (3 m) high for every 17 feet (5 m) of boat length will attract and divert lightning flashes, thus providing a boat with a cone of protection angled downward at 120 degrees. A metal mast makes a good conductor but must be connected as directly as possible to a below-the-waterline ground plate at least one square foot in area. Standing rigging, winches, guardrails, and other large metallic objects, if not tied into the boat's bonding system, should be joined to the ground plate with a stranded copper wire of #8 AWG or larger gauge.

degrees from the top of the conductor.

An aluminum mast on a sailboat makes a good conductor, but a boat with a wooden mast needs a thick, stranded copper wire of at least #4 AWG (or a copper strip at least ¹⁄₃₂ inch or 0.8 mm thick) projecting at least 6 inches (150 mm) above the mast.

This conductor, or the metal mast, must be connected as directly as possible to a lightning ground connection—a submerged metal grounding surface of at least 1 square foot (0.1 m²).

Standing rigging, as well as winches, lifelines, pulpits, and large metal objects that are not tied into the bonding system should be joined to the ground plate with stranded conductors of at least #8 AWG.

See also **Downburst; Thunder and Lightning**.

Lights at Anchor

What the rules say you must show, and where to put them

Vessels less than 50 meters (164 ft.) in length are required to show at least one all-around white light visible for 2 miles while they're at anchor. Boats less than 7 meters (23 ft.) in length don't need to show an anchor light at all, as long as they're not anchored in or near a narrow channel, fairway, or where other vessels normally navigate—but their skippers would be wise to do so anyway.

Some "special anchorage areas" are found in inland waters, typically near yacht clubs and similar facilities, where you can

anchor or make fast to a mooring without a light, as long as your boat is less than 20 meters (65.6 ft.) long.

The white all-around anchor light may be placed "wherever it can best be seen." Because it's convenient to do so, sailboat manufacturers have almost universally adopted the habit of placing the anchor light on the very top of the mast. However, skippers of boats entering an anchorage on a dark night are intent on what is immediately in front of them, not what's hidden high overhead among the stars, so they may not see your lofty anchor light, especially at close range. If you want to sleep peacefully, keep your light reasonably low and visible. The proper place is a few feet off the deck or about a third of the way up the forestay of a sailboat.

Use electricity, kerosene, or anything you like, as long as it's white and can be seen through 360 horizontal degrees for 2 miles.

See also **Anchors, Anchoring; Navigation Lights**.

Lightweight Anchors

Cheaper and easier to handle, but they have limitations

Sheer weight helps an anchor dig into the sea bottom and quickly set itself firmly in place. In fact, many conservative boaters insist that any anchor weighing less than 30 pounds (14 kg) has no place on a boat.

That may be true when anchoring in hard sand or on a bottom covered with dense weed or thick grass, because it will be difficult for a light anchor to break through to the ground—but it's not the whole story.

Lightweight anchors such as the Danforth, the Performance, and the Fortress have no peers when it comes to anchoring in mud or soft sand and clay. Their large fluke areas generate tremendous resistance to being pulled through soft bottoms. Their superior performance depends on their being able to dig into the holding ground in the first place, of course, which doesn't always happen. If that were guaranteed, they would be the perfect anchors. There would be no need for the heavier plows, which—although their holding power is less—will set in anchorages where lightweight anchors are useless.

All light anchors are carefully constructed so that the angle their flukes make with the shank is carefully controlled for optimum penetration and holding power. Some have flukes whose angle you can alter so they open farther— the better to deal with soft mud.

Despite their light weight, these anchors have to be exceptionally strong to endure the strains imposed by high winds and swells. Unfortunately, their strength doesn't always match their holding power. Always choose the type made from high-tensile steel.

See also **Anchors, Anchoring; Anchor Types**.

Lines of Position

Knowing where you are, and also where you are not

In navigation, you'll hear a lot about lines of position (LOP), which are lines drawn on the chart after you've taken an observation or measurement of some kind. They tell you that (1) you're situated along that line *somewhere*, and (2) you're not situated anywhere else—near a reef or a rock, for instance.

If you can obtain another LOP at right angles to the first one, the two will cross—and that will be your *exact* position, known as a *fix*.

It's usually difficult to obtain two LOPs at right angles to one another, but the rule of thumb says you can get an acceptable fix from lines that cross at 60 degrees or better. On small boats in bad conditions, however, you take what you can get. A fix from two lines intersecting at an angle as small as 30 degrees is likely to have some error, but it's better than nothing if you use it with caution and common sense. However, anything substantially less than 30 degrees is hardly worth plotting.

Not all position lines are straight. If you can measure your distance from a lighthouse or other object on shore, you can draw an

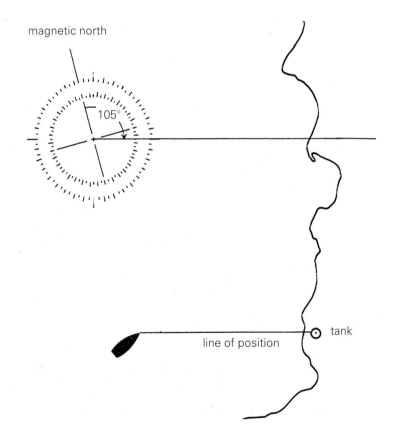

On deck the magnetic bearing of tank has been measured as 105°. On the chart a line at that angle has been drawn through the center of the magnetic compass rose. If that 105° line can be moved parallel to itself to pass through tank it becomes a line of position.

arc or circle with the lighthouse as the center and the distance as the radius—you will be *somewhere* on that line.

You may establish an LOP with a compass bearing, a radio signal, a visual range or transit, a series of soundings, or a sextant sight of a celestial body.

See also **Circles of Position**; **Fixes**; **Piloting**.

Lines Plans

Visualizing the shape of a hull from a set of plans

The lines plans of a boat provide an immediate indication of her looks, performance, and seaworthiness. They typically consist of three perpendicular views of the hull: the profile, or sheer plan, is the view from one side; the half-breadth plan is the view from directly above; and the body plan consists of views from directly in front of and behind the boat.

Horizontal lines pass through the hull parallel to the base line, and are called waterlines. Diagonal lines pass through the plan lengthwise at arbitrary angles to delineate the shape of the hull more completely. Buttock lines are slices through the hull from top to bottom, running parallel to the keel.

When the waterlines, diagonals, and buttocks are in place, you can develop the lines of a hull and create the stations, or sections. There are usually 10 stations along the waterline of a boat; when they're drawn one inside the other, they produce the body plan, which

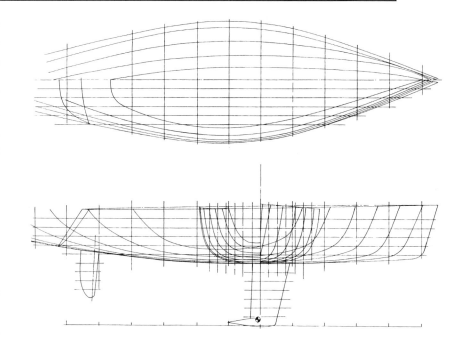

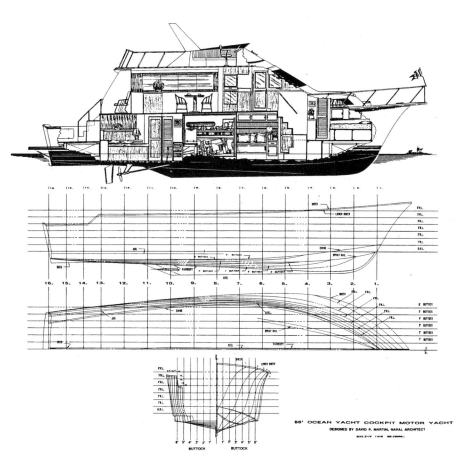

Lines plans for a cruiser-racer designed by Roger Marshall (top) *and for a Dave Martin–designed 56-foot motor yacht* (above).

contains the important midship section.

The stations in the body plan are usually drawn as half-sections, with the after sections on the left and the forward sections on the right. After a little practice, you can easily visualize the shape of the boat from the body plan and determine some characteristics of its behavior.

See also **Length-to-Beam Ratio; Hull Shapes**.

Locating Batteries

Conflicting requirements make this a case for compromise

Batteries present a dilemma for a boat designer: they need to be stowed low to maintain stability—but they also need to be stowed high to keep them away from bilgewater and engine heat and to make them accessible for maintenance.

Batteries need protection from extreme cold, salt spray, and hot sunshine. They need ventilation, so that the hydrogen generated when they're charged is easily dissipated. Because of their ability to make sparks, they also need to be kept well away from areas where gasoline fumes might collect. However, they also need to be close to an engine to avoid excessive voltage drop to the starter motor.

Batteries need to be contained in an acid-proof box in case they spill electrolyte. They should be securely fastened down in case of capsize, but you need to get to them easily for servicing.

These conflicting needs are impossible to reconcile completely on most small boats. Compromise is the order of the day: make your choices and live with them.

See also **Battery Choices; Battery Needs**.

Locks

Changing levels from one body of water to another

A lock is an enclosed basin in a canal, river, or tidal estuary that has opening gates at both ends. Boats are raised after they have entered a lock and the lower gate is closed astern of them. Sluices are then opened to allow water to run in from the higher level, after which the upper gate is opened and boats are free to proceed. Locking downstream is a reversal of that procedure.

Locks controlled by the U.S. Army Corps of Engineers have an established order of priority:

1. U.S. military vessels

2. boats carrying mail

3. commercial passenger boats

4. commercial tugs with tows

5. commercial fishing boats

6. pleasure boats

Noncommercial craft may be locked through with commercial vessels at the discretion of the lockmaster, if a safe distance can be maintained between them and if the commercial vessels are not carrying hazardous cargoes.

You need at least two lines to hold your position alongside a lock wall, and a person to handle each line. The length of the lines should be twice the distance from the deck to the top of the lock, so they can be looped around a bollard above and retrieved or payed out on deck as the boat rises or falls. Some locks have mooring posts recessed into the chamber walls that float up and down with the changing water level and, therefore, don't require an adjustment to your lines.

Have several fenders in place and watch for turbulence as the chamber fills. If you are locked in behind a larger vessel, let her get clear first and wait for her backwash to subside before you take in your lines.

If you're planning to transit the Panama Canal, you'll need four line handlers as well as a compulsory pilot. There is usually sufficient help available from local sources or the crews of other boats waiting to lock through.

According to the Panama Canal Authority, 450 yachts up to 50 feet (15.2 m) in overall length passed through the canal in 1998, 515 in 1999, and 432 in 2000.

Lookouts

Keeping a good watch is fundamental to your safety

Rule 5 of the Rules of the Road is very explicit: "Every vessel shall at all times maintain a proper lookout by sight and hearing."

On large ships, a seaman was stationed on the forecastle or in the crow's nest for this purpose, but on small boats it is usually the duty of the person at the helm to keep an eye (and ear) out for traffic.

This rule is often ignored on small boats. Even vastly experienced ocean cruisers such as Lin and Larry Pardey admit that they often stay below for 10 minutes or so at a time while on watch at sea. Yachting literature reveals that on many occasions, especially during gales, no lookout at all is kept for several hours at a time while the crew rests below. Single-handers have no chance of complying with the law when they cross oceans, of course, so—in theory—their voyages are illegal from the start.

There appears to be no record of any of these transgressors ever having been prosecuted, probably because they are more likely to come off worse in a collision with a big ship. At the same time, the danger to small boats of not keeping a constant lookout is very real, especially at night: a fast modern freighter can appear over the horizon and be upon you in 15 minutes or less.

See also **Rules of the Road; Single-Handed Sailboats; Single-Handed Sailing.**

Lubber Line

A small vertical line that indicates the boat's heading

On a magnetic compass or a radar scope, the boat's heading is indicated by a vertical line known as the lubber line. Many yacht compasses have two lubber lines, one at the forward end of the bowl and the other at the after end, but only one is necessary. A line projected through the lubber lines would be precisely parallel to the boat's fore-and-aft centerline.

There may also be additional offset lubber lines marked to indicate beam bearings of objects at 90 degrees to the boat's heading, or simply to help maintain a course when the person at the helm is standing to one side or the other of the compass.

The origin of the term is obscure, though it may have been applied originally to the vertical line that allowed even a "lubber"—a big clumsy seaman—to steer a precise course by compass.

See also **Compass Types.**

Lying Ahull

Leaving the boat to look after herself in storm winds

When the wind rises above a moderate gale, things become uncomfortable for a sailboat that is hove to. At force 9 on the Beaufort Scale, a wind speed of nearly 50 knots, some sailors believe it's time to start lying ahull.

There is no fancy seamanship involved; you simply douse all sail and lash everything down well. Lash the tiller to leeward so the boat will come up into the wind if she gathers way, and leave her to look after herself.

She will lie broadside to wind and waves, or nearly so, leaving a slick of wake to windward. If you can persuade her to stay directly to leeward of that slick, it may offer some protection from heavy seas by making them break before they reach you.

Shallow draft is an advantage if a plunging breaker hits you be-cause it allows your boat to skid sideways and absorb much of the blow.

The weight of the wind keeps the boat heeled over appreciably, even under bare poles, so that the strong rounded sections of the hull are presented to the seas. If you have a reasonably small watertight cockpit, you will be safe lying ahull until the seas build up to such an extent that you are physically lifted and hurled down sideways. Then it will be time to run off before the wind.

Lying ahull is not a universally endorsed tactic, however; indeed, there seems to be a rising tide of opinion against it. The reason is that even one breaking sea cascading against the side of a boat whose keel is planted in deep water will likely capsize or damage it, even if it's a heavy-displacement hull. There is growing sentiment that a boat is best off with its ends to the seas. When heaving to becomes untenable, many feel it's time to run off, trailing a drogue from the stern.

Lying ahull is a bad idea for most powerboats. With its big saloon windows, high superstructure, and lack of a significant keel or ballast, the typical powerboat lying beam-to the wind and seas is extremely vulnerable to capsize and serious structural damage—a sitting duck. When a gale builds to the point where running downwind imposes serious risk of pooping or broaching, your best option may be to choose a lull between waves and turn quickly to punch your bow into the seas.

See also **Drogue; Heaving To; Heavy Weather; Running Off; Scudding; Sea Anchors.**

M

Mainsail Slides

Curing the tendency for the sail to jam in its track

If you have trouble handling your mainsail because the slides stick in the track, take a look at how the slides are attached to the luff.

Sailmakers have a habit of using stiff Dacron webbing between the slide and the luff, which can result in difficulties if it's seized too firmly.

Most nylon slides have a little bail along their after edge. When the sail is being hoisted, whatever is joining the luff to the bail should be free to run up this bail to the top, so that the pull on the slide comes from its upper half.

Similarly, when you're dropping the sail, the attachment should be able to drop to the bottom of the bail. That way, if you have to pull on the sail, the slide will be dragged down from its bottom edge.

If your slide is held too stiffly, it will tend to pivot as it's being pulled so that its top and bottom edges dig into the mast track or groove.

A small plastic or metal shackle between the luff cringle and the bail will correctly pull the slide from either end instead of from the middle, allowing you to raise or lower the sail without jamming. Shackles tend to create chafe, however, so the areas around the sail cringles must be covered with clear plastic protectors. Shackles also make a lot of irritating noise when the sail is shaking, especially against a metal mast—but they are strong, simple to install, and easy to replace.

See also **Chafe**.

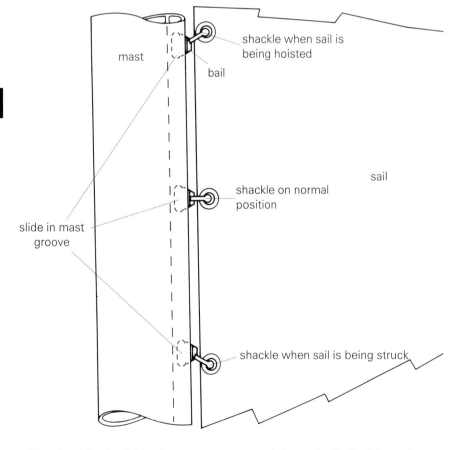

mast

bail

shackle when sail is being hoisted

slide in mast groove

shackle on normal position

sail

shackle when sail is being struck

The shackle should be free to move up and down the bail of the sail slide.

Making Fast

Acknowledging the correct way to say she's tied up

The word *fast* is derived from the Old English *fæst*, which means firm or stable, so when a boat is *made fast*, she is firmly tied up. But we never say "she's tied up," of course, lest we be taken for landlubbers who don't know better; we always say "she's made fast."

There are also further adverbial subtleties for those who really want to be nautically correct. The old rule says a boat makes fast *alongside* a jetty, pier, or wharf. She makes fast *in* a slip, and *to* a buoy or pile.

Man Overboard

See Crew Overboard.

Marine Operators

Expect changes in the way you make phone calls from boats

It used to be easy to make a telephone call from a boat. You simply called the nearest marine operator on the VHF radio and you were patched through to the land-based phone system. There were certain problems, however: anyone with a VHF radio could hear your conversation; and if you hadn't made arrangements in advance or it wasn't a collect call, you had to give a credit card number, which would be broadcast in the area.

The service was improved when MariTel purchased 85 percent of all marine-operator radio stations in the United States a few years ago. Transmissions were electronically blocked to all but the marine operator, so eavesdroppers could hear only the incoming broadcast to you. However, the popularity of cell phones has obviously cut into the marine operators' profits because MariTel cancelled several marine operator

channels; for example, all its public correspondence stations in the Pacific Northwest completely stopped transmissions in 2001. The future of stations in the rest of the country is uncertain.

The present emphasis is on providing a marine telephone service that is a cross between VHF and cell phones, allowing what amounts to direct dialing between radios and phones. The system uses special VHF radios equipped with digital selective calling (DSC), and it offers offshore ranges of between 50 and 100 miles. A nationwide network of 161 towers provides callers with 24-hour service at rates less expensive than those charged by satellite-phone operators.

Nothing seems to last long in the fast-changing world of personal communications, so you can expect phone calls and Internet connections to boats at sea to become cheaper and more readily available in the future. However, the need for VHF radio is not likely to diminish because it is the only method of simultaneously alerting all other boats in the area when you are in distress or simply need information.

See also **Radio Transmitters**.

Masts

What they're made of; their positions in modern sailboats

The Anglo-Saxon word *mæst* refers to a tree trunk, and for many centuries that's exactly what sailboat masts were. Nowadays, most masts are made of metal: aluminum on small boats and steel

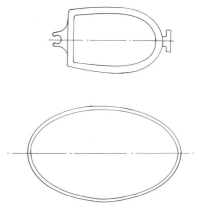

A conventional thin-walled aluminum mast (bottom) *with one or two spreaders requires a section of large diameter. Making the wall a little thicker* (top) *and incorporating multiple sets of spreaders makes a smaller section possible. The result is a lighter, bendier, harder-to-tune spar that allows better airflow over the mainsail of a racing sailboat.*

on large ships. Some gaff-rigged sailboats still have solid, stumpy wooden masts, and many older Bermuda-rigged cruiser-racers have tall, hollow wooden masts, glued together in two long pieces.

Aluminum alloys—especially #6061-T6—have proven successful on pleasure boats, requiring a minimum of maintenance and being comparatively light and long-lived. For these reasons, aluminum largely replaced wood in the masts of boats built after 1960. However, an aluminum mast does require adequate staying because if it bends excessively under compression, it's likely to fold and collapse—unlike a wooden mast, which can take a lot of punishment and spring back unharmed.

In the 1990s, carbon fiber became increasingly popular for masts, to the point that it is now

M

the material of choice for new large yacht masts. Carbon fiber is light, tremendously strong, and more supple even than wood. It is also expensive, more difficult to ground, and can set up galvanic corrosion with metal fittings. For these reasons, many sailors still prefer aluminum.

Thick-sectioned carbon-fiber masts are used without stays in large cat-rigged cruisers, whereas racing yachts use highly stayed, thin-sectioned carbon masts. Strong as it is, a carbon-fiber mast can still break. The 128-foot carbon-fiber mast of the 110-foot catamaran *Kingfisher II* broke suddenly in two places in a 25-knot breeze following several days of storm-sailing in the Southern Ocean in February 2003. The dismasting ended *Kingfisher II*'s attempt in the Jules Verne Challenge around-the-world speed record, which then stood at 64 days.

Pleasure boats mostly have one or two masts, although a large schooner may have three. Following are their relative positions in a boat, according to individual rigs:

- sloop: one quarter of the waterline length abaft the stem
- cutter: one third to one half the waterline length abaft the stem
- yawl: mainmast about one quarter of the waterline aft of the stem; mizzenmast on (or close to) the after end of the waterline
- ketch: mainmast about one third of the waterline aft of the stem; mizzenmast about one sixth of the waterline length forward of the after end of the waterline

- schooner: foremast about 20 to 25 percent of overall length abaft the stem; mainmast 52 to 60 percent of overall length abaft the stem

Multiple masts should not be set up exactly parallel to each other because they then appear to be closer together at the masthead than at deck level. This applies particularly to schooners. To compensate for this illusion, each mast must rake aft a few degrees more than the one ahead of it.

See also **Galvanic Corrosion**; **Sailboat Rigs**; **Wooden Spars**.

Mast Steps

Climbing the mast to check the condition of your rigging

If you don't have your mast removed when you haul your boat every winter, somebody needs to go to the top of the mast at least once a year to check the condition of the rigging.

Many cruising boats fit mast steps to make this trip easier. The steps are made of stainless steel or aluminum and fastened to the sides of the mast with rivets or screws. They are staggered, one to port and one to starboard every 15 to 20 inches (400 to 500 mm), except that two steps side by side are placed so you can stand and work at the spreaders and masthead.

The advantages of mast steps are that you are not dependent on anyone else to haul you up the mast, nor are you trusting your life to a halyard or a snap shackle. You don't have to worry about whether your crew has the skill to

lower you safely in a bosun's chair and, if you're painting or varnishing up there, there's no halyard to drag through your wet work.

The disadvantages are that halyards may snag the steps at awkward times unless you string thin preventer lines from one to another. The steps also create windage and weight aloft, which is detrimental to performance. You will probably have to lower the mast to install the steps properly, and they may be slippery when they're wet. They cost $13 to $17 each and their fittings make a lot of holes in the mast—a minimum of three per step, and usually more.

Some mast steps are designed to trap your foot so that it cannot slide off the end of the step; others have dispensed with this feature to reduce windage and weight. Still others can be folded up flat against the mast after use.

If you use mast steps, wear a chest harness and clip it on at every opportunity.

The most popular alternative to mast steps is the bosun's chair, for which you normally need a crew to winch you up on a halyard. The most sensible alternative is probably ratlines, but whereas some modern boats have two shrouds running up to the spreaders, few have two that converge at the masthead, so there is no way to fit ratlines to the top third of the mast.

Another sensible alternative is a Dacron ladder that is hoisted by a halyard in the luff groove of the mainmast, but it may require removal of the mainsail first. In use, it needs patience and a good aim with your feet.

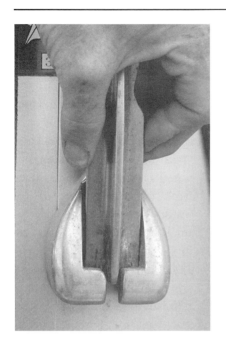

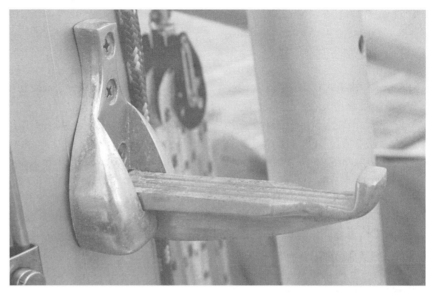

Details of a folding mast step.

Jumars are handheld brakes used by tree surgeons and mountaineers that slide up or down a halyard or other line led from the masthead to deck level. They alternately grip or release the halyard, letting you use your leg power to raise yourself; however, you will need side restraints to prevent a jerky pendulum motion if the boat rolls.

See also **Bosun's Chair; Harnesses; Preventers.**

Mast Vibration

Curing the "pumping" action of a bare mast in a beam wind

When the wind is blowing from abeam, a bare mast will sometimes start to "pump," or vibrate, alarmingly. It occurs in moderate winds (5 to 14 mph or 2 to 6 m per second), and the vibration may become severe when the natural frequency of the mast coincides with the frequency of vibration.

Movement occurs when wind eddies shed alternately from one side of the mast to the other; in theory, it's possible for a mast to vibrate back and forth in winds from any direction. Almost always, though, the mast movement is fore and aft, with the wind coming from abeam or nearly so. You can cure this vibration, or lessen it, in several ways:

- tighten loose stays; then tighten the shrouds if necessary, particularly the fore lower shrouds (if any) and the aft lowers
- add an inner forestay of wire or rod
- hoist a stiff narrow strip of heavy sailcloth in the mast groove to disturb the rhythm of wind eddies; make it at least 4 inches (100 mm) wide
- turn the boat more into or away from the wind
- for temporary relief, lead a nonstretch line from a strong point at the bow, clove-hitch

it around the mast as high as you can reach, take it aft to a cockpit winch, and tighten it as much as possible

See also **Shrouds and Stays**.

Mayday Calls

Calling for help when you're in grave and imminent danger

The spoken word *Mayday* is an internationally recognized distress signal, an English phonetic rendering of the French phrase *m'aider*, or help me.

In an emergency, call for help by radio on VHF channel 16 (156.8 MHz) or SSB 2182 kHz. You can, of course, broadcast a distress signal on any channel that seems sensible, but those two channels are reserved for calling and distress and are more likely to bring results.

Don't make a Mayday call unless your boat or a person aboard it is in grave and imminent danger because it sets off a chain of events that involves a lot of rescue personnel. Getting lost or running out of fuel is not considered grave and imminent danger.

As soon as you make the call, the U.S. Coast Guard or other controlling authority will impose radio silence on the emergency channel by calling Silence Mayday (pronounced *see-lonce mayday*). All vessels that hear the call for silence are forbidden by law to transmit on that frequency unless they are in a position to render aid. Any vessel that hears another transgressing this rule should call the transgressor with the signal Silence Distress and identify herself. Normal radio traffic on the distress channel may resume only when the controlling authority broadcasts Silence Fini (pronounced *see-lonce fee-nee*), meaning "silence finished."

To make a distress call, say the word *Mayday* three times. Say "This is (the name of your vessel)" three times. If you're using a VHF-DSC radio, give your Maritime Mobile Service Identity (MMSI) nine-digit number as well; this registered number will further identify your boat to the coast guard.

Now pass on the distress message. Say the word *Mayday* once again. Repeat the name of your vessel and MMSI number (if applicable). Give your position (latitude and longitude or bearing and distance from a known location). State the nature of your distress and the kind of assistance you need. Add anything else you think might aid rescuers, such as the length, color, and rig of your

boat; and the number of people on board and whether they are wearing life jackets.

Give this information as briefly and clearly as possible. Then say "Over" and wait for a reply. Repeat the call several times if necessary. If there is still no reply, listen for traffic on another channel and break in with your distress call. Ask other vessels with more powerful transmitters to relay your call to the U.S. Coast Guard if necessary. When another vessel retransmits a distress message, the words *Mayday relay* must be spoken three times before the vessel's name, followed by, "The following distress call was received from the vessel . . . "

If you're using a VHF-DSC radio, you can precede the channel 16 Mayday with a channel 70 distress call. An "undesignated" call on channel 70 can be sent within seconds by operating the radio's "Distress" button. If the radio is interfaced with GPS, the call will automatically include your coordinates; otherwise, you have to manually enter your position. After 15 seconds, the channel 70 call must be followed by a channel 16 call, as described previously.

See also **Pan-Pan Calls**.

Miles

Defining the basic unit of distance in marine navigation

Boaters know two types of miles. On the Great Lakes, inland waters, and the Intracoastal Waterway, the statute mile of 5,280 feet or 1,760 yards (1,609 m) is used.

On coastal and international waters, the nautical mile is used.

For many years, the nautical mile was understood to be 6,080 feet, but modern surveying equipment has discovered that it's actually 6,076.1 feet, or 2,025.4 yards (1,852 m). The nautical mile is defined as a minute of arc on the Earth's surface, or $1/60$ of 1 degree.

For all practical purposes on a small boat, you can assume the nautical mile to be 2,000 yards. The cable is $1/10$ of that, or 200 yards. It makes your calculations much easier and navigation doesn't get much more precise than that on a small boat.

Roughly speaking, a nautical mile is $1/7$ larger than a statute mile. To convert nautical miles to statute miles, multiply nautical miles by 1.15—or multiply by 8 and divide by 7.

To convert statute miles to nautical miles, multiply statute miles by 0.875—or multiply by 7 and divide by 8.

See also **Fathoms**; **Latitude, Longitude**.

Mooring

Securing a boat so it's free to respond to wind and waves

Many owners prefer to leave their boats on moorings rather than in marinas, but the steady proliferation of boats places great demands on what little mooring space is left.

A mooring consists of an anchor or a heavy weight on the sea bottom and a chain that rises to the surface, where it is attached to a floating buoy. Mushroom anchors are commonly used singly, or in a triangle when swinging room is limited. The rule of thumb is that the mushroom anchor should weigh at least 10 pounds (4.5 kg) for every 1 foot (300 mm) of the boat's overall length; that is, 300 pounds (136 kg) for a 30-foot (9 m) boat. In some areas where the composition of the bottom is suitable, helix anchors are screwed in to provide secure holding. If you use concrete blocks for weights, they must be very large to be effective—at least three to four times as heavy as mushroom anchors—because they lose so much of their weight when they're submerged.

The riser chain is usually galvanized, although unprotected steel chain that remains underwater does not rust as readily as chain near the surface where more oxygen is available.

The float or mooring buoy must be sufficiently buoyant to support the riser chain at the highest tides. It is often a hollow sphere of steel, plastic, or fiberglass about 12 inches (300 mm) or more in diameter, with a steel rod running through the middle. The riser chain is attached to the bottom of this rod and a mooring pendant of rope—which is taken aboard the boat and made fast at the bow—is attached to the top end.

Because the floating buoy often fetches up against the side of the vessel in light wind or contrary currents—and may damage it if the buoy is not well fendered—some boaters prefer to bring the buoy on board and attach the boat directly to the chain.

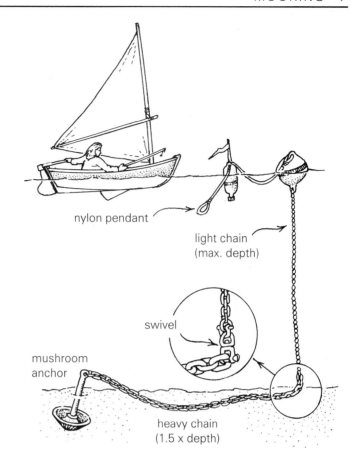

Typical mooring configuration.

In that case, a lighter chain pendant may be used, long enough to reach the bottom at all normal tides.

The pick-up buoy should have a large ring or loop on top so that you can hook it with a boathook, and it should be strong enough to take the weight of the boat temporarily during mooring operations. An alternative to the ring on top is a long rod or "wand" standing up vertically, which may be grabbed by hand from the foredeck.

When you approach a mooring single-handed under sail, it is handy to prepare in advance a fairly light line made fast in the cockpit and running forward to a single pulley block at the bow,

then outside the lifelines and rigging, and back to the cockpit. The line should terminate in a snaphook.

Then you can luff into the wind, stop with your mooring buoy alongside the cockpit, and simply reach over to snap the hook on the ring. Haul in the other end of the line that is made fast in the cockpit; the buoy will move forward and you are immediately made fast by the bow. Drop the sails at your leisure and then finish mooring properly.

The advantages of moorings are privacy, low cost, and the ability to sail on and off without the need for an engine. The fact that a boat almost always faces into the wind can also help with ventila-

M

tion. Furthermore, a boat free to swing on a mooring and dance in the waves is more lively and appealing than one crammed into a marina, at least in most owners' eyes.

Among the disadvantages of a mooring are the swinging space it requires and its dependency on a single line from the bow. If it's a rope pendant, it could chafe badly in heavy weather. The vessel herself usually has less protection from the weather and from other boats maneuvering nearby. Electrical power and fresh water are not available, as they are at most marinas, and you either need a tender (and a place to keep it) or a ferry service to get you to and from your boat.

See also **Chafe**; **Fenders**; **Slips Versus Moorings**; **Ventilation**.

Motorsailers

Improving a boat's ability to sail well and *motor well*

A few decades ago, the term *motorsailer* might almost have been regarded as a derogatory description of a hybrid boat that could neither motor as well as a powerboat nor sail as well as a sailboat.

Motorsailers had large heavy engines, big fixed propellers, and shorter-than-usual masts, so their performance suffered under both sail and power. Of course, had you been an optimist, you could have pointed out that they sailed better than pure powerboats and motored better than pure sailboats. But the concept never really excited the popular imagination.

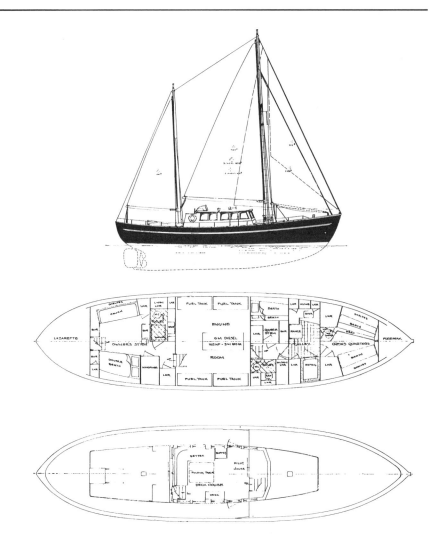

This John Alden–designed 1930s-era motorsailer looks comfortable and seaworthy. The rig is well balanced and easy to handle, and the long, narrow hull will move easily with the single 165-horsepower diesel specified in the plans.

Since that time, marine auxiliary engines have been getting lighter and more powerful, so that many of today's fine auxiliary sailing boats would almost qualify as motorsailers.

One classic definition of a motorsailer by the naval architect Francis S. Kinney appears in Skene's *Elements of Yacht Design.* Kinney painted a background of a wind blowing at force 6 (22 to 27 knots) and raising a short, choppy sea. If a sailboat could make way to windward quicker under shortened sail than under her motor alone, she was an auxiliary sailing yacht, Kinney decided. If she could reach her destination to windward more quickly by continuing under power alone, she was a motorsailer.

It's probable that many modern yachts with high-powered auxiliaries would fall into the latter category, and it's almost certain that today's real motorsailers— with their feathering or self-pitching props—both sail and power better than ever before.

The old-style motorsailer had a sailboat hull with a roomy deckhouse that could have been borrowed from a powerboat. She had an enclosed steering station and possibly a flying bridge. Her accommodations were roomier than a sailboat's but more solidly built than a powerboat's. Today's motorsailer looks more like a pure sailboat, and her impressive ability under power alone often comes as a surprise to those who challenge her.

See also **Yacht Design**.

Multihulls

Sailing around the world nonstop in just two months

A multihull is any vessel with more than one hull. Pleasure-boat multihulls include catamarans (two hulls), trimarans (three hulls), and proas (one hull and an outrigger).

Sailing multihulls are potentially faster than monohulls because their narrow, shallow hulls cause comparatively little wave resistance and their wide beam gives them the stability to carry extra sail. They are also less likely to sink when the hull is flooded

because they don't need heavy ballast keels. They sail almost upright and don't roll downwind to the same extent as monohulls.

In small to medium sizes, their speed advantage over monohulls is largely negated on ocean crossings because of the weight of water and provisions they must carry. Multihulls perform best when they're kept light.

Their biggest handicap, other than the space they take up in port, is the fact that they are difficult to right after a 180-degree capsize. If they don't lose the rig, they are even more stable upside down than right side up. Unlike

M

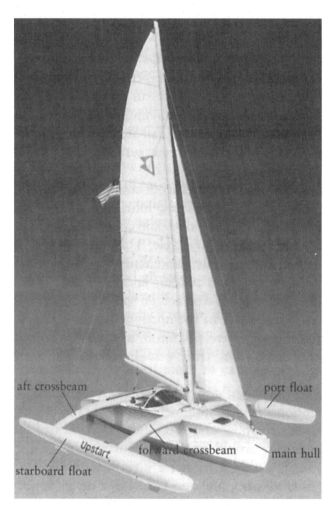

Two modern multihulls for cruising: a Dick Newick–designed trimaran and a Chris White–designed catamaran.

monohulls, multihulls lose stability as they heel.

Of the three types, the proa is potentially the fastest, but also the most unstable. The trimaran is theoretically the slowest, but also the safest. The catamaran, being faster than the trimaran but less likely than the proa to capsize, is usually used in long-distance racing; in fact, a 110-foot catamaran called *Club Med* broke the world record for a circumnavigation under sail in March 2001.

Club Med, the winner of the Race of the Millennium, took 62 days to cover 26,500 miles at an *average* speed of 18.2 knots. In one 24-hour period, she sailed 650 nautical miles—an average of more than 27 knots. No other clipper ship has ever come close to that record; the fastest American-built clippers, such as the *Sovereign of the Seas* and *Lightning,* achieved a mere 420 to 440 miles a day.

Ironically, *Club Med* was not credited with the official record because she did not start and finish at the same port, as required by the official record keeper, the British-based World Speed Sailing Council. She started at Barcelona and finished at Marseilles. As of this writing, the existing record of 64 days, 8 hours, 37 minutes was established by the 110-foot catamaran *Orange* in 2002. *Orange* raced over the official Jules Verne Challenge course, starting and finishing between the lighthouses at Lizard Point in southwestern England and Ushant on the northwestern tip of France. One year later, *Orange* went after the record again—this time as *Kingfisher II* under the command of Ellen MacArthur—but was dismasted in the Southern Ocean.

See also **Hull Shapes**.

N

Navigation Lights

Showing the position and course of your boat at night

Every vessel underway or at anchor must show navigation lights between sunset and sunrise, as well as during times of restricted visibility during the day. An exception to this rule is that boats of less than 65 feet (20 m) need not show anchor lights in an area shown on a government chart as a "special anchorage."

The kind of lights you need and where you place them depends on the type and size of your boat, the rule of the road under which she is operating, and the purpose for which she's being used. As a general rule, green lights mark a vessel's starboard side and red lights mark her port side.

Anchor lights. All vessels less than 164 feet (50 m) in length must show an all-around white light that's visible for 2 miles when anchored between dusk and dawn. That range is reached in clear weather by a 12-watt electric bulb shining through clear glass or plastic, or a $\frac{1}{2}$-inch-deep wick in a kerosene lantern.

Running lights. Underway between sunset and sunrise or in restricted visibility, a powerboat of less than 164 feet (50 m) or a sailboat operating under power must display red and green sidelights, each visible for 2 miles through an arc of 112.5 degrees. The red arc starts at the bow and sweeps to 22.5 degrees abaft the beam to port; the green arc mirrors this to starboard. The boat must also display a white masthead light visible for 5 miles (3 miles if the boat is less than 65 ft. or 20 m long) through an arc of 225 degrees centered ahead, and a white stern light visible for 2 miles through an arc of 135 degrees centered behind. If the boat is less than 39 feet (12 m) long, the masthead and stern lights can be combined

Right: Navigation light requirements and what they look like. A boat less than 39 feet (12 m) long operating under sail alone can dispense with the white steaming light and, as a further option, can show a single tricolor mast-top light in lieu of separate deck-level red and green running lights and white stern light. Any boat of more than 23 feet (7 m) that is operating under power, however, needs the light pattern shown below, though it is permissible on a boat of less than 39 feet to combine the steaming light and stern light into one all-around white light.

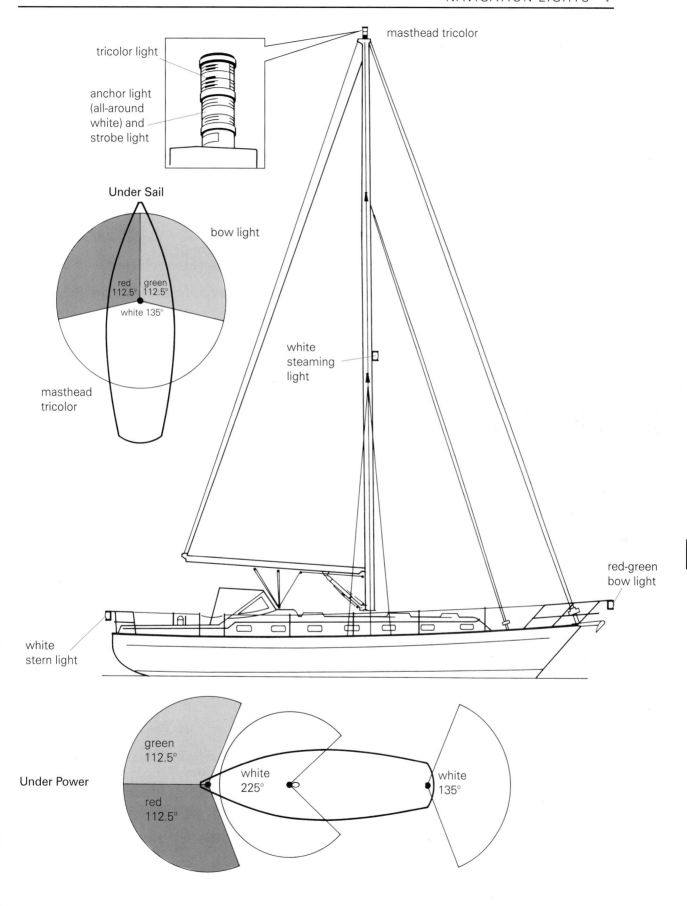

tricolor light

anchor light (all-around white) and strobe light

masthead tricolor

Under Sail

bow light

red 112.5°   green 112.5°

white 135°

masthead tricolor

white steaming light

red-green bow light

white stern light

N

Under Power

green 112.5°

red 112.5°

white 225°

white 135°

Lights for Power-Driven Vessels Under Way

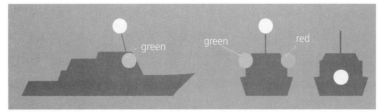

Under 164 ft. (50 m), masthead light, sidelights, and sternlight.

Over 164 ft. (50 m).

Lights When Towing

Under 164 ft. (50 m), two white steaming lights and towing light aft (yellow over white).

Vessel being towed shows sidelights and sternlight.

If tow is over 657 ft. (200 m), three steaming lights.

Lights When Pushing

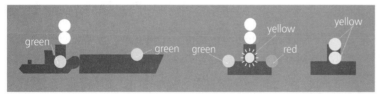

In inland waters only, the lights are as shown, with the yellow bow light flashing. In international waters, there is no yellow bow light, and the two yellow stern lights are replaced by a white stern light.

Deciphering Lights at Night

If you see this at night . . .

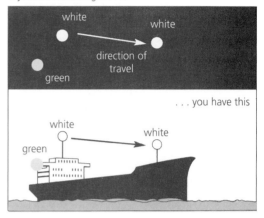

If you see this at night . . .

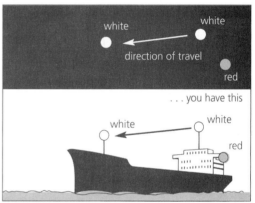

If the two white lights are aligned . . .

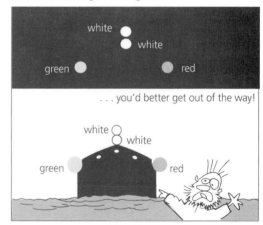

Navigation light requirements and what they look like (continued).

N

into one all-around white light visible for 2 miles. If the boat is less than 39 feet and operating under sail only, the masthead light may be dispensed with and, as a further option, the sidelights and stern light may be combined into one tricolor masthead light. Finally, in a power-driven boat of less than 23 feet (7 m) traveling at less than 7 knots, a single all-around white light will suffice, although sidelights should be displayed if practicable.

The colored glass or plastic of the sidelights absorbs 85 to 90 percent of the light from the bulbs, so you need to increase their wattage to get the needed range. For example, a 24-watt bulb shining through clear glass or plastic is visible at about 3 miles; however, a 24-watt bulb showing through red or green glass or plastic is visible for little more than 1 mile. Interestingly, to increase visibility from 3 to 4 miles, you must approximately *double* the brightness of a lamp.

See also **Lights at Anchor**.

Net Tonnage

Calculating boat size for purposes of documentation

If you want to document your boat with the U.S. Coast Guard, she must measure at least 5 tons net. For practical purposes regarding pleasure boats, net tonnage is understood to be ⁹⁄₁₀ of gross tonnage.

To calculate gross tonnage, take half of the overall length L times overall breadth B times

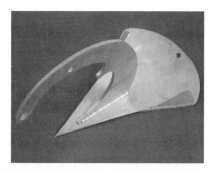

Clockwise from top left: Bulwagga; spade; barnacle.

depth D (the internal measurement of the hull, not the draft), all in feet, divided by 100. In other words: ½ (L x B x D ÷ 100).

Roughly speaking, 5 net tons corresponds to a moderate-displacement boat about 30 feet in length. A heavy-displacement, long-keeled cruising boat could be as little as 25 feet overall but still have sufficient volume below decks to qualify for federal documentation.

A documented vessel must be owned by a U.S. citizen. The captain (and any other officer) must be a U.S. citizen as well, although crew members need not be. Documentation gives you the legal right to fly the special U.S. Yacht Ensign (in home waters only), an authority that is not officially granted to other yachts—although many wear it anyway.

A documented yacht's title is also proof of ownership because it records the liens, mortgages, and other financial liabilities (if any) that she carries.

See also **Flags; Registration**.

New Anchors

Three newcomers challenge the established favorites

Many new anchors are invented but few come onto the market, and even fewer challenge the established favorites. Sometimes a new anchor that is perfect in other respects is simply too bulky or awkward to handle and stow. Perhaps it is too easily dislodged by its own rode when the wind or current changes, or perhaps it is too complicated and expensive.

N

There is no perfect anchor. The favorites that have evolved over the years all have faults, but they have proven *adequate* in most bottoms most of the time.

Nevertheless, there are three new anchors whose credentials pose a challenge to the reigning favorites. In tests conducted by the well-respected consumer magazine, *Practical Sailor*, they all fared well. Of course, no matter how many anchor tests are conducted, they never seem to point to an anchor that is head and shoulders above the rest. The truth is that individual anchors perform best in certain conditions: some are better in rock, some in sand, some in mud. Even then, their performances from test to test may be inconsistent because of variations in the seabed. A clam in the wrong place can prevent a Danforth from setting, for example, and a small patch of rock in a sandy bottom will defy most anchors.

That said, here's what *Practical Sailor* discovered in tests that included the old favorites as well as these three new ones:

Spade. Astonishingly, this modified plow anchor with a fixed head and a curved shank ranked first of 18 anchors tested. A 16.5-pound (7.5 kg) Spade 80 held 1,000 pounds in sand and 660 pounds in mud (454 and 299 kg).

Bulwagga. With its twin triangular flukes joined to a straight shank, this anchor was found to be "clumsy to handle and difficult to stow," according to *Practical Sailor*. But, once again, it performed wonderfully under test. A 17-pound (7.7 kg) Bulwagga held 816 pounds in sand and 680 pounds in mud (370 and 308 kg), ranking it second of 18.

Barnacle. This strange-looking anchor has a single fluke and a curved shank. A 25-pound (11 kg) Barnacle held 355 pounds in sand and 800 pounds in mud (161 and 363 kg), ranking fourth of 18. It also has the great advantage of stowing flat.

Any new anchors that perform as well as these three did against the tried and proven favorites certainly bear watching.

See also **Anchor Types**.

Nighttime Boating

Experiencing the fright and delight of the night

Boating at night requires a set of skills that is more easily learned in the company of someone who has done it before and often. If you rush into it on your own, you may find it more anxiety-provoking than you imagined.

Nothing looks the same at night. Shorelines and headlands you know like the back of your hand might as well be on the back of the moon. Distances are difficult to judge, the waves seem bigger, the wind seems stronger, and every action you take seems to be a little more difficult. But with a little practice, all of this becomes familiar and manageable. Then boating at night can be a wonderful experience, and
one that's reserved for comparatively few people.

On nights when there is luminescence in the water, you float in a marine fairyland, with silver fringes dripping from your dinghy oars and a necklace of burning ice-fire dripping from your anchor chain. Once you've seen the twirling, hollow tubes of fire that dolphins make underwater when they speed toward your boat at night, you'll never forget it.

At sea, there is almost always enough light for you to make out objects on a light-colored deck—even when there is no moon at all—and in clear weather, the stars can be so bright that they cast shadows.

Breaking wave crests often reflect a gentle glow on white sails, but there are occasional still nights so thickly overcast and dark that you literally cannot see your hand in front of your face or make out any trace of a watchmate sitting right beside you. On nights like those, the faint red glow of the compass light is a great comfort.

Coastal navigation is often easier at night than it is by day because it's easy to locate and identify a light by the number of times it flashes. However, because of the confusion of bright shore lights and navigation lights, don't try to enter a strange port at night until you've had considerable experience. Even entering your own port, which you know so well by daylight, can be a harrowing experience the first time you try it in the dark.

There are some areas where boating at night is not a good

N

idea. In Puget Sound in the Pacific Northwest, you could run into a vertical submerged log called a deadhead—you have little chance of spotting one before it's too late. In Maine, where abundant rocks and islets are strewn in swift currents, navigation at night calls for a lot of local knowledge and experience.

Once you get away from land, of course, much of your apprehension will disappear. You will be steering by the stars, getting to know the phases of the moon, learning the names of the planets, and even spotting satellites as they scoot across the horizon. You will feel very close to nature.

See also **Color at Sea; Faint Lights; Navigation Lights**.

Noises in Fog

How sounds and sizes can become strangely distorted

When you're in fog, distant noises mostly sound low and dull; nearer noises are higher and brighter. That's because high-frequency sounds are filtered out over long distances through air, allowing the lower frequencies to predominate.

For instance, nearby thunder crackles and crashes, but faraway thunder rumbles and rolls. The same principle applies to ships' horns and other navigation signals in fog. A loud, high-pitched whistle could indicate another vessel close by, with a chance of imminent collision.

Fog carries sound more effi-ciently than dry air, so even the faintest noises drift for miles. You can never judge distance accurately from the noises you hear in fog because they will probably be distorted in some way.

Size can become distorted too. When visibility in fog is between 30 and 150 yards (about 25 to 140 m), vessels and other objects frequently appear twice their normal size. This illusion effectively doubles the speed of approach and strikes great fear into the heart of cautious mariners.

See also **Fog Types**.

Nonskid Surfaces

Preventing slipping as you move around on slanted decks

To keep your footing on a wet and slanted deck, you need a good nonskid surface. On sailboats, you need the cabintop and cockpit floor to be nonskid, as well as the decks.

Bare wood, especially planked teak, provides an excellent grip, wet or dry, but it becomes lethally slippery if it's varnished or painted. Fiberglass boats normally have a roughened texture or nonskid pattern molded into the gelcoat where needed.

You can apply a special nonskid paint with sand or small plastic beads already mixed into it, or you can paint the deck and then scatter fine sand on it while it's wet. When the paint has dried, gently brush the extra sand off the top and then apply one or two coats of paint over the sand that's stuck down. If the sand feels too sharp to the touch, scour it gently with half a brick and paint it again. You can use fine sawdust instead of sand, but it will soak up a lot of paint and become much heavier than a coating of sand.

On metal boats, as well as fiberglass boats whose nonskid texture has worn smooth, you can apply a specially textured plastic deck covering. Simply cut it to shape and glue it down. It's expensive, but it's attractive, easy to work with, and long-lasting.

Nylon Line

Stretching is what makes this plastic rope valuable afloat

Nylon is a synthetic plastic that was marketed after World War II. In fiber form, its stretchability makes it particularly suitable for anchor rodes, mooring lines, and dinghy painters.

Under a 20 percent load, nylon has a working elasticity of about 22 percent, or more than a fifth of its length. This compares with a stretch of about 9 percent in Dacron, another synthetic plastic fiber. Nylon's high stretch enables it to absorb the shocks a boat generates while at anchor—shocks that would otherwise part the line, unseat the anchor, or damage deck cleats or mooring bitts.

Nylon line is strong for its weight, dries quickly, and is not susceptible to rot. It is, however, prone to deterioration if it's constantly exposed to the ultraviolet rays of sunlight.

N

It's too elastic for halyards or sheets, of course, and for the same reason you should avoid it in webbing form for harness tethers or jackstays if possible. Dacron, when available, is the preferred fiber for all these tasks.

If you have odd lengths of nylon aboard for use as shock relievers on a chain anchor rode, be sure to mark them in some way so they don't get mistaken for Dacron—it's not easy to tell the difference just by looking at them.

See also **Plastics**.

Ocean Currents

Winds create two kinds of giant rivers in the sea

There are two kinds of ocean currents: surface (or drift) currents and stream currents. They are much like rivers in the sea, except that their lateral boundaries are not as clearly defined.

A surface current is the result of wind action. A wind blowing steadily from one direction for 12 hours or more creates a surface current with a speed of about 2 percent of the wind's average speed.

A stream current is a surface

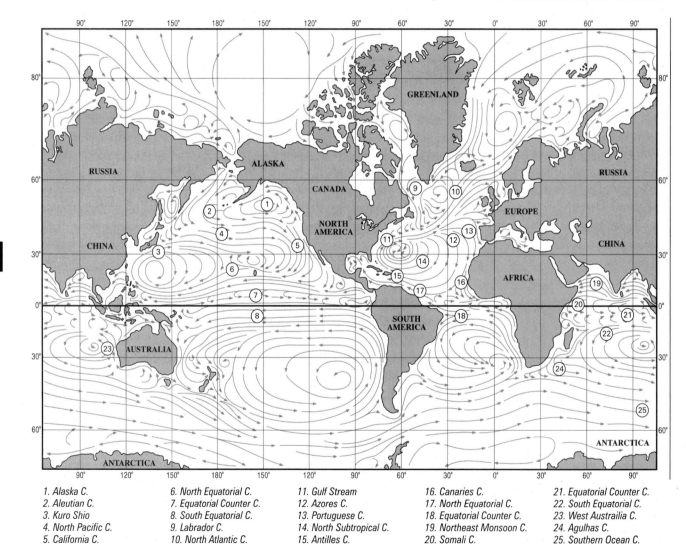

1. Alaska C.
2. Aleutian C.
3. Kuro Shio
4. North Pacific C.
5. California C.
6. North Equatorial C.
7. Equatorial Counter C.
8. South Equatorial C.
9. Labrador C.
10. North Atlantic C.
11. Gulf Stream
12. Azores C.
13. Portuguese C.
14. North Subtropical C.
15. Antilles C.
16. Canaries C.
17. North Equatorial C.
18. Equatorial Counter C.
19. Northeast Monsoon C.
20. Somali C.
21. Equatorial Counter C.
22. South Equatorial C.
23. West Austrailia C.
24. Agulhas C.
25. Southern Ocean C.

The principal currents of the world.

current that has been confined to narrow waters, or one that has been deflected from its original course by the coast or a shallowing seabed.

Currents do not usually flow in exactly the same direction as the wind, however, because of the inertial effects of the Earth's rotation, known as the Coriolis force. In the Northern Hemisphere, the current is deflected to the right; in the Southern Hemisphere, it's deflected to the left.

The amount of deflection varies with latitude, ranging from about 15 degrees to as much as 45 degrees. The nearer the poles, the greater is the deflection. The depth of the water also has an effect: the shallower the water, the greater the deflection.

Ocean currents generally circulate clockwise in the Northern Hemisphere and counterclockwise in the Southern Hemisphere, spurred on by the constant westward push of the trade winds toward the equator. There are exceptions, however, one notable one being the Pacific Equatorial Countercurrent, which runs almost due east to return the vast quantities of water moved west by the Pacific Equatorial Currents to the north and south of it.

Fast currents such as the Mozambique or Agulhas Current, which can reach 4 knots at times, are a source of dangerous seas when strong winds blow against them.

A current is described by its set (the direction *toward* which it flows) and its drift (its speed in knots).

See also **Coriolis Force; Trade Winds**.

Ocean Temperatures, Northern Hemisphere, °F (°C)

Latitude	Atlantic	Pacific	Indian
0 to 10	80 (26.7)	81 (27.2)	82 (27.8)
10 to 20	79 (26.1)	79 (26.1)	82 (27.8)
20 to 30	76 (24.4)	74 (23.3)	79 (26.1)
30 to 40	69 (20.6)	66 (18.9)	—
40 to 50	56 (13.3)	50 (10)	—
50 to 60	48 (8.9)	42 (5.6)	—
60 to 70	42 (5.6)	—	—

Ocean Temperatures, Southern Hemisphere, °F (°C)

Latitude	Atlantic	Pacific	Indian
0 to 10	77 (25)	79 (26.1)	81 (27.2)
10 to 20	74 (23.3)	77 (25)	78 (25.6)
20 to 30	70 (21.1)	71 (21.7)	73 (22.8)
30 to 40	62 (16.7)	62 (16.7)	63 (17.2)
40 to 50	48 (8.9)	52 (11.1)	48 (8.9)
50 to 60	35 (1.7)	41 (5)	35 (1.7)
60 to 70	30 (-1.1)	30 (−1.1)	30 (−1.1)

Ocean Temperatures

Southern oceans are always colder than Northern Hemisphere seas

As a general rule, the ocean waters of the Southern Hemisphere are considerably colder than those in the Northern Hemisphere. The tables above give rough average temperatures for three oceans in both hemispheres at different latitudes.

Ocean Voyaging

Cruising the four seas of the world in small boats

At any given moment, hundreds of small boats up to about 50 feet (15 m) in length are cruising around the world. The overwhelming majority are sailboats, and most of them take three years or more for a circumnavigation.

Statistics provided by the Panama Canal Authority show that 450 yachts up to 50 feet overall passed through the canal in 1998, 515 in 1999, and 432 in 2000. During a circumnavigation, almost all yachts pass through Panama; each year, only a few cruising yachts cross from the Pacific to the Atlantic (or vice versa) by way of Cape Horn.

Sailboats predominate in ocean crossings for several reasons. Powerboats, unless specially designed for long-distance cruising, have difficulty carrying sufficient fuel for an ocean crossing and—whereas the wind is free—fuel costs are considerable. Although cruising sailboats are

O

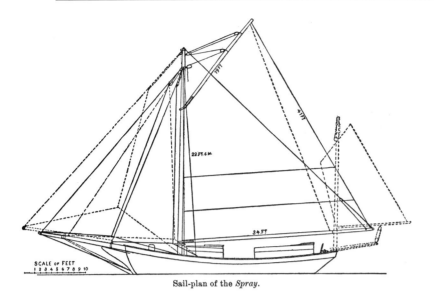

Sail-plan of the *Spray*.

designed to right themselves from a 180-degree capsize, few power-boats would survive a 180-degree rollover without substantial damage to their superstructure, as well as consequent flooding.

The size of your boat is not a reliable indication of her seaworthiness, but a good big boat is safer than a good small boat. Eric Hiscock, the British sailor and author who circumnavigated twice in his 30-foot (9.1 m) *Wanderer III* with his wife Susan, felt that the larger the vessel, the better—provided that management was within the capabilities of her crew and within their financial scope.

In practice, most long voyages have been undertaken by couples, and most have found that a boat of about 30 to 35 feet (9 to 10.7 m) overall, with moderate to heavy displacement, is about right for their physical capabilities. In recent years, spurred in part by labor-saving advances in sail-handling gear, voyaging boats are getting bigger, and the average length might now be 40 to 45 feet (12 to 14 m).

The Hiscocks moved to bigger boats in later years, and found them to be more trouble than they had imagined. They never felt so much in control as they did with *Wanderer III*, nor had so much confidence in their ability to handle emergencies themselves.

The basic needs of an ocean-going sailboat are seaworthiness, comfort, self-steering ability, and speed. Seaworthiness includes stability and self-righting characteristics, as well as brute strength. It also includes the ability to punch your way off a lee shore in

Joshua Slocum wrote the captivating book Sailing Alone Around the World, *which tells of his voyage in the 37-foot* Spray *in 1895–98. The book has been continuously in print ever since. The solid lines show* Spray's *sail plan at the start of the voyage; the dashed lines show her sail plan when she returned to Massachusetts.*

heavy weather and the ability to heave to, lie ahull, or run off safely.

See also **Circumnavigation; Seaworthiness**.

Ocean Water

Looking at the salts and elements that comprise seawater

"The ocean is the Earth's greatest storehouse of minerals," Rachel Carson wrote in *The Sea Around Us*. "In a single cubic mile of seawater there are, on the average, 166 million tons of dissolved salts, and in all the ocean water of the Earth there are about 50 quadrillion tons."

As you might expect, sodium chloride (NaCl, common salt) is the most abundant salt in the ocean, making up 77.8 percent of the total salts. Magnesium chloride ($MgCl_2$) is next, at 10.9 percent; then magnesium sulfate ($MgSO_4$) at 4.7 percent, calcium sulfate ($CaSO_4$) at 3.6 percent, and potassium sulfate (K_2SO_4) at 2.5 percent. All the other salts combined comprise the last 0.5 percent.

More than 50 of the known elements, including gold, have been identified in seawater. The following list shows the number of grams of various substances in every kilogram (1,000 g) of water at a salinity of 35 parts per thousand: chloride, 19.4; sodium, 10.8; sulfate, 2.70; magnesium, 1.3; calcium, 0.4; potassium, 0.4; bicarbonate, 0.1; bromide, 0.067; strontium, 0.008; boron, 0.004; and fluoride, 0.001.

See also **Drinking Seawater**.

Oil Bags

Calming heavy seas may take much more oil than you think

From ancient times, oil has been used to smooth troubled waters. But there is little evidence of its widespread use by small pleasure boats caught in gales.

Captain John Voss records in his book, *Venturesome Voyages*, that he used oil bags in his 19-foot (5.8 m) waterline *Sea Queen* in near-typhoon conditions, but they seemed to become ineffective as time wore on and the seas became larger. Jean Gau hung an oil bag from the weather shrouds of his 30-foot (9.1 m) ketch, *Atom*, when he was lying ahull in a hurricane, and believed that it contributed to his survival. And William Robinson pumped oil through the forward head when *Varua* was caught in what he called the "ultimate storm."

But few others have even tried oil, possibly because the consensus is that it must be used in considerable quantities if it is to be effective—the average yacht doesn't have the room for drums of heavy oil. Ironically, the smaller the boat, the more oil it would need to carry because of the greater need to subdue the seas.

In his authoritative work, *Heavy Weather Sailing*, British ocean racer and publisher Adlard Coles comments: "There seems little evidence to support the textbook theory that a thin film of oil, seeping slowly from a oil bag will subdue really big breaking seas. Nevertheless, a 2-gallon (7.6 L) drum of heavy oil pumped out the head might be useful as a tem-

porary measure when running into a harbor in very rough weather or crossing a bar, though it would be far safer to remain at sea in deep water."

It is important to keep the slick of oil directly to windward, which may not be possible if the boat is fore-reaching. The ideal situation for its use would be when running dead downwind before heavy seas.

See also **Drogue; Heaving To; Lying Ahull; Running Off**.

Osmosis

See Blisters in GRP.

Outboard Motors

Engineering revolution underway in outboard-motor design

An outboard is a portable motor, usually gasoline-powered, that may be attached to the stern of a boat for propulsion. It is a combined engine, propeller, rudder, and (sometimes) gasoline tank.

There is no record of when the first outboard motor was made, but it is known that the Vulcan Company, in Sweden, was manufacturing transom-mounted motors in 1891. A German outboard motor designed by Gottfried Daimler was exhibited at the 1893 Chicago World's Fair. The British manufacturer, Watamota, followed suit in about 1895. The first U.S.-made model came along in 1896; it was powered by either gasoline or kerosene, but found little favor

O

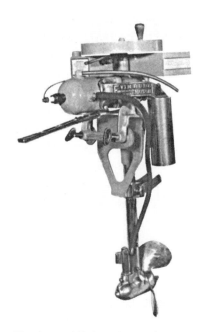

The famed Evinrude rowboat motor, circa 1912, had a wooden "knuckle buster" starting knob on the flywheel. Note the rubber water tube. The steering arm moved only the lower unit assembly, not the powerhead.

among boaters. These motors used a long inclined shaft angling downward into the water some distance aft of the transom.

According to Dave Gerr, a New York naval architect, it was most likely Cameron B. Waterman, a lawyer from Spruce Harbor, Michigan, who invented the first truly modern outboard in 1906, with the help of George Thrall, who ran a nearby boiler factory. Waterman's breakthrough was to make the engine's driveshaft vertical, and have the propeller coming off at right angles at the end of it. The Waterman Porto had one cylinder, produced 2 hp, and weighed 40 pounds (18 kg). By 1917, about 30,000 Waterman Porto outboard motors had been sold.

Another pioneer who started building transom motors soon after Waterman was Ole Evinrude, whose name still appears on outboards to this day. Both he and Waterman introduced horizontal flywheels in place of the early vertical ones, and the modern outboard was born.

Until recent years, almost all outboards operated on a two-stroke combustion cycle. They are simple, compact, relatively inexpensive, and produce a good ratio of power for their weight. The problem with two-stroke engines is that because the intake and exhaust ports are partially open at the same time, some of the gasoline-oil fuel mixture passes through the motor unburned into the water. Simple two-stroke outboards are now recognized as a source of environmental pollution, and federal and state laws have called for remedial action.

The next revolution in outboards, therefore, is in engineering design to make them burn cleaner and more efficient. Manufacturers are following several different paths, all of which have pros and cons.

Four-stroke engines run cleanly and quietly and use far less fuel than traditional two-strokes, but they need valves and are, therefore, heavier, more complicated, and more expensive to buy and repair.

Oil-injected two-strokes use less oil in the fuel mixture and cause less pollution in the water, but they are more complicated than ordinary two-strokes and there is little difference in their exhaust-gas pollution.

Fuel-injected two-strokes, the latest development, cause very little pollution. They use fuel economically, and are quiet and compact. Some are not yet as reliable as they should be (although time and usage will presumably cure that) and, once again, they are more expensive and more complicated than conventional two-strokes.

See also **Drowned Outboard Motors; Twin Screws**.

Overhangs

They're elegant and fast but not basically seaworthy

An overhang is that part of a hull that extends above and past the waterline at the stern or bow. Powerboats mostly have modest overhangs at the bow and often none at the stern. Sailboats are more likely to have overhangs because the action of heeling immerses some of the overhang, temporarily lengthening the amount of hull in the water, thereby raising the boat's potential top speed.

Long overhangs look elegant on a sailboat, but in any kind of a sea they can cause pounding at the bow and slamming at the stern. In quartering seas, particularly, a long overhang hit by an overtaking wave may slew a boat around into a dangerous broaching position.

Excessively long overhangs like those found on some older sailboat racing classes are best suited to calm water. For seagoing boats, short overhangs are safer, even to the point of plumb bows and sterns with no overhang at all.

See also **Yacht Design**.

O

Overloading

Knowing how much you can carry helps avoid accidents

It's easier to overload a small boat than a large one, but even a modest amount of overloading can seriously affect the seaworthiness of a larger craft.

Most drownings attributable to overloading occur in dinghies, yacht tenders, and fishing skiffs. For boats less than 20 feet (6 m) in length, this simple rule of thumb applies: Maximum number of persons on board equals length (overall, in feet) times beam (overall, in feet) divided by 15. In metric terms, that's length (overall, in meters) times beam (overall, in meters) divided by 1.4.

Overloading a larger vessel may affect its stability by raising the center of gravity and reducing the safety margin of flotation. In general, however, you can safely sink a boat of average displacement below its design waterline by an amount equal to 1 percent of the waterline length.

See also **Center of Gravity**; **Dinghy Capacities**; **Stability**.

P

Paint Amounts

Calculating areas and estimating your paint needs

Estimate how much paint you need from the old rule of thumb that said 1 gallon of enamel paint or varnish would cover 500 square feet—or 1 liter would cover about 12 square meters.

Similarly, 1 gallon of antifouling paint would cover 350 to 400 square feet, and 1 liter would cover about 9 square meters. That's the theory. The practice might differ somewhat because modern paint finishes vary greatly in their covering capacity, and most cover less than the enamels of a generation ago. A gallon of two-part polyurethane, for example, might cover 200 to 250 square feet. Refer to the manufacturers' cans or brochures for a more exact idea of the paint required for a certain area.

You can, however, easily estimate the area to be painted. In the following formula, if you measure in feet, the answer will be in square feet; meters give square meters:

$$\text{area of both topsides down to waterline} = (\text{length overall} + \text{beam}) \times 2 \times \text{average freeboard}$$
$$\text{area of bottom of hull to waterline} = \text{waterline} \times \text{beam} \times \text{draft}$$

For heavy-displacement, full-keel cruising boats, use 75 percent of the result. For light-displacement, fin-keel boats, use 50 percent.

$$\text{deck area} = \text{length overall} \times \text{beam} \times 0.75$$

Subtract area of cockpit and deck structures.

$$\text{Spar area} = \text{length overall} \times 2.5 \times \text{average diameter}$$

See also **Bottom Painting**; **Paints**; **Painting Time**.

Painting Time

The best time for painting and when to break the rules

A lot of painting on boats has to be done outside in the open atmosphere in less-than-ideal conditions, so it pays to read the instructions on the paint can about when you can and can't do it.

In general, however, it's safe to paint or varnish between 10 A.M. and 4 P.M. You can bend the rules if you know them, but be aware that the rules vary with the different kinds of "protective coating systems." So whether you've got the type of paint that dries by solvent evaporation or the type that hardens by chemical cross-linking of molecules, first read the instructions on the can of paint. The following general principles apply to almost all kinds of paint or varnish:

The work to be covered must be smooth, clean, dry, and free of anything that is likely to prevent paint from sticking to it, including wax and old flaking paint. You must also have prepared it correctly with primer, filler, and undercoat, if

P

necessary. Most of the work of painting is in the preparation.

The ambient temperature must be reasonably mild—somewhere between 60°F and 80°F (16°C to 27°C)—so that your paint can transform itself from a liquid to a solid without getting so hot that it forms blisters or so cold that it freezes or dries with a dull surface.

It's possible to paint when it's hotter or colder, but you need some experience before you try it to know what the limits are. Starting at 10 A.M. gives the boat a chance to warm up and evaporate the dew. Stopping at 4 P.M. gives the paint a chance to skin over before dew starts to form again. If water comes in contact with newly applied paint, it will probably affect its looks and possibly its integrity.

The 10-to-4 rule is, of course, just for beginners, but if you're out of practice, it will pay to stick to it. Many factors affect the timing—especially your latitude and the season of the year—but the more experience you gain in painting, the more confident you'll feel about breaking the rule. Incidentally, we're talking about real sun time here, not Daylight Savings Time; so in the summer, make that 11 to 5 instead of 10 to 4.

See also **Paints; Paint Amounts**.

Paints

Ask for manufacturer's instructions before starting

Most modern paints are parts of what manufacturers like to call "protective coating systems," which include compatible fillers, putties, fairing compounds, thinners, and undercoats.

If you're planning anything more than a touch-up, ask for the full manufacturer's directions because, all too often, one kind of paint will not stick to another's undercoat, even if it's made by the same manufacturer.

Marine paints can be divided into two groups: topside paints and bottom paints.

There are at least four major kinds of topside paint used on boats, each with its own characteristics and applications:

Alkyd enamel. Marine alkyd enamels are nothing more than formulations of oil-based exterior house paint. On boats, this type of paint is great for interior spaces and makes an inexpensive deck paint. Thirty years ago, alkyd enamel was also the leading choice for topside paint, and it still does the job. But for a fiberglass hull, which—unlike a wooden hull with its constant working—provides a stable platform for a long-lasting paint, polyurethane provides a longer life and a higher gloss.

Single-part polyurethane. This is a urethane-modified alkyd enamel, a compromise between alkyd enamel and true polyurethane, which offers good gloss, three- to five-season longevity, and moderate ease of application.

Two-part linear polyurethane (LPU). This is the best choice for high gloss and a long life, but it's a problem to apply. A professional polyurethane job is sprayed—not recommended for the amateur even if wearing the requisite respirator. Several brands are formulated for application with roller and brush; done correctly, the result is almost indistinguishable from a spray coating. Ideally, it's a two-person job: one to roll on the paint with vertical strokes, the other following behind with a paintbrush to tip the paint with horizontal strokes. As always with marine coatings, preparation is the key to success. The primer will be proprietary to the topcoat.

Epoxy. Epoxy is sometimes used as a primer over porous or crazed gelcoat under a topcoat of marine alkyd enamel, but its high susceptibility to ultraviolet degradation renders it unsuitable as a topcoat.

Bottom paints are mostly antifouling paints; that is, they contain a compound to deter or prevent the growth of marine organisms, such as weed and barnacles, that would slow the progress of a boat or damage the hull surface. There are at least four common types of bottom paint: ablative, sloughing, modified epoxy, and vinyl, all of which usually contain a copper biocide. Teflon paint has no biocidal properties, and is used on racing craft removed from the water after use. Bottom paints may be incompatible, too, so you must find out what type of paint is on your boat's bottom before you paint over it.

See also **Bottom Painting; Paint Amounts; Painting Time; Polyurethane Paint**.

Pan-Pan Calls

Asking for help or warning that you're in difficulty

A system of priorities in marine radio communication has been established to ensure that the three most important types of messages take precedence. They are preceded by the words *Mayday*, *Pan-Pan*, and *Sécurité*. Of these, Pan-Pan is probably the least understood by amateur sailors.

Mayday refers to distress messages and Sécurité refers to details regarding nautical hazards and the safety of navigation in a given area, or it may constitute general warnings about bad weather. Pan-Pan (repeated three times) indicates that an urgent message is about to follow. However, different people have different ideas about what constitutes urgency. To avoid clogging the airwaves with frivolous Pan-Pan calls from boaters, urgent messages are restricted to those concerning the safety of your boat or someone on board. They also apply to the safety of someone you might spot in the water.

For example, you could put out a Pan-Pan call on channel 16 VHF if your engine broke down and a current were sweeping you toward some rocks a few miles away. At the present time, your situation would not warrant a distress call, for a Mayday indicates *immediate* danger, whereas a Pan-Pan call would alert the authorities that a rescue effort might be required in an hour or two. You would then keep in touch on a working channel and periodically inform them of your situation, as mutually arranged.

If you found yourself in dense fog in a narrow channel and you heard a large ship approaching, you could put out a Pan-Pan call identifying yourself and giving your position.

You could also instigate a Pan-Pan call for medical advice if a person on board fell ill or suffered a non-life-threatening injury. You could receive instructions on which medication in the first-aid kit to use, and so forth. Of course, if immediate assistance were required, you would preface your call with a Mayday instead.

A final word: the standard instruction is to pronounce the urgency tag as *Pahn-Pahn*.

See also **Calling for Help; Distress Signals; Mayday Calls.**

Passages, Gangways

Figuring out how narrow you can make a passage down below

Boat designers and amateur builders both need to know how narrow they can make doors, entrances, and passageways in the cramped confines of a small yacht. The need is to keep the measurements reasonably tight without inducing claustrophobia; therefore, some rules of thumb have been established over the years. They apply to average-sized people; depending on your size, you may want to make adjustments accordingly.

For passages and doorways, the minimum width down below is 19 inches (about 480 mm). However, at that width, if you're really broad shouldered you might have to twist slightly sideways to fit through. If you have the space, passages 24 inches (610 mm) wide are more comfortable.

You can make cutouts below the waist much narrower—usually about 14 inches (about 355 mm) wide. Waist level, incidentally, is arbitrarily understood to be 30 inches (762 mm) above floor level.

See also **Hatches**.

Piloting

The art and science of navigating close to shore

There are two nautical meanings for the word *piloting*. The first is the act of guiding a ship through near-shore hazards by a pilot, a person qualified by reason of being familiar with navigational routes and local dangers. A pilot thus engaged is conducting pilotage.

The second meaning is that of finding a vessel's position and directing her course by means of bearings on land or by buoys and soundings when near land. In other words, piloting is the business of inshore navigation as opposed to the celestial navigation used when out of sight of land.

The basic elements of piloting are direction, distance, and time. With the aid of these three elements, plus soundings, a navigator can secure a positive position fix from bearings of charted objects ashore. Similarly, a dead-reckoning position may be obtained, which—when compared with a fix—will reveal the set and drift of any current affecting the vessel.

See also **Compass Bearings; Dead Reckoning; Fixes; Lines of Position; Tidal Streams.**

Pitchpoling

The most dangerous form of capsize a boat can experience

When a boat is thrown stern over bows into an inverted position, she is said to have pitchpoled. Pitchpoling is the most dangerous way a boat can capsize because of the forces involved and the chances of heavy objects being hurled around at great force on deck and down below.

Pitchpoling is rare, but it usually occurs when a boat is running before winds of gale force or more in heavy seas, and when—after running down the face of a wave at high speed—she buries her bows in the back of the wave ahead. This results in her stern being flung viciously into the air, up and over the stalled bows, until she slams down mercilessly, floating upside down on her deck with the keel pointing up into the air. Sometimes a pitchpoling boat

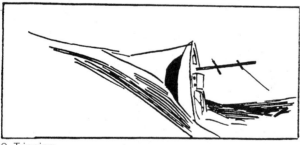
1. Running and towing a hawser.

2. The bow goes in.

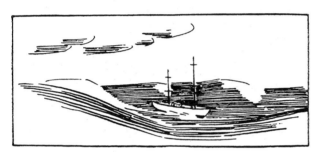
3. Tripping.

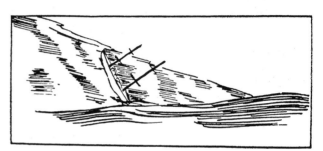
4. Over: falling on to beam ends.

5. Rolling away and facing opposite way.

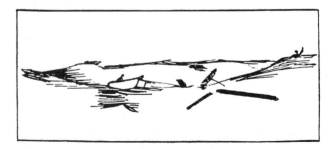
6. Falling away broadside to sea, spars to leeward.

Miles Smeeton sketched this reconstruction of the Tzu Hang *being pitchpoled by a giant wave near Cape Horn for his classic narrative* Once Is Enough.

will twist to one side as she goes over, but she too will end up facing the direction from which she came. Well-documented cases of pitchpoling have been recorded by Miles and Beryl Smeeton in *Tzu Hang*, Erling Tambs in *Sande-fjord*, and others.

Tzu Hang, a 46-foot (14 m) Bermuda ketch, was heading for Cape Horn from the South Pacific when she was caught by a bad storm. While running before it, streaming 60 fathoms of hawser, she was pitchpoled and dismasted by a huge wave. Miles Smeeton's *Once Is Enough* records the ordeal in detail. Beryl Smeeton was washed overboard but managed to swim back to the yacht.

Sandefjord, a 47-foot (14.3 m) gaff ketch designed and built by Colin Archer, was on her way to Cape Town, South Africa, under the command of her Norwegian owner, Erling Tambs, when she encountered a storm and ran off before it under a double-reefed

mainsail only. The seas were so heavy that she needed two men at the helm to control her. An extra-steep sea lifted her stern high into the air; her bow dived deeply into the back of the swell ahead. *Sande-fjord* turned end over end, losing one man and her mizzenmast.

The standard procedure to avoid pitchpoling is to tow drogues to slow the boat and prevent her from getting out of control while surfing down the face of a wave—when that no longer seems safe, start scudding.

See also **Capsize**; **Drogue**; **Running Off**; **Scudding**.

Planing

Skimming the surface of the water for increased speed

There are two basic hull types: planing and nonplaning. When a boat seems to leap out of the water and skim along the surface,

she is planing. You need a lot of power and a fairly flat bottom to do that. Nonplaning boats are mostly known as displacement boats because they displace their own weight of water all the time they're moving. A planing boat displaces less than its own weight of water because it's getting dynamic lift from the bottom of the hull.

Most sailing monohulls are displacement boats. They have keels that protrude down into the water, and curved hulls. As they move forward, they push water out of the way and make a wave. When they reach the maximum speed for their hull length, the wave starts at the bow, dips in the center of the boat, and rises up again at the stern. But they don't have the power or the dynamic lift to rise over their own bow wave and start skimming over the water, as a planing hull can. Thus, a displacement hull is restricted to the speed of the wave it

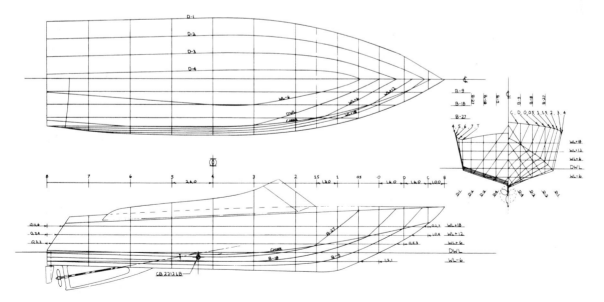

This powerboat design by naval architect Dave Gerr shows a V bottom with shallower deadrise aft for planing and a deeper V forward to reduce pounding in waves.

sits in; the maximum speed of a wave in knots is about 1.34 times the square root of its length, from peak to peak, in feet.

Planing hulls (including those of small centerboard sailing dinghies) have the power to push uphill over their bow waves, and escape the wave trap of the displacement boats. As soon as they flatten out on the other side of the bow wave, they experience a great increase in speed. In fact, their top speed is dependent mainly on the power available—it's the power-to-weight ratio that counts.

For example, a planing powerboat hull should achieve 25 knots when the total weight of the boat, fuel, crew, stores, and everything else equals 40 pounds for every 1 hp delivered to the propeller. If you change that 40:1 ratio to 10:1—that is, if you supply 1 hp for every 10 pounds—the speed increases to 50 knots.

A hull trim angle of about 2 to 4 degrees (bows up from the horizontal) minimizes resistance when planing.

See also **Bilge; Chines; Deadrise; Displacement Ratio; Hull Shapes; Hull Trim; Powerboat Engines**.

Planking

Forming the outer skin of traditional wooden boats

Planking is the collective name for the planks that are joined to each other and to the frames to form the hull and decks of a wooden boat. Several forms of planking were used for small boats in the traditional days of wooden boatbuilding, the following being the most common:

- Carvel planking, in which the ends and sides of the planks were butted to each other to form a smooth outer surface. The seams were filled with caulking cotton and stopped with filling compound.
- Lapstrake or clinker planking, made famous by the Viking long ships, in which each plank slightly overlapped the one below it. This provided great strength with light framing, and no caulking was needed after the wood had absorbed water and swollen.
- Double diagonal planking, consisting of two or more layers of planking laid at angles to one another. The inner planking might be laid from keel to gunwale, for example, and the outer planking from bow to stern. Unbleached calico, well oiled or varnished, was often inserted between the skins; the result was a strong light hull.
- Strip planking, in which thin pliable strips of wood, almost square in section, were laid on top of each other and edge-nailed and glued in place. It made a strong hull without open seams and needed only light frames.
- Marine plywood sheets, which were cut to the shape of the hull and decks and fastened to the frames. This was strong, light, and easy for amateur builders. The glue in the layers of plywood also prevented deep penetration by wood-boring mollusks.

Modern wooden planking is likely to be slightly smaller in section because additional strength is gained by sheathing it in fiberglass or other structural materials soaked in epoxy resin to make a

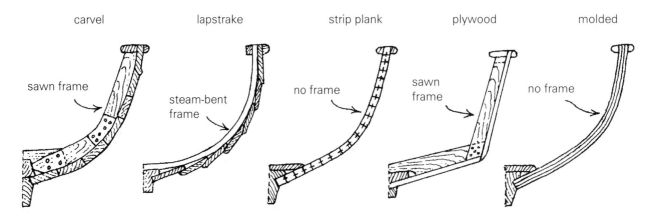

Sectional views of several planking types for wooden boats.

carvel   lapstrake   strip plank   plywood   molded

sawn frame

steam-bent frame

no frame

sawn frame

no frame

strong, light wood-epoxy composite. With epoxy to prevent wood from rotting and to unite many strips of wood in a one-piece, or monocoque, structure, wooden boat building is very much with us, although significantly transformed.

See also **Wooden Hulls**.

Plankton

Investigating the unseen riches of the deep ocean

One of the greatest wonders of the sea is the amount of life it sustains, most of which goes unobserved as we plow our way over it. William Beebe, the ocean scientist, explorer, and writer, asserted in 1927 that "shipwrecked men in an open boat, if their lot is cast on waters rich in plankton, need never starve to death if they can manage to drag an old shirt, net fashion, through the water at night. The great percentage of crustaceans makes plankton a rich, nourishing food, even raw."

Beebe once undertook the laborious task of counting the number of tiny creatures he caught in a net. Following is his account, from *The Arcturus Adventure*: "One dark, moonless evening I put out a silk surface net, the

Examples of microphytoplankton (top), microzooplankton (bottom), and macro- and micro-zooplankton (next page), all to different scales. The copepod (#6 in the drawing on the next page), at about 4 mm long, is some 40 times as long as a diatom (#5 in the top drawing).

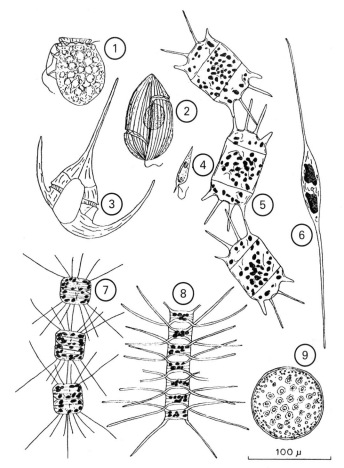

Examples of microphytoplankton: dinoflagellates [Dinophysis (1), Gyrodinium (2), Ceratium (3), Prorocentrum (4)], diatoms [Biddulphia (5), Nitzschia (6), Thalassiosira (7), Chaetoceros (8), Coscinodiscus (9)].

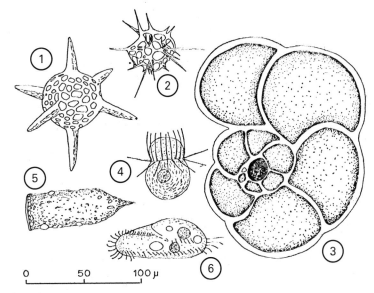

Examples of microzooplankton: radiolarians [Hexastylus (1), Plectacantha (2)], foraminiferan [Pulvinulina (3)], ciliates [Mesodinium (4), Tintinnopsis (5), Amphisia (6)].

P

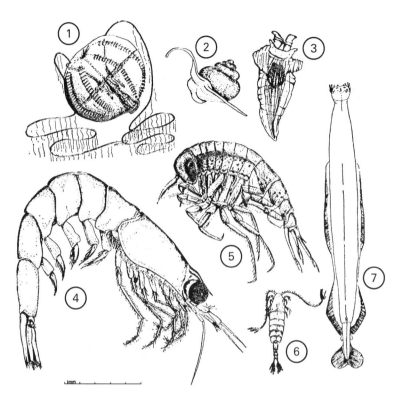

Examples of macro- and mega-zooplankton: ctenophore [Pleurobrachia (1)], mollusc pteropods [Limacina (2), Clione (3)], euphausiid [Thysanoessa (4)], amphipod [Parathemisto (5)], copepod [Calanus (6)], chaetognath [Sagitta (7)].

mouth of which was round about a yard in diameter. At the farther end of the net a quart preserve jar was tied to receive and hold any small creatures which might be caught as the net was drawn slowly along the surface of the water. This was done at the speed of 2 knots and kept up for the duration of 1 hour.

"When drawn in, the net sagged heavily and we poured out an overflowing mass of rich pink jelly into a flat white tray. This I weighed carefully and then took, as exactly as possible, a one-hundred-and-fiftieth portion.

"I began to go over this but soon became discouraged, and again divided it and set to work on one sixth of the fraction on which I had first started."

After many hours of eye-straining counting under the microscope, Beebe conservatively estimated his $1/150$ part of the hour-long plankton haul at 271,080 individuals.

"If we multiply this by 150, we get 40,662,000 individuals . . . a very conservative estimate," Beebe added.

Beebe caught his plankton at the surface on a dark night. He repeated the experiment in full daylight and caught only about 1,000 creatures instead of 40 million. "Plankton will have nothing of the sun or even of moonlight," he observed. Indeed, the word *plankton* comes from the Greek *planktos*, or wandering, and refers in small part to the creatures' habit of rising and falling in the ocean

in response to darkness and light (and in greater part to the fact that they drift with the currents).

The "individuals" Beebe was counting were members of the zooplankton: slightly mobile animals that spend all or part of their lives adrift in the water, and which include tiny crustaceans, swimming mollusks, jellyfish, and the larval forms of many bottom-dwelling worms, crustaceans, snails, and bivalves. Most zooplankton range in size from less than a millimeter to several millimeters. They are the herbivores of the sea, and two kinds in particular—copepods and euphausiids—are basic to the marine food chain. Euphausiids include the krill sought after by baleen whales.

Beebe would have had phytoplankton in his net as well, but these photosynthesizing microalgae—the primary producers on which all ocean life depends—are probably too tiny to have captured his attention. A single-celled diatom, for example, is typically a tenth of a millimeter in diameter, although multicelled chains can make a thread several millimeters long. Phytoplankton, like all plants, needs nutrients as well as light to grow, and that is why nutrient-rich coastal waters and high-latitude waters that turn over seasonally (when surface waters cool and sink, bringing nutrient-laden deep water to the surface) offer the highest concentrations of phytoplankton and zooplankton and thus the richest fisheries.

P

Plastics

Major categories of plastics used in modern boatbuilding

Widespread use of plastic in pleasure boats during the last 50 years has made boats cheaper, more numerous, and practically indestructible. In harbors where a few wooden boats once bobbed gracefully at moorings, there are now huge marinas cramming hundreds of plastic boats into congested berths.

Twenty or more forms of plastic are used in modern boatbuilding, many combined with materials such as glass or carbon fibers for strength and flexibility. Following are some of the major categories:

- acetals: resilient and tough; high melting point; used in water pumps, through-hull fittings, and interior panels
- acrylics: clear and resistant to sunlight; used in port lights, windshields, dodgers, and paint
- alkyds: form tough skins in paint and varnish; make good electrical insulation
- aminos: very scratch-resistant and heatproof; melamine and urea are examples; used for countertops and tableware
- epoxies: tough, gap-filling adhesives; form high-grade laminates with glassfiber and other materials; used extensively in paints and barrier coats, but adversely affected by sun
- fluorocarbons: very slippery, they eliminate much friction; used in engines, blocks, and

as insulating material to prevent galvanic action between different metals
- nylons: very strong, light, but stretchy; used for light-weather sails, anchor rodes, chocks, and bushings
- polycarbonates: tough, stable, and resistant to chemicals; used in windows, pumps, and engines
- polyesters: the resins mixed with fine glass fibers, most commonly used to build boat hulls, and known as fiberglass or glass-reinforced plastic (GRP); also the basis of Dacron fibers for rope and sails that are more stable than nylon but not quite as strong
- polyolefins: best known are polyethylene and polypropylene; very light and strong; used for floating ropes, fuel and water tanks, fenders, and galleyware; adversely affected by sunlight
- polystyrenes: very light; used for flotation, fenders, and insulating and packing material; adversely affected by sunlight
- polyurethanes: best known as tough, flexible sealant-adhesives; also form ultradurable and glossy paints, as well as flotation material and cushions
- silicones: form long-lasting flexible gaskets and bedding for port lights and deck fittings; also used as lubricants and to waterproof fabrics
- vinyls: expensive but very waterproof resin; often used on hulls below the waterline to discourage osmosis; ubiquitous as surface coverings, in-

flatable boats, rain gear, water hoses, paint, and so on

Plow Anchors

Popular modern anchors use an old idea from the farm

Plow anchors are the standard by which other anchors are judged. As the name implies, they are shaped like a farmer's plow, with a long shank ending in two curved flukes. They perform well in sand, gravel, rocks, and coral, but not so well in soft mud or clay, where their smaller surface area may not provide adequate resistance.

The Laughlin plow was an early American model, but the three most popular makes now are the C.Q.R., the Delta, and the Bruce. All stow well in a bow roller, which is just as well because they're very awkward to stow anywhere else.

The C.Q.R. (a poor pun on the word *secure*) is made of hand-forged steel and has a lifetime warranty against breakage. It features a hinged shank; therefore, it will not be unseated by small changes in the direction of pull.

The Delta, a newer design, lacks the hinged neck of the C.Q.R. and is less expensive. It is otherwise very similar and may be slightly superior in holding power. It will launch itself from a bow roller as soon as you release tension on the rode, and its weighted tip makes it roll over into the dig-in position as soon as it hits the bottom.

The Bruce is a modified plow that is more of a winged scoop.

P

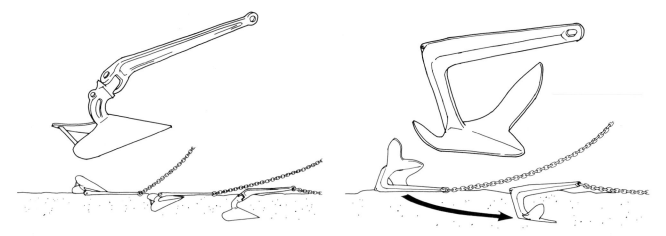

The C.Q.R. (left) *and Bruce* (right) *are both plow anchors.*

Like the other two, it has a solid reputation among cruising sailors. It is simple, rugged, and has the ability to set itself quickly, usually within two shank lengths. It, too, stows well in a bow roller, and a small one fits neatly over a corner of a stern pulpit.

See also **Anchors, Anchoring; Anchor Types**.

Plunging Breakers

Avoiding the dangers of rolling white water at sea

There are two types of breaking waves most commonly associated with heavy weather at sea: spilling and plunging. Of the two, plunging breakers are by far the more dangerous.

Either kind of breaking wave can capsize a small boat, however. Any wave with a height equal to 55 percent of a typical boat's overall length has the potential to capsize her.

If you're caught out in bad weather at sea, the standard advice is to avoid breaking waves or, if you can't, to meet them end-on,

because it's much more difficult to capsize a boat end over end than it is to roll her over sideways. It's not always possible to act on such advice, however, and often the boat must be left to look after herself.

Breakers are formed when the wind pumps too much energy into a wave system in too short a time; the crest of the wave must get rid of excess energy by breaking, or spilling over. The same thing happens when a strong current flows against the wind and the seas are heaped up unnaturally steeply, or when the bottom of a wave hits shallows and is slowed down. It's physically impossible for a wave to maintain a stable form when its face exceeds a steepness ratio of 1:7.

The crest of a wave reaching steeply shelving land can spill over suddenly and with great energy, forming the thunderous plunging breakers we call surf. Or, in deep water, the crest can topple over and pour more gently down the face of the wave, forming a spilling breaker. Luckily, spilling breakers are far more

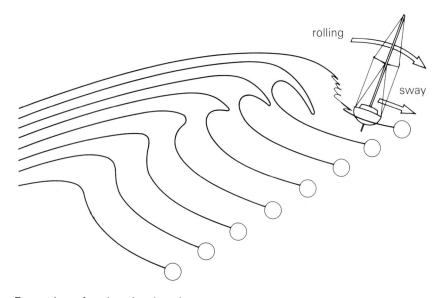

Formation of a plunging breaker.

common than plunging breakers on the open ocean.

The reason plunging breakers are so dangerous is that the speed of the water in what is known as the jet can be as much as four times that of the advancing wave. A boat hit by solid water traveling at such a speed must be very strong to survive without damage. Plunging breakers are common in areas where tidal streams or ocean currents meet sudden gales from the opposite direction. Even fairly small ones—known as overfalls and caused by currents running over inequalities in the seabed—are dangerous to small boats. When you see overfalls marked on the chart, take the warning seriously.

See also **Capsize; Drogue: Pitchpoling; Waves in Gales.**

Polypropylene

Floating line that avoids propeller wraps, stays light

Polypropylene rope is made from artificial plastic fibers. It's a member of the polyolefin family, and a close relative of polyethylene. Its claim to fame is twofold: it's light and it floats. For these reasons, it's popular with water-skiers.

Polypropylene is supplied in several layups, including a conventional twisted three-strand and a 12-strand single-braid line that is often used for dinghy mainsheets because it is soft, light, and renders through blocks without kinking.

It is not used for halyards or headsail sheets, however, because it abrades and is not very strong

—only about 60 percent as strong as Dacron. Some people who have trouble remembering to take in the dinghy painter when they're backing up their boats use polypropylene because it floats on the surface and is not as likely to foul the propeller. Because it does not absorb water, polypropylene always retains its lightness and comes out of the water almost dry.

On the other hand, polypropylene is slippery and does not retain knots well. It is weaker than most other lines of comparable diameter and it's badly affected by sunlight, which turns it brittle and causes it to lose strength.

See also **Rope Strength.**

Polyurethane Paint

Rescuing a shabby hull with a miracle paint job

There is really only one kind of paint to refurbish the gelcoat topsides of a fiberglass boat that have become scuffed and chalky with the passage of the years, and that's two-part polyurethane. No other paint approaches it for brilliance, hardness, and durability. You can expect it to last at least five years in prime condition, and probably much longer.

At least one big marine hardware store states in its catalog that the manufacturers of twin-pack polyurethane recommend that it be applied by professionals only, but that is incorrect information. Some manufacturers go so far as to produce booklets, audiotapes, and videos to promote its use by amateurs.

The marine stores suggest us-

ing a so-called one-part polyurethane instead because it is cheaper and easier to apply (and presumably because they have a good supply in stock). Beware: one-part urethane-modified alkyd enamel is not a *true* polyurethane and does not have the sterling characteristics of its two-part namesake. It behaves more like a high-quality alkyd enamel, at greater expense.

Proper polyurethane comes in two separate cans that must be mixed to start a slow chemical reaction; amateurs should always apply it by brush and/or roller because it is highly toxic when sprayed. The recommended procedure is for two people to apply it, one laying it on quickly with a roller, and the second following immediately behind with a brush to smooth and "tip off" the "orange peel" finish left by the roller. However, many amateurs (including the author) have successfully applied it single-handedly with a brush only.

The trick is to paint fast with horizontal strokes in vertical strips 12 to 18 inches wide, working from gunwale to waterline. The idea is to maintain a wet edge at all times for the next strip to meld with, because the paint starts to set up quickly once it has been applied.

It's of vital importance to adjust the viscosity of this paint so that it is neither so thin that it runs nor so thick that it fails to smooth out the brush marks. Find the exact consistency by testing it on a vertical sheet of clean glass and adding small amounts of recommended thinner until it covers properly.

P

Polyurethane is expensive and it requires more preparation because it emphasizes flaws rather than hiding them, but it will add significant value to your boat, and—with any luck—you'll never have to do it again. As far as color goes, white is the most forgiving; darker colors look even more spectacular, but they make spectacles of all your tiny mistakes, too.

See also **Paints**.

Pooping Seas

Slowing down to avoid the big waves that break on board

The most common definition of pooping is "a sea coming over the stern of a vessel." By that definition, however, ocean racing yachts are frequently pooped when they're running downwind in gale conditions. The head of a wave often breaks over the stern and half fills the cockpit.

The late Adlard Coles, a British sailor and author who had 50 years of experience racing and cruising in small sailboats, felt that a true pooping was something far more serious. "It means being overwhelmed aft by a breaking following sea," he wrote in his definitive book, *Heavy Weather Sailing*. "It may result in a broach-to, which throws the yacht on her beam ends as she rounds to the wind. This can be a dangerous thing if it leads to dismasting or structural damage to the yacht. Genuine pooping is a very rare thing indeed, and I have experienced it only twice in a lifetime."

Before the days of self-draining cockpits on sailboats, a pooping could prove very dangerous and allow a lot of water to get below. These days, it is less of a problem as long as no one is washed out of the cockpit, but it remains dangerous to powerboats with large open cockpits or to sailboats without bridge decks and substantial washboards in the main hatchway.

To avoid a pooping while running before the wind in a sailboat, slow the boat down so that following waves will overtake you rather than hold you captive for seconds at a time while you surf along uncontrollably in their grip—during which time your wake encourages them to break on board.

Ideally, some form of drogue should be towed through the water—with or without a small area of sail up forward—to reduce your boat speed to about 4 or 5 knots, or whatever seems best to maintain good steerageway without excessive speed. That gives you the maneuverability to avoid the worst of the plunging breakers rearing up astern.

In extreme conditions, when a storm has been blowing for a considerable period across a large fetch, the drogue might hamper your boat too much, in which case you'll have to let her run free under bare poles, luffing up to take each big wave at an angle of 10 or 20 degrees on the stern.

See also **Drogue**; **Scudding**; **Sea Anchors**; **Towing Drogues**.

Portholes

Fitting storm shutters to beef up inadequate portlights

A porthole is an opening, usually round or oval, in a boat's hull or cabin side that admits light and air. Another name for a porthole is a port.

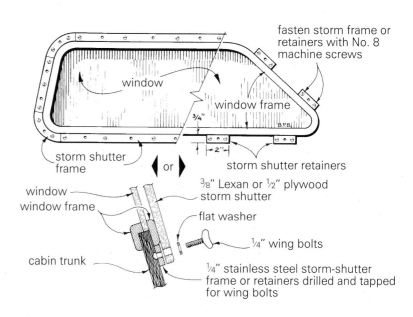

Storm shutters like those shown here should be fitted to all large portlights.

The framed glass used to make the porthole watertight is a portlight if it can be opened or a dead light if it can't. Many portlights on mass-produced boats are made of plastic that is not strong enough for ocean work. If you're planning to go to sea with a boat like that, be sure to fit external storm shutters of Lexan or plywood, especially if the portholes are large.

Portlights are often the source of irritating leaks that dampen bunks and bedding. These leaks are usually the result of aging rubber or neoprene gaskets becoming brittle and inflexible. The answer is to remove them, scraping them out of their grooves with a screwdriver if necessary, and to replace them with new gaskets bedded in rubber cement.

See also **Leaks**.

Powerboat Engines

Below hull speed, a little power does it

It takes surprisingly little engine power to push a boat through the water at modest speeds, but the amount of power you need depends to a large extent on the design of the hull and the speed you seek.

Powerboat hulls fall roughly into three classes: at either end of the spectrum are displacement hulls and planing hulls; in between are semidisplacement (or semiplaning) hulls.

A displacement hull is designed to displace the water it moves through, shoving it outward and downward as it goes. In so doing, the hull creates a wave trough whose two high ends are positioned roughly opposite the ends of the boat when it approaches maximum speed. Below this speed, a displacement hull needs comparatively little power. About 2 hp per ton of displacement is sufficient to propel it at what is known as hull speed—the situation described above—in calm water. The hull speed of a displacement hull (its theoretical top speed) is roughly 1.34 times the square root of its waterline length in feet; the result is in knots. Modern powerboats have considerably more than the minimum power requirement, of course, to compensate for wind resistance and rough water.

A semidisplacement hull with a lot more power can partially rise up over its own bow wave and go faster than the displacement hull, but it can never skim over the surface of the water as a true planing hull does. For example, let's take a displacement hull of 36 feet on the waterline whose twin 120 hp diesels give it a hull speed of 8 knots. A semidisplacement hull of the same size would need almost to double the horsepower to achieve a top speed of about 12.5 knots. Even then it would not be planing cleanly, but rather simply bursting through its own bow wave.

In true planing hulls, the primary factor governing speed is the power-to-weight ratio. With 1 hp delivered to the propeller for every 40 pounds of boat weight (including crew, fuel, and stores, of course), the average planing hull will do 25 knots in calm water. If there's 1 hp for every 10 pounds, the speed increases to 50 knots, and so on.

See also **Bilge**; **Chines**; **Hull Shapes**; **Planing**; **Sailboat Engines**.

Preventers

Acting to stop accidents before they actually happen

Preventers are aptly named: they usually are lengths of rope or wire intelligently placed and artfully attached in the right place at the

P

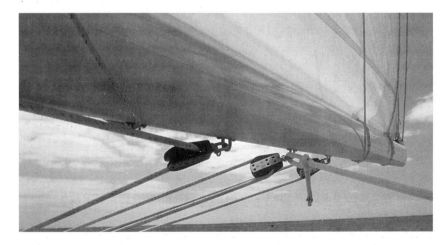

The simplest preventer is simply a line tied to appropriate hardware on the main boom, then led forward to prevent an accidental jibe.

right time to prevent something awful from happening. In other words, an ounce of preventer is worth a pound of cure.

Preventers are, in fact, a measure of a sailor's forethought and ability to anticipate accidents before they happen. A preventer stops the mainsail from jibing accidentally when you're on the run, with all the mayhem that that can cause. A preventer holds a dinghy firmly to the cabintop so that it will not be washed overboard in heavy weather. A pre-venter backs up any other line under great strain so that if it parts, a potential major catastrophe becomes no more than a minor inconvenience.

Some preventers are permanently installed and known by other names. On a sailboat, for example, there's the topping lift, which prevents the boom from falling on your head when the mainsail is lowered. But most preventers are temporary and applied as the need arises; for this purpose, a well-found boat always has available a selection of strong lines of different lengths and diameters.

Privacy

Observing the need for privacy helps preserve peace

It may seem strange to talk about privacy on a small yacht where people necessarily live in each other's pockets, but if you go to sea for a week or more, privacy deserves serious consideration. All crew members need to define their private places and (if necessary) the times they will occupy them.

Professor Michael Stadler, a German sailor and expert in experimental psychology, asserts in *The Psychology of Sailing* that there must be "a place for each member of the crew on board which guarantees this privacy and to which they can retreat as and when they feel like it. A sailor's bunk is naturally the most suitable spot." Stadler goes so far as to recommend that the number of crew members on a long cruise should be determined by the number of fixed berths available. He believes that no one should be expected to share a bunk on a shift basis. It is also vitally important to the success of the voyage that all private areas should be respected by everyone on board, he says.

Territorial behavior defines areas of influence, power, and responsibility. "Traditionally, the captain of the ship is given a cabin to himself, provided, of course, there is such a thing as a single

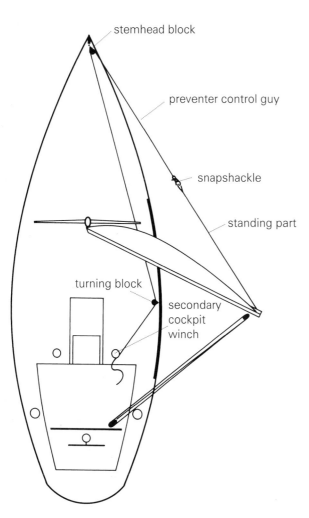

This drawing shows a more elaborate alternative: A rope pendant with stainless steel thimbles at both ends is permanently attached to the end of the main boom and stowed along the boom. In use, the forward end is detached from the boom and shackled to a preventer control guy, which here is led through a block forward, then back to the cockpit.

Labels on drawing:
stemhead block
preventer control guy
snapshackle
standing part
turning block
secondary cockpit winch

P

cabin on board. This is generally considered his due, regardless of his actual needs. Other members of the crew seek to stake out their territory in different ways. Individuals claim, more or less overtly, the galley, the fo'c's'le, sail bags, anchor system, radio system, etc., for their own personal areas of responsibility . . . generally speaking, it is an expression of undefined or unstructured power and authority relations on board."

A skipper contemplating an ocean voyage is advised to consider this subject because territorial behavior can lead to serious conflicts of authority and questions of competence. "A skipper who silently demonstrates in all his actions how capable he is himself, and how incapable the others are, only succeeds in promoting the slow but systematic growth of dissatisfaction on board," Stadler maintains.

Propeller Advances

Turning and slipping is the way propellers create thrust

In the long history of ships, the propeller is a fairly recent invention. The first screw propeller was used in England in 1838, and the first vessel to cross the Atlantic with the aid of a propeller was the British ship *Great Britain* in 1845. The development of propellers has been advancing ever since.

Auxiliary sailboat propellers usually have two or three blades, and most powerboat props have three or four blades. Each blade is twisted so that if it turned in a solid medium, it would bore its

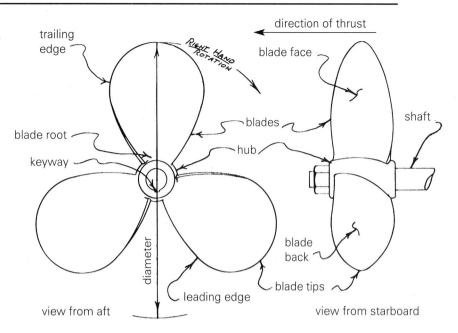

Propeller anatomy.

way through like an auger bit. In water, however, the blades act more like the wings of an airplane in flight, gaining "lift" as they turn, and their rate of advance is reduced by slippage. Interestingly, a propeller with no slip would displace no water and, therefore, generate no thrust. It's similar to the principle that governs the lift generated by a sailboat's keel—if there were no leeway at all, the keel would not generate lift.

The Complete Boating Encyclopedia defines a propeller as "a pump, submerged in the fluid it is pumping. Normal rotation sucks the water from ahead of the propeller, accelerates it, and discharges it astern, creating an opposite reaction that pushes the boat forward."

Two-bladed screws are the most efficient because each blade moves through water that is least disturbed by the passage of the other. But to get the blade area required, the blades must be comparatively long, and often there isn't sufficient clearance between the propeller shaft and the bottom of the hull. Therefore, three or more broader blades of smaller diameter are used instead. Nevertheless, some very fast small powerboats, as well as sailboats seeking to reduce drag under sail, use two-bladed props.

A large-diameter, slow-turning propeller is usually more efficient than a small one turning at high speed, although an exception to this rule is made for boats operating at 35 knots or more. In small craft, "slow-turning" means fewer than 1,000 revolutions per minute (rpm).

The problem for the sailboat is that a big slow-turning propeller creates a substantial amount of detrimental drag when the vessel is under sail alone, so it is usual to compromise with a less efficient, smaller, faster-turning propeller that allows better performance under sail.

P

For a powerboat, a three-bladed prop often produces a higher top speed than a four-blade, but the latter vibrates less and may be more efficient at slow to moderate speeds. With its greater blade area, it may also accelerate better.

The amount of slippage on propellers fitted to different kinds of boats is as follows:

- high-speed powerboats: about 20 percent
- light power cruisers: about 24 percent
- heavy power cruisers: about 26 percent
- auxiliary sailboats: between 40 and 55 percent

See also **Cavitation**; other entries under **Propeller**.

Propeller Drag

There's no consensus on whether or not to lock it

Does a sailboat propeller cause more drag under sail when it's fixed or when it's allowed to rotate? The answer seems to be that there's so little difference, nobody can really tell.

Dave Gerr, a respected New York naval architect and author, asserts: "The simple answer is that a propeller creates less drag when free to rotate." But, he adds, if you can hide a two-bladed propeller from the flow of water by locking it vertically behind a skeg or keel, it produces less drag than when it's rotating freely.

On the other hand, Francis Kinney, an equally well-respected

naval architect, maintained in Skene's *Elements of Yacht Design* that "the shaft should be locked so that the propeller cannot revolve. It has been found that a revolving propeller causes more drag . . . "

Eric Hiscock, a vastly experienced British sailor and author, wrote: "Experiments made by P. Newall Petticrow Ltd. have shown that a two- or three-bladed propeller offers less drag when it is locked than when it is free to spin, and that the drag of a spinning propeller is greatest at about 100 rpm."

Some sailors don't have a choice in this matter; on certain boats, the propeller must be locked under sail because the transmissions will not be lubricated when the engine is not running.

On ocean passages, most sailors lock the shaft for the simple reason that the noise of the racing screw is unacceptable.

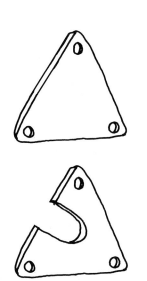

cut two plates from ¼" mild steel

A simple propeller puller.

See also other entries under **Propeller**.

Propeller Facts

More fascinating tidbits about marine propellers

Propellers provide an endless source of discussion for boaters. Following are a few facts to add to the debate:

A right-handed propeller is one whose top half revolves from port to starboard when going ahead; a left-handed propeller works the other way. Most single propellers are right-handed.

On twin-screw installations, one propeller is usually right-handed, the other left-handed, to cancel out "propeller walk." The right-handed propeller is normally the starboard one.

An increase of 1 inch (25 mm) in diameter absorbs more power than an increase of 1 inch

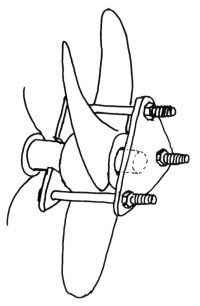

tighten nuts evenly

in pitch, where pitch is the theoretical distance the propeller would advance in one complete revolution without any slippage.

A decrease of 1 inch in diameter is good for an increase of about 300 shaft rpm.

On sailboats, the absolute minimum clearance between the hull and the tips of the propeller blades is 10 percent of the propeller's diameter.

On powerboats, the minimum tip clearance is 20 percent of the propeller's diameter, to reduce vibration.

A propeller is fastened to its shaft with two nuts. Contrary to what you might think, the thinner locknut should be installed on the propeller shaft first, directly against the propeller hub. As the second larger nut is tightened, it assumes the entire load on its own threads.

Boaters in the higher latitudes need smaller propellers. The colder and denser the water, the smaller the propeller needed. The rule, based on a starting temperature of 70°F (21°C), is that normal propeller diameter should be reduced about 1 percent for every 10°F (5.6°C) drop in water temperature.

See also other entries under **Propeller**.

Propeller Fouling

Searching for the magic potion to keep barnacles off

When barnacles and weed grow on a submerged propeller, its efficiency is greatly reduced. Consequently, boaters experiment with all kinds of paints and potions to keep their propellers free of marine growth.

The problem is formidable because no matter what type of coating you put on a propeller, it's likely to be worn off quickly when the screw starts turning in the water. At high revolutions, a propeller experiences considerable stresses, so much so that its surface can become pitted. Nonetheless, boaters keep searching for the answer.

Ironically, most propellers are made of bronze, which contains a large percentage of copper, the basic ingredient in antifouling paint. In theory, then, the propeller itself is biocidal—and it would be in practice, if it were left to itself. Unfortunately, to prevent its gradual erosion through galvanic corrosion, the propeller is almost always furnished with a sacrificial zinc. Although the zinc certainly does a good job of protecting the propeller, it also negates the biocidal properties of the copper. So you are faced with a choice: leave the zinc off the propeller, and the screw will get eaten away slowly, but it will stay clean of barnacles; or protect the propeller with a zinc block and prepare to play host to mollusks and weed.

Many owners cannot resist coating the propeller with something before launching the boat for a season afloat. Some swear by Rutland Liquid Stove & Grill Polish; others use axle grease, paraffin wax, beeswax, or anhydrous lanolin. All are effective for a period, but all eventually wear off. Some racing boats kept in warm waters cover their folding propellers with black plastic bags between outings to keep the barnacles off. A crew member is designated to dive overboard to put the bag on after the boat is moored, and (perhaps more importantly) to take the bag off before the boat tries to go anywhere under power.

Meanwhile, the rest of us keep hoping that someone, some day, will happen upon the magic formula for a biocidal coating that will stick to a propeller through thick and thin.

See also other entries under **Propeller; Zinc Anodes**.

Propeller Options

Different propellers and the reasons for choosing them

Propellers for most pleasure boats are three- or four-bladed, but two-bladed propellers are frequently found on auxiliary sailboats and small outboard motors. Propellers of five to seven blades appear on large motor yachts, where they confer decreased vibration levels in exchange for a higher cost.

A two-bladed propeller is the most efficient for a displacement sailboat, and it causes less drag under sail if it can be aligned vertically in the shelter of the rudderpost. On some boats, a two-bladed propeller causes vibration as the blades pass through the comparatively still water behind the rudderpost and suddenly hit the moving water alongside.

Because two-bladed screws are long and thin, there is often not enough clearance under the hull, so a smaller-diameter three-bladed propeller is used instead.

P

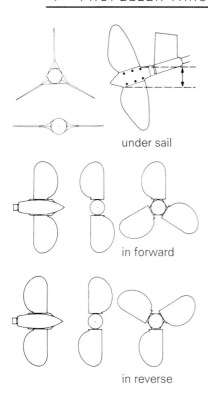

under sail

in forward

in reverse

The Max-Prop propeller feathers to a low-drag shape under sail (top). Under power in forward gear (middle) or reverse (bottom) the blades open to a pitch that matches the throttle setting.

A three-bladed propeller is less prone to vibration, but each blade works in water disturbed by the one before it, so it's slightly less efficient, area for area. Each blade, being shorter and broader, also has a less efficient shape than the high-aspect-ratio blades of a two-bladed propeller.

To change from three blades to two, you'll need a new propeller with a slightly larger diameter and pitch. Multiply your old three-bladed propeller's diameter by 1.05 and its pitch by 1.01 to achieve the same (or improved) performance.

A folding propeller, two- or three-bladed, causes little drag, but is not as efficient as a fixed

propeller. It is more suited to a racing sailboat than to a cruiser because it may not work properly if it is neglected. One barnacle growing in the wrong place can prevent it from opening properly. Folding propellers are sometimes poor performers in reverse gear.

Adjustable-pitch propellers don't need a gearbox or clutch, but the sophisticated gear needed to vary the pitch underway is expensive and prone to malfunction, which is why they're fairly rare.

Automatically feathering propellers, such as the Max-Prop, greatly reduce drag while sailing and are efficient under power, but their detailed engineering makes them too expensive for most small boats.

Self-pitching propellers have proved promising in experiments that showed them capable of adjusting their pitch automatically under power, according to the prevailing conditions. They are fairly simple and cause minimal resistance under sail, but there are still problems to be solved; for example, they seem to take a long time to "bite" in reverse.

A counter-rotating propeller consists of two props, one in front of the other, on a single propeller shaft, rotating in opposite directions. The idea is to cancel the side forces that cause propeller walk and increase efficiency. These props are used on a few stern-drive engines.

See also other entries under **Propeller**.

Propeller Thrust

Diameter and pitch are the main controlling features

The thrust of a propeller depends on its size, the angle of attack of its blades, and the speed at which it spins. By convention, propellers are described by diameter and pitch, in that order. The figures should be punched into the after end of the propeller boss. For example, the figures "12 x 13" indicate a propeller with a 12-inch diameter (305 mm) and a 13-inch pitch (330 mm), which is the distance it would screw itself through a solid block of wood in one complete revolution, if it could.

The diameter of a propeller is governed by its speed of rotation and the power of the engine driving it. For example, a 20 hp engine would drive a 14-inch (356 mm) propeller at about 1,500 rpm. If the propeller had too small a surface area for the power provided, it would overspeed and cavitate at high revolutions, providing little or no thrust.

Pitch is dictated by the propeller's speed of rotation, its percentage of slippage, and the speed required from your boat. For example, a propeller with a pitch of 11 inches (279 mm) and a slippage of 55 percent, working at 1,500 rpm, would drive an auxiliary sailboat at about 6 knots.

If necessary, a propeller shop can alter the pitch of a common bronze propeller as much as 2 inches (51 mm) for a reasonable price. Too high a pitch makes a boat fast in light weather and economical on fuel, but at the expense of extra strain on the en-

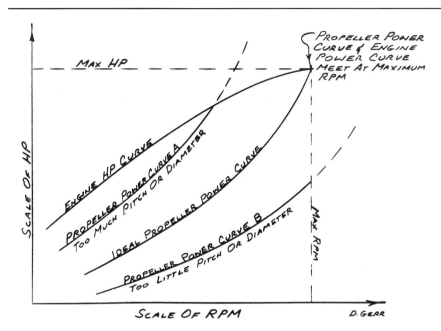

Why the propeller must match the engine. The propeller of curve A has too much pitch, diameter, or both and will overload the engine at higher RPM. The propeller of curve B, on the other hand, lacks the pitch and/or diameter to absorb the engine's full power, and will spin without ever effectively translating engine power into forward thrust.

gine and reduced thrust in headwinds and choppy seas. Less pitch, like low gear on a bicycle, reduces top speed in light weather but is better able to maintain a reasonable speed to windward in heavy weather and eases the load on the engine.

See also **Cavitation**; other entries under **Propeller**.

Propeller Vibration

Curing the problem of vibration with more blades

The most efficient propeller would have one blade because it would be working in water undisturbed by any other blades. But such a propeller would be impossible to balance at speed and would vibrate excessively.

The next most efficient propeller would have two blades, but other than the fact that most boats can't accommodate the large diameter required for effective drive, two-bladed propellers also set up unacceptable vibration when they pass suddenly from free-flowing water to the dead water behind a keel or a skeg.

The answer to vibration is three or more blades to smooth out the thrust. New York naval architect Dave Gerr explains in his book, *The Nature of Boats*: "Vibration is just repeated banging. Every time the blades of your prop pass under your hull or by the strut, they cause a change in pressure that generates a push.

"If the push is strong enough, you get a bang. Lots of bangs equal vibration. If you have a three-bladed prop that turns at

1,000 rpm, then the blades pass under the stern 3,000 times every minute, or 50 times a second—a vibration of 50 cycles per second. Switching to a four-bladed prop, still at 1,000 rpm, would change this to 4,000 times a minute or 66 cycles per second. The more rapid the cycles, the smoother the feel—and the less likely your hull is to resonate (amplify the sound like the body of a guitar) with the vibration."

See also other entries under **Propeller**.

Propeller Walk

Dancing around out of control when trying to go astern

The bottom half of a revolving propeller works in water that is slightly denser than that affecting its top half, so the tendency is for the entire propeller to move sideways—as if it were a wheel on a road taking the stern with it. The larger the propeller, the greater is the effect.

When a boat is moving forward, this sideways walk is easily corrected by turning the rudder a little in the opposite direction; however, when you're in astern gear, strange things can happen. Some boats handle beautifully under power in reverse, but a great many are totally unpredictable.

In theory, a right-handed propeller working in astern gear will walk the stern over to port—that is, to your *right* as you face *aft*. In theory again, you should be able to compensate by putting the rudder over to starboard as you make a stern board. But, in practice, the

P

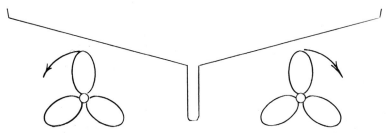

twin-screw rotation viewed from stern

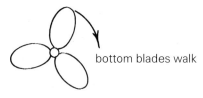

bottom blades walk

right-hand prop walking viewed from stern

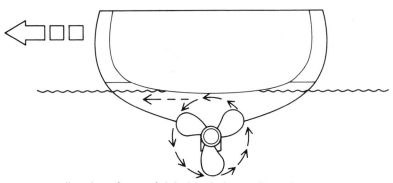

direction of yaw of right-handed propeller going astern

Propellers "walk" in the direction of rotation.

Provisioning

How long you can keep unrefrigerated galley stores

When provisioning a vessel for a long voyage, you'll need to know the shelf life of certain galley stores. Here's how long you can expect various items to keep without refrigeration:

- three months: vegetable oils
- four months: ready-to-eat cereals, sealed; sugar, brown or powdered
- six months: milk, evaporated; nonfat dry or whole milk in a metal container
- nine months: peanut butter, sealed
- one year: baking soda and powder; bouillon products; cereals, uncooked, in paper; cream, instant dry; flour in an airtight container; honey, jam, and syrup; hydrogenated solid shortening; pudding mixes, sealed.
- eighteen months: cocoa, coffee, and instant tea; hard candy and gum; instant potatoes
- two years: granulated sugar; powdered beverages; salt

Canned food gradually changes in flavor, texture, color, and aroma, but will normally be fit to eat for at least a year. Solid-pack meat products and fish preserved in oil last the longest—up to five years. Always discard a can that is rusting, bulging, or damaged—the contents may be deadly.

See also **Ice Boxes**; **Refrigeration**.

stern may go in either direction; even if it does meekly go to port as the laws of mechanics dictate, you may not be able to correct it with the rudder at all. Auxiliary sailboats often "hang" from the propeller and align themselves stern-first into the wind, no matter where you try to steer. Others will do nothing but go around in ever-tightening circles in reverse.

On twin-screw powerboats, propeller walk is tamed by having each propeller turn a different way. On single-screw installations, it used to be fashionable to bring the propeller shaft out of the hull at a slight angle to the centerline to offset the skewed thrust of the propeller. On some powerboats and outboard engines there is a small trim-tab that can be adjusted to offset propeller walk in forward gear.

Propeller walk is individual to each propeller and each boat, so the best you can do is be aware of its effects and plan cautiously for the worst that can happen.

See also other entries under **Propeller**.

Pulling Power

Using skill rather than strength to tighten a line

Sheets on a sailboat generate a considerable pull and need frequent adjustment; hence, the need for cockpit winches to multiply your muscle power. The maximum horizontal pull a person can exert on a line, given a good foothold, is around 150 pounds (68 kg). But when you're pulling downward—on a halyard, for example—your maximum pull equals your body weight.

You can easily tighten a halyard to more than your body weight by swigging it. Swigging (or sweating up) is the old term for putting far greater tension in a halyard that would be possible with a straight pull.

To swig a halyard, hoist it as tightly as you can and then take a half turn around a cleat to prevent its slipping. With one hand, grasp the halyard as high as you can, and pull it out—away from the mast—using your body weight. Then take up the slack you have won in this way by pulling with your other hand as you let the line go back toward the mast. The lower end of the halyard will slip around the cleat and be held in position as you haul tight on it. Repeat the process several times and in a brace of shakes, the halyard will be bar taut.

It requires some dexterity and timing, but it's a valuable skill that comes quickly with practice. On large yachts, two people can work together, one swigging and the other taking up the slack. Swigging can also be used on docklines and anchor lines.

See also **Winches**.

Purchases

Using lines and blocks to provide mechanical advantage

A purchase is any rig of rope and blocks that provides a mechanical advantage. It also refers to the amount of power gained in this manner. The terms *purchase* and *tackle* are synonymous.

When using a tackle to lift heavy weights or exert a strong pull, you need to know how much purchase a certain set of blocks will provide. The rule is that the power gained is equal to the number of lines leading to and from the moving block only, including a line attached to its becket, but excluding a line attached to the load.

It's a fairly simple concept,

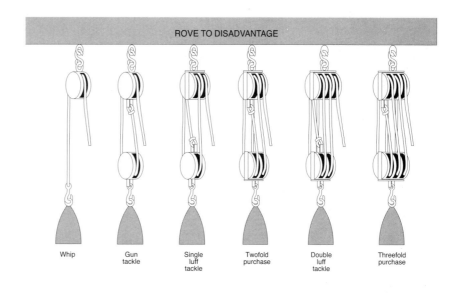

ROVE TO DISADVANTAGE

Whip   Gun tackle   Single luff tackle   Twofold purchase   Double luff tackle   Threefold purchase

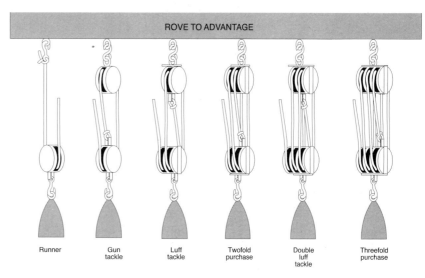

ROVE TO ADVANTAGE

Runner   Gun tackle   Luff tackle   Twofold purchase   Double luff tackle   Threefold purchase

These are the tackle configurations the coast guard might present for identification on the exams for captain's licenses.

P

but many people's minds refuse to grapple with it; perhaps it's more easily understood if you have a tackle in front of you—say, a single block at one end and a double block at the other.

Another way to explain it is to say that the mechanical advantage of a purchase equals the number of parts pulling on the load. In this case, a part means a line leading into or away from the sheave of the moving block or attached to the block's shell. From that, it follows that you get a greater advantage when the part on which you haul is pulling on the weight (i.e., leading from the moving block). Such a tackle is said to be rove to advantage. The emphasis here is all on the moving block for the simple reason that a fixed block adds no power—it merely changes the direction of pull.

Incidentally, if you apply one tackle to the hauling part of another, the total power gained is the power of the first *multiplied by* the power of the second. Thus, a two-part purchase applied to the tail of a four-part purchase results in an eight-part purchase, not a six-part purchase.

There is friction at every sheave the line passes over, of course, so a 3:1 mechanical advantage, for example, as calculated by the previous rule, will actually be a little less. Traditionally, friction is reckoned at one tenth of the load for every sheave. For modern blocks, with improved bearings, that is undoubtedly an excessive figure, but it does automatically provide a margin of safety in your load calculations.

See also **Block and Tackle; Handy-Billy**.

Purifying Water

Making sure your drinking water is safe to consume

There have been a few occasions in my travels when I have had no option but to collect drinking water from a stagnant pool covered in green scum. I was always careful to boil that water for 10 minutes, and after I had filtered out the foreign bodies, it did me no apparent harm.

Sometimes, when you're cruising the more remote regions of the world, sweet fresh water is difficult to find, so you have to learn to purify water from less-than-desirable sources.

Boiling water for 10 minutes kills almost all known harmful organisms, including *Giardia* cysts, but this may be impractical as a long-term solution unless you carry a lot of extra fuel for your stove. Iodine and chlorine tablets, available at drugstores, are reliable and simple to use, although they give the water a foul taste.

You can also use household bleach containing a 5.25 percent concentration of · chlorine, as many world cruisers do. To sterilize 15 gallons (60 L) of fresh water, add one teaspoon of a bleach such as Clorox. The active ingredient, sodium hypochlorite, is toxic to humans as well as to germs, but it does its job swiftly and breaks down about 10 minutes after being exposed to light and air.

Leave the filler cap off the tank for 30 to 60 minutes to be sure the chlorine gas has dissipated into the surrounding air.

Take care when you first taste the purified water, because excess chlorine will burn your mouth and throat. To test it, pour some on the palm of a hand; it should smell no more of chlorine than typical city water from a household faucet.

Filters can remove bacteria, organic chemicals, and protozoa, including *Giardia*, but they can't remove viruses—the most dangerous waterborne organisms that cause fatal diseases, such as polio and hepatitis—unless they also include chemical disinfection.

To clean and flush a water tank, add a cupful (250 mL) of 5.25 percent liquid bleach to every 50 gallons (200 L) of water. After 10 minutes, pump the water through all your faucets and pipes. Save some to pour back down the filler and vent pipes, where lurking microorganisms could reinfect your entire water supply. Then drain the tank and refill it with fresh water.

Chlorine is harmful to stainless steel, so make sure the bleach breaks down quickly by exposing the water's surface to fresh air for at least 10 minutes before sealing the tank. Never add bleach to a water tank connected to a reverse-osmosis watermaker—the bleach will damage it.

See also **Provisioning; Watermakers; Water Needs**.

P

Q

Quadrant

Measuring the angular height of a heavenly body at sea

A quadrant is one of the simplest instruments ever devised for celestial navigation and was well known to the early Arab seafarers. In its crudest form, it's just a 90-degree protractor with a plumb bob hanging from its apex. Its name refers to the fact that it measures one fourth of a circle.

Some of the first quadrants were large, measuring about 4 feet along the sighting arm, and it needed two people to take the altitude of a heavenly body—one to hold and aim the instrument, with the aid of two peepholes, and the other to take the angular reading from the arc.

At best, the quadrant could fix latitude within a degree, or 60 nautical miles, but in bad weather on a heaving deck it was all but impossible to use. According to Dennis Fisher, author of *Latitude Hooks and Azimuth Rings*, Christopher Columbus had a quadrant, but complained in his log about not being able to use it except in a flat calm—and even then it was off by as much as 19 degrees.

Tycho Brahe, the sixteenth-century Danish astronomer, had a quadrant the size of a room to make his chart of the heavens, which Johannes Kepler subsequently used to make his great discoveries.

The quadrant was gradually superseded by the cross-staff and the remarkably efficient backstaff, which was invented by the Englishman John Davis in about 1590 and remained in use, little changed, for more than 200 years. The first double-reflecting octant—the forerunner of the mirrored sextant—appeared around 1730.

See also **Backstaff; Sextant**.

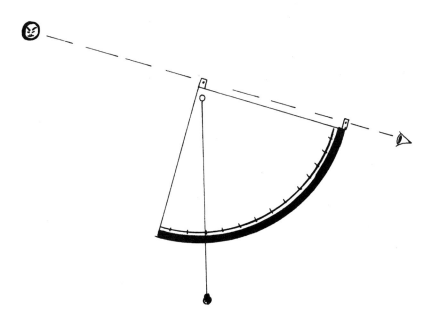

Measuring the angular height, or declination, of the sun or a star with a quadrant.

Quarantine

Dealing with contagious and infectious diseases on board

The word *quarantine* is a corruption of the French *quarantaine*, from *quarante*, meaning 40. In other words, it's a period of 40 days.

In sailing-ship days, that's how long a vessel was forbidden to have contact with the shore if she arrived in port with actual or suspected malignant contagious disease among the people on board. She was sent to an isolated quarantine anchorage, and patients removed from the vessel might be sent to a nearby quarantine hospital.

Today, of course, there is little heard about quarantine in connection with ships, not only because of better disease control and

Q

prevention, but also because few passengers now spend so many months at sea on long passages.

Nevertheless, it is still the correct procedure for a yacht arriving in a foreign port to fly the Q (quarantine) flag of the international code from her port spreader. It's a plain yellow rectangle that signifies "My vessel is healthy and I request free pratique." *Pratique* is derived from the French word *practiquer*, meaning "to practice" (the letter *c* seems to have been omitted along the way). Therefore, *free pratique* means "permission to do business ashore or use a port's facilities."

Incidentally, don't ever use two Q flags, one over the other, unless you're in deadly earnest. The signal means: "My ship is suspect; that is, I have had cases of infectious diseases more than five days ago, or there has been unusual mortality among the rats on board my ship."

See also **Code Flags**; **Flags**.

Quarter Berths

Bringing light and air to a form-fitting sleeping place

In the language of ships, the quarter is the after part of the ship's side; hence, the naming of the quarterdeck. But it is also used to describe the rounded part of a ship's stern, as well as a bearing or direction as you look astern—for example, the lighthouse bears two points (or 22.5 degrees) on the port quarter.

(Incidentally, you can always spot landlubbers by the way they use this description of direction. That's because true sailors never talk about an arc of more than four points on the quarter. As McEwen and Lewis point out in *Encyclopedia of Nautical Knowledge*, "the improper *five points on the quarter* becomes *three points abaft the beam*, there being an arc of eight points between abeam and astern.")

On a small boat, a quarter berth is named not for its size, but rather its position. It's a full-sized bunk aft of the main saloon, in the boat's quarter. It's usually squeezed in between the boat's side and the footwell of the cockpit or the engine compartment; more often than not, it resembles a slightly oversized coffin devoid of light and air.

People either love or hate quarter berths. They are the delight of nautical troglodytes, for whom they represent the epitome of privacy on a small boat—once you're wedged in position, nobody else knows what's going on down there, and your possessions are out of everybody's sight and reach, down by your feet. Other people rebel at the claustrophobic stuffiness and the difficulty of climbing into the berth feet first.

You can improve ventilation with a Dorade box at the aft end of the quarter berth, and you can introduce both light and air with an opening port set into the side of the cockpit footwell, which would be a blessing on still nights in the tropics. Just make sure that any opening port can be firmly closed from the outside by a crew member in the cockpit when bad weather threatens.

Quick-Stop Method

Staying as close as possible to a person in the water

The quick-stop method of rescuing a crew member who has fallen overboard from a sailboat is promoted by the U.S. Naval Academy Sailing Squadron in Annapolis, Maryland. It follows the principle that a fast turn toward the person overboard (no matter how unseamanlike a mess it makes of sails and rigging) is the safest rescue technique because it keeps the victim in sight and close to the boat.

As soon as the crew-overboard alarm is sounded, head the boat into the wind and tack. Don't worry about the jib. Let it back— it will fill again on the downwind leg. Head back toward the person in the water and make your approach so that you're on a close reach, aiming for a point just to windward. Furl the jib if you can; otherwise, let it flap freely—and control your approach speed by trimming and easing the mainsail only. When you're alongside the victim, stop the boat by easing out the mainsail until it is flapping just like the jib. Throw the victim a line with a loop in the end to go under the armpits.

Don't be tempted to use the engine if there's wind; there is great danger of fouling the propeller with trailing sheets, and the risk of hitting the victim with the propeller is unacceptable. Use the engine only in a calm, and then with the greatest caution.

There are other crew-rescue methods that may be equally or more effective—depending on

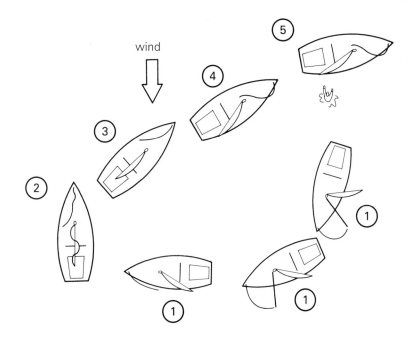

1. Regardless of the point of sail, the boat is brought hard on the wind.

2. The boat is tacked, leaving the headsail sheeted to windward.

3, 4, 5. Sail back to the person, aiming for a point just to windward.

The Quick-Stop Method for recovering a person overboard.

your particular boat and its equipment—including the Lifesling system and the figure-eight method promoted by the American Sailing Association.

See also **Crew Overboard; Lifesling System; Figure-Eight Method.**

Radar Reflectors

Making them bigger, rigging them higher, for best results

Most yachts show up only faintly on ships' radar screens, if at all. To be "seen" properly, you need a radar reflector, a device made of metal vanes set at right angles to each other. It is designed to return a radar signal straight back to its source with little loss of strength.

The bigger the reflector, the better, because its reflective performance is proportional to the fourth power of its linear dimension. In other words, if you double its size, its effectiveness increases 16 times. Thus, if a 12-inch-diameter (305 mm) reflector is the standard, then a 15-inch (381 mm) reflector is about $2\frac{1}{2}$ times better. An 18-inch (457 mm) reflector is 5 times better than a 12-inch one. Incidentally, this measurement is the diagonal quoted by manufacturers. Diagonals of 16 to 18 inches (406 to 457 mm) correspond to sides of about 11 to 13 inches (279 to 330 mm).

The reflector is at its most efficient when you hang it in the "rain-catcher" attitude, with one of the eight pockets facing directly upward. It will not work as well if you hang it from a single corner—although the question of peak efficiency becomes moot when a boat is heeling and pitching.

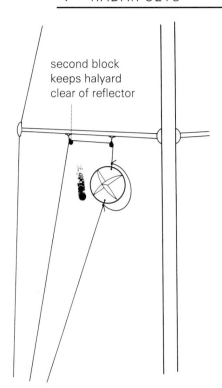

second block keeps halyard clear of reflector

A method for hoisting a radar reflector that prevents it from chafing through its halyard.

Many sailors are skeptical about manufacturers' claims for radar reflectors, and never take it for granted that they will be spotted by ships—especially in bad weather when wave clutter tends to disguise weak returns from small yachts.

Simple reflectors seem to work as well as their fancier cousins, though. More expensive reflectors have multiple facets to collect and return the transmission, or use the properties of concentric layers of plastic material to focus and return a beam. None claims 100 percent efficiency, but they're probably an improvement on the two-piece, slot-together, foil-covered cardboard reflector the skipper produces in times of panic.

Don't forget to raise your reflector as high as possible. Radar transmissions follow the line of sight, so the higher your reflector, the farther away you'll be seen.

If you take action to avoid collision with a ship, and want your change of direction to be noticed on the other vessel's radar screen, you must alter your course by at least 60 degrees. Small changes of course are notoriously difficult to discern, even for experienced radar operators.

See also **Radar Sets.**

Radar Sets

Seeing the invisible with the help of radio waves

The word *radar* is an acronym formed from the initial letters of the words *radio detection and ranging.* Radar detects objects by the echo principle, bouncing radio waves off them and timing their return; it works regardless of darkness or weather conditions. It thus enables you to "see" potential navigational hazards and other ships before you run into them.

The radio waves are transmitted from a revolving antenna. When they return, they're interpreted on a screen that gives a rough representation of land masses and objects such as channel markers, buoys, and other boats. Because this radar display provides accurate bearings and distances, it's a valuable navigation tool.

Small-boat radars are available with ranges up to about 48 miles; however, because of the limited height of the antenna, they're most useful at ranges of 16 miles or less.

The radiation from radar an-tennas is harmful to human beings at close range, so be sure that yours is installed above head level—and make sure it's not operating if you have to pass close by in a bosun's chair.

The horizontal beam width is typically 6 degrees and the vertical beam width is 30 degrees. This means that a radar transmission from a sailboat heeled 15 degrees or more will be aimed at the sky unless the revolving antenna is mounted in a self-leveling radome.

Current draw is usually about 10 watts or less in power-economy mode.

Displays are commonly of three types. The monochromatic cathode ray tube (CRT) is bulky but gives a good green-on-black contrast. It is best used in low to subdued light in a boat's interior.

The monochromatic liquid-crystal display (LCD) works well in bright sunlight or in subdued light with the backlight on, so you can use it on deck near the helm station. It has a thin case that is more easily accommodated on board, and it's the least expensive display type. Its resolution is not as sharp as the others, however.

The thin-film transistor (TFT) screen provides a color display with sharp resolution, but is more expensive.

Radar displays are often integrated with GPS chart plotters, so that one display can fulfill both functions.

Incidentally, although radar is a wonderful asset on a small boat, it's important to be aware of the false sense of security it can give you. It takes a lot of practice to interpret every little blip on the screen. Military radar operators spend weeks at special schools learning how to do it.

See also **Radar Reflectors**.

Radio Direction Finders

See RDF Sets.

Radio Transmitters

Communicating with other boats and land stations

There are no statutory requirements that a private pleasure boat carry any kind of radio transmitter, but for safety reasons as well as for ordinary ship's business, most boats carry a marine very-high-frequency (VHF) transceiver for short-range purposes. Those headed offshore often carry a single-sideband (SSB) shortwave radio for longer-range communication as well.

The effective range of your radio can vary substantially, but there are widely accepted norms for a VHF transmitter operating at 25 watts in the marine VHF band, which has frequencies from 156.050 to 163.275 MHz, as follows:

- range between boats is about 25 miles—but because the transmission is essentially line of sight, it's limited mostly by antenna heights
- range between a boat and a high land station may be as much as 50 miles

- range between a boat and a high-flying aircraft can be up to 300 miles
- range between handheld stations, which are limited to a transmitting power of 6 watts, is about 3 miles

The ranges of SSB transmissions vary from 50 miles on the 4 MHz band to as much as 10,000 miles on the 22 MHz band. Following are some common results:

2 MHz	100 to 150 miles in daylight; 100 to 300 miles at night
4 MHz	250 miles (day); 150 to 1,000 miles (night)
6 MHz	50 to 100 miles (day); 250 to 1,800 (night)
8 MHz	250 to 500 miles (day); 300 to 3,000 (night)
12 MHz	400 to 4,000 miles, late afternoon and all night
16 MHz	1,000 to 6,000 miles day and night, but best during the day
22 MHz	1,200 to 8,000 miles or more, day and night, but unpredictable and dependent on propagation conditions

The distress and calling frequency on VHF is channel 16; on SSB, it is 2182 kHz.

A VHF radio can be used to contact other boats, harbormasters, bridge tenders, marinas, restaurants, and others to conduct the full panoply of ship's business using appropriate channels from the 100 working channels in the VHF band. A basic knowledge of VHF protocol is incumbent on the user. There are also 11 receive-only channels for weather, environmental, and other broadcasts.

Prompted by development of the international Global Maritime Distress and Safety System (GMDSS), VHF and SSB radios are increasingly offering Digital Selective Calling (DSC) capability. If you carry a DSC radio aboard, you should apply to the Federal Communications Commission (FCC) for a nine-digit Maritime Mobile Service Identity (MMSI) number that is unique to your boat. Anyone who knows that number can then call you directly, and your radio will ring like a telephone.

While underway, a non-DSC VHF radio should be tuned to channel 16, the distress channel, and monitored continuously. With a DSC radio, this is no longer necessary. The coast guard or other authority will broadcast weather and safety alerts on channel 70, and the ringing of

R

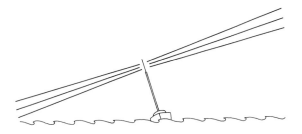

The transmission pattern from an antenna with too much gain (i.e., too narrow a focus) may be directed largely into the sky or water, causing fading and bad reception.

your radio will alert you. More-over, a friend on another boat who knows your MMSI can call you as well. When you respond to the call, your radio shifts to a working channel.

Finally, a DSC radio will broadcast a Mayday at the touch of a button and go on broadcast-ing it while you fight a fire or flooding.

You don't need a ship station license or an operator's license for a VHF transceiver unless you in-tend to use it in a foreign country. License applications for SSBs are available from marine hardware stores.

It's illegal for anyone but a li-censed ham-radio operator to broadcast on the special ham-ra-dio frequencies within the short-wave band, although many SSB transceivers now include the ham frequencies. Even if you are a li-censed ham, you may not use the ham frequencies for commercial purposes—that is, for profit. "Commercial activities" used to include ship's business—ordering spares for your engine, for exam-ple—but these restrictions have been lifted. Ordinary marine SSB frequencies are also fine for ship's business.

See also **Marine Operators; Mayday Calls; Pan-Pan Calls; RDF Sets.**

Rafting Up

Socializing in groups requires common sense and caution

It's great fun to raft up at a ren-dezvous and have a chance to see how other people have outfitted their boats, but it should be done with a certain amount of common sense because it's not exactly sea-manlike.

Rafting is convenient for most boats because often it's only the one in the middle—usually the biggest boat—that sets out an an-chor. Two or more boats simply tie up alongside and swing with her when the wind or current changes. But you should raft up only in daylight in calm, settled weather, because if the wind and waves get up, the strain on the single anchor line will be exces-sive and the movement between boats dangerous, no matter how many fenders are used.

Sometimes you'll see every second boat from the center lay-ing out another anchor, but this can result in a monumental tangle of rodes if the wind shifts. In re-ally organized quarters, at rallies where 20 or 30 boats want to raft up together, they form a large cir-cle with anchors out in all direc-tions. This is probably a better way, as long as you plan to stay for the duration of the raft-up—al-though it takes careful planning and deft execution.

Before you join a raft-up, have a forward-leading aft spring line ready, as well as bow and stern lines. Have your fenders out and, if you have a sailboat, be sure to lie alongside in such a way that your spreaders will not foul your neighbor's.

Stay clear of smaller raft-ups where a half dozen boats lie to one anchor for the night. If the wind rises, there will be trouble for sure. You'll get a better night's sleep if you extricate yourself and go to anchor alone.

If a raft-up forms to wind-ward of you when you're an-chored alone, move away. Find a safer spot where six boats with their lines tangled and their crews in a panic won't come drifting down on you in the night and carry you away with them.

Ranges

Lining up two marks makes for super-accurate positions

Range markers are among the navigator's best friends. The glory of ranges, or transits, is that when you have them lined up, you are absolutely certain that you are on an extension of the straight line that joins them.

Formal ranges are fixed aids to navigation, with a low front marker and higher rear marker that must be lined up exactly to keep you on a safe course in a nar-row channel or among rocks. You can also make your own ranges from any two objects you can identify on the chart, such as a lighthouse and a headland or the edge of an island. When they're in line, draw a line of position on the chart with unparalleled accuracy.

Charted ranges are usually boldly painted with three vertical stripes to make it easy to line them up, and are mostly lighted for use in the dark. It takes prac-tice to know which way to steer when you drift off course and the marks get out of line, but the sim-ple rule is to follow the forward, lower marker. If it moves to the left side of the rear marker, you need to go over that way too, and vice versa.

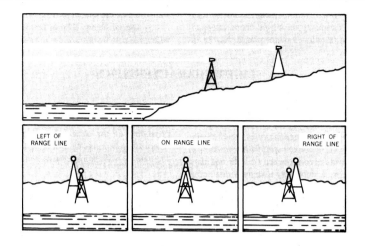

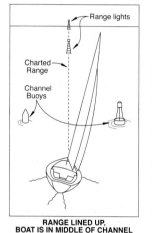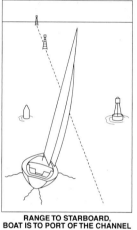

Range lights on shore guide mariners down the centers of some tricky or heavily traveled channels. When the lights line up, you are in the middle of the channel.

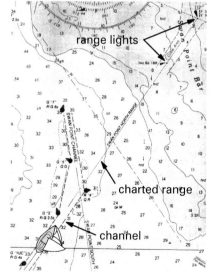

Swan Point North Range is shown on this section of Chesapeake Bay chart 12278.

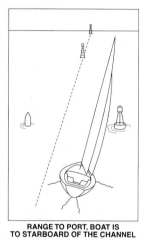

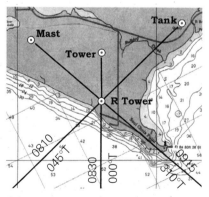

More generally, any two charted objects can be used as a range to generate a precise line of position, assuming you can see them both from your boat. When they line up, you'll know you're somewhere on the line drawn between them and extended out to sea.

The compass direction of most formal ranges is noted on the chart. You can also easily ascertain from the chart the bearing of any informal range or transit points you may choose. If you head your boat directly toward or away from the range makers, you can then check the accuracy of your compass on that course.

RDF Sets

Finding your way home the simple, old-fashioned way

Radio direction finders (RDFs) have largely fallen into disuse, among pleasure boats at least. Few marine stores sell them because their capabilities were overtaken first by loran and more recently by the ubiquitous GPS system of navigation.

The principle of RDF is simple. If you point a ferrite-rod antenna toward the source of a medium-frequency broadcast, you will get little or no reception when the antenna is pointed directly at the broadcast station. That tells you the direction to the transmitter, and if it's marked on your chart, you can lay down a line of position from it. Another plot at right angles to the first will give you a fix.

In an emergency, you can use a cheap AM radio to find your way home at night or in fog, as long as you know precisely where your local transmitter is located.

Most portable AM radios are directionally sensitive and will give a reasonably sharp null (lack of reception) when they're end-on

R

to the transmitter. Just beware that you're not tuned to a repeater station that will lure you onto the rocks.

The cheaper the radio, the better it works as a direction finder. Expensive radios have improved circuits to improve reception in the null zone, which is exactly what you *don't* need.

See also **Radio Transmitters**.

Reciprocal Bearings

Making use of back-to-front compass bearings

A reciprocal bearing is the opposite of any ordinary bearing. In other words, it differs in direction from an ordinary bearing by 180 degrees.

A compass bearing from a vessel to an object on shore, compared with the reciprocal bearing—a compass bearing of the vessel from the object on shore—will reveal the deviation of her compass on various headings.

Light lists are given in reciprocal bearings when they make such comments as: "Shows green from 180° to 200°." Those bearings are not the directions of the sector edges as they emerge from the lighthouse, but rather the bearings of the lighthouse as taken from a vessel. On the chart, the sector would be shown as ranging from 360° to 020°.

A reciprocal bearing of a sailboat's heading—in other words, a bearing extending aft along her centerline—may be compared to the visible wake to find the amount of leeway she is making.

See also **Compass Bearings; Leeway**.

Reefing

Keeping a sailboat under good control in rising winds, seas

Reducing sail before your vessel becomes overpowered by the wind is good seamanship. She will feel more under control with less sail area, she will ride more comfortably, and—if you're making to windward—she'll sail more upright and therefore faster.

The three basic rules of thumb about reefing are as follows:

1. Reef before you have to—in other words, as soon as it occurs to you.

2. When sailing downwind, reef as if you were going to windward in that same breeze.

3. When in doubt, take in a double reef instead of a single.

Rule 1 highlights the fact that it's far easier to shorten sail before things get out of hand. It's kinder to you and easier on the gear.

Rule 2 reminds you how easy it is to misjudge wind speed on a downwind course. It's always blowing harder than you think, and rounding up in big waves to reef becomes more hazardous the longer you leave it.

Rule 3 applies in those many situations when the wind suddenly comes through with a blast and you have no way of knowing whether it's just a passing gust from the leading edge of a cloud or the beginning of a long and fierce gale. When you're not sure, take in two reefs while you're at it—if you misjudged, it's a simple matter to shake one out later.

Reef as soon as you fear losing control of the boat. When you're on a beat, the signs are obvious: excessive heeling, side decks awash, and heavy weather helm. When you're running or broad-reaching, you can easily be deceived. Watch for prolonged surfing and a sloppy, dead feeling to the helm when an overtaking wave passes underneath. Keep an eye on the quarter wave that rears up near the transom and threatens to charge into the cockpit. Watch out for headlong plunges down the faces of waves, when the bow wants to bury itself in the back of the swell ahead. It's all very thrilling, but it's time to slow down.

Reef when you've anchored in an open roadstead where the wind could later blow onshore. Put in a double reef before you go to bed, so you'll be able to sail out to safety if a gale springs up in the middle of the night, and you won't have to do it in pitch darkness in plunging seas.

See also **Reefing Options**.

Reefing Options

Several different ways to reduce sail area in a blow

Reefing is the business of reducing sail area in high winds to reduce heeling and maintain control of the boat.

A headsail may be furled or

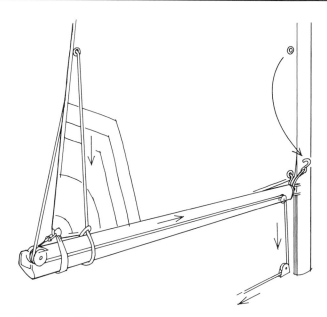

Mainsail slab- or jiffy-reefing system.

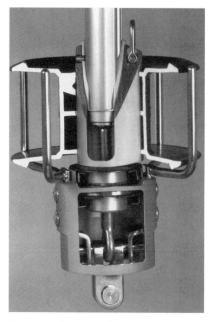

Section through the stem-mounted drum of a roller-reefing headsail. The headstay passes through the luff foil, making the furling unit part of the standing rigging.

reefed quickly and conveniently by means of a foil that surrounds the stay and revolves, rolling the sail up on itself. The foil (usually an aluminum extrusion) is turned by a line on a drum at its foot.

(Very occasionally, the headstay itself rotates.) But most roller furlers are inefficient when used for reefing because the sail becomes fuller and less suitable for windward work. Special padding may be inserted along the luff of the sail to reduce bagginess, but a roller-reefed sail almost always has a less efficient shape when deeply reefed than a smaller sail fastened with hanks.

Some working headsails with hanks may be reefed by reattaching the sheets and the tack fitting to new cringles some way up the leech and luff, respectively, but the better choice is often to drop a working sail altogether and hoist a storm jib in its place.

Modern mainsails may be fitted with jiffy reefing, or slab reefing, which simply involves lowering the sail and making fast the new cringles at the tack and boom-end fittings. Some mainsails use roller-furling systems similar to those found on headsails, but set inside the mast or boom instead. They are expensive, however, and

prone to malfunction. Roller reefing, often seen on older boats, works by rolling the mainsail around the outside of the boom. However, it results in a baggy, less efficient sail and has now been almost entirely discarded.

See also **Reefing**; **Roller-Furling and Roller-Reefing Headsails**.

Refrigeration

Cooling food and drinks on board: some popular methods

The two most popular methods of cooling drinks and food on small boats are iceboxes and mechanical refrigeration.

The first method is simple and cheap, but crude and uncertain. Block ice is heavy and cumbersome, and may not be available everywhere you go.

The second method is complicated, expensive, and prone to breakdowns. If you have mechanical refrigeration on board, you will never have to wonder what to do with your spare time.

Donald Street, a well-known Caribbean charter skipper and owner of the 45-foot wooden yawl *Iolaire*, talks from vast experience when he writes in *The Ocean Sailing Yacht*: "Mechanical refrigeration can break down . . . the original installation is expensive, and mechanical refrigeration is like a chain, the links being the starter motor, the engine, the generator, the water-cooling pumps, the compressor, the condenser, the holding plates, the expansion valves, and so on and on. Failure of a single link renders the whole system inoperable."

R

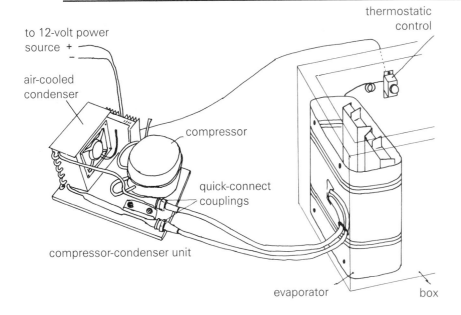

Components of a 12-volt refrigeration unit.

In the same book, Joe Repke, a marine refrigeration engineer, warns: "Anyone intending to do serious cruising must be sure to understand fully the refrigeration system of his boat. He should know the purpose of every component, every valve, and be able to adjust the valves, change the dryers, recharge the system, and so on. Refrigeration experts are few and far between in the middle of the ocean."

Aboard *Iolaire*, Street depends on ice. "The normal routine in the southern islands is to find a small boy with a dinghy, and give him a dollar along with the money for the ice and couple of ice bags," he writes. "Then one can sit back and relax, have a couple of rums, and in no time the ice arrives."

His two 100-pound iceboxes chill fresh food and drinks for 6 people for 10 to 12 days. "The great advantage of an icebox is that it is foolproof. One just fills it with ice, and everything gets cold. There is nothing to break down."

Few small boats can carry 200 pounds of ice, of course, so what works for Street is not good for everybody. Eric Hiscock and others have used small absorption refrigerators worked by a constant open kerosene flame, but they can only be used in port—and then with great caution. The manufacturers strongly recommend against their being used on boats.

You can have a refrigerator and freezer powered by an electrical motor, but the drain on the batteries is heavy and constant. The sad truth is that refrigeration consumes a lot of energy. Boating author Don Casey estimates that adding 12-volt refrigeration to a normally equipped 35-foot yacht will absorb 100 amp-hours per day in hot climates, and triple the demand on the ship's batteries. That means running the auxiliary engine of a sailboat for at least 2 hours a day to charge them.

The refrigerator can be driven directly from the engine, which eliminates battery problems, but

engine-driven systems are expensive—they cost twice or three times as much as 12-volt refrigerators and are more complicated. They are, however, more powerful and, whereas a 12-volt refrigerator cycles on and off all day and night, you need only run an engine-driven compressor once or twice a day to freeze its holdover plate, which is similar to loading the box with ice.

Despite its cost and many drawbacks, many cruisers cannot imagine living without refrigeration. "There is no sweeter symphony to my ear than the susurration of wavelets running along the beach of a deserted cove, mixed with the ringing of ice cubes in slender glasses," writes Don Casey in *This Old Boat*.

The concert may be sweet, but the price of admission is high.

See also **Iceboxes**.

Registration

Signing up with state and federal regulatory agencies

Federal regulations require that all undocumented vessels with propulsion machinery be registered in their state of principal use. Upon payment of the requisite fee, the state will issue you a certificate of number whose numbers must be displayed on either side of the bow of your vessel.

You must carry the certificate of number with you whenever your boat is in use; if you move it to another state, you have 60 days in which to reregister. The certificate is not legal proof of your boat's nationality. In Alaska, the

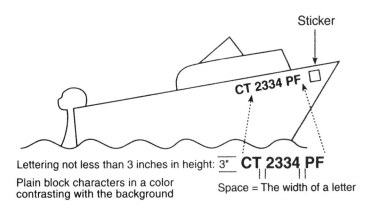

Lettering not less than 3 inches in height: 3" **CT 2334 PF**

Plain block characters in a color contrasting with the background

Space = The width of a letter

Registration display requirements.

U.S. Coast Guard issues the certificate of number.

Documented boats (normally those at least 25 feet or 7.6 meters in length and measuring 5 tons net) are registered with the U.S. Coast Guard. They are not, however, exempt from registration with their home states—the only difference being that they need not display their state registration numbers on the bows. The certificate of documentation must be on board at all times.

Federal documentation provides a form of national registration that legally establishes a boat's nationality and ownership. It also offers her the protection of local U.S. consular officials anywhere in the world.

Net tonnage, in the case of documentation, is not a weight but a volume derived from gross tonnage, which is the total enclosed space or internal capacity of a vessel, expressed in units of 100 cubic feet and referred to as tons.

Net tonnage is gross tonnage minus the volume of interior spaces that will not hold cargo. As far as pleasure boats are concerned, deductions from gross tonnage are made mainly for engine compartments and control stations.

See also **Net Tonnage**.

Renaming a Boat

Doing it the right way staves off the possibility of bad luck

Superstition still plays a significant role in boaters' lives. The sea, hardly changed in all the eons since its creation, is still a source of mystery and wonderment. Half of the Earth's surface is covered by abyssal seas where light never penetrates, but where life nevertheless exists—sometimes in outlandish forms—in conditions of unimaginable pressure and Stygian darkness. Little wonder, then, that frail human beings plying the interface between the unruly atmosphere and the fearsome oceans should seek help by performing certain rituals known to their ancestors, and turning to their ancient gods for protection.

One superstition still widely held concerns the renaming of a boat, which, in the United States at least, is held to be unlucky. The answer is to hold a denaming ceremony before you rename your boat. You can make up your own ceremony, or you are welcome to use mine, which has been used with every appearance of success. It is now widely distributed on the Internet, but it is repeated here for your convenience.

Before you hold the denaming ceremony, you must remove all physical traces of the boat's old name. Take the logbook ashore, along with any other charts, books, or papers that bear the old name. Be ruthless: sand away the old name from the lifebuoys, transom, topsides, dinghy, and oars; painting over is not good enough. We're dealing with gods here, you understand, not mere mortals. If the old name is carved or etched, try to remove it. At the very minimum, fill it with putty and paint over it. And don't place the new name anywhere on the boat before the denaming ceremony is completed—that's just tempting fate.

You can read the ceremony with flair on the foredeck before a gathering of distinguished guests or, if you find this whole business embarrassing and go along with it only because you're scared of what might happen if you don't, you can skulk down below and mumble it in solitude. But the words must be spoken.

The last part of the ceremony, the libation, should be performed at the bow. Use good champagne and spray all of it on the bow—do not presume to save some for yourself. The gods despise cheapskates; buy another bottle for your own consumption.

Here is Vigor's Famous Inter-

R

denominational Denaming Ceremony:

"In the name of all who have sailed aboard this ship in the past, and in the name of all who may sail aboard her in the future, we invoke the ancient gods of the wind and the sea to favor us with their blessings today.

"Mighty Neptune, king of all that moves in or on the waves;

"And mighty Aeolus, guardian of the winds and all that blows before them:

"We offer you our thanks for the protection you have afforded this vessel in the past. We voice our gratitude that she has always found shelter from tempest and storm, and found safe harbor.

"Now, wherefore, we submit this supplication, that the name whereby this vessel has hitherto been known, '[————],' be struck and removed from your records.

"Further, we ask that when she is again presented for blessing with a new name, she shall be recognized and accorded once again the selfsame privileges she previously enjoyed.

"In return for which, we rededicate this vessel to your domain in the full knowledge that she shall be subject, as always, to the immutable laws of the gods of the wind and the sea.

"In consequence whereof, and in good faith, we seal this pact with libation offered according to the hallowed ritual of the sea."

There. Now you are free to christen your boat with a new name. It doesn't pay to be too quick, though. Most of us like to wait at least 24 hours to give any lingering demons time to pack their duffel bags and clear out.

See also **Unlucky Names**.

Resins for Boats

Choosing the right one for the specific layup in hand

Plastic boats are built from liquid resins that slowly harden into solids when they're catalyzed. They're strengthened with fibers of various kinds, and the kind of resin used depends on how compatible it is with the kind of fiber chosen.

Generally, polyester resin is best with the glass fibers known as E-glass (electrical grade) and S-glass (structural grade). The latter is extruded with much finer strands and is stiffer and stronger than the cheaper and more widely used E-glass. The polyester resin most frequently used is orthophthalic, because it's inexpensive and easily worked. Isophthalic polyester resin, although more expensive, imparts

Resin	Tensile Strength psi x 10^3	Tensile Modulus psi x 10^5	Ultimate Elongation	1990 Bulk Cost $/lb
Orthophthalic Atlas P 2020	7.0	5.9	.91%	.66
Dicyclopentadiene (DCPD) Atlas 80-6044	11.2	9.1	.86%	.67
Isophthalic CoRezyn 9595	10.3	5.65	2.0%	.85
Vinyl Ester Derakane 411-45	11-12	4.9	5-6%	1.44
Epoxy Gougeon Pro Set 125/226	7.96	5.3	7.7%	4.39

Orthophthalic polyester resin is the standard choice for production fiberglass boatbuilding because it's the least expensive alternative and produces good results. Isophthalic polyester is stronger, makes a stronger secondary bond with previously cured fiberglass, and is more resistant to osmosis (and is thus sometimes used as a barrier coat under the gelcoat to help prevent blistering). Vinylester resin surpasses orthophthalic in all respects and is used in custom boatbuilding to obtain a light, strong hull.

greater tensile strength and elongation to a laminate and is more resistant to osmosis. It also adheres better to previously cured polyester.

Most factory-produced boats have layups made with polyester resin, but the best repairs, alterations, and additions are made with epoxy resin. Epoxy adheres well to cured polyester. It forms a stronger bond, in fact, than does new polyester on old polyester. Epoxy also grips well to wood and metals and is compatible with all reinforcing fibers, including carbon fiber and Kevlar, but it's more expensive than polyester resin.

Vinylester resin, too, is expensive, but it's increasingly being used in underwater hull laminations because of its superior water resistance. Its greater impermeability helps prevent blistering, or osmosis, and it's usually specified to replace the gelcoat in osmosis repairs.

See also **Blisters in GRP; Epoxy; Fiberglass; Plastics.**

Resistance

Making waves and creating friction slows down your boat

All boats resist being moved through the water. Resistance takes three main forms: skin friction, wave-making resistance, and eddy-making resistance.

Skin friction is naturally greater if the bottom surface is rough, and it varies with the speed of the boat. More friction is experienced in the front part of the boat because it passes through still water, whereas the after parts

of the hull pass through water that has already been given some forward motion. Skin friction is the major portion of resistance at low speeds. The lighter the displacement of a boat, the greater is the proportion of skin resistance to total resistance.

Wave-making resistance is caused by the boat literally pushing aside water as it moves forward. This type of resistance increases with speed until the boat is sitting in the hollow of a wave about the length of her hull, with crests at the bow and stern. Although displacement hulls cannot escape this wave, a powerful planing hull can rise over its own bow wave and increase its speed by shedding most of its wave-making resistance.

Eddy-making resistance is perhaps the most intriguing of all forms of resistance. Whenever the passage of a boat through the water causes eddies—the swirls and little whirlpools you often see in a wake—the boat will be slowed down. It takes energy to create eddies, and that energy is subtracted from the power driving the boat forward.

Anything projecting from the hull, such as a through-hull fitting, a depth-sounder's transducer, or a propeller strut, will cause eddies. On a fin-keel sailboat, speed-robbing eddies often form at the very bottom of the keel, where there is a substantial pressure differential between the two sides. Winglets similar to those seen on the wingtips of commercial jetliners help prevent keel-tip eddies, but also contribute more skin friction at slow speeds.

See also **Hull Shapes; Planing.**

Rhumb Lines

Steering just one course all the way to your destination

If you steer your boat in one constant compass direction, you're following a rhumb line. If your course is due north or south, you'll also be following a meridian; if it's due east or west, you'll be following a parallel of latitude. In all other cases, you will be spiraling toward a pole.

The glory of the rhumb line for the amateur navigator is that one compass course takes you all the way from one port to another. The penalty you pay for this convenience is extra mileage.

The shortest distance between two points on the Earth's surface is a great circle, and (with few exceptions) a rhumb line is not a great circle. Over short distances, the difference in distance is unimportant, but on ocean passages it can be significant. For example, the great-circle distance between San Francisco and Yokohama is 4,517 nautical miles. The rhumb-line distance is 4,723 miles, or another 206 miles.

Of course, it would be impossible for a yacht to make the gradual and minute course corrections a true great-circle course would require. The practical method is to divide the course into straight legs of about 600 miles each, and change course more substantially at the end of each.

The nearer your course takes you to the poles, the greater is the

R

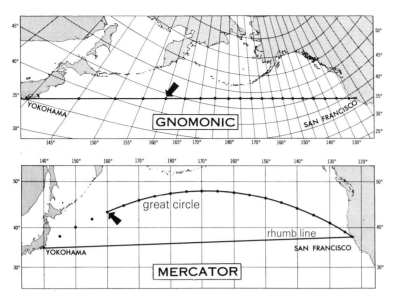

A great circle course plots as a straight line on a gnomonic chart. A rhumb line plots straight on a Mercator chart, but if you follow the rhumb line from San Francisco to Yokohama you will travel substantially farther than you would on a great-circle route.

difference between rhumb-line and great-circle courses. The great-circle course also offers significant benefit if your course is mainly east or west. If you're traveling mainly north or south, you might as well stay with a more convenient rhumb-line course.

See also **Ocean Voyaging**.

Rigging Sizes

Making sure your mast will stand up in a gale at sea

Wondering if your rigging is strong enough is a common pastime for sailors caught in a gale, a worrying thought that lucky powerboaters are spared. Modern rigs are very strong, but they have to withstand severe stresses in heavy weather because of the disadvantageous angle by which the standing rigging is attached to the masts of most monohulls.

Following are some basic rules about rigging strength that have stood the test of time:

Shrouds. The total breaking strength of all the shrouds on one side of the boat should equal about 1.2 times the boat's displacement in fully loaded condition. Racing boats and daysailers can afford to make that about 1.0 times displacement, but serious offshore cruisers should increase it to 1.4 times displacement.

If you have double lower shrouds, assume only one is working at any given moment. In other words, use only one lower shroud for this calculation, and make the other shroud the same dimension.

Load division. In a single-spreader rig, the lower shrouds take 60 percent of the load, the upper shroud takes 40 percent. In a double-spreader rig, the lowers take 48

percent, the intermediate 26 percent, and the upper 26 percent.

Where intermediate and upper shrouds combine at the lower spreader and run to a single turnbuckle and chainplate, the combined intermediate-upper shroud carries 52 percent of the load.

Spreader locations. A single spreader, or crosstree, needs to be between 50 and 52 percent of the mast's height from the deck upward. In a double-spreader rig, the lower spreader should be 37 to 39 percent of the way up the mast, and the upper spreader should be 68 to 70 percent of the way up.

Headstay. Make the headstay the size of the heaviest shroud, or one size bigger.

Backstay. The backstay should be the same size as the headstay or one size smaller.

Turnbuckles. For standard, open-body bronze turnbuckles, the screw diameter should be twice the diameter of the rigging wire. High-strength stainless steel turnbuckles might be a little lighter.

Turnbuckle jaws. The opening between the turnbuckle jaws should be twice the rigging wire diameter.

Clevis pins. These should be twice the rigging wire diameter.

The golden rule. Always use toggles (universal joints) between turnbuckles and chainplates, and between mast tangs and shroud

Diameter of Wire		Breaking Strength	
Inches	mm	Pounds	kg
1/8	3.2	2,100	953
5/32	3.9	3,300	1,497
3/16	4.8	4,700	2,132
7/32	5.6	6,300	2,858
1/4	6.3	8,200	3,719
9/32	7.1	10,300	4,672
5/16	7.9	12,500	5,670
3/8	9.5	17,600	7,983
7/16	11.1	23,400	10,614
1/2	12.7	29,700	13,472
9/16	14.3	37,000	16,783
5/8	15.9	46,800	21,228

Breaking strength of 1 x 19 stainless steel wire. These figures are for type 302/304 stainless steel, the type most commonly used for standing rigging. Type 316, recommended for tropical use because of its higher resistance to corrosion, is approximately 15 percent weaker.

eyes, to cut down on metal fatigue from bending and vibration.

See also **Rigging Tension; Turnbuckles; Wire Terminals**.

Rigging Tension

Adjusting the standing rig for tension and straightness

How tight should a sailboat's standing rigging be? It's a question that often engages the mind of amateur sailors. The old rule of thumb was that when you're on a beam reach under normal working sail in a moderate breeze, the shrouds on the leeward side should *feel* slightly slack, but not *look* slack to the casual observer.

But that's a little too imprecise for most people, especially because it's possible to measure wire tension with a simple gauge you can buy at a marine store, such as

the Loos gauge. By pretensioning the rig, you avoid the sudden shock loads that wind gusts will impose on a floppy rig. But too much permanent tension can cause hogging of the sheerline and drive the mast downward with enough force to distort the cabintop or damage the keel.

The mast should remain perfectly straight under sail unless it's a fractional rig purposely designed to bend or a freestanding mast with no fixed rigging.

Follow these steps to tension the rig:

1. Give the upper shrouds and backstay a tension of approximately 10 percent of the boat's displacement. (You will induce a slightly higher tension in the forestay—which is good—because of the narrower angle it makes with the mast.)

2. Tighten the forward lower shrouds (or babystay) so that the

mast bows forward slightly but noticeably at the spreaders.

3. Tighten the aft lower shrouds to straighten the mast again.

4. Sail for a few hours in moderate winds, allowing the rig to adjust itself.

5. While still in a moderate breeze, straighten the mast from side to side by adjusting the appropriate shrouds, if necessary. Unscrew the turnbuckles on one side a few turns before taking up the turnbuckles on the other side the same number of turns. It usually pays to tackle the lowers first, making sure the mast is middled and straight as far as the spreaders. Then adjust the cap shrouds to straighten things out from the spreaders upward.

See also **Rigging Sizes; Shrouds and Stays**.

Right of Way

Forgoing your rights is the safest way for small boats

One of the most puzzling and worrisome aspects of the collision regulations is that you are bound to hold your course if you have the right of way, so that the give-way vessel can maneuver clear of you if necessary. But the rules also burden you with the responsibility of giving way at the last moment if the other vessel fails to do so in time to prevent a collision.

Obviously, you can't know the maneuverability of every vessel you come up against. You can't possibly know how quickly she can get out of your way, or how

R

late the other skipper is going to leave it, or even if she has spotted you at all. So if your nerve cracks and you start to give way, and the other boat starts to give way at that same moment, you can find yourselves heading for the same spot, causing a swift last-minute collision with no way out.

The rules make no concession to size. In open waters, a large freighter is obliged to give way to a tiny sailing dinghy. Fortunately, sailors themselves tend to apply the rules with common sense, which usually means that small maneuverable boats give way to clumsy leviathans whether or not they have the right of way.

If you find yourself on a collision course with a larger vessel, your safest course is to forgo your rights under the collision regulations and get out of her way. However, you must make this decision early on; don't leave it until the last moment. Change your course early, and change it substantially, so that the other vessel understands your intentions.

And if it irritates you to have to give way to the big bullies all the time, remember the old epitaph:

Here lies the body of Michael O'Day,
Who died maintaining his right of way.
He was right, dead right, as he sailed along,
But he's just as dead as if he'd been wrong.

See also **Collision Bearings**; **Rules of the Road**.

Rodes

Chain and nylon line work together for the best rodes

According to McEwen and Lewis in *Encyclopedia of Nautical Knowledge*, the word *rode* was a term used by East Coast fishermen for a boat's anchor rope. Today, the word is used more widely and is generally understood to include all the gear lying between a boat and her anchor. That may consist of chain alone, or a combination of chain and stretchable nylon line.

Because nylon is easily chafed by coral, rocks, and other underwater obstructions, it's essential to use chain at least for that part of the rode in contact with the sea bottom.

Long-term cruisers usually go one step further and carry one, if not two, all-chain rodes. The major advantage of chain is its weight, which tends to hold the boat in one place at anchor, and lessens her tendency to range from side to side. Chain isn't degraded by sunlight, as nylon is, and it isn't susceptible to being chopped in half by a passing outboard motor's propeller. Furthermore, it's self-stowing and it doesn't tangle.

The weight of chain makes it hang in a loop, or catenary, so that the upward pull of the boat at the bow is changed to a horizontal pull at the anchor, which is exactly what's needed. That means you can often get away with a scope of 3 to 1 in a crowded anchorage—a trick that will limit your swinging circle and endear you to your close neighbors.

It's almost impossible to get a horizontal pull on the anchor with an all-nylon anchor line, so a length of chain extending back from the anchor is used to create a catenary and avoid chafe. Unfortunately, the weight of an an-

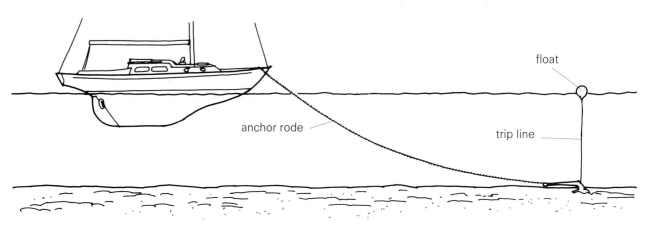

anchor rode

float

trip line

An all-chain rode with a scope of 3 to 1.

chor chain stowed near the bow is detrimental to performance under sail. Although it's acceptable to cruisers, most racers, weekenders, and daysailers try to get away with as little chain as possible.

If you're not going to use an all-chain rode, a good rule of thumb is to combine three-strand nylon line with a length of chain equal to the length of your boat. That's the minimum length of chain; you can, with advantage, make it longer if you want.

Nylon does have its advantages, of course. It's cheaper than chain; it's lighter and won't rust; it can be knotted and spliced; and, most significantly, it prevents snatching and shock loading of deck fittings by stretching to absorb sudden strains.

Never use polyester line (Dacron or Terylene) in place of nylon—it doesn't stretch enough. For the same reason, don't be tempted to use nylon line that's too thick. It won't stretch, which is the whole object of the exercise.

An all-chain rode won't stretch either, naturally, but it has a built-in shock absorber in the heavy loop it forms. If the wind is so strong that it pulls the loop tight, you can reduce shock loading by sending a heavy weight partway down the chain, suspended from a large shackle or a special roller.

In shallow water and very strong wind, however, an all-chain rode probably won't provide the elasticity needed to avoid dangerous snubbing. The answer is to clap on a 20-foot (6 m) length of nylon called a snubber, which will act as a shock absorber.

Incidentally, *rode* isn't the only term applied to an anchor line; it is also referred to as a cable or a warp. A cable may be a rope, a chain, or even a wire. An anchor line, or warp, is usually understood to be rope—although, as you probably know, rope is seldom called rope on a boat. A warp, strictly speaking, is a rope or hawser used in mooring or shifting a vessel. If all this becomes too confusing, ignore it; use the term *anchor rope* or *anchor chain* instead.

See also **Anchors, Anchoring; Scope for Anchors**.

Rogue Waves

See Freak Waves.

Roller-Furling and Roller-Reefing Headsails

Probing the limitations of an old jib-handling system

Roller furling for headsails has been around a long time, certainly more than 60 years, but it has still not achieved the kind of reliability on which many ocean sailors insist.

Back in 1938, British authors Graham and Tew were advising boaters to fit the patented Wykeham Martin roller gear to their jibs, although they warned that it was for furling only, not for reefing. And the gear had been in use for at least 15 years before that.

But 50 years later, after years of cruising in their own small boats and dozens of deep-sea delivery trips, the well-known cruising couple Lin and Larry Pardey wrote: "We haven't yet delivered a boat with a roller furling jib that worked correctly in all situations."

There is a useful distinction to be made between roller furling and roller reefing. Strictly speaking, the former involves a headsail with a wire luff that rolls up on itself independent of the headstay. In roller reefing, an aluminum extrusion, or foil, is fitted around the headstay; the headsail is slotted into the foil, which rotates to wind up the sail. (On a few roller reefers, the headstay itself rotates.) Roller furling does not work well under load and does not provide a good reefed sail shape; roller reefing is much better in this regard, but failure of a roller reefer can cause failure of the headstay—which could lead to loss of the mast. Roller-reefing technology now dominates, and traditional roller furlers are rarely seen anymore.

Manufacturers will tell you that their products have improved since the Pardeys gave their verdict, and it's certainly true that many circumnavigations have been made with roller reefers, but it's also true that they are complicated and still prone to misbehavior. The very thought of having to shinny aloft in a gale at sea to cut away a flogging foresail is enough to deter many conservative sailors. A hanked-on headsail always comes down on cue.

Roller reefing works well for weekend sailors and coastal cruisers with ports close at hand, but

R

shorthanded ocean cruisers are entitled to view it with suspicion despite its siren lure. And no matter what cunning arrangements sailmakers make to take the excess belly out of a rolled-up jib, it still can't be as efficient as a hanked-on storm jib.

You may point to the round-the-world single-handed racers who use roller furling and reefing, but remember that their passages are mostly downwind, and they are the supermen and superwomen of sailing. They think nothing of hoisting themselves up forestays in Roaring Forties gales to slash their headsails free of stuck roller furlers; ordinary mortals would do better to stick to hanks.

See also **Reefing; Reefing Options**.

Roll Times

Ascertaining stability from the time a boat takes to roll

The time it takes for a boat to roll from one side to the other is an indication of her form stability. A reliable rule of thumb is that a powerboat should have a roll time in seconds equal to between 1 and 1.1 times her overall beam in meters—that is, her overall beam in feet divided by 3.28. This is regarded as a good compromise between stiffness and comfort.

Boats with much shorter roll times are very stiff, which means they have great initial stability, but they will have a tiresome, jerky motion at sea. Boats with much longer roll times have less

stability and should be handled with greater care on the open ocean.

Check the roll time of your boat fairly accurately on a calm day at the dock. Gather enough people to press down in unison on the gunwale until the boat is rolling as hard as she can. Everyone should stop pushing when she is at the bottom of her roll toward the dock. Time her roll with a stopwatch from this position back to this position, or as near as she comes. Time it to the nearest tenth of a second. On a boat 10 feet (3 m) wide, the roll time should be close to 3 seconds. You might want to repeat the rolling several times and take an average.

Incidentally, when the waterline beam is less than 90 percent of the overall beam, as in a boat with a large amount of deck flare, the overall beam should be reckoned as the waterline beam plus 11 percent.

Sailboats are more difficult to time accurately because of their greater inertia and the resistance of the keel and skegs, but following are some rough figures (roll times given in seconds per meter of overall beam) for different types of boats:

- heavy-displacement cruisers with a ballast ratio of 25 percent or less, with no high deckhouse: 0.95 second
- heavy cruisers with a ballast ratio of between 25 and 35 percent and nothing unusually heavy on deck: 0.90 second
- medium cruisers with 35 percent ballast or more, no ex-

trahigh cabins: 0.85 second
- cruiser-racers, 35 percent ballast or more, moderate draft and moderate cabin height: 0.80 second
- racing boats, 40 percent ballast or more, deep draft, low cabintops: 0.75 second
- fringe racers with 45 percent ballast or more and extradeep keels: 0.70 second

See also **Stability**.

Rope Strength

Working loads and breaking strengths of modern fibers

The safe working load for three-strand laid line is 11 percent of its tensile strength. That's the opinion of the safety experts, who must bear in mind, of course, the consequences of weathering and fatigue and the fact that human lives may depend on a rope's integrity.

Braided rope, on the other hand, may be pressed into use at 20 percent of its breaking strength, ostensibly because the inner core, which takes most of the strain, is protected by the outer sheath. Single-braid, double-braid, and parallel-core lines may all be considered stronger than ordinary three-stranded line.

All modern plastic lines are tough, resilient, and extremely strong. A $\frac{1}{4}$-inch-diameter (6 mm) nylon line, for example, has a breaking strength of about 1,100 pounds (499 kg). The same size line in Dacron will break at about 1,200 pounds (544 kg), and

General Characteristics of Synthetic Marine Rope Materials

Material	Strength	Stretch	Shrinkage	Flotation	Cost	Common Uses
Nylon	strong	stretches	shrinks	sinks	moderate	mooring lines and docklines
Polyester (Dacron)	strong	low-stretch	low-shrink	sinks	moderate	sheets and halyards
Polypropylene	low-strength	low-stretch	low-shrink	floats	economical	water-ski towlines
Aramid (Kevlar)	very strong	low-stretch	no-shrink	sinks	high	running rigging
High-Tenacity Copolymers	strong	low-stretch	low-shrink	floats	economical	sheets and tackles
High-Tenacity Polyethylene (Spectra and Dyneema)	very strong	low-stretch	no-shrink	floats	high	running rigging

Rope Strength

Diameter	Manila	Nylon	Dacron	Spectra
3/16 in.	450 lb.	850 lb.	900 lb.	1,600 lb.
5 mm	204 kg	386 kg	408 kg	726 kg
1/4 in.	600 lb.	1,100 lb.	1,200 lb.	3,000 lb.
6 mm	272 kg	499 kg	544 kg	1,361 kg
5/16 in.	1,000 lb.	1,800 lb.	1,800 lb.	4,850 lb.
8 mm	454 kg	816 kg	816 kg	2,200 kg
3/8 in.	1,300 lb.	2,600 lb.	2,600 lb.	6,000 lb.
9 mm	590 kg	1,179 kg	1,179 kg	2,722 kg
7/16 in.	1,700 lb.	3,700 lb.	3,500 lb.	9,700 lb.
11 mm	771 kg	1,678 kg	1,588 kg	4,400 kg
1/2 in.	2,600 lb.	5,000 lb.	4,500 lb.	10,800 lb.
13 mm	1,179 kg	2,268 kg	2,041 kg	4,899 kg
9/16 in.	3,400 lb.	6,400 lb.	5,500 lb.	13,600 lb.
14 mm	1,542 kg	2,903 kg	2,495 kg	6,169 kg
5/8 in.	4,400 lb.	8,000 lb.	6,800 lb.	19,500 lb.
16 mm	1,996 kg	3,629 kg	3,084 kg	8,845 kg
3/4 in.	5,400 lb.	10,500 lb.	9,300 lb.	24,300 lb.
19 mm	2,449 kg	4,763 kg	4,218 kg	11,022 kg
7/8 in.	7,700 lb.	14,000 lb.	12,600 lb.	33,000 lb.
22 mm	3,493 kg	6,350 kg	5,715 kg	14,969 kg
1 in.	9,000 lb.	18,800 lb.	16,100 lb.	43,200 lb.
25 mm	4,082 kg	8,528 kg	7,303 kg	19,596 kg

Conservative breaking strengths of three-stranded manila, nylon, and Dacron, and of double-braid Spectra covered with Dacron. Single-braid, double-braid, and parallel-core lines may all be considered stronger than ordinary three-stranded line.

a 1/4-inch Spectra line will break at 3,000 pounds (1,361 kg).

The ordinary 1/2-inch (12 mm) Dacron line so commonly used for sailboat sheets has a breaking strength of 4,500 pounds (2,041 kg). That's far in excess of its normal loads, but it's chosen because anything thinner would be difficult to handle.

Many other lines made of exotic fibers such as Kevlar, Zylon, Vectran, and Technora are even stronger, lighter, and stretch less under load, but their high costs and shorter working lives have restricted their use to highly competitive racing boats. They are now migrating to cruising sailboats, as most racing technologies do sooner or later, but beware: high-modulus ropes like these don't like knots, and splicing them is a pain.

See also **Halyards**; **Rope Stretch**; **Rope Versus Line**; **Sheet Sizes**; **Synthetic Fibers**.

Rope Stretch

Choosing the line with the amount of elasticity you need

All rope stretches under load on board a boat, but some materials stretch more than others, so you have to be careful to choose the right line for the job.

R

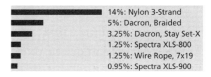

14%: Nylon 3-Strand
5%: Dacron, Braided
3.25%: Dacron, Stay Set-X
1.25%: Spectra XLS-800
1.25%: Wire Rope, 7x19
0.95%: Spectra XLS-900

Approximate stretch in rope under 30 percent of its breaking load.

The three most commonly encountered synthetic materials found on boats are nylon, Dacron, and polypropylene. Their uses are as follows:

Nylon stretches about 10 to 15 percent under a load equal to 30 percent its breaking strength; therefore, it is used for anchor lines, docklines, and towing lines, where its great strength and stretchability are advantages.

Dacron, a polyester fiber, stretches only about 3.5 to 5 percent under the same conditions, so it is used for sheets, halyards, and other applications where stretch would be undesirable. Dacron is known outside North America as Terylene, Duron, Fortrel, A.C.E., and Kodel.

Polypropylene has little elasticity, tends not to retain knots, and has only about 60 percent the strength of Dacron, but it's light and inexpensive and it floats. It's used for heaving lines, dinghy painters, and water-skiers' towlines.

The more exotic ropes made of Kevlar and Spectra stretch about 1 to 2 percent, and even less in some cases. Kevlar is several times stronger than steel, but it's not durable when bent sharply, so it is not suitable for halyards. Spectra is even stronger than Kevlar and accepts bending. It's also good at resisting chafe. Its Achilles' heel is elongation—it tends to "creep" slightly under a heavy sustained load.

See also **Dacron; Halyards; Nylon Line; Polypropylene; Rope Strength; Sheet Sizes.**

Rope Versus Line

Knowing the ropes

Self-styled boating experts will inform you that rope mysteriously turns into line the moment you get it aboard your boat and is never again referred to as rope. But perhaps that is an affectation born of a desire to be more nautical than one's knowledge or experience permits, because there has always been rope on boats. The *Encyclopedia of Nautical Knowledge* defines rope this way: "In marine use, general term for cordage composed of strands, and, as a rule, larger than 1 inch in circumference."

It's true that for practical purposes ropes are given other names on boats, and may turn into sheets, halyards, warps, rodes, pendants, painters, hawsers, strops, cables, mooring lines, docklines, leech lines, heaving lines, downhauls, uphauls, outhauls, guys, reef points, lashings, lanyards, preventers, and vangs, among others.

But there are still also many "ropes" on a vessel, including the bolt rope, the tiller rope, the foot rope, the check rope, the dip rope, and others, including wire rope. Most telling of all, a sailor's own phrase for professional competence was "to know the ropes." Not the lines, you observe.

See also **Rope Strength; Rope Stretch.**

Rudder Loss

Regaining control of your steering with a makeshift rig

Because the rudder is one of the most important controls on a boat, its loss is a serious blow but not necessarily a life-threatening one. Twin-screw powerboats can be steered with the throttle control of one engine, of course, and many sailboats can be made to steer themselves by balancing the sails. Almost all boats can be steered with a jury-rigged rudder of some kind.

Sailboats will most easily sail themselves to windward. Trimming the headsails and easing the mainsail, or reefing it, will usually stop the boat rounding up into the wind. If your course lies downwind, it's important to move the center of effort of the sails as far forward as you can, dropping the mainsail altogether and sheeting in the headsails absolutely flat. A makeshift bowsprit fashioned from a spinnaker pole or the mainsail boom will enable you to extend the sails even farther forward, which will keep the boat heading downwind, at least on a broad reach.

There are many ways to fashion a jury rudder from a boom, oars, or spinnaker pole with a blade made from a floorboard or a locker door. The sweep may then be pivoted at the stern, lashed to the stern pulpit or a quarter stanchion. The actual design and construction of such a crude rudder depends entirely on the material available and the design of the stern.

R

A makeshift rudder. (Stanchions and lifelines omitted for clarity.)

You can also control a boat's direction with a drogue or anything that will cause a fair amount of drag, such as a car tire, a metal bucket, or a bulky sailbag stuffed with clothing and towels. After extending the drogue at least one full wavelength behind the boat, tie a rolling hitch to the drogue line about 15 feet (about 5 m) aft of the stern and take the two ends to cockpit winches port and starboard. Then you can steer by winching in the line on the side to which you want to turn. If necessary, the steering effect can be enhanced by separating the lines more laterally. Lash a spinnaker pole across the after deck or just forward of the stern

pulpit; take the lines through blocks made fast to its outer ends; and then inboard to the winches.

Rudder loss is rare but a good boater will give some thought to how best to handle the situation if should it ever occur.

See also **Rudders**.

Rudders

Controlling the direction of a boat's movement by steering

The word *rudder* comes from the Anglo-Saxon *rother*, meaning a paddle. The first rudders were almost certainly paddles, and the

Viking long ships used modified paddles as steering oars, pivoting them in an upright position at the starboard (Anglo-Saxon *steorbord*, or steering side) quarter and controlling them with a tiller.

Powerboat rudders are typically much smaller in area than sailboat rudders because they work in the "prop thrust"—the fast-moving stream of water directly behind the propeller. The stream that impinges on the rudder of a sailboat under sail only is much slower, so the rudder must make up in size what it lacks in power per unit of face area.

Powerboats and sailboats are rigged so that the top of the steering wheel turns to the same side as the rudder, just as an automobile's steering wheel turns the same way as the wheels. But a tiller moves the opposite way, turning the rudder (and, therefore, the boat) to starboard when the tiller is put over to port.

A sailboat's rudder is dependent entirely on a flow of water across its surface. If the boat is motionless in the water, she cannot be steered, even though that water may be moving over the land in the form of a current and carrying the boat with it.

In general, a deep skinny rudder is more efficient than a wide shallow one, and a rudder supported by a skeg or the after end of a deep keel is stronger (and better protected from groundings) than a spade rudder that depends entirely on its projecting stock for strength. The farther aft the rudder is placed, the greater its turning leverage will be.

A semibalanced rudder, one

R

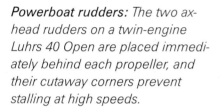

ax-head

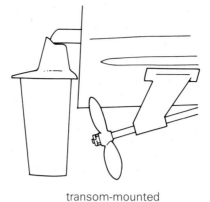

transom-mounted

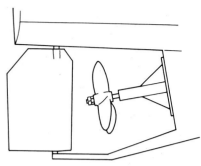

flat stock with skeg

Powerboat rudders: *The two ax-head rudders on a twin-engine Luhrs 40 Open are placed immediately behind each propeller, and their cutaway corners prevent stalling at high speeds.*

The rudders on a Blackfin 29 sportfisherman have to be transom-mounted because the two engines, and therefore the propellers, are so far aft. The rudders have built-in anticavitation plates.

The Mainship 34 Pilot, a single-engine semidisplacement powerboat, supports the bottom of its rudder on a keel projection.

R

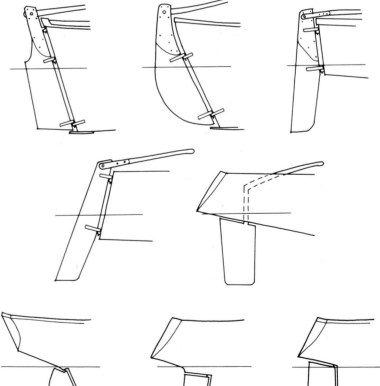

A selection of inboard and transom-mounted sailboat rudders.

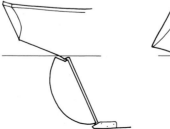

RUDDER SIZE CHART

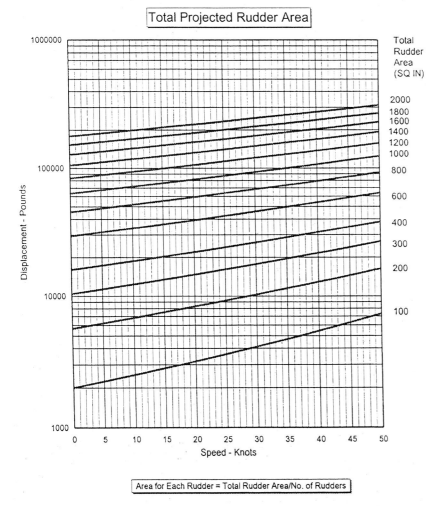

Total Projected Rudder Area

Area for Each Rudder = Total Rudder Area/No. of Rudders

The minimum rudder area needed for adequate steering as a function of boat speed and displacement. A bigger rudder adds responsiveness at slow speeds and drag at high speeds.

with about 15 to 17 percent of its area forward of the pivoting axis, gives a lighter helm and quicker response, but it tends to stall at a smaller angle of attack and often takes a "lead," making the boat wander off course. An unbalanced rudder hung from a skeg or a full keel will not stall as readily, and will center itself when left alone.

Rudders are usually most effective when they're angled at 35 degrees to the flow of water; a higher angle will only result in a stall and much less efficiency—sometimes even a complete loss of control.

With most boats, however, you can increase the rudder angle with benefit after the stern has started to swing in an arc because the angle of the rudder to the water still does not exceed 35 degrees.

See also **Rudder Loss; Skegs**.

Rules of the Road

Applying two sets of collision-prevention rules

There are two sets of collision regulations (what the U.S. Coast Guard calls COLREGs) to guide vessels of all sizes: the International Regulations for Preventing Collisions at Sea and the U.S. Inland Navigational Rules.

The Inland Rules apply to all vessels inside the demarcation lines separating inland and international waters; the International Rules apply outside the demarcation lines. These lines are shown on charts, but in their absence, the International Rules apply within bays, harbors, and inlets; along specified stretches of coasts; and up the connecting rivers to their limits of continuous navigation.

By careful design, there are few differences in the two sets of regulations, and they mostly concern navigation lights and sound signals.

Who, then, gives way to whom? In the following list, every vessel gives way to all other vessels listed before it:

- a vessel not under command
- a vessel restricted in her ability to maneuver
- a vessel constrained by her draft
- a vessel engaged in fishing
- a sailing vessel
- a power-driven vessel

Three exceptions to this list are discussed later in this entry. Meanwhile, be aware that a "vessel not under command" is one

R

ONE-MINUTE GUIDE DECISION TREE

IN-SIGHT SITUATION	WHAT YOU SHOULD DO
TRAFFIC SEPARATION SCHEME — YES	If using scheme, stay in lane in direction of arrows on chart If crossing, do so at 90° and stay clear of vessels in lanes If sailing, fishing, or less than 20m in length, use inshore zones Do not anchor in or near the ends of traffic lanes If risk of collision occurs, use additional rules below
NO	
IN NARROW CHANNEL OR FAIRWAY — YES	If crossing, do not impede vessels using channel If fishing or sailing, do not impede vessels using channel If overtaking, obtain agreement by sound signals Otherwise, keep to starboard edge of channel
NO	
OVERTAKING — YES	If overtaking, stay clear and use sound signals if necessary If in doubt, assume you are overtaking If being overtaken, stand on and respond to sound signals
NO	
POWER-DRIVEN HEAD-ON — YES	Both vessels alter course to starboard and pass port-to-port Use sound signals if you wish starboard-to-starboard (VHF may be substituted for sound signals under Inland Rules)
NO	
POWER-DRIVEN CROSSING — YES	If other vessel is on your starboard, keep clear and pass aft If other vessel is on your port, maintain course and speed
NO	
TWO SAILBOATS MEETING — YES	If on different tacks, port-tack vessel stays clear If on same tack, windward vessel stays clear If on port tack and uncertain about windward vessel, stay clear
NO	

MIXED VESSEL TYPES — YES	Stay clear of vessels higher than you on the list below
	(to claim status, vessels must display shapes or lights):
	  Not under command and restricted in ability to maneuver
	  Constrained by draft
	  Engaged in fishing (not angling)
	  Sailing (engine not running) underway
	  Power-driven underway
	  Seaplane

FOG SITUATION	WHAT YOU SHOULD DO
REGARDLESS OF TRAFFIC	Maintain safe speed, power-driven sound 5 sec. blast @ 2 min. Most other vessels sound one 5-sec. + two 1-sec. blasts @ 2 min.
HEAR SIGNAL AHEAD	Slow to bare steerageway or stop
RADAR TARGET FORWARD	Slow; do NOT turn to port unless overtaking
RADAR TARGET AFT OR ABEAM	Do NOT turn toward target

R

An at-a-glance guide to appropriate responses as set forth in the nautical rules of the road.

that is unable to keep clear of another vessel *through exceptional circumstances.* Such a vessel *must* display the correct signal: two balls or similar shapes in a vertical line, or two all-around red lights in a vertical line by night.

Similarly, a vessel that, from the nature of her work, is "restricted in her ability to maneuver" *must* exhibit a ball, a diamond, and another ball in a vertical line; or, at night, a red light, white light, and another red light in a vertical line.

A vessel "constrained by her draft" *may* show three all-around red lights in a vertical row by night, or a cylinder (with the axis vertical) by day. She's not obligated to make these signals, but if she has any sense, she *will.*

A vessel "engaged in fishing" is defined as one "fishing with nets, line trawls, or other fishing apparatus that *restricts maneuverability.*" This rule specifically excludes vessels fishing with trolling lines or gear that doesn't restrict maneuverability.

Don't forget that a sailboat using her engine in gear is regarded as a power-driven vessel, whether or not she has sail set.

The three exceptions to the previous list are as follows:

- Rule 9 says a vessel of less than 66 feet (20 m) in length or a sailing vessel of any length must keep clear of any vessel that can navigate safely only within a narrow channel or fairway.
- Rule 10 says a vessel less than 66 feet in length or a sailing vessel of any size shall not impede the passage of a power-

driven vessel following a traffic lane in a traffic-separation scheme.
- Rule 13 simply stipulates that the overtaking vessel shall keep clear—which means that if a sailboat starts overtaking a slow-moving powerboat, it's the sailboat's duty to keep clear.

If you're in a powerboat and you intend to overtake another vessel in a narrow channel, you must correctly signal your intention and receive an acknowledgment. In a sailboat, you may overtake without signaling only in waters subject to the Inland Rules.

See also **Fishing Boats; Sound Signals.**

Rum Punch

Doling out rum to compensate for rigors of shipboard life

Rum is an alcoholic liquor made from sugar cane and its by-product, molasses. It has played a large role in the history of navigation and exploration under sail, for it was doled out in prodigious portions to the crews of sailing ships —both warships and cargo carriers.

The rum cask was often broached to reward crews for a job well done in difficult circumstances. Those men of steel presumably had stomachs of asbestos to withstand the pints of fiery rum they consumed.

No doubt one purpose of the rum ration was to take sailors' minds off the grim conditions of

their existence—the danger, the lack of privacy, the harsh discipline, the poor pay, the atrocious food, and so on. There was no man less popular in the British navy than Admiral Edward Vernon (1684–1757) when he ordered the sailors' rum to be diluted with water. His nickname was "Grog" because he wore a grogram cloak—a material made of coarse silk and often stiffened with gum—and sailors thereafter referred to their watered-down rum ration as grog.

The islands of the Caribbean, with their prolific sugar plantations, were famed for the production of rum and for the drink known as rum punch. The traditional recipe for Caribbean rum punch, or Planter's Punch, is "one of sour, two of sweet, three of strong, and four of weak." That translates to the juice of 1 lime or lemon, 2 heaping teaspoons of sugar, 3 ounces of best Jamaica rum, and 4 ounces of dry gin. It is not for the faint of heart.

Running Inlets

Entering a narrow inlet from the sea can be hazardous

An inlet is a narrow channel connecting an inland body of water, such as a lagoon or a river, with the sea. Inlets such as those on the eastern and western coasts of the United States often carve sinuous passages through dangerous shallows. Those channels frequently change position in storms and floods, so they are difficult to mark in the usual way. Entering an inlet from seaward without lo-

R

cal knowledge is often so risky as to be foolhardy.

In most cases, a current flows through the navigable channel, either the outpouring of a river or the reversing flow of tidal movement. When an outgoing current meets heavy onshore winds, it creates steep, close, breaking waves of great danger to small boats.

This hazard is compounded by the fact that it's difficult to see the excessive height of such waves from the seaward approach. Thus, the age-old advice for those thinking of running an inlet for the first time in heavy onshore winds is: Don't. The rule of thumb states: When in doubt, stay out. You'll be safer riding out the gale in deep water at sea.

Sometimes this advice can't be followed, so here are some tips that might make an emergency entry less hazardous:

Have everybody on board don lifejackets.

Call ashore for advice on the present state of the bar or inlet and when conditions might improve. Use channel 16 on your VHF radio.

Study the chart, *Coast Pilot*, and any cruising guide you have at hand. Try to memorize the pattern of buoys, lights, and day marks you will encounter. If the preferred channel is marked by a range, you want to know it in advance.

If you have no success with the radio, take the time to search from seaward for the lowest surf, which indicates the deepest water in the inlet. Approach the surf line with great caution and constantly watch behind for waves threatening to break.

If you possibly can, wait until the flood tide is flowing into the inlet. When the wind and the current move in the same direction, the sea will be much calmer. If the inlet has uniformly shoal water, try to wait for high-water slack.

Look for a pattern to the swells. Often one wave in a series of three to seven is bigger than the rest because of different swell patterns riding on each other's backs.

Stand off until the biggest swell has broken, and then run in directly behind it. Try to stay slightly forward of the trough, matching your speed to the swell (easiest in a fast powerboat), and keep the boat stern-on to the waves—that is, at right angles to them. Do not let her slew around parallel to the waves or it is likely that you will capsize. In a twin-engine boat, alternately increase and decrease power on port and starboard engines to help your boat hold its course.

See also **Seamanship**.

Running Off

Fleeing before a storm: a good strategy against capsize

When sea conditions in a gale become so bad that it is no longer safe for a sailboat to heave to or lie ahull, she must be run off before the wind. Her course then will be perpendicular to the wave crests, so she will be much less likely to capsize. It takes much more energy to tilt a boat head over heels (or mast over keel) than it does to roll her over sideways.

To get a sailboat to run off under bare poles, you may need to temporarily raise a scrap of foresail to pull her head downwind and give her some steerageway. Once she is moving, you will have no trouble keeping her going the right way.

You'll find that you can steer her 20 or 30 degrees to port or starboard of dead downwind. If you keep an eye on what's coming up astern, you'll be able to weave a path through the waves so as to miss the worst of the plunging breakers. You need an alert crew for this, of course, and you must be prepared for a large wave to board from astern and wash heavily into the cockpit. When the helm starts feeling sloppy and you lose control as a wave passes beneath you, the boat is running too fast for safety. It's time to slow her down by towing drogues.

As a powerboat tactic, running off is most likely to be of use in a moderate gale—say, less than 40 knots of wind and seas less than 10 to 15 feet (3 to 4.5 m). Concentrate on running directly downwind and avoiding a broach. Good wheel and throttle work should accomplish this on a twin-screw boat; trailing a drogue may help on a single-screw boat. But when wind and seas build higher, you will need to turn to face the wind and seas in order to avoid broaching or being pooped—that is, you will need to heave to. Because the turn will put you momentarily

R

broadside to the seas—a power-boat's most vulnerable attitude—you must time the turn for a lull between high seas and accomplish it as quickly as possible.

In summary, sailboats heave to in moderate gales and run off in survival conditions; power-boats do the opposite.

See also **Drogue; Heaving To;** **Heavy Weather; Lying Ahull; Pooping Seas; Scudding; Towing Drogues.**

S

Safe Anchorage

Planning where to anchor so the boat always comes first

When you're seeking a safe anchorage, remember the following basic requirements:

- shelter from wind and waves
- room to swing around the anchor
- sufficient depth of water at low tide
- good holding ground for the anchor

These requirements are all for the benefit of the boat. Shore facilities and diversions for the crew are also welcome, but should be regarded as bonuses, to be enjoyed only after the basic needs of the boat have been satisfied.

See also **Anchors, Anchoring.**

Safe Anchor Weight

Why a good anchor needs weight as well as fine design

Although it's true that engineering design makes them effective, anchors still need sheer weight to dig into the bottom. The rule of thumb is that no matter how small your boat might be, you shouldn't leave her unattended on any anchor weighing less than 30 pounds (14 kg).

That's because a change in wind or current will bring about a shift in the direction of pull on the anchor, and probably break it out of the ground. Then it will have to reset itself, something a light-weight anchor of the Danforth type might be reluctant to do if there is any grass or weed on the bottom. There's also a chance that the anchor line will drag across a Danforth during the change and foul itself on one of the projecting tripping palms, in which case the anchor will be useless.

A heavier plow anchor, such as a C.Q.R., a Bruce, or a Delta, will reset itself with more certitude on most bottoms, and is much less likely to be fouled.

All this applies only to boats left to swing on a single anchor, of course. If two anchors are used so that neither can be fouled by either rode and neither will break out after a change of wind direction, then Danforth-type anchors can certainly be used for long-term anchoring. In fact, for insurance purposes, a boat lying to two properly set anchors is moored, not simply anchored.

See also **Anchors, Anchoring; Bahamian Moor.**

S

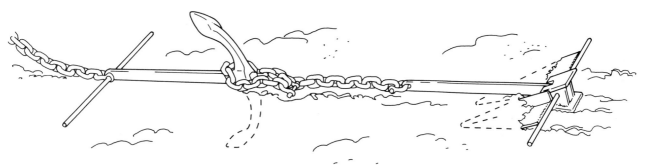

Anchors used in tandem.

Sail Area

Figuring out the amount of sail needed for performance

Because sails provide a sailboat's motive power, the actual area of sail is obviously an important factor in her performance. Sail area on a sailing yacht equates with horsepower on a motor yacht.

The area of sail a boat can spread is limited by many factors, including the waterline length, displacement, and stability afforded by her hull shape and ballast. You can estimate sail required by taking three fourths of the square of the waterline length in feet; that is, multiply the waterline length by itself and take 75 percent of the result. The answer is in square feet.

Racing boats invariably carry more sail than this, and cruising boats probably less, though it's not always a good idea to do so. Experienced cruisers such as Lin and Larry Pardey advise against reducing the size or height of rigs on cruising boats because they are almost always heavily laden and

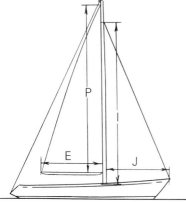

Figuring Sail Area
mainsail = (P x E) ÷ 2
100% foretriangle = (I x J) ÷ 2
total sail area =
    mainsail + foretriangle

need power to keep them moving at a reasonable speed.

About 85 square feet (7.9 m²) of working sail for every 2,000 pounds (907 kg) of displacement is sufficient to produce a boat that is an efficient passagemaker in medium winds.

Another way to estimate a sailboat's performance is to study her sail area–displacement (SAD) ratio, which is a static power-to-weight ratio that makes no allowance for different amounts of power produced by winds of different speeds.

The SAD ratio is calculated as the sail area in square feet (or meters) divided by the displacement in cubic feet (or cubic meters) to the two-thirds power. The following are accepted SAD ratios for different types of boats:

- cruising boats: 16 to 18
- racer-cruisers: 18 to 20
- pure racers: 20 to 22
- extreme racers: 22 upward
- racing multihulls: 28 upward

For ease of handling, a boat's total sail area is usually shared by two or more sails. A sail of about 400 square feet (37 m²) is about the limit for one person to handle with any regularity. Uffa Fox, the British designer and sailor, insisted that one person could "reef or stow a 500-square-foot (46 m²) mainsail in all weathers," but he was an exceptional seafarer, and Sir Francis Chichester decided that his mainsail of 380 square feet (35 m²) was more than he could manage in heavy weather during his circumnavigation.

See also **Horsepower; Sailboat Rigs.**

Sailboat Engines

Matching propeller, shaft, and engine for performance

The British voyager Eric Hiscock maintained that an auxiliary sailboat engine should give a speed of at least 2 knots against a force 5 wind with the weather shore as far as 2 miles distant.

Surprisingly, although many boats will run at hull speed at modest revolutions in calm weather, they fail miserably the Hiscock test in choppy water and headwinds.

The secret to good performance in heavy conditions (when it's most needed) is to match engine power with propeller size and shaft revolutions.

It takes surprisingly little horsepower to push a boat through the water, and vessels that fail the Hiscock test usually have propellers that are too big in pitch and/or diameter for the shaft speed; therefore, their engines lug and fail to reach maximum revolutions—and cannot put out their maximum power.

Engine manufacturers continue to produce models that are smaller, lighter, and more powerful than their forebears, while maintaining and improving pollution and economy standards, so there is little excuse these days for an auxiliary sailboat to be underpowered.

Displacement in the amount of 3 to 4 hp per ton is comforting; any extra is likely to be wasted and wasteful. Wasted, because once you have reached maximum hull speed in a displacement boat, you can't go markedly faster even if you double or triple the horse-

S

power—and wasteful, because a more powerful engine than you require will normally run with a light load, which spells an early demise for a diesel engine. Diesels thrive on hard work.

See also **Diesel Engines; Engine Life; Powerboat Engines;** entries under **Propeller.**

Sailboat Handling

Learning to sail need not be complicated by complex jargon

Children learn to sail easily: put them in a small dinghy and they'll figure it out in an hour or two. But adults who have never sailed before often have more trouble learning how; for many people, sailing is not intuitive. Furthermore, beginners are often overwhelmed by unnecessary nautical jargon. They also fear capsize and, perhaps even more, they fear making fools of themselves.

Sailing is actually a simple sport, but—like many others—it has become so overwhelmed by gadgets and gear that beginners, who cannot separate what's really needed from what's not, might find it complicated.

The best way to learn to sail is in a small dinghy from 8 to 16 feet (2.4 to 4.8 m) in length. If you can sail a dinghy well, you can sail anything. The second-best way is to take lessons in a small keelboat, a daysailer of between 18 and 24 feet (5.5 and 7.3 m). It handles much like a large dinghy but won't capsize. The third best way is to crew on someone else's sailboat.

The basic controls of a sailboat are the tiller, the halyards,

the mainsheet, the jib sheets, and (in a dinghy) the centerboard. To make the boat go, raise the sails by pulling on the halyards. Use the sheets to adjust the sails to the wind. Pull them in until the sails just stop shaking. Lower the centerboard to stop sideways drift. Use the tiller to steer. If the boat heels over too much in a gust, let the sails out.

To stop the boat, turn the bow into the direction the wind is coming from, or let out the sails until they are flapping in line with the wind.

See also **Sails and "Lift."**

Sailboat Rigs

Choosing the best sail plans for boats of different sizes

There is considerable variation in the rigs used by sailing yachts, but

most fit into one of six major categories.

The sloop is by far the most popular. The mast is placed fairly far forward and supports one mainsail and one headsail.

The mast on a cutter is placed farther aft, almost in the middle of the boat, and supports a proportionately smaller mainsail and two headsails: a forestaysail and a jib.

The ketch is a rig usually found on larger yachts. It has two masts, the forward of which is roughly in the same position as a sloop's. A smaller mizzenmast is located aft, but forward of the rudder head. The mainmast supports a mainsail and one or two headsails. The mizzenmast supports a smaller sail akin to the mainsail abaft the mast, and off the wind may support a mizzen staysail, which is set flying with its head at the mizzen masthead and its tack forward on deck.

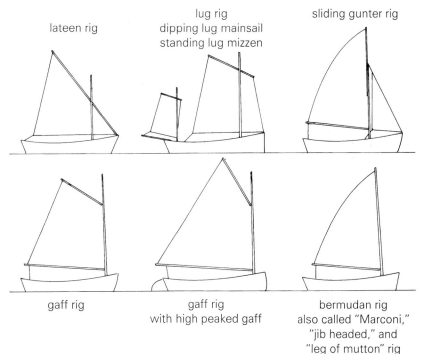

Types of sailboat rigs based on sail shape.

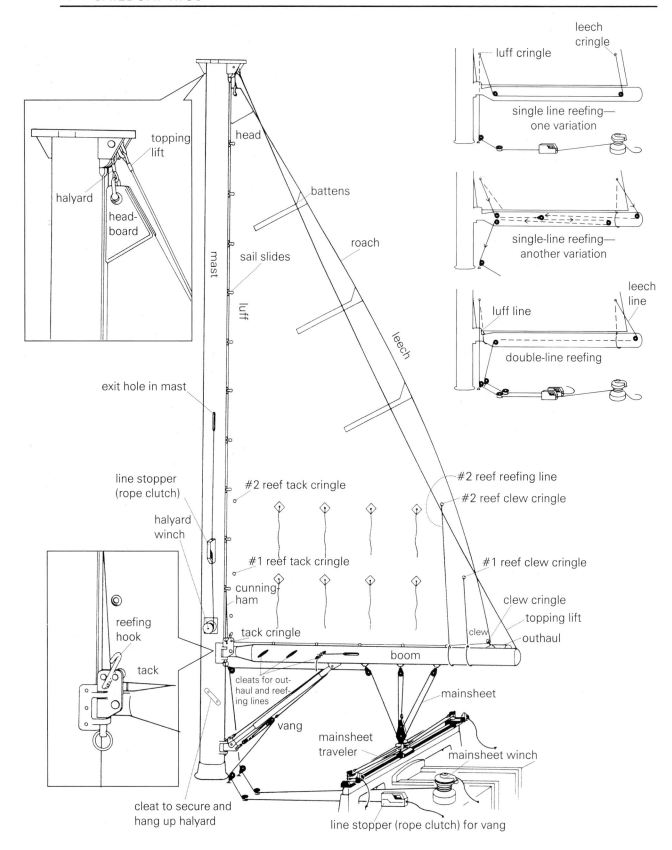

luff cringle

leech cringle

single line reefing—
one variation

single-line reefing—
another variation

luff line

leech line

double-line reefing

topping
lift

halyard

head-
board

head

battens

roach

mast

sail slides

luff

leech

exit hole in mast

line stopper
(rope clutch)

halyard
winch

reefing
hook

tack

#2 reef tack cringle

#1 reef tack cringle

cunning-
ham

tack cringle

cleats for out-
haul and reef-
ing lines

vang

#2 reef reefing line

#2 reef clew cringle

#1 reef clew cringle

clew cringle

topping lift

clew

outhaul

boom

mainsheet

mainsheet
traveler

mainsheet winch

cleat to secure and
hang up halyard

line stopper (rope clutch) for vang

Principal sail and spar terminology. **Upper right:** *cockpit reefing strategies.*

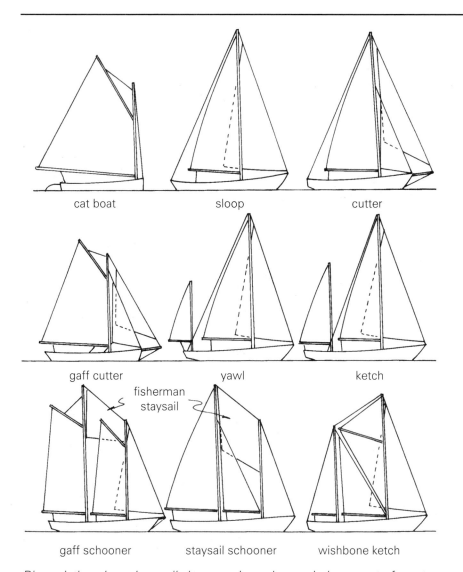

cat boat

sloop

cutter

gaff cutter

fisherman staysail

yawl

ketch

gaff schooner

staysail schooner

wishbone ketch

Rig variations based on sail shape and number and placement of masts.

The yawl rig is similar to that of the ketch, except that the mizzenmast is stepped aft of the rudder head and, therefore, is proportionately much smaller than the ketch's mizzen.

The schooner also has two masts, but the foremast is lower than the mainmast (or, rarely, the same height), so she carries small sails forward and a large mainsail aft. Depending on her size, she may carry one or two headsails.

The cat rig is headless; that is, no headsails are carried—just a mainsail set aft of the mast, which is stepped far forward near the bow. A cat ketch has two masts, the forward one higher than the after one, supporting a mainsail and a mizzensail.

Mainsails are mostly Bermuda-rigged (triangular) and rarely gaff-rigged (rectangular), but mizzensails are almost always Bermuda-rigged. A schooner may have gaff or Bermuda rigs on either or both masts.

Of these six rigs, the sloop and cat are the simplest, the schooner the most complicated. The sloop is more efficient than the cutter, which in turn is slightly more efficient than the ketch or yawl. Sloop rigs are mostly carried on boats up to about 35 feet (10.7 m) in length, but may also suit larger hulls if they have the power to handle the big sails. Cutters start at about 30 feet (9 m); ketches and yawls start at about 35 to 40 feet (10.7 to 12 m) and go up to 70 feet (21 m) or more.

See also **Booms; Gaff Mainsails; Junk Rigs; Lateen Rig; Masts; Sail Area**.

Sail Cloth

Laminating films to maintain the best strength and shape

The majority of mainsails and headsails are made from the tightly woven polyester fiber known in the United States as Dacron. For spinnakers and other light-weather sails, lightweight rip-stop nylon material is used. Sails made from these materials are used extensively on cruising boats and small club racers.

Racing boats, on the other hand—and even some cruisers—are increasingly using sails laminated from newer, stronger, and more stable Kevlar and Spectra materials combined with Mylar, an airtight, thin polyester film. As these technologies become more accepted, other racers seek to push the envelope still farther. High-tech Cuben and carbon fiber are the latest arrivals. Laminated sails do better than polyester and nylon at maintaining their shapes in heavy winds, and typically stretch only a few tenths

S

of a percent under normal working loads. High-quality Dacron stretches about 1 or 2 percent, and nylon much more.

The biggest problems currently facing laminated sails are higher cost and a shorter working life compared with Dacron, although it is difficult to compare their respective values on the sole basis of working life. Whereas laminated sails retain their most efficient shape for nearly all their working life, Dacron and nylon sails usually stretch into permanently inefficient shapes after a couple of seasons' use. It is almost impossible to see the subtle differences that cause the inefficiency, however, so the problem usually goes undetected for years, especially in boats not used for racing.

Different weights of cloth are used for different kinds of sails flown in varying wind conditions, but you can estimate the average weight required for everyday working mainsails and headsails by dividing the waterline length of the boat in feet by 3. The answer will be in ounces of cloth per square yard.

See also **Sailboat Rigs**.

Sailing in Gusts

Maneuvering your sailboat to reduce speed and heeling

It's uncanny how often the wind will start to rise when you're entering a congested anchorage or port under sail. You know you should reef to reduce speed and heeling, but either you can't leave the helm or there simply isn't the space to heave to while you take in sail. What to do?

> In a puff, spring a luff;
> In a lull, keep her full.

That's the old adage. It applies to cruisers as much as to racers. Feather the mainsail in the gusts by giving it some sheet and pointing up close to the wind, and then fall off well to leeward as soon as the gust passes. You'll be carving a zigzag course, and probably alarming your fellow boaters, but you will be averaging the required course and your boat will actually be under much better control.

You can't do this for long, of course—it's a short-term expedient to get you out of immediate trouble. If you're planning to carry on for any distance, you'll have to find a place where you can tuck in a reef or claw down the sails and fire up the engine.

Sailing on Friday

Inviting bad luck is not for superstitious boaters

Superstition still maintains a firm hold on those who go down to the sea in ships and—even in this age of satellites and nuclear power—there are sailors who will not set sail on a Friday.

Friday was named after the Norse goddess Frigg, or Frigga. The goddess of love and fertility, she was the wife of the god Woden, after whom Wednesday is named. In early times, Friday was regarded as a lucky day, and an especially good one on which to get married. But the early Christians turned all that around. They regarded Frigga as a witch, and her day as unlucky. It became a deep-rooted superstition, manifesting itself in many ways. Among sailors, it became bad luck to set sail on a Friday.

"Sailors are more foolish on this point than you can imagine," wrote Mrs. Henry Wood, the Victorian novelist, in 1890, "and I believe . . . that ships sailing on a Friday have come to grief through their crew losing heart. No matter what impediment is met with—bad weather, accidents, what not—the men say at once, 'It's of no use, we sailed on a Friday.' "

This feeling is so strong that there is still today an apocryphal tale with wide currency among boating people about the British navy's attempts to quell sailors' fears. The Admiralty is said to have commissioned a new ship to be named HMS *Friday*. Her keel was laid on a Friday, she was launched on a Friday, and she was put in command of Captain James Friday. She set sail on her maiden voyage on a Friday—and was never heard of again. It's a pity to spoil a good story, but there is no record of a ship called HMS *Friday*, or even of a Captain James Friday, in the British navy.

The fact that countless ships set sail every Friday and safely complete their passage presents a dilemma for those of us who believe the superstition or, at least, are too timid to challenge it. How can this be? Why don't these foolhardy mariners come to grief, as they are supposed to?

Perhaps the answer lies in the Black Box Theory, which states that luck is not fortuitous, but must be earned. In that case, it can only be assumed that skippers who set sail on Friday must have enough points in their black boxes to overcome the bad luck of sailing on that day.

See also **Black Box Theory; Unlucky Colors; Unlucky Names**.

Sails and "Lift"

How a sailboat makes progress against the prevailing wind

There is still a great deal of mystery attached to the process whereby a sailboat makes progress *against* the prevailing wind, but it's possible to state it in simple general terms. A sail would never generate "lift" if it were flat—its curved, asymmetrical shape causes the wind passing over it to be deflected, and that deflection in turn causes small differences in the pressures on either side of the sail, with high

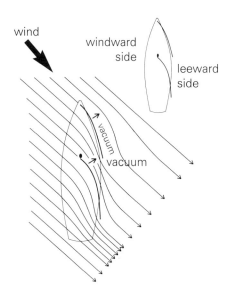

Idealized depiction of airflow over properly trimmed sails.

pressure on the windward side and lower pressure on the leeward side.

The net result is a force acting to leeward at right angles to every part of the sail's surface. In the case of a mainsail trimmed for beating, most of that force is directed sideways, of course, but a small portion is directed forward. The sideways force is counteracted by the boat's keel or centerboard, and the small remaining force is what drives the boat forward. Because of the obvious comparison with the way an airplane wing works, that force is referred to as "lift," even though the drive is horizontal, not vertical.

Naturally, no sail can drive a boat directly into the wind. Modern sailboats mostly beat to windward at an angle of about 45 degrees to the real wind direction, although highly developed racing craft can head up almost 10 degrees more.

Lift occurs only when there is a stream of wind passing across the sail from fore to aft, which is normally the case from a beat to a broad reach. As you turn your boat farther downwind from a broad reach, the cross-flow ceases and the sail becomes a stalled airfoil, blowing before the wind in a manner that is intuitively understood.

When sailing dead downwind with stalled sails, you can't go any faster than the wind. But a boat on a broad reach may exceed the true wind speed because its forward motion creates a faster "apparent" wind against the sails.

See also **Air Pressure on Sails; Wind and Altitude; Yacht Design**.

Saloon

A cabin by any other name sounds not quite so sweet

Many boaters seem to find the word *cabin* rather lacking the elegance and significance they associate with their boats. Therefore, they refer to their cabin as a *salon*, a fancy French term for reception hall or a room filled with perfumed finery.

Hairdressers, beauticians, and couturiers have salons; sailors have a saloon. *The Encyclopedia of Nautical Knowledge* defines a saloon this way: "In a cargo and smaller passenger vessels, the main cabin, or that serving as a dining-room, assembly room, etc." *The Oxford Concise Dictionary* describes a saloon as a "public room for first-class or for all passengers on ship."

The only dissonant note is sounded by *Webster's New World Dictionary*, which allows the use of both *salon* and *saloon* but then confesses that saloon is "specifically, the main social cabin of a passenger ship." Nevertheless, whereas most sailors use the word *saloon*, most powerboaters seem to prefer *salon*.

It's possible that some boaters use the word *salon* because they don't want their boats to be associated with saloons where strong alcoholic drinks are served and rough men indulge in fisticuffs. But a better choice than either *salon* or *saloon* would be *cabin*. What could be simpler or more correct?

See also **Yacht Design**.

S

Salvage

Getting paid for the risk of saving a vessel in distress

By law and by custom, mariners are bound to do everything in their power to save the lives of those in peril at sea, but there is no corresponding onus on them to save a vessel in danger of being lost, or any of the property associated with it. Thus, if you do save a vessel in distress you may qualify as a salvor and be entitled to an award. In general, you have to satisfy the following four conditions:

- the vessel must have been in genuine distress, that is, in grave danger of being badly damaged or destroyed
- you must have offered your help voluntarily
- you must have risked your own life or property to save the ship
- the salvage effort must have been successful

If the owner of a vessel in peril comes to an agreement with a salvor beforehand, the salvor will have no further rights to salvage. To protect yourself from a possible salvage claim, therefore, ask your potential rescuer whether there will be a charge for the service, and if so, how much. Once you have agreed on a price, the rescue effort becomes nothing more than a contract to render help. This contract does not have to be written; a verbal agreement is legal and binding, but it would be wise to record your conversation or have one or more witnesses.

Contrary to popular belief, your acceptance of a towline from another boat does not automatically entitle the other skipper to claim salvage. Neither can you be forced to accept a tow to safety, no matter how desperate the situation is.

The ability to contribute to your own salvation may lessen the amount of any award made to a salvor, so don't abandon your boat if it's not necessary. Do all you can to help the salvor, including giving him your towline, if possible. The less you have to rely on his special skills, knowledge, and equipment, the weaker will be his claim in Admiralty Court. Salvage awards are usually based on the amount by which the salvor's efforts improved the situation, and that amount must be significant.

See also **Groundings**.

Sandpaper

Smoothing and preparing surfaces for paint, varnish

Anyone who has owned a boat of any kind has more than a passing acquaintance with sandpaper, which is used to prepare surfaces for varnishing and painting.

Sandpaper comes in many different sizes of grit and types of backing paper, but you can do almost all your boat work with two kinds of paper and a half dozen grits.

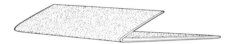

TYPE OF PAPER	IDENTIFYING COLOR	USES	SUGGESTED GRITS/COMMENTS	
Aluminum oxide	Tan or brown	Good all-around sandpaper	60D—rough sanding and paint removal; 120C—surface preparation for painting; 220A—between-coat sanding.	The most useful paper; have plenty aboard
Emery cloth	Black	None	None	Except to prepare aluminum for paint, has no refinishing use; good for polishing metal and sharpening plane irons
Flint	Light beige or light gray	None	None	Dime-store sandpaper; useless—never buy flint paper
Garnet	Red	Hand sanding fine woodwork	None	Expensive and will not stand up to machine sanding; leave to the cabinetmakers
Silicon carbide (open coat)	White	Fine finishing paper; the best choice for sanding disks	180A—between-coat sanding; 400A—pre-polish sanding	Cuts well and relatively long-lasting; good choice for fine sanding
Silicon carbide (closed coat)	Black	Waterproof paper for wet sanding	340A—wet sanding between coats of polyurethane; 600A—pre-polish wet sanding	Called wet-or-dry sandpaper; wet sanding yields the finest finish

Grit numbers roughly represent the number of grains of grit per square inch—the higher the number the smaller the grains must be, so the higher the grit, the finer the finish. The letter code following the grit designation—i.e., 60D or 400A—indicates the weight of the paper. A is the lightest and F is the heaviest (D is the heaviest commonly available for typical boat applications).

Sandpaper types and uses.

S

Use aluminum oxide production paper for all dry sanding. It's backed with brown paper and the grit is sharp, tough, and long-lasting, even on fiberglass. The grits you need are 80 for initial rough sanding, 120 for early sanding between coats of paint or for smoothing wood, and 220 for fine sanding between coats.

Wet sanding is done with waterproof silicon carbide, or wet-and-dry paper, which is the color of charcoal. When you keep it wet and dip it frequently in water, the grit remains unclogged for long periods. It, too, is sharp and long-lasting. Its main use is sanding between coats of paint or varnish for an extrafine finish; for this you should use 340- or 400-grit. It's also used for sanding antifouling paint without causing toxic copper-laden dust that might otherwise be inhaled. Use 40-grit to remove old bottom paint and 80-grit between coats.

See also **Paints**.

Scope for Anchors

Letting out enough cable to allow an anchor to do its job

The term *scope* refers to the length of line or chain between the anchor and the boat's bow relative to the depth of water in which the boat is anchored. Thus, a scope of 3 to 1 indicates that a boat lying in 10 feet of water has an anchor line 30 feet long.

In fact, the scope is measured to the bow roller, so the distance from the bow to water level must be added to the depth of the water. This is not significant on

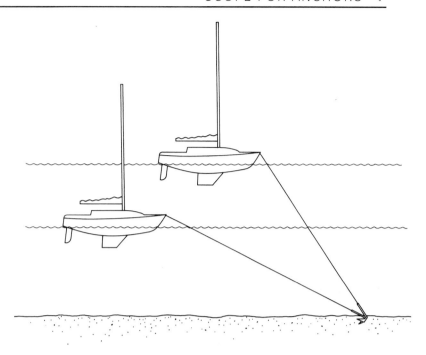

Rising tide reduces scope.

most small craft, but be aware that when depth of water is mentioned in connection with scope, it really means the distance from the bow roller straight down to the seabed.

Also be aware that a rising tide will reduce your scope. This can be an important factor in areas with large tidal ranges.

You should know the scope of your anchor line at all times because too little line will cause your anchor to drag. Under favorable conditions, the minimum scope should be 5 to 1. Under average conditions, a scope of 7 to 1 is considered necessary, and in really heavy weather you'll need as much as 10 to 1.

These scopes allow a nylon line (with a boat-length of chain attached to the anchor) to exert an almost horizontal pull on the anchor, which is important because most anchors break out of the ground if the angle of pull is

higher than 8 degrees from horizontal.

To know your scope, you have to be able to judge how much line you've let out, and there are various ways to gauge it. With nylon three-strand line, it's easy to thread numbered pieces of fabric or plastic through the weave at intervals—every 10 or 15 feet is sufficient. Chain is usually marked with thick and thin bands of paint in one or more colors to represent fathoms. Some anchor winches or windlasses incorporate a mechanical counter that records the amount of chain veered. No matter how it's done, you need to know the length of your rode fairly accurately—guessing just isn't good enough.

On many occasions, of course, you'll find yourself jammed into a crowded anchorage where no one can veer the recommended scope for fear of swinging into someone else. If

S

you have an all-chain rode and the weather is settled, you can probably get away with a scope of 3 to 1, but nothing less. If you have a combination rode of chain and nylon, try a scope of 3 to 1 and hope for the best, bearing in mind that you may have to make a quick getaway in the middle of the night when the wind blows up and dragging boats cause mayhem in the anchorage.

When conditions are crowded, a prudent skipper will set a constant anchor watch and check anchor bearings at regular intervals to detect dragging. Most of us, unfortunately, are only semiprudent. Although we regret that we don't set watches when we should, we gain comfort from the knowledge that if the worst happens, we certainly won't be the only ones panicking.

See also **Anchors, Anchoring.**

Scudding

Running fast downwind to survive the ultimate storm

It was the French cruising sailor Bernard Moitessier who drew attention to the technique of high-speed scudding in a sailboat as a way of surviving "the ultimate storm." Moitessier used the technique to save his boat *Joshua* in the southern Pacific Ocean, but he credits the idea to Vito Dumas, who sailed around the world in the Roaring Forties during World War II in his boat *Lehg II*.

Dumas found that his boat would get out of control in the troughs of really big, long, fast-moving seas when she was blan-keted from the wind. She needed to be moving faster to carry her way and retain maneuverability.

But let's backtrack for a moment. The buildup to the ultimate storm produces short, steep seas in which Dumas, Moitessier, and such renowned scientific experts as C. A. Marchaj believe it's best to stream a drogue that will hold the stern up when the boat is on a breaking crest and the rudder is inefficient. In that sea state, the plunging breakers are close together and it's almost impossible for a small slow boat to avoid every one rolling up astern. But the breaking crests are not yet fully developed, and the occasional one that boards will not greatly harm a well-found boat with a watertight cockpit and lockers and a sturdy bridge deck. The drogue slows the boat down and prevents her from surfing off out of control, broaching, and capsizing.

After a few hours of storm-force winds, however, the seas get bigger. The breakers plunging down their faces become more fearsome. A sailboat pooped by one of these monsters would likely suffer damage. Fortunately, at the same time, the seas lengthen and grow farther apart.

So now it's time to start scudding, or moving faster downwind with greater maneuverability, and therefore with a greatly increased chance of avoiding the worst of the more widely spaced monsters rolling up from astern—or at least that's what Moitessier believed.

First, get rid of the drogues. Moitessier simply cut his free; there was no way for him to retrieve them, which would be the case in most boats under those conditions. He had found that *Joshua* was being held fast while massive breakers boarded her aft and rampaged over the decks; however, as soon as he cut the drogues away, she was free to flee downwind under bare poles.

He would keep her running dead downwind until a steep sea reared up close astern. Just before it struck, he would turn *Joshua* 15 to 20 degrees to one side and try to maintain that course while the sea broke under her and passed by.

If the helm pulled when the wave was underneath, Moitessier released the tiller completely for a few seconds to give her her head. It was important, he said, not to fight the sea at this critical period. Then, when the sea had passed ahead, he would put the helm up again to bring her back on course, dead downwind.

Moitessier confirmed Dumas's theory that taking the seas at an angle like this prevented *Joshua* from getting out of control by surfing too fast and plowing into the sea ahead. The oncoming sea also heeled her to leeward substantially, so that if she did dig deep into the back of a sea, her rounded bow tended to scoop her out.

An active storm-fighting technique like this demands constant attention to the helm, of course, and only works properly with a fresh, attentive crew. Exhausted, shorthanded crews must use passive techniques, such as heaving to or running off, and leave the boat to fend for herself as best she can.

See also **Heaving To; Heavy Weather; Lying Ahull; Pitchpoling; Pooping Seas; Running Off; Towing Drogues.**

S

Sculling

Learning to scull could get you home when things go wrong

Sculling is one of those useful skills all boaters should try to cultivate, even those with inflatable dinghies. It could get you home if your motor is inoperative or if you lose an oar or an oarlock.

It's a knack that comes quicker with practice than by reading about it, but basically all you do is extend an oar over the transom and waggle it back and forth in a vague representation of a fish's tail in action.

You can scull boats of various sizes, from small dinghies to cruising sailboats weighing several tons, but on the bigger boats, the work is heavy and the going slow.

The advantage of sculling is that it provides a steady pull when you're working from a dinghy and towing a larger craft—there is no snatching on the towline as there would be if you were rowing. Sculling may be better than rowing for short distances in rough water and high winds because the blade never comes out of the water to create wind resistance.

Heavy narrow dinghies are the easiest to scull. Light dinghies require short snappy strokes to counteract the tendency of the stern to move sideways.

Every dinghy transom should have a sculling notch or a dedicated oarlock offset to port or starboard if necessary to allow for an outboard motor in the center. The usual dimensions for an egg-shaped sculling notch are $1^7/_8$ inches wide by $2^1/_2$ inches deep, narrowing at the top to discourage the oar from jumping out.

See also **Dinghies**.

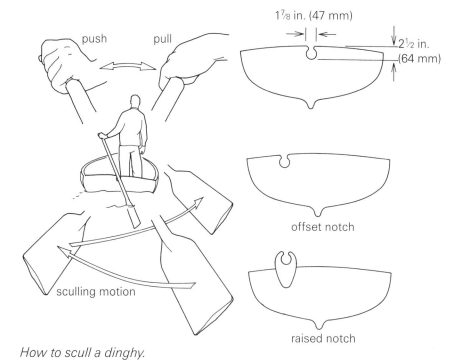

How to scull a dinghy.

Scurvy

Warding off a killer disease with vitamin C in many forms

Scurvy is not a threat to most sailors these days, even those crossing oceans, because it can take months to deplete the body's stores of vitamin C, the lack of which is the prime cause of the disease.

Nevertheless, long-term cruisers living off the ship's stores still need to watch out for it—it's a killer if left too long. The symptoms of scurvy are weakness, anemia, spongy gums, and bleeding from mucous membranes.

Small boats without refrigeration can't keep fresh produce for long, but there are some excellent alternative sources of vitamin C that will last well if they're kept cool and well ventilated. They include cabbage, carrots, celery, winter squash, garlic, grapefruit, onions, potatoes in their jackets, and oranges. You can also take vitamin C in synthetic form, of course. One multivitamin tablet a day will provide all you need.

Nothing, however, seems to supply the vitamin in such concentrated form as fresh or bottled lemon juice. The British navy substituted lime juice for lemon juice as an antiscorbutic in the late nineteenth century but found out the hard way that it contained little or no vitamin C. So British sailors (Limeys) suffered severe outbreaks of scurvy until the Lordships of the Admiralty came to their senses and reinstated lemon juice in 1918.

Another happy source of vitamin C is beer. Dr. Hannes Lindemann, who made two Atlantic crossings—one in a dugout canoe and another in a rubber-and-canvas folding boat—recommends that voyagers should carry plenty of beer to supply them not only with vitamin C, but also with other valuable vitamins and calories. His recommendation, although well received, is not widely practiced because of the difficulty of finding space for bulky beer supplies on a small yacht.

See also **Provisioning**.

Sea Anchors

Holding a boat head-on to the breaking seas in ocean storms

The difference between a sea anchor and a drogue is mainly one of size. A sea anchor, in the shape of a cone or a parachute, should be large enough to hold a boat almost dead still in the water, whereas a smaller drogue towed astern will merely slow her down.

The principle behind the sea anchor is that a boat held head-on to large waves has the best chance of survival in a storm. But the only boats that will lie head-on consistently are those with comparatively shallow hulls and no large keels, skegs, or rudders. This means that although most powerboats and many multihulls benefit from a sea anchor, most monohull sailboats don't unless their underbodies are canoe-shaped.

The famous small-boat voyager John Voss invented a conical sea anchor for his 1920s circumnavigation in his Nootkan canoe *Tilikum*, which was, of course, the ideal shape, and he misled generations of sailors into believing that their deep-keel, conventionally rigged cruisers would fare as well as *Tilikum* behind a sea anchor.

But ordinary sailboats tend to lie broadside to the wind and waves in storm conditions, with or without a sea anchor streamed from the bows. Most sailboats, in fact, lie stern-on to a sea anchor with ease, largely because the windage on the mainmast blows the bows downwind. The problem then is that heavy waves break against the nearly stationary boat, stressing the rudder, flooding the cockpit, and battering the companionway.

See also **Drogue**.

Seacocks

Shutting off water flowing through a hole in the hull

Many sailors still confuse seacocks with through-hull fittings, or through-hulls, as they are commonly called. A seacock is a special tap, or valve, that shuts off a flow of water; a through-hull is a metal or plastic lining for a hole in the hull. Every underwater through-hull hole on your boat should be fitted with a seacock capable of shutting off the flow of water that will result if a hose breaks or pulls away from the fitting.

The seacock attaches to the inside tail of the through-hull fitting. Some seacocks have flanges that are bolted through the hull into the outside flange of the through-hull; others merely screw

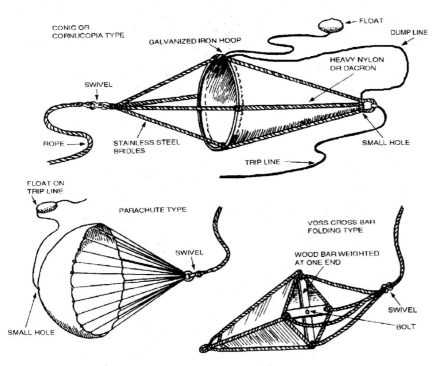

Sea anchor types. The two configurations on the right might also be used for drogues deployed from the stern, but a drogue should be smaller than a sea anchor.

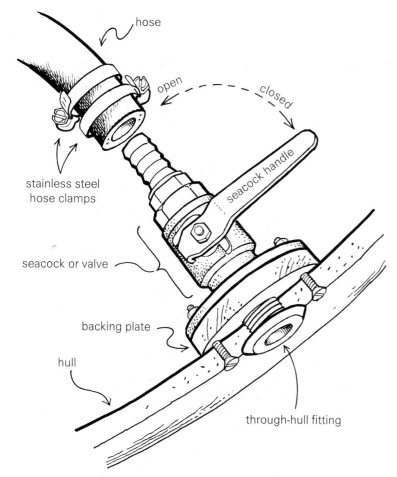

Typical through-hull and seacock configuration.

requiring only a smear of petro-leum jelly once a year or so. Those with bodies made of Marelon, a glass-reinforced nylon, are corrosion-proof and have gained wide acceptance, but they're still not regarded as the equal of the bronze-bodied ones by conservative mariners.

See also **Through-Hulls.**

Seakindliness

Judging the ability of a boat to be kind to her crew at sea

Seakindliness is a term applied to a boat that is gentle with her crew at sea. Her movements are easy and steady, not jerky, and she conducts herself in a seemly way—not hurling her-self against waves and sending spray flying everywhere in brash confrontation, but rather slip-ping quietly among them with little fuss.

Crews of racing sailboats will tell you that seakindliness is just another word for slowness. They maintain that if they were to reef and slow down, their boats would be seakindly too. Al-though there is some truth in that, no lightweight racing boat can ever be as seakindly as a properly designed displacement cruiser.

The same principle applies to powerboats. In *Sorensen's Guide to Powerboats,* author Eric Sorensen gives this rule of thumb: "The wider, flatter, and lighter a boat is—or the more extreme in any one of those elements—the less comfortable it will be, at speed or at rest. If you want comfort,

into the protruding tail of the through-hull.

There are three common types of seacock used on small boats: the traditional tapered-plug seacock, the T-bar type with a swelling plug, and the ball-valve seacock. (Brass gate valves are also used fre-quently because they are cheap, but they have no place on a boat: they corrode quickly, and you can't tell if they're properly closed.)

Bronze-bodied, tapered-plug seacocks are widely used and highly recommended. They need to be dismantled and greased at least once a year, but they have proven over time to be safe and reliable.

T-bar seacocks also have bod-ies of bronze, but instead of a ta-pered bronze plug, they have a cylindrical neoprene plug. A threaded bar shortens the plug when it's turned, forcing it to swell in the middle and make a very efficient seal. Certain chem-icals can make the neoprene swell and prevent the seacock from opening or closing, so be careful if you're directing discharge from the head or the galley.

Ball-valve seacocks with bronze bodies have a hole run-ning through the middle of a chrome-plated bronze or stainless steel ball turning in Teflon seals. They're almost maintenance-free,

S

there's just no substitute for a narrow, deep, and heavy vessel."

He also remembers his first ride in a Dyer 40 (a semidisplacement Down East–style lobster yacht) after a steady diet of high-speed, hard-chined planing boats. "I'd forgotten how comfortable a semidisplacement boat can be. The Dyer rolled easily in the 2- to 3-foot seas, not too deeply, and certainly not stiffly like the average hard-chine planing hull."

Howard I. Chapelle, the eminent naval architect, defined one of the elements of seakindliness as "the ability of a boat to meet heavy weather and remain reasonably dry, shipping no solid water and relatively little spray."

He also believed that few boats under 40 feet (12 m) in length could meet the other requirements: namely, that the boat should provide a comfortable ride through a slow, easy roll, with no jerk or sudden stop at the end of each one, and an equally slow and easy pitch.

Chapelle pointed out that the very design characteristics required to prevent a smaller boat from shipping solid water would make her uncomfortable for the crew. The plentiful buoyancy needed to keep her on top of breaking seas would necessarily cause her to react jerkily, to the extent that it would be impossible to stand or walk without clinging to supports.

Nevertheless, there are degrees of seakindliness, and whereas light displacement and speed often equate with discomfort, heavy displacement usually results in a gentler ride.

See also **Chines**; **Hull Shapes**; **Seaworthiness**.

Sea, Land Breezes

Warming, cooling air results in coastal breezes

On many coastlines in warm climates, a breeze will spring up in midforenoon, blowing from the sea toward the land. It's a response to the sun's warming of the air over the land, which then starts to rise. Cooler air from the sea moves in to replace it.

This sea breeze is common year-round in tropical and subtropical latitudes, but it also occurs in higher latitudes in summer. It usually reaches it peak strength by midafternoon and dies away gradually after sunset.

The greater the temperature difference between the land and the sea, the earlier the sea breeze will start and the stronger it will be.

After dusk, the flow is often reversed as the land becomes cooler than the sea. About 2 hours after sunset, a breeze springs up from the land and blows out to sea to replace the warmer, rising air out there. This land breeze is usually gentler than the sea breeze, and it attains its maximum strength in the small hours of the morning. Although it may reach a distance of 5 miles or so offshore, it is often strongest within a mile of the shoreline—as coastal racers know well.

See also **Wind Systems**.

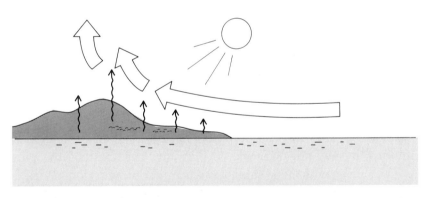

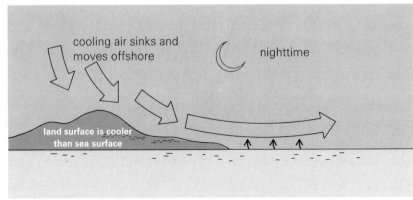

Land and sea breezes.

Sealants

Modern bedding compounds and sealants have many functions

Sealants have many uses on a boat: they form flexible, waterproof gaskets between fittings; they prevent water dropping through fastener holes in the deck; they electrically isolate different metals; and they fill the seams between planks. The sealants most often found on modern boats are polyurethane, polysulfide, and silicone.

Polyurethane is used for joints that require a permanent bond, such as hull-to-deck joints. It is also a powerful adhesive and must not be used on fittings that will later need to be removed. It bonds well to most boat materials and can be used above and below the waterline. It will attack Lexan and ABS plastic, and some polyurethane formulations cannot be painted or varnished.

Polysulfide is available in single packs as well as twin packs, which cure faster. It is used for most kinds of bedding and sealing, and will allow hardware to be removed at a later stage. Polysulfide bonds well to most surfaces except plastic, which it melts. It's used extensively as a seam filler, but when using it on teak or other oily woods, be sure to use the recommended primer. Most polysulfides can be painted or varnished.

Silicone can be used safely on all materials, including plastics. It forms excellent removable gaskets that resist heat and chemicals. It's not an adhesive, like polyurethane, but some hybrid silicones have improved adhesive qualities that can make them more difficult to remove—be sure to read the label. Silicone bonds well to fiberglass, glass, metal, plastic, and wood, but it will not accept paint or varnish.

See also **Adhesives**.

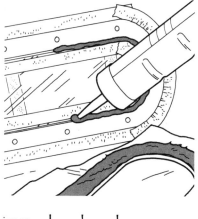

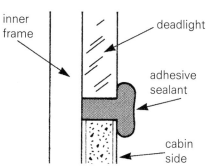

Rebedding a fixed (nonopening) plastic portlight. Up on deck, run a bead of silicone-based adhesive sealant around the perimeter of the portlight, which has been taped into position (with masking tape) against its inner frame. Once the adhesive-sealant is applied as shown, apply more of it to the back of the outer frame, then snug the outer frame in position using the through-bolts or machine screws you removed when you disassembled the unit. Let the silicone cure 30 minutes, then tighten the screws. Finally, trim the excess silicone with a razor knife.

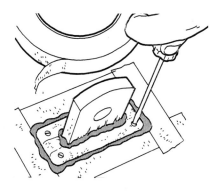

Resealing a chainplate. Having removed the trim plate and cleaned off the old bedding compound, apply masking tape to the perimeter of the job as shown, work a generous quantity of polysulfide adhesive-sealant into the gaps between the chainplate and the deck edge, apply adhesive-sealant to the bottom of the trim plate and its mating deck surface, then reinstall the trim plate and tighten it with self-tapping screws as shown. When the sealant cures, trim the excess with a razor knife and remove the masking tape.

Seamanship

Learning about boat handling is a never-ending occupation

Seamanship is the name for excellence in boat handling, and its scope is so wide that even the most experienced sailor cannot hope to learn everything about it in one lifetime. One of the best definitions of seamanship appears in *The Complete Boating Encyclopedia*: "Seamanship—General word for the arts and skills associated with handling a boat, especially with handling her efficiently and well. Good seamanship embodies thorough knowledge, and intelligent application, of all the principles of operating a

S

boat away from her pier or mooring—getting underway, safety practices, piloting, maneuvering in difficult situations, avoidance of hazards, and so on—plus the constant exercise of prudence, good judgment, and consideration toward others. Perfection in all these things is a goal every thoughtful skipper strives for."

There is much more, of course. So many disciplines are involved in boating, from aerodynamics and celestial navigation to meteorology and plumbing, that perfection in all is practically impossible. Nevertheless, the best skippers have a good working knowledge of all these disciplines, and know where to look or whom to ask for more information when it's needed. Incidentally, the highest order of seamanship is practiced by sailors who know what to do *after* things have gone wrong. They have anticipated possible trouble, and have given thought to how to handle it.

And good seamanship doesn't end with handling your own boat. Knowing how other vessels react in certain situations may be just as important in avoiding collisions and making prudent decisions.

Good seamanship starts in port, with detailed preparation and careful checks—and it never ends. See also **Black Box Theory**.

Seasickness

Finding the right drug to fight off the dreaded nausea

The word *nausea* is derived from the Greek word *naus*, meaning

ship. Between 25 and 30 percent of passengers on the old transatlantic liners became nauseous within the first three days of a *normal* passage. On small yachts, the percentage is much higher. About 60 percent of survivors of shipwrecks cast adrift in inflatable life rafts succumb to seasickness, according to studies carried out during World War II. If sea conditions are bad enough, almost everyone will get sick for at least a limited period.

The cause of seasickness is believed to be a conflict in the brain between what the eyes see and what the inner ear "feels." When you are down below in a seaway, the balance system of your inner ear informs your brain that you are being subjected to accelerations. But your eyes, looking around the cabin, insist that your body is stable. You certainly do not *appear* to be moving, no matter what your inner ear is reporting. This theory does not cover all the bases, of course. People get seasick on deck, too, even when they can see the horizon and there should be no conflict in the brain.

It is also not clear why the eye-ear conflict should result in the brain giving orders to the stomach to empty its contents, except that some of the symptoms of seasickness may be similar to those of food poisoning. The symptoms usually occur in the following order: frequent yawning or sighing, slight headache, dry mouth, unnatural paleness, cold sweat, nausea, and vomiting.

Once you recognize the first symptoms, either stay on deck as

long as possible or lie flat on a bunk down below. On deck, you should stand upright if it's not too rough, with legs slightly apart. Don't sit down—that's the position most conducive to seasickness. Down below, lie face up, eyes closed, as close to the fore-and-aft center of the boat as possible, and keep a supply of strong paper bags nearby.

If you are seasick for a prolonged period—days, rather than hours—your bodily fluids may get seriously out of balance. Drink a half cup of seawater once or twice a day to restore them. You may not keep it down long, but your tissues will absorb enough vital salts to help put things right.

There are about a dozen drugs on the market for controlling motion sickness. Over-the-counter drugs include Dramamine, Bonine, Meclizine, and Marezine. Prescription drugs include Antivert, Phenergan, Phenergan plus ephedrine, Transderm-Scopolamine, and Scopolamine HBR plus dextroamphetamine. Widely used by boaters, Transderm-Scopolamine is manufactured in the form of a dime-sized patch worn behind the ear for 72 hours, by which time you should have adapted to the boat's motion.

The golden rule is to take these drugs well before you go to sea. Before choosing any drug, discuss your plans with your family doctor.

The only good news about seasickness is that extremely few people die of it, though many in its grips wish they would.

See also **Drinking Seawater**.

S

Seaworthiness

Defining the characteristics of a boat that's fit for sea

Seaworthiness in small boats is poorly understood and difficult to define. If it were merely the ability to stay afloat in all conditions, no matter what, then a piece of cork or an old lightbulb would be the epitome of seaworthiness.

A good big boat is undoubtedly more seaworthy than a good small boat. Breaking-wave capsize is the biggest danger in heavy weather, and the height of a breaking wave needed to capsize a boat is directly proportional to boat length. (Any boat may be turned turtle by a breaking wave with a height 55 percent of her overall length.) But in other respects, seaworthiness has more to do with design than with size. In addition to the ability to stay afloat, a seaworthy boat must be able to maneuver clear of dangers in extremely heavy weather—the bigger, more powerful boat scores more points. She also must have enough space down below for the humans who sail her, and she must be able to right herself after being turned upside down.

Howard Chapelle, the famous designer, coined this classic definition of seaworthiness in *Yacht Designing and Planning*: "Seaworthiness is basically the ability of a boat to live in heavy weather without swamping, capsizing, breaking up, or being heavily damaged while underway."

That is a restricted definition; to be truly fit to go to sea and behave well in all conditions, a boat needs additional qualities. Perhaps the following broader definition is closer to what modern designers aim for: a seaworthy sailboat is one that is

- able to recover quickly from a 180-degree capsize without serious damage and without sinking
- strong enough to look after herself while hove-to or lying ahull
- seakindly—free of violent, jerky rolling and pounding
- well-balanced, docile on the helm, and easily handled at all times
- agile downwind and able to avoid most plunging breakers
- able to beat to windward, or at least hold her ground, in all but the heaviest conditions
- habitable—able to carry ample crew with good headroom and comfort, plus water and supplies, for extended periods
- capable of good average speeds on long passages

In *Principles of Yacht Design*, Larsson and Eliasson note that the seaworthiness of a sailing yacht depends on its dynamic behavior in a seaway; dynamic effects, naturally, are much more difficult to measure or predict than static effects. Larsson and Eliasson propose a "dynamic stability factor" that increases with size, displacement-to-length ratio, and righting moment at 90 degrees of heel (a measure of the ability to recover from a knockdown), but is decreased by several factors, among which are excessive beam (which makes a boat undesirably stable upside down) and excessive sail area relative to displacement.

In *Sorensen's Guide to Powerboats*, Eric Sorensen equates seaworthiness with a boat's "survivability, including its ability to resist capsize," and with its behavior in rough seas: Can it be controlled, and does it respond in predictable fashion? Capsize resistance is in turn related to stability, just as it is in sailboats. A heavy-displacement trawler yacht with a low center of gravity will fare better in storm seas than a sportfisherman of the same length with a lighter displacement, big open cockpit, and higher center of gravity. On the other hand, given adequate warning, the sportfisherman will outrun a storm that may catch the trawler. Thus, speed can be thought of as a seaworthy feature in a powerboat.

See also **Seakindliness**; **Stability**; **Yacht Design**.

Self-Steering

Freeing yourself from the tyranny of steering by hand

All boats that set out to sea on long voyages, even coastal voyages, need some form of self-steering device. A good system frees you from the tyranny of the helm and is as valuable as an extra crew member because it will remain on duty 24 hours a day, nonstop.

Powerboats—and, increasingly, sailboats—usually use electrically operated autopilots that incorporate a fluxgate compass to sense direction and a motor that

S

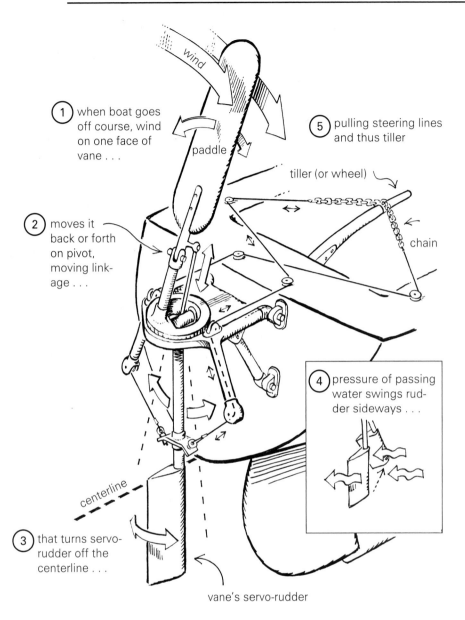

① when boat goes off course, wind on one face of vane . . .

② moves it back or forth on pivot, moving linkage . . .

③ that turns servo-rudder off the centerline . . .

④ pressure of passing water swings rudder sideways . . .

⑤ pulling steering lines and thus tiller

paddle

wind

tiller (or wheel)

chain

centerline

vane's servo-rudder

A servopendulum windvane on the transom of a sailboat.

maintain a steady magnetic course, the many different types of vane gear work by keeping the boat at a constant angle to the wind. So, if the wind direction changes, the boat's course will change accordingly unless the vane is adjusted.

The main types of vane gears are trim-tab gears and servopendulum gears. Trim-tab gears have a long thin tab on the trailing edge of the main rudder. When the wind vane turns a trim-tab to port, the rudder turns to starboard, and vice versa. The popular servopendulum gear develops considerable power by dragging a top-hinged oar at an angle behind the boat, and lines are led from the oar to the tiller or wheel.

Trim tabs work best with outboard rudders, but if you have an inboard rudder, you may use another vane system that drives its own auxiliary rudder. That results in more underwater drag, but it has the advantage of acting as a spare rudder if your main rudder ever suffers damage.

The Achilles' heel of most wind-vane systems is downwind sailing. Most vanes need a flow of at least 5 knots over their surface to work properly. As the boat is headed off the wind, the flow of air over the vane decreases, and it becomes less effective. One answer is to tack downwind, so that the boat's forward speed increases the boat's apparent wind speed. In dead calms, of course, an inexpensive autopilot will do a good job of steering under power.

Newer autopilots integrated with electronic sensors will steer to the wind or to a waypoint. Increasingly, blue-water cruisers

S

moves the rudder quadrant. There are two major kinds of autopilots: the inexpensive kind that mounts in the cockpit where it's exposed to the weather, and the expensive kind that mounts belowdecks, out of harm's way. Powerboats usually install the latter type because they can generate ample power from their main engines while underway.

Most sailboats have the choice of using a cockpit-mounted autopilot when they are under auxiliary power and a wind-vane gear when they are sailing (and when the autopilot would be too much of a drain on the batteries). Recently, however, more below-deck autopilots are appearing on sailboats.

Whereas fluxgate autopilots

who prefer electronic to mechanical complexity and are willing to pay for convenience with high power consumption are depending mostly or exclusively on autopilots, consigning their windvane self-steerers to a backup role—or not carrying them at all. This is not necessarily a step in the right direction.

See also **Ocean Voyaging**.

Selling a Boat

Tips for a quick, clean sale during a time of high passion

It's often tempting to try to sell your boat yourself, and thus avoid having to pay a commission to a yacht broker. But in most cases, it's wiser to leave the selling to a professional.

Brokers bring to the transaction a sensible, impartial balance that many owners find impossible to achieve because of their emotional attachment to a boat.

Brokers can estimate far better than you can how much your boat is worth on the open market. They also have access to extensive lists of prospective buyers. They know the law, they understand the procedures, and they can smooth the way to financing the deal.

Selling a boat can be a time of high passion. You're either distressed at parting with her or overjoyed at the prospect of getting rid of the darned thing. Either way, your judgment is likely to be too clouded to secure the best deal. Here are some hints for a quick sale:

- move the boat as close as possible to the broker
- take all your personal gear off: the buyer wants to visualize his or her stuff there
- have the boat professionally cleaned
- be honest about what works and what doesn't
- don't set an outrageously high asking price, hoping to give yourself some negotiating leeway

Here, in no particular order, are the biggest turnoffs for a prospective buyer: dirt, leaks, rust stains, wood rot, frayed lines, mold and mildew, musty smells, fuel smells, wet and dirty bilges, torn upholstery, peeling varnish, broken fittings, and an engine that won't start.

Remember that it's not a good idea to spend too much on getting a reasonably well-maintained boat ready for a sale; the capital is seldom recovered. Most buyers are interested in low price. But do consider leaving behind any gear such as GPS or VHF radios that you want to upgrade when you get your new boat.

Finally, be aware that few things impress a potential buyer more than newly painted, dust-dry bilges.

Sentinels

Preventing dangerous jolts from an all-chain anchor rode

The use of the heavy weights known as sentinels, or kellets, on anchor chains to prevent snubbing and help the anchor dig in has largely been discontinued. Modern sailors mostly use thin, stretchy nylon lines instead.

Sentinels were slid about halfway down the anchor chain on a separate line so that the chain could not straighten out and create jerks that might damage deck fittings. The weight of the sentinel also reduced the an-

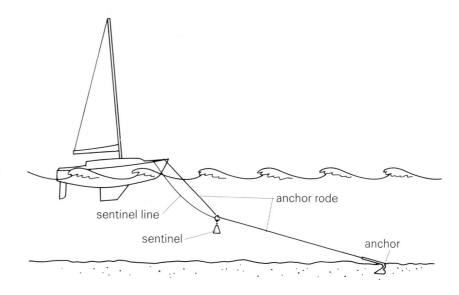

A heavy weight, or sentinel, in use to prevent snubbing and provide a more favorable angle of pull for the anchor.

gle of the rode to the seabed, giving the anchor a better chance to grip tightly.

Although the sentinel is still occasionally seen in use, the majority of sailors with all-chain rodes now use a length of three-strand nylon made fast to the rode with a rolling hitch or a chain hook. This so-called snubber is brought back to the foredeck bitts or cleats where it's made fast. The chain between the attachment point and the bow roller is given some slack and allowed to hang in a loop. The stretchiness of the nylon absorbs the sudden damaging jolts that can occur, particularly when an all-chain rode is used in shallow water.

See also **Anchors, Anchoring**.

Setting Anchors

Learning the right way is important for safety reasons

Modern anchors are surprisingly forgiving of poor handling techniques. We've all seen the shiny new speedboat, fresh from the dealer's showroom, roar into an anchorage. We've all nodded knowingly as the excited, land-lubberly crew hurls overboard a great tangled mess of anchor and line. And we've all been amazed (and perhaps a little disappointed) to see the boat settle down happily for the night without dragging an inch.

Nevertheless, there is a correct way to set an anchor and—even if you don't choose to use it—you should at least know it. Having chosen your anchoring spot, observe how other boats are

lying. Approach your spot so that when you drop anchor, your boat will be lined up parallel to theirs and facing the same way. If there are no other boats, approach into the wind. Alternatively, if there is a strong current running that is likely to push your boat against the wind, approach into the current.

At your chosen spot, let the boat drift backward slightly with respect to the ground, then slowly lower the anchor into the water. There's no need to hurl it far ahead. Let the rode run out handily as you drift back. This method prevents the rode from piling up directly on top of the anchor and possibly fouling it.

When you have let out a length of anchor line about four times as long as the water is deep, make the line fast at the bow. Wait a few minutes while the boat settles back and starts to put a strain on the line. Then put the motor in astern gear and give it half throttle or less, which drags the anchor slowly along the ground at the end of its line, causing it to dig in. Too much throttle may cause it to skip and skate quickly over the seabed.

When you can see (from marks on the shore, or other nearby boats) that you are no longer drifting backward, you may assume that the anchor has started to set itself. Give the engine a burst at full throttle for a minute or so to set it deeply. You may want to adjust the length of your anchor line. If you're in a crowded anchorage and have an all-chain rode, you may want to shorten up to a scope of 3 to 1. If you have ample swinging room, you would be better off

veering sufficient cable for a scope of 7 to 1.

If you don't have a motor, the anchor will still set itself if there's some wind or current to put strain on the line, but it will take longer and you won't be sure how secure it is until the wind really starts to howl.

The most important part of the anchoring drill is to ensure that the anchor isn't fouled by its own line. The second most important part is to test that the anchor is well set by powering in reverse. If you anchor in light weather, there will be no strain on the line to cause the anchor to set, and you could easily start dragging if the wind rises in the middle of the night.

See also **Anchors, Anchoring; Scope for Anchors; Sentinels; Stern Anchoring**.

Sextants

Gaining satisfaction and safety from an old instrument

The advice to carry a sextant as a backup for satellite navigation is repeated so often that it's in danger of becoming totally ignored by a modern generation with implicit trust in the electronic global positioning system (GPS).

Many world cruisers now regard sextants as old-fashioned and unnecessary. In fact, it's becoming increasingly more difficult to justify the considerable expense of a good sextant when GPS sets cost a fourth of the price or less. In any case, even if the whole constellation of 21 GPS satellites were shot down by space aliens in one fell

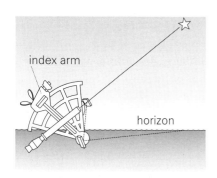

This sextant has been inverted so the observer, looking through the telescope, can view a star or planet while rotating the index arm until the horizon appears in the field of view. At that point the index arm will be at the correct angle for taking a sight on the star or planet in question, making it easier for the observer, having returned the sextant to its upright position, to sight the body in the usual way.

swoop, you would be able to find your way to the nearest large piece of land by dead reckoning if you had enough food and water on board—say a month's worth. The Polynesians didn't have sextants, and neither did the Vikings nor the Phoenicians, nor many of the great maritime explorers who came after them.

Nevertheless, those who feel pride in our maritime heritage and have an attachment to the old self-sufficient methods of navigation still carry sextants. What is often overlooked is the satisfaction derived from handling a beautifully crafted instrument to measure the height of the sun or a star, and using the result to plot your position on the face of the Earth. Celestial navigation has become very simple, thanks to the *Nautical Almanac* and sight-reduction tables that do the math;

you need only be able to add and subtract.

On the other hand, GPS is so accurate and so accessible 24 hours a day, in even the worst weather, that it would be foolish to ignore it entirely in favor of the sextant. Perhaps the best advice is to use GPS for everyday navigation, but to take along a sextant—the best you can afford—for fun. Celestial navigation is a fascinating art and a gratifying pastime; perhaps one day, when all the GPS satellites blow their little transistors, you'll be glad you mastered it.

See also **GPS**.

Sheet Sizes

Figuring out the load on a headsail sheet in a breeze

The polyester fiber from which most sailboat sheets are made is so strong that the size of the sheet is chosen more for ease of handling than for its breaking strength. If

sheets were matched to the loads they have to carry, they would mostly be too thin for comfort. Nevertheless, you can estimate the reserve strength in your sheets by comparing the load with the line's breaking strength.

The strain on a jib sheet can be worked out roughly this way: multiply the square of the wind speed in knots by the sail area in square feet, and divide the answer by 232, which gives you the approximate pull in pounds. For example, in a 20-knot breeze, a 200-square-foot headsail would exert a pull on its sheet of 20 x 20 x 200 = 80,000 ÷ 232 = 345 pounds, or 156 kilograms.

The official working load for polyester line is 11 percent of the breaking strain, so you would need $^7/_{16}$-inch-diameter (11 mm) Dacron with a breaking strain of 3,500 pounds (1,587 kg). But mainsail and headsail sheets on nonracing boats are rarely less than $^1/_2$ inch (13 mm) in diameter because anything thinner is uncomfortable to trim by hand.

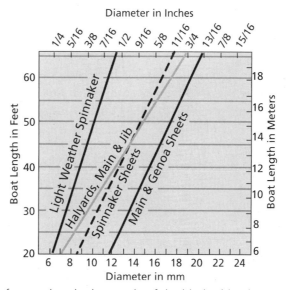

Line sizes for running rigging made of double-braid polyester (e.g., Dacron).

These are conservative figures, of course, because there are enormous reserves of strength in these sheets, even allowing for the weakening effect of knots.

Mainsail sheets led to the middle of the boom need to be about the same diameter as sheets for headsails of the same area. However, for multipart mainsail sheets led to the end of the boom, 1/2-inch (13 mm) Dacron is appropriate for all sail areas up to 500 square feet (46 sq m).

See also **Halyards**; **Rope Strength**; **Rope Stretch**.

"She" Is for Ships

Making the case to retain a time-honored marine pronoun

The Associated Press style handbook, used by all the major newspapers in the United States, warns journalists not to use the pronoun *she* in reference to ships. "Use *it* instead," the handbook says. There is no attempt to explain or justify this peremptory directive, but one suspects it stems from an honest but misguided attempt to eradicate sexism in the written word.

I think we all recognize the need to avoid thoughtless sexist remarks in our speech and writing, which is why most of us no longer use the words yachtsman, man overboard, helmsman, and many others—even at the cost of some ugly verbal juggling. But to ban the word *she* in connection with ships and boats seems neither reasonable nor necessary.

Women themselves refer to boats as *she*. In 1795, Ann Radcliffe wrote in *The Mysteries of Udolpho*: "the vessel was anchored in the bay below, but in so shattered a condition that it was feared she would part before the crew could disembark."

Nicolette Milnes Walker, who crossed the Atlantic alone in her 30-foot (9.1 m) Pionier class sloop *Aziz*, writes in *When I Put Out to Sea*: "I bought *Aziz* from Mr. Carpenter in March 1971. She was in good condition." I have heard famous long-distance cruisers like Susan Hiscock and Lin Pardey refer to their boats as *she*. None of them had any inhibitions about it nor found it offensive.

Furthermore, the International Regulations for Preventing Collisions at Sea, subscribed to by all the major maritime nations of the world, and the Inland Rules of the United States, refer to ships throughout as *she* and *her*.

Logically, a good case could be made for referring to a boat as *it* because a boat is, after all, an inanimate object. By the same token, there's a good case for changing the word *motherland* to *personland*, but it's doubtful that anyone would welcome the change, no matter how logical.

Interestingly, the pronoun for motherland is *it*, not *she*, which just demonstrates that English is an eccentric language, and all the more delightful for it. Boats have been referred to as *she* in English for so long that nobody now recalls why. It's a tradition of the sea that shouldn't be discarded offhandedly at the whim of some lubberly journalist scared witless by the mere suggestion of gender discrimination.

Ship's Log

Making an official record of all the ship's business

It's not compulsory for recreational vessels to keep a log of any kind; it's purely voluntary. However, it's a good idea because it would provide solid documentation in the case of an insurance claim or legal suit that you run your vessel with due regard for national and international laws, and that you practice good seamanship.

A deck log is a record of your boat's travels—a navigational guide. It typically records the time of significant events, such as when you get underway, when you pass charted landmarks, and when your voyage ends. It notes the courses steered, the distance traveled in each watch, the positions (particularly when navigating by GPS, so as to have a starting point for dead reckoning if the GPS fails), the direction and force of the wind, the state of the barometer, and other observations of interest to safety or navigation.

You don't need a professionally printed logbook. You can make your own by ruling lines in a spiral-bound hardcover notebook. Date and number each page. The skipper should sign each page. Never erase an entry, however. If you make a mistake, rule it out without making it illegible, then add the correct entry and initial it.

Two other logs you might consider keeping are a radio log that lists all calls sent and received, and an engine log that records engine hours and mainte-

S

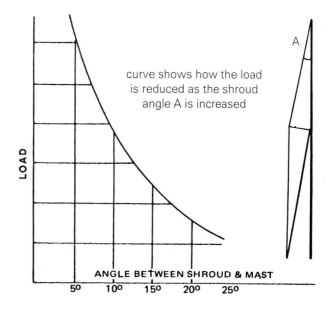

A page from the log kept by the author aboard his 31-foot (9.4 m) sloop Freelance *en route from the Indian Ocean to Florida via Cape Agulhas with a crew of three. These entries were made in the South Atlantic, two days before landfall on the island of Fernando de Noronha. Noon position* (lower right) *was obtained by sun sight using a sextant.*

nance and repair work. You can make a note of important radio calls, such as Mayday calls, in your deck log.

The deck log should be brought up to date at the end of each watch, but—to make things easier—many small-boat sailors, especially navigators, make their entries in a small notebook they always carry. They then transfer the details from this scratch log to the official ship's log when their watch is over and they can go below.

See also **Dead Reckoning**.

Shrouds and Stays

Calculating angles and sizes for mast-supporting wires

Shrouds are the wire ropes that hold a mast up sideways. The wire ropes that hold the mast up fore and aft are known as stays.

The tall masts found on modern Bermuda-rigged sailboats result in narrow angles between the shrouds and the mast. Because the tension in shrouds increases quickly as the angle diminishes, mast designers and riggers try to ensure that the attachment angle of the shrouds to the mast is never

less than 10 degrees, achieving this angle with the help of spreaders, or crosstrees, if necessary.

Interestingly, a sideways push of 20 pounds (9 kg) at the masthead induces a tension of about 240 pounds (108 kg) in a shroud attached to the mast at an angle of 4 degrees. But if you increase the attachment angle to 12 degrees, the tension in the shroud drops to about 80 pounds (36 kg).

All the shrouds on one side of a racing boat should be strong enough to support the total weight of the boat, plus her crew and two thirds of her water, fuel, and stores—her displacement, in other words. For inshore cruisers, that figure should be increased by 20 percent; that is, the breaking strength of all the shrouds on one side should equal the displacement times 1.2. For offshore cruisers, it is prudent to increase total shroud strength on one side to displacement times 1.4.

When you calculate the loads to get the correct sizes of shrouds, you may assume that on a single-

curve shows how the load is reduced as the shroud angle A is increased

Shroud loading decreases dramatically as the shroud angle A increases.

spreader rig the lower shroud bears 60 percent of the load and the upper shroud 40 percent.

On a double-spreader rig, the lower shroud bears 48 percent of the load, the intermediate shroud 26 percent, and the upper shroud 26 percent. When the upper and intermediate shrouds join at the lower spreaders and run to a single turnbuckle and chainplate, the combined upper-intermediate shroud should carry 52 percent of the load.

Where you have double lower shrouds, one leading forward and one aft of the mast, you should assume that only one is working at any one time. The second lower, therefore, should be the same size as the first, and either of them should be capable of bearing the whole lower-shroud load at any one time.

The headstay should be the size of the heaviest shroud or one size larger. The backstay should be the same size as the headstay.

On cruising boats, where the weight of rigging is not crucial to speed, it's convenient to have all shrouds and stays of one size— that is, the size of the heaviest shroud needed.

See also **Rigging Sizes**; **Rigging Tension**; **Spreaders**.

Single-Handed Sailboats

The pressing need for good self-righting capability

Adventurous newcomers to sailing sometimes ask how big a boat they need to cross an ocean single-handedly. A better question would be, "How small a boat can I get away with?"

There are single-handers these days who race around the world in 60-footers, but they are not ordinary people in ordinary boats. That is deep-sea racing at its riskiest, and the statistics show it. The boats deliberately sacrifice seaworthiness for speed, and it's only the skill, experience, and constant attention of their solo crews that keep them upright— and then, as we have seen, not always.

If you're planning to cruise rather than race as a single-hander, the most important characteristic of your boat should be the ability to look after herself in bad weather when you are lying down below exhausted. The primary requirement for a monohull cruiser is, therefore, a large range of stability—that is, the tendency to return to an upright position after having been heeled 130 degrees or more from the vertical. Such stability comes from ample low ballast, reasonably heavy displacement, and moderate to narrow beam.

As far as size goes, there are two limiting factors. The first is the anchor: Can you raise the biggest anchor on board without using a windlass? Even if you ordinarily wouldn't need to do this, there's always a chance that you might have to. The second limiting factor is the size of the largest sail: Can you handle and smother and reef it on your own in the heaviest weather?

If you feel confident about your ability to manage these two factors, you're probably physically able to single-hand the boat. For most people, this translates to a moderate- to heavy-displacement boat of between 28 and 35 feet (8.5 and 10.7 m) overall. These are safe, conservative limits that balance ease of handling and maintenance with reasonable speed and safety, but they won't suit everyone. There will always be the mavericks with boats much smaller or much bigger—and good luck to them.

See also **Lookouts**; **Seakindliness**; **Seaworthiness**.

Single-Handed Sailing

The reasons otherwise sane people do it

Humans are herd animals; we tend to gather together in tribes and maintain close social relationships. Why, then, would someone want to cross an ocean single-handed? What motivates them?

American author and sailor Richard Henderson has closely studied the goals and achievements of single-handers. In his

Captain Joshua Slocum was the first person to sail around the world alone.

book *Singlehanded Sailing*, he suggests ten reasons why an otherwise sane, reasonable sailor would want to sail off into the blue alone:

1. For practical purposes. To test a theory, perhaps, or to gather material for a book or a study. To earn money or to win a race. Sometimes, because the boat isn't big enough for two.

2. Self-significance. To find one's place in the world's pecking order and acquire a sense of belonging.

3. Curiosity and fulfillment. A desire to see and experience the thrills and moods of the sea, and exotic landfalls, for oneself.

4. Recognition. A desire for fame that exceeds the search for self-significance.

5. Independence. The need for the greatest possible freedom and control over one's own destiny.

6. Escapism. This is closely allied to independence, but includes a certain rebelliousness against routine, as well as a possible flight from personal and societal problems.

7. Adventurousness. Adventure has always been strongly attractive to restless spirits with a desire for novelty, travel, and excitement. Solo sailing can provide all of these in large (and sometimes excessive) quantities.

8. Competitiveness. This may take many forms, including personal competition with the ocean and one's inner fears, as well as the desire to win races or set records.

9. Solitude. Some introverts like being alone. Other people may experience the spiritual cleansing of a retreat that makes them more appreciative of subsequent human companionship.

10. Mother Sea. All life came from the sea, and it still runs strongly in our veins. Some deep instinct, dimly felt and poorly understood, draws many people back.

As Henderson points out, all single-handers possess at least some of these motivations in various degrees and combinations. Most are braver than they know, particularly those who do it *despite* their fear of the sea and the unknown.

See also **Ocean Voyaging**.

Skegs

Protecting and strengthening a rudder, lacking a long keel

On a full-keeled sailboat such as a Colin Archer, the skeg is the aftermost and deepest part of the deadwood, or that part next to the sternpost. It's the projecting end of the keel upon which the rudder is stepped.

In fin-keel designs, the skeg is a detached vertical projection, usually triangular in shape, beneath the after end of the shallow hull. The skeg has several functions: it supports the rudder, it provides lateral resistance, and, like the feathers on an arrow, it gives a boat directional stability. The word *skeg* comes from the Icelandic *skaga*, a promontory or headland—something that projects or juts out.

A rudder hung from a skeg is stronger than a spade rudder that depends entirely on its projecting stock for strength, and offers better protection to the rudder when the boat runs aground or dries out. A skeg-hung rudder will not stall as readily as a spade rudder, and tends to hold a steadier course because it will center itself when left alone, rather than take a small "lead" to port or starboard as a semibalanced spade rudder will do.

A short, partial keel on a powerboat is sometimes called a skeg. In the Sea Bright skiff design that developed a century ago along the Jersey Shore, for example, a boxed skeg begins about amidships and runs aft, even as the hull body sweeps up. With its flat bottom and hollow interior, the boxed skeg supports the skiff when it dries out between tides, and allows the single engine to be

S

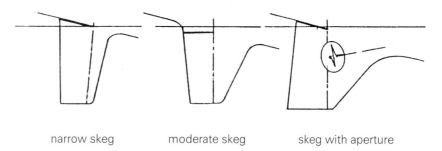

narrow skeg   moderate skeg   skeg with aperture

Three variations of skegs with attached rudders.

placed deep in the hull with an almost horizontal propeller shaft. It also gives the boat added directional stability for launching from and landing on surf beaches.

See also **Rudders**.

Skid Fins

Attempting to cure a power-boat steering problem

Long shallow hulls sometimes present a steering problem on high-performance planing powerboats. In certain states of wind and sea, their bow tends to fly sideways on occasion, causing a sudden, disconcerting change of direction.

A small skid fin placed quite far forward on the bottom of the hull greatly helps restore directional stability. It should be about 90 percent of the rudder area and located between 10 and 15 percent of the length of the boat forward of her center of gravity.

New York naval architect Dave Gerr warns in *The Nature of Boats* that you have to be careful not to make the skid fin too big. "Too much area forward makes a boat too quick on the helm," he says. "In rough seas, such a fin can broach a boat, or cause her to trip and capsize."

Incidentally, if you don't know where the center of gravity is, Gerr says you may assume that on a high-speed planing hull it's about 60 percent of the waterline length aft of the bow, at the waterline.

See also **Hull Shapes**.

Slack and Stand

Why the tidal stream mostly doesn't coincide with the tide

Slack water occurs when you can no longer detect any sideways (horizontal) flow of current at the change of tide. The water is said to stand when the tide is no longer rising or falling. Strangely enough, the two do not usually coincide.

Tidal streams do not automatically quit flowing when the tide reaches its highest or lowest point. There can be a difference of an hour or more between the two—that is, the water level can be falling while the stream is still flowing in the direction of the flood current, and vice versa. In a river mouth, look for an ebb current to continue after the tide begins to rise, and look for the high-water slack to occur before the high-water stand.

There's only one rule that's always true about tides and currents: they're inevitably more complicated than you think.

See also **Tidal Streams**.

Slips Versus Moorings

Weighing the pros and cons of safety and accessibility

In many coastal areas, boats may be left on moorings rather than berthed in marinas. Moorings are permanent anchors to which the boat is made fast by a single line at the bow, so she is free to swing with the wind and current.

Many boaters prefer moorings to marina slips, especially those who haul their boat out for the winter months and those whose mooring is well protected from wave action. The advantages of a slip are as follows:

- water and electricity are usually laid on
- the boat is well protected in all weathers
- access to the boat is easy
- there are often restaurants, toilets, and showers nearby
- it is easy to entertain guests
- consultation with other boat-owners is easy

The disadvantages of a slip are as follows:

- you can't "get away from it all"—a marina is a city of boats
- there is little privacy
- you might have noisy neighbors
- your boat might suffer corrosion caused by stray currents from other boats
- the water is more likely to be polluted

The advantages of a mooring are as follows:

- the boat almost always faces into the wind
- you can raise the sails, make adjustments, or reef before setting off
- you don't need an engine
- it's easier to leave and pick up a mooring than to maneuver into a tight slip in a congested harbor

- a mooring is much less expensive than a marina slip
- you can enjoy your privacy
- usually, there will be more breeze and better natural ventilation throughout your boat
- sleeping on board is more fun

The disadvantages of a mooring are as follows:

- access to the boat means paying for launch service or using your own dinghy and finding a safe place to park it
- if you leave an important tool or chart in your car, it's a long trip to retrieve it
- there is no shore power, nor water for washdowns
- you'll probably have less protection from wind and waves
- you'll need to be on guard for chafe on the mooring line
- if a gale blows when you're at home in the middle of the night, you'll worry about the boat

Finally, as a matter of simple aesthetics, let it be said that a boat looks more natural and alive on a mooring, where the waves chuckle under her bow as she flirts with the wind and dances in the swell. Boats tightly bound up in marinas look sad and misplaced, like prisoners waiting to be freed. If you've ever suddenly stopped rowing away from your boat, lost in admiration for her beauty as she lies to a mooring, you have experienced something wonderful that never happens to people with boats in marinas.

See also **Moorings**.

Smart Regulators

Charging faster with modern multistage regulators

The alternator on your engine generates alternating current (AC), the kind the power company transmits to your home. But your batteries can receive and give out only direct current (DC), which flows in one direction all the time. Luckily, modern diodes and circuits can rectify matters, changing AC into DC with little loss of power, so your alternator can charge your batteries after you've run them down.

The problem for most boaters is that it takes a long time. That's why many sailors are installing new multistage regulators that allow faster charging from larger alternators. For example, if you have two batteries with capacities of about 100 amp-hours each, the constant charging rate with a normal regulator should not exceed 10 percent of their combined capacity, or 20 amps. A higher rate will greatly shorten battery life.

But a "smart" regulator allows the alternator to charge at between 25 and 40 percent of battery capacity, or 50 to 80 amps, which will cut charging time by a half or two thirds. Smart regulators work by sensing the state of the battery and adjusting the flow of charging current in multiple stages, whereas "dumb" regulators allow full charging for only a short while before cutting the flow back to little more than a trickle charge.

Because powerboats run their engine(s) continuously while underway, charging time is not nearly so critical an issue.

See also **Alternators**.

Solar Panels

Transforming the power of the sun into electricity

In bright sunlight, about 6,000 watt-hours of solar energy falls on the deck of a 30-foot boat every 15 minutes. That's sufficient to fully charge five 12-volt, 100-amp-hour batteries from scratch.

But solar panels, which generate electricity directly from the sun's radiation, are only about 12 percent efficient, so the amount of electricity they produce is only about 25 percent of their rated wattage. That is, the number of amp-hours generated in a period of 12 hours = watts x 0.25. That means a fixed, 12-volt, rigid solar panel rated at 35 watts will give a daily output in amp-hours of approximately 35 x 0.25 = 8.75 amp-hours. If the panel is adjusted all day long so that it stays at right angles to the sun's rays, its output may be doubled.

To replace 100 amp-hours of electricity consumed on board daily, you would need solar cells covering an area of about 8 by 4 feet.

The three main types of solar panel are monocrystalline, polycrystalline, and thin-film panels. Monocrystalline are the most efficient and the most expensive. They are almost rigid, as are the polycrystalline panels. Thin-film panels are flexible, which makes

S

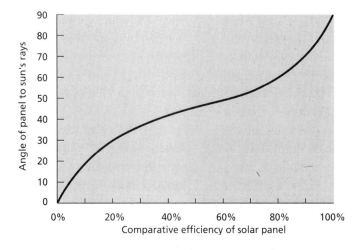

wind generator

Source	Output	Operating Hours	Total Amp-Hours
Water	5.25 amps at 5 knots	12	63
Wind	7.0 amps (15-mph wind)	12	84
Solar	2.64 amps (two 35-watt panels, average day)	12	32

These are rough comparisons, taken from manufacturer's brochures, of the electrical output of alternators—one driven by a propeller dragged through the water behind a boat, the other by a wind propeller—and solar panels.

them more convenient and adaptable on many boats, but they are far less efficient than the other two types.

All types of solar panels are affected by the intensity of the sun's radiation, and their output drops dramatically in cloudy weather or when shadows fall across them. Because the intensity of radiation decreases with increasing latitude, solar cells are less efficient farther away from the equator.

The voltage of individual cells in solar panels is about 0.45. To charge a 12-volt battery, therefore, you need between 32 and 37 individual cells. Panels with 33 cells or fewer will not develop sufficient voltage to charge a 12-volt battery fully. On the other hand, they probably won't need regulation and can be connected directly to the battery.

If your panel has 36 cells or more, the higher potential requires proper regulation and a blocking diode in the circuit so that the battery doesn't drain itself

by trying to heat up the solar panel at night.

See also **Battery Needs**.

Soundings

Differentiating between deep water and shallower

The verb *to sound* comes from the Old French *sonder*, meaning to measure a depth. In the days of sailing ships, sounding was done manually with a lead line. Today it is done electronically by measuring the time it takes a high-pitched noise to travel from the boat, through the water to the bottom, and back again to the depth-sounder, where the depth is displayed digitally on a screen.

But we still use the phrases *on soundings* and *off soundings*. A vessel is said to be on soundings when the water is less than 100 fathoms deep. To seaward of the 100-fathom line, it was inconvenient to sound with a lead line, and when a ship sailed out there she was said to be off soundings.

Incidentally, sound travels

A solar panel generates most electricity when it is angled at 90° to the sun. This graph shows approximate efficiency at other angles.

S

through water four times faster than it does through air. In water, it travels at about 4,800 feet (1,463 m) a second. In air of 32°F (0°C) at sea level, the speed of sound is 1,088 feet (332 m) a second—or roughly a nautical mile in 5 seconds.

See also **Lead Lines**.

Sound Signals

Defining the navigation signals required by law

According to the collision regulations, boats are required to make sound signals under certain circumstances, usually when changing course or in restricted visibility. The signals consist of short blasts, long blasts, and combinations of both.

The rules define a short blast as lasting 1 second; a long (or prolonged) blast lasts between 4 and 6 seconds. These blasts are made with what the rules call whistles, but a whistle is "any sound-signaling appliance capable of producing the prescribed blasts" that complies with the specifications in annex 3 of the rules. Annex 3 gives the frequencies of whistles for boats of different lengths. Basically, the bigger the vessel, the deeper is the note.

Most pleasure boats fall into the "less than 75 meters (246 ft.) in length" category, which means your whistle should blast at a frequency of between 250 and 525 Hz.

If your boat is less than 20 meters (66 ft.) in length, the whistle must be loud enough to be heard for at least half a nautical

mile. Vessels between 20 and 75 meters (66 to 246 ft.) must be heard for 1 nautical mile.

The actual signals you are expected to make are specified in Rules 34 and 35 of the International Regulations for Preventing Collisions at Sea and the U.S. Inland Navigation Rules. It's obligatory to make sound signals in fog and also in snow, rain, dust storms, or any other form of restricted visibility. But not everyone realizes that you must also make the signals when you're *near* an area of restricted visibility, even if you are in bright sunshine.

The object is to inform another vessel feeling her way through a fogbank just half a mile away that you'll be in her path when she emerges from it.

See also **Rules of the Road**.

Speed Limits

Setting physical limits on the top speed of small yachts

There are practical limits controlling the maximum speeds of boats. The speed of nonplaning hulls, under power or sail, is governed principally by their waterline length. The formula for determining maximum speed is 1.34 times the square root of the waterline length in feet, or 2.43 times the square root of the waterline length in meters. This formula applies to average boats in average conditions, and does not include the increased speed that may occur temporarily when a boat surfs down the face of a wave.

When a displacement hull reaches its maximum theoretical

speed, it's lying deep in the trough of a wave of its own making, and there is no economical way to make it go faster.

Planing hulls conform to a different set of rules. They have shallow, flattish underbodies that give the hull dynamic lift, and their maximum speeds are determined almost wholly by the amount of power available. They can rise over their own bow waves and start skimming over the water. The critical factor is the power-to-weight ratio.

A planing hull can achieve speeds of about 25 knots if there is about 40 pounds (18 kg) of total weight for every unit of horsepower delivered to the propeller. To increase that speed to 50 knots, you would need to drop the ratio to 10 pounds (4.5 kg) for every 1 horsepower.

Semiplaning, or semidisplacement, hulls fall between the two types discussed previously. They derive some dynamic lift from the action of the water passing beneath the hull at speed and the rest from the hull's natural buoyancy. The speed of a semidisplacement hull, therefore, depends on how closely related it is to one or the other. In other words, it's a little faster than a displacement hull but not nearly as fast as a planing hull. The semiplaning hull is a compromise that usually creates a gas guzzler trailing a huge wake. It's the worst of both worlds to its detractors; to its many admirers it makes a good cruising hull, combining some of the displacement boat's low-speed efficiencies with a turn of speed when needed to outrun a storm or reach a distant anchorage.

S

See also **Fighting Currents; Hull Shapes; Hydrofoils; Speed of Boats**.

Speed of Boats

Transport on water is a comparatively slow way to go

The speed of vessels on salt water is measured in knots, a term that comes from the days when a ship's speed was measured by the number of knots that ran out in a certain time in a line cast into the water astern. The knot is defined as 1 nautical mile per hour; it is therefore not necessary to refer to boat speeds in knots *per hour*. Vessels operating on the Great Lakes and other freshwater bodies, however, measure their speed in miles per hour—and those are statute, or land, miles.

Compared with many other forms of transportation, speeds on water are slow, particularly those of boats under sail. The fastest run by a clipper ship in 24 hours was 465 miles, achieved by the *Champion of the Seas* in December 1854, west of Cape Horn. That's an average of a little more than 19 knots.

Only in recent years have we learned how to substantially improve on speed. In March 2001, the 110-foot catamaran *Club Med* broke the world record for a circumnavigation under sail. The winner of the Race of the Millennium, *Club Med* took 62 days to cover 26,500 miles at an *average* speed of 18.2 knots. But one day she sailed 650 nautical miles—a 24-hour average of more than 27 knots.

She was a highly specialized

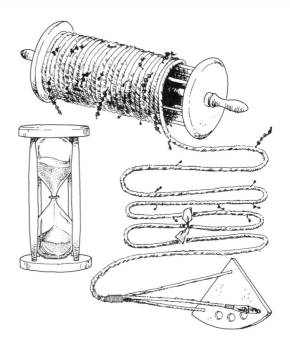

Before the age of electronic knotmeters and GPS, speed was measured with a chip log. The pie-shaped wood, when deployed over the stern, would strip line off a rotating drum as the vessel moved forward. Knots were worked into the line at measured intervals, and the number of knots running out in a given time gave the boat's speed.

boat, of course. Most small sailing yachts average between 5 and 8 knots, making a modest 120 to 190 miles in 24 hours, a distance a family automobile could cover in 3 or 4 hours. For planning and provisioning purposes, the rule of thumb for small sailboats is to allow for progress of 100 miles a day.

The top speeds of displacement powerboats are similarly limited by waterline length, although trawler yachts are increasingly likely to be capable of speeds into the semidisplacement range as diesel engines get lighter and more powerful. Whereas a full-displacement trawler yacht of 40 feet or so might top out at about 8 knots, its semidisplacement counterpart—marked by a fuller bow, wider waterline beam, and tightly radiused or hard-chine bilge to give a flatter bottom for hydrodynamic bearing and lift—offers speeds up to 15 knots or more, the trade-off being less efficient operation at low speeds.

A similar trend toward higher speeds is noteworthy among production powerboats capable of operating at planing and high-end semidisplacement (or semiplaning) speeds. The 40-plus-foot Bertrams and Vikings that topped out at 16 to 20 knots in the 1970s might be capable of 32 knots or more today, speeds at which pounding becomes much more pronounced. To counteract it, the new designs carry more deadrise aft than their forebears, yet they have to remain flat enough in their stern sections to provide lift at high speeds. These boats are not fuel-efficient.

See also **Bilge; Chines; Hull Shapes; Multihulls; Speed Limits**.

Speed Trials

An easy way to check the maximum speed of your boat

In or near many big ports, markers on land indicate measured miles, allowing you to check the accuracy of your speed and distance logs. They're always prominent from the water and they're always marked on the chart.

You can calculate your top speed over such a course very simply, as long as you make the run in reasonably deep water—say, 30 feet (9 m) or more. Shallow water creates a sinking action that holds a boat back, and you won't achieve your top speed. Make sure the course runs at right angles to the markers, and time the boat going one way. Your speed equals 3,600 divided by the number of seconds.

Now time the boat in seconds going the opposite way, as soon as possible after the first run. Find the speed as before, and then average the two speeds to find the true speed through the water. Once again—average the two speeds. Don't be tempted to average the two *times* or you'll get an incorrect result.

The two-way run is necessary to cancel out the effects of tidal currents and winds. If the measured mile is a statute mile of 5,280 feet, your result is in miles per hour; if it's a nautical mile of 6,076 feet, your result will be in knots.

See also **Speed Limits; Speed of Boats.**

Splicing Line

Building character by splicing double-braided line

Splicing three-stranded line is easy; splicing double-braided line is not. In fact, most amateur sailors are so intimidated by the complicated instructions and special tools required for splicing braided line that they never even attempt it.

If you have a cruising boat, there is a good case to be made for using nothing but three-stranded, low-stretch Dacron line for the running rigging. Then you can make all your own splices.

The bowline is a substitute for an eye splice, but it's not always a good one because it weakens the line by about 40 percent—on the other hand, a good eye splice hardly weakens the line at all. A bowline is also bulky and might prevent a sail being hoisted

as high as it should be because the knot cannot pass through the sheave.

You can buy braided line already spliced, of course, or you can have it custom-spliced to your order by a rigger, but even the simplest eye splice is not cheap, and a pair of splices might well exceed the cost of the line.

Because double-braided Dacron has only half the stretch of three-strand Dacron (which stretches about 4 percent with a load of about 15 percent of its breaking strength), most sailors could compromise by using professionally spliced double-braid for the halyards and headsail sheets, and self-spliced three-

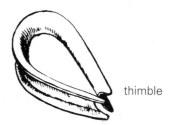

thimble

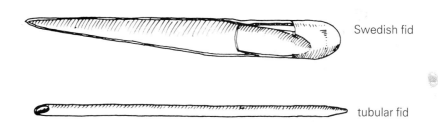

Swedish fid

tubular fid

Tools for splicing line.

Approximate Lengths of Fid Sections, in. (mm)			
Rope Diameter	Short	Long	Full
¼ (6)	2 (51)	3½ (89)	5½ (140)
⁵⁄₁₆ (8)	2½ (64)	4¼ (108)	6¾ (171)
⅜ (9)	3 (76)	4¾ (120)	7¾ (197)
⁷⁄₁₆ (11)	3½ (89)	6 (152)	9½ (241)
½ (12)	4 (101)	7 (178)	11 (279)
⁹⁄₁₆ (14)	4¼ (108)	8 (203)	12¼ (311)
⅝ (16)	4½ (114)	9½ (241)	14 (356)

S

Eye Splice in Three-Strand Twisted Rope

Unlay (i.e., untwist) the rope for 2 or 3 inches (50 to 80 mm) and tape each of the three individual ends or seize them tightly with twine. Tape again at the point where the unlaying should end; for this splice in ¾-inch (19 mm) rope, that would be about 16 inches (400 mm) from the working end for four tucks. Add the amount of rope necessary to form the eye, or loop. Tape again. This spot is called the throat of the splice.

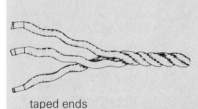

taped ends

Unlay back to the first piece of tape. To avoid a twist in the eye of the finished splice, untwist the rope just half a turn between the pieces of tape.

To do the first tuck, raise a strand just below the tape on the standing part of the rope and insert the middle working strand under it. You can usually do this with your fingers, but if the rope is twisted too tightly, use a Swedish fid. Insert this splicing tool under the strand, and then place the middle working strand

through the fid. Pull the strand into place and remove the tool.

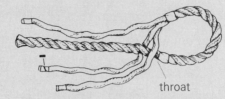

throat

The first time you work the splice, place a single hash mark on the strand that you just tucked. Numbering the working strands should help you to keep track of the tucking process.

Tuck the next working strand over the strand you just tucked under, and under the strand just below it. Mark this with two hash marks.

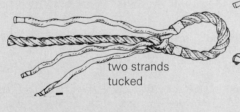

two strands tucked

Turn the entire piece over. You have one working strand left to tuck, and there is one strand left in the standing part of the rope that doesn't have a working strand under it. Make this tuck, continuing to work counter to the lay, or twist, of the rope. Mark with three hash marks.

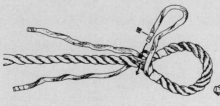

The first round of tucks is now complete. Tighten if necessary by pulling on the strand ends.

Take care when you tuck that you use all three strands in each round, and that you tuck under a strand in the standing part of the rope and not under one of your working strands.

Make three more rounds of tucks unless the rope is nylon, which holds better with five or six rounds.

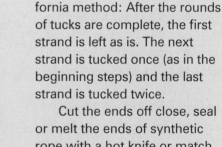

For a smooth, better-looking splice, finish with the California method: After the rounds of tucks are complete, the first strand is left as is. The next strand is tucked once (as in the beginning steps) and the last strand is tucked twice.

Cut the ends off close, seal or melt the ends of synthetic rope with a hot knife or match, and remove the tape.

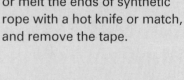

S

Eye Splice in Double-Braid Rope With or Without a Thimble Insert

Trim the end of the rope evenly, cutting off melted ends, or tape the end to be spliced. Using a tubular fid, measure one full fid length from the tape and label this point with an R.

Add the amount of rope necessary to form the eye or the loop around the thimble, if one is used. Mark an X there, at the throat of the splice. This is a complicated splice to complete with a thimble, so measurements are critical.

Move up the rope at least five full fid lengths and tie a tight slip knot.

Return to the X and gently push aside the strands of the coat (the rope's outer covering) to expose its inner core. Pull a small loop of the core through the coat as carefully as possible, and draw a single hash mark across the core. Then continue pulling out the core until its working end is completely exposed, and tape the end. Work the cover down into place to confirm that the X and hash mark are aligned and

equal distances from the coat and core end, respectively.

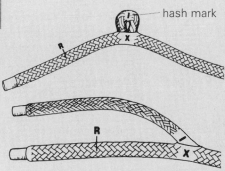
hash mark

Now pull out more core, this time from the standing part of the rope, and measure one short fid length from the single hash mark. (Short and long fid lengths are marked on tubular fids; for the measurement in inches, see the table.) Make two hash marks there.

Continue along the core for one full fid length plus one short fid length, pulling out more from the standing part if necessary. Make three hash marks.

For maximum strength in the splice, you will need to draw the rope's outer coat into its core and then its core into the coat. It will help to remember that the coat is marked with letters and the core with hash marks.

Pinch the taped end of the coat and insert it into the hollow end of the fid, taping it in place. Push the fid into the core at two hash marks and out at three hash marks. Be careful not to twist the coat. Pull until the R comes into view. The core will bunch up as you do

so, but this will correct itself later.

To taper the end of the coat, work toward the fid from R, and count off seven sets of picks, or parallel ribs, that run clockwise; mark this spot with a T. Continue toward the fid, marking every seventh pair with a dot so you will know where to cut.

Now go back to the R, this time marking the counterclockwise picks for tapering. To offset the tapering on these picks, mark your first dot at the fourth pair. From there, mark every seventh counterclockwise pair until you reach the fid.

Remove the fid and the tape. Cut and remove a single strand at each marked pick along the coat.

While holding the core, pull the coat until the T shows beyond the two hash marks. Take care not to lose the end of the tapered coat into the core.

For extra strength, the core end should be drawn through the coat, past the throat of the splice, and into the standing part of the rope. Measure from the X toward the slip knot one short half of the tubular fid; label this spot with a Z.

(continued)

S

Tape the pinched end of the core into the hollow fid end. Insert it into the coat at the T and work it through the coat as far as you can without a struggle. Depending on the size of the eye, the fid may not reach the necessary exit point in one pass. If this happens, bring the fid out of the coat, pulling some of the core with it. Then simply reinsert the fid into the same hole and work it farther through the coat. Continue this snaking process until the fid exits at the Z. Be sure not to snag any strands of coat with the fid at reentry points.

Draw up the slack until the coat-to-core unions formed at the T and two hash marks meet at the top of the eye. Now that this portion of the splice is complete, you should hide the end of the coat by smoothing the coat from the T to the three hash marks. Take your time and be thorough so the tapered end slides completely into the core at the three hash marks.

Remove the fid and smooth the pucker. Poke through the coat at the X to make some visible mark on the core inside. Also mark the core where it exits from the Z. Pull on the core tail until the mark you made under the X exits from the coat at the Z. Unbraid the tail, comb and fan it; then cut it off at a 45-degree angle between the two marks. Hold the rope gently at the union, and ease the coat from there around the eye until the core tail disappears. Trim the ends.

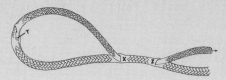

Take a firm grip of the rope close to the slip knot or attach it with a hook to a firm surface. If you measured carefully from the beginning of the splice, there should be enough slack in the bunched coat to roll down of the tail end and the coat-to-core joints.

Bunching may occur at the throat as the doubled core section and displaced yarns are distributed. If it does, roll and flex the rope. Begin this process gently but firmly. As you proceed, you may have to exert more pressure, perhaps to the point of pounding on the throat with a wooden mallet.

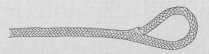

Double-braid splices—like most splices—are easy to take apart because they are designed to be pulled on, not pushed. To hold this splice firm, lock-stitch it in the following way.

Pass a needle threaded with twine all the way through the throat, leaving a tail of about 8 inches (200 mm). Make three complete stitches running along the standing part of the rope. Remove the needle from the twine and thread it with the tail end. Sew three stitches parallel to the first, but 90 degrees around the rope's circumference from them. Bring the two ends together through the standing part of the rope and tie with a square knot.

Turn the rope 90 degrees and repeat the stitches. Trim the twine ends. If you wish to protect the eye with a leather chafing strip, you'll need to apply this before you put in the lock-stitching.

Barbara Merry, in
The Splicing Handbook

S

strand Dacron for the remaining running rigging.

Sadly, though, the inescapable fact remains that any sailor worthy of the name ought to be able to make a splice in double-braid. If nothing else, the learning process is a good character builder and will teach you to deal with impatience, irritability, and the overwhelming urge to curse aloud for extended periods.

See also **Knots**.

Spreaders

Connecting the shrouds to the mast at more efficient angles

Although we use the term *spreaders* nowadays for the two pieces of wood or metal that spread apart a sailboat's shrouds, they were referred to as crosstrees in the days of commercial sail. Their purpose is to obtain a large and efficient angle between the shroud and the mast at the point of attachment.

Obviously, the longer the spreaders and the larger the angle, the better from a mechanical point of view, but the lengths are always a compromise because extralong spreaders interfere with the set of headsails when you're sailing on the wind.

Spreaders should exactly bisect the angle formed by the shrouds where they run over their tips. In other words, the outside ends of the spreaders should be slightly higher than the ends next to the mast. This not only looks more pleasing, but is also structurally stronger as it ensures that the force exerted on the spreader is purely a compression load. A horizontal spreader experiences a bending load under compression, which can lead to flexing and sudden failure.

Short, gaff-rigged masts on sailboats with reasonable beam do not need spreaders, but tall Bermuda-rigged masts are more difficult to keep upright—and need one, two, or more sets of spreaders to keep them in column.

Single spreaders should be lo-

cated between 50 and 52 percent of the mast height, measured upward from the deck. If you have double spreaders, the lower set should be located between 37 and 39 percent of the mast height upward from the deck, and the upper set should be between 68 and 70 percent.

Wooden spreaders are usually painted white or a light color on top to protect them from the sun and weather; however, they are usually varnished underneath so that rot may be spotted before it gains too great a hold. It's important to check the state of your spreaders regularly because the loss of one could easily result in a dismasting.

See also **Shrouds and Stays**.

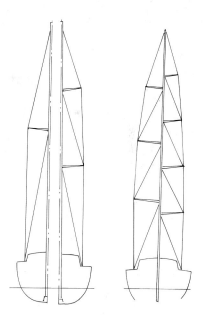

Single-spreader masts have the largest diameter and are the stiffest spars. Double-spreader masts are about as far as a hardcore cruiser should go. Cruiser-racers can benefit from a triple-spreader mast, and extreme racers will make their sails marginally more efficient with a four- or five-spreader rig.

A spreader should exactly bisect the angle formed by the shroud at its top.

Stability

Resisting being heeled over or capsized by wind and wave

When we talk of stability in a boat, we mean her resistance to being inclined or her tendency to return to an upright position after having been heeled. That kind of stability is known as form, or initial, stability because it is derived largely from the form or shape of the immersed hull. A boat that greatly resists being heeled is called stiff; a boat that heels easily is said to be tender, or crank.

But you will often hear reference to another kind of stability called ultimate stability, which is a boat's ability to right herself from a 180-degree capsize. Paradoxically, good form stability often results in poor ultimate stability. The reason is that form stability is mostly derived from wide beam. A beamy, shallow-hulled sailboat feels comfortingly resistant to capsize. When you step aboard, she hardly heels—and when the wind blows hard, she hardly leans over. But if she is capsized by a wave, her beam will keep her upside down for an excessively long time, perhaps long enough to sink her. The point is that beam contributes to stability both in the upright *and* the inverted positions.

It's another paradox of naval architecture that the beamier and more stable a boat appears to be in calm water, the more unstable she appears to be in a seaway. Her wide beam creates a long lever that makes it easier for each passing wave to lift her, and her response even to small waves will be rapid and jerky.

Whereas initial stability comes from wide beam and keel weight, ultimate stability derives mainly from reasonably narrow beam and a low center of gravity—that is, a deep, narrow boat. Such a boat may lack the form stability of a beamier boat and may heel more initially in a breeze—at least until her ballast keel starts to have some effect—but she will also be unstable in the inverted position and will, therefore, roll herself upright very promptly.

Obviously, ultimate stability is not of great importance if you always sail your boat in sheltered waters, but if you plan to go to sea, there is always a chance that a wave will capsize you.

Big boats are better than small boats in this respect, because the initial stability increases with size. The overturning moment varies with the cube of a boat's length, whereas stability varies with the fourth power of her length. Nevertheless, any boat may be turned turtle by a breaking wave with a height of 55 percent of her overall length.

Stability is an important part of seaworthiness, but it's not the prime agent, according to eminent research scientist and small-

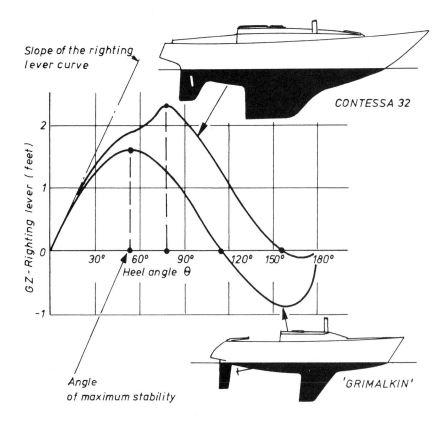

Hydrostatic stability curves for a Contessa 32 footer and the Half-Tonner Grimalkin *in still water. These two boats, similar in length but different in hull shape, displacement, and position of the center of gravity, have different stability characteristics; this is particularly true of their ranges of positive (safe) and negative (dangerous) stability.*

S

boat sailor Tony Marchaj. "Seaworthiness is in fact profoundly affected by a number of interacting factors other than mere stability," he says.

One of those factors is inertia, which is largely responsible for the renowned seaworthiness of some fairly narrow sailing yachts that many people might be tempted to dismiss as being too tender.

In powerboats, as in sailboats, the height of the center of gravity is the final arbiter of ultimate stability, and the center of gravity will be lowest in a displacement powerboat with a comparatively narrow, deep hull and its engine(s) and tankage carried as low as possible. The center of gravity will be higher—up near the top of the engines—in an express sportfisherman; in a planing powerboat with its wide, shallow hull, the center of gravity will be well above the waterline.

The hull shape of the planing powerboat gives it high form stability, so it will *feel* more stable than the more rolling displacement hull—particularly because, at speed, it derives dynamic stability from the hydrodynamic lift its hull form generates. But this is deceptive: whereas a displacement trawler might retain positive stability to a roll angle of 130 degrees—up in seaworthy keel-sailboat territory—a planing powerboat will have an ultimate stability of about 45 degrees or less.

See also **Capsize; Hull Shapes; Inertia; Keels; Seaworthiness; Stability Limits.**

Stability Limits

Calculating the angle at which self-righting ceases

There is an angle of heel for every boat at which positive stability disappears—that is, when the boat no longer tries to return to the upright position. It is a different angle for each design, of course, but for sailboats it's usually well over 90 degrees from the vertical.

It's difficult to calculate the exact limit of positive stability or the actual angle at which a boat inverted in moving seas will still try to right herself. You need to know the boat's displacement, her center of gravity, and the true shape of the hull and deck. You must also be able to estimate the center of buoyancy for the submerged hull.

Designers and builders of sailboats often came up with angles of positive stability that are different from those calculated by the International Measurement System (IMS), a widely used handicapping system for cruising and racing yachts. This seems to be because the IMS calculation does not consider the positive stability of the cabin trunk, which makes its figures substantially lower than the builders' figures—often as much as 20 degrees lower. For example, the makers of the Crealock 37, a well-found long-distance cruiser, give her a range of positive stability of 139 degrees from vertical, but IMS measurement certificates reduce that figure to the mid-120s.

The bulk of offshore racing sailboats have a stability range of between 110 and 130 degrees

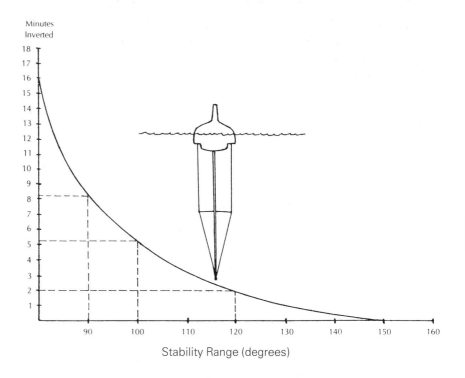

Number of minutes boats with various stability ranges are likely to remain inverted once capsized.

without including the cabin trunk, and some cruising boats have considerably more.

It has been calculated that a yacht with a 120-degree range is almost 3 times less likely to be trapped in the upside-down position than is a boat with only 90 degrees of positive stability; a boat with a 150-degree range, such as the Contessa 32, is 10 times less likely to be trapped.

Among powerboats, trawler yachts can achieve ultimate stability limits near 130 degrees, but a planing powerboat loses positive stability at a roll or heel angle above 45 degrees.

See also **Capsize Screening**; **Stability**.

Stainless Steel

It's an alloy of metals that will sometimes stain and rust

Stainless steel is neither stainless nor rustproof, despite the claims made for it. In fact, it will rust just like mild steel under certain conditions.

It is an alloy of several metals, one of which is chromium. When the chromium is exposed to oxygen, in air or in water, it forms an inert outside layer that protects the underlying metal. But if you deprive stainless steel of oxygen and surround it with moisture, particularly salt water, the oxidized layer of chromium breaks down and the stainless steel will rust just like any other steel.

Thus, you can expect trouble if you enclose a stainless steel propeller shaft in a stern tube—unless there is a slow but steady drip of oxygen-bearing water through the stuffing box. Likewise, keel bolts of stainless steel are always suspect if they have ever admitted water.

Some types of stainless steel are more corrosion-resistant than others, but all are subject to pitting or crevice corrosion when they are starved of oxygen and their protective oxide film.

See also **Electrical Bonding**.

RESISTANCE OF STAINLESS STEEL TO PITTING CORROSION: PITTING INDEX*

Stainless Steel Categories	Pitting Index (nominal)
18-8 (Types 301 to 304)	20
molybdenum-bearing (316, 317)	32
high-performance: austenitics	35.7
high-performance: duplex	39
high-preformance nickel-rich: austenitics	45.2
high-preformance nickel-rich: superaustenitics	44.4

*Pitting index is a function of chromium, molybdenum, and nitrogen content. The formula used to calculate this was devised by InterCorr International, Inc. (www.clihouston.com 15 May 1997).

Stanchions

Keeping the lifelines in place with stainless posts

The word *stanchion* is derived from the Old French *estance*, a stay or support. In small boats, a stanchion is an upright post placed at the outer edge of the deck to hold a lifeline in place. It is almost always constructed of stainless steel tubing.

Stanchions are vulnerable because of their small areas of attachment, and should be bolted

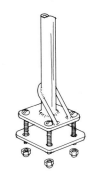

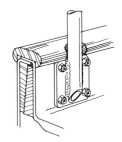

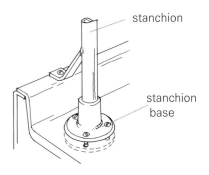

stanchion

stanchion base

Stanchion base installations. If the base is fastened to a vertical support as well as bolted through the deck, it will be much stronger.

S

through the deck (never screwed) and backed up by a large plate under the deck to spread the considerable stress loads. Their proclivity to bend, and to tear open the deck, can be considerably reduced if they can also be firmly attached to a bulwark at a height of several inches above deck.

Instruct your crew—and helpful bystanders on the dock—never to fend the boat off by pushing against the stanchions. The wit of man could hardly have devised a more efficient lever to mutilate the deck. Never be tempted to fasten your safety tether to a stanchion, either, except possibly at the base, because it's not designed to take the heavy jolt of someone falling overboard and coming up suddenly against the end of the tether.

The brown stains that stainless steel stanchions often exhibit after exposure to saltwater spray may be removed quickly with any mild metal polish.

See also **Lifelines**.

Starter Draw

Large flow, but for short time, gives modest demand

Have you ever wondered how much energy your starter motor draws from your battery? Surprisingly little, under normal circumstances. The flow of current is huge, often the equivalent of 7 hp or more, but because it flows for only a few seconds, the effect on a battery is minimal. It's only when starting is difficult and you have to grind away for many minutes that the battery starts to run down.

For example, if you use the starter motor to crank a medium-sized diesel and it draws 4,800 watts for 20 seconds, you're taking about 2.5 amp-hours from the battery. That's about half of what your CD player consumes if you use it 4 hours a day. At a modest 30-amp charge, your alternator will replace the energy in less than 10 minutes.

If you have a gasoline engine, the starter draw is much less—often as little as half the amount required for a diesel—because of its lower compression ratio.

See also **Cranking Ratings**.

Steel Hulls

Using steel for a hull produces a super-strong boat

Steel has many advantages for boatbuilding, among the foremost of which are its strength and resistance to abrasion and impact.

"A small boat built of steel is as close to truly indestructible as it's possible to get," writes naval architect Dave Gerr in *The Nature of Boats*.

Another advantage of steel is that it's easily worked on by welders anywhere in the world, making repairs inexpensive for cruising boats. It is also ductile, or stretchable, which means that if you hit a rock or a half-submerged shipping container, you're not likely to sink. The hull may be dented and deformed, but it probably won't be holed, as a wooden or fiberglass hull might be.

On the other hand, steel vessels are heavy because designers assume that about a fourth of the plate thickness will rust away in 15 or 20 years, so it's difficult to build a reasonably light steel boat that is less than 35 feet (10.7 m) long. In fact, steel craft of less than 90 feet (27 m) are noticeably heavier than similar boats built from wood, aluminum, or fiberglass.

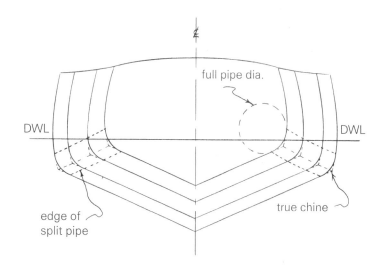

In radiused-chine construction, a split pipe welded between the steel topside and bottom plates softens the chine to imitate a round bilge. Here the combination with a convex curvature in the topside plating makes for a pleasing hullform.

S

Steel is also difficult to form into the compound curvature needed for a round-bilged hull, although modern radiused chines have greatly softened the slab-sided, hard-chined look of older steel sailboats.

The resale value of a steel-hulled yacht drops by almost one half after it reaches the age of 10 years. This is an average figure, of course, and there are many exceptions among those boats that are built to the highest standards and meticulously maintained.

See also **Aluminum Hulls; Wooden Hulls**.

Steering Systems

Wheels and tillers can claim their own distinct advantages

The basic steering system on most boats is a rudder (or a pair of rudders) and some means of turning it at an angle to the flow of water past the boat.

On inboard rudders—that is, rudders located some distance forward of the boat's after end—the rudderstock, from which the rudder is hinged, is extended upward into the hull of the boat where it is invariably turned by an attached tiller or a quadrant—which is a horizontal arc spanning two small tillers fixed about 90 degrees apart.

On a powerboat or a large sailboat, the quadrant is linked mechanically (by means of pulleys and wire ropes, or sets of gears) or hydraulically to a steering wheel. Sailboats up to about 40 feet (12 m) in length can use a long tiller that fits directly onto the rudder head.

Wheel-steering frees up the cockpit space swept by a tiller and gives a mechanical advantage that makes steering easier, but it's complicated and needs frequent checking and occasional maintenance. Some wheel systems also lack the "feel" or "feedback" a good sailor uses to sense the balance of a sailboat. A tiller provides that feeling, and is the simplest and most reliable of all steering systems.

Wheel-steering systems are provided with tillers that fit directly onto the rudder head for use in emergencies.

See also **Quadrant; Tillers**.

Stern Anchoring

Dropping anchor and setting it firmly without an engine

Anchoring by the stern is often a useful maneuver in a sailboat, and many cruising boats have a stern anchor locker with a chain-and-nylon rode ready to feed out. Others have a special reel of nylon anchor line at the stern.

When you sail into a crowded anchorage, the trick is to work your way to the most windward position and strike your mainsail there. Then you can sail downwind gently under a small foresail—or under bare poles if the wind is blowing hard—and ease the anchor over the stern when you reach your chosen spot.

Feed out line until you have a scope of about 5 to 1 and then—and only then—snub the line around a cleat to dig the anchor in. To make sure it's really set firmly, temporarily raise a foresail and let the wind do its work.

Now you are anchored securely by the stern and you can take your time to stow the sails and sort out the gear. When you're ready, take a line from the bow, run it aft (outside all the rigging and lifelines), and make it fast to the stern anchor line with a rolling hitch, just aft of the transom. Then let out a boat-length of your stern anchor line. You will be riding happily to your anchor by the bow, and everybody else will stop looking at you and shaking their heads.

See also **Anchors, Anchoring; Setting Anchors**.

Stern Drives

Combining the features of inboard and outboard engines

A stern drive was the name reserved for the lower unit of an inboard-outboard engine, but it is now commonly applied to the entire hybrid system. It consists of a conventional inboard engine attached through the transom to

A 315-horsepower gasoline engine built by General Motors, marinized by Volvo, and mated to a Volvo SX stern drive.

what is essentially the lower unit of an outboard motor.

Stern drives, also known as inboard-outboards, are best suited to hulls between 16 and 25 feet (4.8 to 7.6 m) in length. They combine the advantages of a powerful inboard engine with the handling and steering properties of an outboard motor. Neither rudder nor trim tabs are needed because the outdrive swings from side to side and tilts up and down.

The engine is placed immediately forward of the transom, and a horizontal driveshaft pierces the transom above the waterline to contact the vertical shaft of the outdrive. The upper part of the outdrive incorporates a clutch and gearbox.

The entire outdrive may be tilted up for towing on a trailer or when the vessel is beached. In the up position it will also clear the water and avoid fouling and corrosion.

Maneuvering with a stern drive is quick and positive, and another advantage is that the inboard engine is more fuel-efficient than an outboard of comparable power.

Stern Glands

Keeping all but a little propeller-shaft water at bay

Despite the availability of modern dripless seals, most boaters still rely on the old-fashioned type of stuffing box to stop water penetrating the boat past the propeller shaft.

This type of stern gland has a small chamber filled with rings of flax packing. The flax is squeezed closely around the shaft by a plunger turned by a large nut.

The pressure on newly installed flax is adjusted so that when the propeller shaft is not turning, the gland will admit a flow of about four drops of water a minute. When the flax has bedded in after 10 or 15 hours of running, it should be adjusted again for a rate of one or two drops a minute when the shaft is still. When the shaft is turning, of course, the rate will be somewhat greater; the water will not only lubricate the gland, but also prevent overheating of the shaft where it passes through the stuffing box. This is a simple and re-

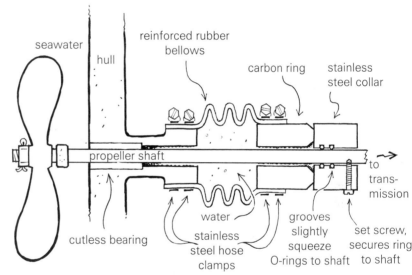

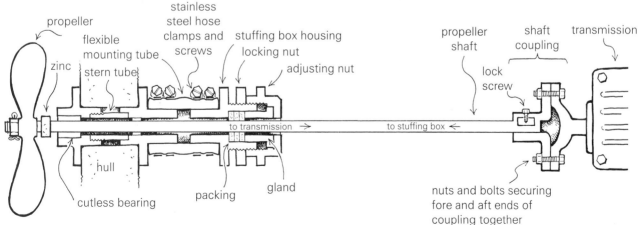

The traditional and still common stuffing box (above) *depends on a few drops of seawater around the rings of flax packing for lubrication. The more complicated dripless shaft seal* (top right) *utilizes a rubber bellows and carbon-graphite ring.*

S

liable system that has been in use for many decades.

Conventional flax packing is square in cross-section. Some brands are impregnated with synthetic lubricants such as polytetrafluoroethylene (PFTE) or Teflon; others are braided from synthetic yarn.

Dripless seals come in two forms: (1) a simple claylike lubricated material that conforms to the shape of the stern gland when you stuff it in, creating a permanent waterproof seal; and (2) a more complicated form that relies on a mechanical seal between the stuffing box and the propeller shaft. This second type holds a stationary, high-density, carbon-graphite flange against a stainless steel flange on the propeller shaft, and the shaft where it passes through the box is enclosed in a nitrile bellows.

Stove Fuels

Choosing the right type of fuel for your galley cooker

It's significant that the most popular type of galley stove, the propane gas stove, is almost the most dangerous. It's a triumph of convenience and marketing over safety and common sense.

There is no doubt that the clean, instant heat of a propane flame is a wonderful asset to the shipboard cook. No other fuel compares with it for ease of operation and control of cooking temperature. It would, in fact, be the perfect galley fuel if it weren't for one major fault: one small leak can blow you and your boat to pieces.

The trouble with propane, or liquid petroleum gas (LPG), is that it's heavier than air, so any that leaks out will lurk in the bilges, ready to be ignited by the smallest spark from a starter motor or an electrical switch. Fortunately, the human nose is an excellent gas detector, and readily discerns even the smallest concentrations of LPG. That fact, together with comprehensive safety devices, keeps the explosion rate low. It is still an unacceptable risk for many boaters, however, particularly because there are several safer alternatives, the most popular of which are alcohol and kerosene.

Stoves using alcohol as fuel fall into two groups: those that rely on heat to vaporize a pressurized supply of liquid alcohol in a special burner, and those that use capillary action to draw alcohol from a container through a wick.

The burners on pressurized alcohol stoves must be heated in advance so that a flow of alcohol fuel will vaporize into a gas when it enters the burner. In most cases, the preheating, or priming, is accomplished by burning a small amount of alcohol beneath the burner. But if the burner is not heated enough, the pressurized fuel entering the burner will flare up if a light is applied or if it catches fire from the burning primer alcohol. This has given pressurized-alcohol stoves a bad name, even though it is usually caused by the impatience of the user.

Nonpressurized-alcohol stoves do not flare up, but they burn with a constant steady flame that cannot be as well regulated as

a pressurized burner's flame and are not quite as efficient because they do not convert the alcohol to gas before burning it.

Neither stove, in fact, is particularly efficient because alcohol for boat use is expensive—roughly five times the price of kerosene—and because it is the coolest burning of all the stove fuels. One claimed advantage is that it is soluble in water, which is said to make it easy to douse an alcohol fire with water. In fact, it is not always easy to douse a large quantity of burning alcohol because the water tends to spread it around to places where it starts other fires.

Kerosene stoves and heaters work with burners under pressure, just like pressurized-alcohol stoves. They are less expensive, hotter, and more efficient, although they need more priming and will flare up if priming is curtailed. They used to be the most popular type of portable stove and heater in the world a few decades ago, with household names like Primus and Optimus, but they are now quite rare. Many world cruisers use kerosene, however, because it's nonexplosive and a six-month supply can be safely stored on your boat. It's available almost anywhere in the world where you can buy gasoline or diesel fuel and, in a pinch, you can substitute diesel for kerosene—although it will be somewhat smellier and smokier.

Kerosene also has many other uses on board. You can use it as a paint thinner, a brush cleaner, and (with a little light lubricating oil mixed in) as a substitute for WD-40. You can top up your compass

S

and remove masking-tape residue with it. Your diesel engine will also run on it.

Diesel-fueled stoves are common on fishing boats, but they run very hot and mostly produce too much heat for yachts, particularly those venturing into the tropics. They are the least expensive to run, with the possible exception of the small solid-fuel heater-ranges installed by some enthusiasts—which run on coal, coke, peat, charcoal, driftwood, and even pine cones—but heat regulation for cooking is a serious problem.

See also **Galley Placement**; **Gimballed Stoves**.

Sun Exposure

Protecting yourself from damaging ultraviolet rays

Boaters are particularly vulnerable to skin damage from the ultraviolet (UV) rays of the sun. By the time you've developed what's known as sailor's skin—dry, wrinkled, inelastic, and leathery—the damage is irreversible. Skin cancer results from cumulative doses of UV radiation over a lifetime.

There are two particular types of UV rays that affect the skin. UV-B, the major culprit, is responsible for 90 percent of sunburn damage. UV-A accounts for only about 10 percent, but it's still important to protect yourself from it in a marine environment.

The problem with UV radiation is that you can't feel it. It's not like sunlight or infrared radiation, which you can see or feel. You can't sense the presence of UV rays; you only know afterward, by the degree of burn they leave behind.

Another problem is that you don't have to be in direct sunlight to get burned. Indirect sky radiation accounts for almost 50 percent of UV rays reaching the Earth on a clear day; you can be badly burned even standing in the shade. An open-sided Bimini top will not protect you.

Sensitivity to sunburn varies among individuals—it depends largely on the amount of pigment, or melanin, you have in the top layers of your skin; that is, your natural skin color. Melanin forms a natural screen against sunburn and is present in large quantities if you have a dark complexion. It's an inherited trait and you can't do anything to alter it.

What we call a "suntan" is your skin's response to being *burned* by UV rays—it starts to produce melanin to protect itself. But if you have very fair skin, you may not be able to produce melanin. Fifteen percent of the U.S. population, in fact, are unable to tan and are the most vulnerable to burning.

UV rays are most intense between 10 A.M. and 2 P.M. local sun time. That's when 66 percent of daily UV radiation reaches the surface of Earth. But you really need protection from 9 A.M. to 3 P.M., when 80 percent of the day's radiation is received.

If you have a dark or medium-dark complexion, your skin will produce melanin in response to the minor burns that result from controlled exposure to UV rays. But remember that UV damage is cumulative over your whole life; every time your skin is tanned, it is burned and damaged first.

It takes about 14 days to develop a tan that offers at least some protection against further burns. For the first three to six days, the only change in skin color is redness—there is no such thing as an instant tan.

Your individual need for sunscreen depends on your skin sensitivity, and you would be wise to consult your family doctor about what kind to buy and how often to use it. In general, if you have dark skin, you'll need little protection; if you have very fair skin, you'll need complete protection, including a broad-rimmed hat, closely woven clothing, and even gloves if you're at the helm.

In *Dr. Cohen's Healthy Sailor Book*, Dr. Michael Martin Cohen says all sunscreens should be applied to clean, dry skin because some of them are not water soluble and will precipitate if you apply them to wet skin, rendering them useless. So if you're wet or sweaty, towel off first.

Dr. Cohen also says to apply sunscreen an hour before you expose yourself to the sun, and that you should apply it again after swimming or exercise that makes you sweat.

Don't forget to cover every area that's likely to be exposed, including the tops of your feet, the tops of your ears, your nose, and your hands; and don't overlook the less obvious places such as the back of your knees, the back of your neck, and your lower lip.

See also **Cruising Lifestyle**.

S

Surveyors

Using a professional makes sense if you're about to buy

It's not easy to tell how well qualified a surveyor is; professional standards vary and your state may not have licensing requirements. Most surveyors are chosen by word-of-mouth recommendation or because their reputations for good work have won them contracts with boatyard proprietors and insurance companies. Every competent surveyor should have a keen interest in boats and a broad understanding of the marine pleasure-boat business. You may need the services of a surveyor when

- you're thinking of buying a boat and want to know her real condition
- you're thinking of selling your boat and want to establish her value
- you want to finance the purchase of a boat and the bank needs an appraisal
- you're buying an old boat and your insurance company calls for a survey
- when your boat is damaged and you need advice on repairs

The old advice to shop around is always sound when it comes to choosing a surveyor. If you have access to a fairly current survey report, it will tell you a lot about the surveyor, too. Reject any surveyor who can't spell simple words like propeller or gunwale.

When you're buying, don't be tempted to do without a surveyor,

no matter how well you know boats. You're too likely to be blinded by love at first sight to be impartial. Console yourself with the thought that although it will cost you hundreds, a survey could save you thousands.

There are various types of surveys, with varying prices, including condition surveys, surveys to establish a boat's fitness for your special needs, and quick appraisals of worth. Make sure you know what you're getting before the surveyor starts work.

Few small-boat surveyors will give you a report on the engine, other than the fact that it appears to be in running order. Most will not climb the mast to inspect the rigging aloft. If you want detailed reports in those areas, you'll have to hire a marine mechanic and a rigger.

See also **Selling a Boat.**

Synthetic Fibers

Man-made lines and fabrics dominate the modern boat

Almost all lines and fabrics used on modern boats are made from synthetic fibers. The best known synthetics are nylon, Dacron, and polypropylene, but hard on their heels comes a new generation of extremely strong yet lightweight fibers known as high molecular weight polyethylene (HMWPE). Among these "high-modulus" newcomers are Dyneema, Kevlar, Spectra, Technora, Twaron, Vectran, and Zylon.

Nylon fibers are stretchy and thus ideal for absorbing sudden shocks. Nylon lines are used for

anchor rodes, docklines, and dinghy painters. Nylon fabric is used for sailboat spinnakers and other light-weather sails.

Dacron, like nylon, is relatively inexpensive, but it is not quite as strong as nylon. Spun from polyester fibers Dacron stretches much less than nylon but is adversely affected by sunlight. Dacron is used for halyards, sail-control lines, and—in cloth form—basic working sails. Both Dacron and nylon lines are available in a variety of layups and can be spliced fairly easily by amateurs.

Polypropylene makes a very lightweight line and it is comparatively inexpensive—but these beneficial features come at the expense of durability. Polypropylene is only about 60 percent as strong as Dacron, and the working life of polypropylene line is greatly shortened by strong sunlight. Nevertheless, it is widely used, especially for dinghy painters, because of one unique characteristic: it floats.

Kevlar and Spectra are the two most widely used modern, high-tech lines. Kevlar is several times stronger than steel and is relatively expensive compared with nylon and Dacron. It suffers degradation when it is bent sharply. It is used in laminate form for racing and cruising sails. In rope form, Kevlar is used on racing sailboats for lightweight running rigging, including running backstays, and some standing rigging.

Spectra is even stronger than Kevlar and less susceptible to damage from sharp bends, chafe, and fatigue. It tends to elongate

S

slightly under heavy sustained loads, but is nevertheless increasingly used for halyards. Spectra line is about twice as strong as Dacron, size for size, and is ideal for sheets, guys, low-stretch control lines, and spinnaker halyards. Like Kevlar, it is usually sold with a braided polyester cover to pro-

tect it from abrasion and ultraviolet degradation. Spectra is also used in laminated racing and cruising sails.

All the high-tech HMWPE lines are expensive—usually more than twice the price of Dacron—and all are seriously weakened by knots, so special terminal fittings

are required. Alternatively, because these lines are extremely slippery, the ends should be professionally spliced.

See also **Dacron; Halyards; Plastics; Rope Strength; Rope Stretch; Sail Cloth; Sheet Sizes; Splicing Line.**

T

Tacking

Improving the angle at which a boat sails against the wind

The word *tacking* is often loosely used to mean beating. It describes the manner in which a sailboat sails against the wind in a series of zigzag courses. Each course is angled at about 45 degrees to the true wind, and the act of coming

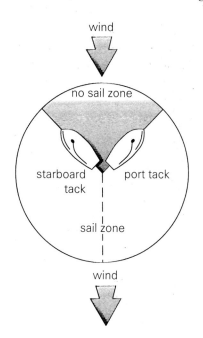

about—that is, when the boat's bow passes through the eye of the wind while changing from one course to the next—is also known as tacking.

No sailboat can make progress directly into the wind, of course, but great advances have been made since the early days of sail. In the seventeenth century, a square-rigged warship could barely make way to windward at all, but by the early eighteenth century, a square-rigged ship of the line could sail at 70 degrees to the true wind. The clipper ships of the mid-nineteenth century were about as handy to windward as square-riggers ever got; they could make 65 degrees.

Smaller vessels such as pilot cutters, rigged fore-and-aft with mainsails hung from gaffs, were beating at 55 degrees to the wind by the late nineteenth century. The Bermuda rigs of the early twentieth century introduced the next big improvement: they gave yachts the ability to sail at 45 degrees to the wind, on average. Today, there are some racing yachts that sail at 38 degrees or even closer to the wind, but only in calm water and ideal conditions.

Sailing a boat as close to the wind and as fast as she will go is a demanding test of skill for the person at the helm, because it is easy to point too high (and lose speed) and even easier to point too low (and lose distance to windward). On average, tacking to a windward destination increases the distance traveled by about 40 percent of the straight-line distance.

See also **Tacking Downwind.**

Tacking Downwind

Taking the rolling out of sailing downwind in the trades

America's Cup racers are not the only sailboats that tack downwind; cruisers do it, too. You'll know why if you've ever rolled your gunwales under for days on end, running dead before the trade winds.

Sailing on a broad reach is usually faster than sailing on a dead run, so if you head off 20 degrees to one side of your rhumb line, you not only enjoy more comfortable sailing, but also gain speed—especially in light weather.

T

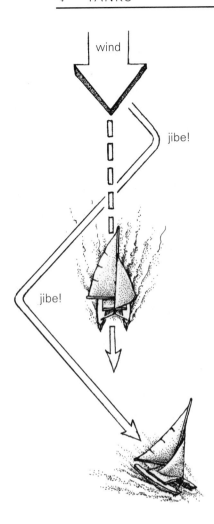

Tacking downwind can get you where you're going more comfortably with little or no loss of time. In some conditions, on some boats, you might even reach your objective faster despite sailing a longer distance.

Sailing on a reach for half a day and then jibing to sail 20 degrees on the other side of your rhumb line does not add as much distance as you might think. Over a straight-line course of 100 miles, you'll only have 6 miles extra to cover by broad-reaching. But thanks to the extra speed you gain on a broad reach, you might get to your destination quicker even if the course is longer. For example, if your speed improves from 4 knots (going dead downwind) to 4.24 knots (on a 20-degree reach), it will take exactly the same time to cover the course. And if your average speed goes up just a quarter of a knot, from 4 to 4.25 knots, you'll actually get there a little sooner—and a lot more comfortably.

See also **Rhumb Line; Tacking**.

Tanks

Tackling the problem of storing various liquids afloat

Tanks are used on small boats to store water, fuel, and sewage. Their size and shape often present problems for installation and maintenance, however.

They should be deep and narrow whenever possible, for stability when the boat is rolling, and the long dimension should lie fore and aft. If you must have wide, shallow tanks, they should be well baffled into sections no bigger than 18 inches (457 mm) square, to prevent surge. Following are some general recommendations about tanks:

- every tank should be equipped with at least one access hatch and a sounding stick
- every tank should have its own shut-off valve
- for convenience and safety, every tank should be easily removable for maintenance, repair, and cleaning

Unfortunately, few tank installations are perfect. Many tanks cannot be removed without destroying cabinetwork or furniture. Others would need to have an engine removed first—and still others, fitted in place before the deck was put on, simply will not fit through the companionway hatch.

Tanks made of ferrous metal or aluminum are likely to corrode from the outside if they are in contact with bilgewater, and they may also be subject to galvanic corrosion if they touch other metals, especially copper. Maintenance is often difficult because they fit so closely to the hull that it's not possible to scrape or paint them in position. Nevertheless, most fuel tanks are aluminum because they're light, inexpensive, and easy for boatbuilders to obtain or fashion in a wide variety of shapes. The aluminum should be at least 0.125 inch (3 mm) thick. Tanks as thin as 0.09 inch (2 mm) are available but should be avoided.

Fiberglass fuel tanks, although heavier than aluminum, will never corrode and, if they are well built, should last the life of the boat. Polyurethane and polyethylene plastic can also be used, especially for smaller tanks (fewer than 75 to 100 gal. or 340 to 450 L).

You can install flexible tanks made of nylon with a neoprene-nitrile coating for diesel fuel, and they will conform to the shape of the space available. They must be positioned carefully to avoid sharp edges, of course, and they must be well secured.

Water and holding tanks are often made of fiberglass or plastic. Flexible water tanks are available with special linings that impart no taste to the water and they, too, will fit in places where hard tanks would be difficult to install.

See also **Fuel Weight**.

Teak Finishes

Looking after one of the finest woods used on boats

Teak is the wood most favored for fine finishes on pleasure boats. The warm honey glow of varnished teak is a sign of quality workmanship. But even if you neglect teak entirely, leaving it exposed to sunshine and salt water, it will endure for years.

Teak is so permeated with natural oils that it does not absorb water and is almost impervious to rot. It is easy to work with and dimensionally very stable. These qualities, together with its long life expectancy, justify its relatively high cost.

It is used extensively above deck for trim on fiberglass boats, to soften the sterile look of large areas of plastic, and it is often used to cover fiberglass decks in the form of thin planks that afford a good foothold when wet. Teak decks are normally left to weather and will bleach almost white in the tropics when scrubbed daily with salt water. They should never be oiled or varnished lest they become as treacherously slippery as inferior wood. Teak decks are, unfortunately, heavy and prone to leaks.

Despite its resistance to rot, teak does need occasional maintenance. Untreated teak will go gray and attract dirt unless you clean it every month or so with a mixture of detergent and bleach. The other alternatives are to paint it, varnish it, or dress it with oil.

Paint offers long-term protection with minimum maintenance, but few boaters can bring themselves to paint such a beautiful wood—sensible as that would be. Nor does teak accept paint well, due to its oily nature. Many boatowners are lured into the trap of varnishing external teak simply because it looks so good. But the sun's ultraviolet rays will make quick work of your varnish unless you sand it down and apply two to four new coats every six months.

A few sailors rendered almost witless by their passion for varnished teak actually invest in covers of acrylic canvas to keep the sun and weather off it. It seems never to occur to them that their gleaming treasures are then hidden from view. Such is the madness teak can create in boatowners.

Dressing teak with oil is another trap. Oil looks stunningly beautiful for a week and then it suddenly begins to oxidize and turn black, especially if salt water touches it. Its single advantage over varnish is that when the time comes to scrape it down to bare wood (as it surely will), there will be no solid residue to fight through.

Down below, teak is best varnished with a matte finish to seal the wood against moisture and the intrusion of mold spores. The varnish will last for many years down there, protected from the sun and water.

Teak is relatively soft, so when you clean it, use a pad rather than a hard-bristled brush. Scrub across the grain; otherwise, you will scour out the softer wood and leave deep grooves.

See also **Brightwork; Varnishing**.

Through-Hulls

Protecting the underwater holes made in the boat's hull

Through-hull fittings are traditionally made of bronze for underwater work. They line and protect each hole made in the hull. They have an external flange and a wide locking nut inside so that they make a firm seal against the hull. Many through-hulls have screw threads so that a seacock may be attached directly; some seacocks incorporate their own through-hull fittings.

Bronze, an alloy of copper and tin, is almost impervious to normal corrosion. Beware of its look-alike, brass, which has no place on a boat. Brass is an alloy of copper and zinc that is quickly attacked by salt water and galvanic corrosion. The zinc is eaten away, leaving only a soft pink residue through which you can poke a finger. It's not easy to tell the difference between brass and bronze, but if you scratch brass, it usually looks bright yellow, whereas bronze looks more pinkish.

Plastic through-hull fittings made of nylon or Marelon are often used to line holes made above the waterline, but don't be tempted to use them underwater.

T

1. head intake
2. head discharge
3. shower drain discharge
4. depth instrument
5. speed instrument
6. galley seawater intake
7. galley sink drain
8. engine cooling intake (2)
9. generator cooling intake
10. electric bilge pump discharge
11. manual bilge pump discharge
12. propeller shaft (2)
13. rudderstock (2)
14. drain for propane locker

A sample through-hull diagram showing types and locations of through-hulls. It's a good idea to carry a diagram like this for your boat.

Hoses attached to through-hull fittings are traditionally fastened with two stainless steel hose clips. However, the barbed pipe for the hose is rarely wide enough for two clips side by side; if you overtighten the outside clip, which is only half on the barb, you can damage the hose. Therefore, tighten the first clip normally, and then go easy on the second one—but don't be tempted to do without the second one. It's something every surveyor and insurance assessor looks for; keep it in place as a spare.

Another thing surveyors like to see next to a seacock is a tapered softwood plug to jam the hole in an emergency. They recommend that a mallet to knock it in with be kept there, too, but that request is rarely gratified.

See also **Seacocks**.

Thunder and Lightning

Protecting yourself and your vessel from thunderstorms

The first indication of an approaching lightning storm is often the rumble of thunder in the distance. You can estimate how far away the storm is by counting the seconds between a flash of lightning and its accompanying thunder. The number of seconds divided by 5 equals the distance in nautical miles.

Almost all lightning activity is associated with the large towering clouds known as cumulonimbus, which often have an anvil shape at the top and can move very fast. Rain squalls and fierce gusts of wind are typical at sea level.

If you can discern the direction in which a thunderstorm is moving, try to put as much distance as possible between yourself and it, especially if you have a fast boat. Move at right angles to its track. The standard advice for those caught in the track of such a storm is to make everything fast on deck and stay below until the storm passes.

Statistically, your chances of being struck by lightning are low, but it does happen frequently enough that protection is warranted. Lightning protection works by offering potential strikes a quick and easy path to ground.

A grounded vertical metal conductor 10 feet (3 m) high for every 17 feet (5 m) of boat length will attract and harmlessly divert lightning flashes. It thus provides a "cone of protection" angled downward at 120 degrees from the top of the conductor. A sailboat's metal mast makes an excellent conductor, of course, but most radio antennas on powerboats will not work unless they are somehow grounded. All the rigging and lifelines should be bonded together and connected to the same ground as the mast or lightning conductor. The ground, in this case, is a metallic object with a surface of at least 1 square foot (0.09 m²) submerged in the water. In lieu of anything better, you could hang a fathom or two of chain over the side from a backstay or, preferably, a shroud.

The wire for bonding and conducting should be copper and not less than #8 gauge. It should take the straightest possible path to ground, with no sharp bends; otherwise, the lightning will take shortcuts and possibly blow a hole through the side or bottom of the boat.

If you have to be on deck during a lightning storm, try not to touch anything made of metal and keep your hands and feet out of the water.

See also **Clouds**; **Lightning Protection**.

Tidal Streams

Sorting out the differences between tides and currents

It takes a sailor to know the difference between currents, tides, and tidal streams, although the rules are simple. A current is a steady, permanent, horizontal movement of water, like a broad river running through the open ocean. A tidal stream also is a horizontal movement of water, but its speed and direction vary frequently and regularly according to the state of the tide. A tide is a vertical movement of water.

You can't pile up water vertically, of course, so when the tide rises, the water has to slip off sideways. This movement is called a tidal stream and, like a current, is described by its set and drift (course and speed).

The average strength of a 6-hour tidal stream is two thirds of its maximum flow. The total drift in nautical miles in that time is two thirds of the maximum rate in knots, multiplied by 6.

In most locations, the ebb (outgoing) tide is stronger than the flood (incoming) tide, and lasts longer. At or near the coast, the ebb and flood don't flow to-ward and away from the shore, but rather run parallel with it. A tidal stream is usually stronger within 2 or 3 miles of the coast than it is farther out.

See also **Ocean Currents**; **Slack and Stand**; **Tides**.

Tidal Waves

Long low swells traveling with great speed and power

Proper tidal waves, or tsunamis, are the result of underwater disturbances such as earthquakes or erupting volcanoes, and are not to be confused with the bores of shallow waters or the heavy sets of rollers that occasionally make anchorages uninhabitable in the South Atlantic and other oceans.

Tsunami waves spread across oceans with little height but great speed so that vessels in deep water will hardly be affected by their passage. Nevertheless, they possess great energy, which is expended with great destruction once they come in contact with the shores bordering the shallow continental shelf.

Although such waves may be no more than a few feet high in deep water, their speed can reach as much as 500 knots and their length may be 100 miles. Tsunamis usually consist of a series of waves with crests 10 to 40 minutes apart, and the highest wave may arrive several hours after the first one.

For shore dwellers, the first sign of a tsunami is the receding of the sea, leaving an abnormally large portion of the beach exposed. This is a warning to take to the hills, for the sea will inevitably return in the form of vast plunging breakers that will inundate the coast and destroy everything in their path. If you're at anchor when the sea starts to recede and you are not immediately set aground, make for the deep water of the open ocean with all haste.

See also **Tides**.

Tides

A mystery to scientists and also a source of agitation

The dictionary definition of a tide sounds quite dull: "the alternate rise and fall of the surface of oceans, seas, and the bays, rivers, etc. connected with them, caused by the attraction of the moon and sun: it occurs twice in each period of 24 hours and 50 minutes (the lunar day)."

In reality, the tide is a source of endless agitation to boaters. The tide hides dangerous rocks and sandbanks. It causes tidal rips that swamp small craft, and currents that either deter the progress of boats or hurl them forward so unexpectedly fast as to confuse bold navigators and frighten meek cockpit hands.

The tide is also a source of great confusion. On America's East Coast, tides are mostly semidiurnal—two high tides each day of roughly equal height, and two low tides each day of roughly equal height. On the Gulf Coast, the tides are mostly diurnal—one high tide and one low tide each day, except that sometimes there are three changes a day instead of one. And on the West Coast, the

T

301

tides are what is known as "mixed"—two high tides and two low tides a day, like semidiurnal tides, but the first and second tide of each day vary substantially in height.

Fortunately, tides are easy to predict with the help of tide tables that list the height above datum level at any given time. However, no guarantees are given about accuracy because strong winds and differences in barometric pressure can affect both the height and timing of tides.

The moon has a greater influence on tides than the sun—about 2.3 times as much—because it is so much closer to the Earth. When the moon is full or new, it is in line with the sun, and the combined pull of these two bodies causes spring tides, which rise to greater heights and sink to lower depths than normal. At half moon, in the first or third quarter, its attraction is at right angles to that of the sun, and we have lesser tides, known as neaps, which do not rise very high or sink very low.

In many ways the tide is still much of a mystery to scientists. This is what the *Encyclopedia of Nautical Knowledge* has to say on the matter: "to simply and clearly present or describe what actually gives rise to the great natural phenomenon, ebb and flow of the tide, with its many variations from month to month, is to attempt the impossible. Indeed, it is doubtful if a satisfactorily lucid explanation ever has been given regarding the prime source of the tidal wave, respect due to the theories of gravitational effect of Sun and Moon combined with cen-

trifugal force of Earth's rotational motion, notwithstanding."

Note that the term *tidal wave* used here has nothing to do with the common (but misleading) term applied to tsunamis.

Spring tides, incidentally, have nothing to do with the season of the year. They have a range (i.e., the difference in height between high water and low water) about 20 percent greater than average.

Neap tides have a range of about 20 percent less than average.

Equinoctial tides around March 21 and September 21 often display an unusually large range, especially when a full or new moon is in or near the equinoctial, and particularly if the moon is at its perigee. Then the sun and moon combine most effectively to attract the seas into the upward swelling bulge that causes tides—or so we think.

See also **Slack and Stand; Tidal Streams; Twelfths Rule.**

Tillers

Specifications for the simplest of steering systems

A tiller is a horizontal beam connected to a rudder for the purpose of turning it for steering. The word's origin is obscure, but was probably influenced by the Middle English *tillen*, to pull. Tillers are now mostly found on small sailboats, although there are still large sailing ships that use tillers moved by tackles.

Any suitable material may be used to construct a tiller, but most are made from solid wood or laminations of wood strips, which are more easily bent into the shape required and glued together.

Most people prefer the handgrip of a tiller to be round in section and about 1¼ inches (32 mm) in diameter. For different lengths of tiller, the square-section size at the rudderhead varies from 2.43 inches (62 mm) for a 4-foot (1.2 m) tiller to 3.08 (78

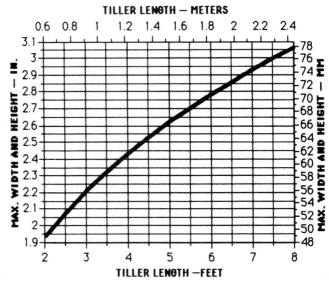

**REQUIRED TILLER SECTION
Square Section Tillers**

Tiller Comb

A tiller comb is pretty much what it sounds like: A blade on the bottom of the tiller drops into the teeth of an upturned comb to hold the tiller in position. A convenient tiller comb is like an extra crew member. It will hold the boat on course while you crank in the genny, adjust the topping lift, or nip below for a spot of tea. Well-balanced boats can sail for hours with the helm locked, which makes watch keeping much less tiring.

Don Casey, in *100 Fast and Easy Boat Improvements*

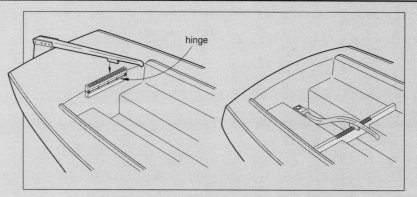

1. Determine the location of the comb. When the rudder is well aft, the comb can often be mounted to the aft end of the cockpit, hinged to fold down when not in use. When the rudder shaft comes up through the cockpit sole, a removable bridge is the more likely mount.

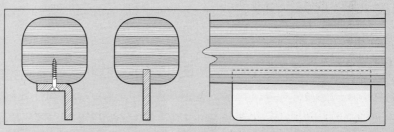

2. Based on the comb location, equip the tiller with the blade stop. The simplest is a length of angle iron screwed to the bottom of the tiller. You might also epoxy thin bar stock into a slot routed into the tiller. Since the tiller travels in an arc, the blade must be long enough to remain over the comb. A blade thinner than the kerf of your circular saw makes comb fabrication easier.

3. Use the stop as a guide to lay out the teeth. Placing the slots close together provides finer adjustment, but the thickness of the stock determines how thin you can cut the teeth and still have adequate strength. Remember that the angle of the teeth changes as you move away from the centerline. With the teeth marked on the blank, you should be able to cut them sufficiently accurately freehand with a circular saw. Make the comb as long as you like, but in use you are unlikely to ever want it to hold the tiller more that a few inches from the center position. (For heaving to, the tiller should be lashed.)

T

mm) inches for an 8-foot (2.4 m) tiller.

From the rudder head, the tiller should gradually taper down to the handgrip. The square section adds strength in a vertical direction. The rule of thumb is that a tiller shouldn't break if a 200-pound (90 kg) sailor falls on it.

See also **Steering Systems**.

Time Signals

Finding an accurate time for navigation with a sextant

If you're planning to cross an ocean and you have a sextant on board for celestial navigation, you'll need the time, accurate to within a second. You don't need an expensive gimballed chronometer in a dovetailed box; since the invention of quartz watches, an inexpensive battery-operated wristwatch will do the trick—provided you can check its rate of gain or loss from a radio time signal.

An ordinary shortwave radio receiver will give you continuous time signals from U.S. stations WWV, near Fort Collins, Colorado, and WWVH, at Kekaha-Kawai. You'll find them at frequencies of 2.5, 5, 10, 15, 20, and 25 MHz. These broadcasts are operated by the National Institute of Standards and Technology.

The time signals of the British Broadcasting Corporation (BBC) are also useful—and you'll get the world news at the same time. The BBC has a "six-pip" countdown to the hour, marking the last 5 seconds; the sixth "pip" marks the exact hour.

Incidentally, don't take it for granted that the time shown on your GPS is accurate to the second, especially when you have just switched it on. Corrections must be made for leap seconds over the years as the Earth's revolutions slow down. Orbiting satellites send out corrections on a regular basis, but they are part of a long stream of signals that takes time to process, and your GPS might not have updated itself yet.

See also **Time Zones**.

Time Zones

Dividing the world into 24 zones with their own times

The world is divided into time zones corresponding to standard meridians 15 degrees—or 1 hour of longitude—apart, with the Greenwich meridian in London, England, understood to be zero.

Each time zone extends $7\frac{1}{2}$ degrees east and west of its meridian. However, in many parts of the world, the borders are bent to include geographical regions with common interests, such as scattered island groups belonging to the same country.

The zones extend for 180 degrees east of Greenwich, and 180 degrees west, meeting at the international date line. If you cross the date line in your boat heading west, advance the date by one day; if you're heading east, subtract one day as soon as you've crossed the line.

When you're at sea, you should adjust the ship's time to correspond with the zones, so that ship's noon is reasonably close to the time when the sun reaches its zenith on your meridian. As noted, the changeover comes every 15 degrees. If you're sailing from England to the East Coast of the United States, for example, you would start off in zone 0, or Greenwich time, also known as Zulu. You would enter zone +1 $7\frac{1}{2}$ degrees west of the Greenwich

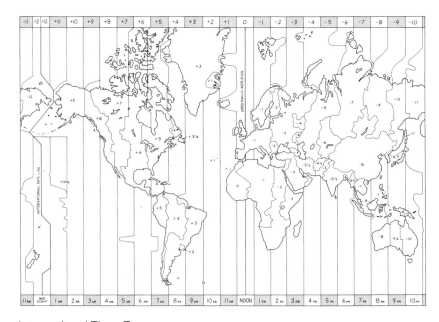

International Time Zones.

meridian, and zone +2 would begin 22½ degrees west of Greenwich. You could conveniently ignore the half degree and change over at 7 degrees, 22 degrees, 37 degrees, and so on, if it suits you better. The difference is only about 2 minutes.

Zones west of Greenwich are designated with a plus sign for a prefix; zones east of Greenwich are designated with a minus prefix.

See also **Time Signals**.

Tonnages

Four main rules define carrying capacity of a vessel

The origin of *tonnage* is from the Old English *tunne*, a large cask for carrying wine, ale, or beer. It had a capacity of about 252 gallons (1,145 L). In those days, a ship of 20 tons was a ship that could stow 20 tunnes in her hold.

The earliest legal act dealing with ship measurement in Britain dates from 1492, but in 1694 it was officially decided that a ship's tonnage would be decided by the simple formula

$$\frac{\text{length x breadth x depth, in feet}}{94}$$

The number 94 was chosen so that the result gave the approximate number of tons of coal a boat could carry. Of course, that wasn't an altogether satisfactory formula because it was difficult to measure the depth of a laden vessel, and the definition of length was often in dispute because of the varying size of overhangs. So

the tonnage rule has been modified many times over the years until today there are four main tonnage rules:

- Gross tonnage. This is a volume, not a weight. It's the total enclosed space (or internal capacity) of a vessel expressed in units of 100 cubic feet, each one of which is reckoned to be a ton.
- Net (or registered) tonnage. This is the gross tonnage less the volume of interior spaces that cannot be used for cargo. On pleasure boats, deductions are made mainly for engine compartments and control stations.
- Displacement tonnage. This is the actual weight of a vessel in long tons of 2,240 pounds each. It can be calculated by finding the volume of the vessel from the waterline downward. The volume in cubic feet divided by 35 equals the tonnage, because 35 cubic feet of seawater weighs 1 long ton.
- Deadweight tonnage. Like net tonnage, this is an indication of cargo-carrying capacity; but whereas gross and net tonnages are volumes, deadweight tonnage is measured in long tons.

By tradition, naval warships are referred to by their displacement tonnage; that is, their actual weight. For the practical purpose of federal documentation of pleasure boats, gross tonnage is measured as half the overall length (L), times overall breadth (B), times depth (D)—which is

the internal measurement of the hull, not the draft—divided by 100. That is:

$$\frac{1}{2}(L \times B \times D \div 100)$$

All the measurements are in feet. Net tonnage is taken to be $\frac{9}{10}$ of gross tonnage, and the minimum size for federal documentation is 5 net tons.

See also **Net Tonnage**.

Tools

Creating a special tool kit for use in emergencies at sea

Boaters are resourceful people and will find a way to make repairs in an emergency at sea, given enough time. But the proper tools make things much easier. Here is a basic list of emergency hand tools for offshore cruisers. You should add to it any specialized tools your engine or rigging might require, as well as basic sail-repair equipment—including a sturdy pair of scissors and a knife.

ax, small
bolt cutters, large
brace, with bits to 1 inch
C-clamps, several
drill, hand, ⅜-inch, and bits
duct tape
electrician's tape
files, triangular, flat, and round
hammer, ballpeen
metal snips
plane, small
pliers, needle-nose, regular, and
    Vise-Grips
rasp, shoemaker's (flat and half-
    round; coarse and medium)

T

saws, regular crosscut and hack-saw with standard and carbide blades
screwdrivers, both flathead and Phillips head
seizing wire, stainless steel
wire clamps
wood chisels, ½ and 1 inch
wrenches, open-ended, plumber's, and socket wrenches

To keep corrosion under control in humid salt air, inspect your tools weekly and spray them lightly with a mixture of kerosene and lubricating oil.

Torque

Harnessing engine power to produce twisting force

The twisting force needed to turn a propeller shaft is known as torque. Slow-turning engines are usually able to deliver the necessary torque at low revolutions per minute (rpm). Fast-revving engines produce less torque, so they need a reduction gear to convert their low-torque, high-rpm power into the high-torque, slow-revving power needed to turn a large propeller.

Slow-turning engines have several advantages. They run more quietly and last longer than fast-revving engines. Unfortunately, their suitability for most pleasure-boat applications is limited because they're also always big, heavy, and expensive. So the great majority of pleasure powerboats and sailboats are equipped with smaller, lighter, fast-revving engines and reduction gearboxes. Because of friction, adding a gear-box reduces the power available to turn the propeller by about 3 percent.

The maximum torque output of an engine occurs well before peak rpm. For instance, a typical 70 hp marine diesel usually produces its maximum torque of about 150 foot-pounds at about 1,800 rpm, after which the figure declines to about 125 foot-pounds at the top speed of 3,200 rpm. Maximum torque is usually produced at between 50 and 70 percent of maximum rpm.

This engine, therefore, will run most efficiently at 1,800 rpm; however, an increase in speed of 25 percent, to 2,250 rpm, will provide greatly increased performance for a relatively small increase in fuel consumption.

See also **Horsepower; Powerboat Engines; Sailboat Engines.**

Towing

Taking precautions when offering another boat a tow

If you ever offer a keel sailboat a tow, be aware that you're in for a slow ride. Most sailboats have

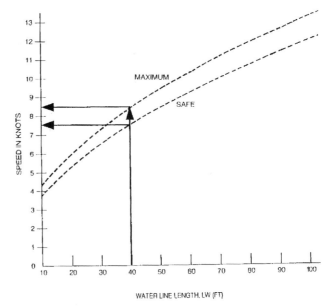

MAXIMUM TOWING SPEEDS

DISPLACEMENT AND PLANING HULL VESSEL TOWING SPEEDS					
VESSELS WATERLINE LENGTH	SQUARE ROOT	MAXIMUM TOWING SPEED	VESSELS WATERLINE LENGTH	SQUARE ROOT	MAXIMUM TOWING SPEED
20	4.5	6 KNOTS	70	8.4	11.3 KNOTS
25	5.0	6.7	75	8.7	11.7
30	5.5	7.4	80	9.0	12.0
35	6.0	8.0	85	9.2	12.3
40	6.3	8.4	90	9.5	13.0
45	7.0	9.4	95	9.8	13.1
50	7.1	9.5	100	10.0	13.4
55	7.4	9.9	105	10.3	13.8
60	7.8	10.5	110	10.5	14.1
65	8.1	10.8	115	11.0	14.7

RECOMMENDED SAFE AND MAXIMUM TOWING SPEEDS OF TOWED VESSELS
(LENGTH IN DISPLACEMENT MODE)

Safe towing speeds when towing astern.

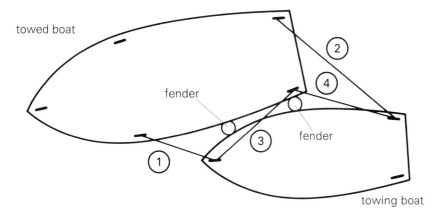

towed boat

fender

fender

2

4

3

1

towing boat

Towing alongside allows the two boats to be maneuvered as one and is the preferred technique when approaching a dock or mooring or maneuvering in congested waters. Make the bow line (1) fast first, then maneuver the towing boat so that its bow angles in slightly toward the towed boat and its propeller(s) and rudder(s) are aft of the towed boat's transom, rudder(s), or stern drive(s). This will give maximum maneuverability. In calm weather rig the stern line (2) next, followed by the tow strap or forward spring line (3) and the backing line (after spring line, 4). In wind, seas, or current, rig the tow strap and backing line before the stern line in order to get the tow underway quicker.

maximum hull speeds of 6 or 7 knots; if they are towed faster than that by sheer brute force, a lot of damage can be done. Similar precautions apply to displacement powerboats; semidisplacement and planing boats are, in this regard at least, easier to tow.

The towing line should be long, between 5 and 10 times the length of the boat to be towed. In the absence of a dedicated towline, a nylon anchor rode will do nicely because it has the required strength and stretchiness. After you've passed the end of your line to the tow, or received the end of the tow's line, take up the slack slowly. If you charge ahead at full speed before the line is taut, you might snap the line or pull out a deck fitting.

Arrange a system of communication with the person at the helm of the boat being towed. If you can't communicate by radio,

at least work out a basic set of hand and flashlight signals that indicate *faster, slower, stop,* and *OK.*

Set up the towline so that the person at the helm of the boat being towed can cast it off at any time if something goes wrong. If the towed boat does not have substantial bitts or foredeck cleats, make sure the towline is secured to the cockpit winches aft, and then led through the chocks or fairleads at the bow. Alternatively, see that the towline is secured in a big loop around the cabintop.

Disregard all advice to suspend an anchor or heavy weight in the middle of the towline to prevent snubbing. It will prove to be nothing but a menace under tow. Bend on extra line instead, to smooth out any jerkiness in the tow.

For a long tow in choppy seas, guard against chafe in the

tow's bow chocks, with sufficient padding lashed in place. You may be able to use a short length of chain from the bitts, through the chock, to the towline.

If you're towing a centerboarder, tell her crew to raise the board completely; otherwise, the board will tend to take a sheer and make the boat heel over dramatically.

Shorten up the tow when you enter port and bring the other boat alongside if necessary, protecting your topsides with fenders.

See also **Salvage.**

Towing Drogues

Dragging devices behind a boat to reduce her speed

Under certain conditions, a sailboat running downwind under bare poles in a bad storm will inevitably lose control and broach to, with possibly disastrous results, if she runs too fast. She must be slowed down by drogues so that overtaking waves may pass beneath her quickly and move out of her way.

A drogue is anything dragged behind a boat to reduce her speed. It is not a sea anchor, which is a parachutelike device that creates resistance enough to bring a boat almost to a complete halt and hardly permits any movement through the water.

Some people use old automobile tires as drogues, on the end of a long line weighed down with an anchor. Others use planks of wood bolted to steel angle iron, or long thick hawsers streamed in a

T

bight from both sides of the stern. Almost all drogues have to be weighted because if they float on the surface, advancing waves will hurl them toward the boat and create slack. The exception is the series drogue, which consists of a long nylon line furnished with 100 or more small cones whose openings face forward. It is streamed straight aft so that most of it is always exerting a pull even if a wave breaks over part of it. The best-known series drogue is that designed by Donald Jordan, consulting engineer for the U.S. Coast Guard Research and Development Center in Groton, Connecticut.

If storm-force winds continue to rise and the swells continue to lengthen and speed up, you may find it difficult to avoid the plunging breakers coming up astern because of your lack of maneuverability. Then it may be time to stop using the drogue and start scudding.

Scudding is running before the wind under bare masts only. The difference between scudding and running off is one of speed. When you first start running off, the seas are slower. But now that they have accelerated and grown larger, you also need speed and maneuverability to avoid them. Scudding is the answer, or so some believe. This topic is controversial, and the weight of opinion often changes. Currently, it seems to be swinging in favor of running off over scudding in that ultimate storm.

See also **Drogue; Heavy Weather; Running Off; Scudding; Sea Anchor**.

Trade Winds

Harnessing the power of two special belts of winds

In the early days of exploration under sail, two large belts of winds were discovered blowing toward the equator: from the northeast north of the equator and from the southeast south of the equator. The word *trade* in those days meant *to advance steadily* and was synonymous with *track* and *path*. The trade winds did indeed allow those unhandy sailing vessels to advance steadily—and, of course, to set up patterns of international trade.

Contrary to common belief, the trade winds are not totally steady in force or direction, but they do trend in the general direction of southwest and northwest at an average speed of force 4 on the Beaufort Scale, or 11 to 16 knots. Their actual speed at any one time varies with the seasons, and can reach force 7 (28 to 33 knots) at times, usually in winter. The trade-wind belts also move north and south as a whole with the sun, covering an area of many hundreds of miles between the approximate latitudes of 30 degrees north and south and the equator, where they are separated by an area of low pressure known as the doldrums.

The trades are suppressed by the monsoons in some areas, mainly the Indian Ocean, the western portion of the Pacific, and West African waters. In sum-

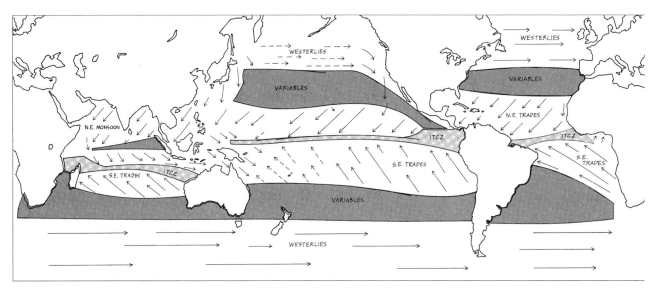

World wind patterns, January to March.

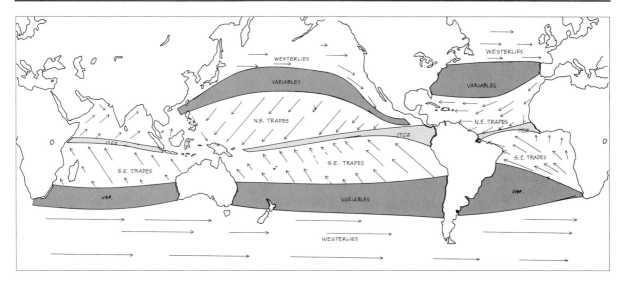

World wind patterns, April to June.

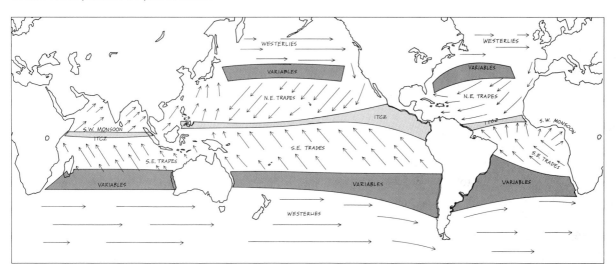

World wind patterns, July to September.

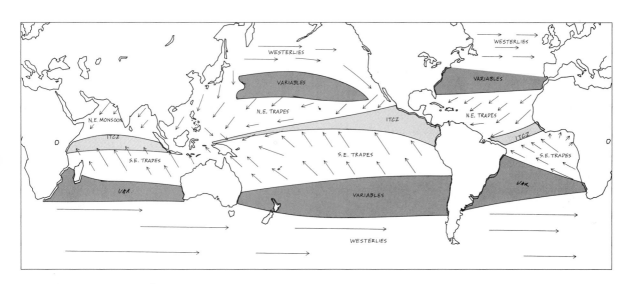

World wind patterns, October to December.

mer, they can also turn into the tropical revolving storms known as hurricanes, cyclones, or typhoons. These storms usually occur in late summer.

In the trade winds, the weather is generally fair and hot. Puffy white trade-wind clouds dot the sky from horizon to horizon, and it seldom rains except toward the western reaches of the trade-wind belts, where thunderstorms become more common as you approach the doldrums.

Off the Portuguese coast, the so-called Portuguese trade wind blows from the north, reaching moderate gale force in summer. Clipper-ship sailors also sometimes referred to the Roaring Forties as trade winds.

Most small sailboats take advantage of the trades when crossing oceans, and many fly special downwind sails that avoid the chafe of the ordinary mainsail-foresail arrangement; they move the center of effort forward to ease the wind vane's task of steering to leeward in light weather. Beating to windward against the trades requires a weatherly boat and a brave long-suffering crew.

See also **Beaufort Scale; Doldrums; Horse Latitudes.**

Traffic Schemes

Organizing the flow of traffic on marine freeways

Traffic-separation schemes are in operation in and near most busy ports to organize vessels into lanes moving in the same direction. They are the maritime equivalent of air traffic control.

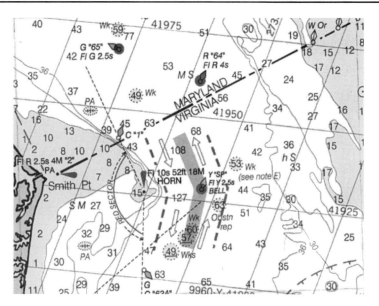

Chesapeake Bay Traffic Separation Scheme (TSS). The outer limits of the area covered by the scheme are shown by dashed magenta lines, the separation zone by a magenta band. The fact that the arrows are solid (not dashed) indicates that the directions are mandatory.

Traffic schemes are intended to make navigation safer and more predictable for large and less maneuverable ships. They are not intended to be used by small pleasure boats. In fact, boats smaller than 66 feet (20 m) in length must give way to larger traffic in traffic-separation lanes and in the zones where the lanes meet or cross.

Although small boats may use the lanes in most cases, they should stay clear of them as far as possible. If you *must* use a lane, go with the traffic flow—never against it—and stay close to the starboard edge. Move outside the lane temporarily if a large ship starts to overtake you. There's usually ample water for small boats on either side of the lanes.

Don't be tempted to use the central separation zone between the two lanes; it's designed to be free of traffic.

You may *cross* a traffic-separa-

tion scheme any time you like, of course, but you're expected to take the shortest route—that is, at right angles to the traffic—and you must keep well clear of any ships using the lanes. Don't underestimate the time you need to cross this marine freeway; some separation schemes are 5 miles wide.

Ships using the lanes are tracked by radar, monitored by a traffic control center, and contacted by VHF radio. The radio frequencies are noted in pilot books; if you're planning to cross a traffic scheme, it pays to listen to traffic control and get a general picture of the traffic pattern. You are not *obliged* to contact traffic control, but you can do so if necessary. For example, if you find yourself in fog while crossing a separation scheme, traffic control will help you avoid collisions with ships in the lanes. You should, of course, have a good radar reflector so that traffic control can detect you on radar and note your position.

Separation schemes are shown on charts but are marked only by occasional buoys, so it's sometimes difficult to tell how close you are to the traffic lanes unless you are using GPS or loran. Don't be deceived by maverick ships that choose not to use the traffic lanes. Although the one-way lanes are intended for use by vessels of 300 tons and more, it's not always obligatory for them to do so. They are, however, asked to stay well clear of the lanes.

See also **Rules of the Road**.

Trailerboats

Opening up a host of boating venues for mass recreation

The swift growth of boating as a recreational sport in the last few decades is due in no small measure to the use of road trailers. Trailers make boating possible for people living far from navigable water, and they open up myriad boating destinations on rivers, lakes, and the sea that are inaccessible to other craft.

Trailerboats are usually fairly small (up to about 23 ft. or 7 m in length) and fairly light (up to about 3,000 lb. or 1,360 kg) but there are always exceptions, of course. Occasionally you will see one that is much bigger, but it will also be a bigger problem to tow, launch, and retrieve.

All kinds of boats can be towed behind a family automobile on a trailer and used for fishing, sailing, water skiing, and exploring sheltered coastal waters. Many have cabins capable of accommodating a family with two small children for a day's excursion or a weekend trip.

Trailerboats are powered by outboard motors, inboard motors, and sails. The sailboats typically have retractable centerboards or daggerboards for ease of launching and towing. Their shallow draft with the boards up also makes it possible for them to be beached like powerboats, so they don't have to carry or tow tenders.

Another big advantage of trailerboats is that you can keep them at home and avoid costly marina mooring fees. Also, unless you're planning to stay afloat a long time, you won't need regular coats of antifouling paint on the bottom.

See also **Yacht Design**.

Trim Tabs

Maintaining the correct trim for minimum resistance

When a powerboat is planing, the minimum resistance lies between 2 and 4 degrees of trim by the stern. In other words, the boat should ride in a slight stern-down attitude.

To achieve and maintain this trim attitude, inboard-engined boats are often fitted with adjustable horizontal plates at the bottom of the transom. At speed, these trim tabs can be moved to make the stern rise or fall, thereby adjusting the horizontal attitude of the boat to best advantage. Trim tabs are usually installed one

A trim tab slightly depressed. Well offset from centerline, trim tabs, or flaps, acting in consort, can lower the bow by raising the stern, or individually correct for a small amount of heel.

at each side and are controlled hydraulically from the steering position.

A slight bow-down trim will help a boat rise onto a full plane more quickly, after which the trim may be adjusted to a slight stern-down attitude for least resistance.

Altering the trim tabs individually can also temporarily correct a list to port or starboard caused by excess weight on one side, but this is only effective when the boat is moving fast.

See also **Planing**.

Trysails

The advantages of a good old-fashioned storm trysail

Many modern deep-sea cruisers have a third set of reef points put in their mainsails in lieu of a storm trysail. The thinking is that the polyester cloth of a mainsail is strong enough to handle the stresses, and it's easier to take in

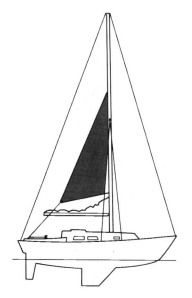

A trysail lowers the center of effort and moves it aft, allowing a boat to point better toward oncoming waves.

a third reef in bad conditions than it is to rig a separate trysail.

But there's a point that is often overlooked. A trysail is shaped like a foresail set on its side. This keeps the sail's center of effort low, and reduces the heeling tendency. It also moves the center of effort aft, which means a boat will heave to under trysail with her bows pointing up well into the waves—the best position of all for medium gales.

When you take in the third reef of a normal sloop's mainsail, however, the center of effort stays high and moves forward, so the bows tend to fall off the wind, leaving the boat vulnerable to waves from the side. It might even be impossible to heave to under a storm jib and triple-reefed mainsail because the boat will tend to bolt downwind unless she is constantly brought up by her rudder.

As always, a lot depends on the underwater shape of the hull and keel. Different boats handle differently in heavy weather, and some might do just fine with a triple-reefed mainsail, but you don't dismiss the trysail until you understand the principle of its operation.

If you do opt to carry a trysail for an ocean crossing, go whole hog and make it easy to deploy. Provide it with a separate track up the mast—or at least a track switch above the mainsail slides—and keep it on its own track, bagged at the foot of the mast, ready for quick action.

See also **Heaving To**.

Turnbuckles

Using screw threads to tighten the standing rigging

A turnbuckle (sometimes known as a bottlescrew) is an ingenious mechanical device used to apply tension to a sailboat's standing rigging wires, lifelines, and so forth. It consists of an elongated metal link, or a tube, with a left-hand thread in one end and a right-hand thread in the other. Thus, when the matching turnbuckle is turned, it will take up slack in an attached wire and maintain tension.

Closed-body turnbuckles are sleek and streamlined, but they are prone to corrosion from water that can enter the center adjustment holes and remain inside. The corrosion will, of course, be invisible until the turnbuckle is taken apart or falls apart at sea. Open-body turnbuckles are much

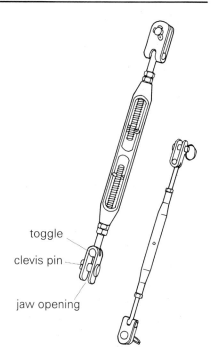

A standard open-body turnbuckle (left) is less prone to corrosion than one with a closed barrel (right).

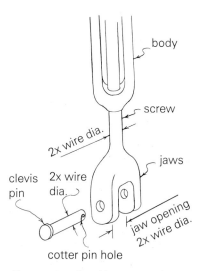

Proper turnbuckle proportions.

safer because they do not hold water and any corrosion will be immediately apparent.

For standard, open-body bronze or stainless steel turnbuckles, the screw diameter should be twice the diameter of the rigging wire. That goes for the opening between the turnbuckle jaws as well, and the clevis pin through the jaws should also be twice the diameter of the rigging wire.

Shroud turnbuckles are normally fastened at their lower ends to chainplates. There is always the possibility of vibration and metal fatigue at that spot, so there should be a toggle, or universal joint, between every toggle and its chainplate. Similarly, there should be a toggle between every mast tang and shroud eye.

See also **Rigging Tension**.

Twelfths Rule

How to estimate the depth of water in between tides

If you know the time of low or high tide and you know the tide's range, you can estimate the depth of the water at any time in between by using the twelfths rule.

A semidiurnal tide rises (or falls) a predictable amount of its total range in every passing hour. After high (or low) water, the tide falls (or rises) the following fractions of its full 6-hour range:

Hour	Amount
1	$^1/_{12}$
2	$^2/_{12}$
3	$^3/_{12}$
4	$^3/_{12}$
5	$^2/_{12}$
6	$^1/_{12}$

The easy way to apply the twelfths rule is to remember 1-2-3-3-2-1, the number of twelfths in correct order. For example, if you are in the fourth hour of a flood tide with a 16-foot range, the water level will have risen 1+2+3+3 twelfths, which is $^9/_{12}$ (or $^3/_4$) of 16 feet, or 12 feet above chart datum.

Interestingly, fully half the tide ebbs or flows in the 2 hours in the middle. Tidal steams speed up accordingly, but not necessarily at the same time as the tide changes height.

See also **Tidal Streams**; **Tides**.

Twin Screws

Second engine adds safety, but at the cost of economy

Generally speaking, two engines are not twice as good as one, whether they be inboards or outboards. Twin-screw installations are comparatively wasteful of power; they also cost much more, need larger fuel tanks, require more servicing, and weigh considerably more.

Twin inboard engines are commonly cramped and leave little room for access, thus almost guaranteeing that they will be poorly maintained.

The reason given for most twin-engine installations is safety: if one engine breaks down, the other will get you home. But it doesn't always work out as well as expected. Many twin-screw planing hulls are almost unmanageable under one engine in bad weather and heavy seas—which is when engine failure is most likely. Furthermore, the most common cause of engine failure is contaminated fuel; therefore, unless your engines draw from separate tanks, you're likely to lose both if you lose one.

A second reason commonly given for twin screws is the added maneuverability they confer. Indeed, in the hands of a skilled operator, a twin-screw boat will turn for docking in its own length or find its way home without operable steering, which are undeniable advantages.

A boat with two 100 hp engines cannot make use of the same amount of power as a boat with one 200 hp engine. There is added weight, added friction in the drivetrains, and added underwater drag from extra struts and rudders—a formidable price to pay, even if you commonly cruise on only one engine.

As a rule of thumb, twin-screw installations use 20 percent more fuel than single engines of the same output.

To overcome the safety problem, many single-engined boats have a separate generator that can be linked with a belt to the propeller shaft. Other, smaller powerboats with single inboard engines carry emergency "get-you-home" outboard motors on the transom, although they will only be effective in reasonably calm weather because of the propensity of the propeller to emerge from the water as waves pass by.

Commercial fishing boats the world over prefer single engines—now you know why.

See also **Fuel Economy**; **Outboard Motors**.

U

Unlucky Colors

Old superstition limits choice of boat colors

Superstition has always played a large role in sailors' lives, and no doubt always will. There is still so much about the sea, its moods, and its inhabitants that is unexplained or incomprehensible that even today it would seem foolish, if not irresponsible, to ignore the superstitious practices of our forebears. That's why it's considered unlucky to paint a boat blue or green, the colors of the sea.

In ancient times, boats were believed to have their own souls (inherited, incidentally, from human sacrifices) and could not presume to identify themselves with the sea or any of the gods who managed its affairs. Punishment would surely follow any boat discovered to have been masquerading under false colors.

Modern skeptics will no doubt scoff at such patent nonsense, but there will always be many sailors who will abide by old superstitions—if only to quell those primordial feelings of unease. And why not? Sailors need all the luck they can get at sea, and heeding the time-honored warnings of yore seems a reasonably convenient way to earn it—and score points for the black box.

See also **Black Box Theory; Figureheads; Sailing on Friday; Unlucky Names.**

Unlucky Names

Beware of naming your boat after fearsome creatures

Just as there are unlucky colors, there are also unlucky names for boats. A vessel with a name that is too presumptuous has long been believed to attract bad luck.

Presumptuous names are those that challenge the sea or the wind, especially those that boast about beating the elements and surviving their meanest blows. To call a boat *Sea Conqueror* or *Hurricane Tamer* is to tempt the fates. The gods of the wind and sea are all-powerful, and they like boat names to be suitably humble.

You may recall from Greek mythology that the most important of the Titans, the vengeful Kronos, cut off his father's genitals with a sickle and threw them into the sea. You can probably imagine how Neptune, god the sea, felt about that.

Yet, in 1912, the British White Star steamship company was foolish enough to name its new Atlantic liner *Titanic*. Not only that, but it claimed she was unsinkable, and it launched her without a proper naming ceremony, thus depriving the gods of their share of the usual libation. Little wonder she was doomed.

In the 2001 edition of *The Mariner's Book of Days*, author Peter Spectre says the all-time favorite names for ships are *Mary* and *Elizabeth*. He warns that to avoid bad luck, you shouldn't name a vessel after any of the following:

- storms: Hurricane, Gale, Cyclone
- fearsome creature of the deep: Kraken, Octopus, Serpent
- cataclysms: Quake, Eruption, Big Bang
- evil characters: Judas, Brutus, Pilate

See also **Black Box Theory; Figureheads; Renaming a Boat; Sailing on Friday; Unlucky Colors.**

V

Varnish Details

*Revealing some of the secrets
of the best varnish finishes*

In their hearts, the owners of boats with traditionally varnished exterior brightwork know full well that they'll have to rub down the varnish every year—without fail—and apply three new coats. But, human nature being what it is, they often procrastinate, claiming that the existing finish is good for at least another couple of months . . . and perhaps a whole season.

Such self-deception can be short-circuited by an easy test. Here's how to tell when your old spar varnish needs to be freshened. Wash the work thoroughly with fresh water to get rid of all grime. Wet an old piece of terrycloth toweling and drag it across the surface of the varnish. If the water left behind forms beads, the varnish is still in good condition. If the water sheets, or lies in flattish streaks, it needs immediate attention.

The first step is to degrease it with a rag dipped in mineral spirits or denatured alcohol. Then sand it down using a fine-grit paper. Before varnishing, wipe the sanding dust away with a tack cloth dampened with varnish thinner. Don't work outside when it's too hot, too cold, too damp, or too windy. Choose your varnishing days carefully.

Some varnishes need to be stirred gently. If so, that instruction will be in the fine print on the can. But be careful not to be too vigorous, or you'll introduce bubbles that your brush will transfer to the work. Stirring usually isn't necessary.

Pour varnish from the can through a fine filter of cheesecloth or an old pantyhose into a small container with a thin collar of cloth rag tied near the top to catch drips, and work from the container. Flow the varnish on—don't scrape it on too thin—using a throwaway foam brush for the first coats. Apply the finishing coat with the finest natural bristle brush you can afford.

You don't need to sand down between the first three coats if you apply the next coat between 10 and 24 hours after the previous one. At that stage, it will be dry enough for overcoating but still "green" enough to form some chemical links with the new coat. After the third coat, lightly sand between each coat—just enough to remove the little specks where you varnished over dust and to scuff away the shiny surface. Use 220-grit dry paper between coats or, for a mirrorlike finish, 360-grit waterproof paper dipped frequently in fresh water.

During the sailing season, keep an old nail-polish bottle filled with spar varnish. Apply it to small scratches and abrasions in your brightwork before water has a chance to soak into the wood and discolor it.

See also **Brightwork**; **Varnishing**.

Varnishing

*Keeping exterior woodwork
looking good is a lot of work*

Nothing on a boat looks as good as exterior wood finished with glossy varnish—and nothing requires more maintenance. Over the years, traditional spar varnish has been complemented with other finishes designed to cut down on maintenance time, but they all have their faults.

Good traditional spar varnish is fairly soft and pliable. If the underlying wood shrinks or swells, spar varnish clings hard and moves with it. It contains additives that protect the wood from the ravages of the sun's ultraviolet (UV) rays, but there is a limit to the amount of protection it can provide and still remain transparent (or nearly so) so that the beauty of the wood shines through.

Spar varnish goes on in thin layers, so new wood requires between 8 and 10 coats for that deep-glowing professional look.

V

After that, it will hold its own for many years if it is rubbed down annually and given two or three fresh coats.

When the sun is shining and a gentle wind and blue seas are beckoning, it's almost a sin to sit in port varnishing your gunwales; so even if the first 10 coats were conscientiously applied, the annual ritual of rubbing down and recoating is often skimped. You can expect fast deterioration of traditional varnish, and you'll be faced with the inevitable task of sanding it down to bare wood and starting all over.

If sailors were any brighter than their brightwork, they would paint the wood instead of varnishing it. Paint forms a solid barrier against UV rays—a principle that has tempted varnish makers to introduce a range of synthetic wood finishes that are almost half paint and half varnish. When first introduced, they were heavily loaded with pigments such as iron oxide that provided good protection from damaging rays, but also gave the "varnish" an orange or brown cast.

These new products were joyfully received because they were fairly transparent, looked almost as good as varnish, and promised to last a long time with just three initial coats and one touch-up every year. Experience has proven that those claims were somewhat optimistic; furthermore, traditionalists disliked the orange hue.

The manufacturers then introduced "light" variations that cut down on the iron oxide and promised a more translucent look, like real spar varnish. However, the more transparent, the less protection there is from the sun, the greater the number of coats needed, and the more maintenance required.

Clear finishes such as urethanes and polyurethanes match the clarity and brilliance of spar varnish, require far fewer coats, and provide a hard impervious finish that is resistant to knocks, scratches, and chemicals. But when the sun strikes through them, the wood eventually changes its dimensions and loses its grip on the tough plastic covering, which starts off more brittle than spar varnish and becomes even more so with age and exposure to sun. Once it starts flaking, it must be removed completely. When it's necessary, you can remove soft spar varnish fairly easily with chemical stripper or a heat gun, but removing rugged urethane coatings is difficult work.

So one way or another, varnished exterior brightwork requires a great deal of loving labor. The option of leaving it completely uncoated, to weather a silvery gray, becomes more appealing with each passing year. Unfortunately, it doesn't stay silvery gray for long. The wood's natural oils start to oxidize and get dark. Dirt collects on it and black mold spores start breeding in its pores. Before you know it, you're thinking what a good idea it would be to rub it down and varnish it.

See also **Brightwork; Teak Finishes; Varnish Details**.

Ventilation

Encouraging a healthy flow of fresh air in a closed boat

The flow of air inside a boat at anchor is usually from aft forward, especially if you have an open forehatch hinged along its forward edge. Air tends to enter through the main companionway hatch and exit through the forehatch. The airflow is maintained when the outside wind is coming from many other directions as well.

If you're adding fans or ventilators, aim to reinforce this natural air circulation, not fight it. Good ventilation is an important part of keeping a boat's interior dry and sweet, but it's often badly neglected by manufacturers of production boats.

Dorade boxes with cowls facing the prevailing wind, combined with louvered hatch slides for air to escape from, will keep a copious amount of air flowing through a closed boat and discourage the growth of mildew and mold in summer and winter.

You should be able to close off ventilators for sea work, of course, but at anchor or in port,

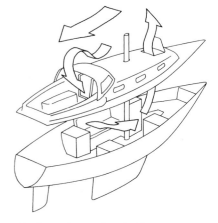

Air flow through a hull.

V

be generous with the size of your ventilator cowls. Perhaps you remember from math class that a 4-inch-diameter cowl provides almost twice as much fresh air as one with a 3-inch diameter—a wonderful bonus for such a modest increase in size.

Voices in the Night

Frightening experience, but with a logical explanation

You're not likely to forget the first time you hear a human voice crying for help from a wave breaking astern on a pitch-dark, stormy night. It's a frightening experience, even when you are sure that no one can be there.

Many people hear voices—and probably more hear snatches of music—when they're alone on a night watch, but it isn't truly an illusion or the result of mental fatigue. Rather, it's a normal and natural occurrence, the result of the ability of the ear and the brain to filter out unwanted noise.

In stormy conditions, the noise created by the wind and the sea contains a broad spectrum of many frequencies in random combinations. Your ear picks up all of them, but in the absence of other instructions, your brain concentrates only on those frequencies of significance to human survival—such as those in the range of human speech—and it suppresses the rest.

See also **Hallucinations**.

Wasted Fuel

Only a fraction of fuel energy propels the boat

Not all the fuel in your tanks pushes the boat forward; not even most of it, in fact. It's estimated that only 13 to 14 percent of the fuel energy you pay for results in forward motion. Here's where the rest of it goes:

- 35 percent is given up to the atmosphere as heat
- 25 percent more goes in heat and vibration absorbed by surrounding water
- 10 percent is used to overcome wave resistance
- 7 percent is used to overcome skin friction
- 6 percent is needed to overcome wave formation and prop wash against the hull

- 2 percent is absorbed in friction at the propeller shaft
- 1 percent (sometimes substantially more) is needed to overcome wind resistance

See also **Fuel Consumption; Fuel Economy**.

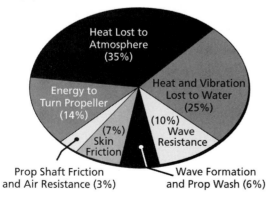

Fuel energy losses.

Watchkeeping

Observing the need for organized sleeping patterns

Formal watchkeeping should begin as soon as your boat has cleared port and is settled down on her course at sea. Long coastal trips or ocean voyages often are started early in the day with all the crew on deck. It's understandable that they should be excited and eager to help with the management of the ship, but a good skipper will make sure that those off watch do not wear themselves out before the night watches come along. They should get as much rest as possible—going down below to their bunks if necessary—even in daylight on the very first day, so they are fresh and prepared to deal with bad weather when their turn comes.

Sound sleep is an important part of cruising. Without it, you lose efficiency; your temper becomes frayed and decisions are difficult. In short, lack of sleep is dangerous.

There are many different watchkeeping systems, depending on the size of the crew. With six people on board, it's possible for pairs to keep deck watches of 4 hours, followed by 8 straight hours off. Most ocean-cruising sailboats have only two people on board, however, and that usually means 4 hours on, 4 hours off. In theory, you get 12 hours of sleep out of every 24 this way, but in practice you don't fall asleep right away and you have to get up before the 4 hours is over to dress and get ready. During your watches below, you will also have to perform the many tasks involved in navigation, maintenance, cooking, and generally running the ship.

Four hours is about as long as anyone should keep watch alone in the cockpit, and cruising couples often limit their time at the helm to two hours, or even one in really bad weather.

Sleep deprivation causes illusions and hallucinations that could affect your ability to make rational decisions, endangering the safety of the boat and the crew. With practice, however, you can get sufficient sleep in short

stretches. Some people are better than others at snatching 40 winks, but almost everybody can improve. Some single-handed racers claim to sleep for 20 minutes at a time, then keep watch for 20 minutes, then sleep another 20 minutes, and so on.

As a general principle, cruisers should be prepared to sacrifice speed for sleep, if necessary. If the watch below has been roused frequently to take in sail, or if the boat has been driven hard in heavy weather so that the motion and noise down below has been excessive, they will be tired, cranky, and inefficient. It would be wise to heave to for several hours and let everyone get some undisturbed rest. The result will be a great improvement in morale, cheerfulness, and efficiency.

The traditional watchkeeping system in the days of sailing ships divided the day into five watches of 4 hours each, plus two dogwatches of 2 hours each, as follows:

- afternoon watch: 1200 to 1600
- first dogwatch: 1600 to 1800
- second dogwatch: 1800 to 2000
- first watch: 2000 to 2400
- middle watch: 2400 to 0400
- morning watch: 0400 to 0800
- forenoon watch: 0800 to 1200

One bell was struck for every half hour of the watch completed, with a maximum of eight bells. At the end of the first dogwatch (1800), four bells were struck as usual but the second dogwatch

was treated a new watch, so at 1830 only one bell was struck. At 1900, two bells were struck; at 1930, three bells; and at 2000, eight bells.

Since 1915, however, U.S. merchant ships more than 100 tons gross have divided the crew into three watches working 4 hours on, 8 hours off, combining the two dogwatches into one evening watch.

See also **Hallucinations; Your Performance**.

Watermakers

Making drinking water from seawater by reverse osmosis

Watermakers work by forcing salt water through a special membrane at a pressure of about 800 pounds per square inch (5,500 kPa). The membrane filters out most of the salt as well as bacteria, viruses, and other contaminants.

If you can afford one, and if you don't mind a fair amount of expensive maintenance, a reverse-osmosis watermaker will reward you with about 1 gallon (3.8 L) of drinking water for every 30 watt-hours of energy its motor consumes.

A compact electric watermaker weighs about 25 pounds (11 kg), makes about 1½ gallons (5.7 L) of water an hour, and can be operated manually if you run your batteries flat. It costs about the same as a 10-foot (3 m) inflatable dinghy. If you're running a big boat with a lot of power to spare, you can buy a watermaker that will provide as much as 800 gallons (3,600 L) a day.

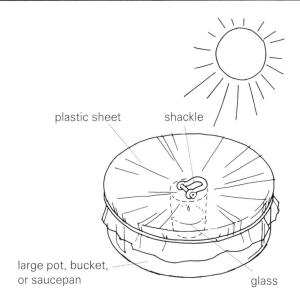

plastic sheet　　shackle

large pot, bucket,
or saucepan

glass

Emergency solar still.

The problem is that they're not foolproof, so you have to carry an emergency reserve of water in tanks anyway; however, that reserve may be smaller the nearer you get to your destination, as long as the watermaker is still working.

A good alternative is a small, completely manual reverse-osmosis watermaker that will keep you alive as long as you can squeeze the handles. An hour of squeezing produces about 2 pints (1 L) of fresh water, which will be worth its weight in gold if you're sitting in a life raft. It costs only about a fourth as much as a 10-foot inflatable and would be a wonderful addition to your abandon-ship bag.

You can also make fresh water from salt water for next to nothing by constructing your own solar still. You need a wide-mouthed saucepan or bucket, some old T-shirts or rags, a tall glass or cup, and a thin sheet of plastic—black is best. Put the glass in the middle of the bucket and place the rags snugly around it. Pour seawater into the bucket until it's about a quarter full, but don't let any spill into the glass.

Tie the plastic sheet over the bucket and make it into an inverted cone by weighing the middle down with a shackle or something else small and heavy. Then leave the bucket in the sunshine.

Fresh water will condense on the inside of the plastic, drip off the point of the cone, and collect in the glass. If the boat is rolling badly at sea, some of the drips might miss the glass; therefore, the wider it is, the better. The deeper you make the cone, the nearer its point will be to the glass.

The deluxe version of this still incorporates a thin plastic tube led from inside the glass, under the plastic sheet, and over the edge of the bucket to the outside—that way, you can suck up water from the glass without dismantling the still. Don't expect too much from a still like this—you'll need one for every per-

son—but it can keep you alive in an emergency.

See also **Catching Water; Water Needs**.

Water Needs

Figuring out how much water you need to carry on a voyage

For drinking only, about a $\frac{1}{2}$ gallon (2 L) of fresh water a day is adequate to maintain good health, even in the tropics. It's preferable, however, to drink more in hot climates. Plan to carry in your tanks the minimum amount of 1 gallon (3.8 L) per person per day for a long voyage, plus a 10 percent reserve in separate cans for emergencies. Good water will remain sweet for at least six months in tightly sealed opaque containers stored in a cool place away from bright light.

Most human beings can survive only three days without water. To merely sustain life in an emergency, you need about $\frac{2}{3}$ of a pint (315 mL) of fresh water per person per day, and 600 calories (2,500 kilojoules) of food, which amounts to about 5 or 6 ounces (140 to 170 g) of hard candy, sugar, or high-fat cookies.

See also **Provisioning; Purifying Water; Watermakers**.

Waterplane Area

Working out how much weight will sink her how many inches

There are several interesting calculations that start with a power- or sailboat's waterplane area, which is

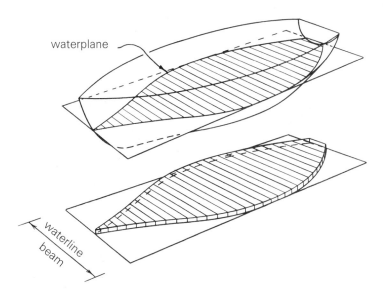

Waterplane area.

Note the bands of wind on the sea surface, spiraling in toward the center of this waterspout.

the area of a horizontal slice through the hull at water level.

If you have a reasonably typical boat, you can approximate the waterplane area by multiplying waterline length in feet (or meters) by waterline beam, and then multiplying the result by 0.76. With the waterplane area, you can calculate how much of a load will put your boat down an inch (or a centimeter) on her marks.

pounds per inch immersion = waterplane area in square feet x 5.34
kilograms per centimeter immersion = waterplane area in square meters x 10.25

For example, let's say you have a 35-footer with a 28-foot waterline. Then:

waterline length = 28 feet
waterline beam = 10 feet, 10 inches
approximate waterplane area = 28 x 10.83 x 0.76 = 230.46 square feet

pounds per inch immersion = 230.46 x 5.34 = 1,231 pounds per inch immersed

See also **Yacht Design**.

Waterproof Clothes

See Foul-Weather Gear.

Waterspouts

Dealing with the maritime version of a menacing tornado

Waterspouts are usually less violent than their lubberly cousins, tornadoes, but they can still be a real danger to small boats. Like tornadoes, waterspouts form beneath thunderclouds, or cumulonimbus.

They start off as funnel-shaped extensions of the cloud base, growing down to a sea surface whipped into clouds of spray. Then they merge with the spray

and join the cloud to the sea via a narrow tunnel.

Most waterspouts measure between 20 and 200 feet (6 to 60 m) across and can stretch from sea level to a cloud 1,000 or 2,000 feet (300 to 600 m) up. Their lives are mercifully short—typically between 10 and 30 minutes—and they become more bent and elongated until the tube breaks open. Then the whole system quickly collapses.

If you're on a sailboat when a waterspout approaches, act quickly. Douse all sail, fold down your dodger, secure everything loose on deck, go below, and slide your hatches tightly shut. If you're on a powerboat, stay clear by turning to a course at right angles to the waterspout's path.

See also **Downburst**.

Watertight Bulkheads

Lessening the risk of flooding after hull damage or collision

Bulkheads on small craft are strong upright "walls" set perpendicular to the keel line. Most are of structural importance, extending from the cabin roof to the inside bottom of the hull and corresponding to the hull shape on both sides.

On most powerboats and sailboats, the bulkheads have openings for people to pass through, but almost all boats also have two smaller collision bulkheads that are completely watertight. One is in the bow, where the greatest risk of flooding the boat from a head-on collision is, the other is in the stern. Such bulkheads prevent water that enters the damaged hull from flooding the entire boat.

Yachts used in extreme conditions often have more watertight bulkheads than those used in calmer waters. For instance, sailboats entered in the Venturer Class (40 to 60 ft. or 12 to 18 m production boats or racer-cruisers) of the Around Alone race must have a minimum of three watertight bulkheads dividing the hull into four approximately equal compartments. The bulkheads must be able to withstand a full head of water on any one side without leaking.

Internal access hatches in the watertight bulkheads are required, and they must also be watertight when shut. The forward bulkhead must not be less than 5 percent of the waterline length aft of the forward limit of the waterline, and the aft bulkhead must be forward of the rudderstock(s). In addition to these bulkheads, Venturer Class boats must have smaller collision bulkheads fore and aft.

See also **Seaworthiness**.

Wave Height

There's just one place for judging the sea's height

It's a difficult business to estimate the size of waves from a small boat at sea. The trouble is that down isn't always down as we know it.

British engineer and naval architect William Froude investigated this phenomenon in 1861 and discovered that waves provide accelerations that combine with gravity to produce a local "down" that is square to the surface of the water. This means that no matter how your boat may be situated on a large swell, straight down will always *seem to you* to be at right angles to the water's surface.

Even when you're aware of this effect, it doesn't help change the sensation you feel because the illusion of down arises from real physical forces to which humans have been conditioned to respond over the millennia.

The practical effect of this phenomenon is evident in a storm, when you look aft and see approaching what appears to be a near-vertical avalanche of water. You cringe and wait for it to break over the stern—but, mysteriously, it suddenly seems to flatten out at the last moment and pass harmlessly beneath the hull.

This is easier to understand if you sketch a boat halfway up the back of a large wave that has just passed. Draw a line at right angles to the surface of the wave, and let it pass through the center of the boat to represent the direction that your body and mind are telling you is down. Then draw another straight line aft, over the trough of the wave and to the crest of the approaching wave. If you now tilt the paper so that the line you drew for down really points down, you'll see why that crest appears to be towering over you.

The rule of thumb forthcoming from these scientific observa-

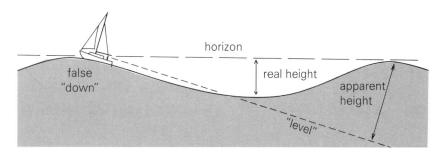

The illusion of wave height.

tions is that the real sea is probably not much more than half as high, or as steep, as it looks at its worst moment.

The only reasonable time to estimate the height of the waves is when you are at the bottom of the trough, midway between crests. During that brief time, most crests will be even with the horizon in all directions, and your perception of the sea's height will not be distorted by illusion.

See also **Waves in Gales**.

Waves

Are any two really the same?

Waves fascinate boaters—and for good reason. There is no better reminder that we are not on land, and that different rules apply, than a vigorous wave train. Fully developed waves can seem monotonous in their similarity yet almost infinite in their detail.

Wind of less than 2 knots generates ripples on smooth water, which disappear as soon as the wind stops. But stronger winds raise gravity waves, which will persist after the wind dies. Because the force of the wind increases with the square of its velocity, a 20-knot breeze imparts four times as much energy to the sea as its 10-knot counterpart. The ultimate size of the seas generated by a wind depends not just on wind speed, but also on the duration of the wind and the unobstructed distance, or fetch, over which it blows.

Storm-generated ocean waves can travel hundreds or even thousands of miles from the gale

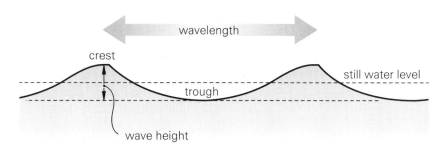

Waves are characterized by their length (the distance from one crest to the next), height (the vertical distance from trough to crest), steepness (the ratio of height to length), and period (the time required for one wave length to pass a stationary observer).

Beaufort force of wind.	Theoretical maximum wave height (ft) unlimited duration and fetch.	Duration of winds (hours), with unlimited fetch, to produce percent of maximum wave height indicated.			Fetch (nautical miles), with unlimited duration of blow, to produce percent of maximum wave height indicated.		
		50%	75%	90%	50%	75%	90%
3	2	1.5	5	8	3	13	25
5	8	3.5	8	12	10	30	60
7	20	5.5	12	21	22	75	150
9	40	7.0	16	25	55	150	280
11	70	9.0	19	32	85	200	450

Wave height as a function of wind strength, duration, and fetch.

that formed them, ultimately settling into the long, smooth, regular wave train known as swell. Although ocean waves propagate ever onward, they do not move water with them. Rather, particles of water describe a near-circular orbit as a wave passes, winding up in a position only slightly different from where they began. In contrast, water is thrown forward in a breaking wave, which is what makes breaking seas so dangerous to boaters. A wave breaks when it becomes too steep to remain stable—that is, when the ratio of its height to length exceeds 1:7. This may happen when

a violent gale imparts more energy to the seas than can be dissipated in a regular wave train, or when two waves from separate wave trains collide to form a rogue or freak sea. In coastal waters (and in the Gulf Stream and other ocean currents), a wind opposing the current can build short, steep breaking seas. In shoaling water, a wave starts to "feel the bottom" when the depth of water equals the wave length, or the distance from one crest to the next. The water becomes progressively shorter and steeper as the friction of the shoaling bottom slows it. When water depth

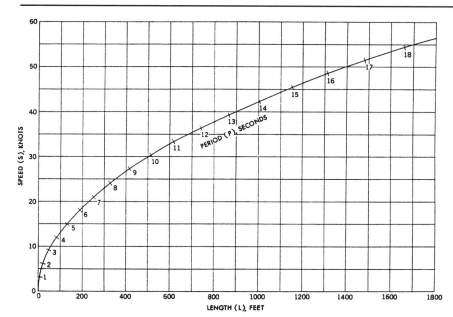

The relationship among speed, length, and period of a nonbreaking wave. Note that period increases with length despite the corresponding increase in speed.

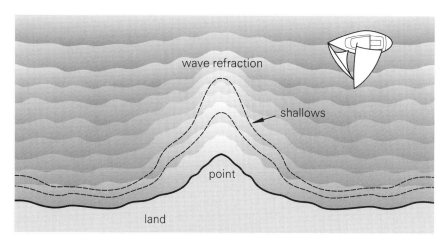

Waves refracting where slowed by friction from a shoaling sea bottom. The resultant convergence can cause rough seas off a point, bar, or ledge.

is about equal to wave height (the distance from trough to crest), the top of the wave finally outruns its base and it falls forward as a breaker.

See also **Beaufort Scale; Freak Waves; Plunging Breakers; Waves in Gales**.

Waves in Gales

The behavior of waves in heavy weather on the ocean

Carefully gathered scientific data indicate that wave heights of between 40 and 50 feet (15 to 15 m) are fairly common in well-developed gales in some oceans. Single waves larger than that are rare but

well documented. A wave 80 feet (24 m) high was observed from the steamship *Majestic* in the North Atlantic at 48°30′ N, 21°50′ W, on December 29, 1922. In 1933 in the Southern Ocean, a 112-foot (34 m) wave was measured by triangulation from the deck of the USS *Ramapo*, a navy tanker. Sea buoys off Nova Scotia have twice recorded 100-foot (30 m) waves, and a 95-footer (29 m) was once encountered by the *Queen Elizabeth II*.

As noted at the Wave Height entry, however, such measurements are difficult to make, not only because of the transitory nature of the wave, but also because of the difficulty of establishing a horizontal surface from which to measure.

For waves to grow to their maximum size, a fetch (a stretch of deep water over which wind can blow unaffected by any land masses) of about 600 miles is required. Thus, there is no reason to suppose that, for the same wind speed, the waves off the coast of Washington and Oregon would be any smaller than those off Cape Horn.

For the waves to become fully developed, the wind must blow in the same direction for a certain minimum time, of course. The rule of thumb is that the time in hours equals the wind speed in knots. Thus, it will take a 20-knot wind about 20 hours to form the biggest waves it can.

Of more interest to small-boat sailors than the size of the waves is the height of the breaking crests on those waves. In an actual gale (48 to 55 knots), it's safe to assume that many 6-foot (1.8 m)

breakers will spill down the fronts of waves.

The relationship between wind speed in miles per hour and wave height in feet is approximately 2:1. This ratio, used by the U.S. Hydrographic Office, suggests that a wind of 50 mph (80 km/h) should raise a 25-foot (7.6 m) sea. The length of a wave, from crest to crest, is about 20 times its height, so a 25-foot wave would have a length of about 500 feet (152 m) and a speed (square root of the length times 1.34) of about 30 knots.

Incidentally, the speed of advance of a group of waves is half that of individual waves. When the wind dies down, the height of waves diminishes rapidly, but the length and speed remain comparatively unchanged. The result is a swell that may travel for hundreds of miles and far outrun the disturbance that caused it.

See also **Beaufort Scale; Freak Waves; Plunging Breakers; Wave Height.**

Weather Fronts

Identifying the restless, roiling borders of air masses

Weather is caused by huge air masses of different temperatures and pressures moving around in

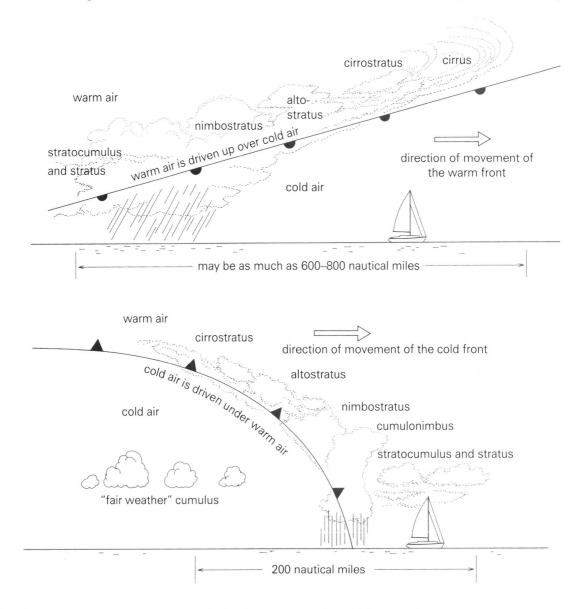

Cloud patterns and weather associated with the passage of a middle latitude warm front (top) or cold front (bottom).

the atmosphere—like globs of wax in a lava lamp. The borders of these air masses, where they touch one another, are known as fronts, and it's here that most storms are formed. Four types of fronts affect boaters.

Cold fronts occur where a wedge of cold air forces its way beneath a bubble of warmer air, creating violent thunderstorms, squalls, and waterspouts—or tornadoes on land. They usually pass fairly quickly.

Warm fronts slide up over a mass of cooler air, bringing a steady drizzle, a low cloud base, and possibly fog. They may take a day or two to pass.

Stationary fronts are those that have nearly exhausted themselves and reached compromise. The differences in their temperatures and pressures have almost equalized. The result is usually little wind but a lot of rain for a long while.

Occluded fronts can be vexatious: they combine the worst of both worlds, occurring when a warm front has been overtaken by a cold front and forced upward. The cold front contributes high winds and unsettled conditions; the warm front contributes steady heavy rain.

See also **Air Masses**.

Weather Helm

Altering the cut or position of sails to improve balance

Weather helm describes a sailboat's tendency to gripe, or forcibly round up into the wind. To maintain a steady course, you have to hold the helm to weather to offset the tendency.

A small amount of weather helm, about 2 or 3 degrees, actually helps a boat sail to windward, but if you have to apply 5 degrees or more, the rudder acts as a brake and slows your progress.

Most boats have weather helm, which is far preferable to lee helm. If you let go of the tiller or wheel for any reason on a boat with weather helm, she will turn into the wind and lose way. If you've fallen overboard, that will give you a chance to swim back. But if your boat has lee helm, she will head downwind at full speed and jibe dangerously and repeatedly.

The main causes of weather helm are

- too much beam, especially beam carried a long way aft
- a mast that is too far aft, or one that rakes aft excessively
- a full-cut or blown-out mainsail
- an asymmetrical hull shape when heeled
- excessive heeling to leeward

Boats with excessive weather helm need to be sailed flat and reefed early. A new flat-cut mainsail will help, as will raking the mast forward (but not beyond upright). If the problem is hull design, it can't be fully remedied, but it can be greatly tamed by decreasing sail area aft of the boat's pivoting point (the center of lateral resistance, or CLR) or increasing it forward of the CLR—by adding a bowsprit, for example.

Excessive heeling increases weather helm because the forces acting on the sails swing out-

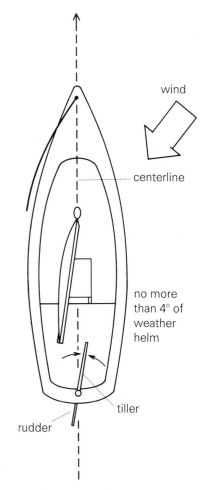

Weather helm is the rudder angle required to counteract a sailboat's tendency to round up into the wind. Anything more than 4 degrees is excessive.

board, thereby gaining leverage to face the boat's bow into the wind.

See also **Balanced Helm; Center of Effort; Lee Helm**.

Weather Information

Receiving meteorological information at sea

Many deep-sea yachts have weatherfax machines that provide information about current weather conditions in synoptic form. Basic information is conveyed by means of weather maps, or charts, on which isobaric lines join areas of equal barometric pressure and various symbols represent fronts, precipitation, wind speed, and other important components of each weather system.

Analysis (current weather conditions) and forecast (projected conditions at a future time) charts are now also available from the Internet for those boats with the satellite telephones (such as Inmarsat) to receive them. These are transmitted as GIF and TIFF compressed files from the National Weather Service website.

But even if you have a weatherfax or satellite receiver, it doesn't guarantee that you'll be able to predict the weather in your immediate area any better than you could by simply observing the clouds, barometric pressure, and temperatures around you. A forecast from a single map is only good for the next 6 to 12 hours; you need a series of maps prepared over regular intervals to deduce much from the latest one. And you need to have a fairly extensive knowledge of meteorology to interpret the clues embedded in the weatherfax synopsis.

You can assume that a front will advance at about 15 or 20 knots in its present direction of movement, as long as there are no highs or lows in or near its path to divert it. Sketch in a new position for the front according to how many hours it has been since the weather map was issued, and then make your own forecast.

But most boaters would do as well to get their forecasts by radio from professional meteorologists who have more data with which to work. Continuous weather forecasts for coastal waters (out to 25 miles from shore) all around the United States and many other countries are available by VHF radio, and several countries transmit worldwide weather forecasts for the high seas several times a day on frequencies you can receive on an ordinary single-sideband (SSB) radio. Offshore marine forecasts for the waters from 25 miles out to the edge of the continental shelf are also available.

The excellent NAVTEX system operated by the International Maritime Organization transmits forecasts in telex text form at 518 kHz. These forecasts—along with Notices to Mariners, search-and-rescue information, hurricane warnings, and so forth—can be received on a dedicated NAVTEX receiver (or an SSB radio cabled to a Windows-based personal computer) 200 miles or more at sea through much of the world.

See also **Air Masses; Clouds**.

Wheel Turns

Assessing the ideal number of turns for the steering wheel

The number of turns for wheel steering depends on the size of the boat and the way she is powered. The ideal number of turns from lock to lock—that is, from 35 degrees port rudder to 35 degrees starboard rudder—for different boats is given as follows:

runabouts, small motorboats, and all sizes of fast powerboats: 1¾ to 2

trawler-type motor cruisers between 30 and 50 feet (9 and 15 m) in length: 2½ to 3½

trawler-type motor cruisers more than 50 feet (15 m) in length: 3½ to 4

sailboats up to 30 feet (9 m) (if it's not feasible to fit a tiller): 1 to 2

sailboats between 30 and 45 feet (9 and 14 m): 2 to 3

sailboats 50 feet (15 m) and up: 3 to 5

See also **Rudders**.

Whistling

Pursing the lips and blowing, in an appeal for better winds

In an old superstition of the sea, whistling was supposed to bring wind. This superstition took two forms. In the first, the rule was that a sailor never whistled on watch for fear of bringing bad weather. He could whistle during his off watch, but the theory was that if he whistled while on watch, it proved that he didn't have enough to do and was idling. Because the gods of the wind and sea disliked idlers in their domain, they would soon provide him with an abundance of labor in the form of a storm. There was one exception to the rule, however. The bosun's mate could whistle with impunity. The rest of the crew viewed him as an agent of the devil anyway, because he wielded the cat-o'-nine-tails.

The second part of the

whistling superstition concerned the practice among sailors in sailing-ship days of whistling for wind when the weather was calm. The *Encyclopedia of Nautical Knowledge* describes the process as follows: "plaintively entreating the winds for a breeze by whistling with the lips in a variety of soft continuous notes while facing the direction from which it was desired that the wind would increase or spring up. Earlier custom required that a group of men occupy a more prominent position, such as the poop, when thus engaged, especially during a lengthy spell of light airs and calms."

See also **Doldrums**.

Winches

Using leverage and gears to handle heavy loads on lines

Winches are used on sailboats to haul on lines that would be too difficult to pull in by hand. They consist of upright revolving drums turned by long handles. Some winches may also be mounted horizontally on masts to set up halyards.

The removable winch handles are usually inserted in the top of the drum after several wraps of line have been taken around the drum. Some winches have handles permanently installed at the base, which allows lines to be placed around the drum more easily. Wraps are almost always put on the drum in a clockwise direction—and the drum will revolve in that direction too—but the handle may be turned either way. Removable handles should be fitted with

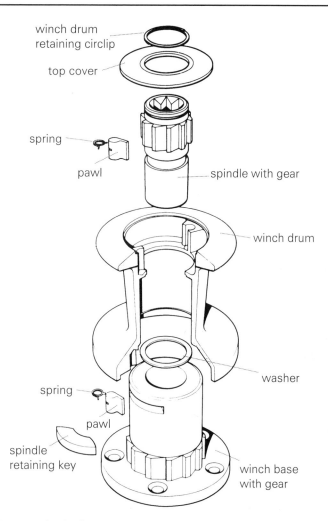

A single-speed winch.

catches to ensure they don't detach from the drums, especially those used on the mast for tightening halyards. Most winch handles lost overboard simply fall out of the halyard winches as the boat heels.

The handle turns the drum through gears that increase the mechanical advantage of the winch, and the handles of the simplest winches—the ones that have only one gear—invariably turn clockwise as well. More complicated winches may have two or three gears that are changed by reversing the direction of the winch handle or by turning switches.

The first gear is usually high so that a lot of line may be brought in while there is still little strain on it. The following gears bring the line in more slowly but exert a greater pull on the line for the same effort of winching.

To keep the line from slipping on the drum, maintain tension on the tail end (the one coming off the winch) with one hand while you turn the handle with the other. When sufficient line has been brought in, simply cleat the tail end. Many modern winches have a self-tailing fitting at the top that grips the line and automatically feeds it off the drum as more

W

line comes on. This allows you to turn the handle with two hands instead of one, and it holds the line in place without cleating.

Most drums accept four full turns of the line, but when an incoming line under considerable strain rides up over turns already on the drum, it can cause a jam that is almost impossible to free until the strain is released. If you're lucky, you may be able to free the tail end by jerking it counterclockwise; otherwise, if you have time, clap a second line onto the standing part with a rolling hitch. Then take the second line to a winch and haul in a few inches to relieve the strain on the working line while you disentangle it. It's possible to get a finger caught in the turns if you're not careful—in such an emergency, you might have to cut the line. To avoid riding turns, make sure the incoming line leads slightly upward to the base of the drum.

When you want to let a line out, uncleat the tail and keep it taut in one hand. When you're ready, ease the tail toward the drum. The drum will not revolve. Feed the line out slowly around the motionless drum until most of the tension is off, then you can safely cast the turns off the drum in succession.

Manufacturers classify their winches according to their leverage, calling it a power ratio. For example, a No. 16 winch pulls about 160 pounds (or kg) for every 10 pounds (10 kg) of force you put into turning the handle. Power ratios vary from 6 to more than 50.

See also **Windlasses**.

Wind and Altitude

How the wind changes speed and direction with height

The speed of the wind rises with altitude, where it is less affected by the friction of the sea. This difference is discernible even over a relatively short distance equal to the height of a yacht's mast.

It follows, then, that if the true wind speed is higher aloft, the apparent wind direction up there is different from the apparent wind down below. It's less affected by your boat's forward speed, so it's closer to the direction of the true wind. This means that the top part of a sail does not need to be sheeted as closely to the wind as the bottom part does.

In theory, the apparent wind direction changes by between 5 and 8 degrees from the bottom of the mast to the top; the top of the

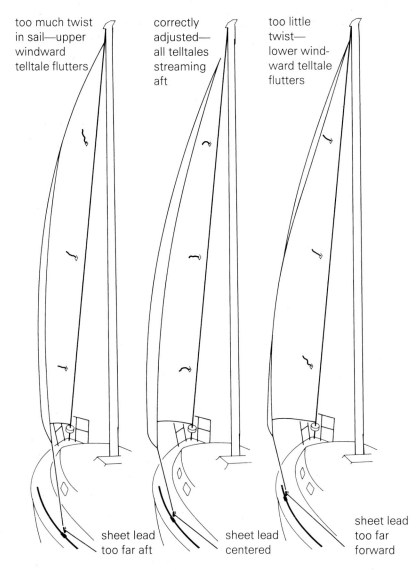

The effect of sheet-lead positions on twist and sail trim. Some twist is desirable because the apparent wind aloft will be slightly freer aft than that at deck level.

sail should be allowed to twist off gradually to leeward accordingly. In practice, you don't have to compensate for this. Your sailmaker knows about it (or should), and has built the correct twist and camber into your sail already.

See also **Apparent Wind; Sails and "Lift."**

Wind Generators

Using the power of the wind to recharge your battery bank

Of the four methods of generating electricity on a small boat, only the internal combustion engine beats the wind generator for efficiency. The advantages of the wind generator are that it's much simpler than an auxiliary engine (or power generator plus an alternator) and the wind is free.

On a good day, two solar panels of 35 watts each will produce about 32 amp-hours. A generator driven by a propeller towed through the water on the end of a line at 5 knots will produce about 63 amp-hours in 12 hours. And a wind turbine will produce about 84 amp-hours in 12 hours if the wind is blowing a steady 15 knots.

The problem is that you can't rely on the wind. As many cruisers have found out, generating electricity in port is often a frustrating business because anchorages are, by definition, well sheltered.

Portable generators may be slung from the rigging in the fore triangle. Permanently mounted wind chargers are mostly set on poles on the aft deck.

When wind speeds reach 30 knots or more, the whirling blades of a large wind generator 4 feet (1.2 m) in diameter make a surprising amount of noise, and constitute a considerable hazard to heads and limbs. Because of this—and the possibility of overheating and/or sending dangerously high levels of unregulated current to the battery banks—most wind turbines must be slowed down, either by turning them away from the wind or feathering the propellers. This is done automatically on new high-tech wind turbines whose blades are computer-controlled and whose output is controlled by internal regulation.

See also **Solar Panels.**

Windlasses

Raising an anchor with the help of a hand or power winch

A windlass is not essential on a boat of 30 feet (9.1 m) or less if you have a reasonably fit crew on board, but it does save a lot of hard work. On boats longer than 30 feet, a windlass is usually

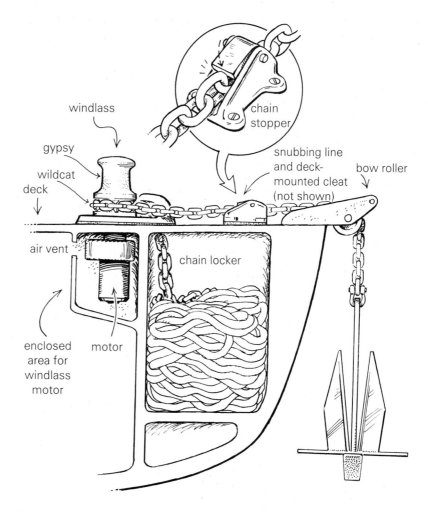

Typical installation of a windlass with a vertical barrel—traditionally known as a capstan.

needed to raise the anchor unless you can use sheet or halyard winches for the purpose—or if you prefer to rely on handy-billies and tackles.

A windlass is a winch with a horizontal barrel, whereas a capstan is a winch with a vertical barrel. They do the same job in the same way, though, and both types are now referred to as windlasses. They may be powered by hand or electricity, and most can handle rope as well as chain. Hydraulic windlasses are mostly found on larger vessels.

Most windlasses are abused. They are not designed to pull a boat up to the anchor in a storm, nor to break out a heavy anchor buried deeply in mud. Their job is to lift an anchor and rode that is not under tension. Nevertheless, because the pattern of abuse has become so established, manufacturers commonly recommend that the pulling power of the windlass should equal three times the weight of the anchor and rode.

If you're prepared to power or sail up to your anchor, and haul it short to break itself out while you wait for 15 minutes, you can get away with a much smaller and less expensive windlass.

You might not need one at all if you fit a chain stopper to the foredeck or a pawl to the bow roller, either of which method will act as a one-way valve and prevent chain running back through the roller as the boat rises on a swell.

Many yacht windlasses have two barrels: a smooth one with flanges for hauling on rope, and known as a gypsy; and one with recesses for links of chain, known as a wildcat.

See also **Anchors, Anchoring; Chain Stoppers**.

Wind Systems

Getting the best from the winds requires good planning

Success in ocean cruising comes from being in the right place at the right time. You need to avoid dangerously bad weather and take every advantage of fair winds. In short, you need to plan a voyage carefully with regard to the wind systems of the world, those that are more or less permanent in character and those that are seasonal. Even the permanent systems move north and south with the seasons, of course, but they do so in predictable, established patterns.

Most small cruising boats make use of fair winds for ocean passages, even if the distance is greater, because beating for any length of time is so much slower and more uncomfortable. Pilot books and charts give full details of the winds you may expect in any part of the world, as do such publications as the British Hydrographic Department's *Ocean Passages for the World* and Jimmy Cornell's *World Cruising Routes*, which is specially tailored to the needs of yachts.

Pilot charts were originated by Matthew Fontaine Maury, a lieutenant in the U.S. Navy, who started collecting material for them in the early part of the nineteenth century.

Basically, the "permanent" wind systems of the world start with the doldrums, at or near the equator, a 300-mile wide belt of frustrating calms, heavy rains, and sudden thunderstorms. The trade winds blow on either side of the doldrums, up to about 30° North and 30° South. North of the equator they blow from northeast to southwest; south of the equator, from southeast to northwest. Trade-wind weather is normally fine and clear, pleasantly warm, and the winds moderate—the trade winds are the ones that fill sailors' dreams.

Outside of the trade winds, toward the poles, are the variables of Cancer (north) and Capricorn (south). These are areas of calms and light or moderate variable winds moving between 25° and 35° North and South—they correspond with the high-pressure belts and are known as the Horse Latitudes.

On the polar sides of the variables, the blustery westerlies reign, becoming more pronounced as latitude increases. They commonly blow from the same direction for many days at a time and often reach gale force.

These are the main systems that affect the course and timing of an ocean passage or a circumnavigation by a small sailboat, but seasonal winds such as monsoons and hurricanes also need to be considered early on in the planning of the voyage.

Almost all ocean voyaging in small yachts is done in winds of 12 knots or less, according to circumnavigators Lin and Larry Pardey. Eric Hiscock said that on

W

his three circumnavigations, the trade winds averaged force 4—between 11 and 16 knots. Gale-force winds lasted less than 2 percent of the time at sea.

See also **Doldrums; Gales at Sea; Horse Latitudes; Trade Winds**.

Winterizing

Preparing your boat for the ravages of icy-cold winters

In cold climates, a boat must be laid up carefully for the winter so that her systems are not damaged by water freezing and expanding. While she is protected from rain, snow, and frost, she must also have a copious stream of fresh air flowing through every nook and cranny to prevent destructive and unsightly mold and mildew growing down below. Good through-ventilation is more important than a roof or cover over your boat, if you have to choose.

Seek out the places where water lurks on your boat—in seacocks, sink drains, holding tanks, and so forth—and drain or pump out as much as you can. Dose what remains with nontoxic antifreeze or a 50-50 solution of vodka and water.

Pressure-wash the hull as the boat comes out of the water, or keep the hull wet and scrape it down as soon as you can. If it's a sailboat, get the mast out and lay it on level sawhorses.

As for the engine, consult the manufacturer's guides. All engines are different, but there are some basic rules:

1. Drain all raw-water systems, including the water-lift muffler. Check the antifreeze in the closed cooling system and renew it now. Also change the engine oil now—you don't want the old oil, full of acids, eating away at your engine's innards all winter. Grease everything that can be greased. Turn the engine over without starting it, and squirt some light oil into the air intake so that it coats the piston heads and cylinder walls.

2. Check sacrificial zincs and replace them now. Plug all openings into the engine from the air intakes, the exhaust system, and anywhere else into which a small creature might be able to crawl. Make a big warning sign reminding yourself not to start the engine until all the plugs have been removed.

3. Disconnect the batteries and take them ashore for steady trickle charging. Take all fresh food off the boat, too. If you own a sailboat, send your sails to the sailmaker for their annual maintenance.

4. If your topsides have been painted with twin-pack polyurethane, beware of shrink-wrapping your boat in plastic. Linear polyurethane often bubbles if it's deprived of air for long periods; gelcoat seems to be immune. If you have a traditional acrylic canvas cover, make sure it has a generous number of ventilators sewn in.

See also **Ventilation**.

Wire Terminals

Finishing off the ends of your standing rigging wires

Wire terminals on yachts fall into two broad categories: electrical and rigging terminals.

As for electrical terminals, crimping is now considered better than soldering. Soldering often produces hard spots that can cause fatigue and breakage when the wire is flexed and vibrated. Solder is not as corrosion-proof as you might imagine, either. Salt air attacks it, leaving a messy white residue with little strength and practically no electrical integrity.

There is only one condition to the crimping process—it must be done with the correctly sized crimping tool specified by the manufacturer of the terminal. After carefully cleaning and crimping the joint, waterproof it and protect it from salt air with an air-drying liquid vinyl or shrink-wrap tubing.

Rigging terminals for the typical 1 x 19 stainless steel wire are mostly permanently swaged in place; that is, they are molded into the weave of the wires by machines under great pressure. Swaged fittings have proven to be long-lived and reliable, but check them monthly for signs of cracks, especially near the joint with the wire. If the wire starts to rust and expand, the swaged fitting will crack and lose its grip on the wire.

The fittings at the lower ends of the stays and shrouds tend to collect salt water and fresh water,

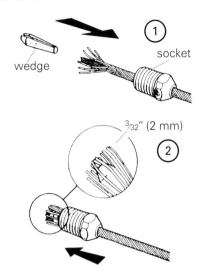

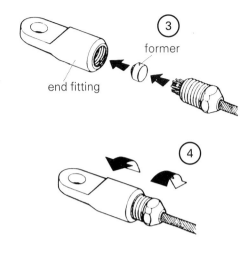

Sta-Lok terminals are designed for use with pre-formed 1 x 19, 7 x 7, and 7 x 19 wire rope. The 1 x 19 wedge is plain, but the wedge for 7 x 7 and 7 x 19 rope has a castellated ring with six gates to take the strands. These are not interchangeable. (1) Cut the cable cleanly. (There should be no protruding wires.) Slip the socket over the end of the cable, and unlay the outer wires or strands to expose a section of the center core equal in length to the wedge. (2) Slip the wedge over the center core of the cable (narrow end first), leaving about ³/₃₂ inch (2 mm) of core and outer wires protruding beyond the wide end of the wedge. Re-lay the outer wires or strands around the wedge, taking care to retain the wedge in its correct position. Carefully pull the socket into position over the wedge to prevent the wires or strands from unlaying. Check the assembly to ensure that the outer wires are spaced evenly around the top of the wedge, and that none of the wires has

slipped into the slot in the wedge. Each of the six outer strands of 7-strand ropes should lie in the "gates" provided (not illustrated). (3) Insert the former into the threaded hole in the end fitting. Screw the end fitting onto the already assembled unit and tighten with a wrench. Too much force can damage the threads; use no more than can be applied with one hand. (4) To waterproof the fitting, unscrew the two parts and insert a raisin-size blob of silicone caulking on the former, inside the bottom of the end fitting. Apply two or three drops of Loctite on the male thread of the socket; screw both parts together again, and tighten. The end fitting may be unscrewed whenever required for inspection or rewiring. When rewiring, cut off and discard the end of the cable and the old wedge. Always use a new wedge when rewiring. The remainder of the terminal parts may be reused a number of times if undamaged.

which might "wick" down the wires into the fitting and hasten any corrosion likely to take place. Some riggers seal the joint where the swage leaves the wire with a small cap of polysulfide sealant; others fear that sealant on the wire will deprive it of oxygen and cause crevice corrosion. The jury is still out on this one, so the best advice is to omit the sealant, wash down the rigging with fresh water after sailing in salt water, and keep a good eye open for cracks.

Use a small magnifying glass to inspect the terminals.

Luckily, swaged terminals on the upper ends of the stays rarely give trouble, probably because they don't collect water. Nevertheless, inspect them for cracks as well at every opportunity.

Serious blue-water cruisers would do better to replace their swaged fittings with screw-on terminals (also called mechanical or compression terminals), such as those made by Norseman and

Sta-Lok. These are designed for easy amateur installation with ordinary tools. Although expensive, they are a lifetime investment because they can be unscrewed for inspection at any time and then reused with an inexpensive new interior cone, if necessary. For emergency rigging, nothing beats them except bolt-on wire-rope clamps, which are regarded neither as permanent nor as strong.

See also **Rigging Sizes**.

W

center strand

cone

terminal body

1–1.5 W

W

terminal end

(1) (2) (3) (4) (5) (6) (7)

To assemble Norseman terminal fittings: (1) Slide the terminal body over the wire rope, and unlay the outer strands from the center strands. (2) Slide the cone down over the center strand, leaving exposed a length equal to 1.5 times the full diameter of the rope. (3) Relay the outer wires or strands, spaced evenly around the cone. (4) Fit all the protruding wires into the blind recess of the terminal end fitting (eye, fork, stud, etc.), and start threading the body and end fitting together. (5) Complete the assembly, turning the appropriate component in the direction of the lay of the rope, as shown in the sketch. Tighten until the resistance indicates that the cone is being compressed into the body of the terminal. Do not overtighten; you may damage the threads. (6) Unscrew the fitting to inspect and ensure that the wires are evenly spaced and closed neatly over the cone. Apply a thread-locking adhesive, such as Loctite, to the threads. (7) Insert a blob of marine sealant, such as 3M 5200, into the end fitting's blind hole and retighten the assembly. Repeat if necessary until the sealant oozes from the body end. Wipe clean.

Wooden Hulls

Building with wood is still the best for one-off boats

Wood is a wonderful material for one-of-a-kind boats. It's stronger—pound for pound—than fiberglass, aluminum, and steel. It floats, it accepts fastenings well, it's plentiful, it's easily worked and repaired with simple tools, and when you're finished with it, it's biodegradable. And there is something about wood that attracts the eye and appeals to the soul, something lacking in plastic or metal.

The big problem with wood is that you can't mass-produce boats from it as inexpensively as you can from fiberglass in reusable molds. So today's dearth of wooden craft is the direct result of economics, not because of anything lacking in the desirability of wood as a boatbuilding material.

In fact, for a one-off hull, there's still nothing to beat wood, especially if it's sealed with epoxy resin and sheathed with fiberglass for long life, low maintenance, and resistance to borers.

Epoxy coatings are not entirely waterproof, but they are efficient at blocking the passage of moisture into wood. Boatbuilding wood should have a moisture content of 15 percent by weight because the fungi that cause decay by feeding on the cellulose between the cell walls prefer a moisture content of between 25 and 30 percent. Without sufficient water, and lacking oxygen, fungi cannot grow in epoxy-coated wood.

Wood does swell if it gets wet, however, and the bigger the cross-section, the more it swells. So it's not a good idea to coat thick timbers with epoxy because if water enters through a small scrape, the wood only has to swell a little and it will expand, causing the epoxy coating to split. Then more water will enter and become effectively trapped in a plastic covering.

The answer is to laminate large timbers from thin pieces of wood, each one individually isolated and encapsulated in epoxy. If the hull is sealed with epoxy and sheathed in fiberglass, there's no reason why a modern wooden hull shouldn't last as long as a fiberglass one.

See also **Aluminum Hulls; Steel Hulls.**

Wooden Spars

Dealing with longitudinal cracks in masts and booms

Wooden masts and booms are still found on many "character" sailboats, from little Stonehorses to large Colin Archers, and most of them tend to develop longitudinal cracks after many years of service. Such cracks do not appreciably weaken a spar, however—in fact, they're a sign that the wood is not "dead."

If the cracks are not deep, there's no need to do anything special, but if you decide to fill the cracks for cosmetic reasons, never use any material that sets hard. Following are two old recipes for homemade filler. The first one can be used cold, like putty; the second one can be poured into the cracks while it's hot if you set the spars up horizontally. Whichever you choose, first thoroughly dry the wood.

- Warm a half pint (227 mL) linseed oil and dissolve in it ½ pound (227 g) resin and ¼ pound (113 g) beeswax. Finally, add 3 ounces (85 g) turpentine.
- Melt together 1 pound (454 g) resin, ¼ pound (113 g) beeswax, and ¾ pint (340 mL) linseed oil. Pour into cracks while mixture is still warm.

See also **Masts.**

X–Z

Xebecs

Low sleek pirate ships with speed and fearsome reputation

The xebec was the big brother of the kind of piratical felucca that chased Joshua Slocum's *Spray* after she had sailed from Gibraltar on his famous single-handed circumnavigation. The felucca was single-masted, with a lateen rig, but the original xebecs had three masts (two lateen-rigged and one square-rigged) and a fearsome reputation. In the eighteenth and nineteenth centuries, they mounted between 15 and 24 guns, and were manned by 300 or more Algerian corsairs—a ragged bunch of Arabs, Berbers, Moors, Blacks, Turks, and others.

The xebecs were low, sleek, and famous for their speed under an enormous spread of canvas. Mariners of other nations were often in awe of the way in which the xebecs were handled. It was said that they could set a third lateen sail on the foremast, in place of the square rig, when they needed to get to windward quickly.

In later years, when coastal piracy was under better control, xebecs were commonly used in the Mediterranean as passenger and trading vessels, particularly for light perishable cargoes that needed to be transported quickly.

See also **Lateen Rig.**

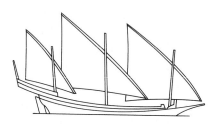

A xebec rigged for windward work.

Yacht Definition

Pinning down the precise meaning of the word yacht

Landlubbers have a difficult time defining a yacht. There seems to be no short answer, and nothing seems to separate a large yacht from a small sailing dinghy. The *Concise Oxford Dictionary* describes a yacht in broad sweeps: "A light sailing vessel kept, and usually specially built and rigged, for racing; similar vessel for travel on sand or ice; vessel propelled by sails, steam, electricity, or motive power other than oars, and used for private pleasure excursions, cruising, travel, etc."

Pleasure is the word that most often occurs in definitions of

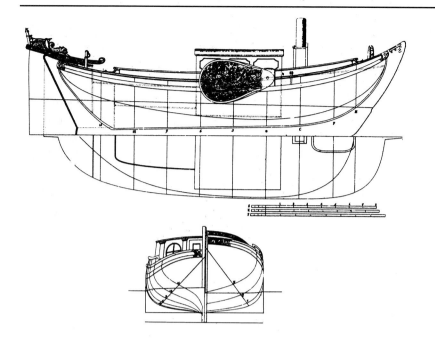

A 25-foot Dutch boier from the eighteenth century.

yachts, separating them from working vessels. This definition from *Chapman Piloting: Seamanship and Small Boat Handling* is probably as accurate as any and has the commendable advantage of brevity: "A yacht is a power or sail vessel used for recreation and pleasure, as opposed to work."

The difficulty of properly defining a yacht is still evident, for this definition also includes sailboards and jet skis, vessels far removed from the original rather grand concept of what a yacht should be.

The word *yacht* comes from the Dutch *jacht*, meaning to hunt or chase. It refers to the kind of small, nimble, Dutch sailing vessel that hunted and chased other vessels. A *jachtschip* was in fact a pirate ship, so it's fitting that modern yachts evolving from its design should still be associated with plunder, even if it is the yachtowners themselves who are plundered these days.

When King Charles II departed from Amsterdam in 1660 to return to Britain after a long exile, the Dutch presented him with a "jacht." It wasn't long before his brother James had one also, but in 1661, Charles won the first yacht race recorded in history.

Perhaps the actual definition of a yacht becomes less important with each passing year as pleasure vessels are more widely referred to in speech and print simply as "boats." Boating books and magazines no longer refer to "yachtsman" and "man overboard"; they have become the more politically correct and gender-inclusive "boater" and "crew overboard."

There are still some traditional words for which no acceptable gender-neutral substitute has been found, however. *Helmsman* is one; *helmsperson* is too clumsy, and *helm* alone is confusing. *Pilot* is a perfectly good word already fully defined in the dictionaries, but has found little favor. Racing

crews often refer to the person at the helm as the *driver*. It has a good chance of becoming more widely accepted, but only time will tell.

See also **Boat**.

Yacht Design

Borrowing from old and established design principles

Designing an efficient boat is part art, part science, and part luck. Besides possessing a vast knowledge of engineering principles, construction methods, and boatbuilding materials, naval architects need to understand the dynamic energy of the sea and its effects on a moving vessel.

Few design concepts are so complicated or call for so many compromises, largely because a boat moves in two media at once: air and water. The hull is half in and half out of the water, with the proportions changing all the time as the boat heels or rolls.

The aerodynamics and hydrodynamics of a modern sailboat are sometimes compared to a light aircraft on its side, with one wing in the water (the keel) and the other in the air (the sails). Both the keel and the sails have to provide "lift" if the boat is to make any progress against the wind. However, water is hundreds of times denser than air, so the design requirements are vastly different and often at odds with one another. Thus, constant compromises must be made, each one tending to make the design more radical and irreversible.

Boats have been designed and

Y

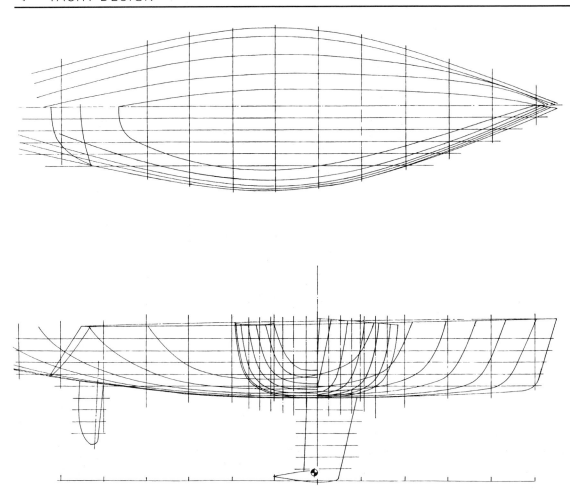

The lines of a 37-foot sailboat designed by Roger Marshall for cruising and racing, showing a deep fin keel with bulb ballast to lower the boat's center of gravity, and a spade rudder aft.

built for thousands of years, however, so the basic principles have been well established—if not by scientific reasoning and mental skill, then by many trials and many errors. Even though computers have rounded some rough edges and made the mechanics of design easier, and electronics have added information and communication, there is little in modern yacht design that hasn't been tried before in the history of sailing—including fin keels, wing keels, solid-wing sails, catamaran hulls, forward rudders, hydrofoils, bendy masts, and many other features that we tend to regard as modern innovations.

In fact, it's a general rule that, in any new boat design, nine tenths is 90 percent borrowed from existing plans of boats of about the same size, and 10 percent is adapted to suit. Of the remaining one tenth, 9 percent seems to fit into place by luck, 1 percent is genuine inspiration, and 90 percent is pure trial and error.

See also **Sails and "Lift"**; **Seaworthiness**.

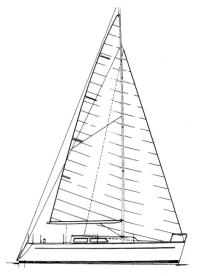

Roger Marshall's 37-foot cruiser-racer sail plan features a fractional rig with the headstay terminating well below the masthead. Running backstays counter the headstay tension.

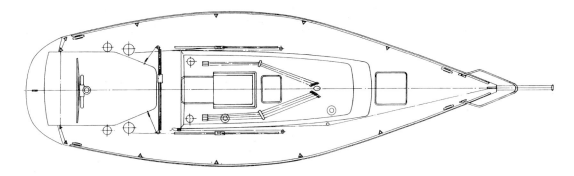

The deck plan shows the functional compromise between cruising and racing. Note how the cabin trunk extends forward of the mast to give headroom below. In a pure racer, this infringement on the foredeck working platform would not be desirable.

Your Performance

How watchkeeping and lack of sleep at sea affect you

Human beings are controlled by a complex timekeeping system known as the circadian rhythm (from the Latin *circa dies*, about a day). The fact that our physical and mental performance varies according to the time of day is of particular interest to boaters who are likely to be at sea for more than a day at a time.

Whether you realize it or not, your performance levels drop steeply between midnight and 3 A.M. They then rise sharply again until 6 A.M. and continue to rise, but more slowly, until about 11 A.M., after which they taper off gradually to another low at 3 P.M. This second low performance level is not as far down the scale as the first one, but it does explain the urge that affects so many of us to have a nap after lunch.

From 3 P.M., there is a gradual rise in performance until 5 P.M., and then it's slowly downhill again all through the evening to midnight, then more quickly to the lowest of the low at 3 A.M.

Your internal and external times are synchronized by environmental clues that include light and darkness, periods of activity and rest, the timing of meals, and so forth. But if you go to sea and begin a watchkeeping system of sleeping, waking, and eating at different times, you will suffer the equivalent of jet lag—and it will take your circadian system between 7 and 10 days to resynchronize fully.

During this period, you will be deprived of your full ration of sleep and fatigue will affect your performance. If you are on deck duty, keeping a lookout, you will experience a lack of vigilance in 20 minutes or less. If you're at the helm, your ability to keep the ship on a steady course will decline after 30 minutes, and until you have fully adapted to your new circadian rhythm, your tricks at the helm should be restricted to a maximum of 2 hours.

Single-handers are affected more severely than others, of course, but they have to find a personal solution to the sleep problem that is compatible with their philosophy about keeping as effective a lookout as possible. Some lone sailors sleep in 20-minute snatches for long periods of the day and night, waking to go on deck for a check of the course and shipping traffic, and then going back to their bunks for another 20 minutes. Others sleep 1 hour in every 3 or 4 around the clock; still others get several successive hours of rest during the day and keep a watch all night, especially when they're in the trade winds and away from shipping lanes.

Industrial psychologists who have studied sleep deprivation suggest that any tasks involving brain work, such as navigation, should be carried out in the late morning, from about 10 A.M. to noon, when performance is at its peak for the day.

See also **Hallucinations; Watchkeeping.**

Zinc Anodes

Suppressing corrosion with sacrificial anodes of zinc

Zinc anodes of various shapes and sizes are used on boats to protect other metals from galvanic corrosion. Dissimilar metals suspended in an electrolyte such as seawater form an electric cell when they're connected by a conductor, and galvanic corrosion eats away the anode—the active electrode—which is the less "noble" metal.

In fact, zinc is one of the least noble metals of all and readily sacrifices itself to protect important structural components made of bronze, copper, and steel, such as propellers, shafts, and through-hull fittings.

Zincs installed on the hull or inside the engine should always meet military specifications or better. The standard is Mil-A-18001 J, but if the final letter is higher, it's better. If your zincs are of lesser grade, they might fail to give the much-needed protection.

Never paint over zincs on the hull—not even with copper-loaded antifouling paint—or you will destroy much of their efficiency. Replace them every year, at least. If they're doing a proper job, they should be at least half eaten away in 12 months; if they're not, make sure they're well connected to the metal they're supposed to protect, either by direct physical contact or by establishing contact with a copper wire.

See also **Galvanic Corrosion**.

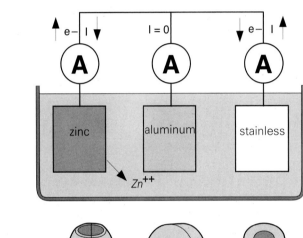

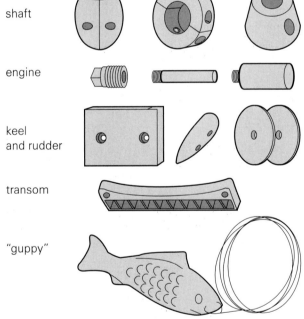

Zinc anode varieties.

Aarons, Richard N. *Small-Boat Seamanship Manual.* Camden ME: International Marine, 2002.

Armstrong, Bob. *Getting Started in Powerboating.* 2nd ed. Camden ME: International Marine, 1995.

The Associated Press Stylebook and Briefing on Media Law. Rev. and updated. Edited by Norm Goldstein. Cambridge MA: Perseus Books, 2000.

Atkin, William. *Of Yachts and Men: An Account of Many Happy Years of Building, Designing, and Living with Small Boats, with Plans and Illustrations of Some of These Boats, and the Circumstances Under Which They Were Conceived.* Dobbs Ferry NY: Sheridan House, 1949, 1984.

Badham, Michael, and Robby Robinson. *Sailors' Secrets: Advice from the Masters.* Camden ME: International Marine, 1997, 1999.

Bauer, Bruce A. *The Sextant Handbook: Adjustment, Repair, Use, and History.* 2nd ed. Camden ME: International Marine, 1992.

Beard, Henry, and Roy McKie. *Sailing: A Sailor's Dictionary.* New York: Workman, 1981.

Beebe, William. *The Arcturus Adventure: An Account of the New York Zoological Society's First Oceanographic Expedition.* New York: Putnam, 1926.

Blewitt, Mary. *Celestial Navigation for Yachtsmen.* Rev. ed. Edited by Thomas C. Bergel. Camden ME: International Marine, 1995.

Brewer, Ted. *Understanding Boat Design.* 4th ed. Camden ME: International Marine, 1994.

Brotherton, Miner. *The 12-Volt Bible for Boats.* 2nd ed. with Ed Sherman. Camden ME: International Marine, 2003.

Butler, Paul, and Marya Butler. *Fine Boat Finishes for Wood and Fiberglass Boats.* Camden ME: International Marine, 1987, 1991.

Burch, David. *Emergency Navigation.* Camden ME: International Marine, 1986.

Calder, Nigel. *Boatowner's Mechanical and Electrical Manual.* 2nd ed. Camden ME: International Marine, 1996.

———. *How to Read a Nautical Chart: A Complete Guide to the Symbols, Abbreviations, and Data Displayed on Nautical Charts.* Camden ME: International Marine, 2003.

———. *Marine Diesel Engines: Maintenance, Troubleshooting, and Repair.* 2nd ed. Camden ME: International Marine, 1992.

———. *Nigel Calder's Cruising Handbook: A Compendium for Coastal and Offshore Sailors.* Camden ME: International Marine, 2001.

Carr, Michael William. *International Marine's Weather Predicting Simplified: How to Read Weather Charts and Satellite Images.* Camden ME: International Marine, 1999.

Carrick, Robert W., and Richard Henderson. *John G. Alden and His Yacht Designs.* Camden ME: International Marine, 1983.

Carson, Rachel L. *The Sea Around Us.* New York: Oxford University Press, 2003.

Casey, Don. *100 Fast and Easy Boat Improvements.* Camden ME: International Marine, 1998.

———. *Sailboat Electrics Simplified.* Camden ME: International Marine, 1999.

———. *Sailboat Hull and Deck Repair.* Camden ME: International Marine, 1996.

———. *Sailboat Refinishing.* Camden ME: International Marine, 1996.

———. *This Old Boat.* Camden ME: International Marine, 1991.

Casey, Don, and Lew Hackler. *Sensible Cruising: The Thoreau Approach: A Philosophic and Practical Approach to Cruising.* Camden ME: International Marine, 1986.

Chapelle, Howard I. *Yacht Designing and Planning.* New York: Norton, 1994.

Charton, Barbara, ed. *The Facts on File Dictionary of Marine Science.* Rev. ed. New York: Facts on File, 2001.

Chichester, Francis. *Gipsy Moth Circles the World.* Introduction by Jonathan Raban. Camden ME: International Marine, 2001, 2003.

Cohen, Michael Martin. *Dr. Cohen's Healthy Sailor Book.* Camden ME: International Marine, 1983.

Coles, K. Adlard. *Heavy Weather Sailing.* 3rd printing. N.P.: Granada Publishing, 1980.

Collier, Everett. *The Boatowner's Guide to Corrosion: A Complete Reference for Boatowners and*

Marine Professionals. Camden ME: International Marine, 2001.

Cooke, Francis B. *Single-Handed Cruising*. London: E. Arnold, 1919.

Cornell, Jimmy. *World Cruising Routes: Featuring Nearly 1,000 Sailing Routes in All Oceans of the World.* 5th ed. Camden ME: International Marine, 2002.

Crawford, William P. *Mariner's Weather.* New York: Norton, 1992.

Crothers, William L. *The American-Built Clipper Ship, 1850–1856: Characteristics, Construction, Details.* Camden ME: International Marine, 1997, 2000.

Curry, Manfred. *Racing Tactics.* Completely rev. by Edward J. Cox and Edward D. Muhlfeld. New York: Scribner, 1973.

Cutler, Thomas J. ed. *The Bluejacket's Manual.* 23rd ed. Annapolis: U.S. Naval Institute Press, 2002.

Darwin, Charles. *Voyage of the Beagle.* Mineola NY: Dover, 2002.

Day, George. *Safety at Sea: A Sailor's Complete Guide to Safe Seamanship.* New York: Putnam, 1991.

Defense Mapping Agency Hydrographic/Topographic Center. *The American Practical Navigator: An Epitome of Navigation* (Bowditch). 1995 ed. Bethesda MD: Defense Mapping Agency Hydrographic/Topographic Center, 1995.

Dent, Nicholas, and Gary Jobson, eds. *The Yachtsman's Pocket Almanac, 1981.* New York: Simon & Schuster, 1980.

Doherty, John Stephen. *The Boats They Sailed In.* New York: Norton, 1985.

Donaldson, Sven. *Understanding the New Sailing Technology: A Basic Guide for Sailors.* New York: Putnam's, 1990.

Eldridge Tide and Pilot Book, 1984 edition.

Eyges, Leonard. *The Practical Pilot: Coastal Navigation by Eye, Intuition, and Common Sense.* Camden ME: International Marine, 1989.

Fagan, Brian. *Staying Put! The Art of Anchoring.* Santa Barbara CA: Caractacus Corp., 1993.

Fisher, Dennis. *Latitude Hooks and Azimuth Rings: How to Build and Use 18 Traditional Navigational Tools.* Camden ME: International Marine, 1995.

Frankel, Michael L., ed. *Gently with the Tides: The Best of Living Aboard.* Camden ME: International Marine, 1993.

Gates, Ernest S. *Sea Navigation: A Manual for Students and Yachtsmen.* London: Harrap, 1968.

Gerr, Dave. *The Elements of Boat Strength: For Builders, Designers, and Owners.* Camden ME: International Marine, 2000.

———. *The Nature of Boats: Insights and Esoterica for the Nautically Obsessed.* Camden ME: International Marine, 1992, 1995.

———. *The Propeller Handbook: The Complete Reference for Choosing, Installing, and Understanding Boat Propellers.* Camden ME: International Marine, 1989, 2001.

Goodman, Di, and Ian Brodie. *Learning to Sail: The Annapolis Sailing School Guide for All Ages.* Camden ME: International Marine, 1994.

Graham, R. D. *Rough Passage: And the Adventure of the Faeroe Islands.* London: Granada, 1984.

Graham, R. D., and J. E. H. Tew. *A Manual for Small Yachts.* 2nd ed. London: Blackie & Sons, 1946.

Gustafson, Charles. *How to Buy the Best Sailboat.* Updated ed. New York: Hearst Marine Books, 1991.

Heaton, Peter. *Motor Yachting and Boating.* Rev. ed. Harmondsworth, England: Penguin, 1976.

Henderson, Richard. *Sailing in Windy Weather.* Camden ME: International Marine, 1987.

———. *Sea Sense.* 3rd ed. Camden ME: International Marine, 1991.

———. *Singlehanded Sailing: The Experiences and Techniques of the Lone Voyagers.* 2nd ed. Camden ME: International Marine, 1988.

———. *Understanding Rigs and Rigging.* Rev. ed. Camden ME: International Marine, 1991.

Herreshoff, L. Francis. *Sensible Cruising Designs.* Camden ME: International Marine, 1991.

Hinz, Earl R. *The Complete Book of Anchoring and Mooring.* Rev. 2nd ed. Centreville MD: Cornell Maritime Press, 2001.

Hiscock, Eric. *Cruising Under Sail: Incorporating Voyaging Under Sail.* 3rd ed. Camden ME: International Marine, 1981, 1985.

———. *Voyaging Under Sail.* 2nd ed. Oxford: Oxford University Press, 1977.

Hollander, Neil, and Harald Mertes. *The Yachtsman's Emergency Handbook: The Complete Survival Manual.* Rev. ed. New York: Hearst Marine Books, 1986.

Hubbard, Richard K. *Boater's Bowditch: The Small-Craft American Practical Navigator.* Camden ME: International Marine, 1998, 2000.

Hunn, Peter. *The Old Outboard Book.* 3rd ed. Camden ME: International Marine, 2002.

Hydrographic Department of Great Britain. *Ocean Passages for the World.* 4th ed. Taunton, England: Hydrographer of the Navy, 1987.

Irving, John, and Douglas Service. *The Yachtsman's Week-End Book.* London: Seeley, Service, 1938.

Jeffrey, Kevin, with Nan Jeffrey. *Boatowner's Energy Planner: How to Make and Manage Electrical Energy on Board.* Camden ME: International Marine, 1991.

Jenkins, O. *True to Compass.* Cape Town, South Africa: Juta & Co., 1970.

Jobson, Gary. *Sailing Fundamentals: The Official Learn-to-Sail Manual of the American Sailing Association and the United States Coast Guard Auxiliary.* Rev. and updated. New York: Simon & Schuster, 1998.

Kent, Rockwell. *N by E.* Hanover NH: University Press of New England, 1996.

Kirschenbaum, Jerry, and Brayton Harris. *Safe Boat: A Comprehensive Guide to the Purchase, Equipping, Maintenance, and Operation of a Safe Boat.* New York: Norton, 1990.

Kroenke, David. *Know Your Boat: The Guide to Everything that Makes Your Boat Work.* Camden ME: International Marine, 2002.

Larsson, Lars, and Rolf E. Eliasson. *Principles of Yacht Design.* 2nd ed. Camden ME: International Marine, 2000.

Mack, William P., Harry A. Seymour Jr., and Lesa A. McComas. *The Naval Officer's Guide.* 11th ed. Annapolis: Naval Institute Press, 1998.

Maloney, Elbert S. *Chapman Piloting: Seamanship and Small Boat Handling.* 63rd ed. New York: Hearst Marine Books, 1999.

Marchaj, C. A. *Seaworthiness: The Forgotten Factor.* Camden ME: International Marine, 1986.

Marshall, Roger. *The Complete Guide to Choosing a Cruising Sailboat.* Camden ME: International Marine, 1999.

———. *Designed to Cruise.* New York: Norton, 1990.

McEwen, W. A., and A. H. Lewis. *Encyclopedia of Nautical Knowledge.* Cambridge MD: Cornell Maritime Press, 1953.

Mellor, John. *Handling Troubles Afloat: What to Do When It All Goes Wrong.* Dobbs Ferry NY: Sheridan House, 1996.

Merry, Barbara, with John Darwin. *The Splicing Handbook: Techniques for Modern and Traditional Ropes.* 2nd ed. Camden ME: International Marine, 2000.

Middleton, E. E. *The Cruise of the Kate.* London: Granada, 1984.

Miller, Conrad, and Elbert S. Maloney. *Your Boat's Electrical System.* 2nd rev. ed. New York: Hearst Marine Books, 1988.

Moore, D. A. *International Light, Shape, and Sound Signals.* 2nd ed. Oxford: BH Newnes, 1993.

Munns, Harry. *Cruising Fundamentals.* Edited by Hal Sutphen. Camden ME: International Marine, 1991.

Nicolson, Ian. *Boat Data Book.* 4th ed. Dobbs Ferry NY: Sheridan House, 1999.

Noel, John V. *The VNR Dictionary of Ships and the Sea.* New York: Van Nostrand Reinhold, 1981.

Noel, John V., Jr. *The Boating Dictionary, Sail and Power.* New York: Van Nostrand Reinhold, 1981.

Norville, Warren. *Coastal Navigation Step by Step.* Camden ME: International Marine, 1975.

Pardey, Lin, and Larry Pardey. *The Capable Cruiser.* Vista CA: Pardey Book, 1995.

———. *The Self-Sufficient Sailor.* New York: Norton, 1982.

Parsons, Timothy R., and Masayuki Takahashi. *Biological Oceanographic Processes.* New York: Pergamon, 1973, 1977, 1984.

Philip, George. *Stars at a Glance: A Simple Guide to the Heavens.* 2nd ed. London: G. Philip, 1976.

Potter, David. *The Care of Alloy Spars and Rigging.* New York: Scribner, 1980.

Pye, Peter. *The Sea Is for Sailing.* London: Grafton, 1957, 1987.

Raban, Jonathan, ed. *The Oxford Book of the Sea.* Oxford; New York: Oxford University Press, 2002.

Radcliffe, Ann. *The Mysteries of Udolpho: A Romance.* Edited by Jacqueline Howard. London; New York: Penguin, 2001.

Reed, Thomas. *Reed's Nautical Companion.* 2nd ed. Boston: Thomas Reed Publications, 1998.

Roberts-Goodson, Bruce. *The Complete Guide to Metal Boats: Building, Maintenance, and Repair.* Camden ME: International Marine, 2001.

Ross, Wallace with Carl Chapman. *Sail Power: The Complete Guide to Sails and Sail Handling.* Rev., updated ed. New York: Knopf, 1984.

Roth, Hal. *After 50,000 Miles.* New York: Norton, 1977.

———. *How to Sail Around the World: Advice and Ideas for Voyaging Under Sail.* Camden ME: International Marine, 2003.

Seidman, David. *The Complete Sailor: Learning the Art of Sailing.* Camden ME: International Marine, 1994, 1995.

Seifert, Bill, with Dan Spurr. *Offshore Sailing: 200 Essential Passagemaking Tips.* Camden ME: International Marine, 2002.

Skene, Norman L. *Elements of Yacht Design.* Dobbs Ferry NY: Sheridan House, 2001.

Slocum, Joshua. *Sailing Alone Around the World.* New York: Century, 1911. Reprint Mount Kisco NY: Regatta Press, 2000.

Small-Boat Seamanship Manual. Edited by Richard N. Aarons. Camden ME: International Marine, 2002.

Smeeton, Miles. *Once Is Enough.* Foreword by Nevil Shute. London: Hart-Davis, 1959. Reprinted with an introduction by Jonathan Raban (Camden ME: International Marine, 2001, 2003).

Smith, Hervey Garrett. *The Marlinspike Sailor.* Camden ME: International Marine, 1993.

Sorensen, Eric W. *Sorensen's Guide to Powerboats: How to Evaluate Design, Construction, and Performance.* Camden ME: International Marine, 2002.

Spectre, Peter H. *The Mariner's Book of Days: 2003.* Brooklin ME: WoodenBoat Publications, 2002.

Spurr, Daniel. *Spurr's Boatbook: Upgrading the Cruising Sailboat.* 2nd ed. Camden ME: International Marine, 1991.

Stadler, Michael. *The Psychology of Sailing: The Sea's Effects on Mind and Body.* Translated by Sally A. R. Bates. Camden ME: International Marine, 1987.

Stapleton, Sidney. *Stapleton's Powerboat Bible: The Complete Guide to Selection, Seamanship, and Cruising.* Camden ME: International Marine, 2002.

———. *Stapleton's Power Cruising Bible: The Complete Guide to Coastal and Bluewater Cruising Under Power.* New York: Hearst Marine Books, 1992.

Steward, Robert M. *Boatbuilding Manual.* 4th ed. Camden ME: International Marine, 1994.

Street, Donald. *The Ocean Sailing Yacht.* New York: Norton, 1973–1978.

Toss, Brion. *The Complete Rigger's Apprentice: Tools and Techniques for Modern and Traditional Rigging.* Camden ME: International Marine, 1998.

Trefethen, Jim. *Inflatable Boats: Selection, Care, Repair, and Seamanship.* Camden ME: International Marine, 1996.

Tryckare, Tre. *The Lore of Ships.* Rev. ed. New York: Crescent, 1986.

Vigor, John. *Boatowner's Handbook: Reference Data for Maintenance, Repair, Navigation, and Seamanship.* Camden ME: International Marine, 2000.

———. *Danger, Dolphins, and Ginger Beer.* New York: Atheneum, 1993.

———. *The International Marine 1998 Daybook and Nautical Desk Reference.* Camden ME: International Marine, 1998.

———. *The Practical Mariner's Book of Knowledge: 420 Sea-Tested Rules of Thumb for Almost Every Boating Situation.* Camden ME: International Marine, 1994.

———. *The Seaworthy Offshore Sailboat: A Guide to Essential Features, Gear, and Handling.* Camden ME: International Marine, 1999.

———. *Twenty Small Sailboats to Take You Anywhere.* Arcata CA: Paradise Cay Publications, 1999.

Voss, John C. *The Venturesome Voyages of Captain Voss.* 2nd ed. Boston: Charles E. Lauriat, 1926. Two of the three stories in Voss's original text are included in *40,000 Miles in a Canoe and Sea Queen* (Camden ME: International Marine, 2001, 2003).

Walker, Nicolette Milnes. *When I Put Out to Sea.* New York: Stein & Day, 1972.

Watts, Oswald M. *The Sextant Simplified: A Practical Explanation of the Use of the Sextant at Sea.* 6th ed. London: T. Reed Publications, 1976.

Weeks, Morris, ed. *The Complete Boating Encyclopedia.* New York: Golden Press, 1964.

White, Charlie. *Living off the Sea.* 2nd ed. Surrey BC: Heritage House, 1998.

White, Chris. *The Cruising Multihull.* Camden ME: International Marine, 1990, 1997.

White, E. B. "The Sea and the Wind That Blows," *Essays of E. B. White.* New York: Perennial Classics, 1999.

Wing, Charlie. *Boating Magazine's One-Minute Guide to the Nautical Rules of the Road.* Camden ME: International Marine, 1998.

———. *Get Your Captain's License: The Complete Study Guide.* 3rd ed. Camden ME: International Marine, 2004.

———. *How Boat Things Work: An Illustrated Guide.* Camden ME: International Marine, 2004.

Wittman, Rebecca J. *Brightwork: The Art of Finishing Wood.* Camden ME: International Marine, 1990.

———. *The Brightwork Companion: Tried-and-True Methods and Strongly Held Opinions in Thirteen and One-Half Chapters.* Camden ME: International Marine, 2004.

Worth, Claud Alley. *Yacht Cruising.* 4th ed. New York: Kennedy Bros., 1934.

Art and Graphic Credits

Full bibliographic information for books is in the bibliography (pages 339–42).

ABYC, in Calder, *Boatowner's Mechanical and Electrical Manual*: 105

Bruce Alderson, in Sorensen, *Sorensen's Guide to Powerboats*: 50, 131

Bruce Alderson, in White, *Cruising Multihull*: 193

Avon Marine, in Calder, *Nigel Calder's Cruising Handbook*: 179

Baja, in Sorensen, *Sorensen's Guide to Powerboats*: 175 (bottom)

Barnacle Anchors: 197 (bottom)

Marty Baron, National Weather Service, in Badham and Robinson, *Sailors' Secrets*: 63 (bottom right), 64

Bennett, in Sorensen, *Sorensen's Guide to Powerboats*: 311

Bruce Bingham, in Spurr, *Spurr's Boatbook*: 216

Donald L. Blount Associates, in Sorensen, *Sorensen's Guide to Powerboats*: 249

Ted Brewer, in *Understanding Boat Design*: 26 (top left), 56 (top), 125, 173 (+ table), 255, 257, 277

Bulwagga: 197 (top left)

Nigel Calder, in *Boatowner's Mechanical and Electrical Manual*: 9 (table)

Nigel Calder, in *Nigel Calder's Cruising Handbook*: 26 (top right), 59 (left), 87 (table), 115, 189, 217

Carolina Yacht Brokers, in Sorensen, *Sorensen's Guide to Powerboats*: 176

Michael William Carr, in *International Marine's Weather Predicting Simplified*: 163 (table)

Don Casey, in *Sailboat Electrics Simplified*: 106 (left), 107 (table)

Don Casey, in *Sailboat Refinishing and Repair*: 260 (table)

Don Casey, in *This Old Boat*: 220, 236

Caterpillar, in Sorensen, *Sorensen's Guide to Powerboats*: 134

F. H. Chapman, *Architectura Navalis Mercatoria* (in Gerr, *The Nature of Boats*): 335

Francis Chichester, in *Gipsy Moth Circles the World*: 148

Everett Collier, in *Boatowner's Guide to Corrosion*: 290 (table)

William Crothers, in *American-Built Clipper Ship*: 120

Datamarine, in Sorensen, *Sorensen's Guide to Powerboats*: 86 (bottom)

Defense Mapping Agency, in *American Practical Navigator*: 54

Defense Mapping Agency, in Hubbard, *Boater's Bowditch*: 322 (table), 323 (top)

Kim Downing, in Hubbard, *Boater's Bowditch*: 15 (bottom), 99, 233, 240, 273 (top), 322 (top), 323 (bottom)

Jim Dugan, in Merry, *Splicing Handbook*: 284 (top left), 285 (top left)

East Penn Mfg. Co., in Brotherton, *The 12-Volt Bible for Boats*: 21

Eldridge Tide and Pilot Book: 93 (right and table)

Dennis Fisher, in *Latitude Hooks and Azimuth Rings*: 227

Thomas Fogarty and George Varian, in Slocum, *Sailing Alone Around the World*: 202, 276

Furuno, in Stapleton, *Stapleton's Powerboat Bible*: 86 (top)

Dave Gerr, in *The Nature of Boats*: 111, 209, 254, 291, 302 (graph), 312 (bottom), 320 (left)

Dave Gerr, in *Propeller Handbook*: 219, 223, 224 (top)

Eric Greene, in *Sorensen's Guide to Powerboats*: 238 (table)

Rob Groves, in Badham and Robinson, *Sailors' Secrets*: 180

Richard Henderson, in *Sailing in Windy Weather*: 24

Richard Henderson, in *Understanding Rigs and Rigging*: 275 (bottom)

Eric Hiscock, in *Cruising Under Sail*: 130 (top)

Hunter Marine, in Calder, *Nigel Calder's Cruising Handbook*: 137 (top)

Lewmar, in Calder, *Boatowner's Mechanical and Electrical Manual*: 327

Joan B. Machinchick, in Goodman and Brodie, *Learning to Sail*: 48, 297

Roger Marshall, in *Complete Guide to Choosing a Cruising Sailboat*: 45 (table), 70, 183 (top), 187, 336, 337

Dave Martin, in Sorensen, *Sorensen's Guide to Powerboats*: 183 (bottom)

Ben Martinez, in Merry, *Splicing Handbook* (drawings only): 283, 284–86

Max-Prop, in Calder, *Boatowner's Mechanical and Electrical Manual*: 222

Barbara Merry, in *Splicing Handbook*: 245 (top table), 283 (table)

Index

Numbers in **bold** refer to pages with illustrations.